The Rise of the Corporate Economy in Southeast Asia

This book surveys the growth of large corporations in Southeast Asia, focusing in particular on corporate organization, methods of finance, the business environment and corporate governance. It details the different phases of corporate and financial development, particularly liberalization and globalization from the mid-1980s, the 1997 crisis, and subsequent attempts at liberalization and the reform of corporate governance. It considers the key themes of the rise of the Southeast Asian corporate economy, and illustrates the theoretical issues through deployment of carefully selected country-specific case studies from across the region. The book examines critical subjects, including the variety of corporate forms found in Southeast Asia; issues of ethnicity; the concentration of ownership, particularly among families; links between the state, the military, banks and corporations; state-owned enterprises and forms of state control; and the role of foreign capital. Overall, this book provides a comprehensive analysis of the rise of the corporate economy in Southeast Asia, and will be an important resource for students of the region and those concerned with theoretical issues of corporate governance.

Rajeswary Ampalavanar Brown is currently Reader in Business History at the School of Management of the Royal Holloway College London. She has previously held positions as Research Fellow at the School of Oriental and African Studies, and as Lecturer in Economic History at the London School of Economics. She is the author of *The Indian Minority and Political Change in Malaya, 1945–1957* (1982), *Capital and Entrepreneurship in South-East Asia* (1994), and *Chinese Big Business and the Wealth of Asian Nations* (2000), and editor of the four-volume *Chinese Business Enterprise*.

Routledge Studies in the Growth Economies of Asia

1. **The Changing Capital Markets of East Asia**
   Edited by Ky Cao
2. **Financial Reform in China**
   Edited by On Kit Tam
3. **Women and Industrialization in Asia**
   Edited by Susan Horton
4. **Japan's Trade Policy**
   Action or reaction?
   Yumiko Mikanagi
5. **The Japanese Election System**
   Three analytical perspectives
   Junichiro Wada
6. **The Economics of the Latecomers**
   Catching-up, technology transfer and institutions in Germany, Japan and South Korea
   Jang-Sup Shin
7. **Industrialization in Malaysia**
   Import substitution and infant industry performance
   Rokiah Alavi
8. **Economic Development in Twentieth Century East Asia**
   The international context
   Edited by Aiko Ikeo
9. **The Politics of Economic Development in Indonesia**
   Contending perspectives
   Edited by Ian Chalmers and Vedi Hadiz
10. **Studies in the Economic History of the Pacific Rim**
    Edited by Sally M. Miller, A. J. H. Latham and Dennis O. Flynn
11. **Workers and the State in New Order Indonesia**
    Vedi R. Hadiz
12. **The Japanese Foreign Exchange Market**
    Beate Reszat
13. **Exchange Rate Policies in Emerging Asian Countries**
    Edited by Stefan Collignon, Jean Pisani-Ferry and Yung Chul Park
14. **Chinese Firms and Technology in the Reform Era**
    Yizheng Shi
15. **Japanese Views on Economic Development**
    Diverse paths to the market
    Kenichi Ohno and Izumi Ohno
16. **Technological Capabilities and Export Success in Asia**
    Edited by Dieter Ernst, Tom Ganiatsos and Lynn Mytelka
17. **Trade and Investment in China**
    The European experience
    Edited by Roger Strange, Jim Slater and Limin Wang
18. **Technology and Innovation in Japan**
    Policy and management for the 21st century
    Edited by Martin Hemmert and Christian Oberländer
19. **Trade Policy Issues in Asian Development**
    Prema-chandra Athukorala
20. **Economic Integration in the Asia Pacific Region**
    Ippei Yamazawa
21. **Japan's War Economy**
    Edited by Erich Pauer
22. **Industrial Technology Development in Malaysia**
    Industry and firm studies
    Edited by K. S. Jomo, Greg Felker and Rajah Rasiah

23. **Technology, Competitiveness and the State**
Malaysia's industrial technology policies
Edited by K. S. Jomo and Greg Felker

24. **Corporatism and Korean Capitalism**
Edited by Dennis L. McNamara

25. **Japanese Science**
Samuel Coleman

26. **Capital and Labour in Japan**
The functions of two factor markets
Toshiaki Tachibanaki and Atsuhiro Taki

27. **Asia Pacific Dynamism 1550–2000**
Edited by A. J. H. Latham and Heita Kawakatsu

28. **The Political Economy of Development and Environment in Korea**
Jae-Yong Chung and Richard J. Kirkby

29. **Japanese Economics and Economists since 1945**
Edited by Aiko Ikeo

30. **China's Entry into the World Trade Organisation**
Edited by Peter Drysdale and Ligang Song

31. **Hong Kong as an International Financial Centre**
Emergence and development 1945–1965
Catherine R. Schenk

32. **Impediments to Trade in Services**
Measurement and policy implication
Edited by Christoper Findlay and Tony Warren

33. **The Japanese Industrial Economy**
Late development and cultural causation
Ian Inkster

34. **China and the Long March to Global Trade**
The accession of China to the World Trade Organization
Edited by Alan S. Alexandroff, Sylvia Ostry and Rafael Gomez

35. **Capitalist Development and Economism in East Asia**
The rise of Hong Kong, Singapore, Taiwan, and South Korea
Kui-Wai Li

36. **Women and Work in Globalizing Asia**
Edited by Dong-Sook S. Gills and Nicola Piper

37. **Financial Markets and Policies in East Asia**
Gordon de Brouwer

38. **Developmentalism and Dependency in Southeast Asia**
The case of the automotive industry
Jason P. Abbott

39. **Law and Labour Market Regulation in East Asia**
Edited by Sean Cooney, Tim Lindsey, Richard Mitchell and Ying Zhu

40. **The Economy of the Philippines**
Elites, inequalities and economic restructuring
Peter Krinks

41. **China's Third Economic Transformation**
The rise of the private economy
Edited by Ross Garnaut and Ligang Song

42. **The Vietnamese Economy**
Awakening the dormant dragon
Edited by Binh Tran-Nam and Chi Do Pham

43. **Restructuring Korea Inc.**
Jang-Sup Shin and Ha-Joon Chang

44. **Development and Structural Change in the Asia-Pacific**
Globalising miracles or end of a model?
Edited by Martin Andersson and Christer Gunnarsson

45. **State Collaboration and Development Strategies in China**
The case of the China-Singapore Suzhou Industrial Park (1992–2002)
Alexius Pereira

46. **Capital and Knowledge in Asia**
Changing power relations
Edited by Heidi Dahles and Otto van den Muijzenberg

47. **Southeast Asian Paper Tigers?**
From miracle to debacle and beyond
Edited by Jomo K. S.

48. **Manufacturing Competitiveness in Asia**
How internationally competitive national firms and industries developed in East Asia
Edited by Jomo K. S.

49. **The Korean Economy at the Crossroads**
Edited by MoonJoong Tcha and Chung-Sok Suh

50. **Ethnic Business**
Chinese capitalism in Southeast Asia
Edited by Jomo K. S. and Brian C. Folk

51. **Exchange Rate Regimes in East Asia**
Edited by Gordon De Brouwer and Masahiro Kawai

52. **Financial Governance in East Asia**
Policy dialogue, surveillance and cooperation
Edited by Gordon De Brouwer and Yunjong Wang

53. **Designing Financial Systems in East Asia and Japan**
Edited by Joseph P. H. Fan, Masaharu Hanazaki and Juro Teranishi

54. **State Competence and Economic Growth in Japan**
Yoshiro Miwa

55. **Understanding Japanese Saving**
Does population aging matter?
Robert Dekle

56. **The Rise and Fall of the East Asian Growth System, 1951–2000**
International competitiveness and rapid economic growth
Xiaoming Huang

57. **Service Industries and Asia-Pacific Cities**
New development trajectories
Edited by P. W. Daniels, K. C. Ho and T. A. Hutton

58. **Unemployment in Asia**
Edited by John Benson and Ying Zhu

59. **Risk Management and Innovation in Japan, Britain and the USA**
Edited by Ruth Taplin

60. **Japan's Development Aid to China**
The long-running foreign policy of engagement
Tsukasa Takamine

61. **Chinese Capitalism and the Modernist Vision**
Satyananda J. Gabriel

62. **Japanese Telecommunications**
Edited by Ruth Taplin and Masako Wakui

63. **East Asia, Globalization and the New Economy**
F. Gerard Adams

64. **China as a World Factory**
Edited by Kevin Honglin Zhang

65. **China's State Owned Enterprise Reforms**
An industrial and CEO approach
Juan Antonio Fernandez and Leila Fernandez-Stembridge

66. **China and India**
A tale of two economies
Dilip K. Das

67. **Innovation and Business Partnering in Japan, Europe and the United States**
Edited by Ruth Taplin

68. **Asian Informal Workers**
Global risks local protection
Santosh Mehrotra and Mario Biggeri

69. **The Rise of the Corporate Economy in Southeast Asia**
Rajeswary Ampalavanar Brown

The Rise of the Corporate Economy in Southeast Asia

Rajeswary Ampalavanar Brown

Routledge
Taylor & Francis Group
LONDON AND NEW YORK

First published 2006 by Routledge
2 Park Square, Milton Park, Abingdon, Oxon OX14 4RN

Simultaneously published in the USA and Canada
by Routledge
270 Madison Ave, New York, NY 10016

Routledge is an imprint of the Taylor & Francis Group, an informa business

Typeset in Times New Roman by
Florence Production Ltd, Stoodleigh, Devon
Printed and bound in Great Britain by
TJI Digital, Padstow, Cornwall

British Library Cataloguing in Publication Data
A catalogue record for this book is available
from the British Library

Library of Congress Cataloging in Publication Data
A catalog record has been requested for this book

ISBN10: 0–415–39559–3
ISBN13: 978–0–415–39559–5

With all my love for Ian, Andrew and Ali

Contents

Tables

Figures

Acknowledgements

In the long process of researching and writing this book, I have been indebted to many people. Chamali Kariyawasam was responsible for the preparation of all the tables in the volume. The scale of work involved was enormous and her wisdom, expertise and friendship are deeply appreciated. I owe Simon Liu Zhuheng a deep debt for his assistance in the final preparation of the tables.

In Indonesia, Niken Laksmita helped with her immense knowledge and good contacts at the Jakarta Stock Exchange. I also wish to thank Peggy Wintin, James Warren, Tharaphi Than and Thuyein Kyaw-Zaw for assisting in the final stages of the preparations. I am grateful for their enthusiastic and skilled assistance.

I also wish to thank Peter Sowden for his confidence and encouragement. My brother Jeyaratna, my sisters Mages, Puvanes, Yoges, Nir and their families have been a source of inspiration. My parents are always there.

I have also found myself in debt to an anonymous but imposing copy-editor and am deeply grateful for this assistance.

In the School of Management, it was the support of Hari, Chris Hitchins, Steve Brown, Jackie, Bob, Romano, Donna and Andrew that convinced me that a monograph is still a valuable contribution and to keep plodding on.

Ian has been a never-failing and wonderfully tolerant support. I also want to record my deepest gratitude to my sons Andrew and Alasdair who staggered around Southeast Asia on my research trips, collecting statistical data wherever possible.

Finally, although friends and family saved me from many errors, those remaining are entirely my own fault.

Raj Brown
London, 5 April 2006

Glossary and abbreviations

ABM	Asian Bond Market
ADB	Asian Development Bank
ADM	Asian Dollar Market
AMB	Arab Malaysia Bank
APP	Asia Pulp and Paper
ASB	Amanah Saham Bumiputra
ASN	Amanah Saham Nasional
Bappenas (Badan Perencanaan Pembangunan Nasional)	National Development Planning Board
BCA	Bank Central Asia
BDNI	Bank Dagang Nasional Indonesia
BIBF	Bangkok International Banking Faculty
BKPM (Badan Koordinasi Penaman Modal)	Capital Investment Co-ordination Board
BNI	Bank Negara Indonesia
BOI	Board of Investments
BOT	build, operate and transfer
BPPN	Badan Penyehatan Perbankan Nasional (Indonesian Bank Restructuring Agency)
BULOG (Badan Urusan Logistik)	National Logistics Agency for Food Price Stabilization
bumiputra	indigenous Malay
CAHB	Commercial Asset Holding Bhd
CAR	capital adequacy ratio
CAT	Communication Authority of Thailand
CDRAC	Corporate Dept Restructuring Advisory Committee
CDRC	Corporate Debt Restructuring Committee
CLOB	Central Limit Order Book
Dakab (Yayasan Darma karya Abadi)	Eternal Work Fund Foundation

DBS	Development Bank of Singapore
Dharmais (Yayasan Dharma Bhakti Sosial)	Social Voluntary Work Foundation
EPF	Employees Provident Fund
FCC	First Capital Corporation
FDI	foreign direct investment
FEER	Far Eastern Economic Review
FPH	First Pacific Holdings
GDP	gross domestic product
GIC	Government Investment Company
GLC	government-linked company
HLC	Hong Leong Credit
HLFB	Hong Leong Finance Berhad
Humpuss	Hutomo Mandala Putra Soeharto Sumahardjuno
IBRA (BPPN)	Indonesian Bank Restructuring Agency (Badan Penyehatan Perbankan Nasional)
ICMD	Indonesian Capital Market Directory
ICULS	irredeemable convertible unsecured loan stocks
IDC	Infrastructural Development Corporation
IFC	International Finance Corporation
IMF	International Monetary Fund
IPO	initial public offering
ISI	import substitution industrialization
JPE	Jaya Perkasa Engineering
KIO	Kuwait Investment Office
KLIA	Kuala Lumpur International Airport
KLSE	Kuala Lumpur Stock Exchange
Kopassus (Komando Pasukan Khusus)	Special Forces Command
KTB	Krung Thai Bank
KTMB	Keretaapi Tanah Malaysia Bhd
KYB	Kwong Yik Bank
MNE	multinational enterprise
MPHB	Multi-Purpose Holdings Bhd
MRCB	Malaysian Resources Corporation Bhd
NBFI	non-bank financial institution
NEP	New Economic Policy
NESDB	National Economic and Social Development Board
NGO	non-governmental organization
NPL	non-performing loan
NSTP	New Straits Times Press
OCBC	Oversea-Chinese Banking Corporation
OUB	Overseas Union Bank

PAB	Phileo Allied Bank
Pertamina	National Oil and Natural Gas Company
PNB	Permodalan Nasional Bhd
pribumi	indigenous Indonesian
PSE	Philippine Stock Exchange
R&D	research and development
RCULS	redeemable convertible unsecured loan stocks
RHB	Rashid Hussein Bank
ROA	return on assets
ROE	return on equity
SCB	Standard Chartered Bank
SCNB	Standard Chartered Nakornthon Bank
SEC	Stock Exchange Commission
SET	Stock Exchange of Thailand
SMEs	small and medium enterprises
SMPI	Sinar Mas Paper Investment
SNF	Siam Nawaloha Foundry
SOE	state-owned enterprise
TAMC	Thai Asset Management Company
TDDBS	Thai Danu DBS
Thai Rak Thai Party	Thai Love Thai Party
TOT	Telephone Organization of Thailand
UAB	United Asian Bank
UEM	United Engineers Malaysia
UMBC	United Malayan Banking Corporation
UMG	United Merchant Group
UMNO	United Malay National Organisation
UOB	United Overseas Bank
USB	United Savings Bank
WTO	World Trade Organization
YPB	Yayasan Pelaburan Bumiputra

1 Introduction

This book is concerned with the growth of large corporations in Southeast Asia, focusing on corporate organization, methods of finance, business environment and corporate governance. These changes in ownership, concentration and governance structure of these family-dominated conglomerates are traced from the immediate postwar period to the present. It is argued that this family-dominated corporate structure exploited banks, capital markets, the state and foreign capital to achieve a dramatic but debt-driven growth. It seeks to understand the dynamism of such a pattern of growth, which, however, had serious impact on corporate governance and corporate stability and was implicated in the economic collapse in the 1997 crisis. The difficulties of restructuring and reforming these corporations after 1997 are, again, linked to this structural and institutional problem.

This concentrated corporate growth is assisted by the rise of multiple holding companies with cross-shareholding held by subsidiaries in the group. Outside capital was tapped to preserve these monopolies, while privatization and financial liberalization, too, pampered the growth of these diversified conglomerates, without sacrificing ownership or control. Only the 1997 financial crisis exposed both the risk in such growth and the increase in corporate and industrial concentration.

The book also seeks to explore the ways in which the region's stock exchanges have determined which industrial and commercial initiatives have found favour, which led to a concentration of ownership and monopolistic power. The broad reshaping of corporate finance through the stock exchanges coincided with detailed changes in corporate structures, the creation of holding companies, integrating newly acquired firms into large multinational enterprises with global ambitions. This rapid growth in economic diversification and globalization was coordinated through large inflows of foreign capital into the region from the 1970s. The effects of large concentrated positions of portfolio capital, in targeting specific sectors of the economy (property, finance and currency market), assisted in the emergence of large diversified corporations in Southeast Asia. With this scale and scope they were confident to expand into Central Asia, South Asia, Africa and Europe and the US, in telecommunications, tourism, infrastructural growth, petroleum refining and banking.

Moreover, an important development in the 1980s and 1990s was the aggressive takeovers and mergers, assisted by the state's privatization programme and inflows of foreign capital and the boom in the stock markets in the region. This further increased concentration in ownership.

In addition, the presence of government participation in Southeast Asia's stock markets and their coteries of crony capitalists have important implications for crony capitalism. This complex, intricate relationship between government and crony capitalists has intrinsic value, both in identifying possible patterns of insider trading, as well as close interlocking ties between major business groups listed on the stock exchanges, and the emergence of institutional shareholders of the state. This dominance of government and large private conglomerates on the stock market is repeated throughout Southeast Asia. In Malaysia it was revealed in large institutional shareholders who were *bumiputeras*; in Singapore institutional shareholders were state investment bodies. In Thailand, the Crown Property Bureau and the military were powerful institutional shareholders; in Indonesia the military and the social, religious foundations prevailed as powerful institutional shareholders. In the Philippines institutional shareholders were nebulous, belonging to private investment groups and to foreign nominees. The major theoretical contribution here is on ownership structure. How far did changes in ownership structure and stock market affiliation, pose important consequences for corporate governance, including that of management, ownership and control, debt structure, and accountability and transparency.

The driving theme throughout is the economic and political importance of concentrated ownership of corporations, the interpenetration of diverse economic, bureaucratic and political institutions within this form of corporate growth. The relationship of this form of corporate growth to the 1997 financial crisis is sketched in detail in all the country studies. In the reforms introduced after the crisis, the role of rising foreign equity in the corporations and the legal reforms in corporate governance and the institutional changes form a parallel and equal grid to the analysis of corporate change.

It would be useful here to outline the major features in the development of equity markets in Southeast Asia in this period, 1970–2000. First, the Malaysian stock market is the largest among the five ASEAN markets, followed by Singapore, Thailand, Philippines, then Indonesia, which despite being the smallest, yet revealed the highest growth rate between 1989–93.[1] Malaysia has the largest number of listed companies, while Singapore, though high in market capitalization, possesses fewer corporations because many are large state-dominated enterprises. Private enterprises are smaller and fewer in comparison to her neighbour, Malaysia.

Second, Malaysia has had the highest influence on the other equity markets; this linkage affords large arbitrage profits, a reflection of the openness of the economies in the region and capital mobility. An interesting element of this growth is on the impact of political patronage on herding, speculation and share price performance. However, a word of caution is necessary. Studies in this volume are embedded not on the literature on efficient markets but on crony capitalism.[2] So there is no direct presentation here of corporate performance against an appraisal of share prices. There is also no identification of share price movements with political factors or events. What is attempted briefly is an analysis of crony capitalists and their direct link to the growth or decline of specific corporations, such as the Salim Group, Renong and the Ayalas. State-connected growth is inevitable, related to this crony capitalism.

Third, the study of the stock market is used to identify the nationality of foreign capital and its volatility. Mention is made of the importance of Middle Eastern capital in some corporations and banks, particularly in Malaysia. However, the largest source of foreign portfolio capital in Southeast Asia has been from Japan, Hong Kong and Overseas Chinese, and, from the 1990s, from Singapore. The closure of the Central Limit Order Book (CLOB) and the imposition of capital controls by Malaysia in September 1998 pushed Singapore more into investing in Indonesia, Thailand and China.

The core argument here is that listed corporations reveal fairly high volatility in certain periods, undoubtedly related to this influx of foreign capital. The stock market is used to tap such capital, achieve diversification, seek entry into capital and R&D (research and development) intensive sectors, and construct joint-ventures with foreign multinational enterprises (MNEs), and establish links with states abroad and with the International Monetary Fund (IMF) and World Bank in investment strategies. Hence, the increased volume in market trading from 1989 corresponded to financial liberalization and privatization in Southeast Asia. This suffered a serious contraction and often collapse in 1997, but recovered because of the massive recapitalization on, and restructuring of, the corporate economy after 1998. Share issuance data combined with data on flow of funds for corporations could be utilized to reveal both contagion effect in these equity markets and existing volatility. However, this volume does not engage in these details. Causes of market inefficiency, such as where there is a lack of correlation between earnings of a specific firm and its share price performance and dividend payments, too, is only occasionally investigated in depth. This is because the complexities of both institutions, the stock markets and corporations, mean any simplistic correlation could produce flawed results.

Hence, it is organizational features and ownership of corporations that are emphasized. Study of stock markets is used only as a background to this institutional analysis of the rise of the corporate economy. The stock markets in Southeast Asia are important but are located within an institutional analysis of the political economy and legal environment prevailing in the region.

Another important focus is on financial institutions and, in particular, the background to the phenomenon of a volatile growth in finance since the 1960s. A critical part of this is concerned with the patterns of financial growth, attitudes to risk, and overall corporate governance procedures. Here, the volatile growth in banking in Indonesia is contrasted with Singapore, where the regional presence of the Development Bank of Singapore (DBS), absorbing majority stakes in Thai and Indonesian banks after 1997, is proof of the diverse investment and growth strategies and differing success of banking in the region.

This is captured in the fundamental differences between Malaysian banking and that of Indonesia. Only financial liberalization and privatization created the conditions for a greater convergence towards a form of 'mixed' banking in Malaysia. This analysis demonstrates two crucial differences with Indonesia. First, state banks were dominant in Malaysia, even into the 1990s. Second, private banks were not always part of a conglomerate. However, with privatization from 1989, there was a rising trend in this confluence of financial and non-financial activities, within large business groups in Malaysia. These were largely through acquisitions of banks. Chapter 5 also introduces a global dimension, where banks mount global moves, first within Southeast Asia and later outside. Much of this global strategy is derived from their financial diversification into investment banking as well as an increase in their stock market activities.

On the theoretical level, models of economic behaviour exhibited by the Singapore corporations and banks verge on a distinct form of state managerial capitalism. This dominance of the Singapore state, associated with intensive activity both at home and abroad is quite distinct from that in the rest of Southeast Asia. Malaysia, Indonesia and Thailand revealed distinct patterns of government–business relations, that were shaped by the larger institutional environment in which the capitalists operated. The pervasiveness of cronyism in business contracts, decision-making, the interpenetration of bureaucrats, politicians and military represented on company boards and holding managerial responsibilities, are complex and different in each of these countries. The historical developments, particularly since the 1950s, determine the sources of this influence. The reform of this cronyism after 1997 involved independent audits, reduction of interlocking ties between firms, reform of state subsidies and preferential treatment, improvement in the laws on insolvency and bankruptcy, all pushing the corporations towards a more regulated, market economy.

The conclusion will provide a theoretical analysis of the empirical data presented on each individual country study. It is this diversity of the economies of Southeast Asia that the study endorses while addressing the similarities in the patterns of corporate and financial evolution from 1950 to 2005. While surveying this diversity and considering common features, one naturally is confronted with the text's overriding concern: are Southeast Asia's institutions different from those in East Asia? The Southeast Asian conglomerates are constantly compared to the *chaebols*, the Japanese *keiretsu* and Taiwan's corporations.

Another nagging problem here is, why has this study neglected the small and medium enterprises? It is beyond the scope of this volume to assess the advantages and disadvantages of small and medium enterprises (SMEs) in reforming the competitive structure of the corporate economy. It is abundantly clear that large corporations were shaping the rapid economic growth of the region, but were distorting market structure, conduct and performance and engaging in collusive or anti-competitive behaviour. In a Schumpeterian sense, they have not driven out competition through efficiency, but become concentrated because of both political and economic advantages.[3]

SMEs in industrial clusters could have provided competition through low labour costs, their inter-linkages with large conglomerates compensating for the latter's volatile growth. Briefly, the historical and institutional circumstances in Southeast Asia do not augur well for such coordinated growth. First, SMEs have been supported by governments as part of a long-run policy to stimulate entrepreneurship, reduce poverty, achieve ethnic economic parity and diversify corporate ownership. However, the institutional structures of finance, human resource management, including education, training and skills as well as marketing support, were ad hoc and fragmented. SMEs faced serious hurdles in upgrading and becoming competitive. They were thus prone to takeover by large domestic and foreign enterprises, so many were easily displaced.

Second, Southeast Asia lacked the Taiwanese networked industrial capitalism where SMEs' supply networks were linked by trust and partial ownership. SMEs had been encouraged by a nationalist government paranoid over political security. SMEs in Taiwan moved from food, clothing, textiles, in import substitution industrialization (ISI) of the 1950s, to technological and capital-intensive, export-oriented production in the 1970s, where with increased international competition they had to restructure and focus on expansion into China. In the 1950s–1980s the SMEs were sustained by the US and Japan as the main anchor, providing capital, R&D and market opportunities. From the 1990s, expansion into China provides the main anchor.

The Japanese *keiretsu* system, which had possessed such loyal networks of SMEs, also confronted corruption and deteriorating economic circumstances after the economic liberalization of the 1990s. Their SMEs were in niche sectors and thus faced difficulties in confronting the need for new forms of foreign processing units for automotive and other industrial components manufacturers.

However, the major reason for neglecting SMEs in Southeast Asia is the overwhelming difficulties in carrying out research on them. It is even difficult to present precisely accurate statistics on SMEs, because of confusion over classification. Exact output figures, particularly for exports, are not easily deduced. Second, there is too much reliance on government industrial statistics which inflate the impact of SMEs. Hence, the fairly ludicrous estimates put forward by Asri Abdullah, that in Malaysia between 1975 and 2000, SMEs accounted for 97 per cent of total establishments in manufacturing and contributed to 80 per cent of total exports.[4]

Asri Abdullah does provide more realistic estimates later. In 1999 in Malaysia, SMEs in the manufacturing sector constituted 3–14 per cent; their concentration is in electrical products at 28 per cent.[5] Here, they were frequently linked to foreign multinationals producing in Southeast Asia. However, with economic liberalization from 1989, they faced serious competition from the relocation of the foreign subsidiaries of these foreign multinationals into Southeast Asia. These foreign subsidiaries were better equipped in R&D, finance, long-term contracts and market access. In 1996, domestic SMEs' share of total exports in Indonesia was 10 per cent, in Thailand 10 per cent, Malaysia 15 per cent, Singapore 16 per cent, and Taiwan 56 per cent.[6] Finally, the high rate of failure or displacement among SMEs in Southeast Asia makes it difficult to trace long-term, linear growth. They had to cope with the erratic, changing investment plans of the East Asian and Western multinationals in this high-growth period. SMEs in agricultural processing rise according to seasonal needs and are therefore easily neglected. We need serious anthropological research to appraise the contribution of SMEs to the corporate economy.

Theoretical approaches

The theoretical conclusions are clear from each of the chapters. An important question in corporate governance is corporate control. In Southeast Asia, concentrated ownership, where the majority of listed firms are controlled by a single shareholder, meant the separation of management and ownership is rare. A second theoretical contribution is that conglomerates held highly concentrated market power. This challenges the view that economies of scope were providing negative returns. The Southeast Asian experience shows that a distinction must be made between related and unrelated diversification. Singapore firms followed a given diversification strategy that built on core strengths, while the Indonesian firms followed an unrelated diversification strategy that increased risks. Third, privatization of state-owned corporations meant the transfer of state monopolies to private entrepreneurs, where such economic diversification was occurring that was unsustainable during the 1997 crisis. The case study of Renong is a clear example of such crony capitalism, distinguished by economic diversification and rapid technologically induced industrialization, that was crumbling in the battering unleashed by the financial crisis of 1997. This book thus attempts a detailed micro-level analysis, chronologically balanced, thematically introduced, both in terms of regions, as well as including the major theoretical debates on financial history and economics.

Historiography

The existing literature on corporations in Southeast Asia has not focused on detailed micro-level analysis. Even articles and reports in financial and business journals on the region's corporations have focused on the overall structure of growth rather than on the institutions shaping their growth and performance. The work of IMF and World Bank economists has concentrated on the macro-economic data.[7] Reports of the IMF and World Bank published in the *Journal of Financial Economics* are empirically weak; models of econometric analysis of corporations are not supported by micro-level data, and analysis. They are also seriously deficient in historical understanding besides revealing a stark ignorance of Southeast Asian economic developments. This book takes the debates on corporations to the level of detailed company analysis and appraisal, and how this assists our understanding of the institutional changes occurring in Southeast Asia. It employs methodologies of business history and economic history.

Other work on Southeast Asian corporations, such as that of Robison, Jomo, Gomez, Hutchcroft, Yoshihara and Ruth McVey are excellent studies in political economy focusing principally on business–state relations.[8] There is, in addition, considerable work on Chinese business and networks, mesmerized by the Hofstede approach.[9] There are, however, significant exceptions to this, including those of Wang Gungwu and Akira Suehiro.[10] There are also some excellent articles on corporate growth in Indonesia by Yuri Sato.[11] However, there is no single comprehensive analysis of the rise of the corporate economy in Southeast Asia that provides a synthesis of intra-regional, intra-periodic study. This book attempts to fill this critical vacuum.

A comment on the statistics

The data series used were both from Bloomberg and Datastream. In addition, I have used individual company reports, which included annual reports, balance sheets, profit and loss accounts, directors' reports as well as those of stockbrokers and investment bankers' analysis of these companies. Cross-checking of these diverse sources was used to correct any visible discrepancies. I have also had access to the archives of HSBC and Standard Chartered, Citicorp, Mercantile Bank and the Oversea-Chinese Banking Corporation (OCBC).

The reports of the Asian Development Bank (ADB) provided another excellent source. These scholars were not only regional specialists but also had access to skilled research assistants in the region. Sadly, the papers prepared for the IMF and World Bank lacked this empirical rigour.

I also took into account differences in the way different countries gathered and presented data, so reliability was affected. Surprisingly, Indonesia presented the most cogent, well-prepared data series, from the Ministry of Finance, Ministry of Commerce and Industry, from Bank Indonesia and Bappenas.

This was in striking contrast to Singapore, Malaysia and the Philippines. Reports here were either highly sanitized or inadequate. In addition, there were difficulties in accessing sources from the Malaysian Ministries of Finance and that of Commerce and Industry and Bank Negara, except for those publications destined for public consumption. The data from the Stock Exchange of Thailand and the different ministries provided substantial data, though only for a limited number of years.

2 Indonesian conglomerates

Ownership, concentration, crisis and restructuring

There is a wide secondary literature that is relevant to the question of industrial concentration and competition in Indonesia. Hal Hill, *Indonesia's Industrial Transformation*, Singapore: ISEAS, 1997, and Kelly Bird, 'Concentration in Indonesian manufacturing, 1975–93', *Bulletin of Indonesian Economic Studies*, 35, 1, 1999, pp. 43–73, are prominent here. These concentrate essentially on macro-economic issues that explain the levels of concentration in industrial sectors, while Stijn Claessens *et al.*, 'The separation of ownership and control in East Asian corporations', *Journal of Financial Economics*, 58, 2000, pp. 81–112, and *East Asian Corporations: Heroes or Villains?*, World Bank Discussion Paper, 409, attempt an analysis of the corporate economy in general and comparisons across the whole of Asia, obscuring some of the complexities and intricate variations persisting among the different corporations in the Asia-Pacific region. While the macro-economic factors and the comparisons in the above literature are important in giving a context to the history of industrial and corporate growth and concentration, it is only by using a number of corporate case studies in Indonesia, in various economic sectors, a micro-economic study of business groups which allows a much sharper level of analysis of this concentration and offers a more precise view of resource misallocation and competitive efficiency. A study of the micro-economic changes within Indonesian corporations exposes the deeper, institutional and financial growth, making possible an evaluation of the relative contribution of different influences and institutions attracting and utilizing state, private, domestic and foreign capital to achieve the high levels of concentration visible in the two decades since 1979. Kelly Bird and Hal Hill demonstrate how this concentration is further reinforced through pricing and distribution arrangements, assisted by the frenzy of mergers and acquisitions unleashed by the limited privatization programme of state-owned enterprises (SOEs) since the late 1980s.[1] What I argue is that only through detailed corporate case histories can one provide the context in which crucial trends in concentration of ownership and monopolies are evolving, contributing to the volatility of 1997.

This chapter therefore seeks to analyse the patterns of this industrial power and competitiveness through a detailed examination of three large conglomerates in Indonesia, dominant in different industrial sectors. The Salim Group's dominance in cement and food manufacturing, Sinar Mas in pulp and paper, and Texmaco in textiles, provide important clues to industrial concentration at home that nurtures elevated ambitions to move abroad and reveals the weaknesses of such a pincer movement. The choice of these conglomerates is partly influenced by their different ethnic backgrounds. Salim and Sinar Mas Groups, being ethnic Chinese, move into Singapore and China with ease, and carve out niches in their pivotal specialisms, in food and pulp and paper respectively.

This chapter traces the crucial changes in ownership and concentration that have occurred since the 1980s, and the restructuring after the crisis of 1997. The focus is on the governance structure of these family-dominated conglomerates; how banks and capital markets were exploited by these large family shareholders who also occupied top management positions in their firms. Here, the role of external capital inflows is analysed in conjunction with the argument that the family-dominated ownership structure, their preference for debt-driven growth, and the prevailing weak corporate governance were implicated in the crisis of 1997 and rendered restructuring difficult. The final section grapples with the issue of corporate reform and restructuring. Was restructuring little more than the rescheduling of debt? Did the restructuring increase the role of foreign equity and ownership? The impact of the restructuring and emergence of foreign ownership on corporate performance and corporate governance is only partially attempted in the final section, since the restructuring was only completed by 2003–5.

Ownership and concentration

Conglomerates in Indonesia are frequently controlled by a single family, with ownership concentrated in the hands of the founding patriarch and sons, or a subsidiary or investment holding company within the conglomerate (see Table 2.1).[2] The conglomerates used multiple holding companies to sustain this concentrated family ownership and control, fortified through solid control by family members, friends and politicians on the Board of Commissioners and Board of Directors. The cross-shareholding held by subsidiaries in the group was high, while the public share was limited. The use of government and institutional shareholders facilitated easy access to outside capital, and preserved this monopolistic strategy of growth. In addition, different Chinese and *pribumi* elite families held stock in each others' conglomerates. Moreover, high-profile politicians and their families held shareholdings and directorships in these corporations. Such concentration was further nurtured by their access to privileges in export-import licences, monopolies in marketing and distribution of essential commodities, including rice, cooking oil, clove cigarettes and timber, as well as government contracts in transport, petroleum, telecommunications, automobiles and media.

Table 2.1 Ownership concentration of publicly listed companies, 1993–7

Shareholder rank	*1993*	*1994*	*1995*	*1996*	*1997*	*Average*
Largest	50.5	48.1	47.9	48.5	48.2	48.6
Second largest	16.6	13.7	14.1	12.0	11.6	13.6
Third largest	3.0	3.9	4.0	4.2	4.4	3.9
Fourth largest	2.1	2.0	1.9	1.8	2.1	2.0
Fifth largest	0.5	0.6	0.8	1.0	1.2	0.8
Total	72.7	68.3	68.7	67.5	67.5	68.9

Source: *The Indonesian Capital Market Directory*, 1990–2000

Privatization, however limited, of SOEs and banks, intensified the concentration within Chinese and select *pribumi* entrepreneurs.[3] The mergers and acquisitions mania of the rapid growth phase of the 1980s and 1990s encouraged further concentration. Patron-client clusters centred around Soeharto and his cronies. Lucrative projects went to those with political and military connections, all sustained by soft loans from the state and foreign investors. Concentration within Indonesian corporate and financial institutions is thus extremely pervasive. Sixteen large family-owned conglomerates with several banks within them possessed 70 per cent of total equity on the Jakarta Stock Exchange between 1989 and 1993.[4] In 1995, 17 per cent of the total value of listed corporate assets could be traced to a single family, Salim.[5] The controlling family exploited the rents associated with privatization, the high rates of protection in certain industries, and capital abundance in the 1990s to launch global initiatives in Singapore, Hong Kong, China and the US. Financial liberalization from 1989 further strengthened these conglomerates while weakening state control over investment decisions and even money-laundering activities. On the other hand, the Indonesian government's optimism in such rapid growth encouraged riskier and more monopolistic, non-competitive participation. Western investment houses, too, applauded such growth and provided optimistic reports that enabled these conglomerates to list free-standing firms in Singapore, Hong Kong, China and the US, and issue high-value corporate bonds. Thus, the five components of this growth: excessive diversification, vertical and horizontal integration and economic concentration, close cooperation with government and business elites in Indonesia, Hong Kong and China, built highly leveraged global conglomerates through capital abundance, in high-risk sectors such as timber, with no effective corporate governance.

These corporate empires often had a family bank. Bank Central Asia (BCA), the largest private commercial bank in Indonesia, formed the core bank in the Salim Group.[6] It was a major recipient of state revenues, foreign aid and foreign direct and portfolio investments, and had access to offshore banks as well as to diverse and innovative sources of finance such as derivatives. This capital abundance intensified corporate economic concentration.

Large syndicated loans arranged through foreign banks not only meant the doubling of external debt between 1990 and 1997 but also assisted monopolistic growth. Industrial concentration exhibited by these conglomerates corresponded to such excessive borrowing.

A further feature of concentration is the high percentage of loans to single individuals or to select groups of conglomerates, the majority of them Chinese. There was also distribution of loans to related firms. When Bank Summa failed in 1992, 55 per cent of its loans were to subsidiaries in the P. T. Astra Group.[7] In June 1995, six banks had made loans to related firms that constituted more than 200 per cent of the banks' own capital, there were 23 banks for whom the ratio was over 100 per cent, and 42 banks had loans to linked companies exceeding 50 per cent of total loans.[8] Hence, almost half of total private banks' debt in 1995 was consumed by loans to their own firms. Such in-house lending introduced prospects for reckless growth and creation of monopolistic advantages.

Such capital concentration also occurred through diversification of financial subsidiaries within their bank: the creation of finance houses, leasing and factoring subsidiaries and insurance companies accelerated in the 1990s. Lippo Group had a securities firm that invested in its own firms, even after being chastised by Bank Indonesia for such malpractice.[9]

Rapid growth and concentration were assisted by foreign partners. Financial liberalization since 1988–9 eased the restrictions on foreign participation in Indonesian conglomerates. Private commercial borrowing, and foreign direct investment (FDI) and portfolio investment became important components of Indonesia's capital account between 1987 and 1996. Private capital rose from US$1,548 million in 1987 to US$11,510 million in 1996: commercial borrowing rose from US$38 million in 1987 to US$3,243 million in 1995.[10] Portfolio investment rose from US$372 million in 1989 to US$1,648 million in 1996. Capital account in total rose from US$3,652 million in 1987 to US$10,988 million in 1996.[11] In 1998, the external debt of private corporations was US$66.8 billion, while their banks held another US$6.5 billion, exceeding that held by public (SOE) corporations and banks of US$68.6 billion.[12]

Finally, this capital and ownership concentration was induced by the growth of the Jakarta stock market. The ability to raise capital both from the state and from domestic and foreign sources on the Jakarta Stock Exchange was exploited without diluting family ownership. The Jakarta Stock Exchange witnessed dramatic expansion in market capitalization, from US$8 billion in 1990 to US$91 billion in 1996, before shrinking to US$29 billion in 1997.[13] An Indonesian government and IMF rescue package in 1999 bolstered the stock exchange with US$64 billion but declined to US$25 billion in 2001. The increase in foreign investors on the Jakarta Stock Exchange rose from 10 per cent of total value in 1989 to 30 per cent in 1993, and, by 1997, the real value of foreign investment on the Jakarta Stock Exchange was 50 per cent, a part of it jointly owned with local conglomerates.[14] Among Asian investors in Indonesia, Japan possessed the highest value between 1968 and 1996, followed by Singapore, then Hong Kong, Taiwan and South Korea. The value of American and European investment in this period accounted for only a third of the total value of investments from Asia. After the 1997 crisis, the top ten investors, in 1999, were Japan, Singapore, Malaysia, Taiwan and Australia, followed by Europe and the US.[15] The popular projects remained the food industry, chemicals and pharmaceuticals, metals, electronics, transport, and pulp and paper. There were dramatic declines in investment between 1997 and 2003.

Another critical source for conglomerate growth was through country and mutual funds. By 1990 there were 16 country funds available for Indonesia.[16] These were frequently directed by the state to its preferred private Chinese capitalists and *pribumi* elite. This increased participation in the capital market sector led to risky diversification in the financial portfolio of these conglomerates. Such highly diverse forms of corporate finance and the accompanying growth of plural financial institutions increased their concentrated growth and volatility after 1989. However, bank loans rather than equity finance continued to be more important for the conglomerates. Banks were central to the growth and concentration of financial capital. In 1990, 84 per cent of the total assets of financial institutions were vested in the commercial banking sector, with the remaining 16 per cent located in investment banks and securities firms.[17] Each conglomerate had a dense pattern of interlocks with state institutions, networks overseas, and domestic investors, intensifying their financial power and influence. Mergers and acquisitions rampant after 1988 added to this cohesion and concentration, with decreasing levels of competition. Indonesian capitalists, euphoric over prophesies of accelerated economic growth in Indonesia circulated by the World Bank and Western investment banks, now sought to go global in the US, Australia, Singapore, Hong Kong and China. The case studies of Salim and Sinar Mas provide clear evidence of these developments.

Foreign capital inflows: corporate growth, concentration and restructuring

As noted earlier, a critical element in the expansion of Indonesian capitalism were the large foreign capital surges, sustaining a boom in their growth, diversification and concentration in capital-intensive sectors. This also provided them with the resources for globalization, creating commodity firms, banks, finance houses and insurance groups in Hong Kong, South-East Asia, China and the US in the 1990s.

FDI into Indonesia, relative to gross domestic product (GDP), rose in the 1990s; in particular, there was an impressive acceleration between 1993 and 1996. A major segment of this increase was private portfolio capital, attracted by higher interest rates in Asia compared to Europe and the US. FDI inflows into Indonesia rose from US$8,751 million in 1990 to US$23,724 million in 1994, then doubled in 1995 but fell in 1997 to US$33,833 million.[18] Portfolio capital rose in 1993, continued to rise again in 1995 and 1996, before collapsing in 1997.[19] There was a slight recovery in foreign investment in 2000, but it was only half that of 1997, and by 2003 it was less than one sixth of the total foreign investment of 1997. However, the number of projects in which foreign capital was involved was rising. In 1997, it was involved in 322 projects; this rose to 615 in 2000, and although it fell to 312 in 2003, it was still a higher proportion to that of new domestic projects.[20] This clearly demonstrates the role of foreign licensees and partners in Indonesia's corporate recovery.

Lending by foreign banks experienced a major rise between 1990 and 1991, with a slight contraction in 1992, followed by an accentuated fall in 1993, before rising in 1994, 1995 and 1996. Volatile inflows were in short-term bank lending. In June 1997, Indonesia held US$58,726 million in cross-border bank lending, of which half were short term (up to a year). The majority of the loans in June 1997 were from Japanese banks (39 per cent), followed by Europeans (38 per cent) and the US (8 per cent).[21] In the years 1991–6, the credit/GDP ratio grew at 5 per cent per annum in Indonesia, and in 1996 was 0.5 per cent, indicating financial vulnerability, but not to a serious degree. What was serious was the cronyistic guaranteed nature of the credit and the moral hazard surrounding this.

This level of bank lending, together with increases in portfolio investment and FDI led to unstable increases in corporate debt nominated in US dollars. Thus, the boom in bank lending in the mid-1990s resulted in serious distortions in growth and the emergence of monopolies. The distortions were made worse by the fact that during this period, asset prices on the stock market and in real estate were falling.

Equity participation by foreigners on the Jakarta Stock Exchange had been slow but accelerated in the early 1990s. In the 1990s, joint-ventures were sought in the new industries of telecommunications and electronics. The involvement of foreigners was high in 1993 (57 per cent) but dropped to 36 per cent in 1999 and 25 per cent in 2000.[22] This mirrored the decline in foreign capital investment. Despite the lifting of restrictions on foreign participation on the Jakarta Stock Exchange in 1999, local investors accounted for 65 per cent of trading volume, in contrast to 1995 when foreign investors accounted for a higher value of investment than local investors.[23]

Foreign equity has been a critical source of funds for corporate restructuring since 1999. While foreign investors were reluctant to invest in Indonesian banks with clear evidence of corruption, as in the Bank Bali episode, they were attracted to resource and capital-intensive sectors, such as petroleum, cement, timber, telecommunications and chemicals. FDI, being attracted to more profitable sectors, can in effect create a two-tier system of corporate structure and monopolistic growth. Product differentiation and specialization in technologically sophisticated industries with financial and technical advantages can lead to displacement of local firms, producing even greater concentration over time and new forms of monopoly. (See the case study of Indofood Sukses Makmur discussed on pp. 21–6.)

Cycle and Carriage of Malaysia–Singapore acquired a controlling stake of 38.4 per cent equity in Astra International in 2000. Toyota Motor Corporation possessed a further holding of 7.56 per cent. The Government of Singapore Investment Corporation, Daihatsu Motor Corporation and Maruberu held further shares. Changes in the management, with John Slack and Kour Nam Tiang being appointed directors, underlined this transition to professional foreign managers and with improved prospects for better corporate governance and corporate social responsibility. What is dramatic is that R&D sectors of the Indonesian corporations are passing over to foreign multinationals. Astra retained its dealerships and distribution networks while the responsibility for production of automobiles was vested in foreign stakeholders. This was accompanied by rapid divestment of loss-making units and successful debt restructuring. The following analysis of Astra International and United Tractors, its subsidiary, reveal the impact of these changes between 1998 and 2002. The diverse modes of FDI entry between 1997 and 2003 are illustrated in the two corporate case studies of the Salim Group and Sinar Mas.

The different modes of entry included acquisition of newly issued shares, acquisition of outstanding shares, long-term loans, mergers and acquisitions, or joint-ventures. Another channel was to target corporations facing severe distress and possible bankruptcy. Cross-border acquisitions became significant new channels for FDI inflows after 1997. A plethora of opportunities for acquisition emerged as distressed conglomerates sold off subsidiaries to reduce their gearing problems.

Rescue funds flowed in from Japanese, Singaporean, Chinese, Dutch and German investors to buy out existing Indonesian partners in joint-venture enterprises, or expand their existing stake, or acquire entire firms. Thus, Heidelberger Zement acquired 61.7 per cent equity in Indocement.[24] Others achieved horizontal mergers through the purchase of marketing subsidiaries from these Indonesian conglomerates. Some even purchased a stake through interlocking equity and directorships as Cycle and Carriage, an automotive group from Singapore did in the restructuring of Astra International and its subsidiaries.[25] Singapore and Malaysia targeted the Indonesian government's investment policies in Riau and Batam to establish food processing companies as well as commodity enterprises. Foreign investors also acquired assets in SOEs in telecommunications, power, petroleum and steel, often displacing Indonesian private capitalists. The acquisition of these corporate assets by foreign buyers means not only deconcentration but also improved corporate governance. But these are occurring in only a minority of listed corporations. Hence the extent of deconcentration is limited in overall volume and impact. On the obverse side, there is the increased prospect of concentrated holdings by foreign stakeholders themselves in individual Indonesian corporations.

The second critical issue in this role of capital in corporate restructuring is the level of private capital outflows between 1997 and 2000. It approximated US$11,828 million in 1997/98, US$9,643 million in 1998/99 and US$8,923 million in 1999/2000.[26] Some of this outflow was suspected to be capital flows mediated by large Indonesian conglomerates, seeking new bases for production and marketing in Myanmar, China, Vietnam, Singapore and the US. The increased global activities of Tirtamas Group, Salim, and Sinar Mas while facing economic distress at home confirms this trend. Tirtamas emerged as a powerful player in Myanmar in 1999, investing in cement, petroleum and timber, while defaulting on loans in Jakarta.[27] The case studies of Salim and Sinar Mas explain further this controversy.

The Salim Group: ownership, concentration and restructuring

The following account of the Salim Group traces its phenomenal growth in the 1980s and 1990s, the devastating impact of the 1997 financial crisis, and the restructuring imposed by the Indonesian government. The Salim Corporation maintained vast industrial and commercial interests in Indonesia and abroad through extensive cross-ownership and inter-relations between industrial firms and their bank, BCA, and First Pacific Holdings (FPH), which was an investment company registered in Hong Kong. In this concentration of financial and industrial power, they were assisted by their close links to Soeharto. Financial liberalization since the late 1980s had led to increased relations with foreign multinationals and foreign capital. Having established firms in government-assisted industries such as food and cement with generous, subsidized credit from state banks, these groups participated in similar industries in Singapore, Taiwan and China. The Salim Group moved into manufacturing and banking in Hong Kong, China, the Netherlands and the US. Privileged access to finance from both domestic and external sources prepared the way for the emergence of concentrated, oligopolistic business in flour-milling, noodles manufacture, cloves, cement, steel and telecommunications in Indonesia and abroad. Its holding company, FPH, had divisions in property (F. P. Davies), telecommunications (Pacific Link, Smart Communications and Indolink), marketing (Hagemeyer, Berli Jucker, Metro Pacific), and finance (Hibernia Bank San Francisco, United Savings Bank California, First Pacific Bank in Hong Kong, Crocker National Bank, and Wells Fargo Bank).[28]

In Indonesia, the Salim Group had diversified through acquisitions, absorbing a whole range of industrial projects through government contracts and procurement policies in essential goods such as flour, cement, steel, tyres and cord (rope). There was horizontal and vertical integration of production and manufacturing, and partnerships with SOEs and joint-ventures with foreign multinationals to maintain this oligopolistic grip in these industrial sectors. This was reflected in corporate performance. Telecommunications, which accounted for 1.8 per cent of Salim's total profits in 1989, had by

1992 risen to 26.3 per cent.[29] The property sector too grew rapidly, with a contribution of 11.2 per cent of net profits in 1989 rising to 19.6 per cent in 1993.[30] Production, marketing and distribution, which accounted for 59.8 per cent in 1989, fell to 48.5 per cent in 1993.[31]

The core family, Liem Soei Liong, his second and third sons, Antony and Andree, dominated the Board of Commissioners and Board of Directors of all the firms in the group (400 in 1996). The ownership and management of FPH was more diffuse, with Manuel Panglinan assuming control, and in 1993 Antony Salim and Indonesian friends departed from that Board.

The explosive growth in banking and finance, with BCA emerging as the largest private commercial bank in Indonesia, was reflected in the corporation's volatility in profitability in the financial sector. Banking, which contributed 10 per cent of total profits in 1975, rose to 27.2 per cent in 1989, but declined to 13.5 per cent in 1991, and only rose to 15.6 per cent in 1993.[32] A partial explanation for this is that the corporation was undertaking risky growth at home and abroad. The result was the spectacular failure of the group in 1997, when Indofood Sukses Makmur faced debts of US$1 billion, Salim Group in Indonesia held debts of US$5 billion, and FPH revealed debts of US$3 billion.[33]

The extensive cross-ownership and the inter-relations between the industrial subsidiaries and banks produced confusion in the monitoring of debt. In this growth both in Indonesia and abroad, financial risk was underestimated. The collapse of the group in 1997 is a direct consequence of this reckless growth in the 1990s. The focus here is how did this oligopolistic growth occur, and what was its impact on corporate performance, 1993–7. The incentives for corporate restructuring of Salim revolved around rehabilitation rather than liquidation, while the proper target of the new competition policy has been to rid the economy of formal and informal barriers to entry and exit, and the extensive vertical and horizontal linkages utilized by corporations to grow and limit competition.

The Salim Group is examined as part of the first tier in restructuring when the Indonesian Bank Restructuring Agency (IBRA) identified the corporation as suitable for reorganization and its assets and core subsidiaries would be attractive for foreign investors. This type of restructuring involved the creation of a new holding company with equity jointly held by IBRA and the Salim Group. The restructuring included the sale of assets to domestic and foreign bidders, issuance of new equity, debt for equity swaps, and streamlining of activities through the divestment of subsidiaries not related to core specialisms, as well as strategies to reduce excess debt.

Growth of concentration

I will now attempt, through a detailed analysis of Indocement and Indofood Sukses Makmur, to identify the high levels of concentration achieved by Indocement in the cement industry and Indofood in food manufacturing. This concentration analysis will be critical to an evaluation of the competitiveness of Salim in certain industrial sectors. The policy interests in these debates on concentration and competition are clear. Both sustain an understanding of how IBRA's strategies between 1999 and 2003 impacted on industrial and corporate restructuring, and the problems in introducing bold reforms in transparency and corporate governance.

The cement industry in Indonesia was dominated by three firms: Indocement (Salim), Semen Cibinong (Tirtamas Group) and Semen Gresik (state owned). Indocement is the second largest domestic producer, with its main markets in Jakarta and West Java. There was a phase of massive expansion in production by the three firms, almost doubling output between 1995 and 1996, and this growth continued into 1999. In 2000, Indocement accounted for 33.8 per cent of total Indonesian production, Semen Gresik 36 per cent, and Cibinong 20.6 per cent.[34] In the same year, the distribution of market share was: Indocement holding 30 per cent of the domestic market, Semen Gresik 45 per cent and Semen Cibinong 14 per cent.[35] Smaller producers were left with tiny pickings – less than a few per cent. These market shares had held since 1989.

Indocement concentrated on the export market and, after the 1997 crisis, increased its export competitiveness as a result of low production costs and lower rupiah values. It exported to South Asia, the Middle East and Africa. Excess capacity in the domestic market meant that prices were low, although an initial doubling of domestic prices occurred just after 1997.

Corporate performance

Indocement's growth was facilitated by generous finance. Since 1988, credit from a consortium of local banks, including BCA, Bank Bumi Daya and Bank Pembangunan Indonesia, sustained its rapid growth. Its foreign loans were secured from European and Japanese banks based in Singapore. Indocement recorded positive net profits between 1993 and 1996, but profits fell in 1997, underwent a brief recovery in 1998 and declined in 1999–2001 (see Table 2.2). Its return on equity was high in 1993, and after this brief spell of positive performance, it declined from 1994 to 1998, made another brief recovery in 1999 but declined again in 2000, followed by another negative return in 2001. Liquidity ratios have seen an increase between 1993 and 1995, but subsequently deteriorated between 1996 and 1998, experienced a moderate, quick recovery in 2000 but fell after 2001, and rose slightly in 2002. The gearing ratios were high since 1993. In 2000 it was particularly high, at 87 per cent.

The 1997 crisis bequeathed to the firm a debt of Rp4.5 trillion (US$1 billion). As part of the debt restructuring, an initial transfer of equity from Indocement to the holding company Holdiko Perkarsa and IBRA occurred. Salim, who had held 62 per cent equity in Indocement, now pledged 19 per cent to IBRA and the government already possessed a further 25 per cent.

Table 2.2 Key financial ratios of Indocement

Key ratios	*1993*	*1994*	*1995*	*1996*	*1997*	*1998*	*1999*	*2000*	*2001*	*2002*
Profitability										
ROE (after tax) (%)	52.16	30.48	18.58	27.59	–42.27	–753.76	46.49	–78.46	–2.28	27.34
EBIT margin (%)	23.53	n/a	n/a	24.98	–16.28	–45.60	53.31	–30.47	11.04	44.63
EBITDA margin (%)	30.27	n/a	n/a	30.70	–5.49	–26.92	62.02	–20.06	22.92	56.69
Operating profit margin (%)	24.34	26.28	26.13	26.62	33.72	27.48	21.09	28.82	19.46	23.55
Net profit margin (%)	10.81	10.86	12.07	12.91	–24.05	–66.23	29.76	–35.87	–1.83	26.37
Operating efficiency										
Asset turnover	0.57	0.61	0.48	0.55	0.24	0.17	0.18	0.21	0.29	0.34
Inventory turnover	8.77	31.49	6.69	7.36	6.17	3.50	3.79	4.36	4.17	4.51
Gearing										
Total equity/(long-term loans + equity)	0.26	0.42	0.45	0.37	0.18	1.00	0.99	0.10	0.25	0.35
Total assets/total liabilities	1.17	1.46	1.68	1.60	1.21	1.06	1.17	1.11	1.30	1.50
Liquidity										
Liquidity ratio (current assets/ current liabilities)	0.70	1.15	2.07	1.74	0.90	0.15	0.23	3.43	2.12	2.82
Quick ratio ((CA-inventories)/CL)	0.42	1.04	1.65	1.31	0.74	0.10	0.18	1.94	0.97	1.45
Cash ratio ((cash + short-term inv.)/CL)	0.04	0.24	1.00	0.75	0.41	0.03	0.12	0.87	0.39	0.73
Inventory working capital ratio (sales/ave working cap.)	–0.92	–1.02	0.71	0.47	0.60	–0.12	–0.07	–0.20	0.96	0.89

Table 2.2 (continued)

Key ratios	*1993*	*1994*	*1995*	*1996*	*1997*	*1998*	*1999*	*2000*	*2001*	*2002*
Growth										
Total income (%)		17.23	16.35	8.35	–63.19	1.15	10.63	39.17	41.05	14.34
Profit before taxation (%)		36.8	15.3	32.7	–143.7	175.6	–171.3	–265.6	–91.5	–1,459.4
Profit after taxation (%)		17.7	29.4	15.9	–168.5	178.6	–149.7	–267.7	–92.8	–1,749.0
Total assets (%)		9.9	47.7	–4.9	–14.6	36.6	8.2	18.3	2.4	–3.9
Total liabilities (%)		–12.1	28.8	–0.2	13.3	55.5	–2.5	25.5	–12.9	–16.5
Equity growth (%)		101.5	112.3	–22.0	–55.3	–84.4	706.0	–0.6	146.9	37.8
Share related										
EPS (net) (RI)	93.15	109.42	140.80	163.15	–156.48	–436.02	216.79	–363.46	–19.11	282.80
Price (RI)	2,750.00	2,258.93	2,741.07	2,571.43	1,800.00	3,175.00	3,100.00	1,600.00	700.00	675.00
PER	29.52	20.64	19.47	15.76	–11.50	–7.28	14.30	–4.40	–36.63	2.39
BV/share (RI)	178.57	357.14	757.82	591.41	370.35	57.86	466.20	450.52	750.59	1,035.00
P/B ratio	15.40	6.33	3.62	4.35	4.86	54.87	6.65	3.55	0.93	0.65
Dividend/share (RI)	44.64	74.29	42.86	85.71	70.00	–	–	–	–	–
Dividend yield (%)	1.62	3.29	1.56	3.33	3.89	0.00	0.00	0.00	0.00	0.00
EV/EBITDA	13.40	n/a	n/a	9.00	–101.44	–35.48	12.32	–27.80	14.62	4.16

Note: The following abbreviations are used throughout the tables: BV = book value; CA = current assets; CL = current liabilities; EBIT = earnings before interest and taxation; EBITDA = earnings before interest, taxation, depreciation and amortization; EPS = earnings per share; EV = enterprise value; NPBT = net profit before tax; P/B = price to book; PER = price earnings ratio; RI = Rupiah Indonesia; ROAA = return on average assets; ROCE = return on capital employed; ROE = return on equity; ROI = return on investment.

Source: Indocement, Annual Reports, 1993–2002

As part of the corporate restructuring, Indocement divested its equity holding in Indofood of 50 per cent, focusing primarily on cement, property and a road toll company.[36] The third phase of restructuring was to find a foreign partner. Heidelberger Zement of Germany increased its stake in Indocement, absorbing a debt of US$150 million for shares in the corporation.[37] Heidelberger purchased the shares that had been transferred by Mekar Perkasa of Salim Group to IBRA and Holdiko Perkasa, Salim's new holding company. Heidelberger held 61.7 per cent. Marubeni, a joint-venture partner since 1991, also absorbed debts of Indocement for equity of 1.9 per cent. The family share was reduced to 13 per cent. The family also lost its position on the Board of Directors and Board of Commissioners. Their cronies, however, remained. Sudwikatmono, a cousin of Soeharto, and Ibrahim Risjad, a *primbumi* Achehnese friend, remained. The rest were now European professional managers.

Its competitor, Semen Gresik, which had concentrated on East Java, West Sumatra and Sulawesi, was able, through this regional diversification, to retain its competitive superiority to Indocement and Semen Cibinong. This SOE still sought a foreign partner in Cemex SA, a Mexican cement producer, selling 14 per cent equity, thereby reducing the government's share to 51 per cent.[38] In addition, Cemex acquired a further 11 per cent shareholding from the public but was restrained from a controlling stake in 2000 by opposition from the provincial government of West Sumatra. Gresik's growth from 36 per cent market share in 1996 to 45 per cent in 1999 was largely due to a decrease in Cibinong's output.[39] Gresik fared better because the bulk of its loans were in local currency. US dollar loans totalled US$250 million, 45 per cent hedged, and were sustained by a low-cost expansion in output. Gresik's turnover rose from Rp309 billion in 1994 to Rp2,315 billion in 1998. Net profit rose from Rp55 billion in 1994 to Rp222 billion in 1998. Return on assets (ROA) rose from 6.8 per cent in 1994 to 10.4 per cent in 1995, but fell to 9.5 per cent in 1998. Return on equity (ROE) increased from 7.8 per cent in 1994 to 10.7 per cent in 1995 but fell to 8.5 per cent in 1998.[40]

The third major cement producer, Cibinong (Tirtamas), held US$1 billion debt, and restructuring was halted by the alleged misuse of US$200 million in cash by Djojohadikusuma, the major shareholder.[41] The restructuring that was imposed by IBRA led to an increase in foreign investment of 36 per cent in 1999, while Tirtamas Majutama, the holding company of the Tirtamas Group, held 41.5 per cent; Holpac held 12.5 per cent, and local subscriptions amounted to 9.8 per cent. Tirtamas suffered net losses of Rp269 billion in 1997, and Rp2,329 billion in 1998.[42] Despite these higher losses in 1998, Tirtamas moved into Myanmar. Further losses of Rp665.6 billion were recorded in 1999. The majority of these were a direct result of foreign exchange losses. Their move into Myanmar reflects not only the lack of efficient networks outside Indonesia but also an entrenched cronyistic response to growth, whether in Indonesia or abroad. Myanmar is not a high-growth area in Asia. Rent-seeking ambitions, perhaps, dictate Tirtamas's move here.

The food industry

Indofood Sukses Makmur had been established by Salim in August 1974, merging with 18 related companies by 1990. In 1994 it was listed on the Jakarta Stock Exchange, and this marked the start of an unprecedented period of growth. It acquired Bogasari Flour Mills in 1995 and oil palm plantations and edible oils in 1997. It was in noodles manufacture, flour milling, edible oils and food distribution. It was one of the largest flour milling concerns in the world, and in noodles manufacture it dominated the market in Indonesia, securing 80 per cent of the total noodles market in 1996.[43] Its flour milling subsidiary, Bogasari, received grain from BULOG (the state marketing board) at fixed prices, and it was disbanded only in early 1999, as part of the new competitive, anti-monopolies policy. Bogasari supplied 80 per cent of Indonesian needs: Indofood alone absorbed 18 per cent of that. Indofood's operations were far flung, covering Java, Sumatra, Kalimantan and Sulawesi. It also had investments in Singapore and Riau.

The key financial ratios for Indofood reveal that 1997 marked a brief period of losses and recovery was swift. Equity growth in 1999 was through a stock split, increasing equity from 1,831.2 million shares to 9,156 million shares (see Table 2.3). This increase in Indofood equity marked the transfer of the majority holding to CAB Holdings from its affiliated company, Indocement. Indofood's positive performance even during and after the 1997 crisis was assisted first by its integrated organizational structure, possessing backward integration into manufacturing and forward into marketing. Such integration reduced transactions costs and provided secure cash flows that helped reduce its foreign exchange debt from US$910 million in December 1998 to US$705 million in December 1999. Its gearing improved to 141 per cent in December 1999 from 645 per cent in 1998.[44] Second, Indofood responded to competition from Western multinationals such as Unilever by segmenting the market, creating new brands to compete on low prices. Nestlé failed to gain a foothold in the domestic noodles market, which helped Indofood.

Third, Indofood sought expansion through acquisition of smaller producers, and acquired related food business assets of other corporations held by IBRA. Thus, despite the existence of foreign exchange losses of US$705 million in 2000, its growth strategy was maintained, and it sought finance through a five-year Rp1 trillion bond listed on the Surabaya Stock Exchange in July 2000. Part of this strategy in growth was through changes in shareholders. The Salim Group reduced its equity to 10 per cent, while First Pacific Hong Kong and CAB Holdings absorbed 40 per cent shareholding, and the state and public subscribed 49.8 per cent. In 2001, Chase Manhattan took over 12.6 per cent shareholding. These changes corresponded with managerial changes. Manuel Panglinan became president, while Antony Salim was reduced to one of the commissioners.

Table 2.3 Key financial ratios of Indofood Sukses Makmur

Key ratios	*1994*	*1995*	*1996*	*1997*	*1998*	*1999*	*2000*	*2001*	*2002*
Profitability									
ROE (after tax) (%)	19.81	22.21	21.10	–247.31	23.67	57.96	21.12	22.15	21.91
EBIT margin (%)	19.94	17.72	17.95	–19.96	10.94	21.92	12.14	11.90	12.47
EBITDA margin (%)	22.66	21.42	22.26	–15.92	13.92	24.40	14.53	14.13	14.67
Operating profit margin (%)	20.58	17.87	18.49	17.14	23.53	19.79	18.86	13.89	11.42
Net profit margin (%)	16.39	14.60	12.43	–24.01	1.70	12.08	5.09	5.39	4.87
Operating efficiency									
Asset turnover	0.94	0.56	0.67	0.63	0.83	1.09	1.01	1.13	1.08
Inventory turnover	10.18	6.07	8.74	7.84	7.40	8.56	6.44	6.85	6.00
Gearing									
Total equity/(long-term loans + equity)	0.94	0.47	0.48	0.09	0.10	0.49	0.40	0.61	0.39
Total assets/total liabilities	4.70	1.60	1.67	1.10	1.11	1.38	1.42	1.50	1.42
Liquidity									
Liquidity ratio (current assets/ current liabilities)	3.34	1.45	1.78	1.40	1.19	0.99	1.30	0.87	1.65
Quick ratio ((CA-inventories)/CL)	2.71	0.97	1.29	1.11	0.88	0.72	0.82	0.51	1.01
Cash ratio ((cash + short-term inv.)/CL)	1.01	0.51	0.83	0.64	0.53	0.45	0.39	0.16	0.40
Inventory working capital ratio (sales/ ave working cap.)	0.27	0.85	0.77	0.92	1.48	3.99	3.38	10.15	2.75

Table 2.3 (continued)

Key ratios	*1994*	*1995*	*1996*	*1997*	*1998*	*1999*	*2000*	*2001*	*2002*
Growth									
Turnover (%)		55.46	35.15	76.54	77.07	30.73	9.98	15.30	12.43
Profit before taxation (%)		13.9	28.2	–376.6	–151.3	271.4	–46.7	14.0	11.1
Profit after taxation (%)		38.5	15.0	–441.0	–112.5	828.7	–53.7	22.1	1.7
Total assets (%)		157.5	14.0	86.9	35.4	–0.4	18.0	3.4	17.5
Total liabilities (%)		654.9	9.6	183.2	34.4	–20.1	15.0	–2.3	23.7
Equity growth (%)		23.5	21.1	–70.9	31.0	279.3	27.1	16.4	2.8
Share related									
EPS (net) (RI)	33.73	37.71	43.38	–130.8	16.41	152.4	70.57	86.32	90.44
Price (RI)	815.04	1,036.46	885.71	360.00	810.00	1,750.00	775.00	625.00	600.00
PER	24.16	27.49	20.42	–2.75	49.36	11.48	10.98	7.24	6.63
BV/share (RI)	137.50	169.74	205.59	52.91	69.31	262.86	334.07	389.66	390.28
P/B ratio	5.93	6.11	4.31	6.80	11.69	6.66	2.32	1.60	1.54
Dividend/share (RI)	66.15	5.46	15.08	9.40	–	–	18.00	–	25.00
Dividend yield (%)	8.12	0.53	1.70	2.61	0.00	0.00	2.32	0.00	4.17
EV/EBITDA	21.37	22.19	13.64	–10.22	11.27	6.89	6.61	5.10	4.72

Source: Indofood Sukses Makmur, 1994–2002

The major pattern of restructuring endured by Salim was the significant scale of divestment of its core subsidiaries. In August 2000, it sold some of its shares in FPH, and by February 2001 it had discarded its remaining shareholding in FPH, recovering a total of US$77.5 million.[45] Subsequently, it sold its interests in oil-palm to Guthrie (Malaysia) for US$350 million, while its property interests were sold to Keppel Land of Singapore. Another subsidiary, Indocoal, was sold in April 2001 to Singapore's Banpu Minerals, and divested Sulfindo Corporation and its mosquito coil company to Reckett Bencheser for Rp610 million. By November 2001, Salim had sold all its interests in steel production and glass. Indocement was sold for US$43.8 million, while Bogasari Flour Mills was sold to an American commodity broker, ATS, for Rp225.3 billion, together with Rp165.9 million and US$5.7 million in debt equity swaps.[46]

These divestments hold important clues to ownership. First, many of these companies were sold to original shareholders, from whom Liem had acquired the firms during the phase of rapid growth in the late 1980s and early 1990s. Some were founding Dutch shareholders, as in the case of the sale of Indomilk in December 2000. A second distinct feature is the rise of Indonesian investment houses and fund managers as potential buyers of these firms. Indomobil Sukses, an automotive, engineering subsidiary, was sold to Trimegah, an Indonesian investment company.[47] In November 2000, Oleochemicals was taken over by Bhakti Investama, an Indonesian securities firm, for US$131 million.[48] The same firm bought Indomaret, a property concern, for Rp162 billion.[49] The media firm Indosair was sold to TDM Asset management for Rp755 billion in January 2001.[50] Two bankers, Djaja Mulia and Irwan Dinata, owned this asset management group.

These investment houses were small, and many had had a volatile existence since the late 1980s. Bhakti Investama had divisions in investment banking and stockbroking. It was established in 1989 in Surabaya by the Tanoesoedibjo family. Briefly, in 1999, ABNAMRO (10 per cent equity), Morgan Stanley (15 per cent), and Goldman Sachs (4 per cent) had been associated with the group but left in early 2000 and the family bought over their shares.[51] The sources of their funds remain a puzzle. The firm's performance remained erratic, recording a loss of Rp98.0 billion in 1998, and a net profit of Rp80.9 billion in 1999.[52] Equally, Trimegah Securities' growth from its establishment in 1990 is shrouded in secrecy. In 2000 it was fined Rp10.5 billion by the Business Competition Supervisory Commission (KPPU) for irregularities in the purchase of Indomobil.[53] Yet because this was not a court ruling, Trimegah claimed that it was not legally binding. It recorded impressive net profits of Rp13.7 billion in 2000, and Rp24.08 billion in 2001.[54]

These investment houses were accumulating company assets in diverse economic sectors; was this another form of concentration since Bhakti Investama was investing in equity in diverse corporations? The painful question is who is actually financing these deals? Are they proxies for more shadowy investors?

Another intriguing aspect of Salim's divestments is the identity of the ultimate purchasers of these companies. For example, the sale of Indofood to FPH appears to be an insider deal, despite the absence of Liem Soei Liong or his sons from the Board after the sale. Equally, the sale of QAF, a food manufacturing company in Singapore in November 2000, had not resulted in a reduction in the family holding.[55] Furthermore, there is clear evidence of these assets being undervalued before disposal.[56] Was this deliberate? First Pacific was sold for US$66.7 million, a ludicrously low valuation for a group with assets in property, finance and trade, and which, prior to the sale, had registered operating profits in 1999 of more than US$180 million.[57] Thus these divestments never recovered more than 40 per cent of their true values.[58] In July 2001, asset sales of 16 corporations of Salim with a book value of US$556.7 million and Rp662 billion of assets produced only US$180.8 million and Rp414 billion, a bare 40.6 per cent of the original book value of these assets.[59]

The final contradictory and confusing development here is that while Salim is disposing of his investments in Indonesia, he is expanding in China. Is this a sign of capital flight from Indonesia? In 2002 his investments in China, Hong Kong and Singapore totalled US$10 billion.[60] He was involved in property development in Shanghai, Hainan and Fujian. He also held equity in Singapore United Industrial Corporation and United Overseas Bank. He used his companies in Singapore to spearhead growth in Vietnam and China. QAF Singapore acquired investment firms as well as food companies in China in June 2000.[61] The 'gang of four', Liem Soei Liong, Ibrahim Risjad (family friend), Djuhar Sutanto (family friend) and Sudwikatmono (Soeharto's cousin), reappeared in corporations in Indonesia, as well as in Singapore, India and China after the restructuring. In fact, Salim was moving into the capital-intensive petrochemical industry in India, with investments of US$30 billion in October 2003. The post-crisis phase now corresponded with aggressive globalization, acquiring Asia Food Property from Singapore, and securing technical arrangements with food production firms in Saudi Arabia, Nigeria and Australia. Meanwhile, independent foreign Australian and Singapore multinationals who had acquired increased stakes in Indofood were now poised to penetrate Western markets.

Finally, the restructuring had not drastically affected the concentration levels in certain industries. For example, Indofood saw a decline of only 7 per cent in its share of the instant noodles market, from 95 per cent in 1998 to 88 per cent in 2003.[62] Competition from other brands such as ABC, Salami, Gaga, Karomah and Mie Duo, was limited. The anti-monopoly law of 5 March 1999, which clearly prohibited monopolistic practices and unfair business competition by price fixing and collusive arrangements between corporations, could succeed only with wholesale restructuring of the conglomerates.[63] The piecemeal method of divestment could not deal with the dominant issue of concentrated ownership. The restrictions placed by the 1999 Act on majority shareholding in corporations by individual families, and the opposition to managers seeking representation on both Board of Directors and Board of Commissioners was again difficult to implement, because of the embeddedness of family, political and bureaucratic networks, in Indonesia.

The effect of these organizational and managerial changes was, first, to increase the presence of foreign ownership. This also marked a regional diversification into the Philippines and China. The third feature was divestment of industrial and commercial interests that were not central to the food sector. Thus, telecommunications was sold, along with banks in the US and Hong Kong. Thus, Salim's diversified growth from 1950 to 1997 had been derived from oligopolistic advantages, maintained through high protection imposed by government and its provision of subsidized credit. These conglomerates, strengthened by this preferential treatment, then embarked on mergers and acquisitions from 1989, reinforcing concentration. The financial crisis of 1997 dealt only a temporary blow. They were reassembling swiftly to carve out monopolies at home and abroad again, despite the 1999 anti-monopoly law and the financial difficulties in Indonesia.

Sinar Mas

Sinar Mas was one of Indonesia's largest conglomerates, and held interests in four major sections: pulp and paper, agribusiness, financial services and real estate. The focus here is on two core firms in the group, active in the wood-based industry: Indah Kiat Pulp and Paper, IKPP (1976) and Tjiwi Kimia (1972). Indah Kiat is the largest and lowest-cost pulp and paper producer in Southeast Asia, and it is this export drive that sustained the growth of these two firms after the 1997 crisis. Asia Pulp and Paper (APP), its parent company, provides a strong global distribution network. However, it remains a capital-intensive enterprise, and this was responsible in part for the traumas in 1997.

The interlocking networks between IKPP and the holding companies APP and Sinar Mas meant that the financial health of others affected IKPP's ability to raise capital. The group's ultimate holding company, Sinar Mas, had massive debts in banking and property. APP, another holding company, was formed in Singapore in 1994 and listed on the New York Stock Exchange in 1995 to consolidate the pulp and paper interests of Sinar Mas. It had debts of US$13.4 billion in 1997.[64] Thus, despite increases in the volume of sales of IKPP and the rise in the prices of pulp and paper, financial restructuring after 1997 was slow and modest.[65]

The advantages it possessed were in size, its integrated structure, low costs, and while 90 per cent of its sales revenue was in US dollars, only 30 per cent of its costs was in US dollars. It has regionally diversified paper production with facilities throughout Indonesia as well as China. It has logging concessions through its affiliate Arara Abadi, and is increasing its planting and pulp production. Eighty per cent of its pulp and paper is exported. Finally, although gearing is high, since 1998 it has reduced capital expenditures on machinery to curtail this gearing ratio. By 2000, its gearing ratio was further reduced through a capital injection of US$700 million.[66] This demonstrated an ability not to raise capital to settle debts but to reschedule debt through negotiations with IBRA and its creditors, and to attract increasing investment from Taiwan and Japan. In September 1999, debts of US$2,146 million had led to a gearing ratio of 75 per cent, but a strong cash flow resulting from expanding production led to gearing falling in 2000.[67] Recovery is also evident from the cash earnings of US$525 million in 1999, a rise from US$114 million in 1998. Despite rises in revenues, foreign exchange demands continued to suppress growth. Net profit rose from US$207 million in 1995 to US$211 million in 1997, to US$263 million in 1998, but fell drastically to US$4 million in 1999. In 2000 it recorded losses. The turnover revenue, however, rose between 1995 and 2000.[68]

Tjiwi Kimia, established in 1972, controls 65 per cent of the domestic paper market through its production in East Java. Exports accounted for 66 per cent of total output in 1999, and in 2000 it was 60 per cent.[69] The markets in Asia accounted for almost half, while the North American market absorbed another 19 per cent in 1999. The domestic demand contracted, leading Sinar Mas to increase production in China and target the Japanese market. It moved into high-quality paper production, and in diversifying paper products. This introduced some volatility into production and prices.

This concentration in production and marketing is matched by the concentration of shareholding within the family firm. Its holding company, Purinusa Ekapersada held 64 per cent equity, while the public accounted for 36 per cent.

Tjiwi Kimia revealed increases in turnover from US$390 million in 1994 to US$706 million in 1997, to US$868 million in 1999.[70] Net profits rose from US$23.6 million in 1994 to US$104.9 million in 1999.[71] Again, in 2000 and 2001, it recorded losses triggered by debt rescheduling and foreign exchange losses. This growth was assisted by a weak rupiah, low-cost production, and a strong demand overseas, despite low consumption in Indonesia where demand fell by 30 per cent in 1997. Despite the threat to the firm from proposed anti-monopoly legislation, there is the prospect of expansion and the benefits of rising prices for pulp and paper. This would overcome any rise in royalties and licence fees. It is the integrated structure of these two firms that provided the core competence in Indonesia, but in the long term this was harmful. APP provided good distribution networks to these two production and manufacturing units. However, the later analysis of APP clearly reveals some of the disadvantages associated with such integrated production: the timing between pulp availability and paper manufacture, the capital costs in maintaining the two sectors, royalties on forest concessions, licence fees, taxes and expensive machinery often nullify the advantages of integration. In Indonesia, Sinar Mas could compensate for these disadvantages because of the tax holidays it had, financial subsidies for development in new regions and abatements in royalties. These privileges and economic assistance ended with the crisis in 1997.

Indah Kiat Pulp and Paper and Tjiwi Kimia both revealed serious difficulties confronting the group in 2000–1. Part of these difficulties were related to their short-term liabilities denominated in US dollars, amounting to US$1.02 billion, due in April 2000.[72] While part of this was settled, the remaining segment was rescheduled. In addition, they encountered obstacles in securing credit at attractive rates because of the failure to meet interest payments on their own debt and the bad publicity surrounding the huge debts accumulated by the parent company, APP, of US$13.4 billion.

IKPP had to settle a yen bond and debt of US$148.6 million to Beloit Corporation, an equipment contractor. Thus, while pulp prices were rising by 28 per cent and paper prices by 14 per cent for 1999–2000, and revenue rose by 12.8 per cent, the net debt of IKPP stood at US$2,146 million, producing a gearing ratio of 75 per cent.[73] It faced foreign exchange losses of US$119.5 million in January 2000. In June 2001, Standard and Poor reduced their rating on securities guaranteed by IKPP from CC to D. This cut in rating was a direct consequence of their repeated failure to make interest payments of US$21.3 million on guaranteed securities, valued at US$150 million and US$200 million, maturing in June 2002 and 2006.[74]

Tjiwi Kimia, too, faced distress in 2000 and 2001. In early 2000 it had a net debt of US$898 million, and a gearing ratio of 98 per cent.[75] Yet, in December 1999, turnover had recorded a 37.5 per cent increase because of rising paper prices. The difficulties in 2000–1 were partly a form of contagion. With the pressures facing APP in China, Tjiwi Kimia was forced to abandon expansion and focus on debt settlement.

The Sinar Mas Group held major shareholdings in both firms, through its holding company and investment firms in the British Virgin Islands, Rotterdam and Mauritius. In 2002, despite drowning in debt, Indah Kiat Pulp and Paper was still held together by the group's subsidiary, Purinusa Ekapersada, which possessed 52.4 per cent of the shares, APP holding 4.2 per cent and the public, 34.8 per cent. In the other company, Tjiwi Kimia, Purinusa Ekapersada held 63.3 per cent and the public 36.6 per cent. Restructuring had not resulted in deconcentration. The only divestment that occurred after 1997 was the sale of companies in Singapore and Hong Kong, and the loss of Bank International Indonesia to BPPN (IBRA) for recapitalization.

The success in restructuring its core interests in the wood industry was partly due to a successful joint-venture with Chung Hwa Pulp and Paper from Taiwan. This partnership had existed in 1976, but had lapsed and was revived in 1999. Hence, Sinar Mas's restructuring was limited. It rescheduled loan payments, reassessed expansion plans, sold major firms in Jakarta which had been established in 1995–6, and sought finance from Japanese banks in Singapore, Chase Manhattan and Deutsche Bank. Its recovery was built mainly on increased export sales. Second, their subsidiaries in Ningbo,

Zhenjiang were profitable and helped sustain their presence in the industry. Their globalization moves in the 1990s into the US, listing APP on the New York Stock Exchange, and into Europe and Australia, met with only modest success. This is discussed in detail later (pp. 31–2).

Between 1970 and 1990, the growth was gradual, and based on domestic expansion. After 1990, the growth was global and fuelled by access to diverse capital. In Singapore, it acquired a partnership with United Industrial Corporation, whose chairman, Lee Kim Yew, was Lee Kuan Yew's brother. This global expansion led to a series of offshore companies in pulp and paper, in the food industry and financial services. In China, Bank International Indonesia had a holding company, China Strategic Holdings, which held equity in 30 state-owned firms involved in beer production and tyre manufacture. In 1995 it acquired *Ming Pao Daily News*. In the same year it moved into property management and financial services in Australia. In late 1996, Sinar Mas moved into the Indian pulp industry with an investment of US$100 million.[76] Many of these ventures abroad were regarded as essential lifeboats in a racially volatile and politically insecure Indonesia. Ironically, it was their domestic interests that saved the group in 1997, not their packaging abroad. Both Indah Kiat and Tjiwi Kimia clearly revealed growth in Indonesia, despite the high volume of debt and high interest payments. In 2002 Indah Kiat Pulp and Paper was held by Sinar Mas's investment company Purinusa Ekapersada (52.4 per cent), and public shareholding was only 34.8 per cent. Purinusa Ekapersada also held a 63.3 per cent stake in Tjiwi Kimia, with the public holding 36.6 per cent. Hence, despite the massive debt overhanging the group, no real reduction in ownership share is achieved. Therefore, restructuring has not produced deconcentration of the family stake.

Globalization and grief

Sinar Mas's global ambitions, particularly in China in the 1990s, held potentially serious repercussions for its survival in Indonesia itself. In the second half of the 1990s, APP was raising huge loans in China, New York and Singapore, investing heavily in the pulp and paper industry in China. APP was listed in Singapore and New York. In China it operated alongside a subsidiary of the parent company, Sinar Mas. Thus, APP Holdings was a free-standing company, and Sinar Mas Paper Investment (SMPI) was a direct subsidiary of Sinar Mas in Indonesia. This organizational structure, the creation of multiple holding companies, obscured the relationship of APP to Sinar Mas, and made it difficult to monitor lending and debt to this group in China.

APP achieved between 1994 and 1999 unprecedented growth in China. In Hainan, Jiangxi, He'nan, Zuhai, Guanxi and Yunnan, which were crucial timber producing areas, it pursued an unplanned expansion, tapping into greedy provincial governments. It attracted US$1.7 billion from Chinese commercial banks alone.[77] Investment in Yunnan in 1994 amounted to US$292 million, in Zuhai it totalled US$29.9 million, in Guanxi US$6.02 billion.[78] In 1995, a joint-venture initiative with Jinhua Forestry led to a total investment of US$5 million, rising to US$428 million in the same year. One single loan from the National Development Bank was for US$132 million.[79]

This growth in debt was one of the main factors contributing to the crisis in 2001. APP used its listing in New York to raise capital there. In April 1995 it raised US$311 million through an initial public offering (IPO).[80] In 1997 a second issue raised US$228 million. In April 1999 it floated an issue for US$400 million.[81] In short, between 1995 and 1999 it had accumulated US$939 million in New York. Many of these investors were attracted by the China connection, and its acquisition of large concessions of tropical hardwood in China, Indonesia, Taiwan and Malaysia. APP was reputed to be the lowest-cost producer of pulp and paper, attributed in part to the integrated production of pulp and paper manufacturing. The focus was on export-led growth, from which it derived 90 per cent of its revenue denominated in US dollars, while raw materials and processing costs were in renminbi.

This growth in debt, the raising of capital from international capital markets, continued unchecked into the late 1990s, and into 2000 and 2001. In June 1999, APP held 22 different bond issues for US$8.7 billion: one was due in December 1999 for US$1.4 billion, another for the same amount was due in 2000, and yet another for US$1 billion was to mature in 2001.[82] There were several more issued in Hong Kong, Shanghai and Jakarta. This volume of debt meant that despite impressive growth, APP's net profitability was in sharp decline.

Between 1994 and 1997, APP registered a rise in sales of 20 per cent.[83] Between 1997 and 1998, the increase in sales amounted to US$2.4 billion, yet net profit fell by 33 per cent in 1998 to US$143 million. Long-term debt rose by 35 per cent to US$8.5 billion, while interest charges increased by 63.2 per cent to US$392 million.[84]

The other important factor responsible for the skewed performance of APP is its gross misunderstanding of the industry. Despite having been associated with the timber industry since 1976, the Widjaja family exhibited a stunning lack of knowledge. For example, in China they concentrated on quality grade paper, when the real demand was for newsprint and packaging paper. It had invested US$4 billion in the manufacture of coated writing paper and carbonless copying paper.[85] APP was also failing to produce the correct fibre pulp required. Its subsidiaries in China were concentrating on producing short fibre from tropical hardwood trees, when long fibre was needed. The lack of coordination between pulp production and paper manufacturing meant that factories were often left idle, with highly sophisticated machinery not being utilized to an optimum level. In Hainan and Guanxi, forestry contracts were all vertically integrated with pulp and paper and were capital intensive: here, profits were a long way off. This, perhaps, was a result of the lack of involvement of forestry experts. This, again, explains why banks and capital markets relied purely on the company's own figures when approving loans. Independent audits were not required, and minimum information on acreage planted, growth rates and yield were sufficient for the approval of these huge loans.

By March 2001, APP was unable to service its debt of US$13.4 billion.[86] The Chinese State Administration of Foreign Exchange and Trade imposed direct suspension of APP's projects. Earlier, in January 2001, the National Development Bank of China had become aware of the risks after APP's share performance on the New York Stock Exchange proved highly volatile, and cancelled all its loans.

The Chinese government was particularly alarmed by the volume of debt in renminbi, and the speed with which it had been accumulated. In 2001, the renminbi debt was equivalent to US$6.7 billion.[87] The almost inexplicable irony was that in October 2002, Sinar Mas raised in China from Chinese domestic banks and Western banks operating in China, investments totalling US$1.57 billion.[88] This confusion can be explained by the existence of multiple holding companies in the Sinar Mas empire. APP was a free-standing firm with no apparent linkages.

Such labyrinthine financial connections aroused suspicions that some of this capital was finance flowing out of Indonesia to appease the Chinese government and banks in China. IBRA made loans to Sinar Mas with striking regularity as part of the restructuring of Bank International Indonesia, the main bank in the Sinar Mas Group. In May 1999 it had guaranteed loans to Sinar Mas for US$900 million.[89]

Money-laundering activities were on the rise among Indonesian conglomerates, and this had prompted the Indonesian government to introduce the Money-laundering Crimes Law, 15, of 17 April 2002.[90] This sought to restrict capital outflows that had no clear economic objective. But Sinar Mas and others had opportunities to overcome such constraints, because of the intricate networks in Singapore, Hong Kong and China.

The growing cynicism among provincial governments in China over Sinar Mas's motives and its viability led to their ban on Sinar Mas repatriating 400 million euros, since the origins of this capital transaction could not be verified.[91]

The major irony in this is that APP was raising capital from international capital markets because of the exaggerated optimism of Western investment analysts. In July 1998, Saloman Smith Barney rated APP as a good stock to buy, and identified the ensuing volatility as short term and that recovery would be swift.[92] In June 1999, Morgan Stanley Dean Witter issued another positive note: 'outperform rating and well-positioned for Asia's recovery'.[93] In November 1999 they repeated the 'outperform' report, when APP had a bond for US$1.4 billion maturing in 2000.[94] This investment bank saw no problem with cash flows, nor did it anticipate any in the future.

What was even more alarming was these analysts were so confident even after the New York Stock Exchange Commission (NYSEC) had suspected serious fraud. The NYSEC attempted in April 1999 a payment settlement. APP then sought to exchange US$800 million zero coupon and convertible bonds for bonds offering a higher rate of interest with a longer period of maturity. This was rejected. NYSEC was wary of APP's efforts to provide a combination of cash, new long-term high-yield bonds, and equity warrants in a scheme aimed at restructuring its debt for US$1.4 billion which was due in early 2000.[95] Now American Depository Receipts (ADR) of APP listed on the NYSE fell from US$5.02 in August 1999 to US$0.17 in February 2000. By March 2001, APP declared a moratorium on its debt for US$13.4 billion. This followed APP's loss of US$220 million from two derivative contracts that had not been reported in its annual accounts.[96] Arthur Andersen, its auditor, resigned, and APP was delisted from the NYSE. The NYSE sued Arthur Andersen and Merrill Lynch, which had acted for APP. Singapore, too, delisted APP. Despite these rejections, APP escaped unscathed in China and Indonesia.

The Oversight Committee appointed by IBRA in 2000 also noted that APP was not to be trusted, since there were no independently audited accounts since 1999.[97] It accused APP of pursuing a policy of selective repayment of debts, using derivatives and other risky financial instruments in its efforts to reduce the debt burden. Both the NYSEC and the Oversight Committee identified APP's strategy of using shares and assets of its Indonesian companies already pledged to IBRA for Sinar Mas's debt, now being used as guarantees for debt in the US, China and Singapore.[98]

The other important factors sustaining APP's financial imprudence and financial chaos, apart from the holding company structure disguising debts, was APP's ability to avoid Indonesian capital restrictions by using networks, and the access to abundant finance because of the optimistic reports by over-excited investment bank analysts. It was ultimately the failure of regulation by governments in China and Indonesia, as well as the restructuring agency IBRA that nurtured such practices. The Indonesian government continued to guarantee loans from state banks and Bank International Indonesia to Sinar Mas throughout the period 1997–2003. IBRA had acquired the debts of the Sinar Mas Group with guarantees from the Widjaja children, when it was the father who owned the majority of the assets.[99] It was also not clear what had been pledged, the value of the assets pledged, and to whom. This debt structure was further complicated by interlinkages between subsidiaries and firms in China, Singapore, Indonesia, Malaysia and the US.

IBRA, faced with this serious 'moral hazard' of not allowing Sinar Mas or APP to fail, identified which debt was to be restructured. In May 2000, IBRA identified that debt of US$1.2 billion could be sustained, arranged for the refinancing of another US$3.0 billion, and labelled as unsustainable debt, only of US$2.0 billion.[100]

In December 2002, debt restructuring in APP involving US$6.5 billion, introduced new partners Nippon Export and Investment Insurance (14.0 per

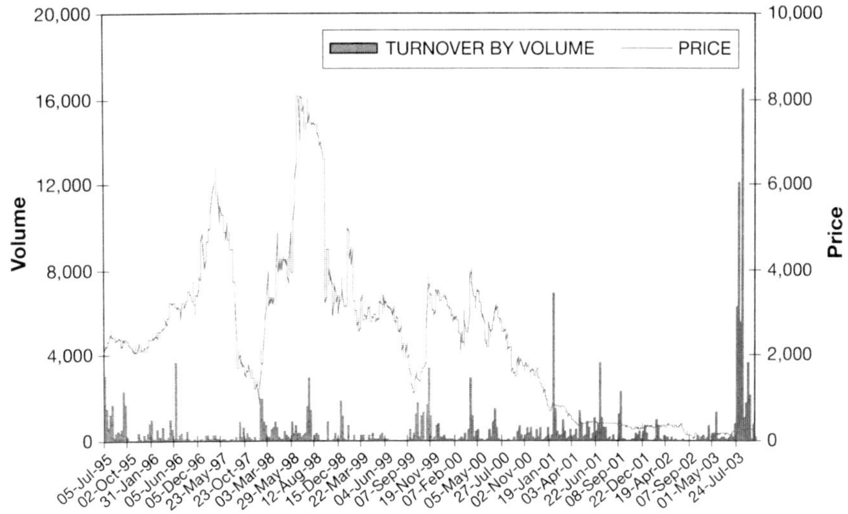

Figure 2.1 Sinar Mas share price and volume
Source: Jakarta Stock Market Productions

cent) and Japanese trading companies Nissho Iwai and Mitsubishi (8.4 per cent). IBRA held 15.2 per cent and bondholders and banks held the remaining 62.4 per cent.[101] APP's debts kept rising in 2003, when a debt of US$360 million had risen to US$420 million. IBRA decided to issue convertible bonds for US$2.4 billion.[102] This meant that the Indonesian government was absorbing this debt in the belief that APP should not be allowed to fail. It was in vital industries, a critical foreign exchange earner, and employees' futures were at stake. So the option was to restructure and refinance rather than liquidate.

In December 2003, APP was transferred to Orleans Investments for US$880 million and Rp7.5 trillion.[103] APP China Holdings in Shanghai was retained with subsidiaries in paper manufacturing and packaging. The members of the Board of Directors were Teguh Widjaja, Mukta Widjaja, Hiroshi Tadano from Sumitomo, Kunihiko Naito from Nissho Iwai, Suresh Kilam from Tjiwi Kimia (Indonesia) and Kenichi Oshitani from Itoh Chu Japan. The president of the Board of Directors was the son, Teguh Widjaja. This retention of crucial family members on the Board of Directors and Board of Commissioners throughout the crisis would dissipate any of the structural reforms, and casts doubt on long-term growth prospects and would threaten the success of the structural reforms, including ownership and potential growth.

In the same month, Bank International Indonesia was sold to Sorak Consortium which included Temasek Holdings of Singapore, Asia Financial

Holdings, ICB Financial Holdings (Malaysia), Barclays Group and Kookmin Bank of Korea as the major shareholders. The purchase price was Rp2.8 trillion.[104] Kookmin Bank alone held 51 per cent holdings. IBRA held 22.4 per cent, and this was sold in the market place. Sorak asked that no special borrowing privileges be permitted for the Widjaja family but IBRA refused to provide that guarantee. Also the consortium wanted the lock-up period of debts to be reduced to six months.

IBRA's difficulties with the Sinar Mas Group have to be understood at different levels. First, it had to concentrate on the restructuring of its bank, Bank International Indonesia. This implied the transfer of all non-performing loans (NPLs) to Bank Mandiri, a state bank. This then freed Sinar Mas to embark on an ambitious programme of expansion in China, unfettered by the debts it had accumulated before the crisis of 1997. Second, IBRA accepted as collateral, assets, land, buildings and machinery that had been overvalued and pledged to more than one creditor. Any serious appraisal of the group was often overturned for inexplicable reasons. Thus, in May 2001, IBRA's highly critical review of Sinar Mas and APP was followed in June by fresh offers of loans guarantees to the group by IBRA.[105] Constantly vacillating policies and decisions made restructuring difficult, and enabled the conglomerate to rake in more debt in the meantime and increase their volatility.

Texmaco Group

This group is used to illustrate how IBRA's protracted method of negotiations in the rescheduling of debt and the subsequent restructuring added to the costs and confusion. Texmaco failed in 1997 with the largest amount of NPLs. This meant it was not attractive to investors for direct purchase. The government, however, felt it was too important to be allowed to fail. Hence, it had to be nursed back to recovery.

The Texmaco Group contained large, vertically integrated textile enterprises, established in November 1970 and listed in March 1994. It possessed 26 firms, included three listed companies, in weaving, spinning, knitting, dyeing and fabric manufacture. It also produced traditional batik from East Timor. It had foreign partners from South India, the Netherlands and Hong Kong. Polysindo Eka Perkasa, established in 1984 and listed in 1991, had Japanese and American partners. Polysindo was integrated into spinning, weaving, chemical production and synthetic fibres. Its fabric interests accounted for 56 per cent of total Indonesian textile production, and it accounted for 28 per cent of total yarn produced in Indonesia in December 1995. The family of Marimutu Sinivasan controlled the entire group. Their competitor, Argo Manunggal (Ning King), also had an integrated concern with 54 subsidiaries in different segments of the textile industry. Its major subsidiary, Argo Pantes, a spinning and weaving company, while securing top place among textile producers in terms of total assets, was shadowing

Texmaco in terms of profitability, enduring losses in 2000 and 2001 because of foreign exchange liabilities. Its franchising with Arrow, Kenzo and all the international garment firms, did not assist in reduction of these massive losses of Rp423 billion in 2000 and Rp167 billion in 2001.[106] Another competitor for Texmaco is Indorama Synthetics, owned by the Lohia family, which has emerged as a large integrated textile producer with significant exports to Europe, the US and Australia. Indorama Synthetics is also a major producer of chemicals, with an expanding polymer division, and downstream activities in fabric and resin production. They were able to survive the 1997 crisis by rescheduling debts and increasing exports.[107]

If the growth of the Texmaco Group between 1970 and 1997 is spectacular, it was marooned with debts of Rp29 trillion in April 2002. It was the largest corporate debtor in the 1997 crisis. Their impressive growth before 1997 is attributable to an inflow of foreign investment into Indonesian textiles. Between 1967 and 1989, 80 per cent of FDI in this sector came from Japan. The US and Europe accounted for only 1 per cent. In the 1990s, there was increased investment from Hong Kong, Taiwan, the US and Europe in the value-added sectors of synthetic fibres and chemicals.

The state also assisted in this expansion. Besides encouraging foreign capital to align itself with large producers such as Texmaco, many of its fiscal, trade and financial incentives were beneficial. The government allowed exemption from import duties on raw materials and equipment forthe first two years, and tax amnesty for the domestic investor. These incentives applied to new factories, to extensions, as well as machinery. Companies were also allowed to carry forward losses in the first six years of operation, and permitted generous depreciation allowances. The net effect, as Hal Hill argues, was to support capital-intensive segments of the textile industry.[108] The over-valued rupiah also stimulated capital-intensive, large, vertically integrated firms such as Texmaco. Capital-intensive groups had advantages from cheaper imports. This large vertically integrated firm was able to overcome difficulties of a fragmented, geographically dispersed domestic market. Garment producers were concentrated in Jakarta, West Java and, to a lesser extent, in East Java. Between 1980 and 1992, the capacity of the garment industry grew 3,000 per cent.[109] Texmaco, with horizontal linkages with suppliers, foreign multinationals, the bureaucracy and the state, achieved increased market share and profitability. However, this changed from 1994.

The companies in the Texmaco Group, Polysindo Eka Perkasa, Texmaco Perkasa Engineering (TPE) and Texmaco Jaya, each reveals a devastating decline in net profit and return on equity after 1997. These ratios were in decline as early as 1994 (see Table 2.4 on Texmaco Jaya). The liquidity rates, too, exhibited a downward pressure from 1994. Short-term borrowings rose in 1996 but were highest in 1998, an obvious indication of financial distress following the 1997 crisis. The engineering subsidiary TPE had endured a serious liquidity crisis since 1994 and collapsed in 1997. Its heavy dependence on debt became clear between 1993 and 1996, while the parent

Table 2.4 Key financial ratios of Texmaco Jaya

Key ratios	*1994*	*1995*	*1996*	*1997*	*1998*	*1999*	*2000*	*2001*	*2002*
Profitability									
ROE (after tax) (%)	16.80	16.80	19.27	–30.95	–12.79	567.41	91.11	45.93	21.13
EBIT margin (%)	22.72	20.59	23.04	–1.34	10.20	–10.77	–39.76	–33.81	–20.15
EBITDA margin (%)	27.47	26.06	28.19	2.98	14.16	–2.21	–29.49	–23.84	–8.27
Operating profit margin (%)	23.83	23.31	25.82	29.09	13.67	–17.53	–24.05	–27.52	–30.96
Net profit margin (%)	11.61	11.70	10.12	–7.78	–1.50	–21.51	–40.84	–34.17	–24.54
Operating efficiency									
Asset turnover	0.71	0.59	0.65	0.80	1.09	0.67	0.69	0.73	0.64
Inventory turnover	5.58	5.08	6.83	9.85	9.25	3.90	3.69	4.44	3.04
Gearing									
Total equity/(long-term loans + equity)	0.91	0.63	0.63	0.32	0.25	–0.10	–58.56	2.51	1.83
Total assets/total liabilities	1.95	1.69	1.52	1.25	1.15	0.98	0.76	0.65	0.58
Liquidity									
Liquidity ratio (current assets/ current liabilities)	1.00	1.14	1.00	1.25	0.77	0.52	0.41	0.38	0.42
Quick ratio ((CA-inventories)/CL)	0.73	0.80	0.79	1.04	0.53	0.27	0.20	0.23	0.23
Cash ratio ((cash+ short-term inv.)/CL)	0.17	0.33	0.36	0.15	0.03	0.02	0.02	0.06	0.01
Inventory working capital ratio (sales/ ave working cap.)	62.64	4.74	4.98	1.66	–5.51	–0.76	–0.41	–0.25	–0.30

Table 2.4 (continued)

Key ratios	*1994*	*1995*	*1996*	*1997*	*1998*	*1999*	*2000*	*2001*	*2002*
Growth									
Total turnover (%)		12.51	37.79	59.57	89.84	–41.46	–5.82	1.86	–18.77
Profit before taxation (%)		–0.5	41.6	–182.7	–63.5	718.3	115.2	–25.0	–41.8
Profit after taxation (%)		13.3	19.3	–222.7	–63.4	738.4	78.8	–14.8	–41.7
Total assets (%)		35.6	24.4	30.2	38.7	–4.9	–9.0	–2.8	–7.1
Total liabilities (%)		56.9	38.4	58.0	51.1	11.9	16.4	14.2	4.8
Equity growth		13.3	4.0	–23.6	–11.3	–118.9	1013.8	69.0	26.8
Share related									
EPS (net) (RI)	211.67	141.00	139.31	–170.91	–62.62	–523.69	–938.43	–801.09	–467.06
Price (RI)	2,333.33	1,150.00	1,200.00	3,200.00	3,350.00	3,125.00	3,000.00	2,950.00	2,950.00
PER	11.02	8.16	8.61	–18.72	–53.50	–5.97	–3.20	–3.68	–6.32
BV/share (RI)	1,227.00	695.39	723.11	552.20	489.58	–92.52	–1,031.00	–1,741.00	–2,208.00
P/B ratio	1.90	1.65	1.66	5.80	6.84	–33.78	–2.91	–1.69	–1.34
Dividend/share (RI)	55.56	60.00	110.00	–	–	–	–	–	–
Dividend yield (%)	2.38	5.22	9.17	0.00	0.00	0.00	0.00	0.00	0.00
EV/EBITDA	10.57	6.70	5.18	70.39	9.53	–97.09	–8.13	–9.65	–34.23

Source: Annual Reports of Texmaco Jaya, 1994–2002

company, Texmaco Jaya, revealed high and rising inventory turnover between 1996 and 1998. While this may imply strong sales, it could also expose the company to falling prices and low profit margins, since companies with high profit margins often have low asset turnover, a consequence of pricing strategies. For Texmaco this was serious, since it had been experiencing problems with working capital for some time. The company by 1998 was unable to finance interest payments. Technically, it was bankrupt. In 2001, 77 per cent of its assets were financed by debt. By 2002, 82 per cent of assets were being financed by debt.[110] Highly leveraged and collapsing under massive debts, the group was unable to return to profitability. And in the light of these negative ratios, it should have been liquidated or nationalized.

This rapid growth prior to 1997 was financed by domestic banks, the Bank BNI (Bank Negara Indonesia, a state bank) accounting for the majority of the loans. There were loans to the engineering group from overseas creditors. In 1998, 90 per cent of these NPLs, denominated in US dollars, were absorbed by IBRA, while IBRA took only 32 per cent of Texmaco's domestic loans. By June 2000, IBRA loans to Texmaco amounted to US$3,079 million.[111] The debt owed to IBRA was only 65 per cent of Texmaco's total debt. Other creditors were owed US$1,649 million. So in June 2000, total declared debt was US$4,728 million.[112] Polysindo Eka Perkasa alone had debts of US$1.5 billion owed to various creditors, excluding what was owed to IBRA.[113]

IBRA justified the restructuring of the group on the basis of the 21,000 workers it employed, and thousands of other workers in other industries who were dependent on contracts from Texmaco. This was crucial since Texmaco supplied approximately 30 per cent of total demand for polyester in Indonesia. The textile industry's recovery was already stunted by new competitors from China and Vietnam, and thus Texmaco could achieve only a modest recovery in sales. The engineering section, which relied on the textile manufacturing division, faced a shortage of working capital.

By August 2002, the debt restructuring of the Texmaco Group was completed. Two new companies were created in place of the old ones. For Bina Prima Perdana, replacing the textile division of Texmaco, IBRA issued bonds for US$41.4 million to absorb dollar debts, Rp2.09 trillion for rupiah liabilities, and US$243 million for another portion of US dollar debt and bonds for Rp3.20 trillion for a further segment of liabilities held in rupiah.[114]

The second company, Jaya Perkasa Engineering (JPE), representing the engineering division, held bonds of US$321 million, US$1.16 billion, and rupiah bonds of Rp2.38 trillion and Rp3.34 trillion. IBRA also segregated the cash flows between the two new companies, eliminating cross-subsidies. IBRA and BNI were represented on the management board, and Sinivasan was to provide a minimum working capital of US$25 million by June 2003 to settle some of these current liabilities.[115]

There were serious complications surrounding the restructuring. First, the repayment dates for the bonds were as late as 2011, even though the restructuring was completed in 2003. Costs of these bonds were rising, the firm's recovery was slow, prices of raw materials were escalating and export demand was falling. China and Mexico threatened to erode the competitiveness of Indonesia's textiles. Texmaco's large capital-intensive facilities, with high fixed costs, added to rising financial liabilities for its engineering division. These liabilities rose from US$20 million in June 2001 to US$29 million in June 2002, and almost doubled in June 2003.[116]

Second, the critical reforms, the end to cross-subsidies between different firms in the group, and the appointment of an independent financial controller, were both seriously compromised by allowing Sinivasan to have 100 per cent equity in the second company, JPE, and his right to repurchase assets that had been transferred to IBRA earlier. The price at which repurchase could be achieved was ignored. This created problems in refinancing repayments.

Third, the government, while absorbing the debts, should have been involved in the micro-management of these corporations, and this would have averted the alleged capital leakages, the corruption and cronyism. Kwik Kian Gie, a powerful bureaucrat during the restructuring, expressed displeasure at the cronyistic relationship between Abdurrahman Wahid and Sinivasan.

The growth prior to 1997 occurring through a concentrated family ownership, reinforced through interlocking holdings by Polysindo Corporation in both Texmaco Jaya (80 per cent) and Perkasa Engineering (95 per cent), was exposed to failure because of massive foreign exchange liabilities. However, this does not exclude the fact that a partial explanation for the earlier growth and subsequent chaos was close links to Golkar and to the politicians. Even in 1998, at the recommendation of Soeharto, Sinivasan's corporation received special credit from state banks to facilitate exports. In 1999 Sinivasan was to accompany President Abdurrahman Wahid on a 16-day trip to Saudi Arabia, India, Europe and Korea, despite the disastrous corporate performance.[117] A former Governor of Bank Negara, Soedradjad Djiwandono, maintained that the trip was purely to assist export growth.[118] Deni Daruri of the Centre of Banking Crisis accused the government of acting as agents for Texmaco. In May 2000, corruption charges against Marimutu Manimaren, brother of Sinivasan, suspected of transferring money to relatives of Tanri Abeng and to Golkar were abandoned.[119] Manimaren committed suicide in August 2003, arousing further suspicion and controversy. Bambang Subianto, too, was accused of failing to exercise control over the recapitalization of Bank Bali.[120]

Whither reform?

From the above case studies it is clear that restructuring was complicated and often ineffective in resuscitating these corporations. The first strategy of reducing debt through the sale of subsidiaries meant that high-performing units, such as Indocement, were sold to foreign investors. However, this was limited and the business landscape was not radically transformed. Foreign multinationals investing in these corporations did introduce greater transparency. But what was incisive was the rise of new Indonesian fund managers, grabbing these assets in fire sales, and the long-term implications of this rise of portfolio capitalists is uncertain. Are these purchases of controlling stakes in too diverse corporations pure speculation? Or is there an industrial economic logic in their random acquisitions of equity in telecommunications, food and property firms? The asset sales, which included real estate as the main component, were ad hoc and lacked clear outcomes. An Indonesian corporation that acquired stakes in failing banks and companies after the 1997 crisis was Djarum, a cigarette manufacturer. In the immediate aftermath of the crisis it expanded into property in hotels and shopping malls, and into consumer electronics. In 2000 the Hartono family (Budi and Bambang Hartono) possessed assets of US$1 billion. They acquired a 51 per cent stake in BCA with an American management group (Fallon Capital Management) for US$500 million. Although Djarum was established in 1951, it was only by 1996 that it became the ninth largest corporation, with an annual turnover of Rp3 trillion.

The second important concern is the issuing of corporate bonds by IBRA. This entangled the government in holding debt, while capitalists were refusing to honour interest payments; the financial infrastructure of these corporations was complicated by these bonds and debt for equity swaps, so they faced difficulties in obtaining credit from the market. A more treacherous outcome was many of these large conglomerates sunk by debt at home were moving abroad, to Hong Kong, China, Singapore and the US, raising capital from foreign banks and Western capital markets. Sinar Mas's resurgence in China, Singapore and the US, and Tirtamas carving out viable economic positions in Myanmar, were surprising moves, and these attracted capital outflows from Indonesia after the 1997 crisis.

Third, and perhaps the most significant, is the failure to transform the institutional structure of the corporate economy. The introduction of the anti-monopoly law in 1999 would have worked in conjunction with the bankruptcy law introduced in April 1998 if the Supervisory Board of the Capital Markets had powers to cooperate with the government and bureaucracy to transform the economy and introduce competition.[121]

In fact, the rather protracted negotiations over restructuring enabled groups to reassemble, increase their loans and mount global initiatives. Corporate bankruptcies were avoided because of the fear of workers bearing the brunt of any liquidation. Furthermore, since each conglomerate had numerous subsidiaries, the financial transactions were complex. The strategy was not simultaneous insolvency but to identify the banks in each group, which bank was to be closed, which to be rehabilitated, and how to dispose of their non-performing assets. Then NPLs were transferred before restructuring the banks, or reforming the corporations. This was, in effect, allowing the status quo to continue, during which time family firms were moving capital out.

Because bank restructuring was difficult, it seriously damaged hopes for corporate restructuring. Often remedies were agreed in private, rather than seeking settlement through the courts.[122]

The result is that the conglomerates are still dominant, asset concentration is still high, and firms are still highly leveraged. An additional fear is that such concentrations could be exploited by foreign multinationals in critical capital and R&D-intensive industries. The rise of domestic investment houses and fund managers with linkages to the conglomerates could further entrench monopolistic market power. In fact, overall concentration rose in certain industries in the immediate aftermath of the 1997 financial crisis; this was because weaker firms collapsed while SMEs faced insurmountable credit difficulties.

The persistent issue is that of corporate governance. Although a law was passed on 19 June 2003 on the restructuring of SOEs, the private sector was the major culprit responsible for the collapse of the economy in 1997.[123]

The sections relating to corporations included the enforcement of independent directors on Boards of Directors and Boards of Commissioners. Half of these members should be voted for rather than be nominated. The Boards of Directors should have enforced legal compliance on corporations holding regular board meetings. The legislation also insisted on the lowering of the number of shares held by a single shareholder. An owner-manager was to be responsible for financial failures, and therefore should maintain improved debt and accounting disclosures. There was a requirement for annual reports and regulation of foreign investment by conglomerates. There had to be independent directors who were not government, military or bureaucrats. The presence of foreign equity led to foreign nationals on Boards of Directors, and this could act as a deterrent to secret deals and fraud. These investors could introduce a strong tradition of oversight and regulation. Above all, corporations had to reduce inter-subsidiary holdings. These recommendations remained merely on paper: no attempts were made to enforce these regulations. The IMF and the World Bank held the view that an endogenous culture of cronyism and a weak legal infrastructure were the scourge of the corporate economy, and that reform was fraught with difficulties.[124] There were also serious doubts about the quality of restructuring undertaken by IBRA.

Comparative policy responses to the crisis and restructuring: Indonesia and Malaysia

This section examines government policies and success in corporate and financial restructuring after 1997, the decision-making processes and achievement of IBRA, and attempts a detailed comparison with the radically different policy responses in Malaysia. The changes in the ownership of banks and corporations led to the entry of foreign investors and their takeover of some banks and firms. Much of what transpired in the restructuring process was the consequence of both economic and political factors. In Indonesia, decision-making and the design of restructuring failing groups were disbursed among many players, domestic and foreign, politicians as well as bureaucrats and technocrats, as well as the IMF and US-Aid. Different political and economic groups influenced the design and implementation of policies. This was in stark contrast to Malaysia where decision-making was more centralized, vested in Bank Negara, the restructuring agencies such as Danaharta, Danamodal and CDRC (Corporate Debt Restructuring Committee), and with Mahatir. In Indonesia a variety of political influences determined the recapitalization and management of corporate debt in each individual case.

First, the seriousness of the 1997 crisis in Indonesia, the levels of bank failures and the extent of corporate distress differed in contrast to Thailand, Malaysia and Singapore. Government intervention was more urgent in Indonesia than in Malaysia. The Indonesian government faced a situation where credit from banks to the private sector had fallen dramatically, accounting for 27 per cent of total bank assets. Government resorted to the use of bonds and securities as credit for the private sector, this accounting for 45 per cent of total financial assets. In Malaysia, government securities contributed only 7 per cent of total financial assets, while 59 per cent was in bank loans.[125]

This strategy of emphasizing the restructuring of banks, in effect, was determining the policies and manoeuvres of Indonesian asset management agencies. Thus, IBRA in 1998 bought distressed assets from financial institutions; the cost of acquiring these damaged assets was exorbitant, yet by the end of 2000, it had restructured only a tiny proportion of the loans that it had absorbed, while sales of the seized assets were slow. Recovery on NPLs of the banks was stagnating; part of this was due to confusion over how assets were valued. Unlike Malaysia, the Indonesian restructuring group took over assets, at overvalued rates, devoid of independent valuation. In Malaysia, assets were accepted at discounted rates, thus the losses were to be borne by the company rather than the government. This enabled Danaharta of Malaysia to restructure and sell the assets without holding on to them and facing huge expenses.

The second flawed strategy was the manner in which IBRA decided on bank closures and corporate restructuring. For example, it nationalized some private banks, then restored them to private ownership. It took over Texmaco when it should have forced it into bankruptcy. This weakness in decision-making meant that the total cost of recapitalization came to US$49 billion or Rp439 trillion.[126]

The use of recapitalization bonds meant that the government was saddled with ownership of failing corporations and banks. In contrast, Malaysia forced the merger of 50 financial institutions into ten groups, and this was finalized by 2002. In Indonesia the situation was more complex. IBRA identified the 50 largest debtors among the failing corporations, merged four state banks into Bank Mandiri, closed 48 banks, recapitalized or merged 20 out of a total of 142 private banks.[127] Yet in 2003 there are still five state banks, 80 private domestic banks and 34 foreign banks. Much of these private banks' equity holding was held by the state; many of the domestic banks were owned by foreign banks. As for the non-financial corporations, they faced equal difficulties in restructuring. Sixty per cent of their finance was derived from bank loans, and these banks were in serious difficulty, so that the decline in bank loans plunged the firms into collapse. Many of these corporations were struggling with debt denominated in US dollars, and were unable to make even annual interest payments. It was estimated in 1999 that 48 per cent of corporate debt was in US dollars, and this level of debt was actually recurring within a small group; part of them formed the top 25 debtors of IBRA in 2000 and are still there in 2004.[128] Many of them were the new *pribumi* elite that had risen during the privatization programme of the late 1980s and early 1990s.

The government organized debt-equity swaps, introducing more foreign owners into the Indonesian corporate economy. Yet, by December 2002, IBRA had restructured only 66 per cent of total debt; even this is highly dubious since scandals continued to rock the corporate economy between 1999 and 2002 on how such recapitalization funds were being diverted to the political party Golkar, Habibie and even Abdurrahman Wahid.[129] Court cases were frequently abandoned halfway because of political embarrassment. In Malaysia, the CDRC, set up in July 1998, had by 2000 restructured debts of 42 companies, rejected 21 and transferred nine others to Danaharta.[130] In addition, it concentrated on only a few large corporations. Those with smaller debts were allowed to disappear. Indonesia attempted for political reasons to support both large and small corporate and retail debtors. This just extended the pain. Bankruptcies of some of the large ones should have been permitted, while smaller retail debtors should have confronted market realities.

A final complicating factor was that much of the decision-making in Indonesia was at different levels, a hierarchy that was distorted by the political turmoil surrounding Soeharto, Habibie in 1998 and 1999, and even into Abdurrahman Wahid's coalition government in 2000. Only Megawati's rise has eased these tensions, though she has had to compromise and conciliate different interest groups. The effect has been a decentralized structure of decision-making. The IMF and foreign multinational banks emerged as influential players in this decision-making, since Indonesia was heavily dependent on external finance, but there were other, competitive actors. This fragmented body or bodies of decision-making is in contrast to Malaysia, where Danaharta, Danamodal and CDRC had precise and distinct tasks. Bank Negara managed Danaharta, Danamodal and the CDRC. There was no conflict between Bank Negara and the Ministry of Finance, and apart from the feud between Anwar and Mahatir, there were no serious political challenges to the designing and decision-making processes of the Malaysian Central Bank (Bank Negara) or the restructuring agencies responsible for resolving the bank and corporate debt of failing corporations and banks. Although Mahatir and his financial advisers were clearly in control, the independence of Bank Negara in its decision-making processes was recognized. Bank Negara, Danaharta, Danamodal and CDRC did not face the political pressures IBRA or Bank Indonesia faced.

Another serious problem was one of personality sabotage through the identification of specific individuals responsible for closures or recapitalization. Bureaucrats Bambang Subianto, Glenn Yusuf and Syahril Sabirin, as well as Kwik Kian Gie faced 'death threats' and media assaults.[131] In contrast, powerful personalities in Bank Negara Malaysia and Danaharta possessed anonymity. Zeti Aziz, as Governor of Bank Negara, was a bureaucrat responsible for mergers but remained in the background. Only Mahatir and the United Malay National Organisation (UMNO) faced criticism over the mergers and restructuring processes from affected parties.

First, IBRA also lacked a coherent structure. It depended on expensive external consultants. Glenn Yusuf and others had been earlier accused of frittering away public funds on these expensive consultants.[132] Second, IBRA faced powerful political and capitalist barons determined to frustrate any moves that would result in personal losses. It is this lack of power, a confusing hierarchy of control, that meant IBRA was faced with constant retractions and compromises on issues. IBRA faced not only recalcitrant banks and corporations but also factions within the Ministry of Finance, Bank Indonesia, IMF, US-AID, and a vitriolic press in the form of *Kompas*, *Tempo* and *Panji Masyarakat*.[133] Third, IBRA often confused the sale of bank and corporate assets, because all major Indonesian corporations possessed their own bank, and the interconnectedness of assets and debts was vast. This was not a problem in Malaysia where banks were separated from non-financial corporate institutions. This confusion and chaos persisting within IBRA was further added to by the frequent changes in its leadership – eight chairmen within just two years.

Fourth, the politically favoured capitalists continued to meddle in Indonesian corporate restructuring: Soeharto, Habibie and Abdurrahman Wahid had cronies who constantly sought concessions. Although it was alleged in Malaysia that Daim Zainuddin was the powerful actor behind the restructuring process, and powerful bankers such as Rashid Hussein and Azman Hashim were implicated in attempting to extract privileges, the final form of restructured banks and corporations revealed less of cronyism because of the powerful position of Mahatir after the 1999 election. Government not only undertook restructuring, it also forced the sale of equity and redistributed managerial positions.

In Indonesia, the Bank Bali scandal, the scandal of the Tirtamas Group, all made recapitalization and mergers difficult.[134] What was remarkable, as seen in the earlier discussion on corporate restructuring, was the ease with which foreign owners moved in. These new owners are multinationals with specific specializations such as Heidelberger Zement in cement. However, it has not been possible to prove that these are efficient. We need to appraise their corporate performance in the future. This selective restructuring in Indocement, Astra International and Indah Kiat had some initial success. Table 2.2 on Indocement (see p. 18) shows that assets have increased and sales have picked up, although profits fell. Texmaco Group and Tirtamas Group have had less success, merely achieving a switch to new Indonesian *pribumi* partners and surviving purely on increased production. There has been little effort to change ownership in Polysindo or in Texmaco Jaya, despite the fact that the Texmaco Group registered the largest debt to IBRA; their firms are still held by their family firm and their investment company. Both the Board of Commissioners and Board of Directors in these firms remained with the family and friends, along with a few token *pribumi* officials. With what was already alleged to be overvalued assets that they transferred to IBRA and the dismal performance as shown earlier, the company should have been declared bankrupt. But instead, in 1998, Sinivasan was reaping credit from state banks, and in 1999 was scheduled to accompany Abdurrahman Wahid on a 16-day trip to India, Saudi Arabia, Europe and Korea.[135]

Sinivasan's family links to Golkar and to Tanri Abeng meant that his companies were reprieved.[136] This meant that corporations remained in control of the assets even after being identified as possessing insurmountable debts and alleged corruption. Therefore, while Indonesia did possess more distressed banks and corporations than Malaysia, and its political landscape was marred by 'palace' intrigue, race riots, student protests, military factionalism and conspiracies, it was both this and the structure, the organization of IBRA, the process of designing and implementing restructuring that were responsible for the tardiness of corporate reform. The legal reforms, the introduction of anti-monopoly laws, the introduction of institutional structures to pave the way for corporate governance and greater transparency were trampled by bureaucratic incapacity. IBRA faced difficulties in extracting repayments, rescheduling debts or restructuring, and won only a few court cases. Although the 1997 crisis caused a slight rupture in previously existing business–political relations, the Salim Group lost control of Indocement and lost its patron Soeharto. A partly successful reform programme now exists because of the presence of foreign corporations and banks who have introduced integrated financial supervision and regulation, which may feed into the Indonesian corporate economy and revitalize it. Indonesia needs to maintain this liberal stance, the partial discipline introduced by the new owners should continue. Sometimes behind the new owners, older owners are still pulling the puppet strings, and this might frustrate the foreign multinationals.

A more serious challenge to sustainable, long-term economic recovery has been the rise of domestic investment groups such as Bhakti Investama and Trimegah Securities, who have acquired as well as mediated the appropriation of valuable industrial assets in timber, food and petrochemicals; the period after the 1997 crisis also ushered in a parallel rise of foreign fund managers and multinationals from Malaysia, Singapore and Taiwan, scrambling for assets in these same sectors. Asset management groups are now being vested with decisions on long-term investments, appropriating assets of high industrial value, and possess the freedom to sell or allocate them to clients not on the basis of competition and competence but, rather, for quick profits. The range of risk of these investments is highly complicated and these asset management companies are merely stacking them up like goods in a supermarket. Decisions on the mix of asset classes, their sectoral allocation and potential volatility are beyond the understanding of many of these private asset management groups, both domestic and foreign. Furthermore, there is an essential need for a defined structure of investment programmes. Many of these asset management groups mushroomed during the privatization boom of the late 1980s and expanded into the 1990s, and are now building up huge fortunes on the restructuring and purchase of these split-off companies. Many of these assets were purchased without appraising their specific risk profiles, and now the groups with these multiple assets and multiple profitability or loss potential face all the attendant risks of portfolio capital. Given the cronyism of the Indonesian economy and Indonesian industries in particular, such passive investors as Bhakti Investama are now playing an active role far above their normal commitments. The possible adverse effects of possessing many such complex diverse portfolios, with the massive swings in performance and profitability after 1997, may introduce a highly dangerous situation in Indonesia. The restructuring of corporations has to play a dominant role in the economic recovery of Indonesia, and asset management groups could thwart this critical transition. Asset management groups should pursue cautious policies to support economic recovery through restructuring rather than aim for their own short-term profits. This form of disembodied capitalism, with serious elements of casino capitalism, could thus have a distorting impact on Indonesia's industrial landscape.

Another significant trend in the restructuring process is the acquisition by a new rising corporation of these failing companies. Often the acquisitions are not an entire conglomerate but the profitable sectors of it. Djarum, an ethnic Chinese cigarette manufacturer, has acquired major assets in property, electronics, paper and finance in the restructuring after 1999. Diah, Michael and Robert Hartono have emerged as powerful corporate predators in this period.

The other main issue for the future is achieving a transition from a system dominated almost exclusively by out-of-court settlements to one mediated by independent courts and judiciary. The out-of-court procedures were complicated by the nature of the workout, by conflicts on the level of payments, the treatment of secured versus unsecured debt, and the distribution of losses among creditors, shareholders, the state and the public. Courts have to be strengthened not just through the introduction of legislation but through strict enforcement. In the absence of this, what the large conglomerates have attempted has been to indulge in high-risk activities both at home and abroad.

The enhancing of the transparency of corporate management and focusing on the accountability of shareholders and managers would eliminate some of this cavalier attitude to debt and capital structure of corporations.[137]

The Indonesian economy has recovered considerably since 2000, and real GDP growth rates of 4 per cent were achieved in 2003. SMEs and many large firms with foreign and domestic capital have made considerable progress over the past three years and profitability is improving. The continuing outflow funds by a few conglomerates – Lippo, Sinar Mas, Gadjah Tunggal and Tirtamas – should not obscure the progress that has been made in restructuring. Salim and others grew in the Soeharto years owing to political cronyism. Thus, the Indonesian crisis could have had a positive impact in checking this cronyistic growth. The corporations that have grown stronger since the crisis, such as Astra International and Gudang Garam, are a direct consequence of refocusing on core specialism, with critical divestment of loss-making sections, and change of ownership and management to successful foreign multinational partners.

The meddling by the IMF in the early phase produced some seriously flawed decisions, such as the transfer of worthless assets to IBRA and the exaggerated ambitions of recovery that were advanced.[138] Ultimately, Bank Indonesia and IBRA lack sufficient autonomy and coherence in what is now a pluralistic, decentralized, politically confusing but democratic environment, vulnerable to serious domestic and external pressures. In Malaysia, a strong political leadership has ironically insulated Bank Negara, Danaharta and Dananmodal from continuous erosion in confidence, and made possible a transition to a coherent policy of restructuring and reform.

3 Irrational exuberance

The fatal conceit of financial capitalism in contemporary Indonesia

This chapter examines an important phenomenon – that of volatile growth within financial institutions in Indonesia since the early 1980s. This volatile growth is scrutinized through a detailed study of Indonesian-Chinese financial-industrial conglomerates – the family business of Salim and Bank Central Asia; Mochtar Riady and the Lippo Bank; Bob Hasan and Bank Umum Nasional and Bank Duta; and Eka Tjipta Widjaja and Bank International Indonesia. One *pribumi* bank, Bank Niaga, is included as a comparison with a non-Chinese private bank.

A critical part of this analysis is focused on financial instability resulting from the patterns of growth and alliances forged by these Indonesian bankers, their attitudes to risk, and the very processes of risk assessment and capital accumulation as important precipitating factors in the 1997 financial crisis. The literature on the Asian financial crisis, while admitting the part played by defects in the corporate economy, provided no detailed corporate empirical evidence or analysis.[1] Stijn Claessens admits to difficulties in securing such corporate data.[2] The primary aim of this chapter, therefore, is to fill this gap, through an examination of Indonesian financial groups and their role in the creation of a volatile capitalism. Crucial here was an 'irrational exuberance' in Indonesian economic growth, driven by highly optimistic domestic and foreign investors, swayed by the 'fatal conceit' prevailing among Indonesian financial groups as they embraced a prodigious growth fuelled by risky capital accumulation. Such positions provided an 'amplification mechanism' to the commodity price falls, trade deficits, declining asset prices and volatile short-term capital flows.[3] These problems were further exacerbated by the 'psychological anchors' provided by the state and Chinese capitalist networks at home and abroad. The crisis and the distorted recovery could have provided 'learning and unlearning' in methods of capital accumulation and risk and volatility inherent in such capitalist growth. But it is not apparent this has occurred even after 1997.

In order to extract the patterns of growth and volatility from these four case studies, we need detailed analysis of performance over the crucial two decades – the 1980s and 1990s. These banks have been chosen on the criteria of size, importance of state connections and ethnic networks, diverse

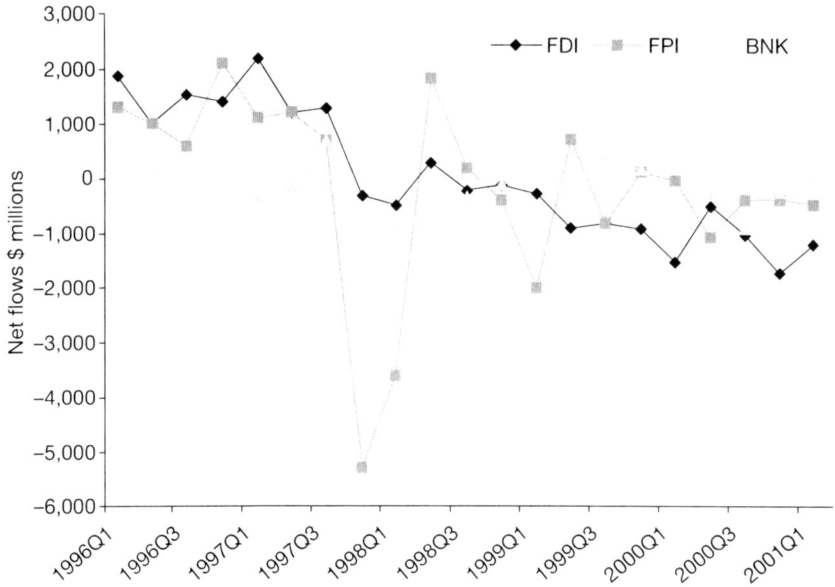

Figure 3.1 Net capital flows to Indonesia, 1996Q1–2001Q1

Source: Reports of Indonesia Investment Coordination Board, 1996–2002

experience during the crisis and subsequent restructuring following the brutal shakeout that occurred in 1997. This sample also includes a *pribumi* bank, valuable in identifying ethnic influences in the growth of the Indonesian financial system. Although this variation in ethnic role and performance may be difficult to quantify, individual or collective strengths and weaknesses of ethnic groups can be crudely evaluated. The most simple and direct observations of the differences in performance between Chinese and *pribumi* banks are sought as part of the broad institutional non-economic factors shaping performance and volatility in finance. This, too, requires verification through the use of detailed empirical data.

Structural factors: corporate organization and concentration

Chinese banks in Indonesia were family controlled, with ownership concentrated in the hands of one large shareholder – the family.[4] This concentration was intensified through cross-holding and pyramid structures, with links to other Chinese corporations, to government and to other capitalist networks. Separation of ownership from management rarely existed because family members dominated the Board of Directors, the Executive Committees and the Audit Committees. This concentration by the family was further strengthened by the fact that 16 large, family-owned conglomerates with several banks within them, owned 70 per cent of total equity on the Jakarta Stock Exchange in the period 1989–97.

Privatization had intensified the concentration within Chinese and *pribumi* entrepreneurs. The mergers and acquisitions during rapid growth in the 1980s and 1990s further encouraged concentration. Patron-client clusters centred around Soeharto and his cronies. Lucrative projects went to those with political and military connections, all sustained by 'soft loans' from the state and through state and foreign capital investments. Concentration within Indonesian corporate and financial institutions is thus extremely pervasive. In 1995, 17 per cent of the total value of listed corporate assets could be traced to a single family, the Salim Group.[5]

Corporate empires were often built around a family bank, as in the Salim Group where BCA was the core family bank in Indonesia with FPH dominating its expansion overseas. Having established themselves in government-assisted industries such as cement and food with generous credit from state banks, these groups participated in the privatization of commercial banking in the 1980s. The private commercial banking sector was a major recipient of oil revenues, foreign aid, foreign direct and portfolio investments. These private banks, as part of large conglomerates also had access to offshore banks as well as to more diverse and innovative sources of finance. Competition from foreign banks was negligible: they had been nationalized under Soekarno while their growth under Soeharto was constrained. State banking dominated throughout and was an important source of funds for private Chinese banks. Until 1983, the government controlled 75 per cent of all bank assets, attracted 75 per cent of all funds and was responsible for 77 per cent of total credit.[6] This dominance of state banking continued into the 1990s. However, it is the proliferation of private commercial banks that is impressive, rising from 70 in 1982 to 162 in 1994 (see Table 3.1).

Table 3.1 Number of banks by ownership category

Type of bank	*1969*	*1982*	*1988*	*1991*	*1994*	*1998*
State banks	5	5	5	5	5	7
Regional and development banks	25	29	29	29	29	27
Private domestic foreign exchange banks	7	10	12	28	51	–
Private domestic non-foreign exchange banks	123	60	51	101	111	130
Foreign and joint-venture banks	11	11	11	29	40	58
Others	12	3	3	3	3	0
Total	183	118	111	195	239	222

Source: Bank Indonesia, *Financial Statistics*, 2000

The state banks channelled cheap credit to a select group of Chinese and *pribumi* financial elites, guaranteeing an uncompetitive banking sector. The consequence of this was that Chinese banking emerged as 'network banking', sustained by state, foreign multinationals and by Chinese conglomerates. The majority of deposits were with state banks while Chinese banks and their clients had access to these deposits through patronage.

Chinese capitalists were also linked to state finance through the interbank money market established by the Soeharto government in 1974 to help banks with liquidity. This was boosted by the establishment of a foreign exchange swap facility in 1979 to help banks attract overseas funds and avoid foreign exchange risks. Bank Indonesia would buy currencies and sell to domestic entrepreneurs at no risk. Foreign exchange earnings derived from oil exports were channelled to private Chinese banks. The subsidizing of funding and preferential credit was highest in the period 1974–90, facilitated by the surge in oil reserves. Chinese and a few *pribumi* financial institutions were the major recipients.

Even with financial liberalization from 1988, state patronage was crucial in determining who had access to large foreign direct and portfolio capital. Thus, state funds and subsidized credit were critical for the growth of Chinese banks in the 1980s and 1990s. Large syndicated loans arranged by foreign banks meant that external debt owed to foreign banks more than doubled between 1990 and 1997, while short-term liabilities to foreign banks rose to 181 per cent of foreign reserves in 1996.[7] Foreign currency borrowings were high and a large proportion were short term and denominated in dollars. The result was unstable gearing ratios for Chinese banks. When the rupiah fell in August 1997, the foreign currency debt of Chinese banks reached unprecedented levels. Corporate borrowing alone amounted to US$38 billion – a large proportion of this was from Chinese banks.[8] The ability of Chinese banks to lend while maintaining a sufficient loan–deposit ratio was possible because of generous support from state funds. The feature of excessive lending, yet preserving smaller reserve ratios accelerated in the 1990s with financial liberalization. Forsaking prudent banking, Chinese banks were less restricted because of increased inflows of foreign capital, in particular short-term portfolio capital.

A further feature was the concentration of loans to individuals or to select groups of conglomerates, the majority of them Chinese. There was also the distribution of loans to related firms. When Bank Summa failed in 1992, 55 per cent of its loans were to its subsidiaries in the P. T. Astra Group.[9] In June 1995, six banks had made loans to related firms that constituted more than 200 per cent of the bank's own capital; there were 23 banks for whom the ratio was over 100 per cent; and 42 banks had loans to linked companies exceeding 50 per cent.[10] Hence, almost half of total private banks' debt in 1995 were consumed by loans to their own firms.[11] Here, the capital–loans ratio exceeded the legal lending limit, particularly on loans to individual clients. In April 1996, 15 banks failed to meet the 8 per cent capital asset ratio, while 41 banks did not comply with the legal lending limit on individual clients.[12] Many banks also exceeded the limits on foreign exchange exposures.

Another source of capital concentration among Chinese banks occurred through the assistance of foreign partners. Financial liberalization from 1988 eased the restrictions on foreign participation in Indonesian banking and these foreign investors found willing partners in Chinese and *pribumi* bankers who tapped into foreign equity to finance new shares issues and grow. Thus, in 1996, 11 listed Chinese banks raised Rp1.6 billion through new share issues. In 1997 they raised Rp3 trillion.[13] Bank Dagang Nasional Indonesia (BDNI – Gajah Tunggal Group) secured expansion through a joint-venture with a Japanese bank. The state, too, directed funds borrowed from Japanese banks to BDNI.

Capital concentration also occurred through the diversification of financial subsidiaries within a single bank: the creation of finance houses, leasing and factoring subsidiaries and insurance companies within single banking groups continued to accelerate in the 1990s.

Chinese corporations were able to retain their core family ownership through the use of the holding company and interlocking shareholding; the only outsiders were government and loyal institutional shareholders facilitating easy access to outside capital and colluding in each others' interests. This concentrated family ownership in listed banks with no separation between ownership and control and management remained even after the crisis. In addition, different Chinese families held stock in each others' corporations. Moreover, high-profile politicians and their families, too, held shares as well as managerial positions in the Chinese corporate groups. There is a core controlling group, comprised of powerful Chinese capitalists, Indonesian bureaucrats and politicians. This concentration persisted throughout the life-cycle of the conglomerate. The evolution of such concentration can be traced to privileges from government: export-import licences, monopolies in marketing and distribution of essential commodities including rice, cooking oil and clove cigarettes, and privileged access in the procurement of large government contracts. This method of collusive growth, aided by preferential cheap credit from government and foreign sources, with direct participation of government officials, bureaucrats and army in banking, distorted the already weak legal, institutional framework and inadequate corporate governance.

Finally, this capital and ownership concentration was further induced by the growth of the Jakarta Stock Market. The ability to raise capital from the state, domestic and foreign sources on the Jakarta Stock Exchange was exploited without diluting family ownership. The Jakarta Stock Exchange witnessed a dramatic expansion in market capitalization from US$8 billion in 1990 to US$91 billion in 1996 before shrinking to US$29 billion in 1997. A state–IMF assisted rescue in 1999 bolstered the Exchange with US$64 billion but declined to US$25 billion in 2001.[14] The increase in foreign investors on the Jakarta Stock Exchange from 10 per cent of total value in

1989 to 30 per cent in 1993, increased the value of foreign investors to double that of local private investors.[15] For Chinese banks, this raising of equity was critical because they could not attract sufficient retail or wholesale deposits to maintain their lending levels.

Another critical source for Chinese financial growth was through country and mutual funds. By 1990 there were 16 country funds available for Indonesia.[16] These were frequently directed by the state to its preferred private Chinese capitalists and *pribumi* elite. This increased participation in the capital market sector led to risky diversification in the portfolio of Chinese financial firms. They now undertook securities business and also participated in bond markets. Such highly diverse forms of corporate finance, and the accompanying growth of plural financial institutions, increased the potential for volatility after 1989. However, bank loans rather than equity finance continued to be more important for corporate finance. Banks were central to the growth and concentration of financial capital. Of the total assets of financial institutions, 84 per cent were vested in the commercial banking sector[17] (see Table 3.1). Each Chinese banking group had a dense pattern of interlocks, with state institutions, networks, overseas and domestic investors intensifying their financial power and influence. Mergers and acquisitions, which were rampant after 1988, added to this cohesion and concentration with less competition. Chinese capitalists, euphoric over prophecies of accelerated economic growth in Indonesia circulated by World Bank economists, now sought to purchase banks in the US, Australia, Hong Kong and China.[18]

Foreign capital inflows and financial volatility

As noted earlier, a critical element in the expansion of Chinese financial capitalism was the large foreign capital surges, sustaining a boom in the diversification of financial institutions. This also provided the Chinese with the resources for global financial moves by creating banks, finance houses and insurance companies in Hong Kong, Southeast Asia, China and the US in the 1990s.

Indonesian-Chinese capitalists mimicked each other in investment behaviour and strategies. Capital became highly sensitive to perceived market potential, and the magnitude of these shifts, both into new industries and new regions, resulted in a phenomenal expansion in finance, ultimately creating great potential volatility. Capital was responding to rumours and perceptions as well as to the inordinate global ambitions of a few Indonesian-Chinese entrepreneurs. This herd mentality, induced and sustained by both rapid economic growth in contemporary Asia and the highly concentrated oligopolies, with increased availability of capital and opportunities, propelled these groups into sophisticated financial ventures beyond their traditional strongholds in commodity production and trade. Chinese nonchalant attitudes to risk and risk management had been nurtured by years of state patronage, while capital inflows fuelled exuberance, an 'irrational exuberance'.

FDI into Indonesia rose in the 1990s; in particular, an impressive acceleration occurred between 1993 and 1996 (see Tables 3.2a and 3.2b). A major segment of this increase was private portfolio capital attracted by higher interest rates in Asia compared to Europe and the US. It is the relationship between this portfolio capital and the unstable, almost precarious, nature of Chinese financial growth that lies at the heart of this chapter. The volatility of both, the magnitude of the impact, need to be understood if Chinese attitudes to risk, to financial capital accumulation and contribution to the financial crisis are to be more accurately grasped. FDI inflows into Indonesia rose from US$8,751 million in 1990 to US$23,724 million in 1994, then doubled in 1995 and even in 1997 approximated US$33,833 million.[19] Portfolio capital rose in 1993, continued to rise again in 1995–6 before it collapsed in 1997 (see Table 3.2a).

Lending by foreign banks experienced a major rise between 1990 and 1991, with a slight contraction in 1992, followed by an accentuated fall in 1993, before rising in 1994–5 and 1996[20] (see Table 3.3). Volatile inflows were in short-term bank lending. In June 1997, Indonesia held US$58,726 million in cross-border bank lendings, of which half were short-term (up to a year). The majority of the loans in June 1997 were from the Japanese, approximating 39 per cent, and Europe, 38 per cent, with the US contributing only 8 per cent.[21]

Table 3.2a Indonesian capital inflows as a percentage of GDP

Year	*Source*	*Percentage*
1990	FDI	1.03
	Portfolio	0.09
	Others	3.29
1991	FDI	1.27
	Portfolio	–0.01
	Others	3.62
1993	FDI	1.27
	Portfolio	1.14
	Others	1.38
1994	FDI	1.19
	Portfolio	2.19
	Others (bank loans)	–0.87
1995	FDI	2.16
	Portfolio	2.04
	Others	1.20
1996	FDI	2.72
	Portfolio	2.20
	Others	0.11
1997	FDI	2.18
	Portfolio	–1.23
	Others	–0.21

Source: IMF, *International Financial Statistics 1998*, cited in Takatoshi Ito, 2000, p. 274

Table 3.2b Indonesia: FDI as a percentage of gross domestic capital formation

Year(s)	*Percentage*
1980–4	10.9
1985–9	1.8
1990–4	3.8
1995	7.6
1996	9.2
1997	7.7
1998	–1.4
1999	–9.0
2000	–12.2

Source: UNCTAD, *World Investment Report*, various years

Table 3.3 The level and variability of capital inflows, 1996–2000, in Indonesia (in US$ million)

	4th qtr					*Coefficient of variation*	
	1996	*1997*	*1998*	*1999*	*2000*	*1994–2001 1st qtr*	*1994–7 2nd qtr*
FDI inflow	6,194	2,702	–356	–2,745	–4,550	1,281.4	102.5
FDI net	5,594	2,551	–400	–2,817	–4,700	2,680.9	109.5
Portfolio flows net	5,005	–3,558	–1,878	–1,792	–1,909	1,008.0	152.1
Bank credit	–758	–117	–2,270	126	–1,420	–229.3	–934.3
Total	9,841	–1,123	–4,548	–4,483	–8,092	–754.6	90.3

Note: The rounding of individual figures implies that the totals may not necessarily be consistent.

Source: Prema Chandra Athukorala, 'FDI in Crisis and Recovery: Lessons from the Asian Economic Crisis', Paper for XIII International Economic History Congress, July 2002, pp. 23–4. See also IMF *International Financial Statistics*, CD-ROM

This level of bank lending, together with increases in portfolio and foreign direct investment, led to unstable increases in corporate debt nominated in US dollars. There was a serious mismatch between Indonesian banks' short-term liabilities and their liquid assets (see Tables 3.4a and 3.4b). Thus, the boom in bank lending in the mid-1990s resulted in serious distortions, which were made worse by the fact that during this period, asset prices on the stock market and in real estate were falling.[22]

Equity participation by foreigners on the Jakarta Stock Exchange had been slow. In the 1990s, joint-ventures were sought in the new industries – telecommunications and electronics. The involvement of foreigners was high in 1993, at 57 per cent, but dropped to 36 per cent in 1999 and 25 per cent in 2000.[23] This mirrored the decline in foreign capital investment. Despite

Table 3.4a Corporate debt composition: Indonesia, 1996

Foreign debt (%)		*Domestic debt (%)*	
Short-term	*Long-term*	*Short-term*	*Long-term*
20.5	19.6	31.4	28.5

Table 3.4b Short-term external debt and international reserves, 2nd quarter, 1997

Short-term debt (US$ billion)	*International reserves (US$ billion)*	*Debt–reserve ratio (%)*
34.66	20.34	1.70

Source: Asian Development Bank, *Asia Development Outlook*, 1999, p. 26

the lifting of restrictions on foreign participation on the Jakarta Stock Exchange in 1999, local investors constituted 65 per cent of trading volume, in contrast to 1995 when foreign investors contributed to a higher value of investment than local investors.[24] Mergers and acquisitions, encouraged by the state after 1997, saw an increase in value from US$36 million in 1998 to US$1,441 million in 2000.[25] The majority of these mergers with foreign capitalists failed because of the persistent suspicion that Indonesian entrepreneurs were not disclosing the true level of financial distress, despite the guarantees offered by BKPM and IBRA.[26]

The impact of foreign capital inflows, in particular, short-term portfolio capital, was crucial in sustaining the casino capitalism of financial growth, speculation on the Jakarta Stock Exchange and the real-estate sector. Indonesian banks did not register a decline in net profits from 1995 as Claessens claims; on the contrary, they were recording net profits until after July 1997. Earlier declines in 1996 were only in their earnings per share (see Tables 3.5–3.10 on banks).[27] My explanation for this continuous growth is that Indonesian banks were exploiting money borrowed from abroad and only the financial crisis of 1997 forced any disclosure of weakness in real earnings. The actual gravity of financial distress was concealed through increased borrowing, most of it from abroad.

The Asian financial crisis, thus, was preceded by a good number of profit rises and asset expansion within the corporate sector. Only stock price decreases were discernible, and those, too, only from December 1996. Thus the crisis was not foreseen. Investors then reacted to the bad news, and asset prices and financial reserves were wiped out in the frenzy.

Besides the volatility created by the short-term, unhedged, private external debt of banks, the lending between banks added to instability.[28] Loans were often concentrated because banks of one conglomerate lent to those of another. This inter-related lending was through political and ethnic loyalties rather than from purely financial motives. Poor risk assessments and further concentration of loans to a tiny elite added to this hazard.

Finally, foreign capital inflows introduced volatility to financial institutions through added volume, mobility, increased risk sensitivity arising perhaps through poor information or just 'irrational exuberance' – a euphoria induced by the high expectations that fuelled Asian economic growth in the 1980s and 1990s.

Banks and volatility

Having established some of the causes of macro-economic vulnerability in Indonesia, this study now focuses on the volatility and inefficiency of six banking groups. This is an attempt to identify and locate volatility, the timing, the areas and long-run causes of disequilibrium. Internal corporate data on earnings, share price performance, dividend payments, liability structure, in particular net income after tax, total assets, return on assets, and capital increases over the 1990s will provide valuable insights on the critical turning points in volatile growth. The banks investigated are BCA, Bank International Indonesia, Bank Duta, Bank Lippo, Bank Niaga and Bank Bali.

First, I will appraise how financial and stock market volatility was reflected in the organizational development of Chinese banks. This includes several political variables, including business links with political leaders, the privatization of SOEs since the 1980s, and the accelerated influx of foreign capital. Second, I need to identify the precise mechanism by which each factor affected financial stability. Third, I will evaluate the alternative plausible explanations for the phenomena, including that of global influence. Fourth, the impact of these factors have to be assessed for the *pribumi* banks too, in order to determine whether Chinese financial groups had greater instability than other ethnic groups or whether the volatility was endemic in Indonesia. Such a comparative approach demands further scrutiny into Chinese strategies of growth and diversification, whether their predatory instincts were innately a Chinese characteristic, and the impact of these on corporate governance. Are these strategies ethnically cast or are they fostered by other market and non-market forces? Fifth, do large block holdings of shares by single owners introduce volatility? Do intimate interlocking relationships between banks and their investment and securities subsidiaries contribute to mercurial growth in a liberated but poorly regulated financial system? The increasing concentrations, polarization of powerful capitalist groups in the Indonesian financial infrastructure need to be explored to understand the lurch to financial collapse in 1997. Finally, the pace and nature of the privatization of banks that took place in the late 1980s gave rise to weak structures in corporate governance, including a weakening bureaucracy and enhanced private sector power in finance, without enhanced public access to information.

The growth and financing strategies of Indonesian-Chinese banks are, therefore, central to this study on institutional volatility of the Indonesian financial system. Therefore, a crucial segment of this analysis will focus on the Asian financial crisis of 1997. An appraisal of the ownership structure, performance, and the political and ethnic networks permeating these financial groups between 1983 and 2000 will assist in identifying the origins of the crisis in banking and the difficulties for a successful resolution there.

Salim, Bank Central Asia and First Pacific Holdings

The Salim conglomerate has been the largest trading group in Indonesia since 1950. Its bank, BCA, was established in Indonesia in 1957. FPH was purchased in 1982 and listed in Hong Kong in1988. The acquisitions of Hibernia Bank in 1983 and United Savings Bank of California in 1986, Wells Fargo Bank and Crocker National Bank in 1985, and Hong Nin Bank (Hong Kong) in 1987 were critical to the group's global and product transformation. From the import-export trade, the Salim Group moved into manufacturing, with the establishment of international manufacturing, first in import substitution industries and later in export-led manufacturing, with the establishment of international manufacturing and financial concerns in Hong Kong, China, the Netherlands and the US. These financial transplants corresponded to the influx of oil revenues, foreign capital inflows (Arab, Japanese and American) from the early 1970s, and the rise of the Soeharto family business empire. Privileged access to finance, both from domestic and external sources, prepared the way for the emergence of concentrated, oligopolistic business groups in strategic industries in Indonesia. Liem carved out powerful shares in flour-milling, cloves, cement, steel and telecommunications, predicated on access to government contracts, state credit and foreign capital. This reinforced the explosion in the banking and financial interests of the group.

From 1957 to 1978, BCA emerged as the largest private commercial bank in Indonesia. The initial period of impressive growth was between 1974 and 1978. In 1973, BCA had no foreign exchange facilities, possessed one branch, and was ranked twenty-third among 58 private commercial banks in terms of total assets. The Indonesian oil boom catapulted the bank into a dominant position. The assets of BCA rose from Rp211 million in 1970 to Rp16,903 million in 1975, Rp1,542,116 million in 1987 and to Rp7,439,999 million in 1990.[29]

Close liaisons with the state introduced Soeharto's family as shareholders. Sigit Haryoyudanto (eldest son) and Siti Hardijanti (eldest daughter) held 6 per cent and 14 per cent respectively. Liem himself held only 8 per cent. The remaining 42 per cent was held by 18 shareholders, mainly foreigners. Indifference to minority shareholders was fostered by the dominance of the Liem family, the Soeharto family and their allies.[30] Mochtar Riady owned 18.7 per cent shareholding in BCA in 1987, but soon left to form his own banking empire – the Lippo Bank.

Table 3.5 Bank Central Asia, 1973–90

Year	*Total assets (Rp million)*	*Total deposits (Rp million)*	*Loans outstanding (Rp million)*	*Paid up capital (Rp million)*	*Net profit (Rp million)*	*Number of branch-es*	*Number of employ-ees*
1973	n/a	n/a	n/a	2.5	n/a	1	n/a
1974	998	24	426	500	39	4	112
1975	12,800	10,766	5,800	1,800	39	4	298
1976	17,523	12,401	8,961	2,500	203	12	620
1977	24,843	19,100	12,607	2,500	203	13	828
1978	37,274	29,045	21,729	2,500	323	15	975
1979	64,628	51,845	27,496	n/a	n/a	n/a	n/a
1980	107,462	88,178	44,239	6,000	1,104	22	1,527
1981	174,462	143,388	68,933	6,000	1,479	24	1,871
1982	240,580	202,121	95,248	15,860	2,050	26	2,207
1983	386,681	290,835	133,649	22,000	5,053	27	2,084
1984	464,798	345,462	287,254	22,000	7,647	29	2,741
1985	707,909	534,047	425,824	22,000	n/a	n/a	n/a
1986	1,045,290	792,088	626,245	32,000	8,276	34	3,474
1987	1,526,283	1,128,929	928,517	32,000	11,023	40	3,904
1988	2,311,055	1,736,229	1,254,755	32,000	16,234	50	4,641
1989	4,172,054	3,409,471	2,327,099	42,678	21,794	173	8,119
1990	7,439,999	5,890,264	4,972,200	42,678	36,714	321	12,883

Source: Yuri Sato, 'The Salim Group in Indonesia', p. 417, citing Bank Central Asia, *Laporan Tahunan Bank Central Asia* (Bank Central Asia Annual Report) (Jakarta), various years

Liem's links to Soeharto date from the 1940s. In the 1950s Liem was involved in the export of primary products. From 1968, Liem held exclusive rights to import cloves for the tobacco industry. In the 1980s, with export-led industrialization, he moved into the manufacture of cement, textiles, steel, aluminium and timber, and mineral extraction. Three-quarters of the group's expansion in the 1970s and 1980s was in manufacturing. The aggressive expansion in manufacturing stimulated a parallel growth in banking.

Multinational banking and investment services were essential to maintain growth. The main argument here is that the expansion and performance of financial interests within the Salim group were sustained by the group's pre-eminence in critical non-financial industries. The Salim Corporation diversified not from its core specialization in commodities but, rather, through acquisitions, absorbing a whole range of industrial projects through government contracts and procurement policies in strategic goods such as flour, textiles, clove cigarettes, cement, steel, tyres and cords. This pattern of state-led growth created appropriate financial structures. There was horizontal and vertical integration of production and manufacturing, and integration with SOEs to maintain this oligopolistic grip. Thus, financial institutions were created to tap into state capital and foreign capital sources. The varying combinations of banking and finance with the non-financial sectors of the Salim Corporation are captured in these figures. Banking contributed 27.2 per cent of net profits in 1989, rising from 10 per cent in 1975. The share declined to 13.5 per cent in 1991, rising slightly to 15.6 per cent in 1993. The relative decline of banking was due to the increased importance of new capital-intensive industries attracting foreign capital. Telecommunications, which accounted for 1.8 per cent of total profits in 1989, was responsible for 26.3 per cent of company profits in 1992. The property sector also grew, with a contribution of 11.2 per cent of net profits in 1989, rising to 19.6 per cent in 1993. Production and marketing and distribution, which accounted for 59.8 per cent in 1989, fell to 48.5 per cent in 1993.[31] Therefore, the growth stages and critical turning points for BCA were contingent on the fortunes of the non-financial segments within the Salim Group.

Multinational banking was also essential for Indonesian private banks because state banks dominated the domestic financial system. To tap into foreign capital as well as channel lucrative earnings available from rising military expenditure in Indonesia in the 1980s, Liem acquired suitable financial institutions in Hong Kong, the Virgin Islands and the US to mobilize and hoard these funds. FPH was typical of this capital movement in the 1980s.

The international ambitions of Liem are covered in some detail in the account of FPH below (pp. 60–2) to illustrate how international expansion increased risk for Chinese capitalists. Under-capitalized Indonesian banks and finance companies borrowed heavily and invested both at home and abroad, confident that the government would bail them out. The hazards behind that guarantee and the privileged access to funds had the most serious consequences in the 1997 crisis. NPLs were the result of poor investment decisions, the collapse of the property market, the decline in exports and the current account deficit and falling reserves. Foreign capital began to flow out, creating a further squeeze on liquidity, which bankrupted financial institutions and the corporate sector.

FPH is principally an investment holding company with four divisions: banking, property (First Pacific Davis), telecommunications (Pacific Link, Smart Communications and Indo Link), and marketing (Hagemeyer, Berli Jucker and Metro Pacific). FPH was acquired in May 1982. Originally called Shanghai Land Investment Company, FPH was incorporated in 1888 by British expatriate merchants in Shanghai investing in land and real estate in China and Hong Kong. Chinese investors bought FPH in 1949. Liem bought and listed FPH on the Hong Kong Stock Exchange in 1983 for HK$1.25 billion, 14 times its original equity. FPH underwent radical restructuring in 1988 with separate listings in Hong Kong and Bermuda, and became an investment company, trading in land, mortgages, equity, currency, bonds and securities, as well as developing banking. The directors of FPH were family members, Chinese and *pribumi*, as well as business associates, and Filipino, American and British bankers and managers.

FPH's largest interest was in banking, with Hibernia Bank and United Savings Bank (USB) in California, and First Pacific Bank (Hong Nin Bank) in Hong Kong. USB was acquired in March 1986, having been established in 1974 in San Francisco as a bank catering for the large Asian population. USB had moved into property development and mortgage lending, but this was risky, and the bank failed in 1986, just prior to its take-over. USB expanded rapidly in its first year after takeover, with a 24 per cent increase in total assets, from US$641 million to US$792 million in 1987. With increased capital in 1988, USB expanded into southern California. FPH had already acquired another bank in San Francisco in 1983 – the Hibernia Bank. After acquiring Wells Fargo Bank and Crocker National Bank in 1986, Salim was involved in corporate finance as well as trade finance in the US. The Hibernia Bank expanded into Hong Kong in 1987, where FPH had acquired Hong Nin Bank and renamed it First Pacific Bank. This was to mobilize capital in East Asia and to specialize in mortgage lending as well as trade financing.

The growth of FPH was impressive. Net profits rose from US$33.4 million in 1989 to US$135.3 million in 1994. Turnover rose from US$1,622.9 million to US$3, 681.9 million in the same period; total shareholder funds increased from US$261.3 million in 1989 to US$439.8 million in 1994. By 1993, it had also undergone another important restructuring, transferring Hibernia Bank to a unit within FPH. The reasons for this restructuring – transferring firms, swapping equities and assets between separate units within the group – are clouded in mystery. In the same year (1993), family members, including Antony Salim, and other Indonesian partners left the FPH Board. Manuel Panglinan, a Filipino executive, rose to the top and FPH strengthened through product diversification, rather than focusing on its major core financial interests. The more flexible joint-ownership and joint-management, with Liem in overall control, had survived until the mid-1980s. Then the directors' own interests conflicted with those of the Board, leading to important restructuring. In contrast, the core Salim family group in Indonesia tightened control and ownership – with Liem, his second and third sons, together with professional managers, the board of directors and 11 divisions, each with a committee, deciding on strategy, and subdivision committees deciding on day-to-day operations. This pyramid controlled 400 companies. In short, there was a centralized ownership – management, with delegation of operations and policy to divisional managers. Domestic and overseas operations could be managed through this system. The ownership and family management of the core financial interests within FPH was more diffused, less dominated by the Liem family. Manuel Panglinan ushered in radical change in growth and diversification in the early 1990s. This change corresponded with increased activity in the Philippines, both in finance and property.

There were dramatic changes in the Salim Group as a result of the currency crisis of 1997. BCA, the largest private bank in 1998, possessing 12 per cent of total liabilities of the Indonesian banks, faced a series of runs in November

1997. On 16 May 1998, it faced more difficulties, with rumours of capital flight by Chinese bankers.[32] Twenty trillion rupiahs were withdrawn on a single day, 6 May 1998. The state provided 30 trillion rupiahs to rescue the bank, after Liem promised to repatriate some of his capital from abroad.[33]

Salim, who had been a close friend of Soeharto, now faced the latter's wrath. Salim, who was already facing a debt of US$3.2 billion to overseas banks, now had to hand over BCA and sell his stake in firms in Hong Kong before the bank could be restructured and returned to the family.

In May 2000, BCA was relisted subsequent to recapitalization and restructuring by BPPN. Foreign investment and state involvement reduced the Salim family holdings to 2.8 per cent held by Antony Salim and 2.1 per cent held by Soedano Salim. Farindo Investment Mauritius possessed 52.6 per cent, the Indonesian government held 6.5 per cent and the remaining 33 per cent was held by the public.[34]

FPH faced a US$3 billion debt. To reschedule this, it had to sell its most lucrative asset – Hagemeyer, the Dutch trading company, in January 1998, for US$1.7 billion. FPH also divested itself of its telecommunications units for US$2 billion and sold USB in California and First Pacific Bank in Hong Kong. These difficulties were closely linked to the crisis in the Salim Corporation in Indonesia, where government subsidies and finance were withdrawn in 1998. Indofood Sukses Makmur alone had debts in foreign currencies of US$1 billion. FPH's turnover fell from US$3,774 million in January–June 1997 to US$2,285 million in January–June 1998. Operating profits fell from US$300 million to US$190 million between January and June.[35] Initially, Salim lost control of BCA to the government and sold his flour-mills, cement factories, oil palm plantations and property. He had debts of US$5 billion. The fall of Soeharto, the riots in Jakarta and the massive debts of the corporation precipitated the sale of its lucrative food interests to an Australian firm. The decline of Liem Soei Leong and sons had already been anticipated by the rise of Manual Panglinan and the shift to the Philippines and a new patron in Estrada.

Changes in performance were reflected in changes in management. For example, in the early phase, family control was maintained, while part management was delegated to executive non-family members such as Sudwikatmono (Soeharto's cousin) and Risjad, and to professional managers – Filipinos, American, British and Japanese. The Board of Directors remained with family and friends. With the rise of Manuel Panglinan, there was a return to increased investment in the Philippines, in property (Fort Bonifacio City), banking, telecommunications and marketing.[36] In 1998, FPH made US$1.7 billion of investment in the Philippines.

The developments in the financial system outlined above contained the ingredients for a crisis. The dominance of state-owned banks and their relations with powerful capitalists – often guaranteeing credit as well as absorbing losses – made it inevitable that during the crisis, NPLs were concentrated in the state-owned banks. The lack of effective state regulation of domestic and offshore banking led to the quadrupling of external debt owed to foreign banks between 1990 and 1997. Short-term liabilities to foreign banks rose by 181 per cent in the same period.[37] The pegging of the rupiah to the US dollar, with only limited movement of 5 per cent, encouraged over-borrowing. Between 1990 and 1997, the real exchange rate appreciated by 8 per cent in Indonesia.[38] The private corporate sector had absorbed much of the domestic credit, which rose by 160 per cent. The domestic corporate sector was therefore over-leveraged, creating a volatile situation. A large proportion of this credit leaked into the real-estate sector, as well as into stock market speculation and investment in new industries, such as telecommunications, throughout Asia. By June 1997, bank lending to the property sector had grown by 40 per cent from 1995.

The de-regulation of domestic financial markets, the liberalization of international capital flows, the rapid innovation in financial instruments and the diffusion of information technology encouraged speculators in both the currency and equity markets. The inflow of short-term portfolio capital created bubbles in asset markets, which, when combined with the dramatic expansion in domestic credit and weakness in accountancy mechanisms, fostered a volatile situation. This volatility was also exhibited by Lippo Bank.

The Lippo Group

The Lippo Bank was founded in 1948 as Bank Perniagan Indonesia but the Riady family was associated with it only from 1989. In 1987 it merged with Central Commercial Bank and in 1989 with Bank Umum Asia. The purchase of Lippo Bank in 1989 coincided with their expansion in global finance. Lippo acquired financial interests in Hong Kong and China. It purchased a bank in Hong Kong to finance and manage infrastructural projects in mainland China. It held 40 per cent equity in China Mercantile Bank, and its branch in Shenzhen coordinated power projects and financed export trade. The Lippo Group used Lippo Bank to finance their joint-venture initiatives in Singapore, Shanghai and Hong Kong. It raised Rp142.8 billion (AU$98.5 million) in 1993 through a rights issue, to fund projects in China.[39] The Group was active in Sydney, Australia, concentrated principally in property, finance and export-import trade. Its fame, however, was in the purchase of Arkansas Bank, and in 1994 President Clinton appointed John Huang, who was the Vice-Chairman of Lippo USA, as the Principal Deputy Secretary of the US Department of Commerce.[40] A major criticism of the Lippo Group in Indonesia was that it was stealthily moving capital away from Indonesia into Australia, Hong Kong and China since 1990 and into the US since 1994.

The growth of Lippo Bank was spectacular between its listing in November 1989 and collapse in November 1997. Its highly impressive expansion occurred in November 1994 and December 1996, but collapsed in July 1997

Table 3.6 Bank Lippo

Key ratios	*1993*	*1994*	*1995*	*1996*	*1997*	*1998*	*1999*	*2000*	*2001*
Profitability									
ROE (after tax) (%)	11.80	15.01	16.55	12.85	12.85	11.78	146.81	–70.90	9.73
Net profit/total assets (%)	0.92	0.95	1.10	1.14	1.14	0.91	–57.87	–6.90	1.09
Net interest margin* (net interest income/average total assets) (%)	6.10	6.28	5.45	5.12	4.48	4.85	–9.08	–5.73	2.84
Net interest margin*(net interest income/average total advances) (%)	17.46	8.52	7.06	6.73	5.99	6.22	–12.51	–16.17	16.65
Capital adequacy									
Total liability/equity	11.79	14.82	14.07	10.23	10.23	11.92	–3.54	9.28	7.93
Total equity/deposits + borrowings (%)	8.97	7.19	7.60	10.70	10.70	9.63	–32.76	13.95	15.28
Total equity/total advances (%)	11.19	8.26	8.53	11.92	11.92	9.61	–60.24	56.61	66.26
Liquidity									
Total advances/deposits + borrowings (%)	80.17	87.00	89.11	89.76	89.76	100.15	54.39	24.65	23.06
Liquid asset ratio (liquid assets/ total assets) (%)	2.49	2.78	3.13	5.44	5.44	9.10	13.76	8.90	10.58
Liquid assets/deposits + borrowings (%)	2.85	3.16	3.59	6.53	6.53	11.32	11.44	12.76	14.44
Net loans/deposits (%)	83.58	88.91	98.74	85.54	85.54	90.94	24.35	16.71	18.26
Free capital/total capital (%)	–38.33	–54.46	–7.57	6.69	6.69	68.44	159.71	–22.09	–65.14
Share related									
Share price (RI)	8,180.36	5,834.94	6,049.46	9,391.26	2,449.89	3,372.68	2,500.00	550.00	450.00
No. of shares ('000s)	1,997,000	1,997,000	1,997,000	2,519,000	2,519,000	2,519,000	1,103,000	856,980	856,980
EPS (RI)	274.22	229.72	293.20	163.14	163.14	137.82	–9,749.00	–80.40	6.29
PER	29.83	25.40	20.63	57.57	15.02	24.47	–0.26	–6.84	71.54
PER (pres. price)	1.6410	0.0000	0.0000	0.0000	0.0000	0.0000	0.0000	0.0000	0.0000
BV/share (RI)	191.90	218.88	253.41	360.09	360.09	398.25	–5,158.00	2,700.00	2,956.00
P/B ratio	42.63	26.66	23.87	26.08	6.80	8.47	–0.48	0.20	0.15
Dividend/share (RI)	4.77	8.58	7.15	20.42	20.42	11.23	0.00	0.00	0.00
Dividend yield (%)	0.06	0.15	0.12	0.22	0.83	0.33	0.00	0.00	0.00

* 1993 ratio not calculated on average assets but on closing assets

Source: Annual Reports, Bank Lippo, 1993–2001

(see Table 3.6). It was taken over by BPPN for recapitalization in December 1998, succumbing to devastating losses in December 1999, before a strong revival in December 2000 and a gradual recovery to June 2001.[41] Throughout the crisis the family retained some equity and Mochtar Riady remained President of the Bank in the course of reconstruction.

Bank Duta

The following account of Bank Duta again identifies the three major factors that contributed to the financial crisis of 1997. The first factor was that links with the state and the Soeharto family complicated the regulation and supervision of financial institutions. The relationship compromised government regulations on capital adequacy rates for banks, tighter rules for loan provisions and, in particular, loans to the real-estate sector. The second factor was the cross-ownership between the bank and industrial firms, which produced further confusion in the monitoring of debt. Large loans and excessive borrowing dominated the Hasan Group. The continuous creation of financial institutions, whereby Hasan had five banks, underestimated risk. The third factor was Hasan's speculation on offshore capital markets, borrowing in US dollars, most of it short-term and unhedged.

Bob Hasan controlled a number of banks largely through acquisitions: Bank Umum Nasional, Bank Umum Tugu, Bank Duta which he rescued in 1995, and Bank Bukopin acquired in 1989. He was also a major shareholder of Bank Muamalat, an Islamic bank formed in the mid-1990s. These numerous banks and their close association to Hasan's corporate interests in timber and newsprint introduced volatility in the financial sector. His monopolies in timber and paper, in the marketing and distribution of these products, were financed by state banks, foreign banks and his personal banks. He secured a giant share of the state's development funds for his regional interests in Kalimantan through his corporation Kiani Kertas.[42] His banks and the credit they secured from the state and foreign interests also helped finance his joint-ventures in shipping, oil exploration and refining, and sustained his contracts with Pertamina, the state oil company. In 1995, 80 per cent of the loans from Bank Umum Nasional had been distributed to Kiani Kertas.[43] In addition, as a Soeharto crony, he had substantial loans from the state, enjoyed tax holidays and had privileged access to government contracts.[44]

As a result of these privileges and uncontrolled borrowing, Bank Duta alone had a bad debt of US$704 million, and all of Hasan's banks were closed in June 1998. To settle these debts he had to sell his companies (33 of them). Bank Duta's failure in 1998 was surprising. Though it had a history of failure, having failed in 1990 and been rescued by Salim and Pangetsu, then failing in 1995 with debts of US$419 million and being taken over by Hasan, collapsing in April 1998 and being taken over by BPPN,[45] between 1995 and 1997, Bank Duta had revealed a spectacular rise in revenues and an increase in net profits before experiencing clear financial distress in 1998 (see Table 3.7 for returns on assets, net income, turnover, capital adequacy ratio and dividend yields).

Bank Duta had been suspected of fraud throughout the 1990s, being linked to three of Soeharto's major charitable foundations and to his prestigious projects.[46] In 1995 it had been listed just three months before its failure, revealing an absence of rigorous supervision by Bank Indonesia and Bapepam (Capital Market Supervisory Agency). Even after the 1997 collapse, Hasan was accused of using the Central Bank's liquidity funds for property speculation and capital transfers abroad between September 1997 and September 1999. Indonesian capitalists had allegedly transferred around US$80 billion to foreign banks in these two years.[47]

Table 3.7 Bank Duta

Key ratios	*1993*	*1994*	*1995*	*1996*	*1997*
Profitability					
ROE (after tax) (%)	12.34	7.42	9.60	10.62	10.65
Net interest margin (net interest income/ average total assets) (%)	3.10	3.47	4.18	3.51	2.75
Net interest margin (net interest income/ average total loans and advances) (%)	5.91	5.94	6.45	5.84	4.34
Asset quality					
Loan loss prov./loans and advances (%)	0.50	0.44	2.60	0.41	1.64
Capital adequacy					
Total liability/equity	9.93	2.83	6.36	10.22	12.55
Total equity/deposits + borrowings (%)	10.07	35.29	15.73	9.78	7.97
Total equity/total loans + advances (%)	16.45	24.86	19.22	14.43	10.12
Liquidity					
Total loans and advances/deposits + borrowings (%)	61.20	141.94	81.82	67.79	78.70
Liquid asset ratio (liquid assets/total assets) (%)	1.93	2.28	2.02	3.07	3.97
Liquid assets/deposits + borrowings (%)	2.25	5.00	2.54	3.64	4.58
Net loans/deposits (%)	72.87	164.52	106.36	97.79	111.43
Free capital/equity capital (%)	–88.84	81.70	88.10	24.32	36.10
Share related					
Share price (RI)	1,053.96	458.24	297.86	366.59	274.95
EPS (RI)	43.63	38.72	48.22	56.47	61.70
PER	24.16	11.83	6.18	6.49	4.46
BV/share (RI)	353.52	477.94	502.51	531.51	579.14
P/B ratio	2.98	0.96	0.59	0.69	0.47
Dividend/share (RI)	45.82	22.91	22.91	28.64	59.57
Dividend yield (%)	4.35	5.00	7.69	7.81	21.67

* Ratios for 1993 calculated on closing assets and not average assets

Source: Datastream and Annual Reports of Bank Duta, 1992–8

Bank International Indonesia

Bank International Indonesia, belonging to the Sinar Mas Group, failed in April 1998 with a debt of US$4.6 billion and was recapitalized through nationalization in April 1999. This was the largest foreign debt owed by an Indonesian corporation in 1997.[48]

The bank was established in 1959 and was only acquired by Eka Tjipta Widjaja in 1982 and was listed on the Jakarta Stock Exchange in 1989. The rise in capitalization occurred between July 1990 and October 1996. Total assets grew from Rp99 million in 1970 to Rp803 million in 1975; to Rp12,249 million in 1980; to Rp102,314 million in 1987; and to Rp388,808 million in 1989. By 1993, this had risen to Rp7,139 billion and by 1996 expanded to Rp17,707 billion (see Table 3.8).

After July 1997, asset growth was through an injection of capital from government and foreign sources. It also undertook recapitalization through a new share issue for Rp967.1 billion in July 1997 to raise the capital adequacy ratio of the bank. This share issue introduced foreign equity of 47.4 per cent, though the family still retained 51 per cent.[49]

Return on assets grew from 2.02 per cent in 1970 to 3.59 per cent in 1980 but fell to 1.97 per cent in 1983, before rising to 2.84 per cent in 1986. In the same period net income as a ratio of assets also rose from 9.02 per cent in 1980 to 13.5 per cent in 1982, falling to 5.9 per cent in 1987. Net income as a percentage of total operating income was 27.53 per cent in 1980, falling to 7.48 per cent in 1984 but rising to 11.82 per cent in 1987. The economic depression of the mid-1980s was responsible for the slight decline in ROA and net income as ratio of assets.[50] (For statistics on growth between 1993 to 2001, see Table 3.8.)

What is clear from the data above is that between 1970 and 1990, the growth was gradual and sustainable, based on domestic expansion. After 1990, the growth was global as well and fuelled by access to foreign capital. This dual growth had serious repercussions for the bank's survival in Indonesia. The globalization of Chinese capitalists was at the heart of the volatility in Chinese capitalism in Indonesia in the 1990s. Ironically, this vulnerability at the close of the twentieth century repeats the demise of Chinese revenue farming syndicates of Southeast Asia and southern China at the close of the nineteenth century.[51] Lucrative global fortunes built on revenue farming by Chinese capitalists in Indonesia and the rest of Southeast Asia disintegrated with the rapid economic diversification and globalization between 1870 and 1914. This cyclical growth in Chinese entrepreneurship is a response to changing political patrons and changing responses to the global economy.

There are three critical factors in Bank International's growth. The first was that the bank had a diverse financial portfolio, in insurance, leasing and corporate banking. More than 70 per cent of its business was with its own firms or with large corporate customers. The second factor was the

Table 3.8 Bank International Indonesia

Key ratios	*1993*	*1994*	*1995*	*1996*	*1997*	*1998*	*1999*	*2000*	*2001*
Profitability									
ROE (after tax) (%)	21.72	16.86	19.07	20.78	9.56	129.97	–108.11	11.44	187.86
Net interest margin* (net interest income/average total assets) (%)	4.06	4.34	4.44	4.14	4.80	–5.00	–3.08	1.98	0.12
Net interest margin* (net interest income/average total advances) (%)	6.22	6.24	6.52	6.23	7.14	–8.51	–7.62	4.98	0.29
Asset quality									
Loan loss prov./advances (%)	0.74	0.46	1.50	0.73	3.15	56.22	4.62	0.14	33.90
Capital adequacy									
Total liability/equity	12.79	10.08	11.80	13.13	8.66	–4.84	19.76	14.91	–14.99
Total equity/deposits + borrowings (%)	10.93	11.77	9.93	10.18	19.31	–30.34	7.26	8.00	–8.14
Total equity/total advances (gross) (%)	11.10	12.41	12.06	10.44	15.51	–48.97	16.40	12.31	–24.66
Liquidity									
Total advances/deposits + borrowings (%)	98.51	94.87	82.29	97.57	124.50	61.95	44.30	64.96	33.01
Liquid asset ratio (liquid assets/total assets) (%)	2.23	1.65	3.07	4.21	4.79	8.59	11.82	10.05	6.79
Liquid assets/deposits + borrowings (%)	3.37	2.15	3.90	6.07	8.93	10.01	17.82	12.79	7.73
Net loans/deposits (%)	104.04	108.71	96.39	91.32	117.41	40.79	38.49	57.89	18.66
Free capital/equity capital (%)	–254.42	–141.47	–138.13	–223.62	–59.55	222.05	–815.50	–110.39	163.80
Share related									
Share price (RI)	5,339.38	3,781.54	5,508.68	10,339.39	1,980.04	1,370.80	1,500.00	400.00	200.00
EPS (RI)	427.00	468.00	608.00	135.00	118.00	–3,038.00	–39.00	3.00	–45.00
PER	12.50	8.08	9.06	76.59	16.78	–0.45	–38.46	133.33	–4.44
BV/share (RI)	1,287.00	1,936.00	2,316.00	2,880.00	4,814.00	–17,088.00	4,988.00	6,025.00	–5,666.00
P/B ratio	4.15	1.95	2.38	3.59	0.41	–0.08	0.30	0.07	–0.04
Dividend/share (RI)	65.51	72.72	72.72	266.82	140.13	0.00	0.00	0.00	0.00
Dividend yield (%)	1.23	1.92	1.32	2.58	7.08	0.00	0.00	0.00	0.00

Note: * Ratios for 1993 calculated on closing assets and not average assets.

Source: Datastream and Annual Reports of Bank International Indonesia, 1992–2002

joint-venture relations; since 1989 with Bank Fuji and from 1993 with Korean Daehan Investment Trust Company. This ability to impress foreign investors added to their hubris. In 1996 it was awarded 'The Emerging Markets Chief Executive Officer of the Year' by the New York International Media Partners and ING Bank. The same year, *Asia Money* ranked it as the best commercial bank in Indonesia, and fifteenth in Asia.

The third factor triggering growth and ultimate decline was rapid globalization. In Singapore it acquired a partnership in United Industrial Corporation, whose Chairman Lee Kim Yew was Lee Kuan Yew's brother. This global explosion led to a series of offshore companies in pulp and paper, in the food industry and financial services. In China, the bank's China Strategic Holdings had equity in 30 state-owned firms involved in beer production and tyre manufacture. In early 1995 the Sinar Mas Group acquired *Ming Pao Daily News*. In the same year they moved into property management and financial services in Australia through the firm Lend Lease. In late 1996 the group moved into the Indian pulp industry with an investment of US$100 million. Many of these ventures abroad were regarded as essential lifeboats in a racially volatile and politically insecure Indonesia. Ironically it was this packaging abroad that undid their fate at home.

Despite the increase in bank revenues, from Rp853,558 million in 1993 to Rp2,332,750 million in 1996, and rise in net profits from Rp112,434 million in 1993 to Rp260,410 million in 1996, the bank collapsed in 1997. The bank's reserves and provision for bad debts rising from Rp125,631 million in 1995 to Rp518,449 million in 1997 could not cover their high exposures to foreign exchange contracts, both in Indonesia and abroad (see Table 3.8).

It was only their stock market performance that hinted at the gathering storm clouds. Bank International Indonesia had seen share prices rising since 1990, with dramatic increases in 1994, and further spectacular rises from 1996, continuous to July 1997, before they collapsed. A precipitous decline continued from 1998 to 2000, with brief recoveries.

The family lost its stake in the bank: the restructuring completed in 2001 resulted in the Indonesian government owning 93.69 per cent. Unfettered ambition abroad had cost the family ownership of one of Indonesia's largest banks.

Bank Niaga

Bank Niaga, a *pribumi* bank, mimicked the same pattern of growth and collapse as the Chinese banks outlined above. The bank was founded in 1955 but only recorded impressive growth after 1974 when it secured a licence to operate in foreign exchange transactions. The bank belonged to the Tirtamas Group (formed by Hashim S. Djojohadikusumo, the brother of Probowo, Soeharto's son-in-law and a relative of the Governor of Bank Indonesia Soedradjad Djiwandono) and expanded into Hong Kong, Cayman Islands and California. This group had four other banks, including Bank

Table 3.9 Bank Niaga

Key ratios	*1993*	*1994*	*1995*	*1996*	*1997*	*1998*	*1999*	*2000*	*2001*
Asset size									
Int. earn. assets/total assets (%)	74.18	78.30	73.74	74.82	84.99	109.97	127.45	39.09	34.56
Cash and reserves/total assets (%)	2.62	2.77	2.45	3.16	3.92	8.67	14.68	8.09	6.30
Contingent/cont. + total assets (%)	0.00	0.00	0.00	0.00	0.00	0.00	0.00	0.00	0.00
Profitability									
ROAA (before tax) (%)	8.84	4.85	4.15	3.95	5.10	25.16	46.53	3.92	2.87
ROE (after tax) (%)	24.99	25.72	30.73	22.84	10.56	127.67	66.56	6.11	6.36
Net profit/total assets + cont. (%)	1.33	1.32	1.41	1.78	0.69	–32.60	–84.26	0.36	0.34
Net interest margin (net int. inc./ave total assets) (%)	8.03	4.30	4.15	4.44	4.77	–10.87	–16.87	–1.03	0.89
Net interest margin (net int. inc./ave total advances) (%)	10.83	5.62	5.48	5.98	5.90	–11.07	–14.53	–1.66	2.43
Asset quality									
Loan loss prov./advances (%)	0.98	1.27	0.86	1.10	2.22	18.87	46.74	–8.96	0.00
Capital adequacy									
Total liability/equity	17.84	18.49	20.79	11.79	14.40	–4.92	–1.79	16.07	17.88
Total equity/deposits + borr. (%)	6.96	6.86	6.01	10.80	9.68	–30.25	–66.94	7.59	6.58
Total equity/total advances (%)	7.16	6.55	6.22	10.43	7.64	–23.22	–99.33	15.00	15.32

Table 3.9 (continued)

Key ratios	*1993*	*1994*	*1995*	*1996*	*1997*	*1998*	*1999*	*2000*	*2001*
Liquidity									
Total advances/dep. + borr.	2.62	2.77	2.45	3.16	3.92	8.67	14.68	8.09	6.30
Liquid asset ratio (liquid assets/total assets) (%)	3.44	3.70	3.21	4.38	5.85	10.26	7.76	10.48	7.83
Liquid assets/dep. + borr. (%)	95.92	103.00	95.21	102.03	123.73	110.98	48.67	43.66	40.03
Net loans/deposits (%)	–113.49	–67.85	–76.54	–44.58	15.71	109.01	105.53	39.66	–8.95
Growth									
Turnover (%)		8.86	58.63	23.80	37.06	93.13	–46.67	13.47	47.67
Net interest income (%)		19.31	24.64	35.00	39.72	–381.75	26.40	–91.81	–241.57
Total income (%)		16.08	25.46	28.24	31.10	–292.37	31.34	–140.69	9.88
Net income (%)		22.28	43.56	51.14	–46.45	–5,438.20	39.75	–101.19	15.62
Operating profit (%)		22.36	10.67	19.83	68.09	509.24	50.63	–88.72	20.33
Total assets (%)		22.91	34.48	19.51	39.29	12.18	–45.93	181.15	22.90
Total loans and advances (%)		29.74	26.65	21.27	58.22	45.16	–37.33	–13.78	8.66
Deposits + borrowings (%)		20.61	37.23	13.09	29.26	41.29	21.12	14.78	28.11
Equity growth (%)		18.79	20.18	103.33	15.86	–541.45	168.07	–113.02	11.04

Source: Bank Niaga, Annual Reports, 1993–2001

Arya Panduarta and Bank Papan Sejahtera. This powerful presence in finance attracted investors such as Rashid Hussein from Malaysia, who in January 1997 purchased a 20 per cent controlling stake in Bank Niaga. This was relinquished in May 1999 when the Indonesian government, through BPPN, acquired 97 per cent equity – in effect, nationalizing the bank. All the other banks owned by Djojohadikusumo were closed. Bank Papan Sejatera held massive bad debts on loans to Semen Cibinong, a firm in the Tirtamas Group.[52] Bank Niaga continued to make serious losses. In 2001, it recorded losses of Rp9.069 trillion and the state announced a new share issue in April 2001 to cover these loans.[53] However, a glance at Table 3.9 shows no indication of impending distress. Positive growth is recorded until 1998.

The descriptions and analyses of the five banks clearly reveal the disastrous misjudgement not only by the state and foreign capital, but also by international financial rating agencies such as Moodys and Standard and Poor.[54] Bank Danamon, which had been ailing for a long time, received a BB rating from both Moodys and Standard and Poor in 1996. Its vulnerable position on long-term and short-term debt and incredible volatilities in net profits and share prices were evident in 1990, 1992 and 1994. It was taken over in April 1998 by BPPN and merged with eight other private banks in June 2000, with BPPN absorbing 99 per cent equity holding. Return on assets for Bank Danamon fell from 5.93 per cent in 1994 to 2.94 per cent in 1995; its return on equity fell from 15.74 per cent to –22.60 per cent in the same years. Net income fell from 61.85 per cent in 1995 to 45.39 per cent in 1996, to –93.46 per cent in 1997, to –151754.15 per cent in 1998, to –81.31 per cent in 1999, to –105.88 per cent in 2000 but rose to 146.33 per cent in 2001 because of recapitalization. Asset quality, too, fell from 0.94 per cent in 1994 to 0.61 per cent in 1995. World Bank economists and international rating agencies were providing the 'anchors' for this continued irrational exuberance and 'fatal conceit'.

The 1997 financial crisis

The following discussion on the crisis again highlights the three major characteristics of the Indonesian financial system: flawed corporate structure, strong political and ethnic networks traversing these organizations and an almost recessive, corrupt economic behaviour by capitalists distorting any attempts by the bureaucracy to achieve reform and recovery. These three characteristics form part of the continuing explanations for Indonesian financial turbulence. The diasporic element of Chinese capitalism merely enhances this endemic volatility; it is neither a cause nor an emphatic factor in determining the nature and course of this turbulence. Indonesian-Chinese bankers were part of this internal endemic volatility; their external diasporic alliances can be said to have only partially influenced this deep-rooted economic instability. My hypothesis is that diasporas become indigenized, almost vernacularized, creating and responding directly to their environment rather than to an ethnic trademark or to diasporic loyalties. This is clear when one compares the upheavals surrounding Indonesian-Chinese financial growth with Chinese banks in Singapore and Malaysia. Hong Leong Bank, Southern Bank, Tat Lee Bank and OCBC were all prudent, sculptured models of their immediate environment, and not simply a product of ethnic entrepreneurial evolution. The phases of financial instability in Malaysia and Singapore, when Chinese banks were trapped, either in the quagmire of the 1930s depression or in the financial crisis of 1997, only revealed critical problems of transitional growth in finance in the 1930s, or the agonies of a global emergency, as in the late 1990s. They were strictly not peculiarities of disaporic Chinese financial behaviour. The severity and length of the crisis reflected the environment, not the ethnic background of the financiers.

The 1997 financial crisis in Indonesia was not precluded by any powerful indication of weak corporate performance or seriously volatile macro-economic factors on the ascendant. The stock market, which peaked in 1995 and 1996, declined only after December 1996. Yet, on 8 July 1997, the crisis thrashed Indonesia with more devastating consequences than in the rest of Southeast Asia, including Thailand. The rupiah was attacked by speculators and continued its downward spiral despite the dedication of Bank Indonesia to support with foreign reserves. Finally, the IMF had to intervene in 1998 with a package of US$43 billion, dependent on trade reform, the dismantling of cartels in essential commodities – rice, flour and tobacco. The IMF also sought the closure of some banks and the restructuring of others.

The causes and outcomes have received the attention of numerous scholars. What this chapter has consistently argued is that it was the serious structural defects in the Indonesian financial system, its macro and micro inefficiencies that provided the environment for a contagion effect to take hold, after Thailand had come under attack in May 1997. The highly positive indicators of economic growth peeled away to reveal nepotistic, fraudulent financial institutions. Iriana and Sjoholm argue that the Indonesian crisis is partly a product of contagion where 'relatively small macro-economic imbalances can generate large economic difficulties if they are combined with regional turbulence . . . economic crises typically spread across borders through changing international investor sentiment'.[55] The account so far has demonstrated the reverse: the major defects in the financial system required only a tiny external pressure for the edifice to crumble.

Hal Hill in his article 'Indonesia: the strange and sudden death of a tiger economy' does admit that weak corporate structures, inadequate regulation, and cronyistic conspiracies and influences created serious moral hazards.[56] However, he emphasizes and concentrates on the critical role of weakening external trade, unstable capital flows and declining manufacturing as critical causes for the crisis. He identifies the role of capital mobility in creating volatility, but concedes that Indonesian external debt 'never reached high levels of most of its neighbours'.[57] Banks only accounted for 8 per cent of Indonesia's total external debt in 1997.[58]

What should be stressed here is the concentrated nature of debt-holding in the hands of a tiny Chinese and *pribumi* elite. High levels of this corporate debt was short-term and nominated in US dollars. The rise in domestic credit by 5 per cent per annum by 1996 was less than that of Thailand, but the density of such holdings in the hands of a preferred few, created the turbulence.[59] This rise in private corporate debt coincided with a phase of decline in the autonomy and rigour of financial bureaucrats in Jakarta. This weakness contributed decisively to and lengthened the Indonesian crisis.

Second, although the stock market did not experience so dramatic an increase in size and value as Malaysia and Singapore, many of the listed companies in Indonesia belonged to this small group; hence, the transfer of risk was further intensified. Public enthusiasm for the Jakarta Stock Exchange was restrained by this dominance and the clear evidence of insider trading. The market index was only 50 per cent higher in 1996 than its 1990 figures.[60]

The volatility here was located in the magnified inflows of foreign portfolio capital in the 1990s and its major recipients, the Chinese and *pribumi* capitalists. Sixty-one per cent of the top listed corporations were in the hands of these 15 families. Their extensive cross-ownership produced further confusion in the monitoring of debt. The links between political, economic elites in Indonesia and foreign capitalists meant that Chinese capitalists could avoid important rules on listing and the protection of the minority shareholder. Risk, too, was underestimated in this vast avenue of capital creation. Bank Duta, which failed in August 1990, had been listed in June 1990. Such cases raise the suspicion that listing was sought to avert immediate default.

Restructuring

The first phase of Indonesia's financial restructuring involved the closure of some banks. Sixty-four out of 237 banks were closed. BPPN took over some while injecting public funds into other failing banks. Bad debt was removed from these banks and taken over by BPPN. There was pressure to create large banks through mergers and foreign investors were encouraged to buy into these banks. Such proposals had two serious implications for Indonesian-Chinese banks with close links to industrial and commercial conglomerates. These banks were not in a position to cover interest expenses from operational cash flows. This proposition of distressed corporations thus rose from 12.6 per cent in 1995 to 40 per cent in 1997, to 58 per cent in 1998, to 63.8 per cent in 1999 and fell back to 57.4 per cent in 2000–2. In contrast, in Malaysia and Thailand, 26 per cent and 28 per cent of corporations were unable to meet interest payments in 1998 respectively.[61] The high leverage of Indonesian bank-corporate groups meant that even a slight contraction in credit aggravated their difficulties in maintaining interest payments.

The bank bail-out that accompanied the crisis pumped in liquidity with no safeguards. The major Chinese capitalists and the Soeharto family benefited initially from this. The total cost of this recapitalization was Rp660 trillion in 1999. In addition, the state acquired overvalued assets from these banks and faced difficulties in selling these assets. They only succeeded in increasing state ownership of the banking structure to 70 per cent, reversing the privatization programme of the early 1990s. At the end of January 1999, BCA had interest repayments of Rp18.3 trillion before recapitalization measures by the state reduced it to Rp8.3 trillion in 2000. Bank International Indonesia recorded interest repayments of Rp3.2 trillion in 2000, half that of its Rp6.2 trillion repayment in 1999.[62]

A second difficulty was in the restructuring of these financial institutions. In April 1998, BPPN took over management of seven private banks, including BUN (Hasan), BDNI (Nursalim of Gajah Tunggal), BCA (Salim), and Danamon (Admadjaja). In return, the banks handed over assets as guarantees. These included land, property, factories and cash. The value of much of these was exaggerated and government reassessment proved this serious shortfall in value.[63]

The banks that were closed were largely those belonging to Soeharto and the *pribumi* elite who had acquired many of these in the euphoric boom of the late 1980s and early 1990s. The restructured banks were largely Chinese banks, with a few exceptions such as Bank Niaga.[64] All this resulted in a reduction of private banks from 212 to 28 by January 1998.[65]

As part of this restructuring of Chinese banks, they were persuaded to repatriate some of their capital from Hong Kong, Singapore and the US through the purchasing of equity by their multinationals. Thus, in June 1999, Salim's Hong Kong subsidiary, First Pacific, purchased 52 per cent equity in Indofood in Indonesia. Salim also streamlined his interests in Indonesia by disposing of equity in Astra, Indocement, Indofood, Indomobil and QAF (Quality Asian Food). This was part of the strategy to reduce the level of bad debt in BCA.

Difficulties in the restructuring of debt arose from the inadequate method of loan classification, and government guarantees on bank liabilities and payments fostered by BPPN. The close links of individual banks to non-financial firms confused these liquidity payments and hampered bank restructuring.

In 1995 the volume of NPLs amounted to 9 per cent of total bank credit; it rose to 10 per cent in 1996, with dramatic increases in 1997 and 1998 to 55 per cent and 65 per cent respectively.[66] State banks held 68 per cent of such bad debt. A major segment of these loans had been distributed through connected, 'memo-lending' by the government to selected Chinese and *pribumi* capitalists.[67] By August 1999, only 13 per cent of NPLs had been restructured. This injection of public funds in the recapitalization of these banks – Rp132 trillion (US$21.7 billion) by June 1998, rising to Rp164.5 trillion by January 1999 and to Rp200 trillion by April 1999, only increased volatility and did not achieve any stability in the banking system.[68] These figures might not be accurate but are useful estimates in appraising the crude level of liquidity support provided by Bank Indonesia.

Another strategy was the issuing of medium- and long-term government bonds at high interest rates of 14 per cent. These bonds were directly exchanged for the worst NPLs. The state was simply taking over useless assets of these banks and corporations. The Indonesians should have emulated Thailand's aggressive strategy of closure of failing banks or provided incentives and guarantees for their safe takeover by foreign multinationals. In addition, the Thai government provided state funds only after restructuring. In contrast, BPPN absorbed the NPLs without securing prior guarantees. Hence, Indonesian debt restructuring was lowest – at 13 per cent of rescheduled debt as a percentage of total bad debt, compared to that in Malaysia of 32 per cent of restructured debt out of the total NPLs, and the Thais succeeded in restructuring 20 per cent of total bad debt.[69]

The third plank in the restructuring platform was mergers and joint-venture alliances. Bank Danamon merged with Bank Tiara and PDFIC in December 1999 and eight other banks, before recapitalization. Bank Buana Indonesia which already held foreign partners – Tat Lee Bank and Development Bank of Singapore – had increased this foreign shareholding with Keppel Tat Lee Bank in 1999. However, by early 2000, the Singapore partners withdrew because of inadequate guarantees and suspicions on unauthorized capital transfers. The Indonesian government then assisted with recapitalization through the Jakarta Stock Exchange in May 2000. This, again, implied increased state ownership. In 1996, 40 per cent of bank liabilities rested with the state; by December 1999, this ratio rose to 70 per cent.[70]

Attracting foreign capital and partnership in bank restructuring was fraught with difficulties. This was constantly marked by prevarication because of the unstable nature of the financial sector and continuing political unrest. Bank International Indonesia, which previously held joint-venture ties with the Commonwealth Bank of Australia, and Inter Pacific Bank, which had ties with French and Japanese banks before 1997, now failed to attract foreign partners. The first was taken over by the state, while Inter Pacific Bank was forced to shed its capital market subsidiaries and concentrate on commercial banking.[71]

However, it was in the debacle over Bank Bali and its foreign suitor, Standard Chartered, that the reluctance of prospective foreign buyers highlighted the three major inhibiting factors in Indonesian bank reform – political corruption, lack of strict corporate governance, and pervasive, confusing inter-bank and inter-corporate linkages.

Bank Bali had been established by Djaja Ramli, but was in serious difficulty in the 1997 crisis. Standard Chartered was persuaded to acquire a 20 per cent stake in the bank for US$56 million in April 1999. This was withdrawn in July 1999 when it was apparent that, because of serious corruption, a higher capital-asset ratio was necessary and recapitalization costs were rising. The level of inter-bank loans, too, was high. The majority of these loans were with banks that had been frozen by BPPN.[72] Bank Dagang Nasional Indonesia alone owed Bank Bali Rp904 billion. Bank Bali had been lending to Golkar and Cabinet Ministers, including Habibie, Rp550 billion for election expenses. There were illegal transfers by BPPN to Bank

Bali to cover these inter-bank losses. This was concealed and only an audit by Pricewaterhouse Coopers revealed this. In September 1999, IMF suspended its loans to Indonesia, further intensifying the crisis. Rudy Ramli and three directors of the bank were arrested the same month, and Standard Chartered withdrew.[73]

This scandal now increased the pressure for checks on how far bankers were using state credit for unauthorized lending – lending to politicians, friends or speculating on the capital market. Bank Bali's net losses of Rp132.2 billion and interest expense of Rp1.2 trillion in 2000 were difficult to reconcile with its positive performance indicators before 1997[74] (see Table 3.10). The Bank was finally taken over by BPPN, after selling its operations in Hong Kong.

This case study again supports my conclusion that endogenous structural factors, rather than ethnic groups and their ethnically determined modes of operations, determined success or failure of financial institutions. Success in restructuring and reform of banks, too, rested on similar endogenous factors in Indonesia. The dramatic but unstable growth in the banking sector corresponded with the inadequate regulatory infrastructure in finance, when in the mid-1980s the Governor of Bank Indonesia lost some of his supervisory power and control, which were then transferred to the Ministries of Planning and Finance. This meant intensification of corruption, collusion and nepotism. Uncertainty and vulnerability, inbred in the dependence on large foreign capital inflows and borrowing from abroad, provided only a mere trigger to the eroding edifice. Historically determined, flawed institutions – political, social and economic – were the culprits.

Pribumi banks such as Bank Niaga were just as exposed to volatility as Chinese banks such as BCA, BUN and Danamon. This emphasis on endogenous patterns of growth is sustainable when we compare Indonesian-Chinese banks with Chinese banks in Malaysia (Hong Leong) and Singapore (Tat Lee, OCBC and UOB) which were successful in restructuring after the crisis.[75] Financial volatility is not a disease of the Chinese diaspora; it is the environment, the institutional framework and levels of regulatory supervision that determined volatility. The financial crisis in Indonesia provided further evidence of this endemic volatility, institutional flaws and bank vulnerability. In 1967, 30 private banks failed.[76] Failures were more frequent following the financial de-regulation in 1988. Bank failures grew with the boom in commercial banking from 112 banks in 1988 to 239 in 1996. Bank Summa collapsed in 1992 with bad debts totalling US$700 million. Bank Duta failed in 1990 owing to foreign exchange speculation. Bapindo, a state-owned bank, collapsed in 1994 after lending US$430 million to Edy Tansil (5 per cent of its total lending) for a single project.[77] This form of connected lending by banks to Chinese capitalists, senior military and political personnel, including Finance Minister Johannes Sumarlin and the Soeharto family, persisted. All this compromised the achievement of an effective reconstruction of banks and financial organizations in contemporary Indonesia.

Table 3.10 Bank Bali

Key ratios	*1993*	*1994*	*1995*	*1996*	*1997*	*1998*	*1999*	*2000*	*2001*
Profitability									
ROE (after tax) (%)	28.52	28.44	24.34	29.13	12.65	149.92	55.44	–235.46	44.99
Net profit/total assets (%)	2.24	2.06	2.05	2.24	0.85	–26.69	–32.04	–9.33	1.78
Net interest margin* (net int. inc./ave total assets) (%)	3.97	4.59	4.60	4.64	4.59	1.97	–5.49	–2.80	0.62
Net interest margin* (net int. inc./ave total advances) (%)	5.67	6.42	6.31	6.57	7.44	3.24	–9.59	–11.75	4.21
Asset quality									
Loan loss provision/advances (%)	0.46	0.51	0.90	0.59	2.69	39.68	15.70	41.14	5.56
Capital adequacy									
Total liability/equity	11.66	12.73	10.82	11.96	13.90	–6.61	–2.72	24.18	24.23
Total equity/total advances (%)	7.86	7.25	8.44	7.70	6.70	–17.80	–57.79	3.96	3.95
Liquidity									
Total advances/deposits + borrowings (%)	81.98	85.56	85.90	84.51	69.13	63.36	34.69	15.93	21.03
Liquid asset ratio (liquid assets/total assets) (%)	2.24	2.70	2.52	3.40	4.19	7.15	13.01	8.46	6.07

Table 3.10 (continued)

Key ratios	*1993*	*1994*	*1995*	*1996*	*1997*	*1998*	*1999*	*2000*	*2001*
Liquid assets/deposits + borrowings (%)	2.62	3.17	2.98	4.19	5.06	6.94	10.11	10.69	7.56
Net loans/deposits (%)	107.65	107.88	105.39	109.62	89.12	40.89	18.48	11.15	19.34
Free capital/total capital (%)	–12.29	–1.03	–5.67	–50.66	–85.62	190.64	110.11	–64.35	–1,302.73
Share related									
Share price (RI)	1,016.45	954.84	638.56	611.58	242.83	179.43	215.31	75.00	40.00
No. of shares '000s	1,208	1,208	1,397	1,404	1,404	1,404	1,404	672	669
EPS (RI)	30.80	30.80	40.47	35.97	61.16	0.00	0.00	0.00	0.00
PER	33.00	31.00	15.78	17.00	3.97	n/a	n/a	n/a	
BV/share (RI)	269.26	298.94	382.70	438.51	600.58	–1,269.00	–2,644.00	704.04	768.63
P/B ratio	3.77	3.19	1.67	1.39	0.40	–0.14	–0.08	0.11	0.05
Dividend/share (RI)	30.81	30.81	34.63	35.96	38.68	0.00	0.00	0.00	0.00
Dividend yield (%)	3.23	5.42	5.88	15.93	0.00	0.00	0.00	0.00	

Note: * Ratios for 1993 calculated on closing assets and not on average assets.

Source: Bank Bali, Annual Reports, 1992–2002

4 Indonesian corporations, cronyism and corruption

The subject of cronyism and corruption permeating the corporate economy of Indonesia has been covered in detail by Richard Robison and Andrew MacIntyre.[1] They have focused principally on government–business relations but not on how far it affected the performance of the corporations. R. Fisman, in his study of the inter-relationship between Soeharto and corporate performance on the Jakarta Stock Exchange, used 'event theory' to assess the impact of political connections on corporations and their fortunes on the stock market.[2] However, without detailed corporate data and analysis, this remains highly speculative. The very assumption of political connections with any one corporation is too rigid and ignores historical changes in the corporate economy. The tenure of Soeharto from 1966 to 1998 was marked by changes in his relationships to institutions – the bureaucracy, the military, *pribumi*, Chinese corporations, state-owned corporations – and Fisman ignores these critical changes and concentrates on the months between the outbreak of the crisis in September 1997 and the ousting of Soeharto in May 1998. Stijn Claessens (1999), too, indulges in broad comparative analysis, forsaking detailed analysis of corporate growth and performance and the influence of political connections in this development.[3]

This chapter uses detailed corporate data to verify the inter-penetration of various political, bureaucratic and economic institutions to ascertain the impact of cronyism and corruption on the corporate landscape of Indonesia. Although the emphasis is on the 1990s, the historical changes since 1950 within the institutions of the presidency, military, private Chinese and *pribumi* corporations and SOEs will assist in identifying the obstacles to sustainable growth and efficiency within the corporate economy.

Pranab Bardhan, in his article 'Corruption and Development', *Journal of Economic Literature*, 30, September 1997, 1320–46, places Indonesia forty-fifth out of 54 in a table ranking the perceived corruption in banking in 1996; on a scale of 1–10, from 'maximum corruption' to 'no corruption', Indonesia scored 1.5.[4] This is derived from questionnaires filled in by *Business International* correspondents in the period 1980–3. Such surveys lack scientific rigour and must remain speculative unless supported by serious empirical data. Concentrating on 1980–3 is risky: these were years of economic boom in the region and perceptions are influenced by such experiences. This is not to deny there is truth in the survey and that the conclusions are fairly robust. It still remains, in Charles Perrow's words, 'The invasion of the body snatchers', where the outline of forms are extracted and maintained while the complexities, the plurality of emotions, values, influence, tensions and paradoxes have disappeared.[5]

The serious dimensions of the problem of corporate corruption and cronyism are entangled in the various institutions in Indonesia: the presidency, the first family, the bureaucracy, the military, the charitable foundations (*yayasan*), dominant ethnic Chinese capitalism, *pribumi* capitalism, SOEs, in particular Pertamina, Bulog and Berdikari, and the legal infrastructure, the judiciary, the courts and legislation relating to corporate affairs. Equally important are foreign agents, foreign investors, World Bank, International Finance Corporation (IFC) and the international accountants, and Standard and Poor and Moodys who provide assurance and confidence for foreign capital markets.

The dual focus is, therefore: what are the institutions that engender cronyism and corruption? How do these institutions foster and promote an economy of entrenched monopolies and privileges with lucrative shares absorbed by a well-connected elite of Chinese capitalists and a tiny *pribumi* elite sustained by ties to Soeharto and the state?

In fact, the resource-rich Indonesian economy has engendered a culture of grab and greed. The development of the timber industry and oil industry, as well as the extraction of minerals has unleashed not just corruption but violence and the displacement of regional populations.

The financial institutions, the banks and investment houses were an integral part of the expansion of the corporate economy from the late 1960s. Their role in contributing to weak corporate governance is acknowledged here. Forms of lending, command lending by state banks to certain groups, access to subsidized credit and the creation of private banks within the conglomerates were a clear source of risk and instability, as demonstrated by the 1997 financial crisis.

The weak and chaotic organization and regulation of the corporate sector, the equity markets, the neglect of minority shareholders, lack of legal rigour on issues of insolvency, bankruptcy and creditor rights confused the rights of stakeholders, and introduced endemic forms of corruption and made corporate debt restructuring almost impossible.

The other important contribution to systemic corruption was the rise of charismatic politicians, technocrats, bureaucrats and military commanders with their visions and ambitions. Soeharto, Habibe, Sudharmono, Ginanjar, Mariie Muhammad, Wiranto, Moerdani, Salim, Prajogo Pangestu, Bob Hasan and Probosutedjo added to the confusion in corporate governance and corporate social responsibility. The civil service, Bank Indonesia and the Ministry of Finance hold an important mirror to these changing pressures on corruption, cronyism and rent-seeking.

Finally, the paradoxical role played by the IMF, World Bank and IFC in shaping the organization and regulation of the Indonesian bureaucracy since 1980 has to be noted. Drafted in to provide effective systems of review and regulation of economic institutions, sometimes they became part of the problem, providing finance and aid cover, while the President and his cronies siphoned off these funds to private ventures, or they provided legitimacy and international credibility to rather ambivalent business practices. The IFC funded large Chinese corporations, SOEs and *pribumi* initiatives, swayed more by their credentials and contacts with 'the palace' than by corporate performance.[6]

These political connections and their direct impact on the corporate economy form the focus of this chapter. In Chapter 2, I covered the major trends responsible for the concentration in ownership of large corporations, their internal governance structures and processes, and how these distorted competition and long-term economic growth. In this chapter, I will concentrate on the external dynamics of this inter-penetration of political, bureaucratic, military and foreign institutions on corporations. As Ito declared: 'Indonesia cannot be understood without investigating the political and social shocks.'[7] This state intervention is traced from 1966, with the rise of Soeharto, from initial planned growth to limited privatization in the 1980s and de-regulation from 1989; each shows high levels of state participation and monopolistic private capital, with multiple interlinks to domestic institutions and to foreign state and capitalist networks.

An important clarification here is that the Indonesian economy experienced an average annual growth of 6.5 per cent from 1967, with no year of negative growth. There was a fall of –13.6 per cent in GDP in 1998, the sectoral effects of the crisis being more pronounced than the overall decline. Agricultural growth remained fairly constant, and only finance, construction and manufacturing confronted serious contraction in 1998.[8] The robust economic growth between 1967 and 1997 is no myth, as in Krugman's sense of growth propelled by increase in the factors of production, rather than total factor productivity; the budget was in balance; inflation was low; the current account deficit as a percentage of GDP was only half that of Thailand; external debt was high but manageable; investment and savings were rising; there was no evidence of an asset price bubble in real estate or the stock market.[9] Trade and investment barriers were declining and Bank Indonesia pursued prudent financial regulation; international reserves were rising in the 1990s and export growth was buoyant. Yet by September 1997, Indonesia was in crisis, with an exchange rate collapse, production declining, sharply rising inflation, declining incomes, rising unemployment and increasing poverty. There was no confidence in the corporate sector and an IMF bailout was essential. Soeharto was toppled by May 1998.

How do we explain this cataclysmic change in 1997? Are we to attribute this to the varying circles of influence: the institutions of the state, the presidency, the military, the foundations, the bureaucracy, formal and informal structures surrounding the large corporations and their family owners? Were these institutions and their relations with business groups central to developmental success? Is Indonesian economic success, too, a complex web of the systematic influence of cronyism? Both state and business display vulnerability to each other. Conglomerates possessed concentrated economic power and were able to control the state, but because state power is centralized in Jakarta, it, too, revealed aggressive power. In the face of the absence of a traditional bourgeoisie, with the *priyayi* an ornamental class with little trappings of economic or political power, Chinese capitalists and a tiny *pribumi* capitalist minority dominated monopolistic growth. There was clear collusion between large business and a coherent state; both found it to their benefit, although in the 1970s and 1980s the state was more powerful than the capitalists. The Chinese conglomerates with global ambitions in the 1990s were able to garner patrons both inside and outside Indonesia. In fact, with economic liberalization since 1989, Indonesian capitalists were able to secure favourable credit, contracts and privileges, and were making an indiscriminate entry into new sectors such as telecommunications and electronics, achieving dominant shares with few structural adjustments. Thus, loan policies, import licensing and export policies all emphasized crucial political connections, but because the state was consolidated and strong, investments were efficient, and thus cronyism and corruption need not stunt growth. There, as Alice Amsden argues for Korea, the state exchanges subsidies for performance.[10] D. Kang makes a serious error in arguing that Soeharto was like Marcos.[11] Soeharto liberalized the economy, state banks were declining, many were privatized, SOEs were large but private conglomerates (largely Chinese) were the powerhouses. As Hal Hill argues, as long as Soeharto was not transferring money into Swiss bank accounts or the Chinese engaging in capital flight, 'growth is feasible with corruption'.[12]

It is, thus, the nature of growth that is unstable: expansion, over-capacity, high foreign debt rather than prudent, efficient growth. As argued in Chapter 2, it was heavy leverage, weak management by the family and the chaotic growth of Salim, Texmaco and Tirtamas that revealed vulnerability. And when the power equation between the state and private capital changed in the 1990s, Soeharto was not sufficiently alert to respond rapidly.

Thus, Chinese conglomerates who had assumed concentrated economic power could not be disrupted or allowed to fail; when *pribumi* capitalists were expanding in a chaotic fashion in the 1990s, Soeharto was struggling to retain control. The majority of the ten largest debtors to IBRA in 1999 were *pribumi*.[13] In their headlong rush for rents, their lack of a product or regional base introduced widespread vulnerabilities.

The interlocks between banking, business, politics, military and Soeharto and his family were intense, high and located within monopolies in cement, oil, timber, telecommunications, media and food, where rents were high. Soeharto, unlike Marcos, did not attempt to divide and rule. Soeharto did not create disorganized business, as did Marcos, who was determined to destroy the existing mestizo oligarchs in favour of Chinese cronies in sugar, coconut and grain monopolies.[14] Bossism in the regional Philippines was intimidating to the centralized economic–political power in Manila. Such powerful barons were absent in Indonesia. It was, instead, the institutions of the military, bureaucracy, Golkar, Soeharto and the large conglomerates with monopolies that could challenge the state. Unlike Singapore and Malaysia with strong states, Soeharto faced diverse institutional threats and his strategy was to corrupt, erode or emasculate them. Thus, Soeharto's form of cronyism could be productive, unlike that of Marcos whose cronyism was riven by factions within Malacanang Palace as well as across the countryside.[15] Soeharto was sufficiently astute to compromise on *pribumi* economic nationalism and support Chinese tycoons, as possessing greater potential as agents of economic growth.[16]

Soeharto exercised enormous power at executive level, rent-seeking was high, particularly with the few *pribumi* capitalists, the first family and Chinese cronies. The weak legal system, which is analysed later in the chapter (pp. 103–7), the weak judiciary and under-utilized courts easily made corruption endemic. Only the bureaucracy, the technocrats, fought for economic efficiency and viable long-term economic growth. In this they were assisted by World Bank consultants.[17]

This chapter, therefore, seeks to analyse cronyism and corruption by identifying who are the critical actors, the power of these actors, and how each extracts benefit from the relationship. The hypothesis of 'mutual hostages' is enunciated in depth in D. C. Kang.[18] In the case of Indonesia, the mutual hostage concept is dynamic, changing, when in different time periods one actor is more or less powerful than the other. Up to the late 1980s, the mutual hostages were fairly contained; thus Soeharto was able to respond effectively to the economic crisis of 1983–5. In the 1990s, with economic liberalization, various economic actors were grabbing economic rents from as many patrons as possible. Chinese conglomerates identified patrons in Indonesia, Singapore, Hong Kong, China, Arkansas and Australia. It is this mobility of capital and over-diversification that rendered rent-seeking more corrupt and corrosive, and brought corporations close to collapse. With economic liberalization, there were opportunities for large firms to determine favourable policy, pursue government contracts, move indiscriminately into new capital-intensive business sectors such as automobiles, telecommunications and electronics. This meant over-diversification, over-capacity and the loss of core competencies, and weak corporate governance in intra-group transactions, magnified by the surrounding weak legal institutions and lack of accountability and transparency.

In effect, the crisis was inevitable. Hal Hill argues that in the 1980s, Soeharto was alert and responsive and averted disaster. But in the 1990s, he was less vigilant and was caught napping in 1997.[19] My own view is that Soeharto was dealing with more elusive hostages at home in the 1990s compared to the 1980s, aggravated by the rising ambitions of his own family.

The following sections will seek to analyse the separate institutions, and how far cronyism and corruption permeated them.

The military and the corporate economy

The major issues to be covered in the discussion on cronyism, corruption and the military are the historical evolution of the relationship between the military and business, the financial, commercial activities of the military, relations to Soeharto and to Golkar, the developments in the regions of Indonesia, connections to Pertamina and natural resources in general, the charitable foundations and the military. And, finally, the role of the military in eroding the efficacy and broad expansion of *pribumi* capital, as a result of its liaisons with Chinese capital. In short, the military secured the growth of a tiny *pribumi* elite capital, while stunting broader regional *pribumi* capitalist caucuses. The corruption in aid and defence contracts, as well as in liaisons with the Chinese led to 'Ali Baba' structures of capitalist development. Finally, the changing relations of the military with Soeharto and Golkar had serious implications for capitalist growth and economic stability.[20]

Soeharto's entrenched view was that Indonesian society possessed serious undercurrents of violence that were tribal, hierarchic, ill-disciplined and disorderly, and lacking in duty. This nurtured in him an excessive emphasis on commercial competence. The army, besides managing its civic social mission, had to undertake wealth-accumulating activities. The remnants of feudal privilege meant that the *Karyawan* (functionality) doctrine permeating the military bestowed military generals with economic privileges, lucrative company directorships and even ministerial posts upon retirement.[21] The culture of *dwifungsi* (dual role in society) bred corruption through random expropriation of land, contracts and licences.

The early rationale for military involvement in the corporate economy was to provide the security services with an economic ability to sustain and expand. Since the state could contribute only 25 per cent of the budget essential for the upkeep of the military, their business was critical. Second, when the Dutch companies were seized in 1958, they were managed by SOEs, but in the New Order of Soeharto, some were handed over to the military. Diponegoro Division, headed by Soeharto, had involvement in agriculture and shipping. These corporate units provided wealth but also a political power base. Many of these business interests remained small and incapable of growth and profit. The only exception remained the military's link with petroleum, which throughout remained a critical source of funding for the military's projects in the oil boom of the 1970s and 1980s. It has been argued that the oil boom coincided with a dramatic increase in cronyism, while the oil recession corresponded with its retreat and with economists rushing in with their economic planning schedules for recovery.

Military-assisted corporations sprouted in natural resource extraction, fishing, finance, real-estate, manufacturing and construction sectors. Not one of their companies was registered in the 20 elite corporations in 1993 or in 2000.[22] It was the Chinese who spun off large companies through their relationships with the military. However, the military's economic strength remained highly visible in the 1970s with domination of Pertamina by Ibnu Sutowo. In 1978 he went bankrupt. The military also developed a network of foundations which received money from the state and was bailed out by the World Bank. Another SOE controlled by the military, BULOG, also became a victim of corruption and had to be rescued by the state.

In 1980, increasing corruption in military business led to compulsory restructuring with heavy losses. Only a few 'strategic' companies were given special protection, in the hi-tech industry, in military projects, in industrial complexes, and with private companies nurturing relations with foreign multinationals such as Free Port, Rio Tinto in Papua and Exxon Mobil in Aceh. Elite components of the different territorial armies (Kostrad, Kopassus) also managed their own private companies, and this was open to fraud.[23] These failed and only the 1997 crisis removed them. Illegal activities, such as smuggling, prostitution and gambling, flourished in this period and the 1997 crisis merely increased their scale.

This accumulation of economic initiatives and the vacillating attitude of Soeharto towards the army introduced not only fraud but also increased vulnerability. In addition, Soeharto's efforts from 1988 to erode the political–economic strength of the military meant that he moved increasingly into the clutches of the Chinese and his own family's business interests.

The economic role was related to the belief that the army could raise funds to finance its initiatives. A corporate culture thus prevailed. This corporate policy, the use of the military in economic ventures, coalesced with the regional structure of the military. In particular, regions such as Aceh, Kalimantan and Papua, areas with high resource endowments, aroused greed and corruption.[24]

Soeharto mediated this territorial structure, maintaining loyalty and stability through a high turnover of regional military commanders to reduce the economic and political power of any single commander. However, the military elite did capture lucrative concessions in minerals, petroleum, timber, land, shipping and reforestation projects. Many of these activities were managed in partnership with major Chinese tycoons. This underlines one significant development: the nexus between the military and Chinese capitalists intensified and created divisions in *pribumi* capital. The military controlled, resource-endowed SOEs, such as Pertamina, Bulog and Bendikari, revealed this connection.

The involvement of the military in two institutions – the SOEs, and the *yayasans* (charitable foundations) and cooperatives – accentuated the existing networks of corruption. The military developed its own foundations which received compulsory contributions from the conglomerates and the state, in addition to voluntary endowments. There is no audit of these transactions and in 1998 they were the focus of enquiries into money-laundering, illegal transfers to personal and Golkar accounts.

These foundations established airline companies, construction and rubber-processing businesses and hotels, and were involved in tourism and fisheries. Inkopad (Army Central Cooperative Board) was the preserve of regional military commanders who exploited their access to state contracts, permits and licences to form joint-ventures with Chinese and foreign multinationals. These connections descended into simple rent-seeking. The military were repeating the actions of the *priyayi* in colonial Indonesia, who absorbed rents in economic relations with the Chinese and political ties with the Dutch.

At the outset it can be asserted that the rise of the *yayasan* introduced a ubiquitous form of fraud because of the interlocking relationships between politicians, bureaucrats, capitalists and the *yayasan*. The transfer of funds from Bank Negara Indonesia to private banks was frequently routed through a *yayasan*. They emerged as an invaluable institution for money-laundering in Indonesia.[25]

There were seven major foundations, belonging to Golkar, the Soeharto family, military and diverse groups: Supersermar (education), Dharmais (orphanages), Dakab (Golkar), Amah Bhakti Muslim Pancasila (Mosques), Dana Sejahtera Mandiri (poor), Dana Gotong Royong (cooperatives) and Trikora. The military possessed several more foundations through which the military elite channelled foreign aid, bribes and illegal activities in the smuggling of arms and explosives, prostitution and gambling.

An important feature of these foundations is that they intensified factionalism in *pribumi* society. Dharmais, established by Sudharmono, was an attempt to divert contracts and charitable funds from the army. Sudharmono, as a bureaucrat in the 1980s, had attempted to isolate the generals from lucrative military contracts.[26] This coincided with the period in the 1980s when Soeharto was prising himself away from the military and eroding their political ambitions. The conflict between Sudharmono and Moerdiono in October 1988 crystallized this growing estrangement from the military. The *yayasan* business interests were closely interconnected with the large Chinese conglomerates, such as Bob Hasan's Nusamba and the Salim Group.

Fourth, many of the *yayasan* owned or held shares in banks. Bank Umum Nasional, a major recipient of *yayasan* financial desposits, was in distress in 1973. In the 1980s and 1990s, Bank Duta, which was owned by the foundations established by the Soeharto family, was in continuous difficulties. In 1990 it recorded losses of US$420 million and was rescued by Soeharto's cronies, Pangestu and Liem.[27]

Many of these foundations received regular payments from SOEs and wealthy Chinese and their corporations. It was estimated that 2 per cent of profits of all major corporations were transferred to the foundations, as well as a proportion of the taxes paid by these corporations.[28]

The efforts of the civil servants to audit these accounts failed. The sums involved were huge, as since the 1970s, some of the taxes on oil revenues had been diverted into these foundations, in addition to some of the foreign aid being absorbed by foundations related to Golkar, the army and the first family. Politically sensitive projects such as reforestation in South Kalimantan, government monopolies in specific sectors, all attracted compulsory donations to these foundations. The foundations' early aims at poverty eradication and the development of *pribumi* entrepreneurship were confused with private greed and money-politics in the 1980s.

Thus, it is justifiable to conclude that these foundations not only increased corruption and cronyism but also stunted the development of an effective *pribumi* capitalist class. Consequently, in the aftermath of the 1997 financial crisis, attention was focused on these foundations. In June 1998 the government targeted the foundations belonging to the Soeharto family, to the military and to Golkar. In April 1998 it was estimated that Dakab (Golkar) had assests of Rp836 billion, Mandiri Rp900 million and Supersermar Rp808 billion.[29] In total, Soeharto's foundations alone had assets of Rp4.5 trillion.[30]

The military had created a culture of bribes and extortion by way of a variety of organizational structures in the foundations, cooperatives and corporations, and managerial roles in state-owned and private enterprises, to extort from the corporations and the communities they defended. Between 1994 and 2001, it was estimated that US$450 million had been diverted from the armed forces budget and US$26 million from that of the airforce.[31]

However, the rise of Habibie in the early 1990s encroached on the role of the military in the procurement of defence contracts. Since 1993, Habibie controlled projects in military technology, aircraft construction and ship building. The over-indulgence of Habibie in hi-tech investment now shifted the conflict to that with the bureaucrats and ministers.[32] All attempts by Mar'ie Muhammad, the Finance Minister, and Bank Indonesia to curb defence overspending by Habibie were thwarted by Soeharto.[33]

However, it was the fraud associated with the SOEs such as Pertamina, Bulog and Berdikari that was critical – a form of corruption initiated by Soeharto and Ibnu Sutowo, and profited from by Salim, Projogo Pangestu, Bob Hasan and a host of other capitalists. In the 1960s, Pertamina provided a third of export earnings, rising to two-thirds after the oil price rise in 1973. The growth between 1968 and 1975 was assisted by joint-venture ties with Shell, Mitsubishi, Caltex, Mobil and Stanvac. By 1975, 35 oil companies were associated with Pertamina. This was the core of its corrupt activities under Ibnu Sutowo. Sutowo had engaged in short-term external borrowing, used for the purchase and charter of tankers, and for diversifying into the steel industry (Karakatau Steel was purchased in 1970) and into industrial property in Batam. In 1975 this debt exceeded US$10 billion which was equivalent to 30 per cent of Indonesian GDP. Sutowo had substantial private business interests and used Pertamina to fund them. Thus, Pertamina represented an institutional form of comprador capitalism of the army and Sutowo.

Although he was head of Pertamina, Sutowo established his own private company, Nugra Santana, in 1969, which was involved in hotels, automobile distribution, shipping (linked to contracts from Pertamina and contracts from local authorities), cattle raising in Timor, and shipyards and engineering, all activities associated with Pertamina. This diversification of Nugra Santana between 1969 and 1973 coincided with the increase in Sutowo's rent-seeking activities with two partners, Sjarnoebi Said (owner of the military business group, Krama Yudha) and Mohammed Joesoef.

In 1970 Sutowo took over Bank Pacific, which constantly violated lending limits to a single borrower, which were his own companies. Before the takeover it had been a successful bank, but in 1970 it faced a serious scandal and in 1982 Bank Indonesia had to absorb 50 per cent of its bad loans. In 1994 it faced bankruptcy.[34]

However, as with the other *pribumi* companies discussed later, one stark feature is that rent-seeking activities produce flawed companies for *pribumi* but highly successful companies for Chinese conglomerates. This is my core argument: that the use of rents produces inconsistent, highly variable, divergent consequences. For example, Nugra Santana had recorded sales revenue of Rp425 billion in 1988, rising to Rp925 billion in 1995; it possessed assets of Rp300 billion in 1988, rising to Rp2,125 billion in 1995. But by 1996 it suffered a decline of 13.5 per cent in sales revenue and a 50 per cent decline in assets, indicating serious problems.[35] There is a bold contrast here to Chinese conglomerates. They are large, have diverse economic interests and receive a more favoured response from foreign investors. Here, it is the size of the corporation, the core product and access to foreign capital. The entrenched nature of Chinese capitalism, its ability to perpetuate concentrated growth and diversification with the assistance of the state and foreign multinationals meant that *pribumi* latecomers could only create a form of clientist, dependent capitalism, a satellite orbiting the state and Chinese capitalism.

Two other corporations revealed this pattern of capital accumulation. One was Bulog (National Commodities Logistics Command), a trading company founded in 1966 and dominated by army officers but providing lucrative contracts and monopoly profits to Salim. Until 1970, Bulog monopolized the purchase of rice for the army and civil service. After 1970 it created buffer stocks to stabilize the prices of essential commodities. This was financed by Bank Indonesia. The purchases were through Chinese middlemen and sales were also through Chinese traders. This introduced two forms of corruption. First, in the distribution of bank loans to support the buffer stocks; most of the loans were leaked to Chinese tycoons and army officers. The first used it to expand in critical economic sectors, the second increased their wealth and social status. Second, there was serious fraud in the commission extracted from the traders. There were, in addition, speculative activities in the pricing and quantity of buffer stocks. Inefficiency and fraud permeated the attempts at the stabilization of essential commodities. Salim was a major beneficiary of this commodity brokerage.

Berdikari, a state trading monopoly, generated more corruption. It had been established in 1966 to absorb two state trading units of Soekarno. The army leadership exploited these monopoly rents. Again, it provided critical profits for the Chinese traders. The head of Berdikari, Suhardiman, collaborated with Taiwanese multinationals, and this use of foreign capital, in addition to the state, remained a dominant feature of *pribumi* rent-seekers.

Pribumi capitalism

This section traces the different phases of *pribumi* capitalist growth in the period since 1949, and considers how that growth unleashed forms of cronyism and corruption that became embedded in the economy. It produces a sharper understanding of weak Indonesian corporate governance and corporate social responsibility. The evolution of *pribumi* capital, therefore, has to be appraised against the developments in five major phases. The Benteng policy of 1949–57, which permitted the entry of regional *pribumi* traders into Dutch enclaves as importers of European goods. But, critically, this was localized: some came from Sumatran trading families located in rubber, tea, coffee and pepper production and trade, and in inter-island trade in textiles and commodities – Agoes Dasaad, Ghany Aziz, Rahman Tamin. These groups thrived on provincial political connections. The rise of Soeharto in 1966 challenged this elite, though some powerful *pribumi* capitalists of the New Order, such as Edy Kowara, were from this group. This group did engage in petty manufacturing and the processing of commodities in this ISI period, built on connections with politicians and bureaucrats. This contributed to a major source of vulnerability, a dependence on a volatile source – that is, changing political factions – and because of such a precarious existence, it encouraged short-term speculation. By 1956 the state assumed more economic power with the creation of SOEs through the nationalization of Dutch corporations. This phase of early economic nationalism led to legislative pressures on the Chinese to leave the rural retail sector and move into urban areas. Ironically, this laid the basis for an aggressive form of Chinese capitalism, moving into lucrative sectors abandoned by the Dutch. They were also able to exploit domestic and external ethnic networks, in Singapore and Hong Kong. In contrast, *pribumi* business was in decline, partly because of civil unrest and lack of patronage, and many were arrested on charges of racketeering and fraud. With the New Order, the *pribumi* capitalists had to adapt or be decimated by the rise of state capital, military and Chinese capital.

In the early phase, both with the Benteng era and the ISI of the 1950s, *pribumi* capital faced serious decline and was unable to compete with SOEs or the large Chinese conglomerates. In 1956, with the end of Benteng privileges, a system of the auction of licences and contracts was introduced. This ushered in the first age of rent-seekers. Under the New Order, rent-seeking and crony capitalism became more pervasive, with aggressive Chinese capitalists and a tiny *pribumi* elite seeking positive and negative rents through Soeharto.

This period, therefore, introduced two extra determinants of *pribumi* capitalism. *Pribumi* groups were riven by factionalism: the moderates pushed for market-led growth, while the extremists argued for greater state control of the economy. Second, the ascendancy of the military in economic activities from the 1960s eroded the power and cohesion of *pribumi* capital. The military preferred Chinese business partners. The model of military-Chinese involvement and partnership in business institutionalized the corruption and cronyistic structures evolving in this period.

From the 1970s, a heterogeneous form of *pribumi* capitalism is discernible, with diverse sites, some embedded in the security services, others through the bureaucracy and in politics, but all were oozing with connections to the state, to Soeharto in particular, and to the dominant Chinese capitalists. As contractors to the SOEs, they were highly influential. Ibnu Sutowo, Sultan Hamengkubowono and Edy Kowara were building family empires for posterity, sealed by ties to Soeharto and rent-seeking activities. Ironically, although the period coincided with one of rising economic nationalism, *pribumi* capital in general was threatened from within by the military's economic aspirations and the technocrats' zeal for the creation of a market-based economy. Soeharto vacillated between intimacy with the Chinese and espousing the economic nationalism of Sudharmono and Ginanjar. This simply intensified the rent-seeking culture and growing corruption.

In the early 1980s, Sudharmono and his Team 10 attempted to promote *pribumi* business interests through the purchase of state contracts valued above Rp500 million.[36] Soeharto again aligned himself briefly with them but this cavorting was brief. He merely exploited this movement to erode the influence of the military in the economy and in Golkar party politics. With increasing Western pressures in the 1980s to liberalize, Soeharto embraced the Chinese camp, convinced that only the Chinese could deliver modernization. This period also coincided with the rising ambitions of his own family and he was hostage to this. Corruption and cronyism intensified. This had a bearing on the emerging corporate landscape.

The privatization programme between 1988 and 1995, which achieved partial privatization where less than 50 per cent of SOEs were offered to the public, was characterized by two developments. First, there was increased FDI: 40.3 per cent of revenues raised through privatization was derived from foreign capital.[37] Second, large Chinese conglomerates and a few *pribumi* families were the major beneficiaries, acquiring banks, lucrative economic units of SOEs and attracting foreign joint-venture partners. Salim, Mochtar Riady, Bob Hasan, Prajogo Pangestu and Nursalim were becoming stronger through acquisitions and mergers of former SOEs, funded by subsidized credit from the state and with massive infusions of foreign investment. Hastily, Soeharto's family and extended groups acquired or established new companies.

Between 1983 and 1996, banking assets were privatized, recording a decline in government banking from 79 per cent to 43 per cent.[38] The Chinese capitalists acquired large banks; the *pribumi* grabbed small banks as part of their business groups and these remained small, inefficient and marked by fraud and insider lending. The institutions pivotal to crony capitalism were strengthened in this period. While the bureaucracy was challenged by Soeharto and by the wealth of an increasingly powerful bourgeoisie comprised principally of Chinese and a few *pribumi* families, the economy was being liberalized. The autonomy of the technocrats was waning, a decline in the military's economic influence was perceptible, and the rise of Soeharto, his family and the Chinese cronies was clear. The Central Bank (Bank Indonesia) was becoming increasingly subservient to the Ministry of Finance and Planning. The tensions increased in the 1990s, marked by closer, corrupt interdependence between Soeharto, Chinese tycoons and *pribumi* barons. Sudwikatmono held the second largest number of board positions in the top 200 Indonesian corporations between 1990 and 1995.[39] Such 'trophy' directorships lacked a serious corporate base. Probosutedjo, Soeharto's step-brother, came into business through close connections with Soedona Salim. He was involved in clove plantations, food, fertilizers and oil-refining by 1995, when it was estimated that he held investments of US$3.5 billion.[40] Edy Kowara's family, whose son, Indra Rukmana, is Tutut's husband, held core interests in construction, oil drilling, food manufacturing and plantations. Sultan Hamengkabowono's family, too, participated in these rent-seeking activities in infrastructure, petroleum and food. The striking feature is that they are small, and they duplicate and compete with each other in the same sectors – contractors to the oil industry, auto distribution, food – all areas either requiring little capital outlay or guaranteed by government contracts and subsidies or assisted by foreign multinationals. Such involvement produces a 'comprador' culture, incapable of transforming into an independent bourgeoisie.

The next section is devoted to identifying and verifying these weaknesses in *pribumi* capital accumulation through detailed case studies of Bakrie Brothers, Bimantara Citra, Humpuss and CMNP. It would be useful now to summarize these weaknesses.

First, *pribumi* entrepreneurship is stunted because of the tripartite structure of capital in Indonesia, with the state, Chinese conglomerates and foreign capital as dominant participants. The *pribumi* remained factional, identified by regional, historical and institutional affiliations, aborting the emergence of a national bourgeoisie. Economic nationalism of the early 1980s was thwarted by the technocrats bent on efficiency and by Soeharto's fervent support of the Chinese and a tiny *pribumi* elite. Soeharto used the technocrats to shield himself from international criticism, as revealed in the recession of the mid-1980s, as pure fire fighters; this manipulation even included the IFC, which funded these cronies. The World Bank and international accountants and foreign multinationals missed the opportunity for the creation of a clear national policy of corporate strategy, corporate governance and corporate social responsibility. Many became innocent pawns in this game of rent-seeking. *Pribumi* corporate ambitions were factured because of the intra-competition for the spoils of rapid economic growth, from the military, bureaucracy, Soeharto and his family, his *pribumi* cronies, and the monopolies and concentrations of the large Chinese conglomerates. *Pribumi* regional capitalists in Sumatra and parts of central Java endured a period of de-industrialization in the 1960s, but it was the regional activities of the army and the provincial governors that further eroded the enclaves of *pribumi* capitalism. This produced one striking feature, the interpenetration of the military, the bureaucracy, the SOEs, *pribumi* capitalists and their alignment with Chinese capitalism and foreign multinationals. This lack of cohesion in *pribumi* capitalism and intra-factional competition easily descended into cronyism and corruption.

Through the three decades since 1970, the *pribumi* did not sustain long-term success. Ibnu Sutowo ruled Pertamina as a fiefdom, and the crisis in 1978 marked his decline. Here one interesting fact emerges. The *pribumi* class, marked by social differentiation and feudal aspirations, now focused on wealth creation, unleashed uncertainties that only patron–client ties with Soeharto and an ambiguous partnership with wealthy Chinese could satiate.

Finally, another institution that reinforced corruption was the *yayasan* (charitable organization or foundation). Although the *yayasan* were established to assist charitable activities, they descended into outright corruption. This is discussed in detail in the section on the *yayasan* (pp. 87–8). The *pribumi* elite, both in the military and in politics, usurped these foundations for personal gain. There were no structures for auditing these foundations, and politicians and the military elite used them as private sources of wealth creation.

The Soeharto business empire

Robison, Schwarz, Claessens, Backman and others focus on the Soeharto business empire and the cronyism and corruption flowing from it.[41] My analysis suggests that the Soeharto business empire is comparatively small and frequently was marked by internal competition, as in the case of Humpuss and Bimantara Citra. Its importance in rent-seeking activities may be excessive but this is again difficult to identify or quantify. Figure 4.1 provides data on the interlocking connections between the Soeharto family and its cronies, but not on corporate size, concentration or importance in the economy. Therefore, my approach is to analyse three major corporations, Bimantara Citra, Humpuss and CMNP, against an evaluation of the industrial sectors in which they are located and their major competitors. This analysis emphasizes core products within these corporations and performance. This intricate analysis of the family corporations and their rivals will provide a more accurate picture of their significance, rather than a simple chart on their interlocking relationships with the major Indonesian corporations that Claessens has provided as proof of Soeharto's wealth.[42] The extent to which rents accrue through these corporate interlocks can only be speculative.

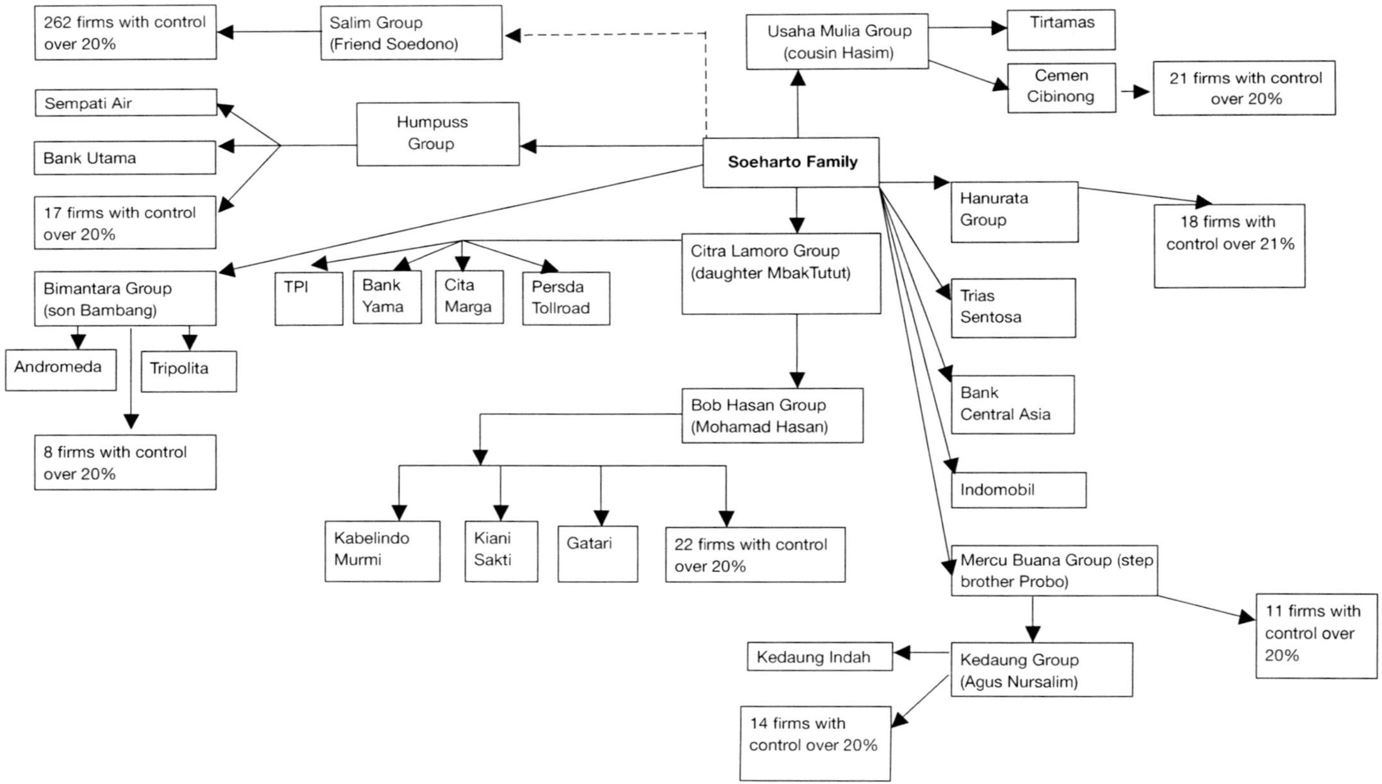

Figure 4.1 The Soeharto Group

Source: Stijin Claessens, Simeon Djankov and Larry H. P. Lang, *Who Controls East Asian Corporations?* Financial Economics Unit, Financial Sector Practice Department, World Bank, February 1999

The discussion so far has revealed the obstacles, the barriers for the successful expansion of *pribumi* capital. Three distinct features characterize the emergence of the Soeharto family business. The family have established business principally in new industries – media, telecommunications, transport infrastructure. Diversification into trading, finance, chemicals, automotive, pharmaceuticals, mining, energy, construction and agribusiness was ad hoc and remained insignificant. The banks within these groups were small: Bank Andromeda remained insignificant and collapsed in 1997.

Bimantara Citra grew between 1981 and 1986 through the creation of 41 new companies and the acquisition of 22 others. From 1987 to 1991, a further 79 subsidiaries were captured. Yet in 1990, 12 firms collapsed and in 1992, 14 more firms failed. This instability resulted from the rapid and chaotic diversification in the 1990s.[43]

Many of their activities were in joint-ventures with foreign capital or as contractors to SOEs. In telecommunications, Bimantara had two foreign partners, Alcatel Telecoms and Scope Trade Malaysia. In automobiles, Hyundai and Ford were major partners. In air transport it was a critical sub-contractor to the Garuda Group, while in shipping it had contracts for bulk cargo transport with Pertamina, carrying 80 per cent of Pertamina oil in 1992 between Indonesia and Singapore, a profit-sharing scheme with Pertamina. It negotiated this transportation with Norwegian bulk carriers. It was also the principal logistics supplier for Pertamina.

However, its largest share of revenue was derived from telecommunications, media and broadcasting. The subsidiaries in oil refining, shipping, automobiles and air transport were faced with losses and high interest expenses through 1995–8. The 1997 crisis forced the group to shed these loss-making units and focus on media, telecommunications and logistics in 2001. In telecommunications, Bimantara Citra's subsidiary, Satelindo, held 32 per cent of the cellular phone market in 1999, while Telkomsel held 47 per cent, Analog 4 per cent and Excelcomindo 17 per cent.[44] Indosat, an SOE, and Satelindo shared the monopoly on international long-distance calls. Telekom and Indosat, both SOEs, remained separate to increase competition.

The growth in the cellular market was impressive even after the crisis. In 1999, subscriber growth of 108 per cent was recorded. There are seven cellular operators, though just three (include Satelindo, established in 1994) held 95 per cent of the market. With regional growth, Satelindo could have achieved impressive expansion and performance but government constraints on pricing remained a hurdle, besides the possible threat posed by a future restructuring by the state-owned telecommunications corporations, while the new telecommunications legislation being proposed could also affect growth. Tariffs are set by the Ministry of Finance and competition between Indosat and Satelindo is purely on quality of service. Satelindo also has more connecting charges to pay, compared to Indosat which has integrated domestic and international lines. Diversification into related products such as the internet and e-business could provide Satelindo with more advantages which Indosat already possesses. Multipolar, another rival to Satelindo, dominates cable television through its subsidiary Kabelvision, and has a stake in internet and multimedia business.

Bimantara thus faces critical competition in this capital-intensive sector and profitability depends on how effectively it can pass on the cost increases to customers. The political and social turmoil in recent years has limited this price rise. Further, the uncertainties fuelled by the prospect of mergers or the restructuring of rival telecommunications groups pose additional challenges to Satelindo.

Bimantara's subsidiary in media and broadcasting has been successful but is located in a highly competitive market, with Salim and Lippo having partners from Hong Kong. A deeper analysis of the performance of Bimantara Citra is contained in Table 4.1 and Figure 4.2.

The serious downsizing imposed on Bimantara by its losses in 1998 and high interest expenses was reflected also in changes in shareholding and in management and control. From its foundation in 1981 until 1998, management had remained with Bambang, Rosana Barack, Indra Rukmana, Mohd Tachril Sapiie and Peter Frans Gontha. The major shareholders had been Asriland, Rizki Abadi and Tejuh Abadi. But the 1997 crisis led to the departure of Bambang and his brother-in-law Rukmana from the Board of Commissioners, though Rosana Barack and Tachril Sapiie remained.

In 2001, new shareholders emerged. Bkakti Investama acquired a 25 per cent holding, with a reduced stake by the existing shareholders.[45] This corresponded with the rise of the Tanoesoedibjo family, on both the Board of Commissioners and the Board of Directors. The rise of these *pribumi* asset managers was noted in Chapter 2 (pp. 45–6), and will be scrutinized at the close of this section.

Another corporation of the Soeharto family is Humpuss, established in January 1984 by Hutomo Mandala Putra, Soeharto's youngest son, and Sigit Haryoyudanto, his eldest son. Their core specialism was in the manufacture of aviation components, telecommunications, shipping, charter flights and construction. Its prestige project was the Timor National Car. All the 12 divisions within the corporation were supplying Pertamina, constructing terminals, providing shipping services and charter flights, telecommunications, and logistics supplier with the help of NEC. This revealed a common trait of *pribumi* capitalism, its heavy reliance on Pertamina and SOEs for contracts. Such rent-seeking activities emasculated prospects for growth in the domestic market as well as abroad. A third common characteristic was its dependence on foreign joint-venture partners: Korean in automobiles, Singaporean in shipping and Malaysian in real estate, properties and national lotteries. The fourth distinguishing feature was its concentration on capital-intensive sectors: telecommunications, shipping, airlines and the acquisition, in 1993, of a 50 per cent stake in Lamborghini. Its global ambitions in

Table 4.1 Bimantara Citra

	1995	*1996*	*1997*	*1998*	*1999*	*2000*	*2001*	*2002*
Growth								
Total assets (%)	27.5	54.1	23.5	–3.8	–29.7	16.6	6.8	
Total liabilities (%)	40.7	111.5	45.0	–2.0	–41.1	1.2	–5.3	
Equity growth (%)	14.9	–1.0	–21.3	–11.3	13.0	58.6	22.3	
Share related								
EPS (net) (RI)	134.00	154.88	11.19	–375.18	–214.76	132.98	335.95	341.55
Price (RI)	1,900.00	3,150.00	1,050.00	525.00	1,650.00	775.00	1,425.00	2,850.00
PER	14.18	20.34	93.83	–1.40	–7.68	5.83	4.24	8.34
BV/share (RI)	946.12	1,087.00	1,077.00	847.78	751.94	849.39	1,347.00	1,644.00
P/B ratio	2.01	2.90	0.97	0.62	2.19	0.91	1.06	1.73
Dividend/share (RI)	–	15.00	20.00	4.50	–	15.00	–	–
Dividend yield (%)	0.00	0.48	1.90	0.86	0.00	1.94	0.00	0.00
EV/EBITDA	9.43	11.59	9.37	105.33	11.51	2.40	2.38	5.60

Source: Annual Reports of Bimantara Citra, 1995–2002

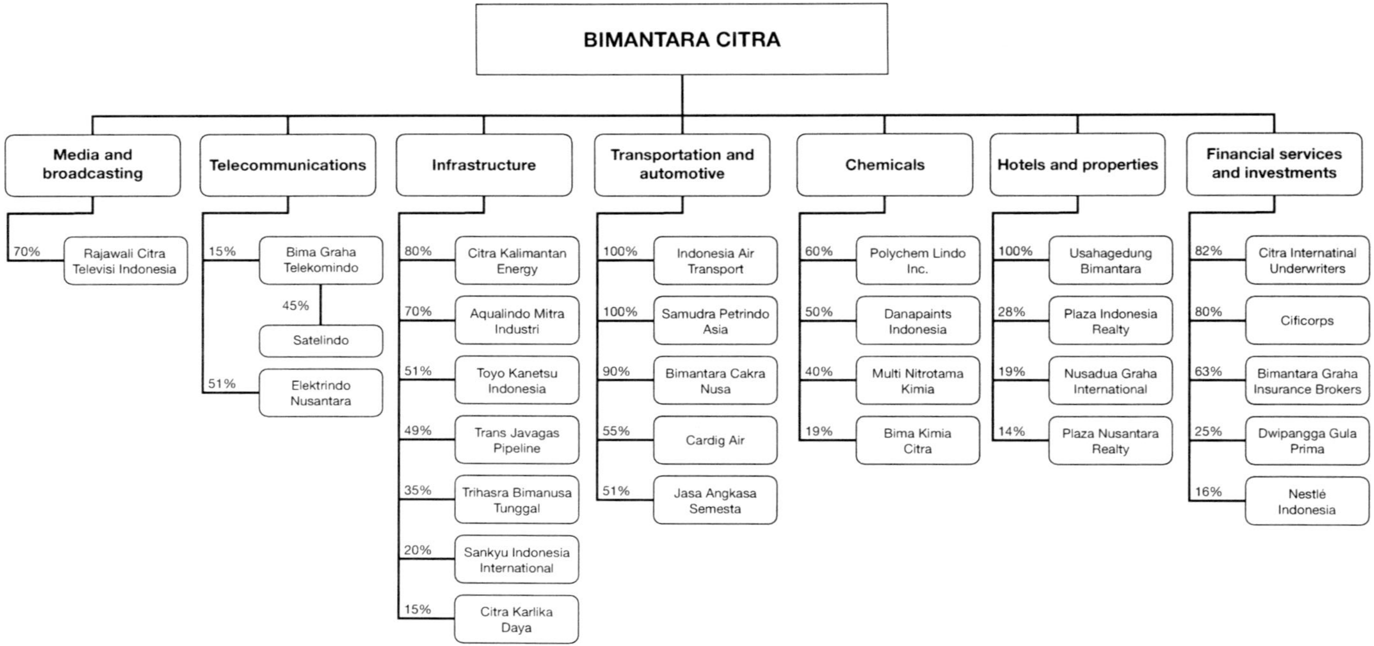

Figure 4.2 Bimantara Citra

Myanmar rather than in China, is, again, a general trait of *pribumi* capitalism: Tirtamas, Bimantara, Humpuss.

Although Humpuss recorded an increase of 14 per cent in turnover of Rp2.05 trillion between 1995 and 1996, by 1998 it was among the top ten debtors. The sharp decline in net profits from Rp74.96 billion in 1998 to Rp11.12 billion in 1999 led to the disposal of 30 per cent of its equity to Sembawang Corporation of Singapore in 2001.[46]

Finally, their sister Tutut (Siti Hardiyanti Hastuti) was associated with transport and infrastructure. Both corporations, Steady Safe and Citra Marga Nusaphala Persada were in transport. The latter had Indocement as a partner and a foundation, Jasa Marga, linked to Soeharto. It operates the Jakarta inner city ring road but raising tolls is a politically sensitive issue. It faced difficulties in raising finance and in settling old debts. Therefore, it lost the licence for other road projects. Finally, it had to issue bonds to finance road construction but the lack of demand for this led to its conversion to floating rate notes.

These three case studies of the Soeharto family enterprise clearly show that they are not predatory but, rather, rent-seekers. Yet, the constant accusation is that they have accumulated huge wealth in Indonesia and Europe.[47] Their financial subsidiaries in Amsterdam are mere shells; there is little evidence of real wealth there. What is striking is that the patrimonial state of Soeharto assisted the concentrated monopolies in food, timber, commodities, and the finance of Salim, Pangestu, Hasan and Riady, while the family was in less lucrative sectors such as airlines, transport and telecommunications, and in volatile rent-seeking sectors. The Chinese attracted foreign capital and exploited Chinese networks, moving into high growth areas – Singapore, Hong Kong, China and the US – while the *pribumi* moved into cement and timber in Myanmar, grappling with the dictatorship and unrest there, all clear testimony to the embedded weakness of *pribumi* capital, whether a blood relative of Soeharto or not.

Claessens and many other scholars have identified Soeharto and his family as the major culprits in the economic crisis of 1997.[48] This Soeharto-bashing is based on the corporate shares carved out by his own children, his stepbrother Probosutedjo, his cousin Sudwikatmono and other relatives. My analysis concludes that their corporate shares are insignificant when compared to Salim, Nursalim, Riady and Prajogo Pangestu. Some of the children's companies reveal improved performance when compared to their immediate rivals in the specific industrial sectors, and also to *pribumi* and Chinese conglomerates in the periods, both before and after the crisis. This analysis of *pribumi* capital will cover first an analysis of Bakrie Bros, a *pribumi* group possessing scanty political connections. The second issue is the rise of investment and fund managers Bhakti Investama after 1997.

Bakrie Brothers was established in 1942 by Achmad Bakrie. The firm was in import-export, and in 1957 it absorbed a Dutch company specializing in

Table 4.2 Bakrie Bros

Key ratios	*1993*	*1994*	*1995*	*1996*	*1997*	*1998*	*1999*	*2000*	*2001*	*2002*
Profitability										
EBIT margin (%)	26.36	25.15	13.72	18.70	−11.13	−38.84	−2.08	−49.66	−147.47	15.55
EBITDA margin (%)	33.64	30.77	16.79	22.74	−6.86	−32.85	6.48	−35.00	−135.29	22.17
Operating profit margin (%)	21.24	16.50	15.03	15.60	5.69	4.63	1.84	2.27	4.51	3.05
Net profit margin (%)	8.48	13.78	9.50	11.90	−14.44	−61.95	−34.14	−67.38	−174.03	1.75
Operating efficiency										
Asset turnover	0.38	0.27	0.37	0.30	0.23	0.33	0.23	0.17	0.24	0.28
Inventory turnover	5.06	10.52	11.83	10.66	5.72	11.05	12.72	10.13	7.08	7.47
Gearing										
Total equity/(long-term loans + equity)	0.29	0.77	0.67	0.46	0.37	−0.62	−3.70	−4.04	0.58	0.59
Total assets/total liabilities	1.30	2.37	2.06	1.57	1.26	0.98	0.96	0.87	1.84	1.86
Liquidity										
Liquidity ratio (current assets/ current liabilities)	0.99	1.60	1.45	1.92	0.52	0.28	0.19	0.12	0.59	0.67
Quick ratio ((CA-inventories)/ CL)	0.83	1.48	1.33	1.81	0.43	0.25	0.17	0.10	0.44	0.48
Cash ratio ((cash + short-term inv.)/CL)	0.18	0.45	0.28	0.33	0.07	0.10	0.14	0.20	0.15	0.16

Table 4.2 (continued)

Key ratios	*1993*	*1994*	*1995*	*1996*	*1997*	*1998*	*1999*	*2000*	*2001*	*2002*
Inventory working capital ratio (Sales/ave working cap.)	–14.41	0.39	0.27	0.19	–0.18	–0.07	–0.02	–0.02	–0.38	–0.46
Growth										
Total income (%)		139.86	69.25	24.47	25.13	79.05	–36.88	–28.16	–14.65	8.36
Profit before taxation (%)		265.4	2.6	65.3	–215.4	584.3	–63.7	37.1	86.6	–107.6
Profit after taxation (%)		289.8	16.7	55.9	–251.8	668.3	–65.2	41.8	120.4	–101.1
Total assets (%)		230.5	25.3	54.2	59.0	25.7	–9.5	–0.9%	–39.4	–9.1
Total liabilities (%)		81.4	43.9	101.8	99.1	60.9	–7.9	9.4	–71.2	–10.3
Equity growth (%)		1,394.9	12.0	9.3	–9.7	–127.7	24.2	178.3	–262.2	–3.1
Share related										
EPS (net) (RI)	55.52	59.50	61.94	97.00	–146.55	–1,126.00	–391.57	–555.27	–473.87	3.64
Price (RI)	698.28	856.25	1,037.5	975	425	225	300	60	50	15
PER		15.42	17.44	15.74	4.38	–1.54	–0.27	–0.15	–0.09	–0.03
BV/share (RI)	194.28	732.56	820.30	896.19	808.98	–224.23	–278.33	–774.42	343.14	332.33
P/B ratio		1.17	1.26	1.09	0.53	–1.00	–1.08	–0.08	0.15	0.05
Dividend/share (RI)	8.62	22.50	18.75	100.00	35.00	–	–	–	–	–
Dividend yield (%)		2.63	1.81	10.26	8.24	0.00	0.00	0.00	0.00	0.00
EV/EBITDA	7.48	9.12	14.54	11.20	–45.67	–8.08	57.17	–15.13	–1.12	5.51

Source: Bakrie Bros, Annual Reports, 1993–2002

wire manufacture and steel pipes. This move into steel pipes and construction materials formed their core success, though from 1982 they diversified into natural oil and gas; the period 1982–92 was marked by an aggressive growth through acquisitions into plantations, farming, mining and chemical industries. Free Port Indonesia was in copper; there was coal mining in East Kalimantan, marble and brick in southeast Sulawesi, and in the chemical industry jointly managed by Mitsubishi and in financial partnership with Saloman Bros. In 1990 they introduced professional managers and by 1995 ventured abroad, purchasing controlling shares in an Australian telecommunications firm, in food manufacturing in China and in Uzbekistan, in telecommunications and tourism, and established financial groups in the Netherlands. The analysis of their performance during 1993–2002 clearly shows instability (see Table 4.2).

Bakrie Brothers was severely affected by the 1997 crisis and, after a series of losses in 1998 and 1999, divested 80 per cent of equity to foreign creditors as part of a debt-equity swap to settle debts of US$1.5 billion.[49] In 2001, recovery was swift after completing its debt restructuring in 2000 and selling some of its subsidiaries, including those in coal mining and chemicals. In 2001 the company formed a consortium with Daewoo to produce and install submarine gas pipes for a natural gas pipeline from South Sumatra to Singapore. It also formed a joint-venture company with Telecom BV Netherlands. Careful divestment, restructuring and foreign collaborations assisted its recovery.

Another interesting phenomenon in *pribumi* capitalism is the rise of asset fund managers after the 1997 crisis. They first emerged in the late 1980s, but since 1997 have taken different forms as investors and owners. The identity of the source of these funds remains a mystery. They purchase assets of failing companies at hugely discounted prices, and it is difficult to track and monitor their investment strategies and patterns. How far have these groups analysed risk before acquiring multiple assets in diverse products and markets? The mix is the worrying issue. Their ability to adhere to strict investment policies is not evident. They appear in diverse industries, in different corporations, and the fear is, do they have long-term ambitions or is this a search for short-term speculative gain? Can they avoid huge losses? The ability to understand particular corporations and the merits of particular industrial sectors and products is revealed by European equity purchases as seen in Indocement, in automobiles. Even Singapore corporations have selected stocks in related industrial sectors such as heavy industry. But Bhakti Investama and Trimegah Securities have not shown such rationality.[50] These predators are selecting stocks in various large conglomerates, and are not clear on competitive positions, on profits, cash flow, shareholder value and prospects for sustainable growth. There is, within a short period, increased purchases of equity. The question here is, are they using more risky forms of finance? Economic recovery in Indonesia is slow, but constant at around 3 per cent since 2000. Therefore, any volatile swings in investment will prejudice the process of recovery and restructuring.

The bureaucracy, legal infrastructure, corporate reform and economic revival

The organization of the bureaucracy was crucial for Indonesian economic growth. Pockets of the Indonesian bureaucracy were staffed with well-trained technocrats and many of the economists were US-trained. The main argument here is: how autonomous was the bureaucracy? Did Soeharto curb the autonomy of the bureaucracy? Was the Indonesian bureaucracy becoming politicized in the last decade of the twentieth century?

From the mid-1970s, Indonesian technocrats had support from international financial institutions, the IMF and the World Bank, and this helped to curb the excesses of cronyism.[51] They maintained a strict policy of avoiding financial deficits but kept an open capital account. The privatization of financial institutions from the late 1980s led to the expansion of commercial banking, promotion of an active money market and expansion of the stock market, and the creation of investment houses and venture capitalists. However, prudent regulations to control and avert irregularities failed because of the concentration of privileges among the elite, which led to economic objectives being co-opted by the special interest groups surrounding the president. Although Bank Indonesia moved from manager to supervisor of a highly diversified financial structure after 1988, its technocrats' role in the formulation of monetary and financial policy was being eroded. Its powers were being challenged by the Ministry of Finance; there was overlapping of authority between Bank Indonesia and the Ministry, which created serious problems.[52] Indonesian decision-making, which was already fraught with a culture of consensus, meant that new bureaucratic tensions and jealousies produced even greater confusion in both the structure and supervision of decision-making. This was further aggravated by the inadequate legal support for introducing effective corporate governance. The struggle for power in capital markets, as well as in the Ministry of Finance, increased the risk of instability in financial institutions. However, the technocratic elite in Bappenas, Bank Indonesia, and the Ministry of Finance and Planning did, to an extent, effectively initiate the successful financial liberalization after 1988, and only the lack of rigorous regulation confused the process. Although decision-making could be centralized under Soeharto, the technocrats were sufficiently powerful to restrain it.

However, it was the weakness of the legal system that Soeharto could skilfully use to thwart the technocrats. The 1997 crisis thus gave fresh opportunities by introducing improved regulatory mechanisms. Bank Indonesia possessed greater autonomy under the 1999 legislation on the Central Bank. Yet, by December 2000, an amendment was seeking a reduction in this autonomy by the appointment of politicians to the bank's Board.[53] The Central Bank had to report to parliament, have foreign consultants and an external audit. The Central Bank was to divest its financial subsidiaries and concentrate on financial policy. A measure of success here is shown by this statistic: corruption and mismanagement of Central Bank funds cost government Rp4.7 trillion in the fiscal year 2000, compared with Rp18.2 trillion in 1999.[54]

Another institution that has sustained rent capitalism is the commercial banking sector. Central to this is banking reform. Private commercial banking became a major source of capital and corruption within corporations. The regulations relating to capital asset ratios, leverage, size of loans to a single borrower and related borrowing were each ignored, and cheap credit fed the appetites of these diversified conglomerates.

Liberalization of the banking system would introduce competition from foreign banks. Such competition could rid the corporate economy of rampant favouritism. Liberalizing foreign investment, permitting foreign ownership of corporations since 1998 has already introduced critical competitive pressures, as well as accountability, transparency and a model of increased corporate governance. Market-oriented, outward-looking policies have curbed the heightened presence of Chinese conglomerates whose importance was owed to a range of special privileges under the New Order. Reform measures remain limited in scope but impetus for reform has come from the bureaucracy and an open press. This leadership of the bureaucracy must be aligned with the creation of a broad political–social coalition capable of long-term economic reform. To challenge the diversified conglomerate (Chinese and *pribumi*), new entrepreneurial elements must be encouraged and assisted. The diversified conglomerate oligarchy itself should abandon rent-seeking in favour of more production-oriented entrepreneurship, particularly in the manufacturing sector.

Positive forms of encouragement of *pribumi* entrepreneurship in the centre and the provinces must be a core policy. In Malaysia's privatization, *bumiputera* (henceforth, old spelling 'bumiputra') bureaucrats were co-opted to manage SOEs.[55] This system needs further enlargement in the Indonesian case, with regional entrepreneurs being co-opted to purchase equity and manage units within these large SOEs, many of which could be privatized gradually, so avoiding the mistakes of the Soviet Union.[56]

The economic and commercial transformation of Indonesia since 1960, while advantageous to the large Chinese capitalist, has reduced the *pribumi* to rent-seeking activities. This produces widespread corruption. A consistent policy of supporting *pribumi* entrepreneurship will help rid this *pribumi* group of such subservient rent-seeking, and introduce dynamism and competitiveness, with entry into manufacturing and industrial production, instead of focusing on the provision of contractual services to SOEs and simply earning rents.

Curbing the state's role is not the only answer, as we see that many SOEs perform better than private concerns. A good example is cement (Semen Gresik) and telecommunications (Indosat and Telekom).[57] A great more research is essential if we are to argue that privatization is the only cure. The state should be more selective. Reform of the legislature, bureaucracy and civil service is necessary, but, ultimately, only the state is capable of controlling private economic power, particularly in the monopolistic form in which it has emerged. The state needs to support SMEs and increase competition. Anti-state ideology has emerged after the crisis; a vociferous advocate is the World Bank and Mark Baird. But this view is not supported in detailed examination of the large private conglomerates in Indonesia. The role of the state in curbing these monopolies, the creation of pluralistic organizational structures (SOEs, private corporations, SMEs, cooperatives) all need to be nurtured.

What is crucial, therefore, is the achievement of some form of regional decentralization, limited privatization of SOEs and to break the economic oligarchs through the elimination of the monopolies, open the protected private sector to foreign multinationals, ease tariff barriers, liberalize the financial institutions by introducing some foreign banks, increase the rigour of regulation of the financial sector while pursuing the liberalization of foreign investment and reform legal institutions. The improvement of corporate governance through the incorporation of professional managers on Boards of Directors of companies and the introduction of consolidated income statements and seeking strict supervision of listed corporations by the state Security and Exchange Commission with meticulous inspections of companies and filings of annual data are urgent.[58] The economic concentration will persist but the worst excesses of rent-seeking could be eradicated through legal reforms on cross-shareholding, command lending, lax loan policies, import-export licences and contracts being distributed to cronies.

Finally, foreign involvement in the reform process meant an active role for the World Bank and IMF. The World Bank launched a review of the civil service and judicial reform to ease corruption. The civil service reform led to a 30 per cent increase in wages in 2000, though 15 per cent was the initial aim. Though limited in securing change, the flow of information about government activities increased, civil service associations expanded and limited legal reform was introduced. The World Bank also insisted that IBRA should be supervised and thus sought the establishment of a nine-member oversight committee with Mari'e Muhammed heading the review.[59] However, IBRA had so many oversight committees that the management of debtors was confusing and conflicting.

Bankruptcy of failing corporations is not an effective solution. Is it to be liquidation, is it a moratorium on debt repayment through court supervision, or is the business to be sold, or should the debt be recast as equity in the offending corporation? These are serious issues, and the judicial system is not sufficiently sophisticated and fair to appraise each case effectively.

Therefore, to achieve improvements in the legal system, continuous legal education and professional training are essential and, particularly, training in commercial law. To preserve the honesty and integrity of judges, salaries need to be raised, and improvements introduced in their selection and recruitment. The commercial courts need to be consistent in law enforcement, impartial, honest, transparent and fair.[60]

First, the Bankruptcy Law of 1998 established a new commercial court to process bankruptcy, petitions and moratoria on debt, and manage general corporate debt problems. However, by November 1998, only 17 cases had been recorded and only two faced bankruptcy. The difficulty here was the lack of well-trained, honest judges; the majority were said to be corrupt.[61] Their lack of knowledge and competence in commercial law, bankruptcy and insolvency procedures made decision-making highly unpredictable.

Second, Indonesian courts faced long delays through the appeal system. Under the new bankruptcy code, a time limit of 30 days for an appeal was imposed.

Third, directors were made liable for a corporation's debts. The rights of creditors were maintained and equal treatment dispensed for all creditors. This was to allay fears of foreign creditors that their rights would be compromised in the resurgence of economic and political nationalism evident since 1997.

However, any attempt at corporate restructuring and debt resolution was hampered by the ineffective commercial courts. Recent court decisions in 2000 left many companies in confusion. For example, the district court ruled in favour of Djoko Tjandra, a defendant in the Bank Bali scandal, and requested IBRA to return to the bank the Rp546 billion held in IBRA's confiscated accounts. The Jakarta court, too, ruled in favour of the Ramli family, and the cancellation of IBRA's takeover of Bank Bali meant continued suspension of Bank Bali, which has reverted to Bank Indonesia. This is serious, since the bank has a negative capital asset ratio of 124 per cent and faces closure if it is not adequately recapitalized.[62]

In another case, the commercial court rejected IBRA's bankruptcy petition for an uncooperative borrower, Tirtamas Comexindo, belonging to Hashim Djojohadikusumo.

In short, the break-up of the monopolies, liberalization of foreign investment, liberalization of foreign trade, devolution of political power from Jakarta to local governments, stock market regulation, infrastructural improvement, eradication of corruption and incompetence of the judiciary, reduction of the spheres of rent-seeking opportunities, creation of a broad pro-reform coalition with diverse stakeholders, including the state, capitalists, SMEs and foreign capital, need to be maintained. It is therefore clear that corporate reform is at the core of the programme for the elimination of corruption, pervasive cronyism and rent-seeking.

The corporate system in Indonesia, with its web of state, family, cronies and banks, is central to understanding the lack of serious corporate governance and corporate social responsibility. The classic separation between ownership and management in joint stock corporations is not clear in Indonesian corporations. First, corporations are not only controlled by families, but also by a constellation of institutions: state, military, foreign capital. Second, large enterprises include financial and non-financial interests, and it is this fusion that is central to Indonesian conglomerates, both Chinese and *pribumi*. Banks are not exercising control in these clusters but the corporations are, unlike the German system, where the centrality of banks in the inter-corporate network has been an advantage both for growth and increased corporate governance and accountability. Large financial institutions hold powerful positions in the corporate economy, in the management of institutional funds, and it is this rational investment holding function that ensures that they do not become part of an extensive corporate web with corruption and cronyism permeating them, as in Indonesia. The weakness of the Indonesian stock exchange has produced a complex inter-weaving of diverse shareholdings, tied into a single network. These high-density linkages are another source of corruption.

Third, the hierarchy of relations within a corporation can assist in increasing market relations. Internal organization of the corporation should reflect the product and capital markets within which it is located and economic conditions. The creation of extensive hierarchies of professional managers in these large enterprises can assist investment, R&D and globalization. Instead, all the Indonesian corporations, irrespective of the product and capital markets they are targeting, are characterized by holding companies. Here, managers occupy weak subordinate positions. Multiple holding companies were adopted as a strategy for growth, and reflect centralized investment and decision-making by the family patriarch. This could have been adjusted by two critical poles of influence: state and bureaucracy. But in the case of Indonesia, the Soeharto-crony nexus was too fused for this to be a positive institution for corporate efficiency and corporate responsibility.

Fourth, the European MNEs organized foreign operations into a matrix system where product specialization was intersected by separate national subsidiaries, co-ordinating their activities in each country. In the last two decades, the move has been to create foreign product divisions, coordinated by distinct home divisions.[63] Indonesian-Chinese movement abroad was through the creation of new companies in Singapore, China, Australia and the US.

The family controlled all the new companies, through the numerous young siblings. This, together with rising concentration and diversification in Indonesia, meant unwieldy corporate structures were emerging and yet no consolidated accounts were being produced for home and abroad. Internal–external transfers of capital were confused by the rapid growth and high rate of acquisitions in the 1990s, and the euphoria and enthusiasm of foreign investors and the Indonesian state. Modernization was parallel with oligopolistic structures, while corruption and cronyism reigned supreme. Reform and revival is urgent, and in this sense the crisis may have positive long-run consequences.

5 Malaysian banking

Organizational control and corporate governance

This chapter examines the growth of banking in Malaysia since the Second World War. It has three important themes. First, it examines how Malaysian Chinese-controlled banks displaced established Western banks immediately after independence. What were their competitive strategies in usurping the position of Western banks? How did they respond to the threat posed by the New Economic Policy (NEP) and the economic restructuring in favour of the *bumiputras*, introduced after the 1969 race riots?

Second, since banking was dominated by the state from the 1970s, how did private banking, both Malay and Chinese, proliferate? The critical changes in corporate shareholding of these banks as a result of this state intervention, combined with the affirmative actions of the NEP for the creation of a *bumiputra* financial bourgeoisie, created powerful state-private banks. Furthermore, it was the rise of powerful local institutional shareholders and a small coterie of politically connected individuals that influenced and shaped the patterns of growth, organizational control and corporate governance of Malaysian banking from 1973 to the present.

The association of banks with differing political caucuses and ethnic backgrounds during various periods distorted linear growth and increased the vulnerability of the financial system. Frequently, changes in ownership from private to state to private coincided with contrasting phases of success or failure, and fraud or scandals. This hampered the linear growth of some banks, despite state assistance and the existence of a disciplined Central Bank with a clear regulatory framework.

In particular, the encroachment of large, non-financial conglomerates into banking during the economic boom of the 1990s slightly disturbed the existing rigid, functional specialism of the Malaysian financial sector. Seeking the creation of a main bank system, these conglomerates confused the existing ownership, control, autonomy and lending traditions of Malaysian banks. Nevertheless, this model of mixed banking still remained less pervasive, in contrast to Indonesia. Since it was controlled by the state and a private financial elite of bureaucrats, accountants and Chinese businessmen, Malaysian banking remained focused on finance and witnessed less of the intertwining relations between banks and industrial corporations that dominated Indonesian banking from 1968.

The rapid growth and consolidation of domestic banking between 1975 and 1990 is revealed in the following figures. In Malaysia in 1959, there were 18 foreign and four local banks. Foreign banks accounted for 89 per cent of all branches, while the largest local bank, Kwong Yik Bank, accounted for just 2 per cent of all bank credit in Malaysia and Singapore.[1] By the mid-1970s, local banks had achieved parity with foreign banks in terms of assets.[2] In 1995 foreign banks possessed only 10 per cent of banking offices and 22 per cent of total banking assets.[3]

The manoeuvres to reduce and undermine the presence and activities of foreign banks were more subtle in Malaysia than in Indonesia, where there was direct nationalization and where foreign banks were only partially readmitted in 1968. The Governor of Bank Negara (the central bank), Tun Ismail, played a crucial role in this process. However, his October 1996 interview with Natasha Hamilton-Hart does not convey the full picture of the attempts to unseat foreign banks in Malaysia after independence. The detailed case study of Malaysian Banking presented later charts the deliberate steps undertaken to displace influential Western banks.

The following overview of the financial systems in Malaysia, the Philippines, Thailand and Indonesia provides figures on foreign banks operating there. The fairly high ratio of foreign-owned financial institutions in Malaysia and Indonesia, in comparison with the Philippines and Thailand, is clear from Table 5.1b. The impressive growth in domestic financial institutions is also captured in both Table 5.1b and Table 5.2.

The dramatic changes in the volume of assets and the subsequent ranking corresponded with fluctuations in ownership patterns. Maybank and Public Bank revealed stable linear growth, fostered by a strong, stable institutional shareholding in the former and a prudent private Chinese ownership in the latter. Other banks that experienced frequent changes in ownership were also tainted by fraud by individual managers and faced hostile takeovers.

Claessens's study of family control of Asian banks and corporations focuses on individual families but neglects the powerful role of institutional shareholdings, both domestic and foreign.[4] Hence, these forms of institutional shareholding may distort the precise proportion of shares held by the top

Table 5.1a An overview of the financial system by country and by sector (as of the end of 1996)

	Indonesia	*Korea*	*Malaysia*	*Philippines*	*Thailand*
Commercial banks	78 (16)	28 (2)	36 (14)	31 (7)	13 (0)
Non-bank financial institutions	9 (2)	30 (14)	28 (3)	5 (1)	25 (4)
Total	87 (18)	58 (16)	64 (17)	36 (8)	38 (4)

Note: Numbers in parentheses indicate the number of foreign institutions.

Source: BANKSTAT

Table 5.1b Ownership structure of financial institutions in the sample, 1996

	Indonesia	*Korea*	*Malaysia*	*Philippines*	*Thailand*
State-owned	10	11	13	4	5
Non-state-owned	77	47	51	32	33
Of which:					
Connected	52	18	36	23	1*
Foreign-owned	18	16	17	8	4
Total institutions	87	58	64	36	38

* The figure for Thailand does not include one bank owned by the government and one bank connected to the Royal Family. The number for Thailand underestimates the number of connected institutions because connections are difficult to trace in Thailand given the habit of local and foreign investors to maintain their shareholdings in the Securities Depository Company (which guarantees complete anonymity) and through nominee accounts.

Source: BANKSTAT

Table 5.2 Malaysian Banks, 1980–95

Bank	*1980 assets (RM billion)*	*Rank*	*1985 assets (RM billion)*	*Rank*	*1995 assets (RM billion)*	*Rank*
Bumiputra	12.82	1	24.97	1	36.46	2
Maybank	9.26	2	24.11	2	66.91	1
UMBC	2.82	3	8.02	3	13.05	4
Public Bank	1.61	5	6.13	4	23.26	3
UAB	2.19	4	5.10	5	–	–
DCB	1.24	6	4.48	6	17.55	4
Bank of Commerce	0.22	15	0.90	16	14.62	5

Note: UAB merged with Bank of Commerce in 1991.

Source: Natasha Hamilton-Hart, *Asian States, Asian Bankers: Central Banking in Southeast Asia*, Ithaca, NY and London: Cornell University Press, 2002, p. 125.

five large shareholders in Malaysia. State control exercised through these institutional shareholders is also augmented through the managerial control and stakeholding exercised by politicians and bureaucrats. Therefore, Claessens' statistical breakdown, which shows the state controlling 17.8 per cent of public listed corporations and 36.3 per cent in the top 20 public listed corporations, is meaningless without a detailed breakdown of share ownership and management over the two decades from 1980 to 2000. Despite privatization from the 1980s, the government still held majority ownership in half of the top 20 listed firms and banks. Equally, the Chinese were still dominant in banking, as well as in non-financial corporations, despite the radical restructuring under the NEP. This neglect of the complexities in ownership and control leads to an incongruence in the analysis and conclusions on what determines success or failure of Asian banking. Survival and success are determined by finance, generous government credit, connections to foreign MNEs and access to large inflows of foreign capital. But, ultimately, it is the nature of institutional shareholding and ownership that shapes a bank's long-term survival and growth. In order to dissect the growth and importance of such institutional investors in the Malaysian financial sphere, the fundamental background to their evolution needs to be charted, particularly after 1970.

Institutional investor: benefit or hazard?

Institutional investors in the form of state unit trusts and pension funds, such as the Employees Provident Fund (EPF), emerged from 1970 as part of this state-directed investment in banks and corporations. The important influence of these investment agencies, such as Permodalan Nasional Bhd (PNB) (which was formed in 1969, was controlled by the Ministry of Finance and acted as an investment holding company for the state), was central in restructuring ethnic ownership in the Malaysian corporate economy. By 1989, ten domestic banks were dominated by the *bumiputras*. PNB monitored this *bumiputra* equity, aware that, while such equity had constituted 60 per cent of the total in 1976 due to state initiatives, it had fallen to 34 per cent by 1980 because of rash divestment by individual Malays. These were absorbed by the Chinese. So the strategy of the PNB was to establish unit trust schemes to hold these shares and increase *bumiputra* participation collectively rather than through distribution to individuals.[5] Thus, PNB shareholding tripled from 841,200 in December 1981 to 2,460,977 by December 1991. PNB soon came to dominate the unit trust industry.

There was also a proliferation of *bumiputra* equity through Amanah Saham Nasional (ASN), founded in 1979 and launched in April 1981, with the provision of interest-free loans for acquisitions. In January 1990, the Bumiputra Unit trust scheme (Amanah Saham Bumiputra (ASB)) was introduced to increase *bumiputra* stakeholding in the corporate economy. Many of these investments were made with bank loans. Thus, PNB was able to control financial and non-financial sectors, emerging as the largest institutional investor by 1990. The distribution of these priority shares varied, with high concentrations in some banks and corporations, and this was also reflected in managerial positions and on the Board of Directors.

Other prominent institutional investment groups were those of the individual regional state financial investment agencies, such as Yayasan Pelaburan Bumiputra (YPB), which was established in January 1978.[6] On behalf of YPB, PNB first evaluated and then selected shares, and distributed them to the *bumiputras* through ASN (unit trust). The majority of these shares were purchased at par value. In this way, PNB held equity in 37 companies by October 1986, rising to 90 companies by March 1990.

Bumiputra equity ownership was 1.5 per cent of total equity of listed companies in 1969, rose to 12.5 per cent in 1980, to 20.3 per cent in 1989, and then to 60 per cent in 1990. This phenomenal increase in *bumiputra* ownership was a result of privatization, an increase in the conglomerate patterns of growth, reverse takeovers, equity swaps, increased state participation, and the wave of takeovers and mergers of existing banks from 1979. The latter was a popular practice because new banking licences were difficult to acquire.

These powerful investment agencies were crucial in the rescue operations of banks that occurred amid the spate of fraud and mismanagement that convulsed some financial institutions such as Bank Bumiputra, the largest Malaysian bank in the 1980s. Institutional investors were tapping into high savings, accounting for 30 per cent of GDP in the 1980s, and thus lubricating the efficiency of the financial sector in the face of these corporate disturbances.

The relationships between these three institutional investors were clearly demarcated. ASN, which was listed in 1991, collected the savings for the share purchases, which PNB selected and managed. In this manner, risk-free investment was offered to *bumiputras*, together with dividends and offers of bonus shares. The second trust fund, ASB, was active in securing equity in privatized firms. While assuming a position as a major shareholder in listed banks and corporations, PNB was, through interlocking shareholding, creating a highly concentrated, almost monopolistic structure within the privatized corporate groups. Its close liaisons with the state, coupled with its access to subsidized credit, introduced weak corporate governance, particularly as it stifled open competition. Resource allocation was state and ethnic driven and, therefore, long-term efficiency could be impaired. According to Adam and Cavendish, PNB and ASN saw the rate of return in their equity holdings fall from 20 per cent in 1981 to 10 per cent in 1987.[7] This had an impact on the Kuala Lumpur stock market since these institutional investors were powerful actors on the KLSE.

The participation in the corporate sector by the pension group, EPF, was gradual and conservative in outlook. By 1993, EPF had gained control of 89 per cent of the workforce's pensions, and 77 per cent of the provident, pension and insurance funds in Malaysia.[8] EPF also held half of the government's domestic debt. From 1991, it participated in capital market investments and in the rescue of failing banks.[9] However, EPF managed to secure autonomy in its decision-making.[10] Prior to 1983, its investments were in safe government securities. Now, with the freedom to participate in the capital market and acquire shares on the KLSE, it was faced with increasing risks, particularly since the government and its cronies dominated the stock market.

This close-knit relationship between the state, banks, securities markets and institutional investors, such as the PNB and EPF, led to the KLSE achieving the highest ratio of growth to GDP in 1993, compared to other Asian countries. These institutional investors navigated the growth of corporations through the phases of privatization, restructuring and denationalization, always providing a steady flow of funds. Since these investments were locked into government investment strategies, there were difficulties in independent management and in effective monitoring. In addition, because they held a diverse portfolio of shares, micromanagement was difficult. However, a more serious issue was that such block investments could distort prices and erode the competition, transparency and efficiency of the stock market. There were also greater opportunities for insider trading. The public was too often swayed by the scale of participation of these elite groups, resulting in bubbles and volatility on the stock market.

Since mutually advantageous relationships existed between these various institutional shareholders, thereby ensuring cooperation, the stock market was less market driven and the corporate economy less competitive. Thus, as many of these institutional holding companies were part of this concentrated network, they were well developed, well funded, and were highly focused on the main priorities in the economy. Influenced and shaped by government connections and objectives, these agents, though well informed, were often unable to act as monitors. It was only the few foreign institutional investors – the HSBC Nominees, Citicorp, and DBS Nominees – that could provide independent monitoring and supervision.[11]

Furthermore, the role of the institutional investor was highly dependent on the existing structure of corporate finance in Malaysia. The state and banks were a major source of corporate funding. The importance of foreign investors remained unpredictable because, though inflows were high, they were not always guaranteed. Historically, banks have not played a role in corporate governance in Malaysia, except in cases of bankruptcies and in rescheduling repayments. Even here, though, the Central Bank usurped these roles. So, typically, the governance framework was exercised through internal mechanisms, with large shareholders, such as these institutional organizations, acting alongside intervention by the Central Bank and the government. This was never free of cronyistic pressures and intimidation.

Since these institutional investors were involved in extensive cross-holdings in banks and major corporations, such high stakes demanded a passive response. Their role remained in ownership. It was only after the 1997 crisis that they sought active representation on the boards of those firms where they held a significant stake. But here, too, ambiguities persisted. For instance, were they fund managers or nominee directors of the company? According to the Price Waterhouse Coopers Corporate Governance Survey of 2002 and the McKinsey Global Investor Opinion Survey of 2002, institutional investors were conscious of good governance and were responsible for the rapid recovery of the stock market in 1998, after its collapse in 1997. Nevertheless, according to opposition politicians, they were open to manipulation by political and cronyistic pressures, and this frequently resulted in the abuse of power, whereby corporate assets were often used by powerful capitalists, such as Halim Saad, Tajuddin Ramli and Daim Zainuddin, for personal gain.[12] Support for Malay entrepreneurship had become so unrestrained that it weakened the traditional economic constraints exercised by the Boards of Directors, institutional shareholders or the internal corporate elite. This 'internal and external contractual architecture' of the corporation,[13] which could have provided stability, was now breached by these cronies and powerful Malay capitalists. Again, in line with the Stiglitz view, such large controlling shareholding, as vested in these Malaysian institutional groups, could have led to greater cooperation with managers and secured greater benefits for the firm.[14] In reality, though, the role of these institutional shareholders in Malaysia was shadowy, constrained by the fact that their share of directors in the corporation was low. Only the 1997 crisis introduced greater incentives for increasing their share of directors, and their direct role was increasingly perceptible.

The earlier, veiled, purdah-like presence of institutional shareholders was due to their perceived role as part of the state privatization programme and protecting *bumiputra* interests. But after the crisis they were confronted by a 'public good' dilemma. They widely diversified their investment strategies and invested long term. Moreover, with the acceleration in mergers and takeovers of banks and corporations as part of a broad rescue and restructure scheme, these investment groups, though still acting on government directive, were assessing and bearing risk better.

Finally, the ultimate success of these institutional investors has been to preserve state assets. Despite the privatization programme of the Malaysian government following the economic recession of 1983–5, the control of financial assets by the government remained high. Indeed, government control of financial assets rose from 37 per cent of total financial assets in 1960 to 64 per cent in 1980, and only declined to 43 per cent in 1995.[15] This slow, limited reduction in government corporate assets was a direct consequence of the activities of PNB, EPF and other state investment groups.

The precise equity stake held by Chinese capitalists in the Malaysian corporate sector was concealed by the level of their crossholdings and investments in offshore financial institutions. Non-*bumiputra* stock ownership, which was principally Chinese, continued to rise from 34 per cent in 1971 to 40 per cent in 1980.[16] The privatization of banks and SOEs in the late 1980s increased some of this ethnic proportion, through mergers and interlocking share ownership.

In addition, the abolition of the mutual listing of companies in Singapore and on the KLSE in 1990, coupled with the establishment of the offshore banking centre in Labuan, acted to increase investments from Singapore and Hong Kong, through Malaysian Chinese private investors or through offshore financial institutional holdings. Thus, non-Malay financial capital increased. This was principally Chinese capital, seeping from diverse sources.[17]

The discussion above has highlighted the importance of political connections for the ownership and management of financial institutions. 'The rise and fall of several Malaysian banks can also be related to levels of personal access to political power holders. There is not, however, so complete a correspondence between private access and success as in Indonesia's banking industry.'[18]

A major part of the political cronyism permeating the banking industry was derived from the Mahatir-Daim plan to reinvent Malay capitalism and entrepreneurship under the aegis of the NEP.[19] They interfered in the distribution of bank licences, guaranteed deposits, contracts etc., thereby ensuring the rise of favoured banks. The dramatic decline in foreign ownership after 1970, along with the privatization of corporations and state-owned banks, and the increase in private banks, ensured that those with political connections acquired lucrative financial institutions.

This conjured up three major attributes in the ownership of Malaysian banks. First, the Malay professional elite, consisting of bureaucrats and accountants, assumed ownership and managerial positions, with individuals often being entrusted with sole dominant ownership. Second, due to repeated failures or the urgency to seek financial diversification, there were constant changes in ownership. Third, banking ownership was dispersed with critical segments held by the state, while others were transferred to the Malay elite and a Chinese capitalist minority. Meanwhile, an Indian-owned bank failed.

There was, in addition, some foreign ownership. Such inclusivity meant there was less concentration in the financial system itself. However, concentration of ownership and management was revealed more in the interlocking directorships within the various financial institutions. In particular, a small Malay elite appropriated these positions, taking advantage of the opportunity to move from public service into private entrepreneurship. Such interlocking webs of ownership, directorships and political connections often meant there was no enduring or linear development of a Malay financial bourgeoisie. Political crises in UMNO and changes in Malay political elites had a direct impact on the fortunes of the newly emerging financial debutantes. Azman Hashim of Arab Malaysia Bank (AMB) and Rashid Hussein of Rashid Hussein Bank (RHB) were both recipients of generous political patronage. As the following account will illustrate, their financial careers were shaped by economic factors as well as by changes in political allegiances and loyalties.

In 1982, Azman Hashim secured Arab Malaysia Development Bank, which had been owned by Malaysian Industrial Development Finance and prominent Arab interests. In 1994, he purchased Pacific Bank and the merged bank was renamed Arab Malaysia Bank.[20] Through interlocking shareholdings and directorships, AMB held several financial institutions.[21] The group cultivated impeccable bureaucratic and political connections, including the Inspector General of Police, Hanif Omar; Rashdan Baba, an academic; and Daim Zainuddin, a politician, though the relationship with Daim was variable. Performance, meanwhile, was volatile. Despite an eightfold increase in turnover between 1992 and 1997, profits were low.[22] The crisis in 1997 deepened the vulnerability of Malaysian banks, with severe losses in property and the stock market. AMB held debts of US$262 million and was recapitalized by Danaharta with a loan of RM1.7 billion.[23] The failure can be traced to a rash surge in acquisitions, many of which were not integrated into the group.

There was also reckless connected lending to large Malaysian conglomerates. In the case of Bank Bumiputra, established in 1966, such connected lending descended into fraud. Due to repeated scandals, control of the bank fluctuated between the Ministry of Finance and the national oil group, Petronas (Petroliam Nasional: National Petroleum Corporation). It grew steadily until 1985, when a sharp decline occurred because of serious fraud by bank officials in the Hong Kong branch. Petronas rescued the bank in 1989 with RM2.5 billion. Its accountability was shielded through its obligations as the fund manager for the government's prestige projects. Less attention was paid to its internal performance, while participation in these state initiatives was guaranteed. During the 1997 crisis it was saddled with the largest share of NPLs.[24] Its NPLs were transferred to Danaharta, and the bank was privatized in 1998 and subsequently merged with the Bank of Commerce, hitherto owned by UMNO and Renong.

This dominance of state and institutional stakeholders in the financial industry only allowed for moderate competition, along with demonstrable government support for certain banks. A major governance problem also arose from frequent changes in bank ownership from 1970. These changes in ownership were often triggered by diverse factors, including, first, the privatization plans of the authorities, second, the constant mergers and de-mergers that occurred during both the economic recession of 1983–5 and the financial crisis of 1997 and, third, the financial liberalization since 1989, which accelerated the processes of financial diversification and the growth of offshore banking. All this occurred without clear and cohesive financial structures.

This constant change of owners is demonstrated in the cases of four prominent banks: United Malayan Banking Corporation (UMBC), a Chinese bank; the Development and Commercial Bank, another Chinese bank; the Bank of Commerce, belonging to Halim Saad of Renong; and Kwong Yik Bank (KYB). The UMBC, the third largest bank, was sold in June 1981 by Chang Ming Thien to the Multi-Purpose Holdings Bank (MPHB) owned by MCA. In 1976, it had been defrauded by some of its directors and been rescued by PERNAS (Perbadanan Nasional Bhd: National Corporation). PERNAS now shared equity with MPHB: 41 per cent each. Later, Petronas acquired another 9 per cent before the bank was sold to the Daim Group. In 1986, the bank was resold to PERNAS and in 1992 it was sold to Datuk Keramat Holdings. In 1995, the state reacquired a controlling stake through its corporation, Sime Holdings.

The case of the Development and Commercial Bank is another example of constant changes in ownership. It was established in 1965 by H. S. Lee, a tin-mining magnate. He later shared ownership with Syed Kecik of Sabah. The government held another 10 per cent equity. In 1984, Alex Lee, the owner's son, misappropriated substantial funds and the bank was sold to the United Industrial Corporation of Singapore, which then sold it to Rashid Hussein in a joint-venture with Mitsui Bussan.

Similarly, the Bank of Commerce was rescued by the state in 1986, recapitalized and sold to Renong. Finally, the case of KYB also shows this irrational transfer. KYB was established in Singapore in 1903 but was liquidated in December 1913. Its branch in Malaysia, however, thrived throughout the colonial period and was acquired by Malayan Banking in 1970. In 1971, the Malaysian government acquired 50 per cent equity and, until his move to AMB, Azman Hashim held another major stake in the bank. The rationale behind the sale of KYB to Rashid Hussein in November 1996 is quite baffling. Its growth had been quite impressive. Shareholder funds rose from RM369 million in February 1995 to RM732.5 million in 1996. Moreover, between 1993 and 1994 the bank produced an increase of 34 per cent in pre-tax profits.[25] Yet it was still sold to Rashid Hussein. This sale had clear political motives. First, KYB had been part of lucrative project finance in domestic and overseas investments. For instance, it had been involved in the financing of the Yangtze toll bridge, was active in Islamic banking and was financing infrastructural projects in Uzbekistan.[26] The sale to Rashid Hussein would enable his group to embark on global projects in Central Asia and South Africa. However, Maybank justified the sale on the grounds that its own subsidiary, Aseambankers, would now specialize in project finance and securities business, which hitherto was dominated by KYB.[27] The sale of KYB to RHB, for RM2.16 billion in cash, improved the capital asset ratio for Maybank, but proved a strain on RHB, which subsequently faced a high ratio of NPLs in 1997.

Maybank: ownership, mergers and multinational banking

This detailed case study of Maybank, the largest bank in Malaysia, reveals similar changes in ownership – specifically, the transition from a Chinese-owned bank to a state-controlled one following serious fraud scandals. Maybank also manifested similar haphazard moves at mergers and multinational banking. The only significant differences from other Malaysian banks were that its growth after takeover by the state was stable and it demonstrated an increased level of competency, skilled management and stable relations with capital markets in Malaysia and Singapore. However, its attempts during the 1990s to become a multinational bank were mired in distress. In its moves into Indonesia, Papua New Guinea and Uzbekistan, Maybank faced high levels of uncertainty constant defaults, and changes in government policies. Maybank also suffered from its limited capacity to create networks overseas and to appraise risk, and the limited variety of services it could offer. Competition from other multinational banks was harsh.

A brief survey of its origins in the 1960s, as the Chinese-owned Malayan Banking, confirms its fundamental feature: a close and enduring relationship with the Malaysian state. The early growth of Malayan Banking can be told in terms of the declining fortunes of the Mercantile Bank, the Chartered Bank, and Hongkong and Shanghai Bank. More significantly, it was the close relationship between Khoo Teck Puat of Malayan Banking and the Governor of Bank Negara that lay at the heart of the bank's rapid growth in the late 1960s. Such ties to the bureaucracy provided a competitive edge for Chinese banking in the 1950s and 1960s, when faced with an established European banking presence. Malayan Banking was established in 1962 by Khoo Teck Puat, the former deputy general manager of OCBC. Its impressive growth in its first decade was assisted by the decline of European banking, principally the Mercantile Bank and the Hongkong and Shanghai Bank. In 1966, domestic banks in Malaysia accounted for just 30 per cent of total bank deposits; by 1972 this had risen to 37 per cent and it reached 70 per cent by 1987. This growth was a result of the economic restructuring that had been introduced to reduce dependence on foreign economic agents.

The 1960s was a period of intense competition. The Malaysian economy was expanding and infrastructural and rural development, particularly in the east coast Malay states, meant that banks were competing for state funds. There was also a rather vague regional specialization among the existing Western banks, whereby the Hongkong and Shanghai Bank and the Chartered Bank dominated the west coast states of Malaysia, while the Mercantile Bank concentrated on the east coast. Malayan Banking was able to dislodge these groups partly through its lending policies and partly through the strong support of the Governor of Bank Negara.[28]

A large proportion of the Mercantile Bank's deposits in east coast Malaysia were derived from the state governments. During the 1960s, there was expansion in infrastructural and rural projects in Malaysia, and much of this funding came from the central government. From 1962, the state authorities were instructed by Bank Negara to transfer these funds from the Mercantile Bank, the traditional bank for the state, to Malayan Banking. The pressure from the Governor was so intense that on 13 February 1963 the Pahang state government withdrew half a million ringgit from the Mercantile Bank and deposited it with Malayan Banking. On 26 February 1963, there was another transfer by the Pahang state government of RM4 million from the Mercantile Bank to Malayan Banking. This money would not be used for the following few months.[29] This loss of government funds in 1962–3 seriously affected the future of the bank. In September 1963, the Mercantile Bank in Trengganu suffered a withdrawal of RM3 million in funds that had been deposited with it. These government funds were critical to the bank because in 1963 they represented two-thirds of the total deposits of the Mercantile Bank in Kuala Trengganu, Kuantan, Kota Bharu and Bentong.[30] Bank Negara was responsible for this shift. In particular, the Bank Negara Governor was assisting Malayan Banking through direct instructions to curb Western banking. The Mercantile Bank in Penang also suffered a 25 per cent decline in deposits between 1960 and 1965.[31]

In addition, the way in which government controls on inter-bank lending were imposed acted in favour of Malayan Banking. The Governor's instructions to Western banks to reduce their borrowing from local banks were calculated to deprive the Mercantile Bank of essential funds. OCBC and UMBC Bank from Singapore had long maintained the practice of building up short- and long-term deposits with the Mercantile Bank. The short-term, often overnight, funds generated an interest rate of 4–5 per cent, while the long-term deposits attracted 6.25 per cent interest.[32] In July 1963, the Mercantile Bank had deposits of RM4.5 million from the local banks; of this, OCBC contributed RM1 million. In January 1963, OCBC held RM21 million with Mercantile Bank. The Governor instructed OCBC to invest surplus funds in Malaysian government bills and securities, or to deposit them with Malayan Banking.[33]

This pressure to hold government debt or to bank with Malayan Banking arose from the Governor's conviction that Western banks were sustained by local banks.[34] For example, in 1965, almost 45 per cent of the resources of the Mercantile Bank in Penang were from other banks.[35] The Mercantile Bank did attempt to soothe the government through increased investment in government bills and securities. Indeed, the Mercantile Bank had expanded into the east coast states to assist in the financing of government infrastructural projects there.[36]

Additionally, the Mercantile Bank and the Hongkong and Shanghai Bank faced difficulties as a result of Khoo's aggressive tactics in securing the accounts of Chinese traders. The Mercantile Bank had been successful in financing Chinese rubber dealers, rice and sugar importers, and importers of light engineering goods. Since he was a shareholder, the most prominent rubber merchant, Lee Kong Chian, transferred his entire account to the OCBC in the 1950s. The smaller rubber dealers and smallholders, however, were attracted by the generous financial terms offered by Malayan Banking. It made large advances to traders, often loans for six months of RM3,000–5,000. This was at a time when, due to a spate of banking crises in Hong Kong in early 1965, the Governor of Bank Negara had insisted on a more conservative capital adequacy ratio.[37]

Malayan Banking expanded rapidly in the 1960s and diversified into real estate and hotel investment. For instance, Khoo purchased Raffles Hotel and Goodwood Park Hotel in 1963. That same year, the bank also acquired a controlling interest in Lombard Central Finance, which was owned by Lombard Banking and Asia Life Assurance. By 1966, Malayan Banking had 108 branches and a 25 per cent share of deposits and advances. Despite allegations of insider lending, which led to a serious run on the bank in 1966, it continued to expand. The Malaysian government increased its equity in Malayan Banking to 50 per cent by 1976, while Khoo retained 20 per cent.[38] In 1988, it had 188 branches, with capital and reserves of RM1,124 million, deposits of RM9,581 million, and aggregate assets of RM14,769 million.[39] Despite the economic restructuring under the NEP, the Chinese still held 15.42 per cent of total bank deposits in Malaysia in 1984 and 13.62 per cent of total bank assets. But the only bank to remain fully in Chinese hands was

Public Bank, the fourth largest, in which Teh Hong Piow held 60 per cent of equity in 1988. Even in 1997, he still held more than 40 per cent.

The sources of growth for Malayan Banking were diverse. For instance, from 1963, it was responsible for the foreign exchange transactions of Muslim pilgrims from Malaysia. This was later directed to Malaysia's state banks. It also held an important share of the rice and rubber trade, as well as of consumer finance. This was a growth area during the 1970s and was managed by its subsidiary, Lombard Finance.

Khoo was evicted from the board of Malayan Banking in 1976. There had been allegations of insider lending, identified by Bank Negara as far back as 1966, and he was forced to resign from his post as managing director. Suspicions of 'insider lending', ostensibly leading to his dismissal, continued to circulate. He sold his shares in the bank for RM50 million and invested in hotels in Singapore. He still retained his equity in Malayan Banking, while investing in other banks in Asia, including Standard Chartered. Nevertheless, Khoo survived. Indeed, in the mid-1980s, he was so powerful as to mount a bid, through a consortium, for the Chartered Bank.

As the bank scandals surrounding Malayan Banking surfaced in the 1970s, the Malaysian government sought a radical restructuring, with a majority holding (55 per cent) being acquired by PNB. The newly reformed institution was called Maybank. It acquired KYB in 1992 and became a major state financier of development projects, both at home and abroad. The dramatic growth of Maybank is captured in the increases in paid-up capital: from RM7.5 million in May 1960 to RM22.5 million in 1968, to RM90.0 million in 1977, to RM225 million in November 1984, to RM562.2 million in November 1990, to RM1.1 billion in December 1994, and to RM2.3 billion in June 1998. A major share of this increase was through rights issues and bonus issues. The leap in capital during the 1990s was particularly striking.

Similarly, the nature of shareholding was changing from the 1980s. *Bumiputra* shares held by institutional shareholders rose to 57 per cent of the total equity, with foreign nominees clearing a further 26.7 per cent.[40] Foreign investment groups included HSBC (8 per cent), Hwang DBS (2.2 per cent), Citicorp (3 per cent) and Chase Nominees (3 per cent). After the 1997 crisis, foreign investors increased their stake to 30 per cent. Amirsham Aziz, the managing director, and Mohammad Salleh Haji Harun, the executive director, held substantial holdings.[41] This pattern of shareholding persevered into 2002.[42]

However, following the 1997 crisis, foreign investors' holdings were distributed in smaller equations, while the directors increased their holdings through further rights and bonus issues. The government still embodied the largest shareholding stake, principally through the restructuring and resolution of NPLs.

This concentrated shareholding vested in a few government agencies was further inflated through interlocking shareholding with financial subsidiaries in the group. These corporate management interlocks and equity holdings were identified with a phase of increasing financial specialization, accompanied by an equally increasing financial diversification and regional dispersal.

The interlocking relation of equity and management also persisted between the foreign and domestic subsidiaries of the group. For example, Maybank held 79 per cent equity in Maybank Nusa International in Indonesia and 100 per cent equity in Papua New Guinea. This was replicated in Singapore and the Philippines. These foreign subsidiaries endured severe losses in 1997 and, as part of the recapitalization, there were mergers within these groups and the absorption of related financial corporations.

Despite the large private shareholding of the directors, dominant ownership remained with the state. This consistency in ownership, by the state and talented directors, ensured the survival of the bank during the 1997 crisis. Only its overseas operations faced extreme difficulties. Maybank's expansion after 1993 had ushered in a period of overseas growth that was unsustainable. Expansion into the Muslim Republics of Central Asia was purely opportunistic. In May 1996, a joint-venture with the National Bank of Uzbekistan was particularly attractive because of support from the IFC and the European Bank for Reconstruction Development.[43] Globalization dragged the Maybank into bad investments in slow growth areas. Its revenue from overseas operations rarely exceeded 6–9 per cent, while the Malaysian operations contributed to 85 per cent of the total revenue of the group.

The barriers to the successful growth of multinational banking were enormous. First, Malaysian banks, including Maybank, lacked international reputations and specialization. Specifically, they had not made the transition from retail banking to investment banking. Second, they lacked regional specialization, having made moves into Indonesia, the Philippines and Myanmar in 1993–4 only through local joint-venture arrangements. Hence, they confronted difficulties in these local environments. They were heavily reliant on networks of ethnic, economic and political elites. Rather than being the leader, Maybank frequently followed Malaysian corporations such as Petronas and Renong into these regions. Third, these difficulties were compounded by the lack of rigorous political and legal infrastructures in the regions that Maybank penetrated. Relations with the host state were often conducted via the Malaysian state. Such banking operations could only be sustained in a period of rapid growth; a slight contraction could spell disaster. Moreover, there was no attempt by Maybank to integrate domestic units with its overseas units. There was only interlocking shareholding, meaning the overseas operations were conducted in a freestanding manner. There were also heavy costs, exaggerated by a lack of customer knowledge in a highly volatile environment.

In these ventures abroad, Maybank targeted certain industries, often public utilities, power and infrastructure. Here, relations were determined by the investment strategies of the Malaysian state, and the World Bank and IMF initiatives. Equally, the services Maybank could provide were not that special, since it lacked links to international capital markets. It also faced difficulties in securing reliable long-term intermediaries in the host nation. This lack of continuity was serious. Maybank faced shifting partners in Southeast Asia as well as in Central Asia.

The lack of continuity in geographical location, organizational structures and business strategies limited Maybank's growth overseas. Maybank moved into Southeast Asia, Mauritius and Papua New Guinea through clear subsidiaries, while in Hong Kong, California and Europe it acquired failing banks. But with both strategies, there were difficulties in penetrating the local markets. In the case of niche collaboration with local entrepreneurs, as in Uzbekistan and Papua New Guinea, it was difficult to sustain long-term expansion. Islamic finance as a niche financial sector failed because of low profits and political instability in Uzbekistan. Aseambankers (a Maybank subsidiary) offered Islamic financing facilities as part of project finance. It was arranged on both the *Murabahah* principle (where profits and losses were shared equally) and on the *Musharakah* principle (where both partners shared in profits or losses in proportion to each one's share in capital). This capital was part of the device to attract finance from wealthy Middle East countries. This was utilized in public utilities projects in China, Mauritius, Uzbekistan and Indonesia. It also issued private debt securities and Islamic overdraft facilities.

Consortium banking could have provided new lines of business, but Maybank was ill prepared and consumer finance was fraught with difficulties. Bad debts and bad collateral increased the risk in these alien markets. Furthermore, innovation in banking services was not viable in such low growth areas. Their strategies of acquiring shareholding in the domestic banks of the host nation also lacked viability. Many of the areas possessed no real market-determined growth since the banks were owned by political cronies and fraud was pervasive, as Maybank's experience in Papua New Guinea clearly demonstrated.

Only the continued strength of the Malaysian economy sustained these adventures abroad. A slight deterioration after 1997 accelerated into record losses, leading to closure and withdrawal from Papua New Guinea and from sections of Indonesian banking. Only Maybank's operations in Singapore remained profitable.[44]

Performance

Maybank displayed gradual growth throughout the 1980s, even during and after the economic recession of 1983–5. The dramatic growth after 1991 reached its peak in 1996; there were no hints of an impending crisis. Particularly impressive was its performance between 1991 and 1995. The background to this growth lay partly in the large inflows of short-term capital, which doubled from RM6.7 billion in 1991 to RM13.9 billion in 1993. Growth was reflected in an increase in deposits of commercial banks, which surged by 20 per cent between 1991 and 1993, and then declined to 13 per cent in 1994–5. This reduced the ratio of NPLs to total loans for commercial banks from 9.4 per cent in 1994 to 6 per cent in 1995.[45] See Tables 5.3a and 5.3b for details.

During this same period (1991–3), however, trading volume on the KLSE fell from 357.9 million units to 191.4 million.[46] In addition, the volume of credit rose by 25 per cent. Between 1994 and 1995, the ratio of loans to total assets rose from 53.8 per cent to 59.8 per cent. There was a marked trend towards financial diversification, in the creation of unit trusts, leasing, venture capital and investment banking. Diversification was also evidenced in the establishment of new financial specialist companies in the Maybank Group. Commercial banking, which accounted for 69 per cent of the group's pre-tax profits, saw a 90 per cent increase in the volume of lending. The merchant bank possessed syndicated loans exceeding RM4.0 billion in 1994–5.[47] The increase in capital market debt instruments by 83.8 per cent in 1995 was part of an increase in project finance. Rapid growth in financial diversification is captured in these statistics. Non-banking activities grew by 58.1 per cent in 1995. Similarly, stockbroking, despite lower profits, grew by 21.9 per cent between 1994 and 1995. The changes after 1997 are revealed in Table 5.4a. Table 5.4b shows the geographical dispersion of activities.

Maybank endured fewer difficulties during the crisis than any other Malaysian bank. Its stability can be traced to the steady rise in net profits between 1994 and 1996. These only contracted briefly in 1998, before a sharp resurgence in 1999–2000. The decline in profits in 1997 was largely due to a deterioration in assets and a narrower return on foreign funds. This trend was repeated for return on capital employed, which collapsed in 1997 but recovered in 1998, and there was no reduction in dividends, just a steady rise after a tiny contraction in 1997. Similarly, shareholder funds expanded from 1994 to 2000, while short-term borrowings saw a dramatic increase from 1996, contracting briefly in 2000. There was no perceptible decline in total asset growth. Maybank had a diversified loan portfolio and better provisions cover, so distress was limited. By September 1999, all the sections in the group, including investment banking, were profitable.[48]

In 1998, Maybank saw losses of US$425.6 million in its overseas subsidiaries.[49] Its bank in Indonesia registered a loss of RM35.1 million, while the Philippines subsidiaries produced a loss of RM0.2 million and those in Papua New Guinea recorded a loss of RM0.7 million. These losses abroad led to divestment and retreat from many of these regions. The restructuring in Malaysia after 1997 involved an emphasis on loans to SMEs. Such loans increased by 19.4 per cent in 2000. Corporate customers' loans, meanwhile, only increased by 1.7 per cent and this was principally in trade finance. There was also an increase in Islamic banking, which registered a growth of 16.6 per cent in 2000. Furthermore, there was an increase in assets through the acquisitions of Pacific Bank, Phileo Allied Bank (PAB), Sime Bank and

Table 5.3a Maybank, performance indicators: balance sheets as at 30 June (in RM '000)

	1994	*1995*	*1996*	*1997*	*1998*	*1999*	*2000*
Profitablity ratios							
Dividends/NPAT	21.80	17.97	15.71	6.44	–110.91	–20.91	–22.13
ROCE	29.17	29.25	29.56	n/a	6.39	10.68	20.11
ROI	0.17	0.18	0.19	n/a	0.01	0.12	0.13
ROE	0.17	0.19	0.20	n/a	0.13	0.10	0.13
Liquidity ratios							
Liquid asset ratio	0.99	0.99	0.99	0.99	0.99	0.99	0.99
Loans/deposits	0.65	0.08	0.70	0.75	0.87	0.83	0.78
Total liquid assets/ short-term liability	1.05	1.05	1.06	1.20	1.04	1.08	1.08
Gearing ratios							
Equity	1,141,383.00	1,143,414.00	1,143,414.00	1,143,414.00	2,286,828.00	2,308,661.00	2,337,975.00
Debt/equity	0.00	0.00	0.00	0.00	0.00	0.00	0.00

Source: Annual Report of Maybank, 1994–2000; Balance Sheets, Profit/Loss Accounts of Maybank, 1994–2000

Table 5.3b Maybank, comparative results (1996–2000) (RM '000)

	1996	*1997*	*1998*	*1999*	*2000*
Operating revenues	258,070	528,007	869,716	875,623	902,228
Profit/loss before taxation	66,536	73,961	–62,603	–64,218	211,372
Shareholders' funds	500,925	526,959	447,439	391,426	635,746
Basic earnings/(loss) per share	13	10	–21	–16	63

Source: Annual Reports of Maybank

Table 5.4a Maybank, revenue derived from different segments (RM millions)

Product	*1998*	*1999*	*2000*	*Ave 2-yr growth (%)*
1 Banking	9,771.03	8,156.44	6,823.61	–16.43
2 Finance company	2,917.37	2,517.10	1,981.07	–17.41
3 Insurance	117.54	157.08	183.39	25.19
4 Discount/factoring	384.49	347.25	171.02	–30.22
5 Stocks/futures brokerage	86.98	63.66	132.51	40.67
6 Others	16.21	43.63	42.34	83.13

Table 5.4b Geographical dispersion of Maybank activities by revenue (RM millions)

Region/country	*1998*	*1999*	*2000*	*Ave 2-yr growth (%)*
1 Malaysia	11,281.58	9,734.05	7,919.52	–16.18
2 Singapore	1,326.36	980.46	383.07	–20.30
3 Others	685.67	624.65	576.34	–8.32

Source: Bloomberg, 22 February 2001

Phileo Allied Securities. These acquisitions also resulted in an increase in NPLs of 32 per cent for the Maybank Group.[50]

The restructuring of debt was slow, partly because economic recovery was slow and the stock market had been disastrously weakened. Thus, the gross NPLs ratio in 2001 was 14.5 per cent for the group and 13.7 per cent for the bank alone, despite increased provisions of RM444.8 million. In addition, there was an increased number of NPLs resulting from the mergers. Some of the subsidiaries were weakened by the decline in the property and stock markets. This meant that the loan loss provisions of the investment banking subsidiary Aseambankers tripled to RM219.4 million in 2001.[51]

In addition, NPLs were reclassified and there was depreciation in collateral values due to deteriorating property and equity prices. The only increase was in the amount of fixed debt instruments, such as bonds.[52] In 2002, asset growth rate was lower than in 2001, which had included the incorporated assets of PAB, Pacific Bank and Phileo Allied Securities. In 2001 it was 10.9 per cent, while in 2002 it had declined to 2.3 per cent. Bad debts were either repaid or converted to equity totalling RM7.0 billion.[53]

The merger of Maybank with other financial institutions was carried out in several stages. First, the mergers, as well as divestitures of financial subsidiaries, were completed before the acquisition and integration of Pacific Bank and PAB were coordinated. Second, there was the regional integration of similar financial components, such as the merging of Maybank Finance Singapore with Maybank Singapore, absorbing the assets, liabilities as well as the branches there. This was completed by May 1999. In Malaysia, Maybank insurance was merged with UMBC insurance in May 1999 and this was followed by the absorption of further financial units into the group. In October 1999, Maybank Finance acquired Sime Finance, a merger costing RM76.55 million. There was a significant interlocking in shareholding, ownership and management within these consolidated firms. The RM1.2 billion acquisition of Pacific Bank in February 2000 was followed by that of PAB in June 2000 for RM1.3 billion. These mergers produced a banking group with total assets of RM147 billion.[54]

These separate processes of restructuring and integration meant the amalgamation of diverse financial units, along functional lines, to constitute strong recapitalized subsidiaries. These mergers introduced a substantial increase in equity, as well as market networks. The internal corporate restructurings that took place prior to a merger, sometimes divesting a core firm in the group before the actual transaction, were not always clear in their objectives. Were they done to enhance the value of shareholder investments so as to secure an advantage in the merger and restructuring discussions? There was sometimes a clear rationalization and streamlining of activities, as evidenced by the merger of Maybank Finance Singapore and Maybank Singapore discussed earlier. This produced an enlarged capital base, as well as a unified but diverse subsidiary in Singapore. Equally, the February 2000 transfer of Maybank Factoring to Maybank Finance Malaysia was a logical step to secure cohesion. However, there were also complicated processes of splitting entire subsidiaries and divestitures of some units, and the creation of new companies with new shareholders. The motives for these were unclear.

Second, during the transitional phase of the merger between Maybank and Pacific Bank, both continued to manage their own accounts and maintained distinct operations. Pacific Bank soon relinquished its commercial banking and concentrated on insurance through its subsidiary Pacific Insurance Bhd.[55] It had paid-up capital of RM65 million and total assets of RM159.3 million. Its commercial banking unit was absorbed by Maybank. This strategic refocusing after mergers produced an increase in group profits, as well as in total assets. The insurance sector of Pacific Bank contributed 19.7 per cent of the group's profits in 1999–2000.[56]

The choice of banks to merge was rather haphazard since it was left to the individual banking groups to select their partners. Indeed, the choice of PAB and Pacific Bank was rather a rigged one. PAB's major shareholder was Mokhzani Mahatir, Prime Minister Mahatir's son, and it had originally been assigned to MPHB. Mokhzani held the shares through Pantai Tongkah Holdings, which owned 28 per cent in Phileo Land. Phileo Land, meanwhile, held 18.4 per cent in PAB. Mokhzani divested his stake following criticisms of his involvement. PAB was controlled by Tong Kooi Ong and had grown through acquisitions into a highly innovative bank; indeed, its securities sector was more profitable than commercial banking. Its involvement in state initiatives and in Islamic debt securities meant there was no serious distress in 1997. The merger was for the long-term rationalization and specialization of Maybank, in particular the improvement of its investment banking sector. In addition, its involvement in project finance, in providing large syndicated loans for major state initiatives, attracted foreign investors.[57]

PAB itself had been established through unusual acquisitions. The acquisition of Peregrine Brokerage (Hong Kong) in 1991 by a little known brokerage firm in Perak led to the creation of Phileo Peregrine Securities. This was followed by a reverse takeover of a publicly listed commodities firm, Wilkinson Linatex Process Rubber Co. The acquisition of this company was part of a strategy to acquire their property assets providing critical collateral for a financial services company. The company was renamed Phileo Allied and soon acquired Overseas Union Bank in Sabah, which had been divested by its parent bank in Singapore. In October 1994, Phileo Allied acquired another failing bank, Cooperative Central Bank. These acquisitions were assisted with funds from the Ministry of Finance. PAB was incorporated in 1994, amalgamating all these banks. Phileo Allied then embarked on a wave of acquisitions to facilitate globalization. The acquisitions of securities firms in Sydney, Hong Kong, London, Jersey, New York, Darulsalaam (Brunei) and Manila were largely to acquire stocks of high value abroad in high growth areas. In 1996–7, PAB's stockbroking activities yielded 51 per cent of pre-tax profits, while the bank only contributed 36 per cent of total pre-tax profits.[58]

After the 1997 crisis, however, there was increased urgency for mergers between the bank and its financial subsidiaries. This consolidation, absorbing the liabilities of the finance company, was completed by 1998. The securities firm in Sydney was sold in early 1999 and, by mid-1999, there were negotiations for a merger with the Maybank Group. These negotiations towards a merger were rather protracted, with frequent changes in merger partner being proposed, including merging with MPHB. However, by May 1999 the first stage of integrating the diverse units within the PAB group was achieved. PAB acquired the assets of Phileo Finance through a new share issue for RM22 million. Maybank then acquired the entire paid-up capital of PAB and recapitalized the bank, disposing of its debt while providing more working capital. This was completed by June 2000. The purchase cost RM1.3 billion.[59]

In the immediate aftermath of this merger, there were crucial changes in shareholding. Before 2000, local institutional investors held 47 per cent, while Avenue Assets held 20 per cent. Avenue Assets (Phileo Land) had tangible links to Mokhzani Mahatir. The only large individual shareholder was Ahmad Abdullah. Tong Kooi Ong and Ng Seng Hin held interlocking shares with other firms in the group and were also directors of the bank. *Bumiputra* shareholding was 44 per cent of the total, non-Malay shareholding accounted for 23 per cent, and foreign investors accounted for another 21 per cent.

Just prior to merger, there was frenzied buying of shares to increase the capital base.[60] After the absorption by Maybank, the shareholding was distributed to Public Nominees (15 per cent), CIMB Nominees (10 per cent), foreign investors (10 per cent), Avenue Assets (18 per cent), Ahmad Abdullah (13 per cent) and EPF (4 per cent). The burden of NPLs persisted because of the weak ringgit, continuous asset deflation, falling consumer demand, lower investments and tight liquidity. PAB held 16 per cent of NPLs in April 1998. In fact, NPLs peaked in 1999.[61] The holding company, Phileo Allied, faced a high interest burden due to heavy borrowings.[62]

Company records for the years 1996 to 2000 clearly reveal highly fluctuating performance for the group in these years. For the financial year ending January 2001, the PAB recorded losses of RM77 million, though its stockbroking unit recorded profits of RM42 million. The losses were high because of the greater provisions made for bad debts.[63]

Management

The management of Maybank had continuity. The managing director, Amirsham Aziz, had been with Maybank since 1977. Mohd Basir Ahmad came from Bank Negara, while Mohd Salleh Haji Harun, the Vice Chairman; Richard Ho, an ex-cabinet minister; and a director of Danaharta, Ismail Shahudin, among others, came from diverse backgrounds – accountancy firms, government ministries and plantation companies. Azman Hashim, who had been involved as executive director since 1971, resigned in 1980 but then rejoined Maybank in 1982. The management changed in March 2000 with more representatives from the institutional investment groups – PNB, ASB and ASN – taking up positions. This rise of state-connected investment directors reflected the increase in direct state involvement.[64]

Background to the 1997 financial crisis

The financial distress in 1997 was far less serious in Malaysia than in its neighbours, particularly Indonesia and Thailand. Indeed, there was little sign of a crisis. Malaysian economic growth was 8.6 per cent in 1996 and this had been the average since 1990. Inflation was only 3.6 per cent, while savings and investment exceeded 40 per cent of GDP. Fiscal surplus was 0.7 per cent in 1996. The current account deficit for the same year was 1.8 per cent, narrowing from 3.9 per cent in 1995. External debt was always low. Total NPLs between 1990 and 1996 was low, declining from 20.4 per cent in 1990 to 8.10 per cent in 1994, to 5.5 per cent in 1995, and to 3.9 per cent in 1996. However, these figures need to be accepted with some caution. In 1997, NPLs were 27 per cent of total gross loans and the decline in NPLs remained weak, registering 18 per cent in 2001 and 17 per cent in mid-2002. The earlier reporting of a low ratio of NPLs could well be a case of under-reporting. Weak methods of disclosure and the ability, up until the crisis at least, to cover up distress through further borrowing which was sustained, in turn, by high capital inflows, meant that the current account surplus, with stable exchange rates and generous government finance, were maintained. The financial crisis exposed these inadequacies.

The liberalization of the capital market in the 1990s corresponded with an increase in the activities of hedge fund providers, institutional investors and speculators. Portfolio investment rose from 13 per cent in 1995 to 45 per cent of total annual capital inflows in 1996.[65] Athukorala argues that financial liberalization, large portfolio capital inflows and the lack of financial prudence were all implicated in this stealthy push towards a crisis. My argument is that the structural, institutional deficiencies in the Malaysian financial industry, aggravated by a global downturn in electronics, which was the main generator of exports, groomed the crisis in 1997. Capital inflows and the lack of a regulatory framework to coordinate these flows can only cause temporary turbulence. It was the institutional flaws, in the form of inadequate corporate organization and culture, that determined the seriousness and length of the crisis. The unhealthy dominance of individual ownership of banks, the propensity for large corporate borrowers to over-leverage themselves, the concentration of bank lending to a few individuals, and the lack of professional managers to curb this form of financial growth and these lending practices provoked the slide towards a crisis. The banks failed to confront the weak internal structures outlined earlier or to improve risk-management strategies. Instead, they relied constantly on a buoyant lending environment. A slight contraction, as seen in the recession of 1983–5, led to immediate difficulties. Rather than narrow interest spreads in the less buoyant lending environment of 1995–6, their response was to borrow more offshore. This lecherous attitude to borrowing, combined with the poor asset quality of the loans, low loan reserves and a lack of adequate provisions – in short, a shameless imprudence – explains the peak of NPLs at 27 per cent in 1997.[66]

The aggressive portfolio capital inflows of the 1990s destabilized the economy, creating bubbles in the property sector and stock market. But it was the organizational, institutional flaws that exacerbated the impact of these capital surges. The share of foreign holdings on the KLSE rose to

30–40 per cent of total holdings in the mid-1990s.[67] This made the KLSE the third largest equity market in Asia, after Tokyo and Hong Kong. Moreover, equity market capitalization (US$200 billion) was 300 per cent of GDP, the highest in the world.

The second pressure was capital inflows into the property sector. In 1996, total bank credit located in this sector amounted to 40 per cent of total bank credit. In March 1997, Bank Negara placed restrictions on bank lending to the property market in order to forestall such speculative growth. Third, residents could maintain offshore foreign currency accounts, where generous terms put pressure on the ringgit. Bank Negara issued restrictions on the external liabilities of commercial banks in February 1994 and these restrained such pressures. However, the restrictions were removed in August 1994.

The role of foreign banks in domestic banking declined between the 1980s and early 1990s. Thus, it was the outstanding credit of the domestic banks that proved to be treacherous, rising from 85 per cent of GDP in 1985–9 to 160 per cent in mid-1997.[68] The government and the private sector were pursuing an ostentatious strategy of infrastructural development, through the creation of the information-technology hub known as Cyberjaya, a new airport and other prestige plans. The excessive credit – indeed, between the mid-1980s to 1997 Malaysia saw the largest credit growth in East Asia, with credit as a ratio of GDP rising from 85 per cent in 1985–9 to 120 per cent in 1994 and to 160 per cent in mid-1997[69] – was unstable, and bore grave consequences because a majority of these loans were to a tiny, politically connected corporate elite, thereby increasing their NPLs. Private sector credit rose from 12 per cent in 1990–4 to 26 per cent in 1994–6.[70] This is an underestimate, however, since many of the elite corporations dabbled in large syndicated loans, bonds and other debt instruments that were concealed within state initiatives and state finance.

This clear corruption and high debt ratios increased the financial fragility of the banks. This fragility persisted, despite the fact that, with the exception of Singapore, their capital asset ratio of 10 per cent in this period was the highest in Southeast Asia. RHB faced a serious crisis in 1997 because of connected lending to Halim Saad of Renong and to the business interests of Transport Minister, Ling Liong Sik. Such profligate lending by RHB at home, along with troubles abroad in the form of weak acquisitions in Indonesia, were hints of impending collapse. Before engaging in a detailed analysis of the crisis and the organizational restructuring that followed, it would be pertinent to elaborate, first, on the dramatic inflows of foreign capital in the 1990s, and, second, on the hectic wave of mergers and acquisitions, and the unstable banking structure that emerged from these activities.

Foreign capital flows

As noted earlier, foreign capital provided another source of financial instability. Foreign capital inflows in the first half of the 1990s averaged 11 per cent of GNP. The highest inflow was in 1993 when it constituted 23 per cent of GNP. Short-term capital inflows were high in the 1990s and much of it fuelled stock market growth. There was also a corresponding increase in FDI whereby foreign equity in the manufacturing sector was 32 per cent of the total paid-up capital by 1989. This increase in foreign equity in the 1990s was striking, since during the 1980s it was only 10 per cent, having fallen from 63 per cent in 1970. Nationalization and the NEP both conspired to reduce foreign equity and it was only after 1986 that foreign ownership was allowed and, then, only if the products were for export.[71]

Between 1980 and 1991, Bank Negara Malaysia constantly appraised the level of foreign assets and liabilities in Malaysian corporations. However, the liberalization measures after 1989 frustrated this reporting by Bank Negara. Hence, details on capital inflows and outflows and geographical distribution of portfolio investment were missed.[72] In addition, outward investments by Malaysian private entrepreneurs (Chinese and *bumiputra*) were encouraged because of limited opportunities at home. Unlike the global initiatives of the Singapore state, where the state led these overseas ventures, it was Malaysian private capital, principally Chinese with some Malay capitalists, that monopolized this move. In short, monopoly rents earned at home were financing expansion abroad. This international diversification also held serious prospects for capital flight, besides the sapping away of profits made in the domestic market.

Hence, what I would emphasize is that globalization often eroded the sustainable growth achieved at home. This was true of the major banking ventures overseas: in Indonesia, Central Asia, Australia, Hong Kong, China and the US. By focusing on foreign capital inflows into Malaysia, one loses perspective on the global inflows and outflows of capital, in particular that of private Malaysian capital outflows, which were often located in deteriorating investments abroad in the 1990s. Table 5.5 illustrates clearly this serious outflow of bank credit between 1993 and 1994.

Central bank governance

Malaysia possessed a good legal framework for regulating financial institutions. The central bank, Bank Negara, possessed appropriate information for regulation, while also maintaining fairly strict autonomy. Its role in industrial policy and in ethnic economic restructuring was conducted in cooperation with other civil service agencies.[73] It did not allow itself to be politicized or to be compromised by business powerbrokers, as happened in Thailand and Indonesia. For details of these two countries, see Chapters 2, 3, 10 and 11 in this volume. Hamilton-Hart sees this autonomy as a direct legacy of Tun Ismail Mohamed Ali, the governor from 1962 to 1980; he had strong views on the bank's impartiality and believed intervention should be limited to the maintenance of discipline and the preservation good practice.[74] Zeti,

Table 5.5 Net capital inflows*, 1990–7 (US$ million)

	1990	*1991*	*1992*	*1993*	*1994*	*1995*	*1996*	*1997*	*1990–96***
Official long-term	–58.7	3.5	–0.9	–3.6	11.8	–1.1	–1.1	60.6	–3.1
Private	158.7	96.5	100.9	103.6	88.2	101.1	101.1	39.4	103.1
FDI	130.6	71.5	78.1	46.4	335.2	55.2	53.7	187.3	69.5
Portfolio	–10.6	–12.6	46.8	92.4	433.6	28.2	37.1	–370.8	53.8
Bank credit	38.7	37.6	7.5	–34.7	–680.5	19.0	10.3	222.9	–15.0
Total***	1,789	5,584	6,607	10,799	1,235	7,612	9,416	2,729	6,149
Percentage of GDP	4.2	11.9	11.3	16.8	1.7	8.7	9.5	2.8	13.9

Notes:

* Net capital inflows comprise net FDI, net portfolio investment (equity and bond flows), and official and private bank borrowings. Changes in national foreign exchange reserves are not included.

** Annual average.

*** Extra figures not included in this table contribute to this total

Source: Derived from Bank Negara Malaysia, Monthly Statistical Bulletin (various issues), cited in Athukorala, p. 55

who took over in 1998 following serious rifts between politicians and the central bank, preserved this aloofness and independence.

Nevertheless, Bank Negara governors have not always been able to avert the clear links between politicians and individual owners of banks. In 1982, Bank Negara introduced limits on loans to connected corporations and, in particular, uncollateralized loans to directors. The 1986 Banking Act, meanwhile, enforced a restriction on the number of shares held by a single shareholder: the limit was 20 per cent for commercial banks and 10 per cent for non-banking financial institutions. Yet, the frequent merging and divestitures of banks confused this regulatory constraint. Moreover, powerful, charismatic politicians and bankers enfeebled the primary role of Bank Negara in averting fraud.[75] The diversification of financial institutions from the late 1980s also complicated the regulatory role of Bank Negara. The financial liberalization of 1989, which provided banks with the freedom to engage in diverse activities and offer a wide range of products and services, unleashed more chaos and destabilized foreign exchange transactions and capital market activities.

Reforms of the stock market were also aimed at greater transparency but, again, there were serious lapses. After the 1997 crisis, the KLSE abolished the nominee system on stock exchange investment. However, in 1998 the government allowed bank loans to be used for the purchase of securities. It even permitted EPF funds to be used to stimulate the stock market. This had volatile consequences for banks, since volatility in share prices was directly transmitted to the banking sector.

Bank ownership and mergers

One important landmark for Malaysian banking was the 1983–5 economic recession. Its main impact was on the ownership of banks. The recession and financial liberalization that followed led to a more diverse ownership, with individuals owning banks along with the state's institutional investors. Prior to 1985, the Malaysian banking tradition had been one of specialization rather than being part of a conglomerate. The 1983–5 recession, however, introduced some powerful conglomerates into banking. There was also a proliferation of new banking groups between 1988 and 1997. Rashid Hussain Banking Group was listed in 1988, while United Merchant Group (UMG) was listed on 18 August 1994. There was also a continuous spate of acquisitions and mergers following the 1985 recession. Rashid Hussain acquired the Development and Commercial Bank in 1990 and in November 1996 took over KYB. Just months later, he took over Sime Bank for RM1.2 billion. In early 1996, he acquired Bank Niaga in Indonesia. The question remains: who exactly is this financial maverick and corporate predator?

United Asian Bank (UAB) merged with Bank of Commerce in September 1990. UAB had faced liquidation in 1986 and Bank Negara recapitalized the bank. After its merger, Renong acquired a 33 per cent stake in Bank of Commerce in October 1990 and it became part of the conglomerate. Meanwhile, UMG, a finance company listed in 1994, acquired Perdana Merchant Bankers and Ban Hin Lee Bank but both had to be divested during the crisis. Many of the takeovers in this period were of well-managed, highly resourced small banks, such as Ban Hin Lee Bank. This raises the suspicion that banks with a good capital base became targets of large failing banks in their desperate attempts to survive. More mergers followed the financial crisis of 1997.

Another structural difficulty that erupted after 1985 was the lack of separation between banking operations and the finance company. There was continuous pressure from Bank Negara for banks to separate their retail activities and to merge their finance companies. Since investment banks are involved in securities and lending, there has to be clarification on who controls which function. RHB had a strong merchant bank: Sakura Merchant Bank. It was active in stockbroking and had acquired smaller securities firms. Such random and diverse activities in the financial sector led to the stock market peaking at 339 per cent of GNP in 1996 and the corporate sector revealing high levels of debt. Prime Minister Mahatir's initial rejection of IMF models for the rescue and rehabilitation of the collapsing economy soon gave way to an acceptance of tax cuts and the raising of interest rates. However, it was his unorthodox adoption of capital controls, a fixed exchange rate with restricted convertibility and a ban on offshore currency trading that aroused serious controversy. These restrictions have since been gradually relaxed.

Restructuring

Table 5.6 clearly reveals the distinct variations in the scale of financial distress across the region.

The restructuring process in Malaysia involved, first, comprehensive bank recapitalization and debt restructuring through Danaharta (asset management company) and Danamodal (capital investment company). This resulted in forced mergers among banks and finance companies, although individual banks were free to choose their preferred partner for merger. By August 2000, Danaharta had restructured and sold RM21.6 billion of financial assets.[76] Danamodal recapitalized ten financial institutions for a total of RM7.1 billion. They were assisted by the government's Corporate Debt Restructuring Committee (CDRC), which by 2001 had restructured the debt of 30 companies, at a cost of RM24 billion. There still remained unresolved debt of RM16 billion. Danamodal also appointed representatives to the boards of firms receiving capital from it.

The second move was a government-encouraged consolidation, in which ten banking groups were formed from 54 financial institutions, accounting for 94 per cent of total assets of domestic banks.[77] This bank restructuring was a highly complicated and long process, partly due to the close and connected lending to large conglomerates. The highly volatile deal between AMB and Utama Bank reached its culmination in August 2000. Following the negotiations, it had to create a new holding company to abort all the smaller firms within both groups. This holding company acquired the entire share capital of the merging institutions and issued new shares. The merger created the fifth largest banking group but, crucially, it increased the significance of the group's role in Sarawak. Bank Utama's shareholders included the Sarawak state government and parties linked to Taib Mahmud, Chief Minister of Sarawak. Taib Mahmud was essential in harnessing local political

Table 5.6 Distress and closure among the five crisis countries

	Indonesia	*Korea*	*Malaysia*	*Philippines*	*Thailand*
Distressed*	44 (50.57%)	31 (53.45%)	16 (24.24%)	4 (11.11%)	25 (65.79%)
Commercial banks	42	18	8	2	11
Non-bank institutions	2	13	8	2	14
Closed*	17 (19.54%)	10 (17.24%)	0 (0.00%)	2 (5.56%)	9 (23.68%)
Commercial banks	17	1	0	0	0
Non-bank institutions	0	9	0	2	9

Note: * Percentage of distressed (closed) institutions.

Source: Danaharta Report on Bank Restructuring, Appendix 1

loyalty for the Barisan Nasional and Mahatir. He had to be coerced into this merger because of his concerns over being swamped by AMB. AMB was controlled by Azman Hashim and the merged group faced a management challenge. Its aggressive over-lending affected investor confidence and share prices.

The merger of RHB also proved fractious. It had already assimilated Sime Bank. Rashid Hussain had also transformed the Development and Commercial Bank and acquired KYB. But the crisis revealed RHB's high ratio of NPLs, and how serious connected lending and the constant changes of ownership had affected growth in the group. Sime Bank possessed the highest level of NPLs in 1998.[78] However, Rashid Hussain had the support of Khazanah Nasional and Malaysian Resources Corporation as major shareholders, and, therefore, recovery and liquidation was possible. RHB recovered by September 1999, recorded a profit, improved its capital base and maintained a loan expansion of 4 per cent per annum.[79]

MPHB, one of the smallest of these core banks, had close links to Daim Zainuddin, the former Finance Minister. It merged with International Bank, Sabah Bank and other financial and investment banks. This was a complex merger of seven major partners, financed through new share issues, share swaps and cash outlay. It also acquired Bumiputra Merchant Banker from the Rothschild Group. The group focused on growth in Sabah through Datuk Musa Aman and Warisan Harta Sabah.[80] Within these group mergers, there was a clear absorption of diverse units, through the cross-selling of units between banks, finance companies and merchant banks. In short, there had been a frantic merging of diverse finance companies before joining one of the ten groups.

The fourth merger involved EON Bank, a unit of Malaysia's largest car distributor, Edaran Otomobil Nasional Bhd. EON Bank merged with Oriental Bank, Malaysian International Merchant Bankers and City Finance. However, these purchases, first of Oriental Bank with debts of RM130 million owed to Malaysian Industrial Development Finance and second of City Finance for RM80 million, ensured resources were stretched to the limit. Moreover, it had already purchased 96 per cent equity of Perkasa Finance and acquired another merchant bank for RM253 million in cash. These acquisitions imposed an excessive burden on its subsequent performance.[81]

The restructuring of Chinese-owned banks was less painful. Public Bank, owned by Teh Hong Piow, was prudent and hence needed no recapitalization of funds from the state. It only transferred a tiny proportion of NPLs to Danaharta.[82] Hong Leong Bank, similarly, required no large recapitalization of funds from the state. Southern Bank merged with Ban Hin Lee Bank and other finance companies to accumulate assets of RM27 million. Three Chinese directors – Datuk Tan Teong Hean, Datuk Goh Eng Too and Steven Yeap of BHL – acquired 20 per cent each in the merged group.[83] This merger was financed through share swaps, funds from inter-bank market and new share issues. The purchase prices were higher than their actual book value because these mergers meant an increase in capital and entitlement to tax incentives. However, these mergers did not result in any substantial increase in foreign equity, as was the case in Thailand and Indonesia.

Foreign banks grew in importance but frequently only in their narrow field of specialization. For instance, Citibank specialized in consumer products, carving out 30 per cent of the credit card market. Standard Chartered specialized in trade finance, while HSBC concentrated on corporate finance.[84] Tables 5.7 and 5.8 summarize the merged units.

Malaysia's response to the crisis was for the state to acquire the debts of troubled institutions and then restructure them to create viable banking groups from among a significant number of private actors. First, it used all the state's institutional investment groups to bear the burden of recapitalization. Second, it sought help from the Japanese government and two Japanese banks. Third, capital controls were imposed. These helped to lower interest rates and improved foreign reserves ratios. FDI was not affected by these capital controls. Despite the fears of many experts, including the Nobel Laureate Merton Miller, these capital controls lowered the cost of domestic credit and improved the competitiveness of its exports through the fixed exchange rate (RM3.80 per US dollar), with seemingly positive consequences in the short term.

There was also a serious impact on the relations between Bank Negara and the government. Despite the rifts and the resignation of the governor in 1998, Bank Negara still retained its autonomy and power. Indeed, the new governor, Zeti Aktar Aziz, with 15 years' experience at the bank, has proved formidable in cruising through these troubled times. Positive developments include a decline in NPLs, from 27 per cent in 1997 to 17 per cent in June 2002. Significant progress has also been achieved in restructuring debt. Other achievements include a continued underpinning of asset quality by loan-loss reserves, which stood at 52 per cent in July 2002, and successful recapitalization of the banks, supported by rising profits. Now the challenges for the sector include how to consolidate and integrate the ten merged banks; otherwise, Bank Negara will have to reduce their number by force. Banks need to improve, their existing NPLs need to be resolved and risk management strategies need to be formulated more precisely and openly. Internal restructuring is essential. Bank ownership is still a worrying issue. Although some banks are owned by institutional shareholders, others remain under the influence of a single individual or family shareholder and, therefore, are lacking in professional management.

Table 5.7 Merged banks, post-1998

Anchor bank	*Banking institutions in group*
Maybank Berhad	Maybank Berhad
	Mayban Finance Berhad
	Aseambankers Malaysia Berhad
	PhileoAllied Bank Berhad
	The Pacific Bank Berhad
	Sime Finance Berhad
	Kewangan Bersatu Berhad
Bumiputra-Commerce Bank Berhad	Bumiputra-Commerce Bank Berhad
	Bumiputra-Commerce Finance Berhad
	Commerce International Merchant Bankers Berhad
RHB Bank Berhad	RHB Bank Berhad
	RHB Sakura Merchant Bankers Berhad
	Delta Finance Berhad
	Interfinance Berhad
Public Bank Berhad	Public Bank Berhad
	Public Finance Berhad
	Hock Hua Bank Berhad
	Advance Finance Berhad
	Sime Merchant Bankers Berhad
Arab Malaysia Bank Berhad	Arab Malaysia Bank Berhad
	Arab-Malaysia Finance Berhad
	Arab-Malaysia Merchant Bank Berhad
	Bank Utama Malaysia Berhad
	Utama Merchant Bankers Berhad
Hong Leong Bank Berhad	Hong Leong Bank Berhad
	Hong Leong Finance Berhad
	Wah Tat Bank Berhad
	Credit Corporation Malaysia Berhad
Perwira Affin Bank Berhad	Perwira Affin Bank Berhad
	Affin Finance Berhad
	Perwira Affin Merchant Bankers Berhad
	BSN Commercial Bank Berhad
	BSN Finance Berhad
	BSN Merchant Bank Berhad
Multi-Purpose Bank Berhad	Multi-Purpose Bank Berhad
	International Bank Malaysia Berhad
	Sabah Bank Berhad
	MBf Finance Berhad
	Bolton Finance Berhad
	Sabah Finance Berhad
	Bumiputra Merchant Bankers Berhad
	Amanah Merchant Bank Berhad
Southern Bank Berhad	Southern Bank Berhad
	Ban Hin Lee Bank Berhad
	Cempaka Finance Berhad
	United Merchant Finance Berhad
	Perdana Finance Berhad
	Perdana Merchant Bankers Berhad
EON Bank Berhad	EON Bank Berhad
	EON Finance Berhad
	Oriental Bank Berhad
	City Finance Berhad
	Perkasa Finance Berhad
	Malaysian International Merchant Bankers Berhad

Source: Danaharta Report on Bank Restructuring, Appendix 1

Table 5.8 Changes in ownership of Malaysian banks after the crisis, 31 December 2004

Bank	*Major shareholders*
Maybank	Amanah Saham Bumiputra (ASB) 34.6%
	Permodalan Nasional Berhad (PNB) 14.7%
	Employees Provident Fund (EPF) 9.3%
	Commerce Bank EPF 27.3%
	Khazanah Nasional 13.1%
	Kumpulan Wang Amanah Pencen (KWAP) 10%
Public Bank	Teh Hong Piow 39%
	EPF 5.3%
Rashid Hussain Bank (RHB)	RHB Holdings 65%
	Utama BG 32%
	EPF 11%
	KWAP 11%
Arab Malaysia Bank	AMCORP 33.6%
	EPF 13.4%
Hong Leong Bank	Hong Leong Credit 50%
	EPF 6.1%
Perwira Affin Bank	Lembaga Tabung Angkatan Tentera (LTAT) 39.2%
	Boustead Holdings 26.4%
	EPF 7.5%
EON Bank	DRB-HICOM 20%
	RH Development Corporation 17%
	Kuala Pura 13%
Southern Bank	Killinghall Malaysia 21.3%
	Hong Leong 7%
	EPF 6.8%
	Lim Siew Lay 5.3%

6 Capital structure puzzle

The Hong Leong Group in Malaysia

This is a study of the capital structure and strategies of growth of a large Chinese corporation, Hong Leong, in Malaysia between 1970 and 2002. The core line of enquiry is how it tapped into capital markets in Asia in order to secure a phenomenal growth extending from Malaysia and Singapore to Hong Kong, China, Australia, the US and Europe. For the sake of clarity and rigour, I will concentrate principally on the Malaysian stock market, from where Hong Leong's core companies were listed and achieved a pincer-like expansion outwards.

The original element in this case study is the impact of political patronage and ethnic links, how these fairly unusual aspects of Malaysia affect the behaviour of the corporation in growth as well as its performance on the stock market. But the analysis is not embedded in the literature on efficient markets but what is more securely argued is crony capitalism, and more pertinently how Chinese family-controlled business sustained phenomenal growth, contrary to the claims of Chandler on personal capitalism.

The focus is on how the stock market was utilized by Hong Leong to acquire and integrate new firms and create a viable multinational enterprise without diluting the existing concentrated family ownership and control. In essence, the main issues in this chapter are first, the factors that facilitated the survival of this highly concentrated family ownership in listed companies; second, the changes in business structure and strategy induced by stock market affiliation; third, the survival and persistence of a form of patriarchal family corporate management; fourth, the impact of government and bureaucratic networks on the corporation's fortunes and effects on its stock market performance: fifth, the targeting by Hong Leong of foreign capital inflows into Malaysia, enabling it to mount a frantic wave of merger activity in the 1980s and 1990s. The effects of such rapid growth through large concentrations of foreign capital produced herding and manipulative activities in several economic sectors – finance, property and infrastructure – which increased speculation and created growth and volatility on the stock market, and only the crisis in 1997 checked this unprecedented, though unstable, growth and diversification. The choice of Hong Leong to demonstrate all the above developments is dictated by its size, economic importance, close liaisons with the Malaysian government elite and its relations with foreign capital, in particular Japanese and Arab capital. All these financial intermediaries influenced and transformed the process of capital accumulation of corporations in Malaysia, as well as in the rest of Southeast Asia.

The Malaysian stock market

It would be useful now to examine the patterns of growth of the Kuala Lumpur stock market in order to identify how this partly reflected the organizational developments of the Chinese family-owned conglomerates.

The Malaysian Stock Market was established in 1960 with separate entities in Singapore and Kuala Lumpur. They were merged in 1964 but split again in 1973 and the KLSE was created. Both exchanges listed stocks from both countries, a practice that ended only in 1989. The Malaysian shares were later traded via an international dealing system in Singapore, the CLOB. The KLSE saw gradual growth until 1989. In the 1990s it witnessed a phenomenal expansion, both in volume and value of transactions of companies listed there (See Table 6.1a and Figure 6.1). The KLSE continued to grow. In 1993, its annual trading volume rose to 100 billion units from an annual turnover of 20 billion in 1992. The increase in market capitalization in Malaysia was higher than that in Indonesia, Philippines and Thailand until 1996 (see Table 6.1b).[1] This intensity in growth was a direct result of the accumulated inflows of foreign capital and the privatization programme of the Malaysian government from the late 1980s. Share issues of privatized corporations usually do not benefit private corporate finance since proceeds typically go to government. However, the structure of privatization in Malaysia meant that funds were often redistributed back to the corporation and to government crony capitalists in large, capital-intensive industries, such as telecommunications, electronics and energy sectors.

The stock market capitalization rose dramatically, reflected primarily in the proliferation of new listings. The number of companies on the KLSE rose from 262 in 1973 to 324 in 1991 and then to 757 in 1997, the most spectacular growth being recorded between 1993 and 1997. The financial crisis of 1997 resulted in a serious decline, though the second board of the KLSE, which was reserved for smaller firms, witnessed a doubling in number after 1996. Thus, while the KLSE had the highest number of listed companies in Southeast Asia, the highest value of market capitalization and the highest price earning ratios between 1993 and 1996, yet much of this enhanced value rested with a tiny minority of large corporations, principally belonging to the state, the Chinese and to a new *bumiputra* elite embracing newly privatized corporations. It is this dominance by a tiny minority that secured stock market performance in the 1990s. This minority of large corporations, with the Malaysian state's institutional caucuses, dominated the Malaysian stock market, and is analysed in detail in the following section (pp. 144–6).

Table 6.1a Value of companies listed on KLSE, 1980–2000 (RM billion)

	Main board	*Second board*	*Call warrant*	*Total nominal value*	*Market value main board*	*Market value second board*	*Market value call warrant*	*Market value total*	*Closing*
1980	7.9	0	0	7.9	43.1	0	0	43.1	366.7
1981	10.7	0	0	10.7	55.4	0	0	55.4	380.82
1982	13.6	0	0	13.6	52.9	0	0	52.9	291.45
1983	16.3	0	0	16.3	80.3	0	0	80.3	401.6
1984	20.4	0	0	20.4	69.3	0	0	69.3	303.56
1985	22.6	0	0	22.6	58.3	0	0	58.3	233.48
1986	23.5	0	0	23.5	64.5	0	0	64.5	252.43
1987	26.6	0	0	26.6	73.9	0	0	73.9	261.19
1988	29.4	0	0	29.4	98.7	0	0	98.7	357.38
1989	34.3	0.03	0	34.3	156.0	0.1	0	156.1	562.28
1990	35.1	0.2	0	35.3	131.1	0.6	0	131.7	505.92
1991	41.2	0.5	0	41.7	159.9	1.5	0	161.4	556.22
1992	52.3	0.9	0	53.2	242.9	2.9	0	245.8	643.96
1993	60.0	1.6	0	61.6	606.1	13.5	0	619.6	1,275.32
1994	73.0	2.9	0	75.9	493.0	15.9	0	508.9	971.21
1995	88.4	3.9	0.07	92.4	542.8	22.7	0.12	565.6	995.17
1996	106.3	5.7	0.05	112.1	746.0	60.8	0.01	806.8	1,237.96
1997	127.7	8.0	0	135.8	354.1	21.6	0	375.8	594.44
1998	130.3	8.8	0	139.1	353.4	21.1	0	374.5	586.13
1999	142.6	9.8	0	152.4	527.6	25.1	0	552.7	812.33
2000	155.0	12.3	0	167.3	461.9	26.9	0	488.8	713.51

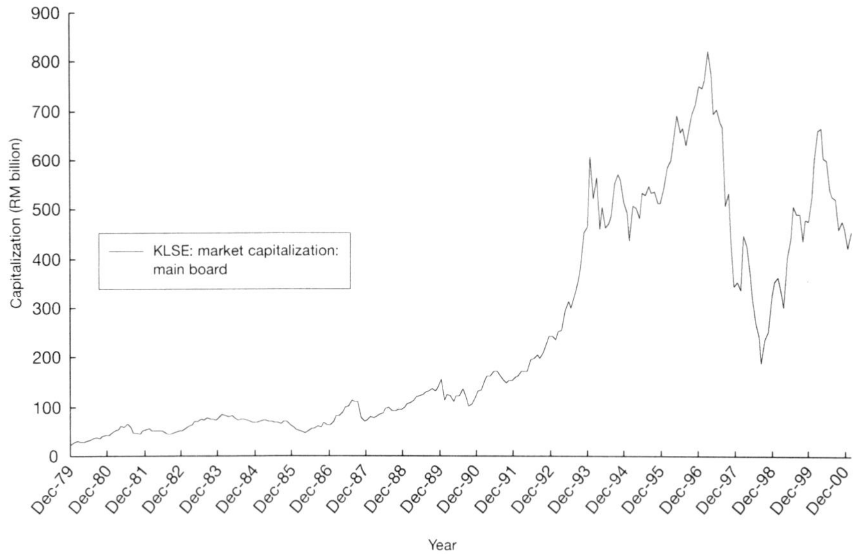

Figure 6.1 KLSE, market capitalization: main board

Source: KLSE Daily Market Data, December 1979–January 2001

Table 6.1b Stock markets in Asia: capitalization as percentage of GNP and turnover rate

	1985	*1995*	*1996*
Capitalization/GNP			
Korea	8.5	40.1	30.1
Taiwan	16.8	74.2	100.8
Hong Kong	103.2	218.0	291.5
Singapore	62.6	233.2	192.9
Malaysia	52.0	248.2	298.7
Thailand	5.0	85.1	55.7
Philippines	2.0	81.1	96.9
Indonesia	0.1	33.7	40.4
Turnover rate			
Korea	61.8	101.1	121.5
Taiwan	48.4	197.7	171.2
Hong Kong	13.7	35.2	40.6
Singapore	25.1	29.6	30.1
Malaysia	13.4	29.1	37.6
Thailand	32.1	43.1	50.9
Philippines	14.1	24.5	31.5
Indonesia	2.9	21.3	35.2

Source: International Finance Corporation, 1997, *Emerging Stock Market, Factbook 1997*, Washington, DC

Sectoral and institutional caucuses

The Malaysian equity market development has been determined by major institutional and ethnic participants. It is generally accepted that the public offering of shares of listed companies on the KLSE went largely to *bumiputra* (Malay) shareholders and to the state's institutional investors (also Malay). However, as Tables 6.2a and 6.2b reveal, the Chinese are still the largest participants on the Malaysian stock market. Private Malay share of corporate wealth rose from 2.4 per cent in 1969 to 18 per cent in 1983, and then to 19.3 per cent in 1990 and 20.6 per cent in 1995, shuffling between 21 per cent and 22 per cent in the years after 1997.[2] NEP initiatives from 1970, followed by the privatization of government enterprises after 1984, did lead to increased shareholding by Malay capitalists and Malay institutional investors, with shares being purchased at special low prices. However, the regulation that 30 per cent of IPOs of listed firms on the KLSE and those of new manufacturing companies producing for the domestic market should be allocated to *bumiputra* groups, has not ensured their overall dominance. Malay share in the entire corporate economy, which includes non-listed firms, rose in the 1990s, although largely as a consequence of increased foreign participation through joint-venture relations with Malay interests in capital-intensive sectors. Thus, the earlier dominance by Chinese capitalists in equity markets that emerged with the nationalization programme of the early 1960s persisted

Table 6.2a Ownership of share capital (at par value) on the KLSE: percentages

	1975	*1979*	*1990*	*1995*	*1996*	*1998*
Bumiputra	18.7	2.3	19.3	20.6	36.7	19.4
Non-bumiputra (principally Chinese)	33.6	28.3	46.8	43.4	44.1	41.1
Foreigners	47.7	63.4	25.4	27.7	19.2	1.8
Nominee companies	–	6.0	8.5	8.3	–	7.7

Source: KLSE, Annual Reports, 1970–99

Table 6.2b Shareholdings of listed companies by type of investor: percentage at year end

	1988	*1990*	*1992*	*1994*	*1996*
Individuals	19.8	16.0	15.4	16.7	13.5
Institutions	42.2	43.6	46.6	42.9	47.8
Nominees	36.2	38.1	35.8	38.6	36.1
Others	1.8	2.3	2.1	1.8	2.6
Total	100	100	100	100	100

Source: KLSE, Annual Reports, 1987–97

throughout the 1980s and the 1990s. In the nationalization phase of the 1970s, when foreigners transferred their shareholding to domestic capitalists, the Chinese benefited, with foreigners losing almost 40 per cent equity stake while the Chinese doubled their share (see Table 6.2a).

The *bumiputra* participation in the stock market is therefore complex. There is a strong institutional holding, together with the transfer of equity from SOEs to private individuals such as Halim Saad, Tajuddin Ramli and Daim. The special allocation of shares to *bumiputras* has serious implications for the growth and efficiency of the stock market in Malaysia. First, these shares were distributed and frequently held by institutions that were government trusts. *Bumiputra* shares were largely distributed through the YPB, established in January 1978, PNB, established in March 1978 and ASN, established in May 1979. The YPB and PNB purchased shares in state and private enterprises, and sold them to the Malays – individuals as well as corporations. ASN participated directly in the stock market, emerging as the largest unit trust in the 1990s.[3] Its role was enlarged in 1991 as the direct shareholder of *bumiputra* holdings through the ASB, which was active in the privatization of SOEs, frequently acquiring shares at below market value.

These institutions created the holding of block shares and the sale of them, to dominant capitalists, with minority shareholders' behaviour being influenced by the behaviour of these large, powerful groups. Second, the government nurtured through this allocation of equity, the rise of an influential cadre of Malay businessmen co-opted from the civil service or state banks. These Malay bureaucrats acquired shares in the newly privatized corporations, transforming themselves instantly into influential capitalists. Halim Saad (Renong), Tajuddin Ramli (Malaysian Airlines, MAS), Daim (the UMNO Group of companies) and Yahya (Proton) were beneficiaries of the state's largesse, and came to dominate newly privatized public utilities in transport, energy, telecommunications and construction.[4]

Third, these agencies and trusts lacked transparency. They possessed no strict accounting procedures and risked being absorbed by the state. Endowing certain elite groups with corporate shareholdings and creating clusters of wealthy Malay businessmen insulated by government patronage saved them from competing in an open, competitive and efficient stock market. Long-term strategies in production, investment, R&D and marketing could not be sustained in this distorted market dominated by crony capitalists. Fourth, and more seriously, it masked the growing foreign share ownership of industrial and manufacturing companies, particularly in capital-intensive, hi-tech sectors.[5] Prior to 1986, 10 per cent of major enterprises had foreign owners. By the late 1980s, 36 per cent of the value of Malaysian corporations principally producing for the export market were held by foreign multinationals. By 1990 the overall number of foreign-owned companies declined. However, in value terms, foreign capital remained substantial. By the middle of 1997 a quarter of the stocks on the KLSE were in foreign hands, another quarter were held by local institutional investors and the remaining half belonged to large private corporations and retail investors. By June 2000, foreign shareholders held 30 per cent of total equity.[6] This had crept in gradually through joint-venture ties and through increased foreign capital inflows.

It is important to appraise further the type of large domestic institutional investor participating in the Malaysian stock market from the mid-1980s. As shown in Table 6.2b, institutions and nominees formed the bulk of the investors on the KLSE between 1988 and 1996. The institutional investor includes a great diversity of corporations: SOEs, state-owned holding companies, private companies, investment groups belonging to particular ethnic communities and pension-fund holders. These groups use their own funds as well as state funds, tap mutual funds and funds of securities companies. Insurance companies were also allowed to participate in the stock market. These groups are integral to the establishment of a strong institutional investor base for Malaysia's capital markets. Since the mid-1980s, the EPF, which includes both categories of pension fund, those from the government (local and central authorities) as well as private corporate pensions which are derived from individual companies, were allowed to invest in the stock market. Prior to this, it invested largely in Malaysian government bonds or cash deposits. The advantages for the private corporation in seeking to raise capital, exploiting these institutional investors, are apparent in the study of Hong Leong, where the presence of institutional investors facilitated the flow of state funds for the large Chinese corporation, which already faced little competition in securing lucrative government contracts and concessions.

Implications for corporate governance

In this analysis of public and private institutions and their involvement in the stock market, it is the level of involvement by banks that has to be stressed. The relationship between banks, finance houses and securities firms are closely intertwined. Banks often had their own finance houses and securities brokerages. This intimate interlocking relationship between the banks and their investment and securities subsidiaries was a lethal combination in the liberalized, but poorly regulated, financial environment of the 1990s. All the major Malaysian banks either possessed a direct securities subsidiary with 70 per cent to 100 per cent shareholding, or were linked to an investment holding company directly engaged in the securities trade. Arab Malaysia Bank and the Arab-Malaysia Merchant Bank together held 33 per cent financial exposure to the stock market in 1997.[7] RHB held 12 per cent exposure to the equity market. This underlines their difficulties and ultimate collapse in 1998, when they required state assistance to restructure and recover.

In a share market where the fund managers and corporate or bank owner were the same and had intimate links to government, the equity market could not develop without more regulation. The interaction of pension groups, banks, securities firms and corporations endowed with free-flowing state and foreign capital does not allow the stock market to allocate resources efficiently. The markets will be cyclical and volatile, reflecting the influence of two factors: foreign investors' belief in the country's economic performance and the government's policies and actions. The dominant role of the state in Malaysia, the power of institutional investors and the perceived role of the stock market in shaping corporate growth at home and abroad meant an increase in moral hazard: the level of regulation was often insufficient to control this, as seen in the volatility and crisis experienced by the KLSE in 1997. However, while speculative attacks resulted in difficulties for Indonesia in the Philippines and Thailand in 1994 and 1997, Malaysia and Singapore endured a serious collapse only in 1997. All these speculative attacks throughout the region were unrelated to trade linkages.

It is clearly evident that the concentration of investment in certain corporate groups with crucial government connections can lead to speculative behaviour on the stock market. Public investors are often swayed by the very scale of participation and choice of stocks invested in by these elites. Even when the fundamentals behind such equities did not justify high prices, the unprecedented purchase of some equities by these large investors and nominees of the government can create baskets of glamour stocks with anticipated abnormal earnings, further fuelling these bubbles. In addition, those with inside information and understanding of key government policies can create pressures and rumours leading to further manipulation of share prices.[8] These signalling trends can emasculate competition and efficiency of the stock market, as well as create volatility in the performance of listed corporations.

The distribution of equity power among a few capitalists with connections to political and bureaucratic elites was further concentrated through the many mergers and acquisitions occurring among these large private firms from the late 1980s. There is an upward trend in internal and cross-border mergers and acquisitions in the years 1994–7 by Malaysian entrepreneurs. Much of this boom was sustained by capital inflows, financial liberalization and the policies of the Malaysian government.

Types of share issues

Besides the distortions introduced by the special allocation of shares to certain client groups in society and an indiscriminate pricing of shares, the Malaysian stock market was also affected by the preference of firms to raise funds more through rights issues rather than public issues. Table 6.3 demonstrates this trend. Throughout the 1980s and 1990s Malaysian companies preferred equity issues via a rights offering to debt issues for additional funds, a ploy to retain existing shareholding structure.[9] In order to entice shareholders to the subscription, the price is substantially below the existing market price. Often the rights issue had the effect of producing abnormal

Table 6.3 Funds mobilized by Malaysian companies and type of share issue (RM million)

Year	*Public issues*	*Rights issue*	*Special/ private placement/ restricted issue*	*Subtotal*	*Offer for sale**	*Grand total*
1973	95.7	37.2	8.3	141.2	–	141.2
1974	12.4	49.6	4.1	66.1	19.6	85.7
1975	13.0	9.5	–	22.5	5.7	28.2
1976	–	22	13.5	35.5	–	35.5
1977	–	95.1	2.9	98.0	21.8	119.8
1978	5.4	24.5	22.8	52.7	46.4	99.1
1979	1.7	134.3	62.2	198.2	16.0	214.2
1980	2.1	103.2	31.8	137.1	14.0	151.1
1981	103.7	598.0	200.1	901.8	28.7	930.5
1982	182.7	286.8	131.6	601.1	27.7	628.8
1983	140.5	638.5	406.0	1,185.0	25.9	1,210.9
1984	174.4	1,347.4	461.4	1,983.2	24.3	2,007.5
1985	164.2	357.5	81.8	603.5	–	603.5
1986	24.0	298.4	97.0	419.4	7.5	426.9
1987	95.8	393.7	386.2	875.7	220.5	1,096.2
1988	53.3	789.3	136.3	978.9	111.7	1,090.6
1989	128.5	1,313.4	166.9	1,608.8	831.2	2,440.0
1990	2,597.1	5,503.0	389.8	8,489.9	1,440.1	9,930.0
1991	230.3	1,672.6	793.6	2,696.5	1,367.2	4,063.7
1992	3,909.6	3,762.5	312.5	7,984.6	2,268.5	10,253.1
1993	171.0	2,429.1	782.0	3,382.1	1,149.4	4,531.5
1994	373.2	5,448.4	1,364.1	7,185.7	2,931.3	10,117.0
1995	1,155.6	5,594.1	2,436.0	9,185.7	4,456.7	13,642.4
1996	1,778.0	7,402.8	8,075.3	17,256.1	3,570.2	20,826.3
1997	2,928.7	9,362.4	4,037.8	16,328.9	2,787.6	19,116.5
1998	346.2	421.9	245.0	1,013.1	698.5	1,711.6
Total	14,687.1	48,095.2	20,649.0	83,431.3	22,070.5	105,501.8

Note: * Includes restricted offer for sale.

Source: KLSE Handbook, 1999, E6

returns.[10] Ariff and Johnson (1990) found that for rights issues, prices continued to rise into the first month after announcement.[11] Such rises could be because investors were chasing such restricted quality stock.

The extensive use of rights issues in the 1990s was to finance the takeovers that dominated the KLSE. By 1996 rights issues accounted for 46 per cent of total funds amassed on the KLSE. In 1992, rights issues had formed 37.4 per cent of the total of new share issues: private placements were significant as well, rising from 0.3 per cent in 1992 to 19.2 per cent in 1993, falling in 1994–5, then rising to 28.6 per cent in 1996 and contracting to 17.6 per cent in 1997.[12] Tapping capital through the congregation of rights issues further empowered the existing small coterie of family shareholders and their Chinese and Malay friends and politicians, who were exploiting the stock market for capital without forsaking the high levels of family ownership or control.

Foreign capital inflows and their impact on corporate finance

The dramatic increase in foreign capital inflows, principally portfolio capital particularly from 1989, held serious implications for corporate finance and patterns of corporate growth. Figure 6.2 on foreign capital inflows, March 1991–September 2000, clearly reveals the high inflows of portfolio capital. Portfolio investments contributed the bulk of foreign capital inflows; the exceptions were brief phases in December 1998, March 1999 and September 2000. Foreign portfolio capital inflows rose to US$25 billion per annum in the early 1990s, falling in 1994, with a further fall in 1997. Net foreign portfolio investment averaged 5.1 per cent of GDP between 1991 and 1995, a third of which was allocated to the stock market.[13] During this period, foreign portfolio equity investment on the KLSE rose from 8.5 per cent to 25.5 per cent of total stock market capitalization.

The large concentrated positions of portfolio capital in targeting specific sectors of the economy (property, finance and currency markets), their herding and manipulative activities, not only increase speculation but assist in creating large diversified corporations in Southeast Asia, which are reluctant to specialize because diversification provided revenues, reduced risks and concealed problems of quality in subsidiaries and connected firms. They were also confident to mount global initiatives in capital- and technology-intensive industries while lacking technological and innovative experience at home. Thus, Hong Leong expanded into Cambodia, Vietnam, India, Europe and the US, in infrastructure, hotels, finance and real estate despite the lack of core competencies in many of these sectors. Second, within this portfolio capital, two important issues need to be disentangled. Who are the providers of long-term portfolio capital, as distinct from the short-term portfolio investors? The source of this portfolio investment in equities, bonds and derivatives is central to clarifying the background to the institutions responsible for the expansion and volatility of the stock market. The volume and patterns of portfolio capital needs to be catalogued, in particular the sources of such capital inflows. Malaysia and Thailand were recipients of larger, long-term portfolio capital inflows from Japan, Singapore, Hong Kong and the Middle East from 1979. Although much of the funds listed in 1990–3 were from Singapore (54.8 per cent) and Hong Kong (33.2 per cent), their ultimate sources were mutual funds distributing capital from diverse sources, including Arab and American capital.[14] The Kuwait Investment Office was an investment trust of the Kuwait government; the investment trust funds of the Saudi ruling elites and the United Arab Emirates channelled portfolio

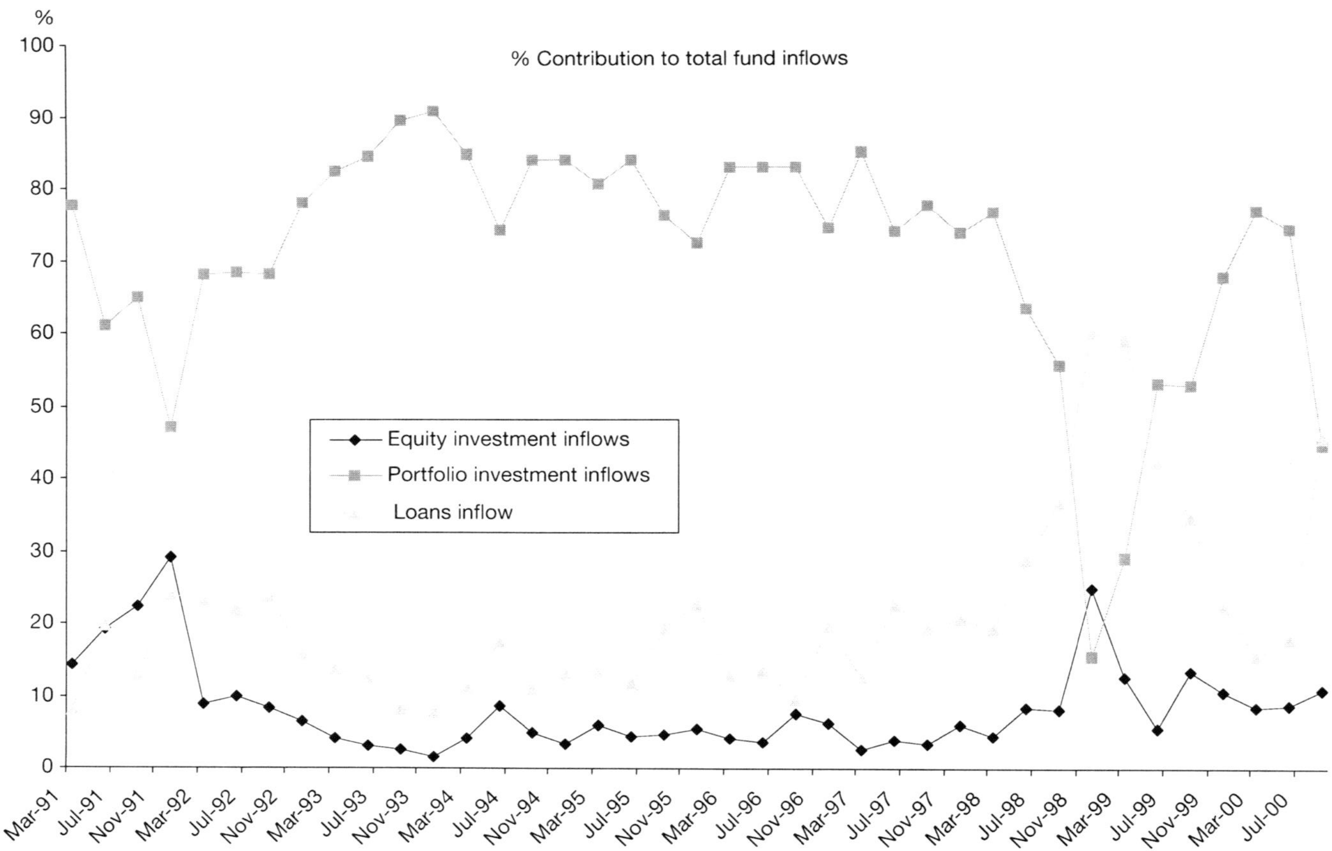

Figure 6.2 Capital flows into Malaysia, 1991–2000

Source: Annual Reports, Bank Negara Malaysia, 1990–2001, and Malaysian Industrial Development Authority, 1990–2001

capital into Malaysia–Singapore, while individual Arab financiers such as Adnan Khasoggi were involved in the Bangkok Bank of Commerce in Thailand. A preliminary survey that I carried out in the summer of 2001 showed that between 1989 and 2001, equities and bonds acquired by Arab investors in public and private corporations in Malaysia increased by 10 per cent.[15] Although this is a small percentage, this investment remained throughout the crisis. Hong Leong received equity finance from Kuwait Investment Office from 1983 to 2001, with little shrinkage after the crisis of 1997. Singapore, Hong Kong and overseas Chinese investors were the largest source of foreign portfolio capital. Japan remained the major source of direct investment into Malaysia.

The core influence of such capital flows on the KLSE is seen in Figure 6.2. The least volatile of the inflows was that of equity inflow, showing a variance of 0.004. This equity inflow does not deviate from the average inflow as much as portfolio investment with a variance of 0.03, while the loans inflow held a variance of 0.02. Examining the overall movement, we can see that the divergence in the percentage contribution between portfolio investment and that of equity investments was wider in the initial phase, 1991–8, and converged early in 1999 to widen again in the latter half of the year. The forward trend seems to be a continuity of this – that is, greater and more volatile inflows of portfolio investment. The close connection of this portfolio investment to the property sector of the KLSE is clear from the bubbles in the property market which had been triggered by foreign capital inflows since the 1980s.[16] However, it was the increase in volume as well as the new, diverse financing strategies that added to the risk. Bank loans, use of bonds and securities and other financial instruments for the precise purpose of purchasing and entering new R&D-intensive industries as well as for investment in the property sector accounted partly for the rise in the volatility in the financial and property sectors of the KLSE in the mid-1990s.

Foreign portfolio capital flows make any thinly traded emerging market such as the Malaysian stock market more volatile, because the added volume, mobility, risk sensitivity and, perhaps, poor information added to the fluctuations. This account attempts to demonstrate that the Chinese have a strong preference for investments in property and the stock market, often treating the latter like gambling casinos, where they play for capital gains rather than dividends. This, together with increased political-business links, increases this interaction.

The emergence of the Malaysian stock market as an important source of capital for large corporations, including that of the Chinese, is further captured and reinforced by the following statistics. The commercial banks' share of total financial deposits fell from 22.8 per cent in 1990 to 13.4 per cent in 1993, rising slightly to 16.1 per cent in 1996. This decline was reproduced in finance companies. Their share of total financial deposits fell from 10.4 per cent in 1990 to 5.3 per cent in 1993 and to 5.7 per cent in 1996. Funds derived from the stock market constituted a rising share of total financial deposits, constituting 48.2 per cent in 1990s, 69.4 per cent in 1993 and 63.4 per cent in 1996. The private corporations absorbed 9 per cent of these stock market funds in 1980–95 but this rose to 19 per cent in the period 1990–6.

A word of caution here is necessary. A rise in the importance of shares as a percentage of deposits does not necessarily imply that companies are more dependent on the stock market. Rather, it may simply reveal that valuations of existing shares may be rising. What is important is that this indicator should be combined with other relevant indications on market growth if we are to quantify the role of the stock market for corporate finance. This is sought and elaborated in the empirical discussion in the following section on Hong Leong. The next section is, therefore, concerned with a detailed empirical study of Hong Leong, and illustrates the main features of stock market affiliation and consequences for growth for a typical large corporation in Southeast Asia.

Hong Leong – the background

Hong Leong was established in Singapore in 1941 as a trading company in collaboration with Mitsui. Both during and after the Second World War there was rapid diversification into cement manufacture, hardware retailing, commodity production, agriculture and shipping. From the 1960s, it emerged as a financier and property developer. The financial focus of Hong Leong was vested in Hong Leong Finance Singapore (established in 1966 and listed in 1969), Hong Leong Credit Malaysia (established 1968, listed in 1969) and Hong Leong Bank Malaysia (acquired in 1993, listed in 1994). In Hong Kong, the major financial subsidiary is Dao Heng Bank, while in the Philippines, Guocco Securities is another important subsidiary.

Hong Leong is a highly diversified conglomerate with manufacturing and property subsidiaries, held together by family shareholding and management ties. The Singapore Group is consolidated through Hong Leong Investment Holdings, a family-owned company. Many of the individual companies within the group are publicly listed, although a dominant controlling interest is still vested in the family. In Malaysia, Hong Leong has ten listed companies, in construction, manufacturing and finance; all were linked to family-owned holding companies, Hong Leong Malaysia and Hong Leong Credit. In Hong Kong, too, the major interests in finance, hotel and property investments were embraced by two holding companies – Guocco Hong Kong and Hong Leong International, Hong Kong. These different holding companies were often operating parallel to one another within the same market, but with separate hierarchy and ownership controls. They were not industry focused but differed in their regional and global ambitions. Thus, Hong Leong Malaysia and Hong Leong Singapore, despite interlocking shareholding and close family ties, often competed with each other in other parts of Asia. The specialized divisions in finance, property and manufacturing also did not separate their specialist objectives from their domestic and their international ambitions. This diverse mix and complexity within Hong Leong has to be understood if the phases of its growth and their links to stock markets in Asia are to be disentangled. Hong Leong grew more through acquisition, merger and various forms of alliance rather than through coordinating investment, technology and innovation, focusing on product specialization or adopting coherent global strategies. Hong Leong, like most Chinese businesses in South-East Asia, was reluctant to specialize because diversification provided revenues, reduced risks and concealed problems of quality. In achieving this growth and diversity, stock markets were critical. To manage and nurture the growth of these interests, stock markets provided the necessary capital. In Japanese industrial groups it was the *sogo shosha*, the trading company, that provided the core. With Hong Leong, it was the financial institution, the bank, and frequently this was a listed company, such as Hong Leong Bank.[17]

The core of the Hong Leong Group is thus located in the bank and the financial firm. The financial division in the Hong Leong Group of Malaysia is Hong Leong Finance Berhad (HLFB), established in Kuala Lumpur in September 1968. In the early 1970s, HLFB was a diversified company, with manufacturing and property subsidiaries. In 1975 it was restructured under Hong Leong Credit (HLC), a holding company. The creation of a holding company was a tactic to absorb existing companies, and thus their assets, and to create new companies and an increased capitalization through new share issues. Thus, HLFB increased its capital base from RM2 million in 1971 to RM49.5 million in 1975 through new share issues and share swaps between firms in the group. Simultaneously, HLC increased its capital from RM7.8 million to RM21.9 million in the same years.[18]

In this expansion, HLC acquired property companies, a development that resulted in an increase in equity from RM72.68 million in 1986 to RM109.01 million in 1988; by 1995, its equity was RM344 million. HLC was involved in a broad spectrum of financial services, including leasing, factoring, insurance, stockbroking and fund management. HLC was linked directly to Hong Leong Industries (Malaysia). The linkages were precise. First, HLC was linked to the private family firm, Hong Leong Malaysia; second, it had direct links with HL Industries Malaysia, financing both short- and long-term loans; third, HLC was attracting foreign capital, from Hong Kong, Taiwan, Korea and Japan which was diverted into its subsidiaries involved in leasing and securities. Thus, the capitalization of HLC rose from RM3 million in 1971 to RM109 million in 1987. Much of this enlargement took place in the 1980s.[19] Its turnover was particularly impressive in the 1990s: RM599 million in 1993, rising to RM1,021 million in 1994, and to RM1,488 million in 1996. Net profits rose from RM92 million in 1993 to RM213 million in 1994, and to RM280 million in 1995.[20]

The financial core of the Hong Leong Group in Malaysia and Singapore was constantly being increased through mergers and takeovers financed through the stock markets in Kuala Lumpur, Singapore and Hong Kong. First Capital Corporation (FCC), a failing investment company in Singapore, was taken over in 1988 with the help of the Kuwait Investment Office (KIO) to attract and assimilate further capital flows from the Middle East. After the takeover, FCC was integrated into partnerships with the KIO and with United Arab Emirates government investment groups. Earlier, in 1980, frustrated by serious obstacles in acquiring banks in Malaysia and Singapore, Quek, the owner/manager of Hong Leong, had moved into Hong Kong, and with the assistance of the KIO, a London-based investment holding company of the Kuwaiti government, had purchased Dao Heng Bank in 1982 from Grindlays. KIO had a 20 per cent shareholding in Hong Leong Hong Kong, as well as equity in Malaysian and Singaporean companies belonging to the Hong Leong Group.[21] Hong Leong paid S$273.5 million to Grindlays Holdings for Dao Heng Bank. Grindlays was divesting itself of its retail banking and moving into merchant banking.[22] The Queks of both Malaysia and Singapore were represented on the board of Dao Heng. This connection with KIO was part of the strategy of Arab capital seeking investment opportunities in Asia following the oil boom of 1973 and the abundant fund of petro-dollars. Quek exploited these flows.

In addition, Hong Leong Malaysia and its financial subsidiaries' activities were influenced and affected by relations with the Malaysian state and Chinese networks. The group, which included financial services, construction, manufacturing, semiconductors and motorcycle assembling plants, had in 1990 total assets of RM2.7 billion, a turnover of RM1.28 billion and profits of RM198 million.[23] It jointly owned and controlled Dao Heng Holdings in Hong Kong. However, its links to UMNO politicians were crucial in sustaining growth. Through the Malaysian government and UMNO, Hong Leong was drawn into infrastructural projects in the 1980s and 1990s. Quek Leng Chan was also moving into infrastructural and tourism projects in China. To finance this, he continued his search for another bank. In 1993 he acquired MUI Bank and renamed it Hong Leong Bank.[24] Quek's aggressive purchase of MUI's financial institutions, in addition to Dao Heng Bank, Hang Lung Bank and Overseas Trust Bank (1993) and Benchmark (1992) was an essential part of the growth of the conglomerate, all facilitated by the booming stock market.[25] This is demonstrated in the detailed case study of Hong Leong Bank in the final section of this chapter (pp. 163–6).

Hong Leong used properties to secure the purchase of these banks, then immediately listed them and so acquired capital for further expansion. Part of his takeover strategy was built on constantly acquiring equity investments in Asian stock markets, building up sufficient equity before constructing an aggressive takeover bid. For example, his purchase of MUI Bank and finance company took place at a time of declining fortunes for that group. Khoo Kay Peng, the owner of MUI Bank, was losing political influence in Malaysia and retreating. Quek's strategy was to purchase and list the bank. He paid RM695 million for the bank, which was renamed Hong Leong Bank, and listed it on the stock exchange in Kuala Lumpur where it attracted a valuation of RM620 million (S$364 million).[26] It became the tenth largest bank in Malaysia in terms of assets. Earlier involvement in securities investment had led to the acquisition of Hoare Govett Asia in 1987.[27]

In 1989, the absorption of Hang Lung by Dao Heng Bank as a fully owned subsidiary increased their presence in retail banking in Hong Kong. Hang Lung had 24 branches in Hong Kong in 1990. Dao Heng became the fourth largest bank in the British colony, having absorbed Hang Lung's retail and commercial banking networks.[28] Here, too, Kuwaiti funds were used, in addition to American capital. Hang Lung Bank had been incorporated in March 1953 in Hong Kong, with HK$6 million equity; by 1973 it had HK$200 million in equity, rising to HK$500 million in 1985.[29] In 1983 it faced serious problems and was taken over by the Hong Kong Government. In 1985–6 it had suffered serious losses on the property market and was ripe for a takeover by Hong Leong.

Quek built his reputation in Malaysia, too, as a corporate raider. But the constant bidding to take over Chinese firms through the purchase of shares (his purchase of shares in Haw Par and Yeo Hiap Seng) constantly threatened the viability of these companies by increasing tensions within these different family firms. He would often entice dissident family members to sell their shares, thus creating instability, and then mount a bid. He used FCC in Singapore to mount takeover bids, frequently competing against his own cousins in Singapore.[30] This form of share manipulation constituted the biggest threat to family firms, including his own. The purchase of these quite successful companies would be followed by continuous restructuring and evolving of new subsidiaries, and subsequently listing them on the stock market in Southeast Asia and Hong Kong to raise further capital.

Network of interlocking shareholdings and state patronage

This section attempts to demonstrate that the pattern of interlocking shareholdings within these numerous firms in the Hong Leong Group further assisted their impressive growth and diversification. Quek himself held direct and indirect shareholdings through the various listed and unlisted firms in the group. For example, he directly held a 0.11 per cent stake in Hong Leong Industries and 0.23 per cent in Tasek Corporation, while owning 51.4 per cent in Camerlin through Hong Leong Industries. Hong Leong Industries directly held 22.2 per cent in Camerlin. Quek indirectly owned 53.6 per cent of shares in Hong Leong Industries through the holding company Hong Leong Co.[31] He possessed a 43.24 per cent stake in Hume Industries, a stake held through the holding company Hong Leong Co. Quek's direct shareholding in Hume Industries was 5.98 per cent.[32] Similarly, his holding in the Nanyang Press Group was 68.27 per cent and in OYL Industries was 62.53 per cent, both held through Hong Leong Co. In Hume Industries,

Quek's indirect ownership of 56.89 per cent was held through Hong Leong Co. In Southern Steel, Quek's indirect shareholding amounted to 21.15 per cent, held through Hong Leong Industries. He used his finance company, Hong Leong Credit, as another holding company with interests in HLG Capital and in Hong Leong Properties. This complexity in inter-firm holding and the use of holding companies as investment vehicles were two distinct strategies in maintaining an increasing concentration in family ownership and management of listed firms.

The second feature of this interlocking shareholding and directorships was the co-opting of prominent Malay bureaucrats, politicians and capitalists as directors with shareholdings. Halim Saad held a 22 per cent shareholding in Hume Industries through his private company, Jaguh Mutiara. Hume, thus, successfully acquired a contract valued at RM500 million from Halim in April 1989.[33] This contract was for supplies of construction materials for the North-South Expressway, a construction project secured from the government by Halim without an open tender. Hume Industries gathered other important Malay elites, including Mohd Samsuddin, a member of the Muslim Pilgrims Management Fund Board, and Zaki Azmi, legal adviser for UMNO. Hong Leong Industries' board had co-opted Nasruddin Mohd from the Ministry of Trade and Industry. He was also a member of the Capital Issues Committee and the Foreign Investment Committee, and director of Petronas Oil Company (1971–83) and Permodalan Nasional Bhd (1971–83), a state investment agency.

In 1991, Quek, with Halim Saad, formed joint-venture projects with Japanese investors and a Japanese transportation firm. This policy of co-opting prominent Malays facilitated Quek's expansion in state infrastructural projects. While securing funds from the state's institutional fund managers, these funds, which were dedicated primarily to aiding *bumiputra* (Malay) entrepreneurs, were thus seeping into Hong Leong. Quek exploited these political ties to access funds from public trusts and pension funds, as well as from foreign fund managers and foreign investment banks. Replenished with such diverse funds, Quek was able to survive the recession of 1985, and expand through mergers and acquisitions in the 1990s, while stalking other listed firms on the stock markets of Southeast Asia, Hong Kong, the US and Australia.

The next section will focus on the main listed firm in the group, Hong Leong Bank, which will assist a closer understanding of the interlinks of the group with the stock market in Malaysia.

Hong Leong Bank: corporate performance and stock market volatility

The primary argument in this section is that the corporate performance of a listed Hong Leong firm is not reproduced in its performance on the stock market. An analysis of the ownership structures and strategies of Hong Leong

Bank is undertaken to demonstrate that interactions between the development of the corporation and the stock market are too complex for the corporation's internal performance to be directly reflected by the swings in its share prices.[34] Clearly, firms such as Hong Leong Bank controlled by families through holding companies, reveal further ambiguity with this participation of interest groups such as politicians and bureaucrats, in an environment of weak legal structure and weak governance. There is no clear separation between ownership and management. Ownership is highly concentrated in the hands of the family patriarch. Finance is provided by related banks, finance houses, by the state, by highly optimistic foreign and domestic investors and by ethnic networks. Further growth is facilitated by acquisitions and mergers sought by stalking groups driven by factionalism or devoid of state support. The protection of minority shareholders rarely entered Quek's thinking because of the weak legal environment in Malaysia, as well as the rest of Asia.

The core argument in this chapter is that while these interactions between the stock market and the corporation are distorting, often the volatile swings in share prices are not directly perceptible in the strong or weak internal performance of the firm. The absence of direct correlations here can be attributed to the fact that the non-market forces in the stock market sometimes have a disproportionate influence in creating these volatile swings. Political factors are as important as the financial indicators of the corporation. It is this paradox that needs to be further verified and understood.

The Hong Leong Bank is the most significant listed firm within the Hong Leong Group.[35] It is a commercial bank with a network of 76 branches. It has a fully owned finance company, Hong Leong Finance, as well as subsidiaries in leasing, property investment and unit trust management. It possesses three major unit trust funds: Hong Leong Bank Growth Fund, Hong Leong Bank Blue Chip Fund and Hong Leong Bank Penny Stocks Fund. In 1999, Hong Leong Bank merged with the Bank of Commerce, Bolton Finance Berhad, and in February 2000 it amalgamated with Wah Tah Bank and Credit Corporation Malaysia. These amalgamations with failing banks were induced by the 1997 financial crisis.

The largest group of shareholders in the bank is the family, the shareholding held through Quek Leng Chan and the two holding companies Hong Leong Credit and Hong Leong Malaysia (see Table 6.4). Throughout the period 1994–2001, 60.08 per cent of the total shareholding was held by Quek and the family's holding companies, Hong Leong Credit and Hong Leong Holding Company. The Employees Provident Fund, a semi-government group, held 7.08 per cent, while other *bumiputra* institutional shareholders held another 5 per cent. Rothputra Nominees Tempatan (Malay) held another 25.5 per cent. Foreign investors held almost 4 per cent equity. Banks such as HSBC Nominees controlled 7.8 per cent equity, Phileo-Allied 6.4 per cent, Chase Manhattan Malaysia 6.4 per cent.[36] Overall, individual shareholders accounted for 6 to 7 per cent of the total between 1994 and

Table 6.4 The top shareholders, 24 August 2002, HLBK-Hong Leong Bank Berhad

Shareholders	*No. of shares*	*% of shares*
Hong Leong Credit Bhd	820,107,168	71.05
Employees Provident Fund Board	81,706,250	7.08
Kurnia Insurans (Malaysia) Bhd	24,912,000	2.16
Kurnia Damai Sdn Bhd	14,530,000	1.26
Permodalan Nasional Bhd	11,109,000	0.96
Siau Teng Chong	7,000,000	0.61
Hong Leong Assurance Bhd	5,978,000	0.52
Government of Kuwait	4,928,000	0.43
Amanah Saham Malaysia	4,000,000	0.35
Kwek Leng Hai	3,955,700	0.34
BHLB Pacific Emerging Companies Growth Fund	2,998,000	0.26
Fidelity Funds Malaysia	2,710,000	0.23
GMO Emerging Markets Fund	2,660,000	0.23
Lembaga Tabung Angkatan Tentera	2,408,500	0.21
State Banks & Trust Funds for Employee Trusts	2,376,500	0.20
Seow Lun Hoo	2,121,750	0.18
Cheng Fu Zay	2,080,500	0.18
The Great Eastern Life Assurance Co Ltd	1,966,000	0.17
Amanah Saham Mara Bhd	1,724,000	0.15
DFA Emerging Markets Fund	1,662,000	0.14

Source: Hong Leong Bank, Annual Report, 24 August 2000. See also HLB, Annual Reports, 1995–2001

1997, and only rose to 9 per cent in 2000.[37] The family retained a major shareholding, while Malay shareholding fell between 1997 and 2000. A consequence of this complicated shareholding structure was the implacable retention of the nucleus of Quek family ownership, while the stakes held by the Malay institutions were lower than the official prescribed limit.

Furthermore, the Malay shareholding was concentrated in blocks within institutions, rather than with individuals. This trend in institutional investors, in particular that of EPF as a major institutional investor, made HLB's stocks more glamorous, attracting speculative funds and thereby adding to the volatility of the Malaysian stock market. These institutional investors, the EPF (pension fund) and ASB (indigenous equity fund), are dominated by the state; government policies, while distorting the valuation of shares through discrimination in favour of certain client groups, were also open to insider trading. Individual retail investors were, themselves, swayed by the scale of participation and the choice of stocks of these government agents. Thus, even when the economic fundamentals behind such shares were weak, there were unprecedented purchases, raising prices and creating asset bubbles. Equally, the reverse was true, when despite the stable financial health of the corporation, the market remained volatile. This is clear from Table 6.5 and Figure 6.3: the decline in share prices is not reflected in a decline in profits.

Table 6.5 Key financial ratios – Hong Leong Bank

Key ratios	*1995*	*1996*	*1997*	*1998*	*1999*	*2000*	*2001*	*2002*	*2003*
Profitability									
ROAA (after tax)* (%)	1.79	1.15	1.11	0.19	0.50	1.25	1.15	1.22	1.34
ROE (after tax) (%)	26.60	17.15	15.60	2.47	6.68	16.57	13.59	14.84	14.86
Net interest margin (net int. inc./ave total assets)* (%)	4.84	3.53	3.32	3.11	2.72	2.99	3.44	2.85	2.63
Net interest margin (net int. inc./ave total advances)* (%)	7.45	5.32	4.91	4.53	4.11	5.01	5.95	4.93	4.91
Asset quality									
Bad debt reserves/advances (%)	6.13	3.83	2.68	4.04	5.40	5.28	4.70	4.59	5.27
Capital adequacy									
Total liability/equity	13.89	16.20	15.61	12.49	12.96	13.37	12.63	11.67	10.15
Total equity/deposits (%)	8.61	7.52	8.31	9.16	8.51	8.60	9.31	9.95	10.86
Total equity/total advances (%)	10.34	8.62	8.87	10.67	11.32	12.25	12.50	13.83	17.83
Liquidity									
Total advances/deposits (%)	83	87	94	86	75	70	74	72	61
Liquid asset ratio (liquid assets/ total assets)** (%)	9	10	9	12	18	21	17	20	18
Liquid assets/deposits (%)	11	12	13	14	22	26	22	25	21
Net loans/deposits (%)	78	84	91	82	71	67	71	69	58

Table 6.5 (continued)

Key ratios	*1995*	*1996*	*1997*	*1998*	*1999*	*2000*	*2001*	*2002*	*2003*
Growth									
Net interest income (%)		–14	33	17	–4	26	47	–1	–3
Total income (%)		–12.32	15.08	37.91	2.32	26.82	43.44	4.00	–4.81
PAT (%)		–24.32	37.34	–78.48	158.15	335.02	29.60	17.00	13.56
Total assets (%)		35.55	45.83	10.20	8.54	19.36	35.01	8.59	1.46
Total loans and advances (%)		42.56	47.52	12.08	–1.84	7.23	39.94	5.61	–10.88
Deposits (%)		36.75	36.10	22.79	12.66	14.65	30.40	9.34	5.63
Equity growth (%)		17.36	50.99	35.71	4.89	15.93	42.39	16.82	15.28
Share related									
EPS (net) (RM)	0.15	0.15	0.19	0.04	0.10	0.29	0.28	0.35	0.40
Price (RM)	3.81	3.46	3.17	1.19	2.52	3.10	3.28	5.35	4.60
PER	25.40	23.07	16.68	29.75	25.20	10.69	11.71	15.29	11.50
BV/share (RM)	0.73	0.86	1.2	1.45	1.52	1.77	2.03	2.37	2.72
P/B ratio	5.22	4.02	2.64	0.82	1.66	1.75	1.62	2.26	1.69
Dividend/share (RM)	0.03	0.02	0.03	0.02	0.03	0.05	0.10	0.10	0.10
Dividend yield (%)	0.8	0.6	0.9	1.7	1.2	1.6	3.0	1.9	2.2

Notes:
* Ratio of 1995 calculated on total and not on average assets.
** Based on incomplete asset breakdown.

Source: Annual Reports, Balance Sheets and Profit and Loss Statements, Hong Leong Bank, 1995–2003

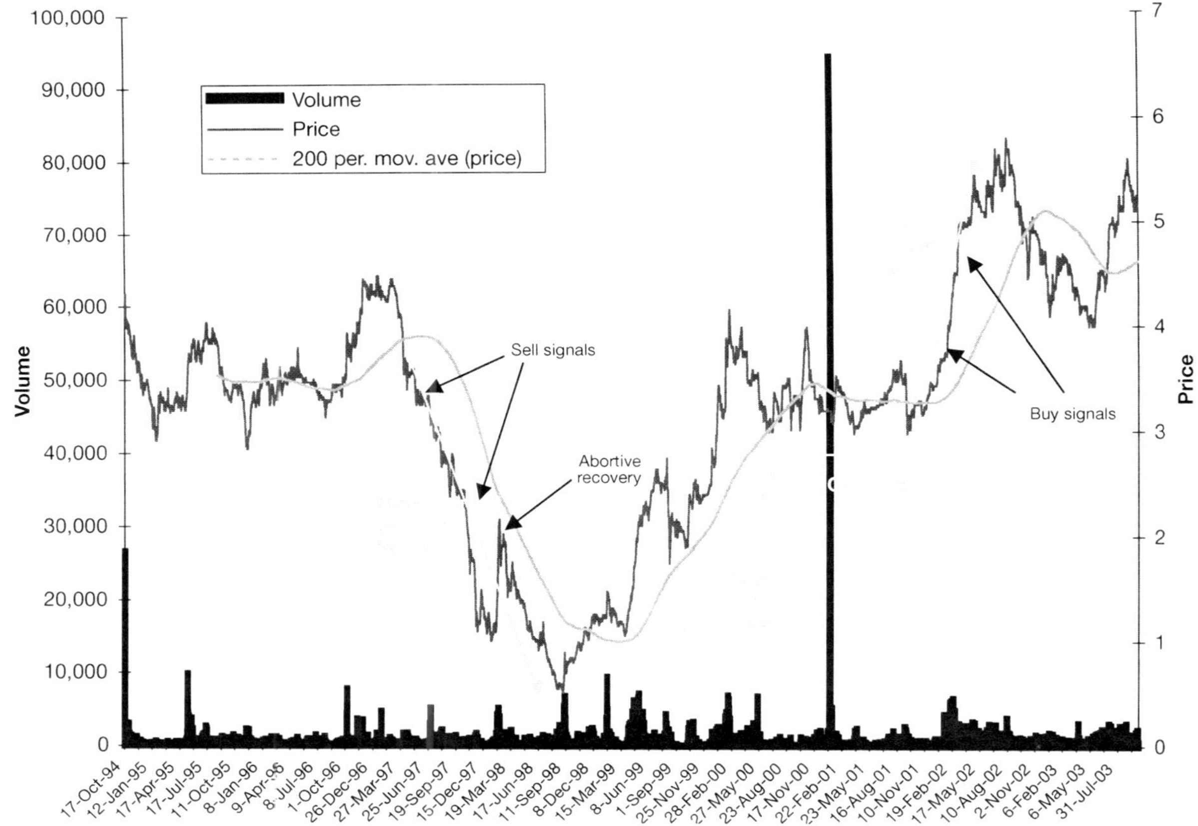

Figure 6.3 Hong Leong Bank, price/volume graph

The discussion so far has revealed that affiliation to the stock market did not dilute the concentrated family ownership of the bank. This was attained through the holding company structure where listing and delisting of powerful units within the group occurred without compromising family control. The listed companies indulged in stock splits, paid low dividends and ignored minority shareholders.[38] However, the core feature central to our analysis and interest is that this maze of firms within the holding company structure encourages the predatorial ambitions of Quek but, equally, it helped sustain his various alliances with political factions in UMNO and dominant Malay capitalists.

The bank revealed impressive growth. Its share capital rose from RM 391.7 million in 1994, to RM696.9 million in 1995, to RM817.9 million in 1996, to RM1,235.12 million in 1997, to RM1,676.01 million in 1998, to RM1,757.6 million in 1999 and to RM2,038.1 million in 2000.[39] A major proportion of this was raised through rights issues. In June 1995 the paid-up capital was augmented through a rights issue of RM158 million. Another rights issue in July 1997 led to an increase of RM64,129,877 in share capital.[40] In addition, Hong Leong Bank offered warrants of 5,650 shares in 1995; in 1996 this was repeated with 43 million shares obtained through a further exercise of warrants. The warrants were sold to existing shareholders at a fixed price. The bank also issued bonds to raise capital – these were taken principally by insurance companies. The bank's equity and debt instruments were rated high. Thus, in 1994 HLB raised the highest amount in a private sector IPO – that of RM620.6 million.[41]

A detailed analysis of Hong Leong Bank's performance from 1994 to 2000 will illustrate the core argument in this chapter that the corporation's economic well-being and its stable growth were not evident in its share value movements. Table 6.5 gives an overview of the bank's performance from 1995 to 2003. Figure 6.3 reveals Hong Leong Bank's share price movements between October 1994 and July 2003. What is sharply clear from these two statistical summaries is the bank's share price movements do not strictly shadow or reflect the corporation's internal financial performance. The table on the financial ratios of Hong Leong Bank reveals steady growth even during and after the 1997 crisis. However, its share price movements reveal volatility that is not prompted in any way by this fairly stable corporate performance.

Despite recording a steady growth in its banking and associated activities, Hong Leong Bank's share performance revealed large volatilities in certain periods. For very small periods between 18 and 20 October 1994, it had three-day runs of negative results. This could be the initial adjustments in the market immediately after its restructuring and floating as part of the Hong Leong Group. The longest positive share performance occurred in January–July 1995, followed by August–November 1996. In the period after April 1997 to October 1998 there was a clear downward trend. This was a direct consequence of the financial crisis, the restructuring of its NPL segment, its predicted merger with other smaller banks and political events in Malaysia, which were all feeding this downward cycle. However, the share price revived in November 1998 and continued its positive growth until April 1999. From June 1999, the bank's share price was falling continuously with the exception of recoveries in tiny fractions. It did pick up briefly in June 2000, but continued a precipitous decline from July 2000.

Second, during the periods, in 1996 and 1999, when positive returns with large price increases were present, the exaggerated rise could be related to the large inflows of portfolio capital (see Figure 6.2 on capital flows into Malaysia, 1991–2000). Here, we could also speculate on possible insider trading. Such volatility clustering, such periodic intense fluctuations are not purely a consequence of economic factors but, more seriously, it is political events, such as changes in the Malaysian Cabinet, that are triggering changes in Hong Leong Bank's share prices. Quek's close links with Anwar may have had some repercussions following the latter's incarceration in September 1998[42] (see Figure 6.3). This chart, however, does not seek to prove the case for market efficiency. There is no direct presentation of profits against share prices, and no identification is sought between share price movements and specific political factors. What is very broadly asserted is that the listings on the KLSE are dominated by the state and its cronies with lucrative government contracts, and hence are influenced by this. However, there is no scope in this chapter for a detailed event study. What is undisputed is that retail investors form a tiny minority, and hence have a limited impact on the stock exchange.

Trends in acquisitions and mergers

The holding company structure was useful for mergers, management takeovers and other strategies for expansion. This rather subtle but complex process of management buy-out, financed through the assets of an almost moribund Hong Leong subsidiary, is evident in the takeover in 1993 of NSTP (New Straits Times Press)/TV3 by four Malay managers of NSTP. The buy-out was arranged through a Hong Leong company, Malaysian Resources Corporation Bhd, where Quek Leng Chan held a majority stake. MRCB was a failing property company, which was being restructured and used to bid for the management buy-out of NSTP/TV3. The strategy is clear: MRCB, a shell company, takes over Realmild, a new company formed by the management of NSTP. This leveraged buy-out in January 1993 of NSTP from Renong for RM800 million by Realmild, which had assets of only RM100,000, was possible because of MRCB and the assets of Quek, as well as the funds provided by the Malaysian state, through HICOM (a powerful group in Malaysia's infrastructural developments), and the Ministry of Finance.[43] The NSTP is an influential media group controlling the largest English language daily and several Malay and Chinese daily papers. MRCB held 48 per cent equity in NSTP and 43.2 per cent in TV3. Later, Quek reduced his stake in NSTP/TV3.

This management buy-out underlines two important facets of corporate growth and restructuring. First, assets of one existing company (MRCB) and one newly formed company (Realmild) are used to finance a management buy-out of a crucial publishing group, NSTP, which, though listed, remains within the orbit of groups favourable to the state. Second, the leveraged buy-out does not introduce a large new shareholder base, which could threaten the company NSTP and which is the main mouthpiece of the government. Third, defunct companies such as MRCB were now revived through acquisition of lucrative government contracts in energy and communications. This proves that client capitalists such as Quek could use units within its group to satisfy such needs of the state without endangering their core firms. Capital could be raised without eroding the family ownership of Hong Leong.[44] Quek also provides capital for *bumiputra* groups at critical phases in the restructuring of Malay corporations in Malaysia in the 1980s and 1990s.

The holding company structure also assisted the retention of family management to dominate the Hong Leong Group. There was a two-tier management structure – the Board of Directors and the Audit Committee. The patriarch Quek Leng Chan and relatives from Singapore, Kwek Leng Seng and Kwek Leng Hai, were permanent members of the management board of Hong Leong Bank. The Board also included Malay technocrats and politicians. Dr Hussain Awang was a director on both the management board and the Audit Committee. In addition, the board included Chinese friends of the family, Tan Kiok Yin, James Lim-Cheng Poh and Seow Lun Hoo. The family members and their Chinese friends maintained their positions throughout the period 1994–2001. Only the Malay representatives changed. Nik Hashim Yusoof, the Executive Director, resigned in 1995 and was replaced by Zulkilfi Hashim who left in 2000. The changes in Malay representatives could be explained by the development and changes of political loyalties to factions within the UMNO. Perhaps the rise and fall of these factions could be linked to changes on the board.[45]

These networks of interlocking shareholding and state patronage created rapid growth in clusters of investment in manufacturing, finance, property and in stock market and in infrastructural projects. The Malaysian government's industrial policies gave priority to larger firms because of their emphasis on heavy industry and export orientation. Hong Leong was a beneficiary of this policy, being responsible for several large infrastructural projects within the Malaysian economy. In addition to its liaisons with the state, it had access to foreign capital, principally Kuwaiti, American, Japanese and European. Much of this was intermediated through the Asian stock markets – Malaysia, Singapore, Hong Kong and China. The sequel to this exploitation of capital markets appears to be an increasing ambivalence by certain Chinese entrepreneurs to ethnic affiliations. Hong Leong's ties with Chinese ethnic networks remained ambivalent. While cultivating Malay political alliances with fervour, Quek Leng Chan, the head of Hong Leong Malaysia, had built a reputation for stalking Chinese firms by using the capital market to finance these, often hostile, takeovers and mergers. This predatorial stance inevitably held a destabilizing influence for some Chinese corporations in Southeast Asia. This is seen in the difficulties confronting Yeo Hiap Seng in the 1990s which were complicated by Quek's adversial activities.[46] The MCA, the main political wing of the Chinese community, felt threatened by Quek's interest in the possible takeover of MPHB in 1989. The MCA succeeded in foiling his ambition and MPHB was acquired by Lim Thian Kiat and his Kamunting Group. Frequently, such random moves by competing Chinese business elites provided significant drifts in share values and company performance. The predatorial instincts of Quek could have been nourished by his close relationship with the Anwar faction in the UMNO until Anwar's political collapse in 1998.

Second, this chapter, through a detailed institutional analysis of the Malaysian stock market and the study of a major listed company, Hong Leong, has revealed some flaws in the 'efficient markets' theory that share prices reflect corporate information, that markets possess all the relevant information to influence share prices.[47] It is very difficult to establish a direct relationship between share prices and corporate performance; the correlation between the scale of dividend payments and risk are fraught with problems. It is this imperfect knowledge which, Mary O'Sullivan argues, leads to fads and bubbles, that characterize the stock market and not efficiency in its responses to information.[48] These fads and bubbles are often a product of institutional interactions rather than just an accumulation of developments in the economy or the company's health. So a corporation's share price and its internal economic performance reveal considerable divergences.

The obvious conclusion is that changes in share prices are a product of complex factors – political and economic – affecting the KLSE. This study of Hong Leong sees only a limited correlation between internal corporate performance and share market performance.[49] First, non-market forces are critical in explaining this disjuncture. The interactions between such corporations and the government make efficient capital valuation difficult. Low pricing of IPOs to attract client groups to become shareholders, the overhang of state-owned shares in privatized companies and the presence of large institutional investment, all hinder the strict pricing of shares and a more efficient operation of the stock market.[50] Second, the frenzied wave of mergers and acquisitions among large private groups since the mid-1980s in a booming stock market has provoked constant financial restructuring, introducing complex strategies for recapitalizing often defunct firms in order to mount new aggressive bids for the takeover of healthy rival firms. This had destabilizing consequences both for the firms as well as for the capital markets, creating waves of 'share fever'. Third, large foreign capital inflows, particularly portfolio investment targeting property and financial sectors of the KLSE, feed on the share frenzies, creating further bubbles.

Therefore, this complex interplay of political and economic influences on the Malaysian stock market has ensured that even a stable, prudent bank, the Hong Leong Bank experiences fiercely fluctuating share prices, mimicking or responding to transactions by powerful operators on the KLSE, including Quek himself. Investors are swayed by political considerations more than by dividend payments, earnings announcements, product or market changes within the corporation. Both the corporation and the stock market need organizational clarity and financial transparency. The broad reshaping of corporate finance since the 1970s through the use of equity, bonds, loans from state and foreign banks, pension funds, insurance funds – such diverse fund-raising measures should have coincided with detailed changes in corporate structure and ownership to provide more transparency and accountability. With the preservation of family ownership, speculators and crony capitalists distort both corporation and the stock market. This degree of non-market forces in the Malaysian stock market is highly visible[51] (see Figure 6.4).

This single case study of Hong Leong is used to argue that it is a firm resorting to growth via acquisition, and is unique in its access to overseas Chinese, Japanese and Arab capital inflows. It also preserved impeccable connections to the Malaysian state and to the *bumiputra* elite. The organization structure of the Chinese conglomerate listed on the stock market exploited the privatization of SOEs, the influx of foreign portfolio capital to support diversification in products, as well as in markets and regions. This diversified growth in a cronyistic environment reveals weak corporate governance. The predatory nature of Hong Leong in its commitment to growth through acquisitions had a destabilizing effect on other family firms such as Yeo Hiap Seng.[52]

Conclusion

The major theoretical and empirical contribution of this chapter has been to demonstrate how the stock market was utilized by a large corporation to acquire and integrate new firms and create a viable MNE, still dominated by a single family. Stock markets provided not just capital, but also opportunities for constructing ties with politicians, bureaucrats, foreign investors, overseas ethnic networks and foreign multinationals, without diluting the existing, solid family control and management. Finally, the interactions between the firm's internal performance and its fortunes on the stock market are not that precise. Performance on the stock market is influenced by more complex factors than the corporation's balance sheets.

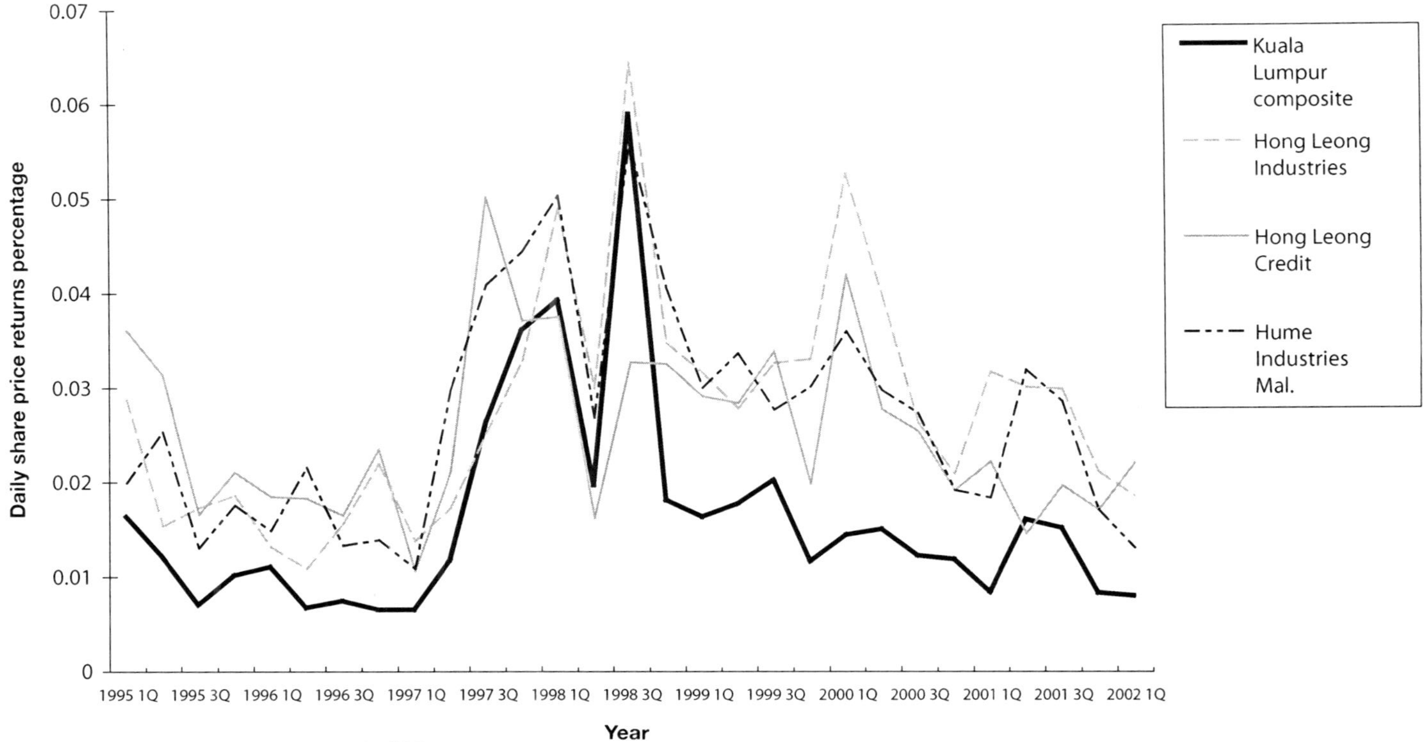

Figure 6.4 Hong Leong Group volatilities, 1995–2002

7 Renong

Privatization bliss and globalization

Renong was the largest industrial conglomerate in Malaysia. Its growth and global initiatives were dictated and shaped by privatization programmes in Asia, South Africa and the United Kingdom. It expanded through links with the state, was funded by tapping into stock markets and through project finance from the World Bank and IMF, and made the transition into capital- and R&D-intensive industries by acquiring appropriate firms and joint-venture partners. All this transformed it from a lapsed mining company into a multinational within a decade from the mid-1980s.

This chapter traces the evolution of this tin-mining company that was founded by British interests in the nineteenth century, acquired by Chinese capitalists in 1957 as a direct result of nationalization, and transformed in 1986 as a critical vehicle of economic restructuring and for *bumiputra* entrepreneurial development. It acquired newly privatized SOEs supported by private projects in infrastructure, public utilities, manufacturing and finance. Having secured highly profitable projects in Malaysia, it identified similar interests in the rest of Asia and Europe through joint-venture alliances with various states and foreign multinationals, and, funded in part by the ADB, the IMF and the World Bank, Renong emerged as a global infrastructural and public utilities corporation.

There are three core questions surrounding this accelerated growth at home and abroad. First, how was this growth achieved and how was it financed? Second, what were the major corporate and industrial structural changes introduced by this growth? And third, what was the impact of the 1997 financial crisis on this growth?

The source of this ubiquitous growth was linked to the privatization programme of the Malaysian Government initiated in 1986. Renong captured lucrative concessions in infrastructure projects in transport, energy and the sewerage and water industries, as well as in the electronics industry. It was a direct beneficiary of the prestige projects of the Malaysian state, with airport expansion, telecommunications, electronics and international sporting events such as the Commonwealth Games held in Kuala Lumpur in 1998. All this led to a continuous restructuring of the group, creating new firms to undertake new priority projects as well as engaging in a wave of acquisitions and mergers at home and abroad.

The increased importance of the stock market for financing, produced further unceasing organizational restructuring, with the creation of new listed subsidiaries to undertake increasingly specialized tasks under the privatization of heavy, capital-intensive, infrastructural and industrial sectors. This growth was also fuelled by the extraordinary stream of acquisitions and mergers, accounting for a significant increase in the volume of stock market capitalization of KLSE, Malaysia. Renong, a conglomerate assembled through major acquisitions and excessive diversification, emerged as the successful option in a booming Asian economy from the late 1980s.

Specialization was achieved through corporate restructuring within the group, sustaining the view that de-conglomeration and specialization were just as pervasive as random diversification. Attempts to absorb related companies in related industries were undertaken more to assert monopoly rights rather than to improve performance or to compete through specialization. Such egregious advances into hi-tech, capital-intensive industries were facilitated through increased shareholding by institutional investors affiliated to the state and to UMNO. Buttressed by this political support, a concentrated individual ownership by Halim Saad and his family persisted. Here it is also important to highlight organizational features assisting growth, such as holding companies, multiple subsidiaries, and the raising of finance from diverse domestic and foreign banks and capital markets.

These factors had a major impact on Renong's growth and performance. Renong had been registered as a public listed company since July 1903; it was engaged principally in tin-mining and was owned by British investors. It remained listed on the London Stock Exchange until September 1976, though with an increased Chinese shareholding. In October 1983, it was deregistered in London and its shares were listed on the KLSE by November 1983. Renong was now principally a property and financial services group, but from 1985 it diversified rapidly into retailing, and yarn and garment manufacture. Indeed, the year 1985 was a turning point for Renong because of the government's programme for privatization of the main public utility companies.

Corporate structure and ownership

A sharp deterioration in the Malaysian economy and the resulting fiscal crisis in 1985 were aggravated by the dismal performance of SOEs in Malaysia. Mahatir sought to promote private investments through privatization, de-regulation and liberalization of the economy, and to engender a belief in competition and in the market. However, this stalled because of the domination by a select few *bumiputra* businessmen who were aided by a continuing state presence in both funding and in the provision of R&D. Renong emerged as a dominant Malay enterprise, possessing critical links to the UMNO and to the former Finance Minister, Daim Zainuddin. Significantly, financial links to major Chinese capitalists were maintained throughout. Even as late as 1996, large warrant holders in Renong were individual Chinese capitalists. In 1999, these Chinese capitalists and state institutional investors retained that niche in financing the conglomerate.[1] Many of these were Chinese tin-mining families, a reminder of the early hegemony of the Malaysian Chinese in commodity production.[2]

An initial change in ownership patterns, occurring between 1986 and 1990, corresponded with two major changes. First, Renong was restructured, diversifying and investing in infrastructural development, construction, telecommunications, property, finance and technical services for the oil and gas industries. Second, Renong and its subsidiaries were listed on the KLSE.

The first major restructuring in September 1990 transformed Renong into a holding company with nine listed subsidiaries, which later rose to 11. In early 1993, Renong disposed of its media interests in Hume Industries and acquired Park May, thereby reinforcing its expanding interests in transport, construction and property. The major projects included the North-South Expressway, the Malaysia–Singapore Second Crossing, the National Sports Complex for international events, Johor New Township development and the local transit system for Kuala Lumpur. This engagement in infrastructure and engineering led, in November 1996, to the acquisition of OPUS International, a firm of architectural planning consultants in New Zealand.

Moreover, in June 1997, Renong expanded into the telecommunications sector through its involvement in the Multimedia Super Corridor of Cyberjaya. Lucrative acquisitions earlier in 1991 included United Engineers Malaysia (UEM), TV3, PLUS and KLOFFE.[3] It now possessed a 30.3 per cent controlling stake in UEM, 43 per cent in TV3 and 50 per cent in Plus (see Figures 7.1a and 7.1b for details). In turn, UEM held six public listed companies with separate functions: in engineering, construction, property development, technology, transportation, and logistics and project management. As for Plus, it coordinated the North–South (N–S) Expressway and was involved in the Kuala Lumpur International Airport and Cyberjaya projects. Linkedua, a Renong subsidiary, was a major concession holder for the Malaysia–Singapore Second Crossing. Renong was also involved in the development of electronic software for transport. The creation of numerous subsidiaries with interlocking shareholding meant the subdivision of functions within one single project. There was also the involvement of several of Renong's subsidiaries in one single project. Thus, Linkedua and Kinta Kellas of UEM were both involved in the Malaysia–Singapore Second Crossing, completed in November 1997 at a cost of RM1.3 billion. With regard to the international airport project, UEM headed a Malaysian–Japanese consortium for the design and construction of the airport, while Kinta Kellas provided technical, management and support services. This project was launched in June 1998, costing RM9 billion.

Within this asset acquisition there were changes in operations, structure and activities. The reverse takeover of Fleet Group by Renong resulted in majority control of the acquiring firm by the acquired firm, through the

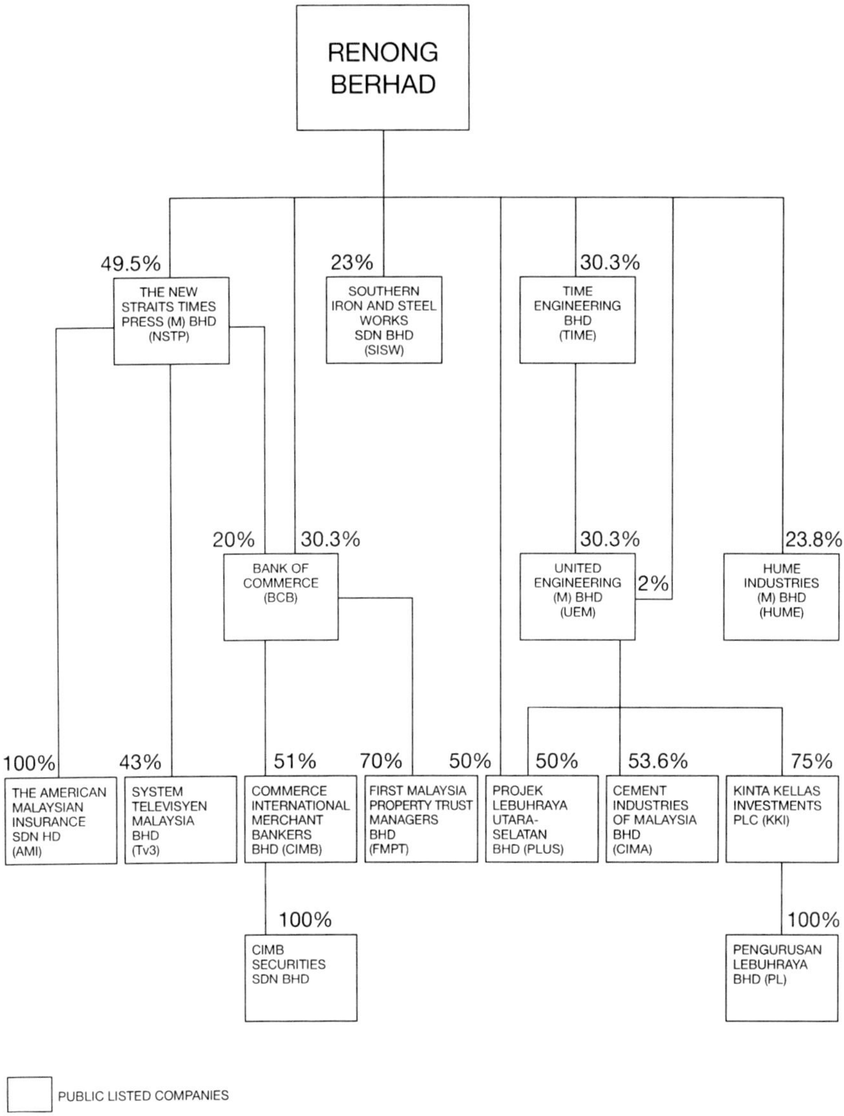

Figure 7.1a Renong Group structure, 1996

exchange of shares. The vertical takeover of related enterprises, whereby producer–supplier relationships were strengthened, was manifested in the acquisition of Cement Industries Corp and a property group by UEM. There were also acquisitions of unrelated business, thus leading to diversification through engagement in new activities. However, even after takeovers, these firms remained separate: the takeovers benefited the large shareholder,

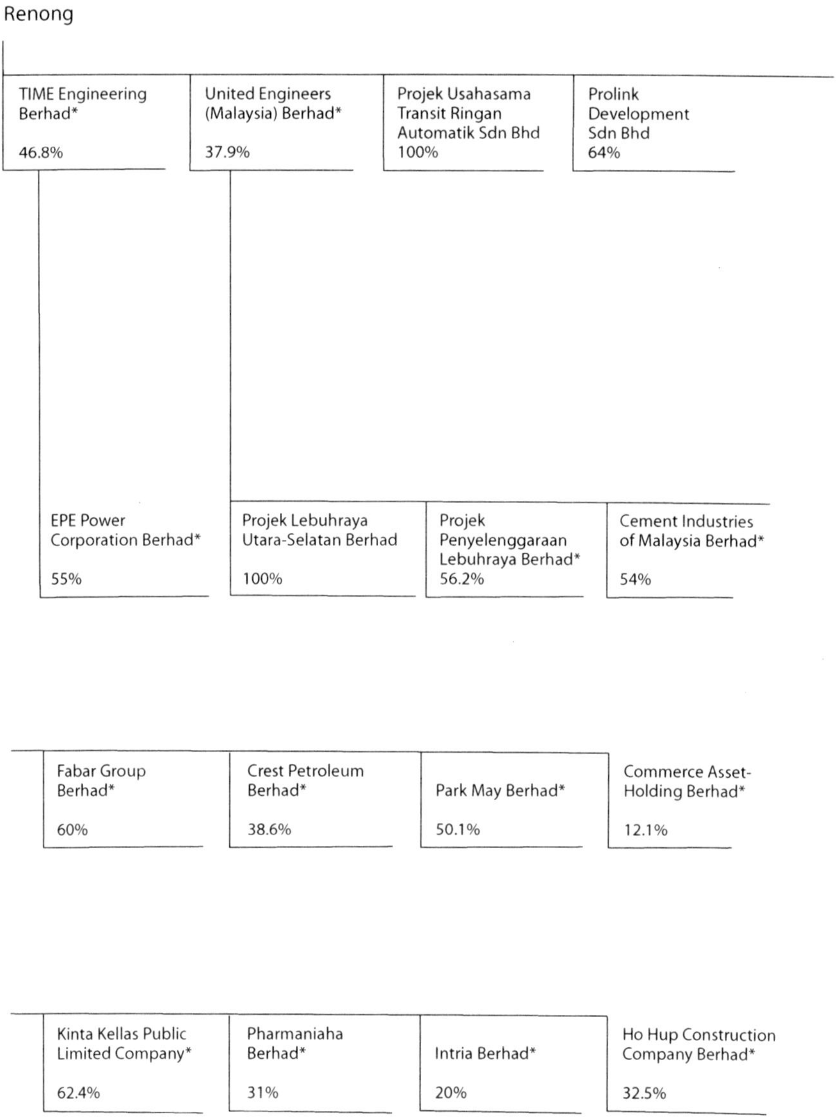

Figure 7.1b Renong Group structure, 2000

namely, the Saad family. Monopolistic market power was achieved through undue collusion between Renong and the government in this concentrated growth in specific industrial sectors and in highly prestigious projects. This confident growth at home explains their global ambitions and initiatives.

Another major interest was in medical services. The privatization of medical services in Malaysia in 1994 produced more subsidiaries for Renong, with more specialist functions. In March 1994, UEM secured contracts for medical supplies to government hospitals in Perlis, Kedah, Perak and Sabah, while another subsidiary, Faber Medi Serve was put in charge of clinical waste, cleaning, engineering, biomedical and pharmaceutical services. By March 1999, UEM, in a joint-venture with Sabah Economic Development Corporation, was in charge of the construction of six new hospitals in Sabah. This continuing privatization of medical services benefited Renong greatly. Indeed, in 1996 another subsidiary, Propel (Projek Penyelenggaran Lebuh Raya Bhd), was placed in charge of the provision of hospital support services.

This process of forming subsidiaries to cater for each concession they secured under the various government privatization schemes continued. However, while what connected the new firm to the concession it was entrusted with was clear, an enormous amount of duplication of functions was inevitable. Thus, Renong's subsidiaries, Prolink (property development), Faber (hotels), Ho Hup Co, UEM and Kinta Kellas, were all in construction. OPUS, a global infrastructural firm responsible for road and dam construction and maintenance, was involved in operations and management with other subsidiaries, such as Plus, Elite and Linkedua. Propel, meanwhile, was assigned the construction and maintenance of hospitals. This continuous breakdown of specialisms continued with Teras Teknologi, which was responsible for software development, specializing in toll collection, traffic management and technology parks.[4]

The corporate structure of Renong also revealed a highly concentrated interlocking shareholding within the individual and separate companies. The substantial shareholdings retained by Renong were as follows: Crest Petroleum (39 per cent), Park May (50 per cent), Probadi (39 per cent), Commerce Asset Holding (20 per cent), Faber (60 per cent), UEM (39 per cent), PLUS (39 per cent), Kinta Kellas (20 per cent), CIMA (18 per cent), Time Engineering (47 per cent), EPS Power (26 per cent), Southern Steel (17 per cent) and Ho Hup (17 per cent).

Such corporate diversification was a drain on resources and in October 1998 Renong attempted an overhaul that focused on four sectors: construction, engineering, transport and property development. Another strategy that was wasteful was the subdivision of tasks themselves. Thus, the N-S Expressway was financed, designed and constructed by Plus through a 30-year concession that will lapse in 2018. Yet Propel, another Renong subsidiary, was responsible for pavement works in this project, while the geotechnical operations were assigned to Central Lab Sdn, a subsidiary of Propel. Propel itself had acquired a construction firm in 1995. Even within Crest Petroleum, which was involved in offshore drilling, marine construction and surveys, there were four subsidiaries. Similarly, Crest owned vessels for soil investigation, while some specialized interests were held by different subsidiaries in the group. Such differentiation was sustained, first, by tapping into the continuing privatization of public utilities in Malaysia and abroad, in Asia and Africa. Second, the operational system of build, operate and transfer

(BOT), whereby private companies could finance and operate these services for a concession period, assisted this random diversification. Under the BOT method, no open system of tender was used in this growth. The politically well-connected were the major concessionaires in this BOT system. Profitability was secured through soft loans, while traffic volume guarantees and exchange rate guarantees were assured by the state. This system induced a private monopoly, protected by the government, and Renong was thereby assured of stable profits with little or no risk.

Financial strategies

Besides globalization that enabled such diversification to continue, there was a fairly sophisticated system of internal restructuring and financing that sustained such a wide dispersal of interests. This incessant financial restructuring was evident from the 1980s. Performance of Renong was modest (see Table 7.1) and capital was sought through the stock market. The company was incorporated in 1982. In 1983, a share issue of RM4.9 million was distributed to the original shareholders. This rights issue was for the acquisition of Kinta Properties, increasing the equity base to RM23.3 million. Another rights issue in 1984 raised capital to RM25 million. By 1990, the capital rose to RM668,162,752, again through another share issue. Much of this was done to finance the acquisition of Hatibudi Nominees. This was a major restructuring, which saw the acquisition of many UMNO companies, including the Fleet Group and Hatibudi Nominees, as well as a stake in the highly lucrative infrastructural firm, UEM. This was also to absorb Renong's own substantial losses in 1989. Renong's strategy was to convert debt into shares. In 1990, Renong converted the RM18.5 million owed to Citibank, Maybank and OCBC into 35.9 million new shares. Dr Chan Chin Cheung purchased a substantial amount of these new shares for RM17.6 million.[5]

The acquisition mania grew simultaneously with the constant issuing of equity. In 1992, the share capital of Renong rose to RM726,894,699 with the issue of 593,124 shares through the conversion of RM946,000 RCULS (redeemable convertible unsecured loan stocks). This conversion continued into 1994 when equity rose to RM822,908,436. The conversion of RCULS was accompanied by the issuing of new equity to finance takeovers, as in the case of Park May in 1994. In May 1996, Renong issued five-year corporate bonds to the value of RM500 million in order to finance its stake in Putra and Prolink. This was followed in December 1996 by the issuing of two further bonds with a total value of RM846 million in order to finance the acquisition of Time Engineering. The bonds were secured on quoted shares in associate and subsidiary companies in the group. This continuous expansion in equity and bonds was essential to finance such an accelerated growth. As shown in Table 7.1, revenues and wealth transfers were limited. This increase in capitalization through the conversion of RCULS, ICULS (irredeemable convertible unsecured loan stocks) and warrants continued. In 1997, share capital rose to RM1,093 million through such issues.

Wide share ownership was absent on the Kuala Lumpur Stock Market because of the strong participation by government and institutional investors, both before and after privatization. The government's role in privatization was in retaining a 'golden' share, partly to hedge against risk. This encouraged newly privatized firms with close connections to the state to ignore minority shareholders and to pursue unrestrained growth through frequent changes in share capital. Within their new acquisitions, their strategy was to exploit the debt capacity of the acquired firm, increase its share capital and alter its market value. This increased the debt equity ratio of both the acquiring firm and the acquired firm. See Table 7.1 for an understanding of the impact of these developments on Renong's gearing ratio between 1981 and 2000.

Besides this complicated system of financing through the issuing of shares and subscribing to rights issues, warrants and bonds, there was the securing of works contracts for each company within Renong. This intensified the flow of project finance. There were complicated financial transfers between subsidiaries. In October 1996, Faber acquired a contract for hospital services. In November 1996, it issued bonds but also sold shares of UEM for RM220 million.[6] Similarly, Park May, an infrastructural unit in Renong, financed three bonus issues (RM18 million), rights issues (RM27 million) and bonds for 120 million, while increasing authorized capital from 100 million to 500 million.

In an attempt to increase capital, Renong utilized bonds as debt instruments in the 1990s. The large bondholders were semi-government institutions such as the EPF (Pension Fund) and *bumiputra* investment companies. This was also done to provide stability and flexibility in structuring cash flow, and borrowing with assets and with clear investment strategies. Because bonds were acquired by institutions with government connections, the complex maze of pricing, selling, supporting and guaranteeing these debt instruments descended into a confusing and relentless search for further additional funds. This constant swapping of shares continued with the increased specialization occurring within the subsidiaries. In addition, there was incessant activity in land and property acquisitions and sales to fund this growth. Globalization was, therefore, pursued in order to increase market share and to access new sources of finance.

In the 1980s, the main sources of finance were bank loans and, to a limited degree, the issuing of common stock. Issuing bonds was fairly constrained. In this way, a staid debt-equity balance was maintained. This is shown in low gearing ratios, which only rose dramatically from 1993 to 1999, as shown in Table 7.1. The Asian financial crisis of 1997 did not dampen this new trend in high borrowing, since Renong's involvement with the central government's economic strategies in infrastructure and electronics reassured bond investors. In addition, there were a variety of bond issues in which

Table 7.1 Performance Renong Berhad: financial ratio analysis for the years ended 30 June

	1980	*1981*	*1982*	*1983*	*1984*	*1985*	*1986*	*1987*	*1988*	*1989*
Profitablity ratios										
Operating profit/turnover	–	–	–	–	30.39	18.8	n/a	n/a	n/a	n/a
NPBT/turnover	–	–	–	–	30.39	18.8	n/a	n/a	n/a	n/a
Dividends/NPAT	–	0	0	11.98	28.62	35.05	0	0	0	0
ROCE	–	0	0	0	9.15	5.34	n/a	n/a	n/a	n/a
ROI	–	0	0	0	0.05	0.56	n/a	n/a	n/a	n/a
ROE	–	0	0	0	0.05	0.04	n/a	n/a	n/a	n/a
Total assets/turnover	–	–	–	–	332.1	351.74	474.58	617.5	295.21	287.52
Earnings per share	–	0	0	0	0.19	0.12	n/a	n/a	n/a	n/a
Liquidity ratios										
Current assets ratio	5.176307	3.738514	7.175687	12.14971	1.511189	1.325332	0.947986	0.915932	0.718621	0.512699
Quick or acid test ratio	5.176307	3.259074	7.175687	12.14971	0.994189	0.868591	0.52085	0.426776	0.273779	0.164018
Ideal level	–	1	1	1	1	1	1	1	1	1
Dividend policy										
Proposed dividend	–	0	0	0	750,000	750,000	0	0	0	0
Dividend per share	–	–	–	–	0.015	0.015	0	0	0	0
Dividend payout ratio	–	–	–	–	28.85	34.97	0	0	0	0
Earnings per share	–	–	–	–	–	0.124469	n/a	n/a	n/a	n/a

Table 7.1 (continued)

1990	*1991*	*1992*	*1993*	*1994*	*1995*	*1996*	*1997*	*1998*	*1999*	*2000*
4.73	0	0	0	22.61	19.68	32.02	37.58	n/a	n/a	n/a
4.91	91.91	105.35	61.13	58.03	84.42	64.04	n/a	n/a	n/a	76
0	0	0	10.14	9.33	10.94	7.21	0	0	0	0
4.56	2.67	5.02	5.76	7.08	4.49	9.36	7.48	n/a	n/a	3.34
0.03	0.02	0.05	0.04	0.05	0.04	0.07	0.05	n/a	n/a	0.02
0.03	0.03	0.05	0.05	0.07	0.07	0.16	0.14	n/a	n/a	0.17
173.72	3,445.41	2,100.66	1,061.28	819.41	1,879.16	684.23	1,119.01	1,142.40	1,394.32	2,277.60
0.03	0.11	0.22	0.28	0.29	0.32	0.73	0.64	n/a	n/a	0.33
1.459599	0.439753	1.670077	5 728239415	4.83520579	0.68134808	0.82607669	0.735008	0.493737	0.586235	2.464481
0.588151	0.332882	1.379544	5.649890319	4.77521419	0.29509773	0.63251248	0.398782	0.437863	0.23155	1.936633
1	1	1	1	1	1	1	1	1	1	1
0	0	0	14,402,000	16,500,000	23,300,000	38,000,000	0	0	0	0
0	0	0	0.0099	0.010236	0.020234	0	0	0	0	
0	0	5.46	3.21	5.83	11.01	5	0	0	0	0
0.028307	0.110536	0.216538	0.280829	0.288213	0.323837	0.726305	0.47154	n/a	n/a	0.327022

Source: Annual Reports of Renong Bhd, 1980–2000

coupon rates varied with the company's acquisition of important development projects, and equity linked bond issues, such as convertible bonds, that offered greater protection to investors. Such a multiple choice of bond issues and securities allowed greater potential for securing investment funds, but also increased the potential dangers to Renong through their overuse. Indeed, this almost brought Renong close to a collapse in 1998. Moreover, it was a particularly serious strategy with overseas bonds that were denominated in foreign currencies and were affected by the exchange rate collapse in September 1997. The only alleviating factors were government support and a steady stream of government contracts for infrastructure and communication projects. Thus, Renong's involvement in the new airport, and road and rail works was used to overcome the difficulties posed by a high ratio of liabilities and a falling exchange rate. Low, stable inflation and interest rates could not halt the decline. However, Renong held valuable assets and, though unable to match debt-assets effectively, was able to sustain growth even after the 1997 crisis.

This profligate financing has to be examined in greater detail. Renong separated bonds from warrants; its bonds were usually guaranteed and taken up by EPF and other prominent institutional investors, such as Syarikat Nominee Bumiputra (28.26 per cent in October 1997), Rashid and Lee Nominees (25.9 per cent), HSBC Nominees (foreign) 8.28 per cent and Citicorp Nominees (foreign) 5.83 per cent. The warrants could be sold to shareholders at a fixed price, increasing the volume of paid-up capital and diluting earnings per share as a result of this enlargement. These warrants often had a maturity span of five years. Renong's warrants were offered as inducements to potential investors to invest on its bonds and were particularly popular in the early 1990s. Renong also held offshore warrants, denominated in foreign currencies and traded offshore, which often carried a maturity of one to three years. These offshore warrants were floated by foreign financial institutions. This practice of raising capital abroad was particularly prevalent between 1994 and 1996. For example, in 1994, offshore bonds and Euro bonds amounted to US$400 million. Domestic bonds in May 1996 accounted for RM500 million.

Besides this issuing of bonds, warrants and shares (right issues), failing subsidiaries were kept afloat by government contracts. In November 1996, Faber faced a crisis and had to abort its plan to raise US$160 million through a bond issue to be purchased by US institutional investors. Yet in January 1997, Faber subsidiary Medi Serve secured a lucrative five-year contract for hospital services. Faber also reduced its failing property interests along with its hotel and banking investments in South Africa, while realigning its interests in the Malaysian government's privatization of medical services. Similarly, Park May, which was seriously affected by the 1997 financial collapse in its property investments, had, by June 1998, secured a contract for the operation of the toll system on Malaysian roads.[7]

Another financial tactic was the swapping of debts, often with the government, through its infrastructural consortium IDC (Infrastructural Development Corporation). Bonds issued by this state agency increased government equity in subsidiaries involved in major projects such as LRT and Malaysian Railways. Besides this swapping of debt, the government also guaranteed debts of important subsidiaries such as UEM. Crucially, in the restructuring of Renong in 1997–8, the government provided core finance, purchased equity and issued bonds to avert the liquidation of Time Engineering, Plus and UEM. By October 1998, Renong was defaulting on its debts and was now unable to subsidize its subsidiaries through its system of loans, a practice that had been pervasive since 1994–6.[8] Faced with liabilities of RM20 billion, it had to promise repayment by 1999, but ultimately it failed to do so. The largest losses were within Prolink, Putra and UEM.

In spite of its huge liabilities in this period, Renong possessed a high credit rating because of the assets it held, and many of these bonds were taken up by the domestic *bumiputra* and state investment agencies. Because of this patronage, Renong's bonds, warrants and other loan stocks revealed only slight fluctuations in returns between 1996 and 2000.

The over-leveraged position of Renong and, in particular, the subsidiary UEM, increased risk but did not deter investors. The optimism of the early 1990s when firms issued complex securities, misguided by the large capital inflows and predictions of high growth, were not eroded even after 1998. The dominance of institutional shareholders, along with the large personal shareholding held by Halim Saad and the substantial inter-firm shareholdings, ensured that Renong did not suffer a reduction in agency costs with their shareholders and bondholders, despite erratic growth. The globalization of Renong and its dramatic expansion both at home and abroad only appeared to justify adding more options to this growing debt. This strategy of growth, based on debt expansion, introduced high risk, particularly in phases of economic recession, but capital-intensive sectoral growth in infrastructure and electronics, assisted by the state, ironically sustained this heady expansion. Briefly, funds derived from internal sources, such as profits and reserves, remained small, and capital transfers from the Malaysian government and bank borrowing, both long and short term, remained high.

Performance

This fluctuating corporate performance amid high growth is further confirmed by the statistics below on Renong's performance between 1981 and 2000 (see Table 7.1). The 1980s were marked by characteristic prudence by the Chinese owners. Reserves of RM7 million in 1981 rose to RM49 million in 1984. However, the recession in 1985 reduced this to 3 million and by 1986 Renong recorded a negative result of –4 million. This negative reserve rose in 1988 to –27 million and by 1989 to –33 million, a deterioration caused more by increased growth rather than just macro-economic constraints.

However, by 1991 these reserves had grown to RM644 million, rising to RM1,196 million in 1993. Between 1998 and 2000, there was another serious deterioration.

Return on capital employed was similarly impressive in the 1980s, despite a dramatic fall in 1986. The gearing ratio also rose slowly in 1988–9, then fluctuated, before rising from 1993 for six years, and then slightly dipping again in 2000. The liquidity ratio, meanwhile, was high in 1981–4 but fell between 1984 and 1991, rose in 1992 and 1993, then fell between 1994 and 1995 and remained low between 1995 and 1999 before slightly rising once more between 1999 and 2000 (see Table 7.1). This fluctuating liquidity ratio was partly a result of investment plans but, more seriously, it revealed a lack of prudence in matching investment strategies with a more cautious appraisal of debt.

Thus, the ratio of turnover against net profits also remained erratic in the 1990s. There were sharp rises in 1996–7, which then dipped into serious negative figures in 1998–9, with a slight recovery in 2000. What is particularly impressive is the ratio of total assets to turnover, which rose dramatically in 1991, contracted between 1993 and 1994, recorded a slight recovery in 1995, and then saw a serious decline in 1996. However, 1997 saw a rise that was maintained through to 2000. This was directly related to Renong's involvement in several prestige programmes, including the new airport and the construction of Cyberjaya.

Overall, Renong experienced a high profitability ratio in 1997, followed by major losses in 1998, after which it achieved a net profit of RM246.1 million in 2000, a profit derived largely from its subsidiary UEM (see Table 7.2).

Table 7.2 Performance of the different segments of Renong, 1994–5

	Turnover (RM million)		*Profit/loss* (RM million)*		*Asset (RM million)*	
	1994	*1995*	*1994*	*1995*	*1994*	*1995*
Financial and advisory services	115.7	127.0	35.1	52.1	244.9	289.6
Expressway and toll	110.9	165.4	40.6	96.4	198.9	1,814.7
Engineering and construction	312.9	561.8	35.7	47.5	880.9	943.7
Telecom and information technology	112.1	186.4	13.4	11.6	504.0	545.4
Oil and gas	175.8	165.3	27.6	7.1	83.9	93.1
Hotels and properties	38.9	44.8	2.4	2.5	815.4	2,849.5
Transportation	17.0	59.7	7.5	8.8	89.3	775.0
Others	95.6	178.9	11.1	(3.2)	66.1	82.0
Corporate and head office	101.0	128.4	58.9	46.6	971.0	603.8
Total	1,079.9	1,617.7	232.3	269.4	3,853.9	7,996.8

Note: * Before tax.

Source: Renong Annual Reports, 1993–6

Renong shares also performed well. Share prices rose in 1993, slightly dipped in 1995, but then rose again in 1996. From February 1997 they were plunging until February 1999, when prices made a slight recovery. This recovery continued into October 2000. Renong share prices often responded to information on government contracts and credit for the group. This saw episodic rises in May 1999 and January 2000. Earnings per share were high in 1995–7, then declined and were positive in 2000. As for dividends, they were paid only in 1984, 1985 and 1994–6, when a huge dividend was distributed. After 1997 no dividends were paid.

Industrial concentration

The concentration of Renong in the Malaysian industrial sector was captured in the interests and activities listed in Tables 7.2 to 7.4 which, in turn, provided them with the appropriate industrial profile to manoeuvre into similar, newly privatized industrial segments abroad. Tables 7.2 to 7.4 capture the individual importance of the subsidiaries and their operations. A major share of profits was derived from financial services (CAH),

Table 7.3 Performance of the different segments of Renong, 1996–7

	Turnover (RM million)		*Profit/loss* (RM million)*		*Asset (RM million)*	
	1997	*1996*	*1997*	*1996*	*1997*	*1996*
Financial and advisory services	276.06	217.49	87.03	64.13	416.37	263.32
Expressway and toll	359.00	295.03	209.73	198.15	1150.23	1084.44
Engineering and construction	1258.13	920.87	69.03	47.98	178.09	322.26
Telecom and information technology	318.34	453.16	(15.20)	24.05	1381.65	395.43
Oil and gas	73.46	56.06	9.29	3.41	147.78	74.79
Hotels and properties	123.90		14.29		163.16	3667.60
Transportation	139.44	107.46	5.68	7.87	3665.64	2214.19
Others	119.49	117.69	48.92	0.46	292.49	348.61
Corporate and head office	121.31	106.52	144.84	19.38	1218.91	182.83
Total	2789.13	2274.28	573.41	365.43	8614.32	8553.47
Turnover of associated companies	(2265.24)	(1953.04)				
Group turnover	523.89	321.24				
Group profit before taxation			573.41	365.43		

Note: * Before tax.

Source: Renong Annual Reports, 1995–8

Table 7.4 Performance of the different segments of Renong, 1998–2000 (RM million)

Product	*1998*	*1999*	*2000*	*Ave 2-yr growth (%)*
Construction	1,096.53	678.43	631.48	–22.52
Expressway/toll	411.57	401.26	489.07	9.69
Hotel and properties	231.46	438.75	326.21	31.95
Oil and gas	157.83	233.62	232.83	23.84
Transportation	143.21	107.54	151.24	7.89
Financial advisory	391.58	365.76	54.80	–45.81
Investment holding	126.42	116.68	45.98	–34.15
Others	92.16	104.65	14.92	–36.10
Telecommunication	548.13	–	–	–
Healthcare	257.92	–	–	–

Source: Renong Bhd, Annual Reports, 1994–2001

engineering and construction (UEM) and road tolls. The profits from interest on loans extended to the associates were substantial.

First, KLIA (Kuala Lumpur International Airport), the new international airport, was opened in June 1998. It was designed, constructed, managed and provided with support services by Kinta Kellas. Second, the National Sports Complex and Games Village for the Commonwealth Games, which opened in July 1998, was built by UEM and Kinta Kellas. Furthermore, Kinta Kellas was project manager for the construction of the Multimedia Super Corridor in Cyberjaya, which was opened in May 1997 and is scheduled for completion in 2011. This consists of residential, recreational and commercial facilities. Through its involvement in these grand projects, Renong's subsidiary in cement captured 13 per cent of the total cement market in Malaysia.

The privatization of Malaysian railways in August 1997 was also transferred to Renong; its subsidiary, Marak Unggul Sdn, managed this with KTMB (Keretaapi Tanah Malaysia Bhd). Other aspects of their success were in the telephone network, in the fibre optics linking the North–South Expressway in Malaysia and in the sub-marine cable system linking the Asia Pacific with the US. The latter was a joint-venture with the American long-distance telecoms carrier MCI. This enabled Renong to expand into the Philippines through involvement in the Manila–Cavite Expressway, which was completed by Kinta Kellas and UEM in December 1994.

Such concentrations were partly financed by the stock market, where a combination of rapid growth and substantial rates of acquisitions appealed to the investor. This increase in concentration, achieved merely through the conversion of existing government monopolies into private monopolies, was also attractive to the stock market. Rights issues were the preferred choice, concentrating ownership further within the existing large shareholders, specifically, the Saad family and institutional investors.

Concentration was inevitable, first, because government policies favoured large powerful firms that possessed the funds for necessary changes in technology. Second, the pressures for the rapid modernization of the industrial sector also favoured these oligopolies. Hence, the privatization programme in Malaysia, particularly in public utilities, nurtured the creation of private oligopolies with private entrepreneurs holding large shares together with government and institutional investors, while retail investors were limited. These oligopolies were highly concentrated in structure with price guarantees, profits ensured and risks hedged by government financial support and with identifiable market shares. Renong had thereby carved out economies of scale, introduced technological changes and achieved increased levels of investments. Debt levels remained inordinately high. There was a small magic minority of *bumiputra* entrepreneurs who, together with a select band of non-Malays, were able to maintain complex investment strategies that eased out competition and rivals through collusive arrangements with politicians. This resulted in institutional weaknesses and a lack of accurate information for investors. Licences, contracts and government subsidies further distorted any allocative efficiency or fairness. Soft loans from state-owned banks assisted such monopolies, while FDI and inflows of direct sources of capital were also channelled to these oligopolies. Tables 7.5a,

Table 7.5a Sources of foreign investment in Malaysia (US$ million)

Country	*1994*	*1995*	*1996*	*1997*
United States	478	721	1,157	853
Japan	674	839	1,843	770
Germany	250	60	59	644
Taiwan	1,097	577	310	479
Singapore	406	404	1,906	456
Korea	156	242	258	241
UK	36	76	152	74
Switzerland	27	755	45	–
Australia	67	56	54	32
India	2	189	25	9
Hong Kong	36	70	5	8
France	19	39	6	1
Finland	65	1	–	–
Others	1,107	355	224	469
Total	4,328	3,657	6,795	4,082
Domestic	4,432	4,690	6,853	5,107
Foreign share	49%	44%	49%	44%

Note: Manufacturing investment only, does not include the upstream oil and gas industry or services.

Exchange rates: 1994 US$1.0 = RM2.62; 1995 US$1.0 = RM2.5; 1996 US$1.0 = RM2.51; 1997 US$1.0 = RM2.81.

Source: Malaysian Industrial Development Authority

Table 7.5b Foreign manufacturing investment by sector (US$ millions)

Sector	*1994*	*1995*	*1996*	*1997*
Food manufacturing	77	48	51	62
Textiles	465	189	137	50
Paper, print	32	39	626	170
Chemicals	429	730	87	260
Petroleum	90	157	1,000	1495
Rubber products	23	31	23	32
Non-metal	307	502	259	41
Basic metal	150	190	244	249
Fabricated metal	94	114	230	215
Electronics	1,842	949	3,681	1,023
Transport	95	185	133	100
Other	724	523	324	386
Total	4,328	3,657	6,795	4,083

Source: Malaysian Industrial Development Authority

Table 7.5c Malaysian investment abroad (US$ millions)

Country	*1994*	*1995*	*1996*	*1997*
United States	239	226	571	832
Singapore	861	969	845	658
Hong Kong	792	505	328	302
Indonesia	38	131	165	220
United Kingdom	193	302	540	200
Australia	245	241	216	175
France	4	7	40	157
China	83	132	204	112
Philippines	85	258	151	103
Others	601	635	1,090	749
Total	3,247	3,464	4,559	3,508

Note: Investment data include equity investment, purchase of real estate abroad and extension of loans to non-residents.

Sources: Cash BOP Reporting System, Bank Negara Malaysia

7.5b and 7.5c show the sources of foreign investment in Malaysia in the specific sectors that Renong captured between 1994 and 1997.

Foreign capital inflows increased between 1990 and 1996, when they amounted to 9 per cent of the GDP in Malaysia. Much of this was portfolio capital flowing into real estate and the stock market, and driving up equity prices, particularly that of corporations with close political connections. Frequently, the share price returns of Renong were related to direct capital inflows (see Tables 7.1, 7.5a and 7.5b).

Concentration was increased through the following interactions. First, there were dense and complex interactions between the holding company and its subsidiaries. Second, the concentrated shareholding of Halim Saad, and his ties to government trusts and financial institutions and to other crony capitalists, increased this power. The prevalence of Saad's cross-holdings increased the concentrated structure of ownership. Ownership of a large block of shares could reduce liquidity as well as affect monitoring. This increased cronyism and corruption, and posed a serious moral hazard in corporate governance. Moreover, the Board of Directors and the Audit Committee were chosen by Saad and his political allies. The manner in which they were chosen and held tenure did not provide transparency or accountability or efficiency. Third, the ownership of shares and stock options by management did motivate growth but increased concentration rather than prudence. Fourth, takeovers and mergers also increased concentration but these were frequently overpriced, with managers being over-ambitious and undisciplined. Fifth, management was so entrenched that it possessed information that facilitated further concentrated incursions into capital-intensive industrial sectors. Sixth, the legal and regulatory constraints on Saad were limited. Political factors were crucial in the growth and any monitoring was warped by this political interference. Seventh, the lack of competition was particularly serious. In a dynamic market with constantly changing products, processes and prices, management should be more disciplined. In Renong, managerial arrogance was encouraged by the lack of a clear organizational structure and responsibility. The role of information as a benchmark for managers to increase or decrease efforts, adapt and meticulously select appropriate risk-averse or risk-prone strategies was absent here.[9] This market was influenced more by takeovers; no evolutionary process of growth was evident or perceptible. This distorts performance, at least in the long run. Only an external shock such as the Asian financial crisis of 1997 could discipline Saad and other managers like him. Ultimately, they were evicted. The entire board was replaced in 2001.

The code of conduct for management defined the firm's long-term strategy, the goal of which was to create a class of *bumiputra* entrepreneurs, accompanied by rapid economic growth and globalization. Any attempts to protect minority shareholders were sacrificed at the altar of unadulterated ambition. Zingales defines corporate governance as a complex set of constraints that shape bargaining over rents generated by the firm and its cronies.[10] Corporate governance not only has efficiency implications but also determines distribution of rents within the firm. The situation in Renong was one of excess investment, aggravated by cross-subsidies by the state or better-performing units within the conglomerate, leading to gross inefficiency. For instance, Kinta Kellas had record losses, particularly after 1998, and yet its expansion continued, its losses being offset by Renong's profits in other sectors. Such misallocation of resources could be aggravated by globalization into unknown markets. Above all, the alliances with the state reinforced managerial power, a power not always used in the interests of minority shareholders or institutional investors.[11]

Concentration in ownership and management

There were critical changes in ownership between the 1980s and the 1990s. The management in the 1990s was comprised of professional groups, a transition from the Chinese merchants and Chinese professionals who had dominated this corporation in the 1980s. Halim Saad (an accountant) was appointed director in May 1990, along with Zakhir Siddique Sidek (lawyer and accountant), Ramli Mohammed (engineer), Dr Chan (medical doctor) and Lee Siew Choong (lawyer). The Audit Committee was packed with people from the same group. Indeed, the only omission was Halim Saad. This change in ownership and management coincided with influential changes in industrial specialization, as well as in state business relations. The pre-1991 dominance of Chinese and Arab shareholders, owners and managers was replaced by the family dominance of Halim Saad and his wife, and by government and *bumiputra* institutional investors.

In 1985, the substantial shareholding ownership was distributed between Arab–Malaysian Nominees, with 31.02 per cent; Kuwait Asia Bank Nominees with 10.6 per cent; Ng Song Choon Enterprise, replacing the Yap Group, with 11.79 per cent; and the remainder was held by individual Chinese and commercial banks. Retail shareholding only absorbed less than 19 per cent.[12] This continued into 1989. In 1990, the Kuwait investors left, while the holdings of the Arab–Malaysia Nominees fell to 1.45 per cent and those of the Ng Song Choon Group declined to 1.82 per cent. There was now a rise in *bumiputra* shareholders. This also coincided with the emergence of an important stake held by Renong within companies affiliated to UMNO.[13] Renong acquired 100 per cent equity in Fleet Group, 100 per cent equity in Hatibudi Nominees and 2 per cent in UEM, together with 12 million convertible unsecured loan stocks in UEM. This marked a turning point for Renong. It was moving into major state infrastructural projects; Halim and his wife were appointed directors on the board in October 1990. The complex interlocking shareholding of Renong with former UMNO companies and with Malaysian investment groups increased the corporation's profile in state development. Foreign banking cliques were absorbing just tiny stakes. It was only in October 1997 that HSBC, DBS and Chung Khiaw Bank acquired substantial stakes. Earlier in the 1990s, Rashid Hussein Nominees had taken 2.58 per cent and Syarikat Nominee Bumiputra 12 per cent. In June 1991, Halim Saad held only 15.07 per cent, yet by October 1997, he and his nominee firms, including Ikral Capital, held a direct holding of 21.73 per cent. This interlocking shareholding between Renong and other subsidiaries was intensifying by February 1991 when it had bought a 31 per cent stake in UEM and 43 per cent in Sistem Television Malaysia, and had become part of KLOFFE, a derivatives consortium on the KLSE.[14]

Halim Saad had direct and indirect holdings (through nominee firms) in three companies in the Renong Group. Indirectly, he held 60.02 per cent of total shares in Faber Bhd.[15] In Renong, he indirectly held a 21.73 per cent stake through nominee companies. He was also a substantial shareholder in, and director of, both Hanuma and Peri Bakti.[16] He thereby emerged as the single largest shareholder of Renong. In addition, he possessed indirect holdings in Park May (50.06 per cent), in Renong's associated companies and Fleet Group (100 per cent), Jaguh Mutiara (100 per cent), Cantuman Bahagia (100 per cent) and Hatibudi Nominees (100 per cent).[17] Saad's indirect holdings in Time Engineering were 55 per cent, held through Hatibudi Nominees and EPE Power. In Crest Petroleum, he had 38.56 per cent through Renong and 38.56 per cent indirectly through Ikral Capital Sdn. In Commerce Asset Holding, he held 19 per cent through Fleet Group Sdn, and in Southern Steel and EPE he had a 55 per cent stake held through Time Engineering. In UEM, Saad indirectly owned 37.09 per cent through Renong, while Renong itself owned 6.4 per cent directly and held a further 30.69 per cent indirectly.[19] His indirect interests in UEM were also through Fleet Group (13.51 per cent), and his private company Cantuman Bahagia Sdn Bhd, a wholly owned subsidiary of Fleet Group, was, in turn, a subsidiary of Renong. Halim held a 100 per cent stake in Plus, 62.4 per cent in Kinta Kellas, 53.9 per cent in CIMA, 23.9 per cent in Intria, 33 per cent in Ho Hup Construction, 5.2 per cent in MetaCorp and 7.2 per cent in ACP Industries.[20] He indirectly held 62.4 per cent in Propel, a subsidiary of Kinta Kellas.[21] Ultimately, Saad's stakes in Renong made him the largest single shareholder, while the institutional investor EPF only held 5.19 per cent. Besides these links, he enjoyed crucial political and personal ties to Prime Minister Mahatir, the former Finance Minister Daim Zaunuddin and former Deputy Prime Minister Anwar Ibrahim. His meteoric rise and fall within two decades is charted below.

Halim Saad rose through UMNO in the early 1980s, when he was manager of Peremba, a private firm linked to UMNO. His role was to manage corporations for the party and this often involved the rescue of debt-ridden sections, such as Fleet Holdings and the construction firm UEM. He was also director of several other companies linked to UMNO. In 1984, he was appointed director of Daim's business. In 1988, he left UMNO's and Daim's firms, having already acquired many of UMNO's companies.[22] His rise revealed the importance of connections to Daim and to UMNO's business interests. It was through Hatibudi Nominees that he came to control a disparate group of companies, ranging from manufacturing, construction and property development to media and telecommunications.

His ties with Quek Leng Chan in the 1990s were through two firms: Hume Industries and Southern Steel, both of which he sold to Quek. He was also a non-executive director on many of the firms in the Hong Leong Group. His links to government should now be clear. He also had access to support from foreign multinationals. The N–S Highway Project involved Mitsui, Dragages et Traveaux Publics France and Taylor Woodrow UK in 1986–7.

The corporation was highly concentrated, with well-established monopolies supported by the state. The various firms in the group did not pursue rationalization of capacity because of the absence of a competitive spur. When faced with economic difficulties it only restructured, splitting into more diverse subsidiaries in diverse sectors and diverse regions abroad. This movement, associated with an intense wave of merger activity, affected a wide range of investments in Malaysia during the 1990s. Bloated through the accumulation of all the major privatization projects in the 1990s, Renong faced mixed performance and its inefficiency persisted. But only the Asian financial crisis of 1997 exposed its weaknesses and led to the exit of Saad from Renong in 2001. The group was restructured, Renong was delisted and UEM World succeeded as the parent company in 2003.

Globalization

It was the privatization of SOEs throughout Asia in the 1990s, along with the breakdown of the Soviet Union, and the increased involvement of the World Bank, the IMF and ADB in this industrial transformation, that provided Renong with the opportunities for global growth. This led to its involvement in infrastructural projects in Vietnam, such as the creation of Noi Bai industrial zone, an engineering concession managed by Kinta Kellas. Kinta Kellas also built and managed the Hanoi Expressway, an airport and some factories.

Some of these overseas projects helped rescue failing companies in the Renong Group. For instance, Ho Hup was facing difficulties in 1997–8 but saw a revival of its fortunes through its involvement in waste-management projects in Shanghai. In contrast, Renong's property diversification into South Africa, through Faber, failed but the subsidiary was saved by successes in Malaysia and Singapore. Some indication of Renong's global reach is given by the fact that its healthcare group operated in Brunei, Samoa, Iraq, Singapore, the Philippines, Kenya, Papua New Guinea, North Korea, Macau, Sri Lanka and South Africa. It distributed medical products and equipment for laboratories.

From 1995, there were 16 infrastructural projects in India that were managed by a consortium of 12 Malaysian firms led by Renong. For instance, the Ahmedabad Vadodara Expressway in Gujarat was initiated in 1996. Similarly, Crest, Renong's subsidiary, held contracts for offshore petroleum exploration in Indonesia, Vietnam, Thailand and China in 1997–8. Petronas assisted Crest in this sector. Renong's exploration and production of petroleum in Central Sumatra and Uzbekistan were declining by the end of 1997, owing to competition from BP. Many of these overseas investments in South Africa, the Philippines, Indonesia, Uzbekistan, Vietnam and New Zealand were reduced after 1997. These global ventures often proved premature and ill-thought out. Renong was exposed by its lack of specialist knowledge and R&D, and was unable to sustain contracts with the state in these volatile and changing overseas environments. Frequently, its moves overseas were through a takeover. For instance, in 1998, Renong secured a contract to provide highway network services in the UK through its acquisition of OPUS

(New Zealand), a road maintenance company which already held 80 per cent of the market share in infrastructure in New Zealand.

Renong was also involved in World Bank infrastructural projects in Papua New Guinea, Tonga, Samoa and the Maldives. In July 1996, a joint-venture with Bank Rakyat Indonesia created a venture-capital group to invest in securities and development projects in Indonesia. This creation of a structure of myriad global projects, centred on specialist subsidiaries in the group, began to unravel in the wake of the 1997 crisis. Global ambitions had raised highly risky financial joint-ventures and failure now confronted Renong.

The financial crisis and corporate restructuring

The 1997 financial crisis produced a landslide of defaulted payments within the major subsidiaries of Renong. In 1999, Renong revealed a debt of RM20 billion (US$5.3 billion) and was unable to meet interest payments. Halim Saad, the vice-chairman, owed RM2.4 billion (US$633 million). Unable to repay this, he sought deferment. He stepped down from the board of UEM in July 2000 and was sacked from Renong in October 2000. In March 1999, Park May defaulted on payment of principal and interest on a loan of RM135.6 million. To avert total collapse, they sold land to sustain the initial debt payments.[23] This was followed by the motor transport firm Putra defaulting on a syndicated loan of RM44.6 million in September 1999. The government then assisted in restructuring loan repayments.[24] In December 2001, the government aided Putra with a loan of RM1,032 million. The Faber Group faced a similar predicament in September 1999. Renong had sold KLOFFE in December 1998 for RM27 million to KLSE and in June 1999 it sold major equity in Teras Teknologi, a hi-tech subsidiary, for RM11 million.[25]

This debt overhang often proved difficult for certain subsidiaries. Time Dotcom, a subsidiary of Time Engineering, sold its shares to Khazanah Nasional, a state investment agency, for a 30 per cent increase in paid-up capital. Khazanah assisted in the raising of a total of RM2.1 million.[26] Time Dotcom also entered into a partnership with Andersen Consulting to enhance customer services and a joint-venture with telecoms partners for voice and global data services. Time Internet Services and Time Cel dominated mobile phone services and technology. This push into technology was part of a joint-venture with new electronics groups. They maintained a policy of share swapping and financial restructuring in order to maintain rapid expansion in capital-intensive sectors. The second phase of restructuring involved assistance from Danaharta, the government financial restructuring agency. In March 1999, Danaharta assisted Prolink in the restructuring of its NPLs, which were worth RM785.778 million.[27] The government also provided direct loans, secured on assets.[28]

This restructuring also involved the sale of hotels in Malaysia, Vietnam and South Africa, and it delayed property projects in Johor, Malaysia. In addition, Renong reduced investments in South Africa, the Philippines,

Indonesia, Uzbekistan, Vietnam and New Zealand. This divestment and restructuring reduced some of the interlocking ownership and operational management that existed between the subsidiaries in the group.

However, there were inherent difficulties in the rescue of many of these firms. First, the issuing of new capital was hampered by the slump in the stock market. Moreover, the sale of assets was difficult, as was bank borrowing. Hence, a feasible strategy was the issuing of bonds and warrants to state investment trusts. The disposal of subsidiaries, such as Commercial Asset Holding Bhd (CAHB), was to reduce the unsustainable gearing level in Renong.[29] This reduction of stake in CAHB followed the merger of Bank Bumiputra Malaysia and the Bank of Commerce.[30] The Bank of Commerce had increased its capital from RM1 billion to RM2 billion in 1997, before acquiring MBF in 1998. This type of recapitalization and acquisition was a common tactic in Renong's restructuring programme.

Despite the seriousness of the financial crisis, Renong went ahead in 1998 with the Malaysia–Singapore Second Crossing, the North–South Expressway, the Central Link, the Light Rail Transit System and the Cyberjaya projects. This was facilitated by the substantial anticipated revenue yields, along with guarantees from the government for fund raising in domestic and foreign capital markets. One serious predicament here was how to reassure foreign investors of Renong's viability and survival as the Malaysian state's main project manager. It was increasingly clear that Renong should be delisted and be substituted by UEM, the main infrastructural firm with the potential for stable growth. In September 2001, UEM was acquired by the state for RM3.8 billion (US$1 billion). The closure of Renong dragged on until March 2003, when UEM World was incorporated as a parent holding company and then listed in September 2003. The new shareholders were Khazanah Nasional and its subsidiary Syarikat Danasaham, which held 63.6 per cent of equity, with UEM holding 25.92 per cent. The rest was held by HSBC and foreign institutional shareholders.[31] UEM World had six subsidiaries: UEM Builders, which focused on engineering and construction; Kinta Kellas, a project management firm; Pharmaniaga, a health-care group; UEM Environment; UEM Land; and Cement Industries Malaysia (see Figure 7.2). UEM World continued its joint-ventures in infrastructure projects in South Africa, the United Kingdom, New Zealand, the Philippines, India, Central Asia and the Middle East. In Central Asia, the funds and expertise came from the World Bank. In the United Kingdom, it brought equity and partnership in Thames Water, Wessex Water and Yorkshire Water.[32]

It was now imperative for the corporation to adopt improved corporate governance if it was to attract foreign investments, as well as succeed in its overseas initiatives. Three independent non-executive directors were appointed. One was a member of Petronas, the petroleum group which bore the financial burden of restructuring these large, failing corporations after the crisis. The appointment of this member was to create greater transparency in finance.

- 51.7% **UEM Builders Berhad***
  Engineering and construction
  - 100% UEM Construction
  - 100% PATI Sdn Bhd
  - 100% Projek Penyelenggaraan Lebuhraya Berhad
  - 100% Intria Blna Sdn Bhd
  - 100% Penang Bridge Sdn Bhd
  - 100% UE Development India Pvt Ltd
  - 33% Castain Group plc
- 62.37% **Kinta Kellas Public Limited Company***
  Project management
  - 100% Pengurusan Lebuhraya Berhad
  - 100% Pengurusan LRT Sdn Bhd
  - 100% OPUS International Consultations Limited
  - 27% Africon Engineering International (Ply) Ltd
- 30.34% **Pharmaniaga Berhad***
  Healthcare
  - 100% Pharmanlaga Manufacturing Berhad
  - 100% Pharmanlaga Logistics Sdn Berhad
  - 100% SAfire Pharmanlaga (M) Sdn Berhad
  - 100% Pharmanlaga Solution Sdn Berhad
  - 100% Pharmanlaga Marketing Sdn Berhad
  - 100% Pharmanlaga Diafnotics Sdn Berhad
  - 100% Pharmanlaga Blomedical Sdn Berhad
- 100% **UEM Environment Sdn Bhd**
  Environment services
  - 100% Kualiti Alam Sdn Bhd
  - 100% Opti Arena Sdn Bhd
  - 50% E-Idaman Sdn Bhd
  - 50% Environment Idaman Sdn Bhd
- 100% **UEM Environment Sdn Bhd**
  Property
  - 64% Bandor Nusajaya Development Sdn Bhd
  - 100% Mahisa Sdn Bhd
  - 25% Setia Harumon Sdn Bhd
- 53.97% **UEM Environment Sdn Bhd**
  Cement manufacturing
  - 100% Negeri Sembllan Cement Industries Sdn Bhd
  - 100% Pemasaran Simen Negara Sdn Bhd

Figure 7.2 UEM world corporate structure, 31 March 2005

Conclusion

It might be thought that this case study of Renong fits in with Mushtaq Khan and Jomo's model that rents can contribute to economic growth.[33] Their hypothesis is that Malaysia is a developmental state that creates an institutional framework conducive to this so-called 'productive' use of rents. Their model emphasizes that in a developmental state, rent-seekers who exploit opportunities for rapid industrial change and innovation are successful primarily due to these crucial economic rents provided by the collusive state. But their analysis is ahistorical. What is ignored is that Malaysia's and Renong's growth was occurring in a decade of phenomenal infrastructural transformation both at home and in the rest of Southeast Asia.

This burgeoning growth was achieved through diverse economic opportunities and diverse sources of finance, both domestic and foreign. Moreover, the growth was through the creation of monopolies. The assembling of this diversified conglomerate proved unwieldy and inefficient. Only continuing state projects and globalization sustained the group. Monopoly rents cannot be sustained indefinitely. It is this lack of an historical, evolutionary, linear explanation that makes Khan and Jomo's hypothesis unsustainable.

The individual case studies used to support their hypothesis are based on macro-economic detail but only specific micro-economic knowledge, in particular that of corporations and corporate governance issues, can illuminate and clarify the validity of their arguments. The complexities underlying the growth of these large conglomerates that survive on these so-called 'productive rents' has to be taken into account. They are vulnerable to global economic changes, to the regulatory constraints of GATT and the WTO and, crucially, to changing domestic economic demands and competition.

Their analysis of institutions is also limited. The developmental state is not a monolithic institution. It has to confront changing institutional pressures on the state: the corporate economy, capital markets and differing product markets and variant forms of entrepreneurship. Investments are complex. Speculative capital nurtured by the security of crony capitalism carries its own risks, particularly in a highly competitive global economy. In their haste to argue that in some cases rents can be productive, Khan and Jomo ignore issues of corporate governance. The long-term destructive potential of rents cannot be disguised as promoting sustainable economic growth, even in the short term. The future calamities caged in such growth have been unravelled by this detailed corporate case study of Renong. Corporate growth in Indonesia (as shown in Chapter 2) and Thailand and the Philippines (Chapters 11 and 12) also reveal this calamitous use of rents.

8 The emergence and development of Singapore as a regional/international financial centre

Can Singapore develop into a regional financial centre, embedding itself as the core in an Asia-Pacific version of the OECD? In the three decades after independence in 1965, Singapore did move from a concentration on trade and commercial activity to an active money and capital market, an increasingly sophisticated stock market linking gold, commodity, capital and foreign exchange transactions of Asian markets with markets in Australia, Europe and the US. If using different categories of financial transactions to identify this emerging international financial centre of Singapore, the primary achievement would be in commercial banking and, in particular, the regional presence of the DBS, absorbing majority stakes in Thai and Indonesian banks and its role as banker for the Singapore government in China, the US, and South and Southeast Asia. Important, too, here is the number of international banks operating in Singapore with the rise in foreign financial assets and the utilization of the city-state as a base for investment projects in Southeast Asia. The range and scope of these financial strategies is important for innovations in investment strategies and modes of entry into these economies in an era of rapid economic growth in the 1980s and 1990s.

Another critical institution to this transition to an international financial centre is the growth of the stock market. Did Singapore attract listings from countries other than Malaysia? Were Singapore's domestic securities and money markets sufficiently developed? Crucial here are the capital flows into Singapore, partly assisting the expansion of international trade and investment in the region, but also diversified into financial institutions providing a package of short-term, as well as long-term credit, access to equities, derivatives and innovative financial products.

Does Singapore fit into a model of an International Financial Centre, or is it just an elaborate, grander version of its historical role as international commercial entrepôt? In order to define this evolutionary position of Singapore we need to appraise the success of its dominant financial institutions: the stock market, the derivatives and financial futures market, the money market, the foreign exchange market, the Asian Dollar Market (ADM) and commercial banking. The role of the state in the development or stagnation of these separate institutions is important, as well as trends towards the creation of financial stability through regional cooperation, as in the Chiangmai initiative of 1999. The changing institutional and regulatory environment since the 1997 crisis imposes new challenges to a city-state obsessed with national over regional aims, stability over innovation.

The Singapore stock market

The Singapore stock market was operated jointly with Malaysia until 1973, and until 1989, Malaysian companies were listed on both stock exchanges. Later, Malaysian and international shares were traded through electronic trading in the CLOB, which was closed after 1998. The growth is gradual; the increase in market capitalization is high, though dominated by a small number of enterprises of the state or statutory boards. Singapore, therefore, has large companies but fewer than those listed in Malaysia. The majority of the shares in these SOEs were held by one of the four government holding companies.

At the close of 1999, there were 370 companies listed on the stock market with total market capitalization of S$434 billion, 3.4 times the GDP for that year. Of this market capitalization, 27 per cent is held by one single government holding company, Temasek Holdings.[1] This domination by the state has persisted from the 1970s. The few privatizations undertaken since 1987 have helped to stimulate trading. This was particularly keen in 1993 with the listing of SingTel. Thus, market capitalization leapt from US$48.8 billion to US$132.7 billion between 1992 and 1993.[2] Between 1990 and 1994, trading value had risen from US$20.2 billion to US$81.0 billion. Foreign counters accounted for 20 per cent of the total market capitalization in 1988–92.[3] In addition, there was secondary listing of foreign stocks denominated in foreign currencies.

The conservative growth in Singapore's equity market is clear from Tables 9.5 and 9.6 in Chapter 9. The growth, though more gradual than that of its neighbours, Malaysia, Thailand and Indonesia, was less volatile. It faced two serious blows: the first in 1985 when the Singapore Stock Exchange faced a case of fraud committed by the Pan Electric Group of 13 firms; the second in 1987 when the world stock market crash caused shares in Singapore to plunge further. But recovery was swift. The high growth between 1993 and 1994 dipped in 1994–5, but regained its buoyancy in 1995–6 because of continuing privatization with IPO issues and secondary flotations. Growth is still limited and this retarded growth of the stock market is further explained by abundant budget surpluses of the government, which could be channelled to these state and semi-state listed corporations, and their overall dependence on bank finance and own retained profits. These corporations only occasionally resort to the use of bonds.

The stock market has listed equity warrants, convertibles and other hybrid products, but again trading is limited, the market is small and is not exploited by large corporations such as Keppel and Sembawang. Derivative options traded in the offshore market are often those relating to banks, hotels and property, all three highly lucrative products. Many of these covered warrants can be traded only by financial institutions or reputable individuals. This has discouraged the growth of secondary listing in Singapore, unlike Hong Kong where trading in derivatives is high and is frequently used to hedge risks. The Monetary Authority of Singapore (MAS) has discouraged the use of domestic derivatives while they can be exploited in the offshore market. This constraint on the domestic market and the lack of integration between this and the offshore market prevails throughout this period and explains slow growth in any transition to an international financial centre.

The Singapore government's focus was always on scrutiny, without providing a clear institutional framework on regulating the derivative market; it increased controls but often without supervising them. This explains the Barings scandal of February 1995.[4] This is not surprising since domestic speculative activity is strictly controlled, while the auditing and supervision of the activities of brokers in offshore markets is fairly lax. In addition, the focus was often on some listed derivatives and thus overlooked fraudulent overtrading in Singapore's International Monetary Exchange in Nikkei and Euroyen futures, resulting in massive losses for Barings.

Another explanation for such distortions is in the clear historical biases within Singapore's derivatives growth. Singapore is an established centre for the trading of spot, forward and swap contracts on energy because of its entrepôt and shipping history and as the world's largest fuel oil bunker in the contemporary period. Its reputation is in oil-refining and processing, and hence its derivatives market in energy, is particularly strong. By the 1980s Singapore ranked third as a trading centre for over-the-counter energy products, after London and New York. Though limited in scope in terms of other commodity options, Singapore's reputation in energy futures has grown in tandem with growth in industrialization, shipping and the accelerated economic changes in Southeast Asia since 1980.

Again, this historical bias has resulted in Singapore attracting gold and currency brokers and traders. Since 1970 Singapore has consistently featured as the largest importer of gold in Southeast Asia, though illicit gold smuggling into Vietnam and Bangkok may cast a different perspective on this.[5] However, Singapore still remains an important gold distribution centre.

Another crucial source for this transition to an International Financial Centre is derived from its investment strategy from the mid-1980s, which focused on the creation of a growth triangle in Riau, Batam and Johor, similar to Hong Kong's position in relation to Special Economic Zones on China's coastal areas. Singapore indulged in global ambitions in China and California, with joint state and private corporations funding and acquiring niches in infrastructure, food, telecoms and finance. In this global expansion, it was the interaction of the Singapore state with the Chinese diaspora in Southeast Asia that helped in acting as a conduit for Chinese capital flight from Indonesia, even Malaysia, as well as acting as a clearing house for investors from the US and Europe. Singapore, though not an important base for international corporations, did attract these investment houses because of its location, its good corporate governance and political stability. In 1994 portfolio capital flows into Singapore accounted for only 3 per cent of total capital investment, further evidence of such direct interactions between the state, Western and Chinese capital.[6] Between 1989 and 1994, Singapore had also witnessed an impressive increase in financial operations and a higher incidence of Western banks relocating themselves from Hong Kong to tap into Asian economic growth. Singapore also experienced a spillover from Japanese financial liberalization, when Japan concentrated on long-term financing, especially in China, while Singapore's advantage was in short- to medium-term financing. The section on commercial banking in Singapore and the emergence of DBS as a global investor, reveals this specialization (see pp. 199–207). Though in the 1990s, SIMEX, which had concentrated on interest rates, currencies and stock indices, did attempt to develop futures on long-term debt instruments, regional currencies and regional stock indices.

There is a complication here. Singapore's monitoring of domestic firms is intense, but because of the secrecy surrounding the distribution of loans or deposits made through the offshore market, and even though the monetary authorities are aware of the sources and destination of capital flow, it does not have the regulatory infrastructure to monitor the geographical distribution of the operations of foreign firms listed on the Singapore stock exchange. Thus, Sinar Mas, the Indonesian conglomerate, listed APP in Singapore as a free-standing company, involved in paper production in China. Yet it had multiple holding companies, conducting labyrinthine financial deals. Only the New York Stock Exchange suspected fraud and forced its delisting in April 1999.[7] Only then was Singapore alerted to this financial chaos. Though APP was able to avoid Indonesian capital restrictions by using networks, and was favoured by the over-optimistic analysis by Western investment banks, it was ultimately the failure of the Singapore and China governments that allowed APP to weave such an expansion into a capital-intensive industry in China. Too much deliberate planning by the state in Singapore overlooks the scandalous developments in certain foreign enterprises. This disjuncture in corporate governance and social responsibility between domestic and foreign enterprises is a continuous feature of Singapore's regulation and supervision. The 1997 crisis has alerted it to this gap.

Internationalization of the Singapore dollar: prospects or panic?

Singapore escaped the harsh shocks of 1997; it endured a depreciation in the Singapore dollar of 15 per cent in July–December 1997, though the dollar deteriorated further in 1998 because of the Indonesian connection, when it suffered a 5 per cent depreciation in January 1998. MAS intervened in the foreign exchange market with reserves falling by US$3 billion in January.

However, this intervention was not sufficient because the offshore market in London and New York accounted for two-thirds the size of the onshore market, and speculators took advantage, causing the differential in offshore and onshore interest rates to widen to 13 per cent. Ironically, the imposition of capital controls by Malaysia helped steady the Singapore dollar's market stability against the US dollar. In short, MAS pursued formal and informal controls to limit speculation, assisted by the rapid recovery of the Singapore economy by 1998.

In the light of these developments, what prospects are there for the transition to a global financial base? In April 1998, Singapore accounted for 7 per cent of global foreign exchange activity, with the average daily foreign exchange turnover of US$139 billion.[8] Yet trade in the Singapore dollar was equal to only 13 per cent of this. This is a direct result of MAS limiting activities in the Singapore dollar. Non-residents are only allowed loans, currency swaps, securities and repurchase agreements to the value of S$5 million. They also need permission from MAS to deal in Singapore dollar options. This is to prevent speculation, but it also hampers the growth of the currency and limits innovation in currency options. Before 1998, Singapore's currency market was less active than even Malaysia.

A few random statistics will help disclose the immaturity of Singapore's capital market. The financial sector accounted for 10–12 per cent of GDP between 1993 and 2000. Stocks, futures and commodity brokering contributed 9 per cent of assets in the financial sector, while banking accounted for 46 per cent of output in the financial sector, insurance added 18.5 per cent and investment 3.8 per cent. Though foreign assets in finance rose from 24 per cent in 1960 to 26 per cent in 1990, foreign banks' share of total banking profits fell from 49 per cent in 1974 to 28 per cent in 1995.[9] In 1998 there were 145 foreign banks, 58 merchant banks and 12 finance companies. The four local banking groups, DBS, Overseas Union Bank (OUB), United Overseas Bank (UOB) and OCBC dominated the financial sector. These figures provide a dismal perspective on Singapore's chances to evolve into an International Financial Centre, challenging Hong Kong and Tokyo. While the creation of an ADM in 1968, a non-resident gold market in 1969 and an Asian dollar bond market in 1971 provided advantages in acting as a collection point for Asian dollar deposits, the over-regulated market weakens growth and innovation. Singapore, despite being ranked fourth in foreign exchange transactions behind London, New York and Tokyo, possesses an attenuated secondary market in the currency trade.[10]

The strict regulation by MAS has meant that foreign exchange market deals are monopolized by the US dollar. The volume of transactions of the Singapore dollar against the US dollar remains small. Cross-country currency trading of yen, Deutschmarks and sterling became large, with the creation of SIMEX as a major futures and options base in 1984. By 1993 there were 16 futures and options contracts, which included currency and interest rate futures. The US dollar has dominated currency transactions in the

Asia-Pacific economy. In 2000, the US dollar was dominant, the Singapore dollar was insignificant. The bulk of the transactions are in US dollars, though the yen has increased in circulation since the 1980s. Since 1987, yen-denominated external debt for Thailand has exceeded that of debt nominated in US dollars. The core analysis here is, can Singapore evolve into a major money market? Does the island state possess the conditions for the creation of an international currency and the institutions to assist such a dramatic transition?

Liberalization of the financial system has not released impressive growth. In July 1973, the Singapore dollar was floated. In August 1973, gold dealing was liberalized. In June 1978 exchange controls were relaxed and in July 1995 the cartel system for fixing interest rates was abolished, and despite Singapore emerging as an important funding centre for Southeast Asia and China, the currency remains limited in circulation. The liberalization in December 2000 and the lifting of restrictions on foreigners borrowing dollars and investing in dollar assets may stimulate growth in the future. Singapore was also forced in 1998 into disclosures on the distribution of loans and deposits made in the offshore market. This could lead to greater integration between the domestic and offshore markets, and offshore interests could be allowed access to domestic capital markets and to the Singapore dollar. This would increase international trade, reduce costs for Singapore multinationals investing abroad, increase markets in swaps and derivatives, and develop a market in Singapore dollar debt both in securities and bond issues.

Parallel to these developments have been major initiatives for achieving monetary integration in Asia to protect the Southeast Asian currencies from the fluctuations in the US dollar and the yen. One idea was the creation of a basket of currencies that could offer protection not only from outside currencies but also from each others' volatilities. Second, there was intra-bloc currency flotation. The third aim was to anchor regional currencies against the US dollar and seek convergence through a single Asian currency.

There has been a flurry of activity since March 1999 in Chiangmai, Kobe in January 2001 and again in Chiangmai in May 2001, pressing for monitoring to limit exchange rate fluctuations. Singapore is central to this, despite suspicions surrounding her intentions. There are formidable obstacles to currency integration. First, there is little similarity in economic structures and policies to create compatibility. Monetary integration would have to overcome the poor–rich dichotomy before any correlation in inflation rates, interest rates, stock prices, unemployment levels, budget deficits and, even, types of business cycles, can be achieved. The 1997 crisis revealed the huge disparities in economic fundamentals and the diversity in political, bureaucratic and economic institutions. Although individual Southeast Asian economies were duplicating manufacturing and trade items and competing with each other, there was insufficient economic cooperation. There is a protective streak in all. Singapore is conservative in all respects. To become global, it needs to shed its protective culture, adapt to new risks, absorb new innovative financial products, and gear towards regional strategies. Second, differences in historical, institutional developments are embedded and create difficulties in integration. The most stark contrast is in the banking developments in Singapore compared to Indonesia and Thailand.

Banking: prudent growth and globalization

Four main banks have dominated the commercial banking and finance sector in Singapore since the 1960s: DBS, OUB, OCBC and UOB. A fifth group, Keppel Tat Lee, emerged in the 1990s. Western banks, which had been active in international trade and finance until the mid-1960s, were threatened by the emergence of powerful Chinese banking cliques formed through the merger of smaller banks catering to the various Chinese dialect groups in Singapore. The OCBC, the only pre-war bank to survive, began operations in 1949. Chung Khiaw Bank of the Aw Boon Haw family was established in 1947 and absorbed by the UOB Group in 1971, one of the four major banking cliques in Singapore. The mergers and acquisitions of the 1970s and 1980s created further financial concentrations. OCBC, for example, acquired Four Seas Communications Bank and the Bank of Singapore.

UOB was the most active in its take-over strategy. Besides the take-over of Chung Khiaw Bank in 1971, Far Eastern Bank in 1984, and the Industrial and Commercial Bank in 1987, UOB possessed a joint-venture bank in Indonesia from 1990. UOB was the second largest banking group. DBS was the largest. OUB was the only Teochew banking group; the others were Hokkien. UOB absorbed Asia Commercial Bank in 1983 and International Bank of Singapore in 1984. The fourth group, the DBS, was formed in 1968, on absorbing the Economic Development Bank. Only Tat Lee Bank remained independent, concentrating on Singapore and Indonesia.

The concentration of financial activities in the four groups was intensified through the incorporation and assimilation of finance companies within them. The three main financial groups – OCBC, UOB and Keppel – emerged through mergers between 1976 and 1988. The inclusion of finance companies into the large banking groups increased the oligopolistic pattern of finance in Singapore. In 1989, there were 13 bank-affiliated finance companies in a total of 28 finance firms.

Between 1965 and 1988, the number of independent finance companies had declined from 96 to 31. Finance companies had grown in the 1950s and 1960s in consumer finance-housing mortgages and hire purchase loans. They were also involved in business finance, in lease finance, investments in real estate and stock markets. There were more legal restraints on consumer finance than on business finance.

It would be useful here to analyse in detail the growth of DBS both from the perspective of its global activities from the 1980s and particularly after 1997, acquiring distressed banks, finance houses and securities firms in Thailand and Indonesia as well as entering into joint-ventures with foreign banks in the US, India, Sri Lanka, China and the Philippines. Increasingly the banking cliques, DBS, UOB, OUB and OCBC, moved from commercial banking to a diversified financial structure, including merchant banking, securities and insurance. The increased flow of international funds from Japan, the Middle East, the US and Europe led to increased interaction with stock markets, and with regional and global financial institutions.

DBS was incorporated in 1968 with more than 40 per cent equity held by the state. A real-estate company was formed in 1969, followed by a merchant bank and finance subsidiary in 1970, and a securities firm in 1986. DBS had access to state and offshore funds, and its main aims were to finance manufacturing, undertake urban renewal programmes and promote tourism. From the early 1970s, DBS engaged in raising capital through the ADM and Asian Bond Market (ABM), holding critical joint-ventures with Japanese and American finance houses. Overall, in the early 1980s it was responsible for a third of the issue in the ADM and ABM.

The regional expansion by DBS was achieved through the creation of branches in Asia, as well as in the US and Europe, while the establishment of joint-venture banks through equity holdings and mergers with domestic banks in Indonesia, Thailand and the Philippines gained pace in the 1990s. In 1977, the first overseas branch of DBS was opened in Tokyo and by 1986 there were 589 correspondent networks in 72 countries. The emphasis was on financing manufacturing. In Singapore, a third of DBS's loans in the 1970s and 1980s were for manufacturing. DBS engaged in offshore banking; in February 1985, negotiable certificates of deposits to the value of 3 billion yen were issued with Daiwa in Singapore. DBS was also active in Japan's financial markets by the middle of 1985 and in 1986 another 4.85 billion yen were raised.[11] DBS also established relations with American merchant banks operating in Tokyo. In absorbing the National Discount Company in 1986, DBS became a major dealer in underwriting issues of government bonds and treasury bills.

This involvement in the Asian market, dealing in debt securities, bonds and undertaking facilities in the 1980s, was crucial in establishing the bank as a major participant in the yen bloc.[12] This brisk trade accelerated in the 1990s. DBS had an 11-year link with Daiwa Securities, Sumitomo Bank and Nomura Merchant Bank from 1972, which was crucial for raising funds for industrial finance in Southeast Asia. This enabled DBS to become the first non-Japanese bank to issue yen certificates of deposits, leading in the 1990s to its involvement in fund management in northern Asia for Chinese manufacturing.[13] A third of DBS revenues in 1996 were derived from these regional activities in Asia.

From 1988, DBS acted as banker for the Singapore Government in China. The consortium of DBS with Keppel Corporation and Sembawang Corporation was critical in innovative financing of Chinese development. In 1993, DBS and Tat Lee Bank provided a loan of US$420 million for automobile production in China. This was a joint-venture between Volkswagen and the

First Automobile Works, a Chinese SOE.[14] DBS fitted in with Singapore's ambition to construct a regional role in Asia that would ultimately neutralize Malaysian antagonism towards the island republic.

DBS's involvement in Indonesia and Thailand constituted its first moves into multinational banking. In 1990, DBS bought a 42 per cent equity stake with Tat Lee Bank in Bank Buana Indonesia. This secured entry into corporate and retail finance in Indonesia. DBS's interests remained in international trade financing for large corporations. In 1991, DBS Merchant Bank had revolving credit facilities to the value of US$40 million in Indonesia. P. T. Gadjah Tunggal was the major corporate debtor and DBS issued substantial credit for its expansion. Gadjah Tunggal, a tyre manufacturer, saw a growth in sales revenue from Rp269,652 million in 1992 to Rp746,824 million in 1995, and to Rp986,880 million in 1996.[15] The 1997 crisis brought serious difficulties for Gadjah Tunggal and a takeover by Pirelli was launched. DBS faced serious defaults in Indonesia during the crisis. In Thailand, DBS had purchased equity in Thai Danu Bank, which led to a merger in 1997, following the crisis. In 1997, DBS injected US$137.5 million into Thai Danu Bank, increasing its stake from 3.4 per cent to 50.27 per cent, although management control remained with Thai executives.[16]

The wish of DBS to emerge as a pre-eminent financier of hi-tech industries in Asia led to the creation of the Venture Capital Fund in August 1986 to finance investments in both domestic and foreign hi-tech industries.[17] In 1983, DBS expanded its stockbrokering activities from Singapore to Hong Kong, Sri Lanka and other countries in Southeast Asia. In 1984–5, DBS was responsible for securing 30 per cent of the total funds raised on the Singapore Stock Exchange and in 1987 it was responsible for 83.6 per cent of the new share issues, amounting to S$670.8 million. DBS also became the lead manager for share issues on Singapore's second securities board, the SES DAQ, introduced in February 1987. With the creation of its own Asset Management Unit in 1990, DBS aggressively targeted the Asian stock market.

DBS formed joint-ventures or acquired existing securities firms in Asia; it acquired its own securities firm in Singapore in 1987, while in 1993 it formed joint-ventures with Sri Lanka, Thailand, Korea, India and the Philippines. The joint-venture with Sri Dhana Finance and Securities in Thailand was finalized in 1994 with a 30 per cent stake. In February 1995 DBS held a majority stake of 75 per cent with Capital Trust to form the largest Indian stockbroker firm. In Indonesia, DBS operated a joint-venture arrangement with Tat Lee Bank and Bank Dagang Nasional Indonesia. P. T. DBS Securities Indonesia saw a growth of 30 per cent in 1995. DBS also expanded into Shanghai where it was permitted to trade in 'B' shares. In Malaysia, there were serious obstacles to its entry. However, close ties were established with Public Bank. In the Philippines securities sector, DBS was assisted by its acquisition of fully licensed banking facilities in June 1996.[18]

DBS achieved spectacular growth within two decades in its capacity as a state bank, with a broad regional mission in Asia to participate in innovative financing of industry and corporate growth. By 1994, it was the largest Southeast Asian Bank with assets of US$39.3 billion. In comparison, Bangkok Bank, had assets of US$30.65 billion. Sumitomo, the largest Asian bank held assets of US$486.9 billion.[19] DBS's business in Singapore recorded impressive profits (see Table 8.1) and these profits and large reserves enabled DBS to compensate for its losses in Indonesia and Thailand incurred as a result of the currency crisis in 1997.

It was this regional presence in Southeast Asia, prior to the 1997 financial crisis, that enabled it to participate in the restructuring of troubled banks in Thailand and Indonesia after 1988. DBS was able to take up majority

Table 8.1 DBS financial performance

Key ratios	*1998*	*1999*	*2000*	*2001*	*2002*
Profitability					
ROAA (before tax) (%)	0.09	1.01	1.54	1.04	0.96
ROE (before tax) (%)	0.12	0.85	1.47	0.85	0.94
ROE (after tax) (%)	1.45	12.42	16.60	8.73	9.53
Net profit/total assets + cont. (%)	–0.02	0.44	0.89	0.52	0.53
Net interest margin (net int. inc./ave total assets) (%)	2.86	1.97	1.87	1.72	1.76
Asset quality					
Loan loss prov./advances (%)	1.29	1.31	0.06	0.35	0.54
Capital adequacy					
Total liability/equity	11.92	11.34	12.29	10.09	10.10
Total equity/deposits + borr. (%)	8.87	9.37	8.72	11.18	11.96
Total equity/total advances (%)	10.06	10.67	9.66	12.49	13.53
Liquidity					
Total advances/dep. + borr. (%)	88.21	87.86	90.27	89.48	88.391
Liquid asset ratio (liquid assets/ total assets) (%)	18.40	17.93	16.77	15.55	13.68
Liquid assets/dep. + borr. (%)	21.09	20.74	19.44	19.28	18.16
Net loans/deposits (%)	89.00	90.09	93.34	94.89	93.68
Free capital/total capital (%)	46.58	33.01	31.31	–15.21	–39.17
Growth					
Turnover					
Net interest income (%)		42.28	0.23	10.67	17.19
Total income (%)		123.01	–10.32	43.00	11.45
Net income (%)		61.47	–3.23	20.50	15.12
Operating profit (%)		620.57	81.09	–20.88	8.68
Total assets (%)		6.43	4.47	36.17	–1.38
Total loans and advances (%)		5.06	7.09	26.26	–9.01
Deposits + borrowings (%)		5.49	4.23	27.37	–7.90
Equity growth (%)		11.42	–2.98	63.22	–1.45

Source: Development Bank of Singapore, Annual Reports, 1998–2002

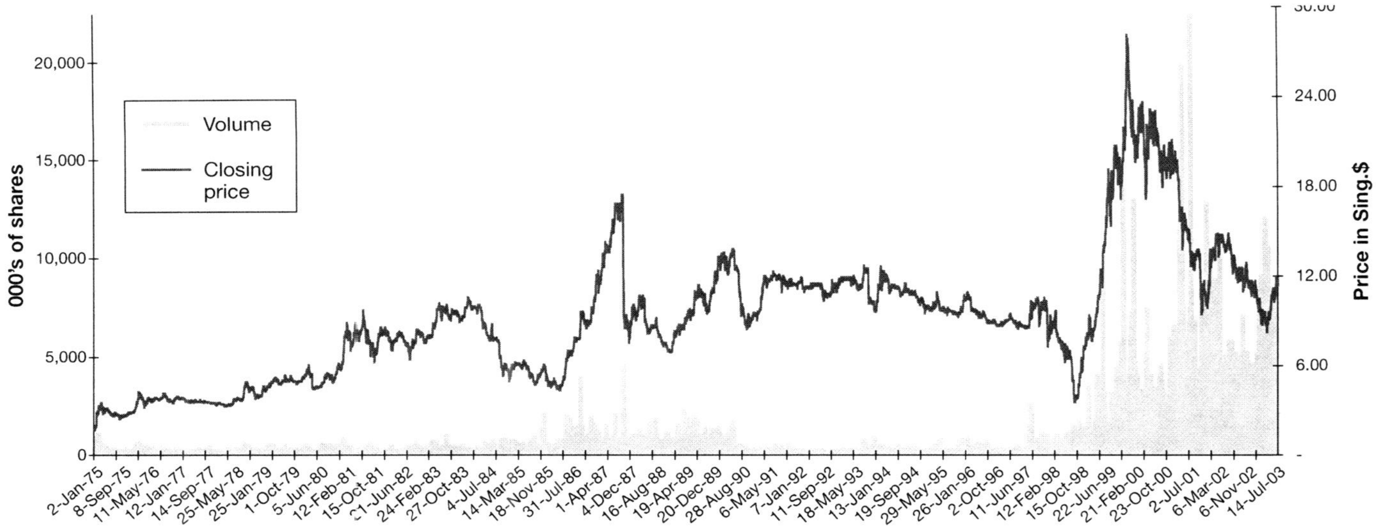

Figure 8.1 DBS share price/volume

stakes in Thai and Indonesia banks, assist in their recapitalization and introduce new managerial hierarchies. This involvement resulted in losses for its headquarters.

DBS had to face losses of US$260 million in 1998 over Thai Danu Bank, together with another loss of US$132 million in connection with revenue reserves, and another US$137 million because of depreciating asset values. Tables 8.1–8.5 illustrate the difficulties faced by Singapore banks as a direct result of the economic crisis in 1997 and their role as knight-errant for erring banks in the region.

Table 8.2 OCBC financial performance

Key ratios	*1998*	*1999*	*2000*	*2001*	*2002*
Profitability					
ROAA (before tax) (%)	1.09	1.63	2.02	1.35	1.07
ROE (before tax) (%)	0.95	1.39	1.56	0.91	0.89
ROE (after tax) (%)	9.10	12.67	13.50	11.34	9.21
Net profit/total assets + cont. (%)	0.67	0.97	1.05	0.66	0.57
Net interest margin (net int. inc./ ave total assets) (%)	5.03	2.34	2.21	1.92	1.78
Asset quality					
Loan loss prov./advances (%)	2.11	1.15	0.29	0.81	0.81
Capital adequacy					
Total liability/equity (%)	9.71	8.98	8.60	11.45	10.61
Total equity/deposits + borr. (%)	11.18	12.26	12.49	9.84	10.65
Total equity/total advances (%)	11.36	12.18	12.80	10.76	11.79
Liquidity					
Total loans and advances/dep. + borr. (%)	98	101	98	91	90
Liquid asset ratio (liquid assets/ total assets) (%)	11.18	11.25	10.28	11.38	11.88
Liquid assets/dep. + borr. (%)	13.40	13.76	12.32	13.94	14.67
Net loans and advances/ deposits (%)	98.45	100.66	97.54	91.39	90.31
Free capital/total capital (%)	68.83	68.41	54.13	10.13	9.82
Growth					
Turnover					
Net interest income (%)		–8.80	–2.33	10.43	8.45
Total income (%)		–11.67	–8.34	76.18	–13.34
Net income (%)		–9.63	–4.03	28.19	0.36
Operating profit (%)		41.98	23.47	–16.52	–4.28
Total assets (%)		–3.43	9.98	43.05	–1.60
Total loans and advances (%)		–3.26	8.76	31.14	–3.61
Deposits + borrowings (%)		–5.38	12.23	39.98	–2.46
Equity growth (%)		3.71	14.33	10.24	5.57

Source: OCBC, Annual Reports, 1998–2002

Table 8.3 UOB financial performance

Key ratios	*1997*	*1998*	*1999*	*2000*	*2001*	*2002*
Profitability						
ROAA (before tax) (%)	1.48	1.02	1.91	1.93	1.33	1.30
ROE (before tax) (%)	13.06	8.78	15.48	17.00	9.13	11.20
ROE (after tax) (%)	8.98	6.32	11.47	13.09	7.05	8.69
Net profit/total assets + cont. (%)	0.74	0.46	1.01	1.03	0.59	0.75
Net interest margin (net int. inc./ave total assets) (%)	2.24	2.41	2.11	1.95	1.59	1.96
Asset quality						
Loan loss prov./ advances (%)	1.17	2.41	0.95	0.32	0.28	0.78
Capital adequacy						
Total liability/equity	7.84	7.68	7.57	8.51	7.68	7.39
Total equity/deposits + borrowings (%)	13.43	13.66	14.04	12.27	13.56	14.33
Total equity/loans and advances (%)	19.53	21.42	24.84	23.67	21.97	22.14
Liquidity						
Total loans and advances/ deposits + borrowings	0.68	0.63	0.56	0.52	0.62	0.65
Liquid asset ratio (liquid assets/total assets)	0.36	0.40	0.44	0.48	0.36	0.32
Liquid assets/deposits and borrowings	0.42	0.47	0.53	0.56	0.42	0.39
Free capital/equity capital	0.74	0.76	0.69	0.68	0.55	0.50
Growth						
Net interest income (%)		8.41	–5.70	5.80	19.25	51.78
Total income (%)		–4.12	23.63	7.91	12.43	14.49
Net income (%)		4.24	3.28	6.58	16.72	38.45
Operating profit (%)		–29.97	86.73	11.21	7.24	19.39
Total assets (%)		2.24	12.49	16.82	71.71	–5.64
Total loans and advances (%)		–5.06	–1.76	10.47	102.49	–3.11
Deposits + borrowings (%)		2.36	10.91	19.58	69.97	–7.54
Equity growth (%)		4.12	13.94	5.26	88.00	–2.39

Source: United Overseas Bank, Annual Reports, 1997–2002

In March 1999, DBS undertook further recapitalization of Thai Danu, having lost 8.1 billion baht in 1998. The recapitalization involved raising up to 10 billion baht through a share issue. The Thai Danu debts had meant that DBS suffered the worst losses among the four big banks in Singapore – S$7 billion. DBS's links to large Chinese capitalists, such as Ng Teng Fong, also meant serious losses in financial and property markets. The bank's involvement in the international expansion of Singapore state enterprises and

Table 8.4 OUB financial performance

Key ratios	*1996*	*1997*	*1998*	*1999*	*2000*
Profitability					
ROAA (before tax) (%)	2.61	1.00	0.58	1.47	1.67
ROE (after tax) (%)	9.51	6.16	4.28	9.28	10.28
Net profit/total assets + cont. (%)	0.55	0.47	0.26	0.70	0.69
Net interest margin (net int. inc./ ave total assets) (%)	4.04	2.23	2.05	2.06	2.32
Capital adequacy					
Total liability/equity	9.23	8.39	9.27	7.12	7.79
Total equity/deposits + borr. (%)	11.29	12.35	11.21	14.74	13.32
Total equity/total advances (%)	11.54	12.58	11.42	15.23	14.14
Liquidity					
Total loans and advances/dep. + borr. (%)	98	98	98	97	94
Liquid asset ratio (liquid assets/ total assets) (%)	12.03	11.93	9.12	11.71	10.86
Liquid assets/dep. + borr. (%)	6.44	5.56	3.69	5.49	5.68
Free capital/equity capital (%)	93.11	94.17	82.57	77.60	61.15
Growth					
Net interest income (%)		19.32	4.23	0.95	17.34
Total income (%)		21.19	4.09	9.94	5.53
Net income (%)		–18.24	–29.26	149.48	21.11
Operating profit (%)		–17.41	–33.87	134.61	18.86
Total assets (%)		15.98	11.19	–9.01	18.37
Total loans and advances (%)		15.81	12.08	–13.73	17.79
Deposits + borrowings (%)		15.42	12.01	–12.53	21.06
Equity growth (%)		26.27	1.69	15.06	9.35

Source: Overseas Union Bank, Annual Reports, 1996–2000

investment groups, such as Singapore Technologies and Temasek Holdings, were lucrative compared to its joint-ventures with private corporations, domestic and international, particularly in Indonesia and Thailand. The foregoing analysis illustrates the risks faced by even the most prudent of banks in Southeast Asia. Even DBS in the highly regulated banking environment of Singapore could not escape the crisis.

A brief look at its performance between 1999 and 2001 captures this dilemma. In 1999, net profits of the DBS group were S$223 million, after providing S$1 billion to cover non-performing loans. Total non-performing loans leapt from S$1 billion to S$7 billion between December 1997 and December 1998.[20] Forty-one per cent of this was for Thai Danu. About three-quarters of the total provision of US$752 million in 2000 was for losses in Malaysia, Indonesia, Thailand, South Korea and the Philippines. Thus DBS's role as a regional bank had catapulted it into losses, a direct consequence of the rescue of these troubled banks in Southeast Asia. UOB acquired

Table 8.5 Keppel Tat Lee financial performance

Key ratios	*1997*	*1998*	*1999*
Profitability			
ROAA (before tax) (%)	0.81	0.51	1.54
ROE (before tax) (%)	0.74	0.42	1.37
ROE (after tax) (%)	–16.66	73.69	35.25
Net profit/total assets + cont. (%)	0.42	0.31	1.13
Net interest margin (net int. inc./ave total assets) (%)	1.97	1.59	2.09
Asset quality			
Loan loss prov./advances (%)	1.80	0.92	0.78
Capital adequacy			
Total liability/equity	–30.31	33.43	31.90
Total equity/deposits + borr. (%)	–4.18	3.67	3.86
Total equity/total loans and advances (%)	–6.42	5.07	5.99
Liquidity			
Total loans and advances/dep. + borr. (%)	65	72	65
Liquid asset ratio (liquid assets/total assets) (%)	41.26	36.43	41.68
Liquid assets/dep. + borr. (%)	50.56	46.07	52.96
Net loans and advances/deposits (%)	65.09	72.38	64.52
Free capital/equity capital (%)	104.95	91.90	84.51
Growth			
Turnover			
Net interest income (%)	6.29	12.63	76.45
Total income (%)	51.96	–7.86	95.40
Net income (%)	16.53	6.64	81.23
Operating profit (%)	–31.45	–12.33	295.97
Total assets (%)	19.12	55.84	20.59
Total loans and advances (%)	24.79	67.89	6.98
Deposits + borrowings (%)	22.07	50.99	20.00
Equity growth (%)	–129.20	–232.64	26.22

Source: Keppel Tat Lee, Annual Reports, 1997–9

Radanasin Bank in November 1999. Both DBS and UOB had acquired medium-sized banks, so held only less than 7 per cent of the total capital and assets of the Thai financial sector. Their market share is low and they possessed branches located largely in Bangkok. However, it has improved services incorporating new technology and internet banking and acted as a catalyst for improved corporate governance in Thai banking. These foreign banks have achieved a swift recapitalization of Thai banks, and by July 2000 had restructured NPLs and losses, reduced employees, improved marketing, and diversified through the introduction of new and innovative products. Competition has intensified as a result of the activities of DBS, OUB and Standard Chartered, and also produced improvements in corporate governance. The insider knowledge of Thai banks held by DBS assisted in the screening and monitoring of the banks' lending relationships.

As reiterated earlier, this regional role of rescuing banks produced some negative results for performance at home. Subsequent to the acquisition of overseas banks in 2000 and 2001, the capital asset ratios of Singapore banks declined slightly. This led to the mergers among the five banking groups in 2001. They were merged into three large banking clusters to achieve economies of scale and scope. The view was that while earnings were stable, it was unlikely to return to pre-1997 levels of profit. Hence, expansion abroad was essential.

The corporations in Singapore were not over-leveraged and hence their debt burden was moderate which enabled the banks to recover quickly from the 1997 losses. See Tables 8.1–8.5 for evidence of this swift recovery. The fairly efficient regulatory framework and the conservative practices of the Monetary Authority of Singapore and a stable currency had further eased any difficulties following the economic slowdown even after 2000.

The difficulties that remain are its small domestic market and a serious lack of competition in the financial sector because of the existing banking monopoly. Furthermore, there is a lack of access to diverse revenues since the capital markets are immature and underdeveloped. Their clear strategy has been to expand abroad, particularly into China, where in 2005 DBS had acquired some equity in Chinese banks. This could increase risk as the financial regulations in China are lax.

Finally, for Singapore to build a credible international reputation, it needs an internationally competitive bank, involved in the corporate growth of Southeast Asia and China, funding an innovative R&D presence in the region and globally. This corporate growth and innovation are analysed in the next chapter.

9 Dead calm

State entrepreneurship in Singapore: prospects for regional economic power

Introduction

The corporate economy in Singapore in the past three decades has been characterized by the rise of a few large and often monopolistic corporations owned and controlled by the state and its investment groups. This increasing concentration in the industrial and corporate structure is clearly evident from the following statistics. In 1963, large firms accounted for 3.8 per cent of the total number of firms; by 1988 this rose to 10.4 per cent. Manufacturing output of large firms contributed to 36.6 per cent of total output in 1963 but rose to 81.5 per cent in 1988. Value-added manufacturing attributable to large firms in 1963 was 47.8 per cent, rising to 73.4 per cent in 1983 and 81.6 per cent in 1988.[1]

This concentration in production within large firms intensified by 2000–1. Large government-linked corporations and foreign-owned firms produced 67 per cent of the GDP in 2001.[2] This industrial concentration was also reproduced by corporate concentrations where, in 1999, 27 per cent of the total market capitalization of the Singapore Stock Exchange was held by a single investment company – Temasek Holdings. Temasek Holdings, in turn, held a dominant stake in the top 20 companies, listed on the Singapore Stock Exchange.[3] These 20 corporations alone accounted for almost 40 per cent of the total manufacturing output in 1999–2000.[4]

The second critical feature is the level of foreign participation in this concentrated growth between 1968 and 1990 and after 1990 with the increasing substitution of these foreign firms by large government-linked corporations. In 1968, wholly local-owned firms formed 80.5 per cent of the total number of firms, while wholly foreign-owned firms accounted for 11.7 per cent; their respective shares in total output that year were 41 per cent produced by local firms, and 46 per cent attributable to foreign firms. By 1990, this had transformed to local firms accounting for 67.7 per cent of the total number of firms and share of foreign firms contracted to 23.4 per cent of the total. Their output, however, remained higher than that of local firms, with foreign firms contributing to 75.9 per cent of total output and domestic firms only 15.1 per cent.[5] This disparity was also produced in their capital expenditures. In 1968 local firms invested 33.2 per cent, while the share of foreign firms was 42.5 per cent. By 1990 the share of capital expenditure of local firms was 17.8 per cent and foreign firms' share rose to 70.7 per cent. However, this was to change in the 1990s. The one major factor for change was the rise of the government-linked companies (GLCs) deepening concentration and influence. GLCs numbered 361 in 1981, rising to 720 in 1994 and declining to 592 in 1996.[6] The decline in number between 1994 and 1996 was largely because of the incidence of mergers and acquisitions within them, creating even larger conglomerates. By 2001 these GLCs were dominant despite staggered attempts at privatization after the recession in 1985. Companies owned by Temasek, the state holding companies alone, accounted for 10 per cent of GDP and 27 per cent of total stock market capitalization in 2000.[7]

The aim of this chapter is to identify the systematic factors facilitating the growth of these large firms in successive periods after 1965, with the emphasis on the final decade of the twentieth century. The focus here is on the four large GLCs: Keppel Corporation, Sembawang Corporation, Singapore Technologies and SingTel. In addition, a private electronics firm, Creative Technologies, is used to identify distinctive and differing organizational structures and growth variations, contrasting with that of the GLCs.

State entrepreneurship

The industrial changes since independence in 1965, from the entrepôt economy specializing in the trade in textiles and electrical goods to the development of a regional manufacturing base with an aggressive involvement of the state assisted by foreign capital, produced the transition in the 1980s and 1990s to a skill-intensive manufacturing specialism in electronic and hi-tech products and financial services. In the year 2000, electronic goods alone contributed to almost 60 per cent of total domestic exports, while the chemical industry provided another 10 per cent.[8] The rising importance of state and foreign capital in a capital- and skills-intensive export-led growth dictated the eclipse of domestic private capital, except in the niche industries of electronics, software, real estate and private Chinese banking.

Since 1980, Singapore has received 12 per cent of the total FDI destined for developing countries.[9] This share of global FDI only fell after 1989, when China presented serious competition for foreign investments. This decline in FDI for Singapore intensified after 1996 with Singapore receiving only 3 to 4 per cent of total FDI planned for developing economies. This is reproduced in a corresponding decline in the share of FDI in Singapore's gross fixed capital formation from 30 per cent between 1985 and 1990, to 20 per cent in the 1990s.[10] Japan and the US were the major foreign investors, with Europe's share rising to 30 per cent in 1997. The electronics sector was the major recipient of foreign funds. In 1997, it absorbed 50 per cent of the inward direct investment. Technology transfer remained minimal (see Table 9.1).[11]

Table 9.1 Stock of foreign investment in Singapore by country (end of period) (S$ millions)[a]

	1987	*1992*	*1993*	*1994*	*1995*	*1996*	*1997*
Total (I + II)	34,540.3	65,351.0	73,285.2	86,811.7	99,215.7	115,648.0	138,960.6
I *Direct equity investment*	29,946.9	56,660.9	62,766.9	74,605.2	84,267.0	94,005.3	112,130.6
United States	7,954.6	9,646.6	11,251.3	12,051.7	14,253.0	15,775.8	20,679.4
Australia	1,541.1	2,943.9	3,128.1	3,281.2	3,131.6	3,214.9	3,258.2
Europe	8,519.2	16,385.1	17,847.6	22,383.5	24,815.7	29,734.1	33,833.0
European Union	6,240.3	13,083.2	13,777.5	15,828.3	17,385.3	20,548.8	22,735.9
United Kingdom	3,651.1	6,020.5	6,165.9	6,616.8	6,666.3	7,011.1	8,305.8
Germany	760.7	1,032.5	1,069.4	1,345.3	1,894.9	1,967.6	1,773.7
Netherlands	1,483.2	4,078.5	4,056.6	4,194.6	4,397.2	6,921.8	6,941.8
Others	345.3	1,951.7	2,485.6	3,671.6	3,868.2	4,648.3	5,714.7
Switzerland	1,780.4	2,634.2	3,348.1	5,753.5	7,106.7	8,642.6	10,418.7
Others	498.5	667.7	722.0	801.7	323.7	542.7	678.4
Asia	8,434.9	20,176.3	21,965.6	25,800.9	28,388.4	31,016.9	33,717.7
Japan	4,578.2	13,186.3	13,471.1	15,806.3	16,969.5	19,132.2	20,266.0
Hong Kong	1,941.0	3,461.9	3,758.7	3,623.1	3,910.4	4,172.4	3,772.4
Taiwan	103.5	360.3	503.3	725.2	927.9	1,037.4	1,842.7
ASEAN	1,614.1	3,041.9	3,843.5	4,928.6	5,676.9	5,907.7	6,763.3
Malaysia	1,295.8	2,220.7	2,462.5	2,910.9	3,523.9	3,868.9	4,656.3
Indonesia	174.1	61.3	170.6	575.0	788.0	873.0	1,092.4
Philippines	26.4	150.3	167.8	351.0	356.7	135.2	128.5
Thailand	44.3	516.9	951.1	904.3	801.8	823.2	716.3
Brunei	73.5	92.7	91.5	187.4	206.2	206.4	168.0
Vietnam[b]	–	–	–	–	0.4	1.1	1.8
Others	198.1	126.0	388.8	717.7	903.7	767.2	1,073.3
Other countries	3,497.1	7,509.0	8,574.3	11,087.9	13,678.3	14,263.6	20,642.3
II *Portfolio and other equity investment*	4,593.4	8,690.1	10,518.3	12,206.5	14,948.7	21,642.7	26,830.0

Notes:
a All figures calculated to two decimal places.
b With effect from 1995, Vietnam is included in ASEAN total.

Source: *Yearbook of Statistics*, Singapore, 2000

Despite these increases in capital inputs, there were no significant increases in total factor productivity.[12] Neither were there gains in value-added share of gross output. In electronics there was a fall in both total factor productivity as well as in the value-added component in gross output. Increases in manufacturing output were essentially achieved through increases in scale and increases in the use of capital and labour, and the state targeting of the electronics sector stimulated diversification within the industry. The heterogeneous growth of the electronics and telecommunications sector, in semiconductors, data storage devices, computer peripherals, printed circuit board, wafer fabrication and medical-related computer technology was possible because of the involvement of Seagate, Toshiba and Matsushita.[13] Between 1986 and 1996, Singapore emerged as the world's largest producer of hard disk drives, with Seagate enjoying a monopoly in this production until the early 1990s.

This focus on the electronics industry accelerated after the economic recession of 1985 when Singapore sought the creation of a regional hi-tech sector, penetrating global markets. This concentration on electronics, where it absorbed 50 per cent of total FDI in Singapore, created a high dependence on the global economy. Yet the demand was highly volatile.

The policy of the government remained the creation of these hi-tech clusters and also sought to transfer to these same industries abroad, in electronics, telecoms and chemicals, through the acquisition of foreign specialists in these industrial sectors. Singapore, possessing no endogenous advantage in this, faced serious competition and risk. R&D expenditure in electronics constituted 1.02–1.87 per cent of GDP between 1991 and 1999.[14] This implied increased dependence on foreign multinationals and foreign capital, with the state contributing some capital, derived from high savings and surplus financial reserves. This led to local firms' share in direct exports in 1990 amounting to 7.8 per cent, while foreign firms' contributions, both solo and in joint ventures with the state, approached 85.8 per cent.[15]

The discussion so far has revealed the critical role of the state in the corporate economy of Singapore. Both in 1996 and 2001, as in 1985, state-owned corporations dominated; private enterprise remained small, limited in scope and influence despite some, hesitant, steps towards privatization after 1985. How did the state achieve such concentrations in ownership and control?

The state carved out dominant shares in electronics, semiconductors, marine services, heavy industry, in transport and infrastructure as well as in banking. This was achieved in three ways. First, through state investment holding companies which were responsible for identifying and funding national champions within strategic industries. Second, there were tightly knit, interlocking ties of ownership and management within many of these GLCs, increasing state concentration within the corporate economy. Third, monopolistic structures and practices became an important feature through the merger and acquisitions rampant since the 1970s. The state and foreign

MNEs swallowed up small private firms; such amalgamations were combined with price controls, strict inflation controls and non-tolerance of unemployment, all essential safeguards against any criticism of profiteering and monopoly.

In this atmosphere of a strong government-led capitalism, only a blind faith in the virtues of private enterprise was circulated without any questioning of the increasing suffocation of competitive institutions and capabilities. Statutory bodies such as Singapore telecommunications, Port of Singapore Authority and Public Union Board were corporatized and ownership transferred to Temasek Holdings. Keppel Corporation arose from the reorganization of the Singapore Harbour Board, while Sembawang Corporation evolved from the conversion of the British Naval Base. Singapore Technologies was conceived and constructed from existing defence interests.

The important dimensions of the rise of state investment companies, their role in the rapid and substantial readjustment of the structure of industry, steering the GLCs into concentrated and diversified growth are palpably clear from the analysis below.

State holding companies

Temasek Holdings, formed in 1974 from the restructuring of the Economic Development Board, was a wholly owned unit of the Ministry of Finance. It is presided over by the President of Singapore. It was a highly secretive organization and did not publish any accounts until October 2004. It had access to large government reserves and its financial prudence secured a triple A debt rating from Standard and Poor. In 2004 it held investment funds totalling S$90 billion.

In the 1970s, Temasek concentrated on investments in Singapore, acquiring a dominant stake in SingTel (63 per cent), Singapore Technologies (100 per cent), Singapore Power (100 per cent), Keppel Corporation (31 per cent) and Sembcorp (51 per cent). From 1989, Temasek focused on investments both in Singapore as well as overseas. Its global strategy was aggressive verging on impetuous purchases of health firms, electronic firms in the US and financial institutions in India, Indonesia, Korea and Southern Ireland.

In 1974, Temasek Holdings managed S$345 million equity distributed in 36 companies.[16] By 1983 it held S$2.9 billion direct investments in 58 companies.[17] These companies, in turn, held 490 either wholly owned or partially owned firms in Singapore. By the 1990s Temasek focused principally on global opportunities. Its investments in China were high. Between 1993 and 1995, FDI from Singapore into China grew fivefold from S$444 million to S$2.4 billion. In 1996 this rose to S$5.3 billion and China became the third largest recipient of Singapore's investments. Temasek was the main conduit for these capital flows into China.

A breakdown of Temasek's sectoral investments in 2004 revealed a 21 per cent interest in telecoms and media, another 21 per cent in finance,

6 per cent in property, transport and logistics accounted for 14 per cent, energy 7 per cent, infrastructure and engineering 10 per cent and miscellaneous interests of 21 per cent. In the same year, a regional dispersal of investments indicated that 52 per cent of its total interests were in Singapore, while Australia absorbed 16 per cent, China had 6 per cent, ASEAN absorbed a further 9 per cent, India and Pakistan and Japan accounted for only 1 per cent each, while Europe and the US each held a 7 per cent share.

One-fifth of its overseas investments were in real estate, three-fifths in manufacturing where a major proportion was dedicated to electronics and telecommunications; the remaining one-fifth was in a mix of investments in utilities, media and retailing. Temasek's ambitious strategy in electronics led to acquisition in the Silicon Valley (US) and into OEM outsourcing arrangements for American hi-tech firms. Some of these investments were failures.

The Suzhou Industrial Park fiasco in China was the result of bureaucratic muddle and fraud, while the takeover of Ansett Airlines of Australia faced serious industrial disputes besides being an overvalued purchase itself. Equally, Temasek was confronted by a spate of failures of dotcom firms in Australia in April 2000. Temasek also saw low returns from its acquisitions of telecoms firms in China, Hong Kong and Indonesia.

Ho Ching, head of Temasek in 2002, was not inhibited by these misjudgements. She purchased equity in the failing Global Crossing, took a stake in China Aviation Oil which was listed on the Singapore Stock Exchange in 2001 and by November 2004 faced bankruptcy. She had, while head of Singapore Technologies in 1996, blundered in the acquisition of the American Micropolis Corporation which closed in 1998 with debts of S$575 million. She now embarked on the purchase of Asian banks: Bank Danamon (Indonesia) in 2003, Bank International Indonesia, Kookmin Bank (Korea), Indian ICICI Bank, Hana Bank and China Mingsheng Banking Corporation in 2004.[18]

The strategy was to use acquisitions to build core technology in the Singapore corporations. The earlier policy of state provision of R&D had limited success because of its dependence on foreign multinationals for this expertise. The second crucial change was in focusing on the US for this expertise. The third strategy was to change the managerial structure and incorporate engineers and corporate leaders. Ho Ching, an engineer was joined by executives co-opted from Singapore Airlines, Fraser and Neave, and Exxon Mobil Asia Pacific. The stable ownership structure vested in the state combined with the technical experts did lead to an improvement in the performance of Temasek. It accumulated profits of S$7.4 billion on an annual revenue of S$56.6 billion during 2003–4. This was an improvement on the earlier profits recorded for March 2002–March 2003.

The second major investment company, Government Investment Company (GIC), was established in 1981. The Chairman was Lee Kuan Yew, Vice Chairman B. G. Lee, and the directors were Richard Hu (Minister of Finance) and Tony Tan (Deputy Minister for Defence). The divisions of the group were first in strategic investments, second in special investments and third in real estate. There was no clarity as to the different functions of these three divisions. It had originally focused on overseas investments but this demarcation became increasingly obscured by changes in government attitudes and changes in the portfolio of Temasek, Singapore Technologies, Raffles Holdings and Capita Land.

It was funded principally through government reserves which in 1999 amounted to US$77 billion; a large proportion of this was in gold and foreign exchange reserves.[19] By 2000, it revealed an investment portfolio of US$100 billion with investments in 30 countries. It held interests in Chinese power projects through joint-ventures with Chinese SOEs. It purchased Dao Heng Bank (HK), Optus (an Australian telecoms firm) and it joined Capita land, a Government of Singapore property group, to promote property investments in China.

The striking feature of GIC is its involvement in bond investments. By May 2001 it had entered the derivatives market, using pension funds to expand investments overseas. Its use of Singapore's reserves, which amounted to US$140 billion by 2001 was quite revealing of the dynamic changes within the hitherto conservative, prudent Ministry of Finance.[20]

The third investment arm was MND Holdings, a direct unit of DBS. The two property specialists, Raffles Holdings founded in 1979 and Capita Land established in August 1995, were aggressive in Australia, the US and Europe, often competing with Prince Alwaleed of Saudi Arabia. Capita Land was formed through the amalgamation of DBS Land and Pidemco. DBS had to divest its property interests in the 1990s because of the legislation restricting banks from ownership of non-financial interests. Capita Land secured more than half its profits from investments overseas. Raffles Holdings is principally involved in the luxury hotels sector in Singapore as well as in the US and Europe.[21]

These individual investment holding companies possessed interlocking shareholdings in each other as well as in the corporations they financed. For example, Temasek has equity in Capita Land through its subsidiary ST Property; Raffles, too, held a 6 per cent stake in Capita Land followed by DBS Nominees with a 9 per cent stake. The remaining major shareholder in Capita Land was Singapore Technologies.

Such interlocking networks of shareholdings left the government as the single largest shareholder, possessing both direct and indirect holdings. These links provided not only finance but also furnished information on investment opportunities and created an integrated, cohesive investment apparatus. Management personnel further articulated close links and unions between these separate investment groups. The President or Chairman was inevitably linked to the Lee family or a loyal acolyte, a trusted bureaucrat or member of the Cabinet. Such memberships created an armoury of stereotypes, reliable, stable and subservient, revealing national ambitions and patriotism, and some expertise. The combined use of debt, equity and managerial control created a hierarchic governance structure dominated by the state. The state in this respect was these loyal individuals guided by patriarch Lee.

The ability to create industrial and sectoral specialism within these investment groups persisted till the 1980s; not until the 1990s did such segregation of functions become more blurred. Autonomy was compromised by increasing intersections between these investment holding companies and their changing functions and their original specialisms. These investment groups were often competing with each other in directing the GLCs into ambitious expansion and diversification.

The significance of this creation of large, highly concentrated, almost monopolistic corporate organizations owned and managed by the state is seen in the euthanasia of competition and of private enterprise. The increased merger activity that accompanied this growth intensified this concentration. The moves towards some privatization of enterprise after the economic recession of 1985 remained stunted. Given the trend of increased capital and R&D intensiveness in industry in Singapore, the elimination of private companies was inevitable. The restructuring of industry by the state proceeded with rigid guidelines, and emphasized the pre-eminence of electronics, chemicals and biomedical sciences. This further ensured the decline of private enterprise and the proliferation instead of capital-intensive large corporations, with access to state and foreign capital. This industrial policy led to the GLCs unscrambling some of their R&D-intensive subsidiaries and effecting rational links and matches with analogous units in other state-owned corporations. Keppel, Sembawang, SingTel and Singapore Technologies divested unrelated units and merged with related firms within the group and outside it. By 2000, the electronics industry possessed a 48 per cent share of fixed assets in manufacturing, a 55 per cent share of the value-added component of manufacturing and a 60 per cent share in total employment.[22]

These two dominant trends outlined above: the emergence of large GLCs and the emphasis on electronics and hi-tech industries are evident in the study of the four large government corporations: Keppel, Sembawang, Singapore Technologies and SingTel.

Diversification and specialization: the Keppel Group

The Keppel Corporation was created in August 1966 through the incorporation of the dockyards of the Port of Singapore Authority. It was listed in 1986, a diversified conglomerate embracing financial institutions throughout Southeast Asia. It is involved in offshore oil-rig construction, energy projects, shipyard repairs, shipbuilding, marine-related activities as well as banking, financial services, telecommunications, transportation and property management. By 2000, the banking and property divisions of the group contributed to 40 per cent and 30 per cent of total profits, respectively. Marine activities produced only 20 per cent of total profits, with communications adding the remaining 10 per cent (see Figure 9.1).

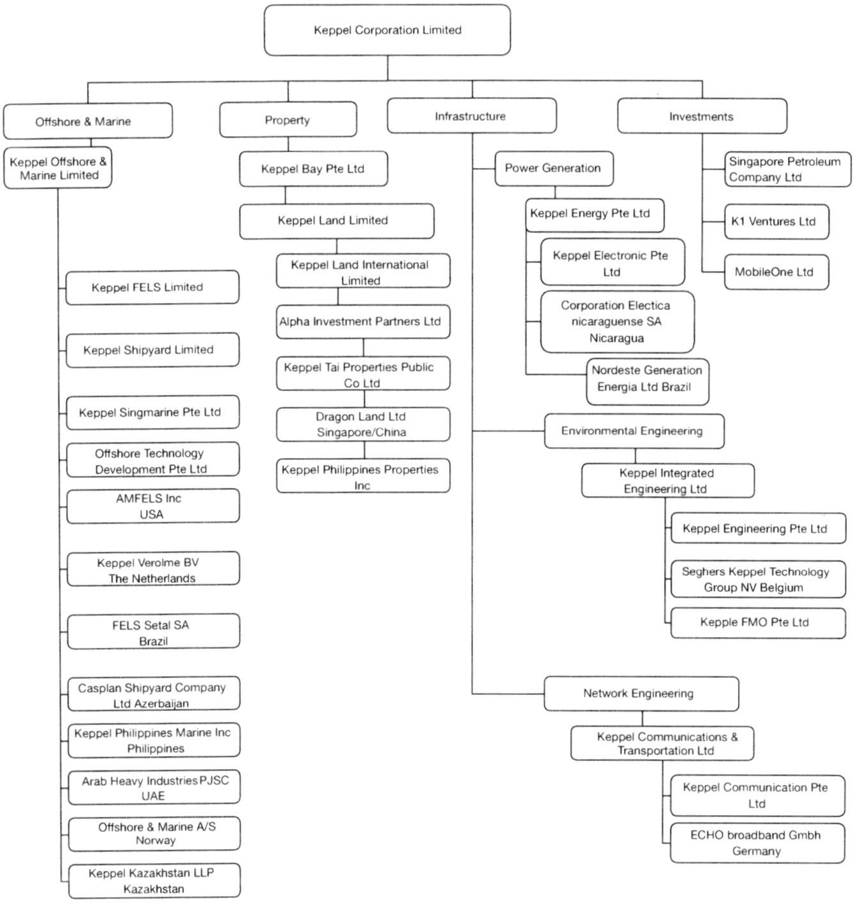

Figure 9.1 Keppel Corporation

Source: Annual Report of the Keppel Corporation, 2003

The decline in the share of profits derived from marine interests was a direct consequence of the divestment of some unprofitable shipping assets. It was increasingly clear that with the powerful presence of Sembawang in marine infrastructure and engineering, Keppel had to diversify into finance and property management. However, offshore oil-rigs, projects in energy and engineering and marine salvage still remained as core functions. The ship repair activities had been the primary interest of Keppel Hitachi Zosen, listed in 1992 with Temasek as a major shareholder, with 61 per cent equity, and Keppel Corporation and Hitachi Zosen holding the rest. The focus was on the Philippines.

Keppel Land, created through the acquisition of Straits Steamship Company in 1980, absorbed other property groups in Singapore, including

Dragon Land in 2001. It refashioned itself as a global property group, pushing into China, Australia, Vietnam, Burma, Hong Kong, the Philippines and Indonesia.

Keppel Telecoms and Transportation is engaged in communications relating to shipping, freight, warehousing and containerization. Telecommunications formed the core of this division in 1998, absorbing 71.9 per cent of its total interests, while logistics accounted for 14.2 per cent, shipping 11 per cent and e-business another 2.7 per cent. Its major cellular phone and pager operator is Mobile One Asia, whose satellite company, KSAT, is listed in Vancouver Canada and operates a satellite network for Chinese telecommunications. Keppel also acquired an American company, Computer Generated Solutions, to assist in the technology-intensive sector.

The fourth division of the Keppel Group is in finance, an interest secured primarily through the acquisitions of Tat Lee Bank, Tat Lee Finance, Southern Bank and Bank Buana Indonesia after the 1997 financial crisis. Many of these acquisitions were made after the 1997 financial crisis. Keppel also moved into Ireland, acquiring a crucial stake in Allied Irish Bank.

This parallel and almost concurrent growth in diversification as well as increasing specialism in this period is no paradox. These continuous organizational, product and industrial changes are part of Singapore's corporate strategy to move into new value-added, hi-tech industries while accruing the benefits of economic diversification.

The organizational structure of Keppel Corporation assisted in this dualism – the intensification of R&D interests along with economic diversification. The separate firms still retained operational autonomy, were specialized and used internal finance. However, the separate units were linked to each other in Keppel group as well as with related units in Sembawang and SingTel through functional links as well as common ownership and managerial control vested in the state. These links varied as new firms were incorporated and as others ventured abroad to overcome the limitations of a small domestic market or to acquire appropriate technology.

The conglomerate structure was maintained through the creation of new independent companies while maintaining its core interests in offshore energy and engineering infrastructure. Although these companies were listed, their major shareholding was held by the parent company, while the significance and needs of these separate units were legally retained as separate entities. There was no possible conflict among shareholders since public shareholding remained an insignificant minority. Such interlocks vested in both the state and in the group were accentuated through the proliferation of mergers and acquisitions by Keppel, a strategy heightened by the Asian financial crisis of 1997.

The growth of Keppel Corporation through these global initiatives is clear from Figure 9.2. Keppel Corporation is the holding company of these overseas divisions; the major shareholding remained with Temasek, GIC and DBS. China was the main regional focus of these investments in property,

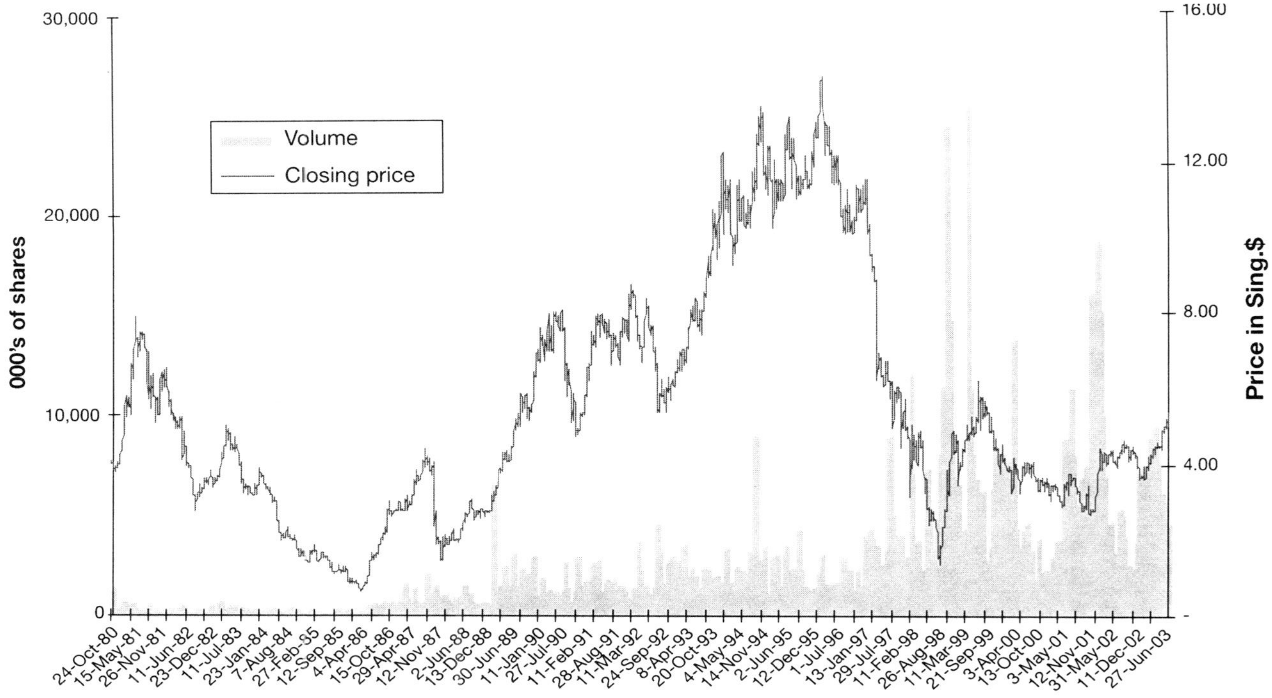

Figure 9.2 Keppel Corporation share price and volume

Source: Singapore Stock Exchange Publications

transportation, communications, engineering, infrastructure, environmental development, trading, petrochemical, power projects, tourist resorts, logistics, shipping, management consultancy relating to the marine sectors and energy.

Keppel Land possessed investments in China totalling US$320 million, 40 per cent of its total assets abroad, and contributed to 30 per cent of its total profits in 2004.[23] Dragon Land focused on real estate and the development of shopping malls and golf courses in China. In 2001, through a joint-venture with Creative Technologies, a private electronics firm from Singapore, Dragon Land, developed hi-tech industrial and media parks in Qingdao.

Keppel Logistics was active in shipping, warehousing and distribution in China, Hong Kong and Sri Lanka. Keppel Logistics Foshan alone held investments of US$20 million; the majority shareholding was held by Keppel Telecommunications and Transportation (70 per cent). while Sinotrans Guangdong possessed the remaining 30 per cent equity. The newly invigorated strategies of diversification, multinational expansion and investment in R&D and marketing were not uniformly successful, but the parent company, Keppel Corporation, exhibited stable growth, both before and after the Asian financial crises. We do not have the requisite data to assess how far the growth in turnover profits and assets seen in Table 9.1 can be attributed to these structural and organizational changes, which were pervasive since 1985. There is, however, a strong circumstantial case for arguing that Keppel's performance in this period and the structural changes are linked. The diversification could have contributed substantially to this underlying increase in growth and productivity improvements, which are clearly present, as seen in Table 9.2.

Keppel's performance on the Singapore stock market is only slightly bullish during certain phases up to 1997 (see Figure 9.2). In the post-1998 phase, there is an increasing trend in a higher volume of activity, while volatility is also on the rise. However, there is evidence of a rapid response and efforts to stabilize quickly, perhaps an indication of increased state and institutional interference and activity here.

Heavy engineering: Sembawang Corporation

Sembawang Corporation is a heavy engineering group. It possessed traditional interests in ship repairs, shipbuilding, chartering and salvage operations. Semb-Corp Marine absorbed the Jurong Shipyards in 1963 and grew through a joint-venture with Ishikawajima Harim, a Japanese conglomerate with interests in heavy industries.

In May 1998 Sembawang Corporation merged with SP Technologies Industrial to form SembCorp Industries, creating the largest engineering and construction group in Southeast Asia, with five core interests: utilities, engineering and construction, environmental engineering, logistics and marine

Table 9.2 Key financial ratios of Keppel Corporation

Key ratios	*1996*	*1997*	*1998*	*1999*	*2000*	*2001*	*2002*
Profitability							
ROAA (before tax) (%)	2.68	1.99	–0.78	2.13	2.14	2.66	4.41
ROE (before tax) (%)	7.86	5.55	–2.82	8.52	9.90	16.54	13.20
ROE (after tax) (%)	3.27	2.21	–3.17	2.95	2.87	9.41	9.25
Net profit margin (%)	7.31	4.77	–6.34	5.58	3.52	6.44	6.48
Operating profit margin (%)	16.70	10.55	–5.77	14.69	11.32	7.87	11.31
Operating efficiency							
Asset turnover (S$ m)	0.15	0.15	0.12	0.12	0.16	0.50	0.48
Inventory turnover (S$ m)	12.71	9.62	35.88	14.93	19.13	2.41	2.13
Gearing and related							
Total equity/(long-term loans + equity) (S$ m)	0.81	0.80	0.77	0.82	0.77	0.63	0.61
Total assets/total liabilities (S$ m)	1.52	1.49	1.33	1.30	1.25	1.52	1.51
Liquidity							
Liquidity ratio (CA/CL)	1.13	1.11	1.10	1.06	1.00	1.05	1.22
Quick ratio ((CA-inventories)/CL)	1.11	1.09	1.10	1.05	0.99	0.57	0.66
Cash ratio ((cash + ST inv.)/CL)	0.50	0.47	0.43	0.48	0.41	0.22	0.23
Inventory working capital ratio (sales/ave wkg cap.)	2.11	53.74	14.15	–14.73	–9.26	58.80	15.05
Growth							
Turnover (%)		19.5	2.3	16.0	54.6	–7.0	–6.0
Operating profit (%)		–24.5	–155.9	–395.3	19.1	–35.4	35.1
Profit before taxation (%)		–18.3	–148.1	–430.8	16.5	–13.3	–23.2
Profit after taxation (%)		–24.6	–188.4	–287.3	14.2	–46.5	31.4
Total assets (%)		19.7	26.7	16.1	15.5	–69.5	–2.1
Total liabilities (%)		21.9	42.4	18.2	20.2	–74.9	–1.2
Equity growth (%)		15.6	–5.3	9.5	0.3	–48.1	–3.7

Source: Annual Reports and Balance Sheets of Keppel Corporation, 1996–2002

engineering. This merger was part of the corporate restructuring that was widespread in Singapore after the Asian financial crisis, aimed to create focused specialist units through the divestment of unrelated interests, with the precise aim of becoming multinational.

SembCorp Logistics, which had been established in 1987, was part of this increasing transition into specialist hi-tech industry. It specialized in supply chain management and offshore logistics, while reducing its activities in marine salvage and port development, which were less profitable and also faced decline in international demand. This expansion into capital-intensive, sophisticated technology, and the divestment of low-value, unrelated activities, remained a prime strategy of GLCs in the 1990s. In 2000, Sembawang negotiated an alliance with Kuehne and Nagel International to offer global integrated logistics solutions. Its interests in offshore logistics contributed to 11 per cent of its entire activities, while supply chain management contributed 70 per cent and marine services accounted for only 18 per cent in the same year. As part of this move towards a focused specialist core, there was a merger between SembCorp Logistics and Kimtrans Singapore, seeking to integrate mining, marine, oil and gas infrastructure.

Prior to the 1990s there was a tendency to absorb unrelated interests in food, finance and light industries; it was highly predatorial, stalking private enterprises such as Haw Par, Salim and Hong Leong. This reorientation of Sembawang towards a more focused corporation intensified with pressures for these state corporations to be privatized after the economic recession of 1985. The prompt response was for the state to divest less profitable unrelated concerns within the group and preserve strategic, capital-intensive industrial interests at home and expand into similar or corresponding niche markets in shipping, and energy abroad in Indonesia, China and India.[24]

The ownership structure revealed two patterns of interlocking shareholding. The state remained the major shareholder through Temasek Holdings, held both in Sembawang Corporation as well as in its subsidiaries and affiliates. Temasek had 51 per cent equity while Singapore Technologies held 39 per cent. Second, through mergers between related units of Sembawang and Singapore Technologies, particularly after October 1998, these interlocks intensified. Capital Group, Kuehne Nagel International, Schroder Investment and Morgan Stanley were there to provide capital, R&D and investment expertise. SembCorp Industries remained the most aggressive among the GLCs in global strategy. As well as the five core interests mentioned above, it is also active in turnkey construction, design, consultancy and infrastructural development. It builds public housing, industrial parks, toll roads, bridges, golf courses and tourist resorts.

It began operating in China in 1988 and has carried out lucrative construction projects throughout China from Beijing to Guangzhou. It builds and operates power plants in China. SembCorp Logistics, in a joint-venture with Shenzen ST-Anda Logistics, is the largest transportation company in South

China. SembCorp Marine has three shipyards in China. Its chemical power installations in Nanjing and Shanghai and its three leading environmental firms in Shanghai are profitable concerns. SembCorp Marine had Dalian Shipyard specializing in the conversion of vessels. This provided an 8.3 per cent increase in net profit and its turnover rose by 22 per cent in 2002.[25] Much of this increase was due to rising demand for oil and gas in China. However, this demand was volatile. In December 2002 it had to sell Bohai Sembawang Shipyard in Tianjin because of a collapse in demand. Bohai Sembawang Tianjin was the only foreign shipyard in Northern China and was in joint-venture with China National Offshore Oil Corporation. This strategy of continual acquisition and swift divestment was a persistent feature of Sembawang's involvement in Chinese corporations.

However, its ambitions in Australia, India, Indonesia, Sri Lanka as well as in Brazil and the Middle East were more stable and long term. It acquired the second largest environmental group in Australia. Second, while its operations in China were vast in comparison, possessing three and later five shipyards in China, it possessed one in Indonesia and one in Brazil in 2001. Third, the greatest disincentive for retaining these acquisitions in China was the managerial difficulties in China, besides the poor financial results of many of these acquisitions. Therefore, the haste in expanding into China, the fluid and active market for acquisitions in China's booming economy meant that they had to come to terms quickly with the problems of over-expansion and seek a more rational and considered approach of creating a credible presence in certain specific sectors rather than squeeze in anywhere. This chaotic experience in China was also a direct result of the centralization of investment funds in Temasek Holdings, while pursuing a decentralized operational approach to local opportunities in diverse provinces in China. There was, in addition, duplication in acquiring and divesting companies abroad between Sembawang, Keppel, Singapore Technologies and SingTel. Possible benefits of their focused drive and strategy were frequently squandered by such duplicating and competing actions of the GLCs abroad.

Table 9.3 on SembCorp's performance clearly reveals stable though modest growth, with contractions in turnover in 1998 and 1999, though recovery was swift. The graph on stock market performance (Figure 9.3) does reveal volatility after 1997. However, a rapid recovery is seen in September 1998. The period prior to 1997 was marked by occasional short phases of heavy trading but there were little price fluctuations. The latter part of the graph shows heavy trading. Its stocks are still weak compared to stocks of other GLCs. Overall, the impression is one of high volatility only for short periods, as in post-1997 years. Also, low volume of trading is a common feature of Singapore stocks because of the dominance of the state and cautious attitude and overregulation of the stock market. This means prices recover very quickly because speculative activity is almost absent.

Table 9.3 Key financial ratios of SembCorp Industries

Key ratios	*1998*	*1999*	*2000*	*2001*	*2002*
Profitability					
ROAA (before tax) (%)	1.11	4.67	4.61	5.89	4.95
ROE (before tax) (%)	3.51	11.72	18.18	20.14	13.99
ROE (after tax) (%)	–28.66	17.89	8.48	10.29	8.26
Net profit margin (%)	–0.52	4.90	5.72	7.62	5.89
Operating profit margin (%)	4.23	5.89	7.64	3.82	1.56
Operating efficiency					
Asset turnover (S$ m)	0.68	0.67	0.54	0.52	0.70
Inventory turnover (S$ m)	13.64	12.03	7.89	7.54	8.57
Gearing					
Total equity/(long-term loans + equity) (S$ m)	0.71	0.74	0.62	0.56	0.63
Total assets/total liabilities (S$ m)	1.46	1.69	1.34	1.38	1.56
Liquidity					
Liquidity ratio (CA/CL)	0.90	1.12	0.86	0.86	1.04
Quick ratio ((CA-inventories)/CL)	0.80	0.99	0.74	0.72	0.83
Cash ratio ((Cash+ ST inv.)/CL)	0.19	0.28	0.25	0.14	0.20
Inventory working capital ratio (sales/ave wkg cap.)	–12.96	–433.24	–47.23	–8.00	–26.99
Growth					
Turnover (%)		–6.3	–20.8	11.4	30.3
Operating profit (%)		30.5	2.7	–44.2	–47.0
Profit before taxation (%)		313.0	–4.2	36.1	–11.3
Profit after taxation (%)		–982.8	–7.5	48.4	0.7
Attributable profit (%)		–177.3	–70.7	49.1	2.6
Total assets (%)		–4.5	–1.2	14.5	–2.1
Total liabilities (%)		–17.5	24.4	11.6	–13.4
Equity growth (%)		23.8	–38.2	22.8	27.7

Source: Annual Reports, SembCorp, 1998–2002

Hi-tech industries: Singapore Technologies

Singapore Technologies grew out of a series of mergers and acquisitions of specialist electronics and aerospace firms, many already existing since the late 1970s. Singapore Technologies Engineering, a major subsidiary, was formed in 1997 through the amalgamation of Singapore Technology Aerospace and Singapore Technology Automotive. In late 1999 it acquired Chartered Semiconductors, which had been established in 1987. This assimilation of hi-tech firms continued with the acquisition of CSE Systems and Engineering established in 1985 for the development of information technology in energy, chemicals, petrochemicals, health, finance and public

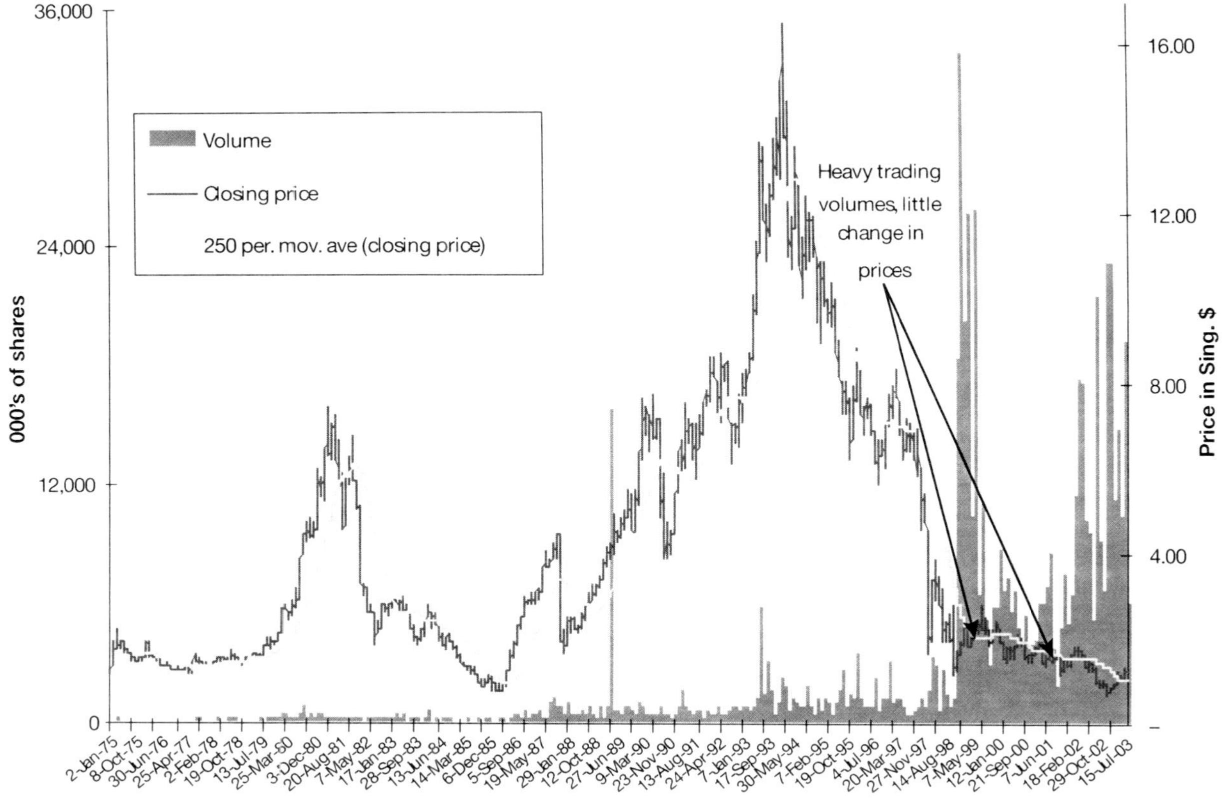

Figure 9.3 Sembcorp share price and volume

Source: Singapore Stock Exchange Publications, 1975–2003

administration. This amalgamation of related firms intensified after 1997. The accelerated growth after 1998 was predominantly in the military weapons sector, concentrating on robotics, micro-electronics and sophisticated engineering equipment.

These independent companies became wholly owned subsidiaries of Singapore Technologies, with the latter converting itself into an investment holding company. The four major divisions of the group are:

- ST Aerospace involved in aircraft maintenance and engineering with operations in Singapore, Australia, US and UK;
- ST Kinetics specializes in design, development and manufacture of speciality vehicles, weapons systems and maintenance and munitions;
- ST Marine designs, upgrades and builds naval and commercial vessels; and
- ST Electronics is in communications systems and software for traffic control.

Singapore Technologies is the largest electronics system firm in Southeast Asia. The contributions of these separate sectors to the group's activities were as follows. In 2000, the aerospace unit contributed 42.3 per cent, the land systems accounted for 23.3 per cent, with electronics another 18.2 per cent, marine 15.8 per cent, and other activities contributed 0.27 per cent.

The subsidiaries in the group were jointly owned by Temasek Holdings and Singapore Technologies. It was listed on the Singapore Stock Exchange and on NASDAQ seeking capital and sophisticated technology. ST Assembly Test Service, another semiconductor subsidiary, was listed on NASDAQ in January 2000 with corporate units in San Diego, Japan, Taiwan and France. Endogenous growth of technology was limited and uncertain despite serious efforts by the state to create a knowledge-intensive economy, that would be globally competitive, producing high value-added products. The prime strategy, therefore, was to acquire technology through global acquisitions. The acquisition of Global Crossing with Hutchison Whampoa reveals this hasty, ill-advised extravagance.

The management structure of Singapore Technologies is clear evidence of technocratic aspirations. Chairman Ho Ching, who was managing director of Temasek Holdings, is an engineer, while her husband, Lee Hsien Loong, a director of Singapore Technologies, is a computer specialist. Lucien Wong and other influential bureaucrats provided further expertise.

Figure 9.4 reveals the magnitude of interlocking ownership and functions between Singapore Technologies and Sembawang Corporation and Capita Land. Singapore Technologies is an investment holding company with critical financial links to Temasek Holdings and Raffles Holdings. It also preserves inter-firm links with the other major GLCs such as Sembawang Corporation.

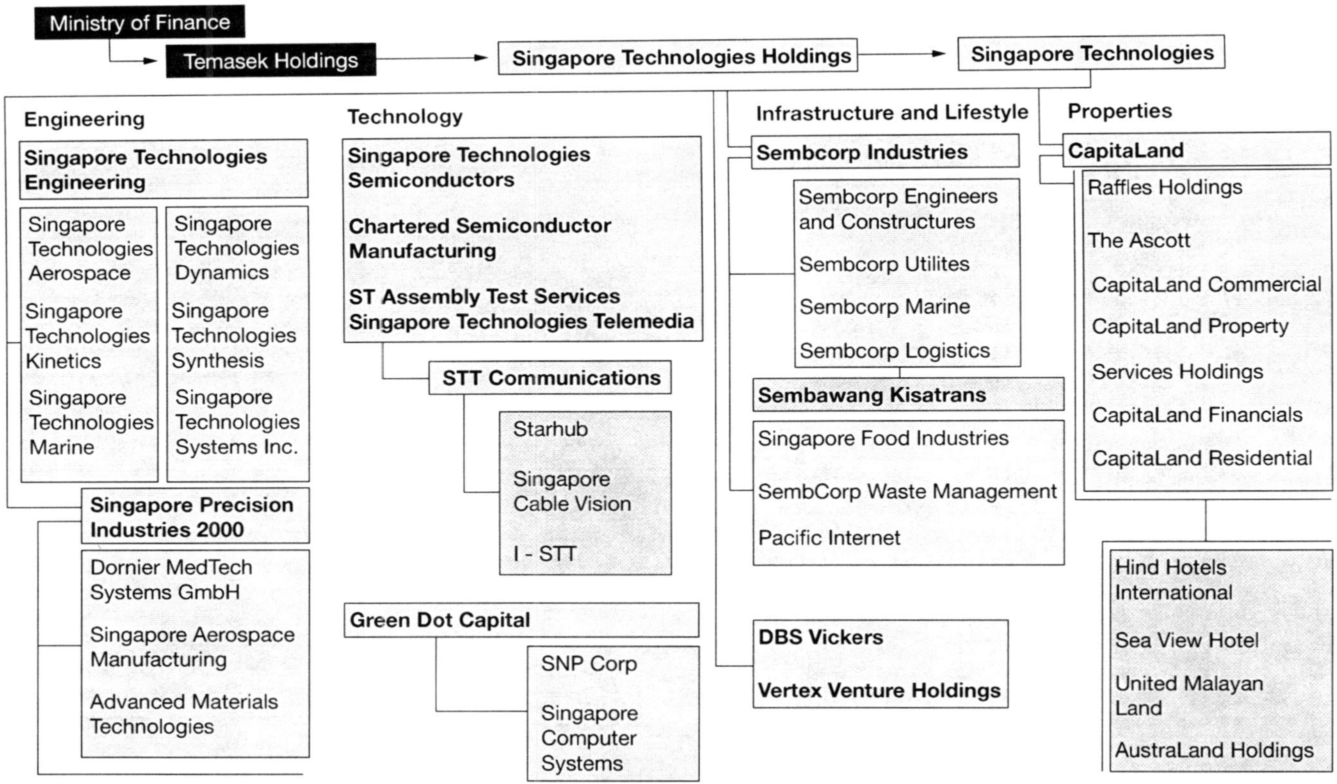

Figure 9.4 Group structure of Singapore Technologies

Source: Annual Report of Singapore Technologies, 2003

Table 9.4 Key financial ratios of STEng

Key ratios	*1996*	*1997*	*1998*	*1999*	*2000*	*2001*	*2002*
Profitability							
ROAA (before tax) (%)	6.22	7.89	8.26	8.97	10.50	9.94	9.23
ROE (before tax) (%)	19.81	24.03	29.05	34.66	44.08	31.52	27.75
ROE (after tax) (%)	12.71	14.34	18.03	23.17	30.79	24.51	22.23
Net profit margin (%)	7.62	8.18	9.31	11.37	12.75	13.86	12.63
Operating profit margin (%)	12.68	16.36	16.21	15.05	16.00	15.72	14.89
Operating efficiency							
Asset turnover (S$ m)	0.52	0.54	0.51	0.52	0.51	0.56	0.58
Inventory turnover (S$ m)	12.11	12.82	4.84	5.61	4.60	4.39	4.17
Gearing							
Total equity/(long-term loans + equity) (S$ m)	0.97	0.95	0.96	0.98	0.99	1.00	1.00
Total assets/total liabilities (S$ m)	1.46	1.44	1.35	1.34	1.27	1.46	1.49
Liquidity							
Liquidity ratio (current assets/current liabilities)	1.09	1.20	0.99	0.99	0.95	1.34	1.41
Quick ratio ((CA-inventories)/CL)	0.52	0.81	0.51	0.41	0.56	0.79	0.84
Cash ratio ((cash + short-term inv.)/CL)	0.67	0.51	0.52	0.58	0.40	0.55	0.58
Inventory working capital ratio (sales/ave working cap.)	8.93	13.24	–8.67	1,123.47	–31.59	5.15	46.48
Growth							
Turnover (%)		18.4	12.5	6.2	28.0	9.3	6.0
Operating profit (%)		52.9	11.5	–1.4	36.1	7.4	0.5
Profit before taxation (%)		36.7	23.2	20.4	37.5	6.7	–6.2
Profit after taxation (%)		27.1	28.4	30.2	41.4	19.0	–3.9
Total assets (%)		15.5	19.5	3.7	30.7	–1.1	3.1
Total liabilities (%)		16.8	27.3	4.7	38.4	–14.5	1.5
Equity growth (%)		12.7	1.9	0.9	8.1	49.2	6.6

Source: Annual Reports, STEng, 1996–2002

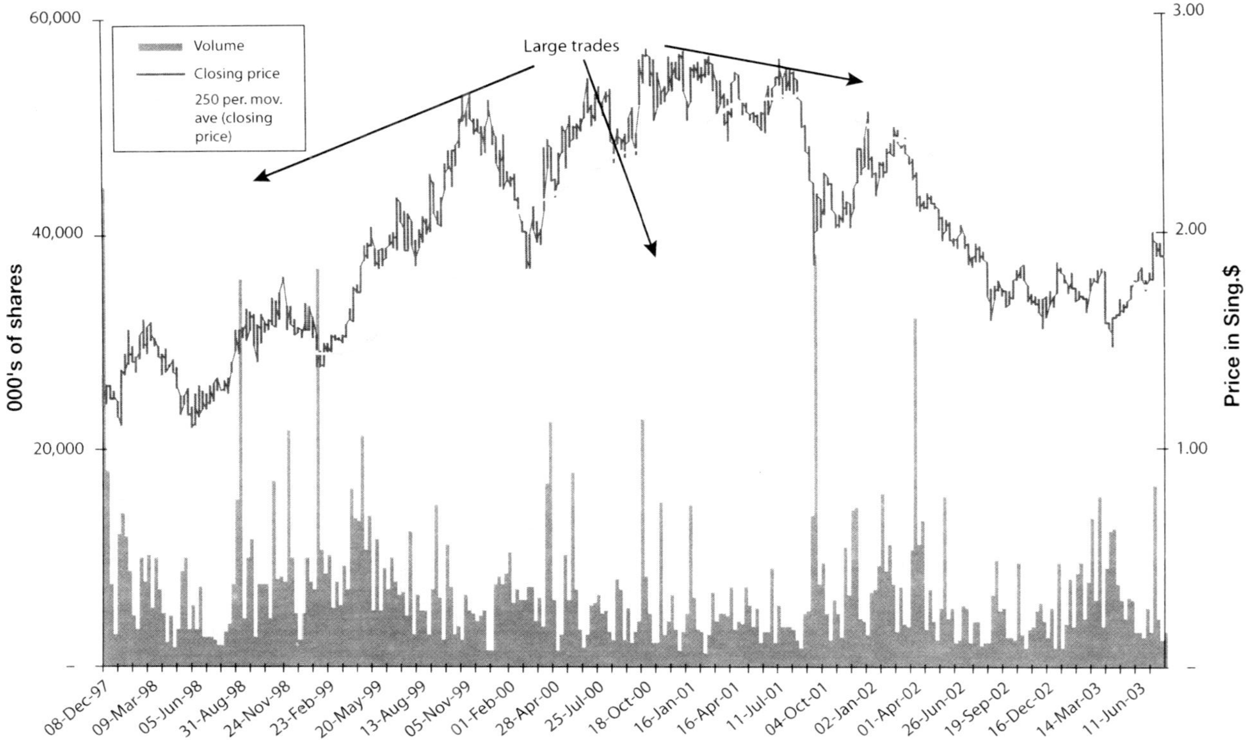

Figure 9.5 STEng share price and volume

Source: Singapore Stock Exchange Publications, 1997–2003

Its main listed firm, Singapore Technologies Engineering, revealed clear stable growth between 1996 and 2000 (see Table 9.4). There was an increase in total assets throughout 1996–2002, but there was a weakness in operating efficiency, despite these healthy profits and almost a doubling of its net assets between 1996 and 2002. Singapore Technologies Engineering revealed the same stability on the stock market. Its trading volume was adequate and there were only short-term falls in price (see Figure 9.5). The occasional large volumes of trading could be because of purchases by the state or institutions. It could also result from an increased interest owing to stock splits.

This trend in increased factor inputs without an equivalent improvement in efficiency is hardly surprising for corporate performance in Singapore. Peebles and Wilson, Krugman, Bloch and Tang have highlighted this low or negative element of total factor productivity in Singapore's growth. 'Factor accumulation, in particular capital growth accounts for almost all rapid output growth in Singapore's manufacturing.'[26]

The Swiss-based Institute of Management Development, *World Competitiveness Yearbook 2001*, placed Singapore as the most competitive Asian economy and even ranked it second to the US. This was based on 297 criteria and a survey of 36,000 top global and local executives. Their focus was on transparency, investment and state strategies. But total factor productivity analysis clearly reveals weakness in technical capacity and efficient use of factor inputs. This is a direct result of the lack of endogenous growth of R&D, as exemplified in the patterns of growth of hi-tech clusters such as Singapore Technologies, Sembawang Corporation and Keppel Corporation. The transfer of technology through state sponsorship or the acquisition of mediocre or failing foreign technology firms is flawed; neither approach can replicate the advantages of endogenous innovation.[27]

Telecoms: Singapore Telecommunications (SingTel)

SingTel is a specialist firm involved in telecoms systems and services: postal services, sale and maintenance of telecoms equipment, provision of mobile phone and paging services, data communication services, value-added network and IT services. It secured a monopoly on fixed national and international services to March 2000 and this was to continue on a non-exclusive base until March 2017. SingTel also possessed exclusive rights to mail services until March 2007.

There were hesitant steps, not at privatization, but attempts to introduce some competition. One attempt, albeit weak, was the duopoly in telecommunications services which ran from April 2000, whereby SingTel had to share its terrestrial services with Star Hub, a consortium of corporations from Singapore, Britain and Japan.[28]

SingTel is owned and controlled by Temasek Holdings. By 1999 Temasek held a stake of 79.7 per cent. It had sold a tiny number of shares to the public in 1993. By 2004 this non-state holding increased to 37.29 per cent. The integrated corporate structure in Singapore and its affiliated companies overseas are shown in Figure 9.6. It possessed a market capitalization of S$40 billion in January 2004, emerging as one of the largest telecommunications groups in Asia. More than a third of its total sales revenue in the same year was earned outside Singapore. Its increase in turnover between 1995 and 2000 was fairly modest, rising from S$3,516 million in March 1995 to S$4,865.8 million in March 2000. Its net profits of S$1,325.3 million in 1995 rose to S$1,852.3 million in March 2000. Its return on equity was

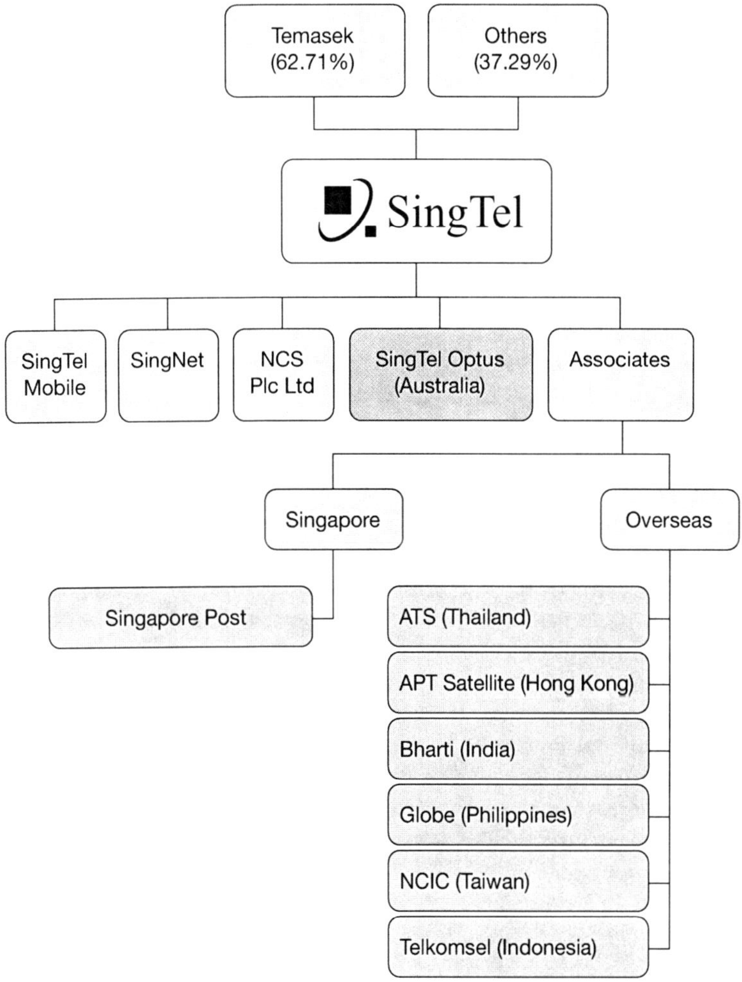

Figure 9.6 Structure of SingTel and its overseas expansion

Source: Annual Report of SingTel, 2003

30.8 per cent in 1995, falling to 28.4 per cent; its profitability ratio fluctuated between 0.381 and 0.400. Its organic efficiency growth ratio was between 22.38 per cent in 1995 to 17.84 per cent in 2000. Its performance on the Singapore Stock Exchange was stable though modest. Share prices fluctuated very little; gross earnings per share mediated between S$0.162 to S$0.168 between 1998 and 2000, and registered price earning ratios of 20.7 per cent to 22.4 per cent in the same years. Between 2003 and 2004 a share price rise of 13 per cent was recorded.

SingTel pursued an ambitious policy of global expansion with joint-ventures and strategic alliances in 20 countries, although the main focus has been in Asia (see Figure 9.6). APT is the largest mobile communications group in Thailand with a 57 per cent market share in 2004. The Bharti group possesses an integrated service of fixed line, national–international as well as mobile, and it is the largest mobile phone service provider in India. Telkomsel is a leading cellular telecoms group in Indonesia, absorbing a market share there of 51 per cent in September 2004. NCIC in Taiwan operates the fixed line network. Its interests in China are substantial. SingTel has operated in Beijing since September 1994, in Shanghai since 1996 and in Guangzhou since May 2002. In 2001 it acquired Cable and Wireless Optus of Australia, the second largest phone company in Australia. It has an agreement with Virgin to create a regional mobile network for Asia, excluding Japan. These overseas acquisitions have provided lucrative profits. In 2004 overseas investments contributed 14.6 per cent of its pre-tax profits.

In Singapore it has retained its dominance, offering an integrated product and services package in telecommunications which accounts for 85 per cent of total interests. Foreign competition in Singapore is negligible, and SingTel's advanced technology and monopoly of government contracts has ensured its increasing monopoly. SingTel reveals a concentration in shareholding with the principal shareholder being the state and Temasek Holdings. This is replicated in a privileged access to finance and R&D, while intra-group trade and interlocking management links result in a further concentrated institutional ownership and power and influence. SingTel, though focusing on a narrow sector of the telecoms industry, has carved out a monopoly share of the market. It faces few internal or external threats so the performance of the company is steady with little uncertainty, particularly since competition is neutralized by state ownership and state control. Would more flexibility and less rigidity through the loosening of this near monopoly improve performance? Since the domestic market is small, competition may not be a boon.

The shortcomings of the GLCs

These discussions of the four major GLCs clearly reveal their patterns of search for dominance both in the domestic market and overseas. Their concentrated growth in essentially capital-intensive sectors has had little effect on their performance but has crucially squeezed out competition, in essence domestic private enterprise. Second, the state has, with their dominance, become an important and constant source of R&D and information. Such centralized sources of innovation have further smothered private entrepreneurial innovation and risk taking. Third, the combined use of equity, finance and board control by the state has created a hierarchic governance structure that is composed of the Lee family, Cabinet ministers, bureaucrats and a tiny elite of foreign experts. Such an entrenched elite imposes business efficiency with an absence of fraud, but offers little radical thinking and adventure. The interdependence of the major corporate groups prevails with board membership being held by the same tiny cohort of co-opted individuals. Philipp Yeo, for example, was Chairman of EDB, Singapore Technologies, Sembawang Corporation, Sembawang Industries, and of Pidemco and Capita Land at various periods of the 1990s and in early 2000. The First Family, too, carved out permanent managerial positions.

In short, Singapore needs not just different organizational structures to meet operational needs but also flexible structures suitable for short- and long-term plans. The divisional managers crucial for monitoring operations as well as financial plans need to be monitored by a heterogeneous managerial elite, responsive to changing environments.

The GLC, though diversified, possesses individual firms that are highly specialized and because of well-integrated suppliers and customers in the domestic market, they face less uncertainty except in electronics with its highly fluctuating demand. Here, too, the state intervenes to introduce stability. Each group (GLC) thus operates across a number of industries with distribution of sales across these industries and a degree of relatedness among the product segments of each industry with preferential access to the state, to finance and to international markets. With their existing managerial talent, it is difficult to launch new business in a variety of industries.

Privatization since 1985 has had little impact. The sovereignty of the GLCs remains unchallenged. The paucity of local businessmen with the expertise to manage the knowledge-intensive new industries is serious. One cannot bemoan the absence of a culture of entrepreneurship, where an interlocking group of civil servants, politicians and the Lee brotherhood command influence in all sectors of the corporate economy. Institutions that regulate, not control the corporate sector, such as the bureaucracy and political party, have become omnipotent, creating further barriers to creative individual private enterprise. The government, reluctant to privatize strategic industries such as defence, electricity, power and telecommunications, has also been slow to be market led. Prices are not competitive. There is a failure to create 'brands', despite the frenzy for specialism within corporations. The dominance of foreign multinationals since the 1970s has further squeezed out local firms. The continuing insecurity of domestic private enterprise in a sea of dominant GLCs and foreign multinationals, now has had to confront an aggressive booming Chinese economy in the 1990s. Finally, Temasek's indifference to the funding of these small and medium private enterprises has led to them grouping in niche markets in food, textiles, or as subcontractors in electronics to foreign firms. A brief case study of a private firm will assist in understanding the background to the failure of private enterprise in Singapore in this period.

Creative Technology: a case study of a private enterprise

Creative Technology (CT) was founded in 1981 by Sim Wong Hoo, a former employee of a foreign multinational. CT develops, manufactures and markets an array of multimedia solutions for the PC, both for entertainment and education purposes. It was listed on the Singapore Stock Exchange and, in 1992, on NASDAQ. CT's products are marketed through OEM arrangements as well as through retail channels. It has its headquarters in Singapore, but its divisions for R&D and sales distribution are based in subsidiaries in North America, Europe and East Asia.

Since 1984 CT has been involved in producing locally designed personal computers, Cubic 99 and, in 1986, Cubic Multilingual multimedia PC with voice and music. In 1989 it produced Sound Blaster for IBM computers. Its focus was on multimedia hardware and software products for PCs both for home entertainment as well as education. Its difficulty was the lack of access to hi-tech clusters in Singapore, which remained the provenance of the state. CT ventured overseas where it could tap into niche markets through joint ventures or acquisitions.

The major acquisitions by CT between January 1993 and September 2000 provide a serious insight into its strategies for growth. In January 1993 it purchased E-Mu Systems and in May 1993 it acquired Share Vision Technology, both in California, followed by Digicom (California), and Aureal Semiconductor. This wave of acquisitions briefly produced chaos on its share prices between 1993 and 1995. There were also rumours of a takeover by Samsung.

The two major shareholders are Sim Wong Hoo, the proprietor, and a direct holding by Capital Group Companies. The growth was modest, but crucially its stock market performance was volatile. Although it saw a dramatic increase in sales between 1999 and 2000, it failed to develop durable subcontracting contracts for the GLCs as well as with foreign multinationals.[29] The lack of a stable technological infrastructure in Singapore for CT meant it was unable to consolidate itself in the domestic market. The government-led structural transformation in manufacturing was so rapid and targeting of industrial sectors so excessive,[30] that CT, like other private firms, could not develop appropriate links between the different sectors being targeted by state finance and preference. Sim Wong Hoo's second firm, Media Ring, a telecom software company could not develop sub-contracting ties with SingTel because GLCs were interacting with other GLCs' related units rather than evolving loyal, long-term, sub-contracting relationships that were a fundamental feature of the Japanese *keiretsu*. This was particularly severe after 2001 when entry opportunities for domestic private enterprise became increasingly difficult, with GLCs creating manufacturing clusters with foreign multinationals in Singapore and in foreign countries. This, however, did not lead to a hollowing out of these industries in Singapore, since the GLCs still maintained a grip on the domestic expansion.

The stock market and corporate economy

The emphasis here is on institutions that nurture entrepreneurial initiative, assist with finance and encourage risk taking. The small stock market in Singapore, again dominated by the GLCs, failed to promote such dynamic private enterprise.

The stock market could have supplied the necessary financial resources to assist the private family firms. The Singapore stock exchange remained small with GLCs credited with more than 50 per cent of its market capitalization and Temasek Holdings as the largest single investor. The high profile of the GLCs had serious implications for private firms and for healthy competition and trading on the stock market.

The market capitalization of the Singapore Stock Exchange grew from US$50 billion in 1988 to US$119 billion in 1993, to US$207 billion in 1999, falling to US$174 billion in June 2000. Hence, between 1988 and 2000, the stock market registered only a threefold increase (see Tables 9.5 and 9.6).[31]

The percentage change in market capitalization between 1988 and 1995 is small even in comparison with the rest of Southeast Asia. Singapore recorded a change of 517 per cent compared with 856 per cent for Malaysia, 1,270 per cent for the Philippines, 1,508 per cent for Thailand and 3,320 per cent for Indonesia. Singapore also had the lowest number of listed companies in the ASEAN, while Malaysia had the highest, followed by Thailand, the Philippines and Indonesia.[32]

Equally, Singapore's trading on the stock market between 1988 and 1995 was lower than its neighbours. It recorded only 1,244 per cent growth in stock trading while Malaysia revealed a percentage growth in trading of 2,854 per cent, Philippines had 1,533 per cent, Thailand had 918 per cent and Indonesia 3,599 per cent. It is clearly evident that Malaysia, Indonesia and the Philippines had larger liquidity and more listings than Singapore.[33] This limited growth persisted despite financial liberalization since 1968. Capital controls were lifted and by 1978 foreign exchange transactions were encouraged in any currency. The Singapore International Monetary Exchange was established in 1984 for derivatives trading and over the counter trading in foreign shares, broadening the base for share trading. Malaysian shares dominated this CLOB but after the 1997 financial crisis this fell because of constraints on trading in foreign currency in Malaysia. The Singapore Stock

Table 9.5 Singapore Stock Exchange: turnover of stocks and shares, 1968–95

	Total		*Industries*		*Finance*		*Hotels*		*Properties*		*Mining*		*Plantation*	
Year	*Units*	*S$ m*	*Unit*	*S$ m*	*Unit*	*S$ m*	*Unit*	*S$ m*	*Unit*	*S$ m*	*Unit*	*S$ m*	*Unit*	*S$ m*
1968	479.8	874.5	355.4	739.2	–	–	34.3[a]	50.1[b]	86.5	77.4	1.6	5.7	2.0	2.1
1970	449.6	740.9	405.4	698.9	–	–	19	17.6	18.4	11.5	2.2	6.2	4.6	6.5
1978	1,477.2	3,365.2	886.7	1,944.5	152.4	637.1	116.8	163.9	142.9	216.4	61.4	129.6	117.0	273.7
1980	2,222.2	7,824.7	1,311.2	4,615.3	229.7	1,295.7	143.2	275.5	325.2	1,030.4	60.3	196.7	114.0	392.6
1983	3,605.2	11,807.1	2,193.4	1,205.1	340.5	2,108.0	212.6	524.1	317.6	1,033.3	125.3	256.6	170.1	502.5
1985	3,024.7	6,319.3	2,144.8	4,338.0	286.2	1,227.5	109.1	153.4	159.0	246.5	151.4	105.2	86.2	203.3
1989	21,646.0	39,149.9	9,773.6	19,654.5	1,342.0	4,799.3	811.2	1,472.9	4,031.3	7,117.4	200.1	397.8	784.0	1,261.8
1990	18,487.0	36,756.0	8,921.7	19,177.4	2,394.3	6,172.8	882.0	1,583.2	2,966.9	5,978.7	51.0	95.7	1,061.7	1,385.9
1993	66,398.2	127,796.9	33,170.9	67,663.9	6,585.0	20,027.6	2,925.9	5,626.5	12,563.5	20,468.1	133.4	277.4	3,509.1	5,823.7
1995	33,918.6	83,866.3	19,272.4	46,450.6	3,506.8	15,843.9	1,106.3	2,212.5	3,764.7	11,391.3	87.8	251.4	899.5	2,093.2

Notes:
a Figure prior to 1973 includes Finance.
b Figures exclude first seven months of turnover and value.

Source: Stock Exchange of Singapore publications, including Company Handbooks for various years

Table 9.6 Turnover on the Singapore Stock Exchange (equities)[a]

	1998	*1999*
SGX Mainboard (S$ trades)		
Volume (million)	35,938.1	96,608.8
Multi-industry	5,751.1	7,861.8
Manufacturing	6,574.1	26,855.2
Commerce	2,149.5	9,302.1
Transport/storage/communication	3,926.1	9,823.2
Finance	5,173.5	5,991.8
Construction	1,686.5	8,587.9
Properties	6,908.4	7,889.6
Hotel/restaurants	302.8	1,629.5
Services	882.2	2,560.9
Electricity/gas/water	–	202.3
Agriculture	–	1,131.7
Debentures, bonds and loan stocks	2,583.8	14,772.7
Value ($ million)	74,479.4	151,107.5
Multi-industry	8,834.0	13,804.1
Manufacturing	13,199.6	33,248.7
Commerce	1,982.1	7,762.4
Transport/storage/communication	11,079.0	20,532.3
Finance	32,278.9	40,043.2
Construction	861.3	5,637.8
Properties	12,999.1	18,196.8
Hotel/restaurants	204.4	1,156.3
Services	1,221.7	3,789.3
Electricity/gas/water	–	64.5
Agriculture	–	433.3
Debentures, bonds and loan stocks	819.3	6,438.8

Note:
a All figures calculated to two decimal places.
Source: Turnover on the Singapore Exchange, *Yearbook of Statistics*, Singapore, 2000

Exchange allowed foreign firms to own up to 49 per cent of equity in local firms and could increase this to 70 per cent after three years. MAS even increased this ceiling on foreign ownership of local banks to 40 per cent from 20 per cent in 1990. By 1996 non-resident firms were permitted to list in Singapore and issue bonds in Singapore currency as long as 35 per cent of the revenue would be earned locally and management and regional headquarters would be located in Singapore.

These measures, though liberal and attractive to foreign investors seeking to list corporations in Singapore, were craftily restricting these groups from entry into strategic industries. Thus, while providing unrestricted access to all investors, they shielded those critical sectors that were the dominant provenance of the state. This left the stock exchange in the hands of the state.

Privatization could have increased the depth and scope of the stock market, creating new counters as well as adding to existing counters. However, the divestment of the late 1980s when GLCs were shedding unprofitable firms and diversifying into more lucrative hi-tech sectors could have produced valuable swaps for domestic private enterprise. But this did not happen. The government's share of the corporate economy was only reduced by 10 per cent between 1985 and 1989. The sincerity behind the encouragement of an increasing role for SMEs through an increase in government grants, loans and tax incentives had limited impact since no protection was offered to the SMEs. In reality, the emphasis on capital-intensive industrial sectors produced over-capitalization in such stocks that were already the monopoly of the state. The weakness of venture capital in the domestic market encouraged private hi-tech firms to list abroad. This desire for a higher profile and to attract institutional investors meant that the only recourse was to go abroad. This is seen in the case study of Creative Technologies.

Singapore could have improved market liquidity and encouraged more diverse firms and improved trading and settlement of transactions through the creation of a regional stock market. This was broached by Brigadier-General Lee in March 2000.[34] There was an awareness that the composition of stocks on the Singapore Stock Exchange could be improved through a regional collaboration. The high ratio of technology stocks in Singapore, with Malaysia's high incidence of industrial, plantation, banking and property stocks together with Indonesia's emphasis on agricultural commodities and banking stocks, and Thai banking and property stocks could form the basis for serious collaboration and perhaps a common regional stock market index. Such transnational networks could overcome the limitations of size, trading volume, narrow ownership, limited performance, in the Singapore stock market.[35] However, political sensitivities as well as the highly differentiated experience of these individual countries during the Asian financial crisis aborted any progress towards such regional cooperation. Hence, when Malaysian authorities froze all trading of Malaysian shares on the Singapore Stock Exchange in September 1998, the number of companies trading on CLOB immediately declined from 130 to 18. So the only option for Singapore was to seek markets in the US and Europe.

This move was a rational one since corporate governance standards were high among Singapore corporations. Accounting standards are high; there is comprehensive and continuous disclosure of price/equity fields, financial reports of Singapore corporations are released twice a year and there is ease of operations because of the electronic coverage provided by the Singapore Stock Exchange. There is little speculative activity, growth is slow but gradual, little volatility was observed even during the 1997 financial crisis. Such uniformity of stock market experience is seen in Figures 9.2, 9.3 and 9.5 on the performance of Keppel, Sembawang and Singapore Technologies on the stock market. The trend was for the ST index to closely shadow the share prices of the stocks of these elite GLCs, displaying little volatility (see Figure 9.7).

Figure 9.7 Straits Times Index movement

Source: Singapore Stock Exchange Publications

Globalization

In view of the small domestic market and the state's clear ambition to create a knowledge- and capital-intensive economy, the distinct option was for global growth. The investment groups Temasek, GLC and Capita Land identified the opportunities for investment, identified the possible partners and assisted the GLCs to establish the plants overseas. However, control could often remain with the headquarters of these firms in Singapore.

In 1992, direct equity flows abroad from Singapore averaged S$17,741 million, rising to S$53,515 million in 1997. China absorbed S$28.3 million in 1992; in 1997 this rose to S$6,777 million.[36] In 1999 Singapore was the fifth largest investor in China after Hong Kong, Taiwan, the US and Japan.[37] In 2000, 16.6 per cent of total FDI from Singapore went to China; of this, three-fifths was allocated to manufacturing and one-fifth to real estate. Malaysia absorbed 10 per cent of the total FDI from Singapore, with Europe accepting another 8.9 per cent and the US 6.5 per cent. Between 1999 and 2000 there was an increase, too, in portfolio investments, largely to the US.[38]

Between 1990 and 1998 Singapore's share of investment in China rose from 1.8 per cent to 16.8 per cent of the total investments overseas from Singapore. The 1990s was a critical phase for the regional growth and only the crisis in 1997 forced a redirection of capital flows from Singapore to the US and Europe. The expansion into China, however, was not a total success. The reform of the Chinese state enterprise led to the rise of local economic elites and entrepreneurs from the ranks of the local party. This introduced a diversity of organizational and decision-making institutions. There was already confusion over the different laws relating to property rights and tax reforms which allowed individual local governments to retain varying proportions of the taxes. Singapore GLCs accustomed to a centralized, state control of business were now confronted by diverse and often conflicting political and economic institutions. Responsiveness and flexibility were crucial in dealing with Chinese administrative and business structures. Singapore firms in China frequently lacked autonomy in decision-making. Their headquarters were slow to delegate this autonomy to local managers. Hence, Singapore corporate transplants in China had to amend structures and deal with new intermediaries locally. Such local mediation is particularly important since good *guanxi* at the local level was paramount for co-opting suitable partners for successful operations in China. Property companies from Singapore adapted more easily than electronic firms, infrastructural and logistics groups, who faced difficulties over the management of R&D and on how to transfer technology without losing control. Hence, value-added industries faced high risks in an uncertain political environment with weak corporate governance. Singapore GLCs with highly concentrated, interlocked ownership and financial institutions now faced serious agency problems in an alien environment characterized by a weak regulatory framework and unstructured information channels. Thus, all the four GLCs used property units to secure profits and offset the risks in other sectors. For the Singapore government the losses in Suzhou Industrial Park in 2001 amounted to US$77 million. This was after seven years of difficult operations there.[39]

Their experience in Indonesia, too, was fraught with difficulties. Again, an uncertain political environment and weak corporate governance muddled the ambitions of Singapore to emerge as a regional economic power. The investments from Singapore to Indonesia totalled S$328 million in 1992, increasing to S$4,669 million in 1997.[40] This increased even after the crisis, despite economic weaknesses, lawlessness, uncertainties over devolution of power to the provinces and political unrest. Reforms after 1997 were gradual and offered little guarantee of economic recovery. Singapore concentrated on the purchase of Indonesian banks and lucrative sectors in agriculture. Their long-enduring links with Chinese capitalists in Indonesia continued even though the latter had accumulated massive debts. Indonesian-Chinese capitalists used Singapore as a safe haven for capital transfers during and after the crisis.

Investments in Malaysia included the growth triangle of Singapore, Johore and Riau. This consumed almost 20 per cent of Singapore's total direct investments abroad in 1990; it was reduced to 12 per cent by 1998. Malaysia still maintained its position as second in importance to China for FDI flows from Singapore.[41]

Conclusion

On the theoretical level, models of economic behaviour exhibited by the Singapore Corporations verge on a distinct form of state managerial capitalism. There can be no doubt that corporate concentration increased at a rapid pace since the 1980s because of the dominance of the state. This period is also associated with intensive activity abroad. While mergers and acquisitions in Singapore were a factor in the increasing dominance of the GLCs, their activities abroad, too, were marked by such predatorial ambitions. Substantial economies of scale were achieved by the GLCs through these twin strategies of concentrated domestic growth and a move abroad to increase this influence. The elimination of small companies, further mergers and the progressive concentration of output under fewer producers are clear from our analysis of Keppel, Sembawang, Singapore Technologies and SingTel.

As a result of this increasing move towards larger-scale enterprises, the vogue for restructuring in the 1990s was for the four GLCs to create greater concentration through interlinks between the four, further eliminating any competitive pressure from private enterprise.

Mergers and acquisitions were also used in this period as a means of gaining access to technology with the government's ambition of creating a knowledge economy. Singapore Technologies emerged as a major player in this 'scientific revolution'.

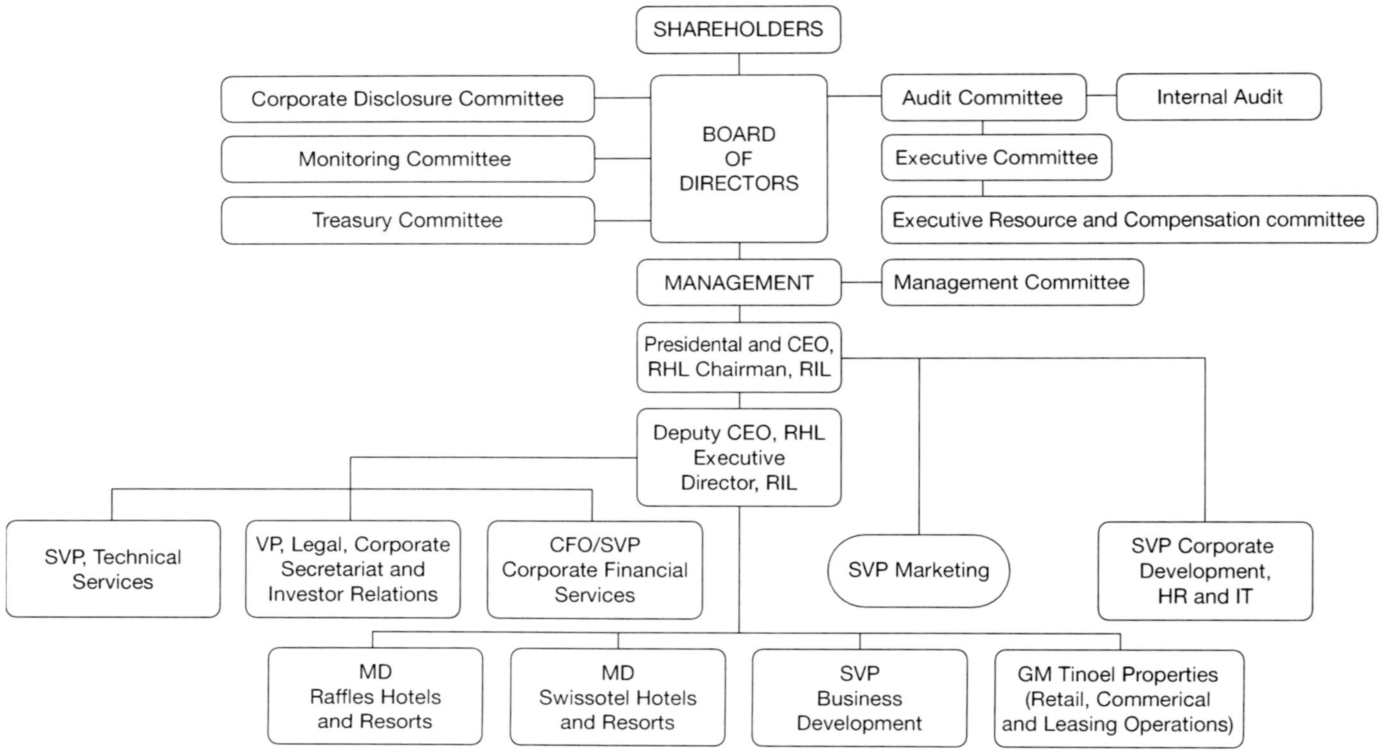

Figure 9.8 Raffles Holdings management structure

Source: Annual Report, Raffles Holdings, 2003

The adoption of a multi-divisional organizational structure meant these large firms could grow within their own specialist industries but also permitted a substantial programme of diversification. Much of this diversification into property and marketing was largely to subsidize these core R&D-intensive sectors in electronics, telecommunications and infrastructure.

After the 1997 crisis and with a sluggish stock market and the lack of venture capital, moving abroad, principally to the US closer to American fund managers, became a major priority. Singapore sought American companies as part of their research strategy. This strategy has serious implications for factor productivity in Singapore.

As argued earlier, the total factor productivity debate for Singapore has attracted a vastly contrasting spectrum of views and estimates. However, it can be consistently argued that capital accumulation accounted for a large proportion of growth, while factor productivity and efficiency proved to be of lesser significance to growth. This implies that Singapore is not a very efficient economy. Between 1973 and 1996, capital input produced 66.5 per cent contribution to real GDP growth, while labour input accounted for only 20 per cent.[42]

This skewed growth is a direct result of Singapore's industrial policies, driven by the GLCs, creating too rapid a structural transformation without appropriate institutional changes. This lack of coordination between the 'old and new industries', the missing symbiosis, is deepened by the insufficient progress in endogenous technological development. The pursuit of technology through foreign capital and the acquisition of foreign hi-tech firms further endangers this domestic progress in industrial research and development. Second, this produces the high import content of capital goods in Singapore's exports. The international competitiveness of Singapore trade is affected by this deficit. Third, the economy is emerging as too specialized in electronics and heavily dependent on Asian markets, since they cannot compete with the more industrialized nations in this capital-intensive manufacturing. The erosion of competition by the highly bloated GLCs, squeezing out SMEs increases such vulnerability.[43]

Throughout there were clear management difficulties, although none were publicized. Dependence on politicians and bureaucrats to manage these large enterprises accounts for the disappointing performance of the GLCs. Their growth is stable but gradual, not impressive in terms of organic growth efficiency, or in increase in R&D growth internally. A segment of their overseas acquisitions on R&D-intensive sectors failed.

De-regulation, disengagement from such aggressive state intervention and an emphasis on enhanced competition as generators of efficiency must be emphasized if Singapore is to achieve its ambition of becoming a regional economic power in Southeast Asia.

10 Thai financial institutions

Concentration, crisis and restructuring

Introduction: banking, growth and concentration

The principal aim of this chapter is to examine the structure, organization and performance of Thai financial institutions and the punishing impact of the financial crisis of 1997 on this sector. A brief comparison with Korea helps to uncover embedded structural features that determined the devastation of the impact as well as the speed of recovery.

Growth of concentration

The oligopolistic character of Thai banking since 1904 was derived from the dominance of a few large domestic banks and the exclusion of foreign-owned ones. This concentration, represented by the share of total assets and share of deposits of the top six Thai banks, increased from 45 per cent in 1964 to 78 per cent in 1983 and to 80 per cent in 1996.[1] This consolidation and control of market share by a few continued even after 1997, when the bulk of financial assets were still held by the five largest banks despite the easing of restrictions on foreign ownership following the crisis.

This dominance by a few large banks was matched by the concentrated, almost impenetrable holdings of certain important families. In Thailand, as in Indonesia, the total shareholding of the top five shareholders was high, being 56 per cent in 2002, with one single shareholder usurping 35.3 per cent of total shareholding.[2] This ownership concentration was inherited from the 1930s and persisted into the 1990s. The top five listed corporations with banks possessed concentrated family ownership of 52.4 per cent in 1990, 68.9 per cent in 1993, 56.6 per cent in 1997 and 57.5 per cent in 1998.[3]

Such concentrations in ownership were achieved in diverse ways. First, the organizational structure of banks facilitated the preservation of monopolistic ownership and control. Typically, the founding family owned and controlled listed banks through holding companies and affiliated subsidiaries in financial and industrial sectors. The largest shareholder was frequently the holding company. In 1990, the typical holding company in the banking group absorbed an average of 27 per cent of total shareholding. In addition, individual family members held 18.5 per cent. Consequently, the family emerged as the majority shareholder, a situation that persisted after 1997. Financial and securities firms in the group held a further 1.5 to 5.5 per cent of the total shareholding. The insignificance of institutional shareholding, both domestic and foreign, persisted throughout. The state as an institutional investor did increase between 1990 and 1998 but only from 1.1 per cent to 2.5 per cent. Pension funds, meanwhile, remained the second major institutional investor, followed by mutual fund groups, which made short-term investments in the hope of short-term trading profits. Public (retail) investors could possess up to 40 per cent but because it was distributed among a large number of them, it ultimately accounted for a tiny proportion.[4] The significance of a crucial minority shareholding had already been eroded by the 1987 removal of the requirement that 30 per cent of IPO shares on the Thai Stock Exchange should be held by small shareholders.

This concentration was further intensified through the absence of any separation between ownership and management in these large Thai banks. The founding family, their friends, relatives, political and bureaucratic cronies would pack the Board of Directors and Executive Committees. Ironically, the Public Limited Company Act of 1992 conspired in this coalescence of family ownership and management because it eased existing stipulations on the appointment of independent directors to the board. This legislation also repealed critical sections on the prosecution of bank owners. Audits were lax. It was only the 1999 regulations that enforced strict audits and better provision for bad debt. This desire to maintain existing family ownership was not disturbed even after the increase in foreign equity in these family banks after 1998. Only Nakornthon Bank lost a significant share of family ownership.

Profligate financing patterns clearly coincided with high ownership concentrations. The founding family owned, managed and used bank debt to finance the growth of banking and non-financial subsidiaries. A large amount of domestic and foreign capital was channelled through the group's own holding companies. The ratio of total debt to total assets increased from 50.8 per cent in 1990 to 52.7 per cent in 1996. Short-term debt was the dominant portion of this.[5]

To illustrate this concentration of family ownership and management, it is worthwhile analysing the interlocking family holdings of Bangkok Bank and Bangkok Metropolitan Bank. Bangkok Bank increased family ownership and control throughout the period from 1960. Family dominance of the bank was maintained despite the increasing number of public shareholders, which amounted to 261 in 1965; 24,194 in 1993; and 26,255 in 1996.[6] The holding company, Bangkok Bank Cayman Islands, was surrounded by several affiliated companies such as Bangkok First Investment and Trust, Bangkok Insurance and Robina Credit Overseas (Hong Kong), which owned shares in Bangkok Bank. These clusters of firms increased family ownership of the main bank. Thus, when the Thai government attempted, through legislation enacted in 1987, to curb the large private ownership of banks, the Sophonpanich family increased its shareholding through family-owned holding companies, which subsequently accounted for an increase of 11.4 per cent equity in the bank. Private investment firms in the group held another 19.4 per cent equity in the bank. The holding company structure was complex. Indeed, there were multiple holding companies operating in Hong Kong, the Cayman Islands, Liechtenstein and New York. Activities and information were decentralized but ownership and governance were retained by the family and executive board members, who were nominated from the Thai army, political elites and the bureaucracy. This use of a holding company to secure new markets and new capital without the weakening of family control was mimicked by Bangkok Metropolitan Bank and the Bank of Asia. The holding company linked the core bank, its subsidiaries, affiliates and other mutual shareholding groups involved in real estate, securities and other diverse financial interests. The bank was designed not only to concentrate and secure family ownership but also to coordinate upstream and downstream activities in finance. Thus, while the Bangkok Bank created vast financial networks in Thailand, Indonesia, Vietnam, Hong Kong and China, the connections with Li Ka Shing and other major Chinese capitalists were useful in securing rent-seeking activities and concessions in the Pacific Basin.

Bangkok Metropolitan Bank, in which the Techapaibul family held 40 per cent equity, pursued a similar policy of rapid internationalization following the boom of the 1980s, despite the collapse of its subsidiaries in 1979 and again in 1983. It opened branches in the Cayman Islands, San Francisco, New York and Hanoi. Although its American branches were closed in April 1996, the bank continued to expand into Vietnam. This growth and concentration were assisted by links with politicians and bureaucrats and through patterns of connected lending to family, relatives, elite capitalists, the army and politicians. Preferential credit distributed by the big five Thai banks to politicians, the army and bureaucrats ensured the continuity of these concentrations.

Bangkok Bank possessed powerful ties to the military elite in the 1947–57 period when the Ratchakhru Group was in power and they had access to Japanese capital. This ceased when Field Marshall Sarit Thanarat seized power in 1957. Between 1964 and 1973, close ties between Chin Sophonpanich and Thanom Kittikhachon, Prime Minister and Defence Minister, and General Praphat Charusathian, Deputy Prime Minister, assisted the revival of Bangkok Bank following Sarit's tenure. Boonchu Rojanastian, the Managing Director of Bangkok Bank, became Deputy Prime Minister in 1980, with the ambition of creating 'Thailand Inc.'. Moreover, Chatri Sophonpanich was a close friend of Prem Tinsulanond, prime minister from March 1980 to April 1988, and this helped the rescue of Bangkok Bank in Hong Kong. By the 1990s, senior executives of the bank were in the Cabinet, for instance, both Dr Amnuay Viravan and Dr Vichit Suraporigchai were in

Chuan Leekpai's first government (September 1992–July 1995). The latter was also Finance Minister during the Chavalit Yongchaiyudh government (November 1996–November 1997). The bank transferred its loyalties to the New Aspiration Party and then to the Thai Rak Thai Party of Thaksin Shinawatra. These ties with the state enabled the bank to retain family and friends as major shareholders, while absorbing foreign equity as part of the recapitalization of the bank in 1998.

Other banks also forged close links with bureaucrats and politicians. Tarin Nimmanhaeminda of Siam Commercial Bank was the Minister of Finance in both Chuan Leekpai governments (September 1992–July 1995 and November 1997–February 2001). Others also held office during Chuan's tenures: Lamsam of Thai Farmers' Bank was Deputy Minister of Commerce, and Pornthep Techapaibul of Bangkok Metropolitan Bank was Deputy Minister of Science and Technology.

The major issues here are as follows. First, does this concentration of ownership in terms of family, political cronies and bureaucrats affect performance? Second, does this affect leverage decisions? Third, does this ownership and capital concentration have implications for these corporate groups' expansion into diverse financial sectors, as well as into capital-intensive industrial interests such as telecommunications, petroleum and electronics?

These questions on performance are addressed by our detailed case studies of these banks. At the outset, though, it is possible to draw some brief conclusions on the linkage between concentrated ownership and performance from a few financial indicators. In the early 1990s, these five banks possessed high debt to equity ratios: an average of 148.3 per cent. By 1997, this had increased to 200 per cent.[7]

Long-term debt to equity ratio was 42.4 per cent and total debt to assets ratio was 52.8 per cent. Long-term debt to assets ratio was 14.8 per cent. Net working capital to assets ratio was 28.0 per cent and operating capital to assets ratio was 64.3 per cent.[8] The product innovation that took place within these banks from the mid-1980s increased this concentration and instability. Bangkok Bank had its own asset and fund management subsidiaries and tapped into diverse markets through joint-ventures with foreign investment banks including Lehman, Mitsubushi, DBS and Morgan Stanley Asset Management. By January 1994, Bangkok Bank had global investments of US$5 billion.[9] Bangkok Metropolitan Bank, imitating such moves, formed fund management and leasing companies with South Korean firms and other Thai financial institutions. This transition into leasing, factoring, mortgage loans and investment banking increased its asset base as well as its financial vulnerability.

Bangkok Bank combined commercial banking with capital market operations, enabling it to increase its size while eliminating any competition. In an environment of imperfect competition and during a period of rapid growth, this non-segmentation of financial interests was a distinct advantage.

Bangkok Bank opted for the internationalization of its wide-ranging activities, assisted by the cooperation of the Thai state, which greatly reduced risk. From the 1960s to the late 1970s, it was a major recipient of American military funds. From the late 1970s, foreign capital inflows, particularly from Japan, further bolstered its resources. Assisted by trading in mutual funds and debt instruments, this concentration persisted with little restraint. The abundance of foreign capital only served to nurture such diverse and risky ambitions.

Thus, the dominance of the fully private Bangkok Bank in Thailand was maintained. In 1950, its deposits accounted for 5 per cent of total bank deposits in Thailand; by 1994 they constituted 25 per cent. In the same period, the Siam Commercial Bank, which was dominated by the Thai state, saw its market share of loans fall from 21 per cent to 8 per cent.[10] However, even for Bangkok Bank, risks remained high because of the concentration of loans. Bangkok Bank's close relations with Thai industrial corporations has parallels with the Japanese main bank system. But while the Japanese networks were more stable and enduring, the linkages of the Bangkok Bank were ad hoc and changing. The Bangkok Bank acted as an agent for corporate borrowing, issuing bonds, underwriting securities and intervening in the stock market. Its clients were in a changing pool, selection often being determined by political factors.

Although Bangkok Bank was never part of an industrial conglomerate, from the 1950s it was closely involved in Thai industrialization. In the 1980s, this involvement was extended into China and Southeast Asia, often shadowing the expansion of Thai industrial corporations abroad. In 1992, the Bangkok Bank was financing Charoen Pokphand's activities in China, as well as Thai state initiatives in China's petrochemical industry. Bangkok Metropolitan Bank, in contrast, combined industrial and financial interests within the group. This diversification increased the risks. Moreover, the functional and institutional specialization of banks became blurred. Bangkok Metropolitan Bank made the transition into multi-product, innovative banking and industrial activities without the appropriate changes in corporate governance, and this increased the perils of diversification.

Another risk for the Sino-Thai commercial banks arose from their transactions with the stock market. With the growth of the Thai Stock Exchange and an increase in the volume of capitalization, the commercial banks were drawn into financing securities, often with disastrous consequences. Another source of instability was the borrowing by domestic corporations and banks from offshore financial markets.[11] Such borrowing rose from 126 billion baht in 1993 to 331 billion baht in 1996. Indeed, Thai banks' foreign currency loans in 1996 amounted to US$31.5 billion, or 17 per cent of private sector loans. By the first half of 1997 such private capital flows, particularly bond issues and syndicated loans, had fallen from US$6.5 billion in the first half of 1996 to US$4 billion.[12]

Bangkok Bank also increased its involvement in offshore finance. It raised US$31 million in April 1995 for Thai infrastructural development and in the same year it borrowed US$482 million from American fund managers.[13] Moreover, in July 1994, the Bangkok Bank had received two licences from the United State Securities and Exchange Commission to underwrite debt investments. In April 1995, the bank secured membership of the Hong Kong Liquidity Adjustment Facility, which enabled it to engage in purchase agreements with the Monetary Authority of Hong Kong. Last, the Bangkok Bank financed electricity and transport projects in Laos and Cambodia, in cooperation with Southeast Asia governments and state enterprises.[14] However, this privileged position with the state and foreign multinationals did not mean Bangkok Bank was able to escape the 1997 financial crisis unscathed. Indeed, during the crisis, it had a serious bad debt position. Through economies of scale it had spread risks. It had pursued a strategy of foreign market penetration, offering financial services not fully developed by local competitors in China and Indonesia, such as assistance in corporate restructuring, Eurobond issues and syndicated loans. Bangkok Metropolitan Bank also expanded in this direction but with less support from the state or foreign capital. Its involvement in derivatives, often as principal rather than as agent, and its exposure to fluctuating exchange rates and asset prices all added to its volatility. Having built its competence in traditional banking, the Bangkok Bank made the hazardous transition, while the Bangkok Metropolitan Bank plunged in without experience or patronage.

Another major contributing factor to this concentration is the difficulty faced by foreign banks that wish to operate in the domestic retail and investment banking sector. Indeed, domination by a few domestic banks continued with little competition from foreign banks. In 1983, foreign banks owned 4.57 per cent of total assets of the commercial banking sector and 2.12 per cent of total debts. Indeed, there was no single fully owned foreign bank until 1998. Foreign banks had 14 branches in the country in 1993 and this rose to 21 in 1998.[15]

Concentration was further assisted by foreign capital inflows.[16] For foreign capital inflows into specific sectors between 1994 and 1999, see Table 10.1. The impact of foreign capital is analysed in greater detail in the next section. For the varying proportions of external debt during the same period, see Table 10.2. Private debt formed a large share of this external debt. The central argument of this chapter is that the increasing concentration within the Thai financial sector, along with the changing sources of capital for these commercial banks, contained the roots of an unstable and unrestrained growth.

Table 10.3 on corporate finance clearly shows that over time internally generated funds contributed only half of the investment funds of corporations. On a more detailed level, internally generated funds contributed 40 per cent in 1970–4 but only 22 per cent in 1990–4. In contrast, in Japan between 1970 and 1994 internally recycled profits accounted for 70 per cent of investment.[17] Long-term bank loans were a critical source of corporate

Table 10.1 Net flow of FDI classified by sector (millions of baht)[a]

Sector	*1995*	*1996*	*1997*	*1998*	*1999*
1 Industry	14,114.3	17,941.8	58,337.0	83,505.0	21,248.0
2 Financial institutions	642.8	1,822.7	3,725.0	20,776.0	5,985.0
3 Trade	11,111.6	13,797.6	33,947.0	34,222.0	16,687.0
4 Construction	906.1	1,782.5	5,786.0	6,167.0	–167.0
5 Mining and quarrying	1,418.6	489.6	653.0	2,451.0	–405.0
6 Agriculture	232.3	51.2	37.0	19.0	53.0
7 Services	2,186.1	3,162.2	9,082.0	12,110.0	13,282.0
8 Real estate	21,245.8	19,054.0	3,467.0	20,421.0	1,823.0
9 Others	–1,970.6	–629.6	2,655.0	19,595.0	4,740.0
Total	49,887	57,472	117,689	199,266	63,246

Note:
a All figures are calculated to two decimal places.
Source: Bank of Thailand, Annual Reports, 1995–2000

Table 10.2 External debt, 1986–99 (US$ billion)

	Government		*Private non-bank*		*BIBF*		*Commercial bank*		
Year	*Long-term*	*Short-term*	*Long-term*	*Short-term*	*Long-term*	*Short-term*	*Long-term*	*Short-term*	*Total*
1986	12.0	0.1	3.1	1.9	0.0	0.0	0.3	0.9	18.3
1987	13.9	0.1	2.8	1.7	0.0	0.0	0.3	1.2	20.0
1988	13.0	0.3	3.0	2.3	0.0	0.0	0.3	2.2	21.1
1989	11.9	0.2	4.6	2.9	0.0	0.0	0.3	0.3	22.9
1990	11.3	0.3	7.3	6.2	0.0	0.0	0.3	3.9	29.3
1991	12.1	0.7	10.0	10.5	0.0	0.0	0.3	4.1	37.9
1992	12.5	0.6	11.5	12.8	0.0	0.0	0.7	5.5	43.6
1993	14.2	–	12.7	12.3	1.4	6.4	1.3	4.0	52.1
1994	15.5	0.2	13.7	7.4	3.0	15.1	3.5	6.4	64.9
1995	16.3	0.1	23.9	18.6	3.8	23.7	4.4	10.0	100.8
1996	16.7	0.1	31.2	18.8	10.7	20.5	2.3	8.4	108.7
1997	24.1	0.0	32.1	13.9	10.9	19.2	3.9	5.2	109.3
1998	30.9	0.2	34.8	10.9	6.9	14.9	3.9	2.5	105.1
1999	35.9	0.1	31.6	10.4	5.3	7.8	3.0	1.6	95.6

Source: Bank of Thailand, Annual Reports, 1986–2000

finance in Thailand because Thai corporations were part of bank clusters. Despite the growth in equity and bond markets since the mid-1980s, banks remained the main source of corporate finance in the kingdom. My hypothesis is that there is little empirical evidence of this dependence on bank finance being later overtaken by funding from the stock market. Southeast Asian corporations do not conform to the European model as advanced by Collier and Mayer.[18] This greater dependence on bank finance can be interpreted as part of their undeviating, unwavering commitment to 'personal

Table 10.3 Thailand, sources of funds in the corporate sector, 1970–94 (as percentage share of the total)

	1970–4	*1975–9*	*1980–4*	*1985–9*	*1990–4*	*1970–94*
Internal finance	39.4	44.0	37.4	35.3	21.5	27.6
Bank finance	19.5	25.1	22.6	25.2	22.8	23.2
New equity	16.0	9.0	6.7	8.6	6.2	7.3
Bonds	0.3	0.4	0.4	0.7	0.9	0.7
Trade credit	1.9	0.2	1.0	0.6	0.1	0.4
Foreign credit	22.1	20.4	30.7	29.4	49.3	41.1
Other	0.7	0.9	1.3	0.2	–0.9	–0.3

Source: Varapat Chensavasdijai, 'The effects of financial liberalization on investment behavior of Thai manufacturing firms', D.Phil. thesis, University of Oxford, 1999, p. 80

capitalism' throughout. While British capitalism was conscious of the need to move away from 'personal capitalism' from the early twentieth century, Southeast Asian capitalism revealed a more pragmatic, opportunistic approach to the capital markets even at the close of the twentieth century.

The increased use of foreign credit by Thai corporations should be stressed. High domestic interest rates of 15 to 19 per cent in the 1980s and 1990s meant that funds were sought from abroad. Foreign credit secured by Thai corporations rose from 22.1 per cent of total borrowing in 1970–4 to 49.3 per cent in 1990–4.[19] Between 1990 and 1994, when FDI into Thailand slowed, the search for overseas loans by Thai commercial banks rose from 60.5 per cent to 90.7 per cent of total borrowing.[20] The increased use of short-term, unhedged dollar funds proved treacherous. When the Thai baht fell in 1997, these debt liabilities destroyed several corporations, commercial banks and finance firms that had borrowed heavily from offshore banks. Their high leverage meant that collapse was inevitable.

The exploitation of the bond market by private corporations was limited before 1990. Indeed, before 1979 there was no bond trading in secondary markets. By 1994, however, bond market issues approximated 10 per cent of GDP.[21] More than half were in government bonds, one quarter were corporate bonds and 18 per cent were bonds issued by state enterprises. More significant, though, was the phenomenal rise in the issue of corporate bonds, from 3 per cent in 1992 to 26 per cent in 1994.[22] Part of this increase was attributable to large infrastructural projects and capital-intensive initiatives in telecommunications and electronics undertaken by Thai corporations in Thailand, Vietnam and China.

Foreign capital inflows

The lack of sequence in financial liberalization in the 1980s – whereby prudent regulation of the banking structure was not introduced before lifting controls on capital flows and expanding offshore banking – seriously threatened the viability of the financial system. The Bank of Thailand's insistence on adequate asset and capital ratios was either ignored or compromised by the legislation of the mid-1980s. In 1991, foreign exchange controls with respect to trade and foreign remittances were lifted. Banks and finance companies were allowed to trade in mutual funds, bonds, debentures and negotiable certificates of deposits. With the establishment of the Bangkok International Banking Facility (BIBF) in March 1993, Thai financial institutions began a frenzied search for offshore capital at lower interest rates.

McKinnon and Shaw have argued that the liberalization of a financially repressed economy will improve the growth and efficiency of the financial system, by securing increased mobilization of resources and their more efficient allocation.[23] The removal of interest rate ceilings and capital control will assist the development of domestic capital markets and reduce the scale of state-directed credit programmes. However, they also stressed that liberalization of the capital account should come only after the de-regulation of the domestic financial sector had been completed. In Thailand, as well as in the rest of the region, controls were lifted without the introduction of necessary regulation and, instead of securing a rigorously competitive financial sector, the reforms simply worsened existing institutional weakness – that is, the reforms strengthened the tradition of government–business links rather than introduced competition. The lifting of controls reduced the liquidity constraints on large corporations. The BIBF's concentration on wholesale banking and offshore financial institutions introduced new sources of funds for large corporate clients, often denominated in foreign currencies. The government also increased its underwriting of debt instruments for these large Thai corporations.

Attracted by high domestic interest rates, portfolio investment rose by 130 per cent between 1989 and 1991. Portfolio equity contracted in 1991 and 1992, and then soared from 1993 to 1996, while direct investment stagnated.[24] Much of the portfolio equity between 1985 and 1991 was derived from Japan. From the 1960s, Japanese direct investment led to the relocation of Japanese subsidiaries in Thailand and the formation of joint-ventures. Japanese joint-ventures with Sukree in textiles, with Charoen Pokphand in agribusiness and with Pornprapha in automobile assembly, assisted Thai import-substitution and export-oriented industrialization from 1960. The appreciation of the Japanese yen in 1983 forced the pace of this industrial transformation. Registered capital of Japanese firms in Thailand grew from 2,836 million baht in 1986, to 38,755 million baht in 1991, and to 125 billion baht in 1996.[25] Loans by Japanese banks to Thai companies accounted for 20 per cent of their total loans in Asia in 1996. Japanese loans also accounted for 54 per cent of total Thai private debt. In May 1997, Bank of Tokyo Mitsubishi had an exposure of US$9 billion to the Thai private sector: Siam Cement alone had received US$100 million.[26] Japanese bank lending to Thai banks was usually through the BIBF, in which Japan's share grew to 80 per cent in 1993, amounting to US$40 billion. Between 1993 and 1996, Japanese banks lent Thai banks US$63 billion.[27] This upsurge occurred while Japanese affiliates in Thailand were reducing output by 29 per cent and Thai exports to Japan fell by 6 per cent.[28] This increase in lending undoubtedly encouraged speculative activities.

Much of this foreign finance was short-term and required no collateral. Between 1993 and 1996, loans secured through the BIBF rose to US$31.2 billion, half borrowed by the Thai private sector.[29] The Bank of Asia secured bonds worth US$4 million in 1993 and US$51 million in 1995. An almost uncontrolled investment surge took place. Between 1988 and 1995, the average annual inflow of funds to Thailand was 12.3 per cent of the kingdom's GDP, and the cumulative inflow by the end of 1995 was equivalent to 51.5 per cent of GDP, the highest ratio among 20 countries studied by the World Bank in 1997.[30] Yet, NPLs were 24 per cent higher in July 1994 than in July 1993. Moreover, in July 1996, the amount of NPLs rose to 40 per cent.[31] Thailand's bank credit in 1996 was more than the current account deficit and, as a share of GNP, it rose from 5.8 per cent in 1994 to 8.3 per cent in 1995. The investment surge took place against a backdrop of declining trade values. Between January and August 1996, with the rising US dollar, the costs of capital goods imports rose – this at a time when Thai companies were moving into capital-intensive activities. The rising costs of labour added to growing inefficiency in manufacturing.

Much of the investment was channelled into the large capital-intensive infrastructural projects of Charoen Pokphand and Siam Cement, or joint state–private enterprises in telecommunications, highway construction and petroleum refining in Thailand, China, Vietnam, Burma, Indonesia and India. Thai corporations borrowed freely, bought the technology and embarked on a global offensive. Investment in capital-intensive industries was securing meagre returns. The stock exchange index for these firms declined from 26.6 per cent in 1990 to 7.7 per cent in 1996.[32] The flood of capital also fed short-term speculation. Cheap offshore funds secured by corporations grew from US$20 billion in 1992 to US$75 billion in 1995.[33] Much of these were directed towards property and real estate and into stock market speculation.

Much of this capital was derived from portfolio investments from East Asia. However, in the early 1990s, European and American investors were also attracted to the Thai Stock Exchange. The net effect was to push up the price of securities and increase the demand for shares. Banks and non-financial corporations became addicted to reissuing shares, thereby exaggerating the value of their assets. They used their stronger equity base to increase borrowing. Inflation was rising, the economy was overheating and speculation continued unabated. The privatization of public utilities from the mid-1980s augmented the equity market, which had important implications for the liability structure of firms: their debt-equity structure was unbalanced and unstable, and failure was inevitable. The development of mutual funds and asset management was also rapid. Within two years from 1992, mutual fund-holders had attracted US$6.5 billion.[34] Twenty-nine funds established in 1993 attracted 59.7 billion baht (US$2.5 billion). In 1994, another 21 new funds accumulated a total of 63.9 billion baht (US$2.8 billion).[35]

Increased exploitation of diverse financial instruments – stocks, bonds and derivatives – occurred at a time when Thai corporations were expanding internationally. Tapping into various international capital markets, while not being monitored by any single authority, was a recipe for disaster. Corporate profligacy and volatility produced the crisis in 1997. Corporations were moving into a form of institutional capitalism in which they diversified from internally generated capital to innovative and multiple sources of finance but they had not shed the paraphernalia of proprietary capitalism, in terms of company organization, ownership, accounting practices and financial transparency, and executive non-family management. Paradoxically, they used securitization and bonds to entrench their form of proprietary capitalism, which was sustainable only in periods of financial abundance and generous state patronage. In recession, patrons and partners absconded.

Such abundant capital inflows were not reproduced in a wave of mergers and acquisitions within banking. Hence, concentration in Thai banking was not achieved through mergers and acquisitions. From the 1970s, the preferred pattern was through the proliferation of financial subsidiaries within these four large banking cliques, in both consumer and corporate finance; embracing both industrial and property firms, and thus creating large conglomerates, like the Japanese *keiretsu*. The difference between the Japanese and the Thai corporation was that the Thai subsidiaries held no interlocking shares in the parent company or in the main bank; this lack of crossholding meant the Thai group was centralized and control was vested in the family.

In summing up, we can safely assert that Thai banks expanded too rapidly and without becoming properly integrated. Diverse forms of finance were sought, much of it in US dollars, so that when the exchange rate fell in 1997 massive debts were accumulated. The central role of the family, along with state patronage, encouraged this risky diverse growth. Traditional banking activities were now combined with risky speculative activities which brought the system into further jeopardy. Name-based, connected lending with personal guarantees, weak collateral, weak credit analysis and chaotic reporting of impaired loans, ultimately brought chaos to the banking sector.

The proliferation of finance companies

The proliferation of finance firms since the 1970s, in both consumer and corporate finance, contained crucially unstable elements. While only 10 to 25 per cent of their loans in the 1990s were channelled into retail consumer finance, principally into hire-purchase, another 10 per cent went to manufacturing. The remainder was absorbed in funding land and property firms, a sector which then suffered 20 per cent losses between 1990 and 1995. Despite these losses, finance company loans to real estate were 360 billion baht in 1997, with another 140 billion baht in hire-purchase finance.[36]

These finance companies lacked a stable base of retail deposits: they relied on promissory notes and other short-term devices, and thus were borrowing short-term and investing long-term in land and property. Then, in the 1990s, investment in bonds, particularly global bonds, became popular.[37] However, this issuing of bonds by a group of finance companies was open to abuse. The use of Japanese floating rate notes, with a maturity of 7–15 years, was particularly risky, because of the fluctuations in the yen.[38] Employing high-cost financial instruments such as corporate bonds to sustain a firm's growth was, ironically, rife during periods of poor performance. These firms also invested in bond markets in Southeast Asia, Latin America and Europe, often utilizing funds borrowed from offshore capital markets.

The risks were increased by poor management and a lack of transparency on the part of Thai financial corporations. Finance One, the largest finance firm in Thailand, collapsed in 1997, after concealing debts since 1993. Finance One's hire-purchase operations alone contained 5,809 million baht of non-performing loans.[39] Exposure in volatile sectors of the economy meant that even a small downturn in business could result in serious difficulties for financial institutions. A minor finance company in 1970, Finance One, was transformed in the 1980s by Pin Chakkaphak, a member of the Yip In Tsoi clan, owners of the Thai Farmers' Bank. By 1987 it had expanded through mergers and acquisitions, and had the largest securities firm in Southeast Asia. It also became one of the three largest shareholders in the Bank of Asia, although it failed to purchase the concern outright. However, Finance One did succeed in securing Thai Danu Bank. The interlocking ownership of Finance One and Thai Danu Bank led to share manipulation.[40]

Finance One's holding company, Holding One, provided for the vertical and horizontal integration of its subsidiaries. The management structure of each subsidiary was independent, but Pin's control provided critical centripetal tendencies. In fact, this was the source of its distress. From 1992, Pin used the holding company structure to conceal the difficulties of Finance One. Finance One's shareholder funds increased by 90 per cent between 1994 and 1997, yet its net profits in the same period declined by 30 per cent.[41] The gap between real profits and the capacity to raise funds, either through shares, bank loans or bonds, was a recurrent feature of the Thai financial structure in the 1990s. The hype surrounding Asian economic growth further encouraged borrowing by large Thai businesses. Unfortunately, the Thai public and foreign investors were unable to distinguish between real and apparent growth.

The stock market and financial instability

The growth of the stock market was partly responsible for this financial diversification, fragility and instability. The stock market, although of limited importance as a source of finance, still threatened financial equilibrium. Ironically, it ensured the rigid maintenance of family ownership, and thereby destabilized strict corporate governance. The absorption of foreign capital in the more risky sectors – such as electronics, property and finance – was frequently mediated through the stock exchange. For details on the Stock Exchange of Thailand (SET), see Table 10.4.

The SET was established in May 1974 to attract and mobilize foreign and domestic capital for an ambitious programme of rapid industrialization. Between 1975 and 1995 the number of listed firms grew from 21 to 416. There were 601 companies by 2000. Market capitalization as a proportion of GDP was only 3.9 per cent in 1980 but reached 31.4 per cent in 1990 and 87.8 per cent in 1995. However, the Asian financial crisis dealt a blow to this growth. Total market capitalization in Thailand fell from US$141.5 billion in 1995 to US$30.7 billion in 1998. Furthermore, the stock exchange index fell from 1,281 points at the end of 1995 to 356 points in December 1998, a fall of 72 per cent.[42] The percentage change in the volume of turnover on the SET ranged from 153.36 per cent in 1990 to 26.46 per cent in 1991, to 167.12 per cent in 1992, to 70.26 per cent in 1996, to 54.46 per cent in 1997, to 136.89 per cent in 1998 and to 39.64 per cent in July 2000.

The financial sector was the dominant sector on the SET with 1.4 trillion baht registered capital and 791 billion baht paid-up capital in 1992. Manufacturing came second with 350 billion baht registered capital and paid-up

Table 10.4 The growth of the Stock Exchange of Thailand

	1975	*1980*	*1985*	*1988*	*1990*	*1992*	*1993*	*1995*
SET Index: 100 = 30 April 1975	84.1	124.7	135.0	386.9	612.9	893.4	1,682.90	1,280.8
Number of listed companies	21	74	93	136	209	305	347	416
Number of securities[a] (million)	27	85	100	165	261	359	408	538
Market capitalization (US$ billion)	0.3	1.3	1.8	8.7	24.0	58.5	130.8	141.5
Market capitalization (% of GDP)	1.8	3.9	4.7	15.4	31.4	65.0	134.5	87.8
Market turnover (US$ billion)	0.1	0.3	0.6	6.2	24.5	73.2	86.9	61.2
Foreign investment (US$ billion)	n/a	n/a	0.1	1.6	7.2	10.7	29.7	32.2
Market P-E ratio	5.0	6.4	9.6	12	13.8	16.3	26.1	19.8
Market dividend yield (%)	10.2	9.4	8.2	3.8	3.6	2.9	2.0	2.3

Note:

a Includes ordinary shares, preferred shares, unit trusts, debentures, convertible debentures and warrants.

Exchange rate: 1970–81, US$ = 20.64 baht; 1982–95, US$ = 25.14 baht.

Source: Varapat Chensavasdijai, 'The effects of financial liberalization on investment behavior of Thai manufacturing firms', D.Phil. thesis, University of Oxford, 1999, p. 80

capital of 261 billion baht.[43] This financial-industrial distribution was partly determined by the flow of foreign capital into these sectors; thus, between 1993 and 1998, securities trading reveals a preponderance of foreign investors over local investors. Hence, in 1993, foreign investor purchases accounted for 34.77 per cent of total securities trading. Industrial domestic investors absorbed 53.48 per cent of the total trading volume, while mutual fund managers and securities firms purchased a further 10–12 per cent. This changed little in 1997 when foreign investors' average purchase rose to 42–51 per cent, while that of local institutions accounted for 6–11 per cent and individual domestic investors took 34–50 per cent. The decline in trading was marked in 1998 when foreign investors' trade fell by 50 per cent. Domestic investors' trading remained high, supported by state measures for the recapitalization of failing banks and corporations.[44]

This fluctuation in the volume and the value of turnover on the SET in the years 1993–8 is reflected in the volatility of share prices in banking, finance, securities, and property and real-estate sectors. Of the top 20 most active stocks on the Bangkok Stock Exchange between 1990 and 1999, Bangkok Bank remained highest – even in 1996, 1997 and 1999 – only falling to second place briefly in 1998. It was the only banking stock among the top 20 most actively traded stocks. The others were in telecommunications, property, airlines and the cement industry.[45]

The rise in total funds in equities, securities and debt instruments was quite dramatic between 1992 and 1999, rising from 6.4 billion baht in 1992 to 599.6 billion baht in 1999. The increase was particularly sharp between 1998 and 1999, when total funds jumped from 174.1 billion baht to 599.6 billion. This increase was assisted by state measures for the recapitalization of banks, along with the increase in foreign equity in domestic banks and a series of foreign purchases of Thai banks.[46]

This increase in market capitalization between 1990 and 1996, with foreign shares in this increase rising from 17 per cent in 1993 to 43 per cent in 1997, was occurring against a decline in the profitability of corporations in the same period. Thus, ROA, ROE and gross profit margins all rose in the 1980s but declined from 1989 to 1996. Corporate indices all revealed a downward swing. ROA of listed corporations dropped from 10.3 per cent in 1989 to 3.4 per cent in 1996. ROE, meanwhile, fell from 21.4 per cent to 5.8 per cent over the same years. Equally, there was a decline in interest earned from 10.5 per cent in 1987 to 5.1 per cent in 1996. This is clearly indicative of a lack of connection between corporate performance and stock market growth. Part of the explanation is that this growth was in equity debt instruments, both domestic and offshore, and the accumulation of funds through the issuance of hybrid financial instruments.

The stock market was characterized by boom and bust: it experienced a boom in 1986, followed by a crash during the Gulf Crisis of 1990, and then a rise in 1993 before a decline. This is reflected in the deterioration of price to earnings ratio from 19.5 per cent in 1994 to 12 per cent in 1996 and to 6.6 per cent in 1997. Between 1994 and 1997, the value of assets of principally industrial companies almost doubled. However, asset growth in petrochemicals, construction, telecommunications and property development was not accompanied by an equivalent surge in earnings. On the contrary, there was a decline in return on assets of a third from 1994 to 1996 and a fall in stock prices in the second half of 1996.[47]

Therefore, while earnings fell, the debt to equity ratio rose in the chemical and property sectors with disastrous implications not only for the stock market but for banking as well. This was because banks remained the main source of finance for large and small firms, despite the boom in the stock exchange. Debt to equity ratio in the chemicals industry rose from 1.1 per cent in 1994 to 5.4 per cent in 1997 and then only fell to 2.59 per cent in 1999.[48] In the property sector debt to equity ratio rose from 1.66 per cent in 1997 and continued to escalate into 1999 at 9.7 per cent. Throughout this period of increase in the vulnerability of the stock market, the deterioration in price to earnings ratio continued: from 19.5 per cent in 1994 to 12 per cent in 1996 and to 6.6 per cent in 1997.[49]

A major factor was the impact of foreign investors on the SET. Between 1994 and 1997, the aggregate share of foreign investors in bank ownership and equity declined but it increased in all other sectors. In electronics, the increase in foreign ownership was from 23.1 per cent to 62.5 per cent between 1994 and 1997; in media the change was from 5.7 per cent to 37.6 per cent; in energy from 13.1 per cent to 35.7 per cent; in transport from 4.7 per cent to 19.8 per cent; and in pulp and paper the adjustment was from 13.2 per cent to 30.6 per cent.[50] By 1995, foreign investors had already become net buyers on the SET and Thais were net sellers.

These changes in patterns of ownership, manifested as aggressive buying sprees by foreign investors, were particularly evident after 1997 when – due to the depreciation of the baht, cheaper securities, and the increased privatization of banks and financial institutions – foreign ownership rose dramatically, particularly in banking and manufacturing. This is discussed in the section on restructuring.

The secondary market was weak. Bonds played only a marginal role in Thai corporate finance. Indeed, in 1996, only 11 per cent of total loans were accounted for by bonds. The Thai bond exchange market was smaller than that in Malaysia where bonds amounted to 56 per cent of GDP while in Thailand it was only 9 per cent of GDP in 1994. Between 1960 and 1980, bonds were utilized for infrastructural projects; this declined in the 1990s. Private corporations preferred bank loans from domestic and offshore banks, short-term promissory notes or bills of exchange. State-owned corporations faced with borrowing difficulties did resort to bonds, though. But this reluctance to use them or secured debt instruments meant that between 1992 and 1996, unsecured corporate debt was 60 per cent while the use of secured debt instruments was only 10 per cent.[51]

Thai corporations preferred the use of retained earnings and reserves, or bank loans; an option determined by their desire to retain ownership and management control, while exploiting low interest rates. The stock market was used to raise additional capital without losing this control. The critical argument here is that there was little change in Thai corporate structures even after listing on the stock exchange. The stock market provided capital, from both domestic and foreign investors, for Thai corporations but family ownership remained intact. Stock market capitalization in Bangkok peaked in 1993–4, when crisis-ridden companies, including Finance One, were borrowing more, thereby stimulating greater hot money inflows. This lack of efficiency and market responsiveness in the equity and financial sectors derived from the idiosyncratic political and cultural risks facing Thai corporations. The fluctuating fortunes of their political allies were often of greater importance to their stock market performance than their actual balance sheet figures. The new capitalists in finance, telecommunications, media and real estate, who emerged in the 1980s, were now displacing manufacturing and commodity producers. Foreign capital investments on the SET in these new sectors boosted the fortunes of the new entrepreneurs.

These developments on the Thai stock market raise two important points. First, there was little evidence of the earlier dependence on bank finances being overtaken by funding from equity markets – the argument advanced by Collier and Mayer.[52] Their hypothesis – that firms rely heavily on bank finance in the early stages of development but turn to the securities market once they are established – ignores critical historical and institutional features. Stock market growth is best understood through a combined use of economic, historical and institutional disciplines. In Thailand, the multiple links between industrial groups, banks, the state and foreign capital were too complex to plot a simple evolution from dependence on banks for finance to dependence on the stock market.

Second, although the stock market was of limited importance as a source of finance, it still threatened financial equilibrium. It ensured the rigid maintenance of family ownership, and thereby destabilized corporate governance. The absorption of foreign capital in the more risky sectors – such as electronics, property and finance – was frequently mediated through the stock exchange.

The institutional structure of the stock market, and the regulatory framework governing its operations, further compromised corporate governance. Before 1975, the Ministry of Commerce was the sole supervisory agent for corporations. In the 1990s, however, the supervisory system became fragmented; with supervision split between the Stock Exchange Commission (SEC, established in 1989) and the SET. Neither institution had clearly defined responsibilities or the power to enforce the law. In 1992, the Stock Exchange Act also separated the primary and secondary markets, with the SEC regulating the primary market, and this created further segregation between trading in securities, clearing house functions and registration. Legal enforcement remained in the hands of the Ministry of Finance and the Ministry of Commerce. The muddled responses of the SET to changes in exchange rates, portfolio capital flows and government privatization, all emerged from these institutional and structural deformities and ensuing confusion. Unsurprisingly, powerful corporations exploited these inadequacies. In short, the stock exchange lacked transparency, revealed insufficient minority shareholder rights, and preserved inadequate accounting rules and methods of disclosure. Until the crisis, unrestricted crossholdings within corporations were permitted and insider trading was pervasive, encouraging political interference and corruption.

Property bubbles

Real-estate investment also increased financial insecurity. Property investments were inherently unstable because of fluctuating prices. Moreover, the methods used by property companies to finance growth proved highly unstable.

The first point to be made is that the use of property or land as collateral was central to the Thai credit market: in 1993, two-thirds of all bank loans were secured on land.[53] Falling prices after 1995 had diminished the value of these assets. Second, property developers were major clients of finance companies. A quarter of their funds were derived from finance houses, another 10 per cent from banks, and the remainder from equity and bond markets.[54] Third, property firms derived substantial finance from offshore banks: their bonds and debentures were nominated in US dollars, which carried exchange rate risks.[55] The relationship between property firms, financial institutions and equity markets held ominous consequences for the stability of corporate and financial structures. Real-estate developments in Thailand proved to be the accelerator in propelling the economy towards collapse. Involvement in property magnified the initial shocks precipitated by financial market imperfections. The following section provides a detailed analysis of the financing strategies of two major Thai property companies.

Land and House was established in 1983 and listed in 1989. The company was involved in high-quality housing projects in Bangkok. Foreign loans, bonds and debenture issues were major sources of finance. Land and House's long-term loans were secured from Thai finance companies and foreign banks. In April 1993, it sold convertible bonds valued at US$60 million in foreign capital markets with a ten-year maturity. In December 1996, the company then issued debentures varying in value from 208 million baht to 1.5 billion baht.[56] These greatly increased the burden of debt and interest payments. The reissue of shares was frequently deployed to repay short-term loans: Land and House reissued shares in 1992, 1994 and 1995, increasing capitalization by 2 billion baht in 1992 and by 3 billion baht in 1994 – an increase of almost 12 billion baht between 1991 and 1996. This was done largely to cover debts. Land and House saw net profits decline by 29 per cent between 1994 and 1995, and by 15 per cent between 1995 and 1996.[57]

Overall, the six largest property companies saw their debt to equity ratios rise from 1.44 in 1993 to 2.06 in 1996, and their interest coverage fall from 1.39 to 0.71 in the same years. Furthermore, these companies suffered an operating cash flow deficit of 38.3 billion baht in 1994 and 25.4 billion baht in 1996.[58] The majority of property firms saw a radical decline in net profits. Some recorded a negative profit rate of 40 per cent between 1993 and 1996.[59] Profits were declining even as sales were increasing. The costs of repayment swallowed up much of the gross profit. The critical year was 1993, when the property companies could not repay debts from internal profits and were forced to seek more and more funds from offshore banks.

Bangkok Land was established in 1973 by the Kanjanapas family. The family also owned another property group, Tanayong, which had been established in 1968. The expansion of Bangkok Land and Tanayong was based on state infrastructural projects, private housing programmes, the creation of satellite cities and resorts in Thailand, and a proposed international airport east of Bangkok. Another of Tanayong's initiatives was the Bangkok Sky Train, financed by Credit Suisse and First Boston. The Thai military and political establishment assisted in all these projects.[60] As early as January 1995, both companies were confronted with serious problems in completing projects and repaying loans. Tanayong had to secure a 3.2 billion baht bond through Peregrine Capital to repay its mounting debts. It had seen its share price fall from 7.21 baht in 1991 to 1.73 baht in 1993, and then to 0.82 baht in 1994. This was followed by a slight recovery that can be partly explained by Tanayong's involvement in the mass transit system for Bangkok, a prestigious rail project. Bangkok Land, meanwhile, was responsible for many of Thailand's largest commercial and residential projects in joint-venture with the French firm Bouygues. It faced difficulties from 1993. In December 1995, it had to repay 31.2 million baht to prospective buyers because of its failure to complete residential building projects. This was followed by the abandonment of its housing projects in Bangkok.[61] In 1997, the group faced liabilities of US$3.7 billion.[62] Its two largest creditors were Bangkok Bank and the Siam Commercial Bank. The group was thus forced to restructure, reducing the family's equity in Bangkok Land to 33 per cent, and within Tanayong to 30 per cent. This achieved a reduction in debt of US$1,000 million in Bangkok Land, of US$882.5 million in Tanayong, and of US$102.5 million in Steleux Holdings Hong Kong. The Muang Thong Thani initiative, a building project in Bangkok modelled on Shatin in Hong Kong, had incurred debts of US$1 billion, and 80 per cent of its housing remained unsold.[63] It was purchased by the Thai military in 1998 in order to prevent the family group from losing ownership and control to foreign investors. The family was able to restructure through the aid of the Thai military, the Thai government and the China International Trust and Investment Company, an investment group based in China.

In brief, capital abundance drove feverish speculation. Loans to property developers tripled between 1993 and 1996: 45 per cent of these loans came from finance companies, while 54 per cent came from commercial banks.[64] Bad loans to the property sector in Thailand amounted to 300 billion baht by March 1997.[65] The disastrous impact of the exaggerated growth in property and stock markets was a direct result of the failure of Thailand's technocrats to regulate the kingdom's financial institutions, particularly given the proliferation of new financial instruments and intermediaries.

The financial regulators

The discussion so far has demonstrated that financial liberalization introduced greater distortions rather than greater efficiency in the allocation of investment. The larger Thai financial groups faced little competition when tapping into and securing large capital inflows. The theoretical literature analysing financial factors in investment decision-making emphasizes the significance of capital market imperfections. In Thailand, imperfect decision-making by firms compromised the structure and operation of capital markets: their management of risk distorted capital allocation. The other major factor in this distortion was the failure of Thai financial technocrats to regulate the capital market. Powerful state–business relationships in Thailand and throughout Southeast Asia seriously weakened the capacity or willingness of officials to impose market discipline. In this context, it is important to note Ammar Siamwalla's view that 'while the root cause of the Thai crisis was the excessive borrowing by the private sector, its effect has been multiplied by misguided policies, particularly those emanating from the Bank of Thailand'.[66]

There were four institutions responsible for financial and fiscal policies in Thailand: the Ministry of Finance, the Bank of Thailand, the Budget Bureau and the National Economic and Social Development Board (NESDB). Complex relations between civil servants and the Thai military, politicians and capitalists further complicated decision-making and undermined the autonomy of the technocrats. The Bank of Thailand was formed in 1944. Puey Ungphakon was its governor from 1959 to 1971 and tried to maintain the bank's strict autonomy. However, from the 1960s, this autonomy was threatened by rapid economic growth and major political changes. Moreover, the governor had no fixed term of office and could be dismissed by the Minister of Finance. Indeed, in the 1980s, two governors were dismissed for political reasons. The NESDB, meanwhile, was responsible for Thailand's five-year economic plans. Staffed with Thai graduates from American universities, it was also responsible for infrastructural projects, the majority of which were funded by the World Bank. The NESDB was a conservative institution and maintained a policy of direct intervention until 1988 when Pisit Pakkasem changed the board's approach to favour the free market.

Ironically, this led to financial privileges being accumulated by those with direct access to government and the military.

In this period, technocrats were either seconded to business or moved to the private sector on retirement. For example, Tongchat Hongladarom left the state enterprise, Thai Petroleum, for Charoen Pokphand. The role of the NESDB as an economic watchdog was seriously eroded when businessmen and the military controlled government contracts in defence and public utilities. In the 1990s, the Prime Ministers Anand Panyarachun (February 1991–April 1992 and June–September 1992) and Chuan Leekpai (September 1992–July 1995 and November 1997–February 2001) attempted to reduce the influence of the military in state enterprises and to restore professional bankers to the civil service. This had a limited impact because the quality and autonomy of technocrats were in decline and they had become highly politicized. Vijit Suphinit, Governor of the Bank of Thailand in the 1990s, epitomized this latter trend. Rapid economic growth, accompanied by massive capital inflows, did not lead to a tight monetary policy. In fact, Vijit encouraged foreign capital in the privatization of public utilities. In December 1995, he supported the Bangkok Stock Exchange through an injection of US$1.18 billion from government sources in order to maintain high share prices.[67] The technocrats had long abandoned the attempt to provide effective supervision.

The autonomy of technocrats had been waning since 1973, a decline that coincided with the demise of Thai militarism and the rise of parliamentary politics. The Thai military, anxious for increased military budgets, had supported the rigorous management of the economy by technocrats but, from 1973, that alliance came under strain. The Bank of Thailand was riven by factionalism as its technocrats became increasingly subservient to the Ministry of Finance. The tensions increased in the 1990s, with the rise of regional political and business barons.[68] In general, the 1990s saw a flourishing of money politics and a closer, corrupt interdependence between political and business elites.

The Bank of Thailand's mismanagement of the exchange rate mechanism in 1997 contrasts sharply with its effective management in the mid-1980s. As Thitinan Pongsudhirak has argued, the technocrats, undisturbed by the political regime in the 1980s, secured successful devaluations in 1981 and 1984 that improved Thailand's export competitiveness and industrial prospects.[69] The devaluation in 1981 was prompted by a widening trade deficit, triggered in part by the second oil crisis of 1980. The 1984 devaluation was a response to the alarming trade and current account deficits caused by a boom in private investment and consumer spending, and was accompanied by tight credit controls in an attempt to restrain imports. After the 1984 devaluation, the baht was tied to a basket of other currencies, instead of just the US dollar. The Thai financial authorities took this action despite strong pressure from the military and business communities; the Bank of Thailand held firm with the support of the Prime Minister, Prem Tinsulanond, and the Finance Minister, Sommai Hoontrakul.

The bending of its technocrats to political pressures after 1985 seriously eroded the management structures of the Bank of Thailand and, thereby, its ability to regulate the macro-economy. The very high volumes of foreign borrowing led to a rise in the real exchange rate. Current account deficits rose to some 8 per cent of GNP. The increasing imbalance on current accounts took place as export growth slowed, under the influence of the rise in the real exchange rate. In these circumstances, the bank should have pushed for a break with the US dollar by 1996 or 1997, to allow for a modest devaluation. But the governor, fearing criticism from political interests, failed to act, and in late 1996 and early 1997 the bank found itself being forced to defend the baht against heavy speculation. The kingdom's foreign exchange reserves dropped from US$40 billion in January 1997 to US$33 billion by the end of June that year.[70] By the beginning of July, insufficient reserves were on hand to defend the currency, and on 2 July the baht was unpegged from the dollar, losing more than a third of its value against the US currency by November that year.

This is not the only example of a critical failure of resolve and independence on the part of the Bank of Thailand in the 1990s. Earlier, in 1996, the bank had failed to suspend the Bangkok Bank of Commerce and instead committed US$7 billion to support a fraudulent bank, owned by members of the Thai elite, the Saudi arms trader Adnan Khashoggi and the Indian Rakesh Saxena.

Financial crisis and meltdown

The financial fragility stemming from this financial concentration is clear. The Asian financial crisis began in Thailand with a 20 per cent devaluation of the baht on 2 July, after efforts to defend the exchange rate through increases in interest rates, along with restrictions on speculation, had failed. Thailand committed US$8.7 billion from its foreign reserves to defend the baht and took a further US$23 billion in forward contracts maturing in the following 12 months.[71]

As argued earlier, Thailand's currency crisis of 1997 had its roots in the rapid growth of Thai financial institutions and in their relationship with foreign capital. Massive capital inflows from the 1970s produced booms in both the public and the private sectors. The institutional structure of Thai capital and its response to that capital flood was the underlying problem, while the web of institutional connections between Thai finance, industry, the bureaucracy, the political establishment and the military further distorted investment priorities. A highly concentrated finance sector orientated itself towards costly short-term capital, and made short-sighted, opportunistic investment decisions.

However, this does not fully explain the currency meltdown of July 1997. Beyond the institutional perspective, certain long- and short-term factors need to be noted. In other words, the analysis needs to go beyond the causal mechanisms. This is not to override the historical and empirical data presented earlier, but theories of business cycles and of chaos can be used to further explain the essential structures of the Thai economy and the origins of the crisis.[72]

The first significant explanation for the crisis derives from the cyclical nature of growth in Thailand. Since the 1950s, the average growth period for Thailand has been 44 months, although some cycles were as long as 51 to 70 months. The only long cycle was that of 1976 to 1982, which was dictated by Japan's restructuring of its domestic industries and the transplanting of labour-intensive firms to Thailand. Textiles, automobiles and electronics were the main sectors of growth. The boom was brought to an end in 1983, when a serious trade deficit led to a credit squeeze. The recession was brief, though. Between 1987 and 1989, Thailand attained growth rates of 9.5, 13.2 and 12.2 per cent per annum.[73] An increase in manufactured exports resulted in a domestic consumer boom. Moreover, FDI increased dramatically after 1987, augmented by financial liberalization, which included the creation of BIBF in March 1993. This unleashed over-borrowing by private corporations, which were unable to confront the economic difficulties that were taking hold around this time, due, in part, to increasing competition from mainland China and an over-valued baht.

The causes of this cyclical growth lie, essentially, in fluctuations in agricultural prices, changes in manufactured exports and movements in the money supply. This last factor was particularly crucial. Changes in money supply, credit volumes and interest rates affected the investment behaviour of corporations and contributed to fluctuations in growth. If cycles are autonomous processes responding to movement in agricultural prices and manufactured exports, in the 1990s the Thai economy was responding more strongly to heavy foreign investment inflows and to financial liberalization. Also important in this period was the impact on Thailand of the fortunes of the Japanese and US economies. The Japanese recession of 1992 and the American boom of 1993–7 had major impacts on Thai finance and Thai industry. After 1992, Japan was unable to re-ignite the intra-Asian economic links that had been so expansionary for Thailand, while the appreciating US dollar brought a rise in the external value of the baht.

In growth cycle analysis, the turning points are crucial. The major turning point for Thailand came in 1993. This is illustrated in the tables on the performance of Thai banks, which all saw a sharp decline in net profit after 1993. The debt-equity ratios of banks and finance companies increased in the period after 1993, accompanied by the decline in net profits. With drastic changes in company performance and demand, effective financial regulation was now necessary. But the state lifted credit ceilings and foreign exchange controls, and embarked on huge infrastructure projects with the Thai private sector. The convergence of an unrestrained financial regime, a huge inflow of portfolio equity and the financial capriciousness of corporations deepened the trough of the cycle.

A second observation to be drawn from this growth cycle analysis concerns the changes in Thai capital, particularly between 1977 and 1997. As a late industrializer, Thailand had telescoped several stages of capitalist development since the 1950s. The private corporations that emerged in the 1950s consolidated in the boom of the 1980s: buying technology from foreign multinationals and becoming international enterprises. In three short decades, they had undergone the transformation that Western multinationals had taken almost a century to complete. Connections with the state and the military were critical in this process. Foreign multinationals added to the web of privilege and ramified increasingly uncompetitive structures. Thus, Finance One grew from a small family business focusing on tin-mining and pawnshops to become the largest finance firm in Thailand with hugely diverse interests. As it moved from retail finance into portfolio equity, bonds and offshore bank transactions, Finance One did not undertake any significant changes to its own structures that might ensure transparency in accounting and financial rigour. The diversification was inherently unstable. In this way, the speculative boom spread from one sector to another – and from consumption to real estate, to the stock market. That transmission locked sectors together, creating strong aggregate, but often unstable, movements. Technocrats should have identified these transmissions – the hot money flows, the almost endless cycle of reflotation and share reissue – and regulated them. No orderly governance was sought, largely because the technocrats themselves were the beneficiaries of alliances with business. Foreign investors, in turn, were caught up in the euphoria.

Key to the cycles was credit expansion and the lengthening of investment phases. The upswings were amplified by real-estate growth and stock market capitalization. Demand for credit continued unabated because of shrinking profits, high domestic interest rates and difficulties in servicing debts. Banks were increasingly forced into involuntary lending. While the economy expanded, the asset bubbles could be accommodated and the impending rupture postponed. The crisis only struck when Soros identified an overvalued baht, a widening current accounts deficit and over-priced stocks. Real-estate prices were artificially inflated, corporate debt was rising and company performance was fluctuating. Soros noted sensitive changes in stock prices and currency values, and also identified the precise volatile points. What appeared as random speculation between January and May 1997 disguised clear identifiable weaknesses. 'Cycles are not like tonsils – separable things that might be treated by themselves – but are like the beat of the heart, the essence of the organ that displays them.'[74] Thus, the Thai economy faced collapse. Regular and random causes were interwoven in the 1997 meltdown not only in Thailand but in many Southeast Asian countries.

Restructuring

The legislative reforms of 1998–9 produced only faltering success. The attempts to amend the Public Limited Company Act of 1992 – which sought to protect minority shareholders through their representation on the board, effect a substantial reduction in minimum shareholding for individual shareholders including the family-owners, separate control and ownership functions, reduce directors' protection, and reinstate the use of cumulative voting, all with the aim of further eroding single family dominance – were ultimately compromised and confused by the persistent lack of corporate transparency.

In 1999, the SET introduced international standards of accounting and disclosure in the form of annual company reports prepared by internationally accredited accountants. Yet it still lacked the necessary powers to discipline erring corporations. This act also sought to exclude major shareholders from being the chief executive. This, too, met with little success; the embedded business–state links compromised any efforts to enforce the law. In addition, pressure to limit the powers of the holding company in ownership and finance failed. Indeed, the holding company should have been made illegal as it was in post-1945 Japan.

Nevertheless, amendments to the 1940 Bankruptcy Law, first in April 1998 and then in March 1999, did improve bankruptcy procedures, through the institution of special courts, and enhanced the voting powers of creditors. It also strengthened their role in auctions of foreclosed assets. Reform in bankruptcy was crucial for improved corporate governance. However, the mere threat of external controls produced different configurations of power among controlling shareholders and managers. They resisted the weak bankruptcy laws on the grounds that they had supposedly been engineered by the IMF, and that these bills could 'blow up the whole country'.[75] Weak bankruptcy laws thus combined with nationalist rhetoric to allow Thai corporations to harbour unsustainable debts, and avoid radical reform and possible closure. The 1999 amendments to the 1940 Bankruptcy law outlined clear procedures for bankruptcy; it was firm on contracts, payments, voting by creditors, clarification on exchange rates when debt is in foreign currency, and when to auction assets. It also provided protection for unsecured creditors. The insolvency reforms outlined above also provided for out of court settlements, as well as informal workouts, and only resorted to liquidation as a final resort.

Similarly, the creation of the Corporate Debt Restructuring Advisory Committee (CDRAC) for debt restructuring had firm timetables on rehabilitating debt and provided for arbitration between debtors and creditors. The legal priorities between creditors and debtor were clarified with enormous flexibility. The times, schedules and frameworks were also mapped out. Even collateral was clearly defined. All this was in line with the American corporate culture of rehabilitating failing companies as opposed to liquidating them.

The institutions responsible for monitoring debt restructuring included the Bank of Thailand, the Board of Trade, the Thai Bankers Association and the Foreign Bankers Association.[76] However, the decline in corporate debt was slow. It only fell from US$153 billion in 1997 to US$140 billion in 1999.[77] By September 1999 a successful restructuring of 62 per cent of private banks and 19 per cent of state-owned banks had been achieved. For precise details, see Table 10.5 on NPLs outstanding, classified by financial institution. However, these results do not reveal the whole picture. The brief case studies of banks below disclose the chronic problems in restructuring.

Bangkok Bank maintained its position as the largest bank. Even after restructuring in 1998, it was responsible for 16 per cent of loans and 19 per cent of all bank deposits. Asset quality remained poor and the bank transferred 24.8 billion baht of impaired loans to the state-owned Thai Asset Management Company (TAMC). The restructuring of its NPLs only resulted in a slight improvement by 2002. However, the ratio of NPLs had risen from 25 per cent to 28 per cent by 2003.[78] See Table 10.6 for details on Bangkok Bank.

Bangkok Metropolitan Bank faced acute difficulties in June 1997. It had the highest ratio of bad loans and was taken over by the Bank of Thailand. It was then merged with Siam City Bank, creating the fifth largest bank in terms of assets. The government reduced its holding from 99.9 per cent to 49 per cent and was keen on swift privatization.[79]

The Bank of Asia, another failing bank, was taken by ABNAMRO. It had already sold its impaired loans of 6.3 billion baht to TAMC and its NPLs fell by 9 per cent, with impaired reserves ratio rising from 9.6 per cent in 2001 to 20 per cent in 2002. ABNAMRO then issued a new rights issue in 2002, which improved its equity to assets ratio.[80] See Table 10.7 for details on the Bank of Asia.

Bank of Ayudhya, with a 6–7 per cent share of domestic loans and deposits, also sold bad loans to TAMC as part of its capital restructuring. The Krung Thai Bank (KTB), the second largest bank, also transferred impaired loans to the state-owned asset management companies, TAMC and Sukhumvit Asset Management, between 1999 and 2002. KTB, which was state owned, held more than 500 billion baht in bad loans and endured four years of losses between 1997 and 2001, before recovering in 2002.

The Thai Military Bank, which was partly owned by the Ministry of Finance, negotiated with ANZ bank for a 20 per cent stake. It revealed a high ratio of NPLs, and weak provisioning and capitalization.[81] Siam Commercial Bank, the third largest bank, also suffered from poor quality assets, despite transfers of NPLs to TAMC.[82]

Frequently, the restructured debt would slip again into impaired NPLs due to corruption and the use of concessions, such as reductions of interest rates and extensions given for repayment.[83] Thus, in 1999, only three cases, in a sample of 40 monitored by CDRAC had their principal reduced, while 33 had been granted extensions. Moreover, in November 1999, out of 240,000

Table 10.5 NPLs[a] outstanding – classified by financial institution (million baht)

	1998		1999		2000		2001		2002	
Private banks	1,149,512.09	(36.47)[b]	1,191,029.13	(39.70)	669,960.67	(24.25)	463,348.67	(17.55)	373,962.50	(14.43)
State-owned banks	910,193.77	(54.74)	1,136,434.86	(67.44)	801,077.00	(49.13)	179,110.83	(12.68)	76,265.04	(5.84)
Foreign banks (full branch)	63,022.72	(7.56)	81,736.69	(11.49)	46,674.50	(7.48)	24,893.08	(4.26)	12,319.98	(2.32)
Total commercial banks	2,122,728.10	(37.55)	2,409,200.67	(44.64)	1,517,712.17	(30.27)	667,352.58	(14.43)	462,547.51	(10.45)
Finance companies	290,417.10	(60.90)	163,426.67	(63.37)	67,446.00	(40.33)	25,420.08	(16.80)	14,441.83	(9.37)
Grand total	2,413,145.67	(39.37)	2,572,627.34	(45.52)	1,588,195.33	(30.47)	697,822.08	(14.38)	479,846.94	(10.37)

Notes:

a NPL = Over three months past due loans.

b Figures in parentheses are percentage of NPL to total loans.

Source: Bank of Thailand, *Annual Economic Report*, 2002

Table 10.6 Key ratios – Bangkok Bank

	1990	*1991*	*1992*	*1993*	*1994*	*1995*	*1996*	*1997*	*1998*	*1999*	*2000*	*2001*	*2002*	*2003*
Profitability														
Return on equity (%)	0.86	1.16	1.50	1.69	1.93	1.91	1.79	0.30	–3.92	–5.06	–1.51	0.52	0.50	0.83
Net interest margin (%)	3.98	3.85	4.46	4.65	4.86	4.48	4.51	3.72	0.92	0.85	2.50	2.76	2.75	2.98
Asset quality														
Provisioning (%)	1.3	0.7	0.9	0.8	0.7	0.5	0.6	2.2	4.5	6.3	3.5	0.5	–0.8	–0.1
Capital adequacy														
Liabilities to equity	19	16	15	11	23	10	10	13	12	25	36	28	21	12
Equity to deposits and borrowings	0.35	0.42	0.47	0.62	0.26	0.64	0.63	0.34	0.60	0.30	0.24	0.42	0.56	0.94
Equity to advances	0.06	0.07	0.08	0.10	0.05	0.11	0.11	0.08	0.10	0.05	0.04	0.05	0.07	0.12
Liquidity														
Total loans and advances to deposits and borrowings	5.55	5.68	6.14	6.18	5.22	5.91	5.55	4.08	5.89	6.01	6.71	8.44	8.16	7.53
Growth														
Net interest income (%)		15	36	17	19	6	11	6	–80	–13	197	2	–6	9
Net income (%)		55	45	32	25	14	5	–80	–1,283	20	–69	–135	–3	81
Total assets (%)		15	12	17	10	15	12	22	–10	–7	5	1	0	9
Total loans and advances (%)		19	17	12	14	15	11	28	–20	–6	1	–7	–5	1
Deposits + borrowings (%)		16	8	11	34	2	18	75	–44	–8	–9	–26	–2	9
Equity growth (%)		40	20	47	–44	150	16	–4	–3	–55	–25	28	29	84

Source: Annual Reports of Bangkok Bank, 1990–2003

Table 10.7 Key ratios – Bank of Asia

	1991	*1992*	*1993*	*1994*	*1995*	*1996*	*1997*	*1998*	*1999*	*2000*	*2001*	*2002*	*2003*
Profitability													
Return on equity (%)	5.01	8.27	13.91	19.34	19.04	15.98	–4.52	–87.79	–95.96	–34.97	–44.11	–25.83	12.46
Net interest margin (%)	2.46	4.06	3.60	3.84	3.58	3.65	3.13	0.29	1.33	2.27	2.84	3.14	3.39
Asset quality													
Provisioning (%)	0.8	2.1	0.8	0.4	0.4	0.4	1.2	4.7	8.2	3.9	3.6	3.4	0.0
Capital adequacy													
Liabilities to equity (ratio)	15	14	13	12	13	10	16	15	12	12	17	13	11
Equity to deposits and borrowings (ratio)	0.07	0.08	0.08	0.09	0.08	0.10	0.07	0.07	0.08	0.08	0.06	0.08	0.10
Equity to advances (ratio)	0.08	0.09	0.09	0.09	0.09	0.11	0.07	0.08	0.11	0.10	0.07	0.10	0.13
Liquidity													
Total loans and advances to deposits and borrowings	0.89	0.92	0.92	0.95	0.89	0.96	0.91	0.84	0.75	0.85	0.79	0.80	0.75
Growth													
Net interest income (%)		74	10	33	13	26	5	–92	335	89	21	11	6
Net income (%)		89	118	74	18	23	–124	1,789	40	–63	–7	–21	–160
Total assets (%)		4	25	18	26	17	25	–6	5	–1	2	1	6
Total loans and advances (%)		6	24	25	21	24	22	–12	–6	11	–3	0	–2
Deposits + borrowings (%)		2	25	20	31	14	29	–4	5	–1	4	–1	4
Equity growth (%)		40	20	47	–44	150	16	–4	–3	–55	–25	28	29

Source: Annual Reports, Bank of Asia, 1991–2003

cases of NPLs, only 300 were referred to the bankruptcy courts.[84] There was an excessive reliance on persuasion, rather than just liquidating the bank. This gradual approach led to an increase in EBITDA from 14 per cent in 1998 to 23 per cent in 1999. Debt-equity ratio also remained high and net profits were lower in 1999 than those in 1994.[85]

These difficulties in restructuring were located in the legal framework, relating in particular to bankruptcy and liquidation. First, Thai banks preferred repayment, rescheduling, the debt being written off, or extensions with interest rate reductions. Second, Thai economic growth was slow due to these burdens of debt dragging it further down, often resulting in the multiple restructuring of the debts of a single bank.

One can contrast this with Korea where the recovery was fast. By 1998, the decline in debt of the corporate sector in Korea had been achieved and banks now concentrated on small retail customers, away from the connected lending to large *chaebols*. The Korean Asset Management Corporation seized the bad loans and disposed them swiftly. It liquidated bad debtors and in 2002 achieved a NPL recovery rate of 47 per cent.[86] Thailand, meanwhile, formed the TAMC in July 2001 to manage distressed bank assets. By 2003, only 50 per cent had been restructured through equity injections, debt to equity conversions and through maturity extensions. Yet, of these restructured NPLs, 45 per cent were deteriorating. The most impaired were those belonging to Thai state banks. TAMC was becoming a warehouse for distressed loans instead of disposing them through sales or through debt equity, as the Korean Asset Management Corporation did. The lack of transparency, combined with the weakness of the Bank of Thailand, meant these bad loans persisted and slippage of loans to NPLs was pervasive. Collateral seizure provided little redress since these were bad assets. Thai banks also struggled to dispose of foreclosed properties because of the collapse in the property market.

A third difficulty for Thai banks was their high exposure to large commercial and manufacturing corporations. Indeed, 46 per cent of their total loans were to these large corporations.[87] In contrast, Korean loan recovery was swift and concentrated on transforming loans to SMEs and on consumer finance. Fourth, the Thai stock market was sluggish so recapitalization was difficult except through state or foreign investors. Fifth, the weakness of the regulatory environment, combined with difficulties in loan and asset classification and provisions, meant that legal redress was lengthy and expensive.

Sixth, a few domestic banks possessed entrenched market positions. Five of the largest banks controlled almost four-fifths of the entire banking sector and two-thirds of total financial assets. In contrast, finance companies' assets had declined from 10 per cent of the total financial system in 1994 to only 2 per cent in 2003. These structural deficiencies made restructuring difficult.

One major consequence of these restructuring developments was a number of mergers of banks, both small and large. In 1998, for instance, Union Bank of Bangkok and Laern Thong Bank were merged with Radanasin Bank and

Krung Thai Thanakit Finance Company. In 1999, all of them were then merged into Bank Thai. The second merger was that of First Bangkok City Bank and KTB. Another major consequence of restructuring was an increase in state-owned banks, from one to four, and this produced a threefold increase in financial assets held by state banks, rising from 10 per cent in May 1997 to 23 per cent in November 1999.

Crucially, there was an increase in foreign investment in the Thai financial sector,[88] though the four Thai Banks acquired by foreign multinational banks were small. In 2000, they only accounted for 7 per cent of the total capitalization of Thai banking, and 9 per cent of loans and deposits in the Thai banking sector. Nationalistic fears of a foreign takeover were unfounded.[89] What is clear is that the Thai government's actions, unlike those of the Indonesian one, were subtle and indirect, avoiding outright bail-outs as was the case in Indonesia.

Foreign capital and restructuring

The most poignant fears during restructuring were of eroding state assets and losing control of banks to Western capital. Foreign shareholding in Thai banks took two forms. The first was outright acquisition, as with Bank of Asia where recapitalization by ABNAMRO raised the level of foreign equity from 6 per cent in 1997 to 77 per cent in May 2000. Equally, DBS Thai Danu saw an increase in foreign investment from 9 per cent in 1997 to 62 per cent in 2000. Standard Chartered Nakornthon Bank (SCNB), meanwhile, revealed an increase in foreign shareholding from 6 per cent in 1997 to 75 per cent in 2000. Last, UOB Radanasin Bank held 75 per cent foreign equity by May 2000. These acquisitions by foreign banks were initially for ten years, after which they could restructure with Thai investors.

The second form of penetration by foreign investors was purely to increase shareholding, while allowing ownership to remain principally with Thai bankers. Bangkok Bank, which had a 25 per cent foreign shareholding in 1997, had an increased foreign equity holding of 49 per cent by May 2000. Similarly, Bank of Ayudhya, which had 25 per cent foreign shareholding, saw an increase to 32 per cent by 2000. The Government of Singapore Investment Corporation held 15 per cent equity in Thai Farmers' Bank.[90]

In order to trace the impact of foreign capital on Thai financial institutions, a more detailed analysis of those banks acquired by foreign multinational banks follows. Wang Lee Bank was founded in 1933 and, upon listing on the SET in 1978, was named Nakornthon Bank. It had been part of the financial networks that had emerged from the Thai rice trade and Chinese remittance business in the early twentieth century. Five major Chinese trading families had established banks and, in the process, attracted state patronage and capital. Wang Lee Bank thus emerged as part of the credit distribution network of overseas Chinese in Southeast Asia and Hong Kong.

In 1993, it was restructured with Citibank as a partner. It pursued a clear strategy of connected lending to large capitalists, such as the electronics magnate Charn Asawachake of Alphatec Electronics, who faced bankruptcy in 1997. This lending to families and relatives, combined with inter-group lending within the Wang Lee trading and manufacturing concerns, added to the bank's woes. It also faced a high debt exposure to real estate and to the declining currency markets in 1997. The bank had seen an increase in turnover between 1989 and 1996 but its return on equity fluctuated between –7.8 per cent to –20.76 per cent. Moreover, its loan deposit ratio was 9.14 per cent between 1991 and 1996. The gearing ratio, meanwhile, remained under 20 per cent until 1997, but in that year it was burdened with impaired loans amounting to a third of its total loans. See Table 10.8 for a clearer perspective on Nakornthon's performance.

Nakornthon Bank was one of the medium-sized banks chosen by the government for sale to a foreign bank. This decision was controversial because its level of distress was lower than that of the Bangkok Bank. However, the larger banks had to be saved because of a moral hazard problem. In July 1999, the Thai state intervened with a capital injection of 7 billion baht prior to the bank's sale to Standard Chartered Bank (SCB), though the Thai state would still guarantee 85 per cent of any future loans for a period of five years. SCB would take responsibility for the remaining 15 per cent. By December 2001, the top five shareholders were from SCB: SCB had a 75 per cent shareholding, Standard Chartered Holdings held 1 per cent and the Financial Initiative Development Fund (belonging to the Thai state) possessed 24 per cent. The remaining shares were absorbed by the Thailand Securities Depository Co., the Crown Property Bureau and the Wang Lee family. The latter also were allowed to retain their managerial position.

The takeover resulted in a dramatic overhaul of the existing organizational structures. The Board of Directors was usurped by SCB, with the appointment of David George Moir as Chairman, Chandru Hassaram Narwani as President and CEO, and Lee Boon Huat, Thippaporn Gertphon and Salinee Wangtal as directors. New senior managers were appointed to critical sections within the bank. Customer banking, Corporate and Institutional banking, Finance, HRM and Risk Management all had new heads.

There were critical changes in capitalization and in new technology. Soon after the takeover in September 1999, 16.7 million baht were invested in technology. Another 5 million baht, meanwhile, were allocated for internet banking. Indeed, by 2001, SCB had invested 1 billion baht in technology. Significant changes were also introduced in the client base. The parent company, Standard Chartered, absorbed the large Thai corporate clients, while SCNB concentrated on the small retail borrowers. Multinational banking activities and business in treasury bonds and wholesale products became the preserve of SCB.[91]

The influence of the family and its networks were eroded in favour of efficiency and merit. The spurt in technology, with automated operations

Table 10.8 Nakornthon Bank/Standard Chartered Nakornthon Bank (1989–2001)

Key ratios	*1989*	*1990*	*1991*	*1992*	*1993*	*1994*	*1995*	*1996*	*1997*	*1998*	*1999*	*2000*	*2001*
Profitability													
Return on equity (%)	4.41	8.57	12.91	15.56	15.34	15.63	4.42	6.39	–67.96	–34.97	26.41	56.23	17.56
Net interest margin (%)	3.22	3.06	3.46	3.24	4.58	3.65	3.46	2.49	3.33	4.27	2.24	3.64	3.79
Asset quality													
Provisioning (%)	0.15	1.10	0.40	1.30	0.60	1.40	1.20	3.70	6.20	3.90	3.60	3.40	2.00
Capital adequacy													
Liabilities to equity (key ratio)	14	15	15	16	13	14	13	16	17	14	13	16	13
Equity to deposits and borrowings (key ratio)	0.56	0.47	0.34	0.5	1.65	0.23	0.46	4.67	2.76	3.01	3.76	2.2	2.84
Equity to advances (key ratio)	0.28	0.12	0.16	0.25	0.23	0.21	0.07	0.08	0.29	0.1	0.19	0.28	0.12
Liquidity													
Total loans and advances to deposits and borrowings	3.34	3.75	3.7	3.76	3.99	4.44	21.35	36.78	8.26	46.49	24.45	21.65	22.89
Growth													
Net interest income (%)		69	21	5	74	10	89	21	11	6	41	11	6
Net income (%)		33	7	24	79	98	63	17	–21	–10	37	53	42
Total assets (%)		1	2	25	4	25	16	12	1	6	1	1	6
Total loans and advances (%)		11	3	22	6	24	11	23	0	–2	3	0	2
Deposits + borrowings (%)		46	68	75	10	46	36	48	–28	–8	8	8	8
Equity growth (%)		26	25	16	40	20	10	14	–48	–29	25	28	29

and e-banking, was accompanied by recruitment and promotion based on merit and ability rather than seniority or family connections. Staff training initiatives were rigorous. By 2001, an aggressive marketing programme, with branches in supermarkets and retail stores, had ensured rapid growth. This occurred against a drastic downsizing, through employee redundancies and substitution with technology. The close interaction between SCB and SCNB ensured efficient diversification in products and technology.

The success of these reforms was reflected in the decline in impaired loans. NPLs, which had peaked at 45.52 per cent of total loan structure in 1999, now declined to 30.47 per cent in 2000, to 14.38 per cent in 2001, and to 10.37 per cent in 2002.[92] Return on capital employed improved between 1999 and 2001.

Similar changes occurred after the takeover of Thai Danu by the DBS. Thai Danu was founded in 1949 with major stakes held by the Thai royal family, prominent bureaucrats and merchants. In 1997 it was failing, with a high proportion of NPLs. DBS, meanwhile, had nurtured ambitions of regional growth, even acquiring 3.4 per cent equity in Thai Danu before the financial crisis. In April 1999, DBS increased its stake to 52 per cent and by 2000 held 62 per cent. In September 1999, it provided 81 per cent of debt recovery provisions against the existing NPLs. Nevertheless, impaired loans still haunted the bank, averaging 40 per cent between 1999 and 2000. Furthermore, Thai Danu DBS (TDDBS) reported a loss of 12.9 billion baht in 1999. Despite these losses, the bank increased its lending. Out of a total 13 billion baht in new loans, 8 billion baht was allocated to large corporations in 2000. In addition, the bank reduced operating costs by 15 per cent between its takeover in January 1998 and the end of restructuring in December 1999. This was achieved through the closure of some branches (indeed, almost a third were closed by 2000), a reduction in the workforce, and an increase in e-banking.[93]

There was also a radical change in loans policy. The connected lending system with no guarantees and collateral of disputed value was abandoned. The bank now focused on small retail customers, including SMEs. It also diversified into housing mortgagees.

The influence of foreign capital and the involvement of foreign banks in Thai banking is clear. While the NPLs of the banks acquired by foreigners were high, recovery and recapitalization were accelerated. TDDBS had an NPL ratio of 41 per cent, Bank of Asia 45 per cent, SCNB 56 per cent and Radanasin Bank 51 per cent.[94] The foreign banks completed the restructuring swiftly, with high investments in the initial phase. They increased the customer base, and offered a wider range of products and services. Significantly, they also reduced employment by 13 per cent and aimed for a reduction of 35 per cent by 2004. Indeed, Thai banks had almost three times as many employees as Western banks. The takeovers resulted in new technology and the introduction of e-banking, as well as advanced technology for marketing purposes.

Crucially, they replaced existing senior managers and created an effective leadership, one that was not dominated by family and cronies. The targeting of SMEs and retail customers helped to widen and secure the client base. However, as Table 10.9 shows, the foreign banks held only a tiny sector of Thai banking, with the five largest Thai banks carving out 75 per cent of the market, even in May 2000. This oligopoly hampered innovation and competitive growth. Thus, while the initial impact of foreign capital was great and led to some improvements in corporate governance, the long-term

Table 10.9 Foreign shareholding in Thai commercial banks, 1997–9

Name of bank	*Ownership*	*Foreign share*
Bangkok Bank	Controlling interests post crisis Sophonpanich family	49%
Thai Farmers Bank	Lam Sam family	49%
Siam Commercial Bank	Crown Property Bureau	49%
Bank of Ayudhya	Rattanarak family	40%
Krung Thai Bank	Thai Government	–
Thai Military Bank	Thai Army	–
Thai Danu Bank	Tuchinda family	Acquired by DBS 51%
Bank of Asia	Phatrapraisit family	Acquired by ABNAMRO 75%
Nakornthon Bank	Wang Lee	Acquired by Standard Chartered
Bangkok Bank of Commerce	Jauchandra family	Closed down, good assets transferred to Krung Thai
Siam City Bank	Mahadamrongkut family	Taken over by BOT (Bank of Thailand) for merger with BMB
Bangkok Metropolitan Bank (BMB in 2002)	Techapailbun family	Taken over by BOT merged to form SCIB
First Bangkok City Bank	Charoen Siriwattanaphakdi	Merged with Krung Thai
Lawmthong Bank	Chansrichawla family	Sold to UOB (Singapore) after merger with bank
Union Bank of Bangkok	Chonwichan family	Merged with 13 finance companies as Bank Thai for sale

Source: Standard and Poor, Report on Thai Banks, 2003; Pasuk Phongpaichit and Chris Baker, 'The Thai Economic Crisis: New Ideals of Liberalism and the Reaction of Thai Society', in Praipol Khumsap (ed.), *Articles Commemorating the Sixtieth Anniversary of Acharn Ammar Siamwalla*, Faculty of Economics, Thammasat University, 1999, p. 222

impact on profitability was determined by structural and institutional factors, and these were difficult to change.[95]

In a World Bank Working Paper of May 1998 entitled 'How does foreign entry affect the domestic banking market?', Stijn Claessens *et al.* made some dramatic assertions on the impact of foreign entry into 80 countries between 1988 and 1995. They concluded that foreign equity and foreign ownership reduced profitability for these domestic banks. There was improvement in corporate governance but this was not reflected in profits. My detailed research does not uphold such sweeping conclusions. First, it is clear that net profit alone is not a serious indicator. Foreign involvement in Thai banks, which was only allowed after 1997, has led to substantial improvements as outlined above.

Second, Claessens' use of the period 1988–95 is unsuitable for Southeast Asia because there were serious constraints on direct foreign involvement in banking during this period. Foreign banks were often attracted to large

Table 10.10 Total capital and total assets of commercial banks

Commercial banks	*Total capital*[a]				*Total assets*			
	Dec-96		*May-00*		*Dec-96*		*May-00*	
	Rank	*Share %*	*Rank*	*Share %*	*Rank*	*Share %*	*Rank*	*Share %*
Thai major shareholders								
First five largest banks[b]	1–5	68.2	1–5	74.9	1–5	68.4	1–5	74.8
Foreign major shareholders								
A Viable private banks								
Bank of Asia	11	2.5	10	2.9	11	2.5	10	2.9
DBS Thai Danu Bank	12	2.3	11	1.9	12	2.3	11	1.9
Sub-total (A)	11–12	4.8	10–11	4.8	11–12	4.8	10–1	4.8
B Privatized banks								
Standard Chartered Nakornthon Bank	14	1.3	12	1.2	14	1.3	12	1.2
UOB Radanasin Bank	15	0.8	13	1.1	15	0.8	13	1.1
Sub-total (B)	14–15	2.1	12–13	2.3	14–15	2.1	12–13	2.3
C Banks on privatization process								
Siam City Bank	8	4.6	7	4.8	8	4.6	7	4.8
Bangkok Metropolitan Bank	9	3.9	9	2.9	9	3.8	9	2.9
Sub-total (C)	7–8	8.5	9–8	7.7	7–8	8.4	9–8	7.7
Sub (A) + (B)	11–15	6.9	10–13	7.1	11–15	6.9	10–13	7.1
Sub (A) + (B) + (C)	8–5	15.4	8–13	14.8	8–5	15.3	8–13	14.8

Notes:

a 15 banks in 1997 and 13 banks in 1998.

b Bangkok Bank, Thai Farmers Bank, Krung Thai Bank, Siam Commercial Bank and Bank of Ayudhya.

Source: Bank of Thailand, Annual Reports, 1996–2001

well-connected banks. In this period of financial liberalization, the latter were embarking into highly risky sectors such as real estate, stock markets and financial derivatives. All displayed a serious lack of prudent behaviour. Additionally, an increased moral hazard persisted, with government bail-outs of these large banks.

In contrast, following the crisis, foreign involvement has led to the injection of new capital, lower costs, new products and services, staff training, rigorous competition in the small bank sector, improved corporate governance and improved profitability. Despite domestic institutional constraints, direct foreign involvement could have contagious effects, producing long-term improvements throughout the Thai financial system. Such improvements through osmosis cannot be discounted. Claessens *et al.* should undertake

Table 10.11 Loans and deposits of commercial banks

Commercial banks	*Loans*[a,b]				*Deposits*			
	Dec-96		*May-00*		*Dec-96*		*May-00*	
	Rank	*Share %*	*Rank*	*Share %*	*Rank*	*Share %*	*Rank*	*Share %*
Thai major shareholders								
First five largest banks[c]	1–5	68.1	1–5	74.2	1–5	71.4	1–5	75.3
Foreign major shareholders								
A Viable private banks								
Bank of Asia	11	2.5	10	3.0	11	2.3	10	2.9
DBS Thai Danu Bank	12	2.4	11	2.2	12	2.3	11	1.7
Sub-total (A)	11–12	4.9	10–1	5.2	11–12	4.5	10–1	4.6
B Privatized banks								
Standard Chartered Nakornthon Bank	14	1.2	12	1.3	14	1.3	12	1.0
UOB Radanasin Bank	15	0.8	13	0.1	15	0.8	13	0.9
Sub-total (B)	14–15	2.0	12–13	1.4	14–15	2.1	12–13	1.9
C Banks on privatization process								
Siam City Bank	8	4.4	7	4.3	8	4.6	7	5.1
Bangkok Metropolitan Bank	9	3.8	9	3.3	9	3.9	9	3.5
Sub-total (C)	7–8	8.2	7–9	7.8	7–8	8.5	9–8	8.6
Sub (A) + (B)	11–15	6.9	7–13	6.6	11–15	6.6	10–13	6.5
Sub (A) + (B) + (C)	8–5	15.1	7–13	14.4	8–5	15.1	8–13	15.1

Notes:

a 15 banks in 1997 and 13 banks in 1998.

b Loans, less allowance for loan loss.

c Bangkok Bank, Thai Farmers Bank, Krung Thai Bank, Siam Commercial Bank and Bank of Ayudhya.

Source: Bank of Thailand, Annual Reports, 1996–2001

serious research in individual countries before making sweeping hypotheses. Many of their findings remain unsubstantiated and highly speculative. Indeed, their conclusions are dangerous because World Bank policies and initiatives may be influenced by such rumour-mongering. Perhaps they should follow the standards set by ADB or Standard and Poor in their evaluation of Asian financial institutions.[96]

11 The power of large single shareholding and industrial concentration in Thai corporate structure and performance

By the 1970s there was, in a number of respects, a movement towards the development of large-scale business structures and higher industrial concentration. The growth of the stock exchange comprised only one small factor in this grouping of industrial assets – textiles, automobiles and telecommunications – into a few large firms. This was not an evolutionary process, nor was it always a rationalization strategy. The dimensions of this corporate and industrial concentration were complex and form the core analysis of this chapter.

The first factor assisting concentration was the phenomenal growth during this period that was followed by organizational changes to further conserve these monopolistic structures. Second, new investment was possible because of large foreign capital inflows. The more oligopolistic markets created by this trend in the domestic economy also encouraged firms to acquire a stake in markets abroad. This clear shift towards a diversification of large-scale operations and multinational expansion was pervasive among an elite few in Thailand during the 1980s and 1990s. These dynamic enterprises were able to secure favours from the government and this complementarity between the firms' growth and government links will be unravelled in the detailed case studies below. Finally, in the Thai case there appears to be no direct correlation between concentration and any merger activity, unlike in Malaysia.

Thailand experienced a period of impressive and sustained economic growth after 1945, despite difficulties in both 1985 and 1997. Its GDP saw an increase to 7 per cent between 1965 and 1980, which then fell slightly to 6 per cent between 1980 and 1991. This growth was part of the fundamental shift to manufacturing and rapid industrialization from an essentially agrarian economy. The manufacturing sector was diversified and assimilated an increasing share in overall growth. By 1990, production in food, textiles and garments accounted for 36 per cent of value-added within manufacturing.[1]

Exports of manufactured goods contributed to 42 per cent of total GDP in 1993, while their composition in exports alone rose from 6 per cent in 1965 to 28 per cent in 1980 and to 73 per cent in 1993. This coincided with a decline in primary exports, including minerals, from 97 per cent to 36 per cent between 1965 and 1990.[2] This impressive export growth in manufactured goods concealed an important ingredient, namely, a high import content that averaged between 27 per cent in the 1980s and 23.7 per cent in 1992.[3]

The restructuring of these corporations into larger organizations was arguably one of the preferred options, given the huge foreign capital influx, generous government subsidies and increasing development of the capital markets in the four decades after 1950. Moreover, the development of the stock market facilitated the raising of capital from domestic and international capital markets. Thus, on a number of fronts – technical, commercial, financial and political – there were strong pressures for concentrated corporate growth. All this created barriers to competition and weakened small and medium enterprises. It is therefore difficult to accept Doner and Ramsay's argument that there is a strong prima facie case for the view that this Thai political clientelism has produced competitive market structures.[4] Rather, the constantly changing power relations between Thai capitalists, on the one hand, and the state and the bureaucracy, on the other, combined with the intra-elite rivalry between these separate segments of power and money, has initiated a powerful, monopolistic, family-dominated corporate structure that even the crisis of 1997 has had difficulty in dismantling. It is this single large shareholding structure and dominance that forms the central theme of this chapter.

Growth in concentration

Thai listed firms exhibit features of a large, single shareholder, which is often a family patriarch or the family's holding company; a concentration that is more pervasive and more dominant than in Malaysia or even in Indonesia. The absence of strong, viable and enduring state or institutional shareholding only partially explains this concentration. This large shareholder concentration is also reproduced in specific families dominating certain industrial sectors: Shinawatra in telecommunications, Pornprapha in automobiles, Sahaviriya in steel and Sukree Photiratanankul in textiles.

This large shareholder analysis is, therefore, examined against an evaluation of how this affects methods of corporate financing, corporate performance, levels of investor protection, managerial behaviour, relations with the state and resulting deficiencies in corporate governance. The existing literature on corporate economy in Southeast Asia, including Claessens' cross-country study,[5] is not based on serious empirical case studies. The causes and consequences of these linkages between corporations and institutions in each state or economy are not only highly complicated, as our case studies in this volume clearly demonstrate, but also change over time. The corporation interacts in a complex, dynamic system with the market, the network of investors and alliances, technology, government and global developments. Thus, concentration in Singapore has widely differing causes and consequences from those in Thailand.

The proportion of shareholding held by certain families in Thailand is high. Individual family members hold a significant amount of shares, normally an average of 18.5 per cent. Between 1990 and 1998, the top five shareholders held 56.4 per cent of total shares; the top three held 50 per cent[6] (see Tables 11.1a and 11.1b.

How does this concentrated ownership occur or evolve? The first major factor is the use of holding companies. The holding company, which is fully owned by the family, sets up affiliated firms. These affiliated firms are held by the parent company but do not own shares in the parent company. Thus,

Table 11.1a Top-five shareholder composition of public listed companies in Thailand, 1990–8

Year	*Company*	*Bank*	*NBFIs*[a]	*Individuals*	*Government*	*Other*
1990	28.3	2.1	6.9	13.9	0.7	1.1
1991	27.6	1.8	7.2	15.2	0.5	0.9
1992	25.4	1.6	7.5	18.0	0.8	0.7
1993	22.8	1.6	2.9	17.9	0.7	n/a
1994	23.3	1.4	6.5	18.9	1.3	1.3
1995	27.3	1.2	5.1	19.4	1.3	0.5
1996	27.8	1.5	4.7	20.0	1.2	0.5
1997	28.6	1.3	5.6	19.3	1.5	0.4
1998	28.5	1.6	5.2	20.0	1.4	1.0
Average	26.7	1.5	5.5	18.5	1.1	3.3

Note:
a NBFIs denotes non-bank financial institutions, including finance and investment companies.

Source: Stock Exchange of Thailand, *Comprehensive Listed Company Information, Information Database*; Piman Limpaphayom, 'Chapter 4 – Thailand', in Asian Development Bank (ADB), *Corporate Governance and Finance in East Asia: A Study of Indonesia, the Republic of Korea, Malaysia, the Philippines, and Thailand.* Volume 2: Country Studies, edited by David Edwards, Juzhong Zhuang and Virgina A. Capulong, Manila, 2001, p. 243

Table 11.1b Top-five shareholder concentration of publicly listed companies in Thailand, 1990–8

	Average[a]	*1990*	*1991*	*1992*	*1993*	*1994*	*1995*	*1996*	*1997*	*1998*
1st largest	28.1	26.2	26.3	26.8	32.3	26.4	27.7	28.1	28.5	28.9
2nd largest	12.0	11.4	11.4	11.0	16.5	10.7	11.3	11.7	11.7	12.1
3rd largest	7.4	6.6	6.8	7.1	9.9	6.9	7.0	7.1	7.3	7.3
4th largest	5.2	4.9	5.0	5.2	6.4	4.9	5.0	5.1	5.1	5.2
5th largest	4.0	3.9	4.0	4.0	4.6	3.9	3.9	3.9	4.1	4.2
Top five	56.4	52.4	52.4	53.8	68.9	52.6	54.3	55.6	56.6	57.5

Note:
a Average for 1990–8 period.

Source: Stock Exchange of Thailand, *Comprehensive Listed Company Information, Information Database*; ADB, op. cit., p. 241

separation is maintained, unlike the case in Japan where cross-shareholding is common. Another distinction is that usually the parent company is not the holding company. Through such devices, the family can own 62 per cent of the voting stock and thereby control the firm.

Second, listed companies in the group are often capital-intensive firms, which possess a critical family stake. Therefore, listing does not necessarily dilute family ownership and even acts as an essential tool for raising funds in capital markets both at home and abroad. See Tables 11.2 and 11.3.

Table 11.2 Public companies registered, 1987–2000

Type of business	*Number of companies*	*Registered capital (baht billion)*	*Paid-up capital (baht billion)*
Agriculture, hunting, forestry and fishing	5	1.9	1.2
Mining and quarrying	6	16.6	11.9
Manufacturing	245	350.1	261.0
Electricity, gas and water	5	30.9	19.6
Construction	13	34.5	23.3
Wholesale and retail trade, and restaurant and hotel	129	111.0	83.1
Transport[a], storage and communication	22	110.9	78.5
Financing, insurance, real estate and business service	194	1,394.5	791.0
Community, social and personal service	42	50.6	21.6
Total	661	2,101.0	1,291.2

Note:
a The data for 2000 is as of October 2000.

Source: Department of Commercial Registration, Ministry of Commerce, Thailand

Table 11.3 Public offerings of securities, 1992–9 (baht billion)

Type of securities	*1992*	*1993*	*1994*	*1995*	*1996*	*1997*	*1998*	*1999*
Equity	1.2	34.0	82.1	64.6	65.2	15.7	136.4	277.2
Debt instrument								
Domestic offering	5.2	20.5	54.7	39.3	40.4	12.2	31.1	286.8
Offshore offering	–	1.0	27.8	31.3	51.9	25.9	–	26.5
Hybrid instrument								
Domestic offering	–	1.6	7.5	8.7	5.7	0.3	6.7	9.1
Offshore offering	–	39.3	22.4	7.9	37.8	2.5	–	–
Total funds raised	6.4	96.3	194.6	151.8	201.0	56.6	174.1	599.6

Note:
(–) not available.

Source: Securities and Exchange Commission of Thailand, *Key Capital Market Statistics*, 1990–2000

Third, government and institutional shareholders often hold less than 2 per cent of the total outstanding shares in the listed company.[7] This is in direct contrast to Singapore and Malaysia where institutional shareholding, particularly by the state and state-linked companies, is high. In Thailand, though, government shareholding only arose in petroleum, the airline industry and other capital-intensive sectors.

Minority shareholding was limited and diffuse;[8] their rights were difficult to uphold because of the rarity of public meetings for shareholders. This was also due to the fact that the roles and responsibilities of government agencies regulating shareholder rights were confused, partly as a result of the diffusion of authority and resulting discord within the relevant state institutions, namely, the Ministry of Commerce, the Stock Exchange Commission, the Stock Exchange of Thailand and the Bank of Thailand. Moreover, control by creditors was weak because of long-term cronyistic relations between commercial banks and the large listed firms. This made the monitoring of debt confusing and chaotic. Consequently, the valuation of collaterals remained difficult and loan repayments were neither structured nor secure. Finally, weak bankruptcy laws meant there were few checks on corporate financial profligacy.

The regulatory legal framework that had been designed to control this growth of concentrated ownership, in fact, favoured this trend towards ownership concentration. The Public Company Limited Act of 1978 limited the proportion of large shareholding but this was relaxed under the 1992 Amendment, which stipulated a large shareholder could now hold up to 70 per cent of the total outstanding shares. Cumulative voting was made optional and punishment of recalcitrant managers was relaxed. This meant external monitoring or any other form of deterrence was weakened. The 1992 Act also relaxed rules on the elections of directors leading to a situation in which the CEO and chairman were often close relatives.

This concentrated family dominance faced little threat from outside since the market for corporate mergers and acquisitions was weak. Between 1978 and 1990 there were only a few acquisitions and mergers. Between 1994 and 1995 there were 41 cases of tender offers. In 1996 this declined to six and the situation remained sluggish in 1997[9] (see Table 11.4 for details). After the financial crisis, however, there was an increase in mergers and acquisitions prompted by the rescue packages initiated by the government and foreign multinationals. The potential for takeover was weak because of the limited presence of investment banking groups and the lack of pension funds that might be used for investments. It was only after the 1997 crisis that the state broadened the provision of pensions.

Table 11.4 Merger and acquisition activities, 1993–9

Year	*Tender offer value*[a] *(baht billion)*	*Purchase value*		*Number of companies*
		baht billion	*% of tender offer value*	
1993	5.4	4.6	84.1	8
1994	23.1	17.3	75.1	27
1995	19.2	11.2	58.1	14
1996	8.3	6.9	84.0	6
1997	6.2	3.5	55.8	9
1998	7.7	6.2	81.3	13
1999	11.0	6.7	60.8	23

Note:
a Tender offer value refers to the minimum offer value.

Source: *Reports of Securities and Exchange Commission of Thailand*, 1993–2000

Corporate performance and risks

What are the consequences of this concentration of corporate ownership and control? First, does this concentrated ownership affect how corporations choose forms of financing? The orthodox view is that family-dominated firms prefer internal forms of finance, namely, the recycling of profits. However, these Thai family firms sought risky finance, in the form of unhedged foreign currency borrowing, in their relentless search for rapid growth and diversification. When seeking external finance, listing on the Bangkok Stock Exchange, as well as on the regional stock markets, was an attractive option. State and foreign investors remained indulgent towards these large firms and, hence, they could be reckless in their borrowing and in the riskiness of their debts. In Thailand, as in most of Asia, levels of sanctioned borrowing may be determined more by the status of the family than by the value and riskiness of the firm's assets.

The utilization of loans from commercial banks and financial houses remained high. Between 1990 and 1996, short-term loans accounted for 40 per cent of total liabilities of corporations, while long-term loans constituted 20 per cent of total liabilities for these same years. Retained earnings accounted for 30 per cent of finance used. Despite this increase in debt, equity finance rose as well. The proportion of external debt also rose from 34 per cent in 1986 to 84.5 per cent in 1996, while external debt as a percentage of GDP grew from 42.2 per cent in 1986 to 251.9 per cent in 1997.[10] Most of these loans were from foreign banks, denominated in foreign currency, and more than half of this was not hedged, thus dramatically increasing the risks. Furthermore, despite these increases in capital and the diverse forms of finance used to achieve growth, these corporations posted disappointing performances.

The financial ratios of listed corporations deteriorated in 1990. Return on assets, return on equity and gross profit margin, all of which had risen throughout the 1980s, stagnated in 1990 and then declined through to 1996. For instance, ROA declined from 10.3 per cent in 1989 to 3.4 per cent in 1996. Similarly, ROE fell from 21.4 per cent to 5.8 per cent in the same period. Although the decline in gross profit margin was not as dramatic, the times interest earned was down from 10.5 per cent in 1987 to 5.1 per cent by 1996.[11] See Table 11.5 for more information.

Financial leverage also deteriorated. Long-term debt increased as expansion was funded by external borrowing rather than by internally generated profits and reserves. The extreme dip in profitability and asset turnover, from 117 per cent in 1985 to 65 per cent in 1996, clearly revealed that while serious weaknesses were apparent throughout the 1990s, increased foreign borrowing sustained expansion on a wave of financial flamboyance and euphoria[12] (see Table 11.6).

This was a powerful cocktail for the SET, which saw a decline in its index from 1,360 in 1994 to 1,281 in 1995 and to 831.6 in 1996, with the SET index reaching its lowest point in 10 years in 1998. Price to earnings ratio declined from 19.5 per cent in 1994 to 12 per cent in 1996 and then to 6 per cent in 1997.[13] The slight increase recorded in 1998 was due to the forced recapitalization of failing companies by the Thai state and foreign multinationals.

However, one should not exaggerate this decline. Performance was stable in the 1980s and impressive growth was recorded in the 1990s. It was only the high leverage after 1987, due to heavy borrowing, that proved destabilizing.

Table 11.5 Average key financial ratios by company size, 1985–96

	Company size by assets			*Company size by sales*		
Item	*Small*	*Medium*	*Large*	*Small*	*Medium*	*Large*
Return on assets (%)	6.5	6.2	5.9	5.1	6.8	6.7
Return on equity (%)	12.6	12.8	13.3	10.1	13.6	14.9
Gross profit margin (%)	26.3	23.8	25.7	30.1	25.1	20.6
Time interest earned (times)	6.5	7.2	6.3	5.4	8.2	6.3
Total debt-to-equity (%)	121.3	135.0	176.8	134.8	142.6	164.3
Long-term debt-to-equity (%)	20.1	29.3	62.3	30.6	31.8	49.4
Total debt-to-assets (%)	43.3	49.6	52.2	47.0	48.6	52.3
Long-term debt-to-assets (%)	7.7	10.5	18.0	10.2	10.6	15.4
Asset turnover (%)	94.3	88.6	83.1	61.5	87.7	116.7

Source: Pacific-Basin Capital Market Database compiled by the University of Rhode Island, US. See ADB, op. cit., p. 239

Table 11.6 Common-size statements for companies listed on SET, 1990–6 (%)

Items	*All years*	*1990*	*1991*	*1992*	*1993*	*1994*	*1995*	*1996*
Assets								
Cash	2.3	2.3	3.2	2.9	2.4	2.2	1.7	1.9
Marketable securities	0.8	3.3	1.6	0.5	0.7	0.6	0.6	0.3
Account receivable	12.9	16.2	15.0	13.6	13.1	13.0	10.9	12.0
Inventories	15.2	17.9	14.6	15.9	14.9	14.7	14.9	15.0
Other current assets	12.4	6.8	9.0	10.2	12.0	14.6	14.8	14.2
Total current assets	43.8	46.4	43.5	43.2	43.2	45.2	42.9	43.6
Net fixed assets	36.1	36.5	37.8	37.6	38.8	34.2	34.3	34.8
Other assets	20.2	17.1	18.8	19.3	17.9	20.6	22.6	21.6
Total assets	100.0	100.0	100.0	100.0	100.0	100.0	100.0	100.0
Liabilities and equity								
Account payable	6.9	10.8	9.8	6.9	6.1	5.9	6.3	6.2
Short-term loans	22.2	17.6	18.8	25.3	25.4	21.8	21.3	21.8
Other current liabilities	7.8	10.5	9.4	8.0	7.4	7.6	6.7	7.7
Total current liabilities	36.9	38.8	37.9	40.3	38.8	35.3	34.2	35.6
Long-term loans	10.1	7.8	8.5	9.6	8.7	9.6	11.6	12.0
Debentures	2.2	2.2	1.6	0.2	2.1	2.9	3.2	2.5
Other liabilities	1.5	1.3	1.6	2.0	1.8	1.2	1.5	1.3
Total liabilities	50.7	50.1	49.7	52.0	51.4	49.1	50.6	51.4
Capital stock	17.3	18.3	18.2	17.9	17.1	17.7	16.2	16.8
Paid-in capital	17.7	16.7	17.7	18.2	16.9	18.4	17.9	17.4
Retained earning	14.3	14.9	14.5	11.9	14.5	14.7	15.3	14.4
Total equity	49.3	49.9	50.3	48.0	48.6	50.9	49.4	48.6
Total liabilities and equity	100.0	100.0	100.0	100.0	100.0	100.0	100.0	100.0

Source: Pacific-Basin Capital Market Database compiled by the University of Rhode Island, US. See ADB, op. cit., p. 258

State–business networks

A further issue is to what extent this concentrated corporate growth was assisted by politics and political networks. Business groups were carving out monopoly niches through their access to state contracts, licences, finance and marketing assistance. Did this Thai clientelism produce competitive market structures, as argued by Doner and Ramsay, or were state–business relations nurturing large-scale monopolies as the mainstay of the Thai corporate economy?[14] That we can find evidence for both these views is hardly surprising for any generalizations and oversimplifications cannot be sustained in the light of the continuous regime changes in Thailand since 1956, as well as changes in institutions such as the bureaucracy. Types of rent-seeking and corruption varied through the decades because of the differing impact of institutional constraints and global challenges. It is this changing relationship that is emphasized in this chapter. A fluid institutional environment and fluctuating personal ties between the government, the bureaucracy and the industrialists shaped corporate growth. Particularly crucial in this respect was the declining power of the Thai military. Divisions within the military stemming from differences in service structure, class and academic backgrounds were accentuated by the curtailment of American aid following the end of the Vietnam War. Although the military controlled the government between 1976 and the late 1980s, and then briefly in the early 1990s, it did so with the support of businessmen, in particular the Bangkok Bank. This changed with the movement towards greater democratic governance in the 1990s.

Relations between capitalists and the state changed in the 1990s when bankers and industrialists were a rising power. The independence of the bureaucracy had been eroded by financial liberalization as well as by intra-elite rivalry and competition among the various ministries, the Bank of Thailand, the Board of Investment and other state economic agencies. The transition to more democratic politics from the 1980s undermined both the bureaucracy and the Central Bank, while powerful political pressure groups emerged. Simultaneously, the Bank of Thailand was seduced by powerful businessmen. In 1996 Vijit Supinit, Governor of the Bank of Thailand, accepted shares in a finance company, while the handling of the failing Bangkok Bank of Commerce further compromised the existing independence of the Bank of Thailand.[15]

Competition between the government departments was intense. There was increasing fragmentation, too. The Board of Investment, the Ministry of Finance and the Ministry of Industry controlled trade and the corporate economy. In addition, five departments divided among these three ministries controlled access to contracts. This overlapping of jurisdictions, the diffusion of industrial policy-making powers and its separation from macro-economic policy-making, combined with the maintenance of low inflation, stable exchange rates and sustainable policies towards foreign investment, to encourage clientelism and, ultimately, corruption.[16]

These developments were further aggravated by the increasing politicization of the bureaucracy from 1989 onwards, with various political parties securing cooperation with certain ministries. For instance, in the 1990s the Chart Thai Party had a powerful influence over the Industry Ministry, while the Social Action Party was dominant within the Ministry of Commerce. The critical transformation of the Bank of Thailand from an efficient, prudent institution in the 1950s to a highly politicized organ by the 1990s is sketched in detail in Chapter 10.

Electoral politics introduced difficulties for consistent government policies, which were confounded further by global capital flows. Moreover, patron–client relations between business and the government were in constant flux. On the one hand, Prem Tinsulanond's government of the late 1980s introduced a liberal period of dialogue, when corruption was held in check, and ushered in impressive growth. Similarly, in the early 1990s Anand Panyarachun twice presided over a technocrat-dominated government

(February 1991–April 1992 and June–September 1992) with greater transparency in the bidding process for the allocation of government quotas, licences, contracts and funds. On the other hand, under the premierships of Chatichai Choonhavan (April 1988–February 1991) and Banharn Silpa-archa (July 1995–November 1996) contracts for railways and telecommunications projects went to cronies.

The rise in the mid-1990s of rural provincial business barons marked the further decline of the bureaucracy. Their loss of control over economic policies was obvious. Banharn, for instance, dismissed bureaucrats at his whim. Under the government of Chavalit Yongchaiyudh (November 1996–November 1997), technocratic influence rose as technocrats were co-opted into politics. Overall though, since the 1980s, politics has been subservient to businessmen and technocratic influence has declined. All this has impinged on corporate governance.

Ironically, the move towards more democratic governance saw an increase in corruption. Despite the increase in labour union activity, student politics and media interventions, and the rise of public interest groups, rent-seeking was rife. This was due to fundamental changes in the bureaucracy and the government that compounded their subservience to corporate power and to foreign capital. Democracy merely meant there were more patrons to satisfy, and thereby led to greater corruption and greater uncertainty. In a strong state, rent collection is clear and predictable and patrons identifiable. In a weak state where there is greater political competition, rent-seeking is more diffuse. Since 2001, Thaksin Shinawatra has created a more concentrated political party with clear policies.

An important player in these changes was foreign capital. The following case studies of automobiles, telecommunications and textiles reveal the interplay of domestic and foreign capital in achieving not only a highly concentrated corporate economy but in pushing for regional and global presence through joint-ventures with foreign partners. Chris Dixon's argument is that foreign capital increased foreign ownership, particularly after 1997, but did not achieve efficient corporate growth. My focus, meanwhile, is that foreign capital aided the concentrated monopolistic growth of corporations before 1997 but domestic capitalists faced more competitive pressures from foreign capital as a consequence of the post-1998 corporate reforms. The nationalist rhetoric and hysteria about foreigners supposedly plundering Thai assets is partly corporate paranoia coupled with an inability to face competition.

The automobile industry

The pattern of growth in the Thai automobile industry, though fairly concentrated, exhibited vastly different structures from those prevailing in telecommunications and textiles. From the 1960s, automobiles, principally from Japan, were assembled locally and this accounted for 40 per cent of vehicles sold in the country in the early 1970s.[17] In addition, from the 1970s, components were manufactured locally. At the heart of this programme was a clear strategy of moving away from ISI to export-oriented industrialization, and from labour-intensive production to large, capital-intensive projects. Throughout this process, there was an implicit acceptance of Japanese technology and expertise.

There were five large Thai specialist automobile corporations. The largest was Toyota Motor Thailand, whose major shareholders were Toyota Motor, with a stake of 59.6 per cent, and Siam Cement, possessing a 10 per cent stake. This group had three subsidiaries producing engines, auto bodies and parts, while Siam Cement also held component-manufacturing firms that produced brake drums and disc brakes. One of the component firms, Siam Nawaloha Foundry (SNF) was involved in technological upgrading, moving swiftly up the technology chain. Indeed, it was the largest component firm in the late 1970s and 1980s. Having acquired experience in the production of agricultural machinery, it moved into automobile components manufacture in 1979.[18] Its success was derived partly from the localization policy of the mid-1980s when the Board of Investment and the Ministry of Industry promoted the diversification of car models and export expansion. The first strategy attracted more Japanese automobile firms, while an export strategy was essential due to a small domestic market. This also increased the scope for the expansion of component firms. SNF held interlocking shareholding in three engine firms and by 1989 was dominant in the creation of a *keiretsu* complex of technologically related Thai firms. In this it was assisted by powerful Thai political and aristocratic links; indeed, the Crown Property Bureau was an influential partner. In addition, between 1984 and 1985, the pace of localization increased due to the intervention of the new Minister of Industry, Ob Vasuratna. His resignation and the economic recession in 1985 dampened this mood for local production.[19]

This localization policy was highly complicated. First, it led to local firms producing components as suppliers to multiple assembly firms. Second, from the mid-1980s, Japanese component manufacturers moved to Thailand, establishing joint-ventures and technical arrangements, and producing superior components for exports. Hence, by the 1980s, Japan absorbed 90 per cent of automobile sales in Thailand, and a high proportion in Malaysia, Singapore and the Philippines. There had to be a change to local production. The Thai government thus promoted the use of local products, greater technology dispersion and local production for export.

The second major automobile company was Siam Motors, owned by the Pornprapha family. It was associated with Nissan Motors who had become the major investor by 1984. However, following the recession in 1985, a restructuring left Nissan responsible for 25 per cent of the assembly operation and global technological costs. This led to Siam Motors establishing nine component firms through joint-venture arrangements, with Nissan Japan producing batteries, shock absorbers and engines. The firms were dominated by family ownership until 1990 when Nissan acquired a 25 per cent stake.[20] Siam Motors was established in 1952 when it was contracted by the Thai military to produce vehicles. It also maintained close ties with the Bangkok Bank, which remained the main financier. From 1962 onwards, the local assembly of cars was through a technical assistance programme with Nissan, which also provided long-term loans. Due to serious family disputes in 1995, the group divested its majority stake of 83.6 per cent in Siam-Yamaha to a relative.[21] However, this did not seriously affect its market share, which was 22 per cent in 1985, and in 1996 was 15.8 per cent of the entire Thai market. Of its competitors, Toyota Thailand held 28 per cent of the local market, MMC Sittiphol absorbed another 8 per cent and Isuzu had 21 per cent, largely because the market for trucks was higher than for saloon cars. Although Siam Motors concentrated on Nissan cars, whereby Thailand ranked second to the US in Nissan car sales outside of Japan, it also distributed Fiat and other European cars.[22]

The third main firm, Isuzu Motors Thailand, was predominantly involved in the assembly of trucks for Isuzu and Mitsubishi. The shareholding was distributed, with three Thai family firms holding 51 per cent and Isuzu and Mitsubishi absorbing the remaining. The three Thai families were Sarasin, Chansue and Boonsoong, though the Boonsoong family was the dominant partner.[23] In the assembling of commercial vehicles the content of local procurement was high. There was also a greater push for exports. Thus, Isuzu Thailand exported to Egypt, Cyprus, Indonesia, Malaysia, Kenya and Algeria. In the 1980s it diversified into real estate, hotels, food and electronics.

The fourth major automobile firm was MMC Sittiphol, which assembled Mitsubishi vehicles. The Kanok Lee Isranukul family had been involved in the manufacture of bicycles before moving into automobiles in 1961 and into truck assembly by 1964. Mitsubishi had a 40 per cent stake and held senior managerial positions. By 1985, the recession had led to corporate restructuring and to the merging of firms within the group. The Kanok Lee Isranukul family still possessed a 52 per cent stake, while Mitsubishi held the rest. The group had investments in two Japanese components firms as well as three associate firms. These had joint-venture arrangements with Mitsubishi Motors in Japan.

This corporate structure of interlocking shareholding and technical arrangements has several characteristics. First, it produced a *keiretsu* which, while displaying high concentration, is more competitive. Second, each component firm belongs to multiple cooperation clubs deriving investments from Thai families, as well as from Japanese multinationals. This scheme of multiple arrangements means component firms are highly competitive, supplying multiple assembly groups. Third, component firms are small, since they produce small quantities of a great variety of components. The market share for each vehicle is small so component firms have to be competitive in terms of cost and technology. Fourth, the assembly firms have linkages with Japanese component firms who possess higher technology, meaning the pressure to diversify and compete is high. Fifth, the economic liberalization of the 1990s further increased competition, with the entry of new assemblers and the opening of new locations in Thailand and abroad. Moreover, the lifting of protective tariffs meant competition between the assemblers was high. This was accompanied by a Japanese strategy of export-led growth. Thus, MMC Sittiphol embarked on the Asian Strategic Car Project in 1993 with Nissan and focused on exports to ASEAN. The boom in automobile manufacture is clear from 1994 when Toyota held 26 per cent of the local market, Isuzu 20 per cent, Mitsubishi 14 per cent, Nissan 13 per cent, Mazda 4 per cent, Benz 2.3 per cent and American/European cars 6 per cent.[24] Sixth, there was the burden of having to comply with impending WTO regulations. Thus, there was pressure to upgrade technology and improve the skills of the labour force.

Moreover, the 1997 financial crisis introduced new pressures and engendered a new scenario. Before the crisis, Thailand's automobile industry was the fastest growing sector in Southeast Asia, accounting for 40 per cent of the total car sales in ASEAN in 1996. However, it had grossly over-expanded and there was excess capacity. Indeed, in 1996, there were 1,200 automobile components firms and six major assembly firms. Yet sales dropped by 70 per cent in 1997 and continued to decline in 1998. By January 1999, only half the firms remained.

The firms were faced with heavy debts. For instance, the Somboon group saw a drop in earnings from 1.3 billion baht in 1997 to 750 million baht in 1998. It sold 46 per cent of its 52 per cent share to its Japanese partner and offered 49 per cent of its four component firms to its creditors.[25]

The entire automobile industry acquired foreign partners as part of its debt restructuring programme. Mitsubishi bought out its Thai partner MMC Sittiphol, while Honda injected new capital into the Isuzu group, acquiring a larger stake there. Toyota also pursued a similar strategy of recapitalization, injecting 4 million baht of new capital and thereby reducing the share of local industrialists. In addition, Toyota bought three component firms of Siam Cement. The latter was forced to divest most of its auto business and focus on its core interests in cement, paper, pulp and chemicals. Ultimately, Siam Cement was left with only 1 per cent in its automobile assembly group, while Toyota, through its recapitalization of 4 billion baht, took over the company. Yamaha also bought a majority stake from its Thai partner. Somboon faced a reduction in its shareholding from 51 per cent to 5 per cent. However, there were agreement guarantees on buy-back options within ten years and at an agreed value.[26]

The result of these changes was a reduction in family dominance in ownership and management. It also reduced concentration, increased competitiveness and absorbed higher technical inputs, thereby improving prospects for global competition, while also improving corporate governance and business practices.

Telecommunications

The main focus in this section is on the emergence of Shinawatra Communications as one of the five major business groups in the telecoms sector in 1994. It not only survived the 1997 crisis but flourished in its aftermath due to the decline of its rivals. The sector consequently became more concentrated. The emphasis in this section is on the mechanisms by which it grew in Thailand and in regional markets in Asia. The state was critical in this expansion: in securing concessions, providing finance and promoting global ambitions assisted by foreign telecommunications specialists. First, the privatization of the Thai telecommunications industry in the 1980s increased the monopolistic position of a few corporations, in direct contradiction to the aims of increasing competition, and promoting efficiency and wider ownership. A natural monopoly already existed in telecommunications whereby a provider in one area could link to several regional operations. Second, it was easy for all technologies – landlines, mobile phones, satellites etc. – to be fused into one. However, there were more complicated reasons underlying the emergence of Shinawatra as a major telecommunication specialist in Thailand and parts of Asia.

Family dominance has characterized the growth of Shinawatra. A privately held holding company, Shinawatra Holding had 50 per cent equity in the public listed firm Shinawatra Satellite, 58 per cent equity in Advanced Information Services, 55 per cent in International Broadcasting Corporation and 100 per cent in Shinawatra International, a private company. A range of associated firms was held by each of the listed corporations in the group. These revealed Shinawatra family links through equity holdings, directorships and managerial positions. Non-family members were technocrats acting as advisers. Decision-making remained entirely within the family.

The creation of separate companies to correspond to particular areas of specialism and for regional specialization did not disturb the interlocking family shareholding and financial linkages. This concentrated organizational structure was feasible because of technological differentiation which encompassed digital networks, transport networks, intelligence networks, software and satellites. The core technology was provided by the state or foreign joint-venture specialists, meaning the family firm could combine all these separate functions without incorporating R&D divisions. Multilayered subcontracting created prospects for Shinawatra to expand in Asia through the creation of shared monopolies. It thus expanded into Vietnam, Cambodia, Laos, the Philippines and India. These global initiatives often disguise the limited scope, along with rising costs and low performance, in the domestic environment. Although domestic competition did exist, securing the right patron at home and abroad often helped overcome any difficulties.

The methods of financing were complex. State finance was paramount, while foreign partners, the World Bank and the IMF also provided crucial assistance. Financial liberalization, meanwhile, provided generous access to bank credit, syndicated loans, and long-term loans from offshore markets. The stock market was also important. Listing on the Thai Stock Exchange was principally intended to raise capital; apart from the adoption of a technocrat executive in charge of operations, little adjustment was made to the organizational structure. Shinawatra had four registered companies on the Thai Stock Exchange. Its competitors – Jasmine, UCOM, Samart and Telecom Asia were listed on the stock market but concessions were constantly being negotiated between them through their political ties. These political alliances were highly fluid due to frequent changes in ministers. Indeed, between 1991 and 2001 Thailand had nine different governments. Furthermore, telecommunications were dominated by two bureaucratic institutions: the Telephone Organization of Thailand (TOT) and the Communication Authority of Thailand (CAT).

The concentration of influence and power within a tiny group of service providers is clear from the statistics below. Between 1988 and 1991, Shinawatra secured seven concessions in phone services and a cable television licence. Meanwhile, of its competitors, Telecom Asia had three concessions in Bangkok and Jasmine International held five. UCOM held a 27-year wireless phone concession. By 1993, Shinawatra's satellite services had expanded into Vietnam, Laos, Cambodia, the Philippines, Indonesia and India.

However, it was the 1997 crisis that gave Shinawatra critical economic advantages in comparison to its rivals. Shinawatra possessed far less foreign debt than its rivals, and it was these debts that were to be so devastating. The restructuring that followed involved greater participation by foreign investors and specialist groups. Among the telecommunications big four, UCOM had the highest ratio of liabilities. Its debt was converted through equity participation by Somers, a British investment enterprise, which subsequently became the largest shareholder with a 46 per cent stake. In May 2002, Telenor Asia (Norway) purchased 24.8 per cent of the stocks from Somers, and 22 per cent of stocks held by UCOM, in addition to 15 per cent of the newly released stocks.[27] Single family stakes in the mobile phone sector were drastically reduced by sales to British and Norwegian telecommunications groups. UCOM also had to cancel a proposed global mobile phone network with Motorola.

Similarly, Telecom Asia faced severe problems. It held debts of 94,415 million baht.[28] It pursued a debt-equity swap with its creditors. It sold overseas interests to maintain its Thai position and attempted a merger of its cable television network with Shinawatra. However, it expanded into mobile phone services to prop up its less profitable sectors in telecoms services.

Meanwhile, Jasmine International held debts of 19,871 million baht. It was restructured under the supervision of the Bank of Thailand and the state restructuring agency, CDRAC. In December 2000, 95 per cent of its debt still remained so it was transferred to the Central Bankruptcy Court in December 2001. Some of its debts were to Ericsson and Alcatel, others were owed to Krung Thai Bank, Credit Lyonnais Bank and Sumitomo Bank. The difficulties in restructuring were because the major shareholders of the group, namely Loxley and Phatra Thanakit, were themselves in crisis and could not present a viable investment plan. The government's insistence on a maximum shareholding by foreigners of 25 per cent also deterred foreign investors, such as Nippon Telegraph and Telephone.

In contrast to these inextricable circumstances, Shinawatra, despite liabilities of almost 100,000 million baht and foreign debt of 30,000 million baht, was able to restructure and expand. Thaksin had hedged 70 per cent of his group's foreign exposure prior to devaluation. The suspicion was that he had been tipped off about this imminent devaluation by the Finance Minister,[29] who later joined the corporation. The price of Shinawatra shares also rose just prior to its flotation in July 1997.[30] By 2001 the corporation only had debts of US$92 million.[31] Shinawatra's new strategy involved diversification into related industries and in the rescue of failing institutions.

This effective restructuring of Shinawatra's debt led to its rescue of the Thai Military Bank in 2000.[32] The acquisition of telecom companies was part of a strategy of integrated operations, hence the purchase of a 46 per cent share in Smart's Digital Phone Co., with Telekom Malaysia. Although the Shinawatra group was a minority shareholder, it still held a top managerial position. Furthermore, its alliance with Singapore Telecoms in the SingTel Yellow Pages Co. introduced new technology, the internet and e-commerce.[33] The regional growth of Shinawatra accelerated in 2000 with the launch of a terminal for a new satellite, iPSTAR, worth US$390 million. It expanded its mobile phone services, and acquired influential groups in wireless and internet services. The convergence of these diverse sectors increased the concentration already present in the industry. Shinawatra's move into media through the takeover of television services was part of a strategy to secure the personal political ambitions of Thaksin Shinawatra, who has been Prime Minister since February 2001. This further convergence of telecommunications, television stations and cineplex entertainment centres, all created a consolidation of interests that proved devastating to Shinawatra's rivals. This improved its prospects abroad where it emerged in India as the biggest foreign satellite telecoms provider. It has expanded into China since 1996 and into Burma since 1998.[34] Moreover, its profits in Cambodia in 2003 were US$24 million.[35] As Prime Minister, Thaksin pushed the ideology of Asia for Asians and the creation of a free trade zone with an Asian-centred growth. His strategy was to concentrate on Burma and Cambodia, where he has close ties to the governments, creating telecoms for education, business and banking. His venture into India was less successful. It concentrated on mobile phone services in a few Indian provinces, providing satellite services for Indian Television and leasing transponders to Indian Space Research. Shinawatra's satellite division had the largest market share in India, Pakistan and the Maldives until 2002 when India's new satellite usurped its position.[36] Shinawatra's experiences in China were more mixed. Most recently, the

January 2006 sale of Shin Corporation to a Singapore Government investment corporation for £1.14 billion (77.3 billion baht), without paying any tax, has ignited the simmering controversy over foreign capital incursions into strategic industries amid clear corruption within the Shinawatra family.

It is clear from the above discussion that there was little competition, especially after the 1997 crisis. Indeed, since the 1980s there has been little transparency in the bidding processes: successive governments and bureaucrats have typically colluded in awarding contracts, licences and concessions to their cronies. Moreover, decision-making in economic policy was highly concentrated within the Bangkok government elite with little decentralization of policy-making powers to other regions in the country. Thaksin acquired further power through his rescue of the Thai Military Bank whereby his family became an important shareholder. The rescue of Thai Petroleum, meanwhile, was followed by further acquisitions of equity in critical industries, including Thai Steel.[37] Large corporations with unsustainable debt have grouped around Thaksin for survival since the government restriction on majority holding by foreigners has made foreign investors wary.

The crucial point here is that foreign firms can assist these failing firms in returning to solvency. For example, Alphatec Electronics, a producer of integrated circuits and semiconductors, faced insurmountable debts in 1998. The acquiring firm, AIG Investment Corporation (US), and Investor AB, the holding company of Ericsson, invested US$40 million and each acquired 40 per cent of equity. The remaining 20 per cent was held by its creditors. This strategy was crucial in its recovery. The acquisition not only led to recapitalization but also resulted in improved corporate governance and less cronyism.[38] In the light of the increasing concentration within Thai strategic industries, these mergers and acquisitions by foreign multinationals have afforded the only scope for competition.[39] Though Thai capitalists who appealed to nationalist sentiments were a serious obstacle to effective corporate restructuring, frequently whipping up paranoia over a suspected mass foreign takeover of Thai corporations, this did not ultimately inhibit the emergence of a leaner, more efficient creation in sectors such as banking and textiles. Thus, Krugman's portrayal of Thai capitalists as 'heads I win, tails the taxpayers lose' is only partially true.[40]

The textile industry

The textile industry also exhibited a highly concentrated structure with two corporations, Sukree and Saha Union, dominating the upstream and downstream activities, including manufacturing. These large, monopolistic firms integrated different segments of the industry: spinning, weaving, dyeing, printing and garment manufacture. In 1978, 25 per cent of spinning activities rested with three large firms. In weaving, three firms accounted for 14 per cent of the total. By 1990, Sukree's share of spinning had risen to more than

35 per cent of the total. There was also integration into the chemical and electronics industries, with the support of Japanese and French multinationals.

The need for technology, along with constant changes in demand and taste, and the growth of synthetic fibres, assisted this concentration, displacing small and medium enterprises. This concentration was further assisted by the 'quota hopping' tactics of Japan and others, who sought reliable Thai partners to form supply chains. Through these joint-ventures, Sukree and Saha Union increased their investment and technological inputs and came to hold serious global ambitions. This accumulation of knowledge, information, and R&D, combined with marketing collaboration with the Thai state and foreign multinationals, led to increased market shares, thereby reducing competition. For its part, the state provided finance and tariff protection and assisted with capital goods imports. Thus, the share of small-scale producers fell from 50 per cent in 1961 to 16 per cent in 1979, largely in the domestic market. The export sector remains the preserve of four large Thai firms and foreign MNEs.

From the early 1950s to the early 1970s, the two groups, Saha Union and Sukree, benefited from ISI. The transition to export-oriented industrialization, and to higher technology and synthetic fibres, also benefited larger corporations. Their relentless expansion into various segments of the industry was partly in response to the investment strategies of quota hoppers from Japan, Hong Kong and Taiwan in the 1970s and 1980s.

This vertical and horizontal integration was made feasible by state support, particularly that of the Thai military. Thus, by 1986, Sukree dominated spinning and garment manufacture and was emerging as the world's largest garment producer. Their clusters and concentration made the textile firms aware of new market information. Unfettered competition would have eroded their advantages in responding to international quotas and trade constraints. Sukree had joint-ventures with Shikibo, Nomura Trading and Rhone-Poulenc. R&D rested totally with its foreign partners. However, since 1959 its relations with foreign partners have been tempestuous because of financial irregularities in the group. Furthermore, the constant swapping of joint-venture partners left the group vulnerable.

The textile firms' concentration was assisted by their linkages with banks, particularly the Bangkok Bank. Though owned by the Darakanonda family, Saha Union shared equity with the Bangkok Bank of 4 per cent.

Even though both corporations had pursued similar strategies of globalization and diversification into utilities, power and petrochemical in Thailand and China, the 1997 crisis affected Sukree more than Saha Union. A partial explanation is that Saha Union used managerial hierarchies, while Sukree, in contrast, was tightly controlled by the family patriarch, Sukree Photiranakul. His conflicts with the Thai bureaucracy, in particular with the Board of Investment, are legendary. The second factor in its collapse in 1997 was its expansions, from the mid-1980s, into land and real estate. Two of its subsidiaries, including Thai Melon Textile Co., were closed in July 1998. This was due to their failure to upgrade manufacturing equipment. One can also infer that difficulties with joint-venture partners in the 1980s and the 1990s produced difficulties in technological innovation and coordinated growth.[41]

Restructuring and outcome

The acquisition of Thai firms by foreign investors was the core issue in the restructuring and probable recovery of Thai corporations following the financial crisis of 1997. Net inflows of foreign capital between 1997 and 2001 totalled US$24.6 billion, with an annual average of US$4.9 billion.[42] This is almost a doubling of the inflows that occurred between 1990 and 1996, which totalled US$14.1 billion with an annual average of US$2 billion.[43] Between these years, only 9.6 per cent of foreign investment involved the acquisition of firms. This is in direct contrast to the 1997–2001 period when 61.0 per cent of foreign investment involved the acquisition of holdings of more than 10 per cent of total equity.[44] Thus, while majority control by foreign investors is limited, there was a noticeable increase in foreign equity within Thai firms. However, the trend was arrested in 2001–2 with the slowing down of recapitalization, while the year 2002–3 saw a short spurt in disinvestment, particularly in electronics. See Table 11.7 for details.

Between July 1997 and mid-1999, 45 large listed companies offered their equity to foreign investors. There were seven banks, eight securities firms, three insurance firms and 27 industrial firms. Firms purchasing majority stakes in Thai firms were Merrill Lynch, Vickers Ballas, Société Générale Crosby, AIG Group, ING Barings, Indosuez W1 Carr, Lehman Bros, BNP, Bankers Trust, DBS, Kim-Eng On and LG.[45] Foreign ownership of property was severely restricted despite the liberalization of leasehold arrangements. A breakdown of these foreign acquisitions in specific economic sectors provides the following figures: the automotive sector saw an acquisition of equity by foreign multinationals amounting to 40 per cent; agri-business, 7 per cent; metal, 8 per cent; service sector, 6 per cent; light industry, 9 per cent; electronics, 13 per cent; and chemicals, paper and plastics, 17 per cent.[46] See Table 11.8.

The consequences of this foreign equity stake are clear. First, an UNCTAD report on World Investment in 1999 found that such Thai firms had their debt to equity ratios reduced dramatically. Their capital formation had improved as well.

Second, many of these firms that restructured with foreign equity were refocusing on core interests and divesting non-performing subsidiaries.

Third, they were introducing international accounting standards with greater reliance on professional managers. Their global ambitions were sharper and more focused, improving the legal framework in which they operated and leading to an alertness to risk and internal corporate change.

Table 11.7 Share of domestic investors' (Dom.) and foreign investors' (Int.) ownership on the SET by economic category (%)

	1995		*1996*		*1997*		*1998*	
	Dom.	*Int.*	*Dom.*	*Int.*	*Dom.*	*Int.*	*Dom.*	*Int.*
Agri-business	84.7	15.3	83.3	16.7	84.1	15.9	82.0	18.0
Banking	77.5	22.5	84.4	15.6	84.9	15.1	90.5	9.5
Building and furnishing	80.2	19.8	86.9	13.1	86.6	13.4	83.1	16.9
Chemical and plastic products	84.4	15.6	82.8	17.2	80.1	19.9	81.3	18.7
Commerce	76.8	23.2	74.7	25.3	74.1	25.9	72.7	27.3
Communication	68.5	31.5	64.0	36.0	60.1	39.9	59.2	40.8
Electrical appliances	59.7	40.3	61.9	38.1	55.1	44.9	53.9	46.1
Electronic components	76.9	23.1	57.8	42.2	46.4	53.6	37.5	62.5
Energy	86.9	13.1	81.1	18.9	77.8	22.2	64.3	35.7
Entertainment	94.3	5.7	89.8	10.2	70.3	29.7	62.4	37.6
Finance and securities	87.6	12.4	88.7	11.3	76.0	24.0	66.0	34.0
Food and beverages	84.3	15.7	84.0	16.0	82.8	17.2	76.7	23.3
Healthcare services	89.5	10.5	93.5	6.5	93.6	6.4	94.6	5.4
Hotel and travel services	74.3	25.7	79.6	20.4	71.2	28.8	67.1	32.9
Household goods	78.8	21.2	83.8	16.2	84.7	15.3	75.8	24.2
Insurance	83.5	16.5	83.6	16.4	80.9	19.1	80.0	20.0
Jewellery and ornaments	85.9	14.1	89.6	10.4	91.2	8.8	91.5	8.5
Machinery and equipment	82.0	18.0	91.7	8.3	85.5	14.5	87.3	12.7
Mining	84.6	15.4	84.5	15.5	84.6	15.4	83.2	16.8
Packaging	90.2	9.8	83.6	16.4	85.9	14.1	87.9	12.1
Pharmaceutical and cosmetics	76.0	24.0	77.4	22.6	76.2	23.8	75.8	24.2
Printing	84.6	15.4	80.1	19.9	75.8	24.2	75.6	24.4
Professional services	65.7	34.3	68.1	31.9	68.0	32.0	68.0	32.0
Property development	83.6	16.4	85.7	14.3	85.1	14.9	84.1	15.9
Pulp and paper	86.8	13.2	85.3	14.7	81.0	19.0	69.4	30.6
Textile, clothing and footwear	70.8	29.2	74.3	25.7	72.2	27.8	70.3	29.7
Transportation	95.3	4.7	88.1	11.9	82.3	17.7	80.2	19.8
Automobile and parts	75.4	24.6	76.8	23.2	77.7	22.3	81.4	18.6
Warehouse and silo	93.7	6.3	95.2	4.8	93.4	6.6	93.2	6.8
Others	96.4	3.6	97.1	2.9	93.3	6.7	94.6	5.4

Source: Constructed from primary data at the Securities Exchange of Thailand

Fourth, while it is difficult to assess improvements in performance since restructuring and downsizing continues to this day, it is apparent that within the 20 corporations with increased foreign equity there was some increase in profitability. For example, in 1997 Siam Cement, which faced a debt of US$4.2 billion in foreign loans, largely unhedged, offered a third of its total assets for sale, including its electronics and automotive companies. It sought to return to profitability through downsizing. It also converted existing dollar loans into local debentures. Its success was in stark contrast to Siam City Cement which struggled despite the sale of 25 per cent equity to Holderbank. Jalaprathan Cement, meanwhile, was sold to Cemente Français.[47] The largest steel producer, Sahaviriya, sold a majority control of two of its three core

Table 11.8 SET capitalization and foreign ownership, 2002

Sector	*Share of paid-up capital (%)*	*Share of paid-up capital that is foreign owned (%)*	*Number of companies with majority foreign ownership*
Agri-business	1.0	12.7	
Banking	27.3	38.0	4
Building and furnishing	1.9	20.8	2
Chemical and plastic products	3.2	20.4	1
Commerce	1.3	29.2	
Communication	6.8	34.6	
Electrical products and computer	1.5	69.5	3
Electronic components	0.7	53.6	3
Energy	1.5	24.6	
Entertainment and recreation	1.6	11.4	
Finance and securities	33.5	3.7	1
Food and beverages	0.5	24.5	
Healthcare services	0.35	3.2	
Hotel and travel services	0.83	28.9	
Household goods	0.52	35.4	
Insurance	0.30	13.5	
Jewellery and ornaments	0.04	6.8	
Machinery and equipment	0.04	3.6	
Mining	0.2	49.0[a]	
Packaging	0.95	11.1	
Pharmaceutical and cosmetics	0.18	17.9	
Printing and publishing	0.1	23.4	
Professional services	0.1	25.3	
Property development	12.8	9.8	
Pulp and paper	0.88	35.5	1
Textile, clothing and footwear	0.62	19.6	3
Transportation	2.1	14.9	
Automobile and parts	0.22	19.7	1
Warehouse and Silo	0.06	0.4	
Others	0.19	12.7	
Total	100	20.3	20

Note:
a Only one listed company.

Source: Calculated from Stock Exchange of Thailand, *Investment Information, Listed Companies*

companies to Japanese partners.[48] Shinawatra reduced its shareholding in the directories business, delayed the launch of a satellite and sold firms in India and the Philippines. It also diverted a 20 per cent stake in AIS to SingTel, while acquiring a digital phone project from Samart and bidding for other failing telecom firms. Last, Charoen Pokphand shed a number of domestic and overseas subsidiaries and concentrated on its core agri-business.[49]

Fifth, these mergers and acquisitions, stimulated by foreign capital, increased prospects for survival and increased value-added activity. Sixty-four per cent of mergers and acquisitions in this period revealed an increase in profit and sales ratio[50] (see Table 11.9).

The fear of dominance by foreign MNEs was widespread, particularly of fire sales when foreign investors snatched lucrative business at low prices. But the reality was that corporations transferred good assets internally and then just left the shell for disposal. The problems in valuation were formidable and, since the government was reluctant to allow bankruptcies, rescue operations dragged on.

Moreover, there was an increasing awareness that foreign acquisitions were short- rather than long-term. Hence, such buy-outs secured assets that would otherwise have sunk to junk status.

There was also increasing evidence that these mergers and acquisitions by foreign corporations helped rescue firms that were not fit for survival, with the foreign firm risking all to secure a local base in Southeast Asia. For instance, Matsushita bought out its Thai partner, as did Samsung, NEC and Acer. Indeed, Acer's purchase of Sahaviriya Computing firm was largely intended to get a foothold in Thai electronics. It took 51 per cent while Epson took 10 per cent.

Finally, the Thai families often retained managerial control. Table 11.10 clearly shows that finance possessed the highest ratio of foreign intervention.

Table 11.9 Economic growth and foreign investment, and cross-border mergers and acquisitions in Thailand, 1990–2001

	Net FDI (US$ bn)	*M&A (US$ bn)*	*M&A as % of FDI*	*M&A in the banking sector*		
				US$ bn	*% of M&A*	*% of FDI*
1990–6	14.09	1.35	9.6	0.15	11.1	1.1
1997	3.9	0.8	20.5	0.2	25.0	5.1
1998	7.3	5.4	74.0	2.2	40.7	27.9
1999	6.2	4.6	74.2	2.6	56.5	41.9
2000	3.4	3.1	91.2	0.5	16.1	14.7
2001	3.8	1.1	28.9	0.1	9.1	2.6
2002	1.1	0.25	22.7	n/a	n/a	n/a
1997–2001	24.6	15.0	61.0	5.6	37.5	22.8

Note: The FDI and M&A figures include the banking sector. While the Bank of Thailand collects the data on the banking sector, it excludes it from tabulations of FDI. Similarly, UNCTAD, which draws its M&A data from the Bank of Thailand, excluded the banking sector until 2003.

Source: Bank of Thailand; IMF, *Balance of Payment Statistics Yearbook*, Washington, DC: IMF, various issues; UNCTAD, *World Investment Report 2000: Cross Border Mergers and Acquisitions and Development*, Geneva: UNCTAD, 2000; UNCTAD, *World Investment Report 2003: Transnational Corporations and Export Competitiveness*, Geneva: UNCTAD, 2003

Table 11.10 Sectoral distribution of mergers and acquisitions in Thailand, 1997–9

Sector	*Distribution of M&A (%)*
Finance	38
Business	15
Trade	10
Electricity, gas and water	7
Non-metallic manufacture	8
Communication	6
Other manufactures	11
Mining, petroleum	2
Other services	3

Source: Derived from primary data at SET

Legal reforms and restructuring

In November 1998, 11 bills were passed as part of the IMF proposals. Two of these made adjustments to allow for wider foreign ownership. Eventually, on 4 March 2000, the Foreign Business Act replaced the highly restrictive Alien Business Law, which had prohibited foreign ownership of Thai corporations and banks. The only exception had been the small US companies permitted under the 1966 Thai-US Treaty of Amity and Cooperation. Not surprisingly, there was strong opposition from Thai conglomerates to this new act.

Two bills were introduced to improve the laws on bankruptcy and liquidation, and to facilitate more effective debt restructuring. The 1999 Bankruptcy Amendment established bankruptcy courts and the Central Bank supervised restructuring. This was modelled on US law, specifically the Chapter 11 clause which favoured rehabilitation. It was highly complicated, and thus exceedingly expensive and difficult to train Thai judges for this process. Indeed, even in the US only 5 per cent of such cases were successful and yet they absorbed 90 per cent of the court's time. The Amendment to the Foreclosure Act passed in 2000 was more successful. It settled default claims and disposed of assets at public auctions. By November 2000, 50 per cent were cooperating in debt restructuring, and of these, 82 per cent were successful, while 5 per cent were in negotiations.[51] The remaining cases were to be adjudicated by bankruptcy courts.

In addition, there were moves to improve the supervision of corporations, principally by reforming the existing system whereby the Ministries of Industry, Commerce and Finance, and the Bank of Thailand had duplicate functions and overlapping jurisdictions. There were also to be powers for the enforcement and disciplining of corporate misbehaviour. Large conglomerates, nourished by a Thai culture of law avoidance, were difficult to control, particularly with the decline of the independence of the bureaucracy and Bank of Thailand since 1989.

The threat posed to good corporate governance and transparency by the holding company structure was glaring and obvious. There was little distinction between a Board of Directors and a Board of Commissioners. Indeed, some individuals might have a position on both. There was also a need for the reform of shareholding; minority shareholding had to be accepted. Reform of audits and greater compliance were sought as well. All this was difficult, though, because of the close state–business ties. It was necessary to use banks to monitor debt accumulation while diversifying debt through the increased use of debt instruments, such as bonds and debentures, and the secondary capital market to discipline as well as to expose weaknesses within corporations.

The composition of the Board of Directors and the Board of Commissioners came under scrutiny. The 1992 Act had stipulated rules on the election of directors, the need for regular meetings and the need for independent directors, as opposed to family or cronies, but all these provisions were flouted. Indeed, the CEO and the Chairman were often close relatives. Remuneration of directors varied but most decisions were made by the family.[52] The audit committee was regulated under the 1999 Act which stipulated that independence of auditors had to be guaranteed. Control by creditors was weak because of the intimate links with banks, so monitoring of debt was difficult.

In April 1999 there was a bill seeking privatization. The focus was on heavy industries, such as petroleum. Opposition to this provision for the sale of a 32 per cent stake to a single foreign investor drew support from large corporations, such as Thai Petroleum, along with public workers and non-governmental organizations (NGOs), an odd alliance that exploited neo-colonialist fears and Thai Buddhism to push its agenda.[53]

Conclusion

Thai corporations were large, monopolistic and family owned, but less diversified than the conglomerates in Malaysia and Indonesia. Their increasing concentration was achieved through the use of holding companies, while ownership and decision-making remained highly centralized within the family. Institutional shareholding, by both the state and foreign fund managers, was small in these private corporations. Moreover, their structure remained unchanged despite operating in different products, different markets and different regions.

Specialist corporations such as Shinawatra, Siam Motors and Siam Cement did absorb some unrelated businesses, but rapid privatization from 1986 onwards led to specialist growth at home and expansion into other Southeast Asian countries and China. Globalization was a natural strategy because scale economies were essential to sustain profitability. The high levels of debt incurred, particularly through offshore borrowing, precipitated the 1997 financial crisis. This has been analysed in Chapter 10. One major consequence of the crisis has been the significant rise of foreign ownership of Thai financial and non-financial corporations. This large foreign presence in the Thai corporate economy can be contrasted with its limited presence in other Southeast Asian countries, especially Malaysia.

12 Philippines' corporate and financial institutions

Straggling continuity in an erratic environment

There is a basic continuity in the evolution of the Southeast Asian corporate economy from the middle of the nineteenth century through to the present. Important, here, is the dominance throughout this period of the family, of ethnic groups and of the state in the structure of ownership and in corporate activities. This does not mean that significant changes did not occur. However, the comparative explorations within the region undertaken so far – Indonesia, Malaysia, Singapore, and Thailand – have demonstrated the limited variety of corporate structures, each with a concentration of family and kin group ownership, and with strong links to the state and the military, and with an important role for foreign capital. This chapter will examine the distinctive features of Philippine corporate growth. Those distinctive features might be characterized as follows.

First, the small number of capitalist families controlling agriculture, trade and finance have survived since the Spanish period. How did they – the Ayala, Soriano and Lopez families – achieve this enduring linear growth? Was this rooted in the peculiar historical circumstances of the Spanish and American periods of Philippine history? Second, it can be argued that the regional disparities of the Philippine Islands fostered these autonomous political and economic oligarchies. Third, Chinese competition was restrained until the Marcos era, when internal and external Chinese networks nurtured the rise of a powerful clientelist Chinese bourgeoisie. Fourth, the state was relatively passive in the capitalist transformation of the Philippines. The bureaucracy was weak and subservient, as was the Central Bank, in comparison with the independent policy-making bureaucratic institutions of Thailand, Indonesia and Malaysia, though it must be said that the latter became increasingly susceptible to politicization after the financial liberalization of the late 1980s. Finally, it will be argued that the rent-seeking culture of the Philippines was different from that in the rest of Southeast Asia, and this would appear to explain in large part the Philippines' less dramatic economic and corporate success. These distinctive features will be demonstrated through a micro-level investigation of Philippine business and, in particular, its responses to internal and external forces, which took place within substantial political, economic and global constraints. The consideration must start with the Spanish period.

Spain's rule of the Philippines – the galleon trade, the land-holding patterns and the tax demands – produced a rural capitalist elite that has, in essence, dominated the Philippine corporate economy from the middle of the sixteenth century. The pattern of monopolistic economic structures that evolved within the colonial enterprise has persisted to the present. Spanish, and Chinese have reproduced the enduring capitalist houses of Ayala, Soriano and Lopez, along with the nouveau riche of Lucio Tan and Gokongwei. This commercial elite was regionally dispersed in agriculture, processing, manufacturing and banking.[1] Much of this export-led growth was volatile, affected by global price movements and international competition, by erratic market conditions and commodity speculation. The agricultural, commercial and industrial activities tied to the export economy have inevitably experienced great concentration. The agro-commercial elite constituted 10 per cent of the population but commanded 70 per cent of the wealth around 1950, and was found principally in Manila but also Iloilo, Cebu City and Davao in Mindanao.

There is remarkable continuity in these capitalist family groups. Out of 28 top capitalists identified in 1903, 14 were still present in the 1980s and 1990s.[2] In 1997, out of 757 major corporations, 216 were owned by just 39 groups.[3] This economic weight, combined with political leverage, has created powerful, enduring economic concentrations.[4]

American rule reinforced the socio-economic structures of the Spanish period, since it favoured the interests of the established elite. The continuity was persistent: it was not seriously challenged even when the Marcos, Aquino and Ramos governments sought to diversify and decentralize corporate power. This persistence needs to be explained.

First, the corporate history of the Philippines was shaped by the different political eras. The Spanish centuries, 1521–1898, were marked by a focus on extractive industries – agriculture and mining – in which religious groups and the landed elite owned vast segments of the archipelago, mainly on the island of Luzon. The Spanish were followed from 1898 by the Americans. The US administration lasted until 1946, except for the brief interlude of Japanese occupation, 1942–5. Despite the coming of political independence in 1946, the economy remained overwhelmingly agrarian, with only modest food processing and manufacturing sectors. Although the manufacturing sector grew from 3.2 per cent in 1949 to 70.8 per cent in 1980, food processing, and the processing of agricultural production more generally, remained an important element of the sector. Agricultural exports declined from 38 per cent of the total in 1949 to 11.2 per cent in 1980.

Thus, the capitalist oligarchs built their wealth from the produce of the land. The Lopez family began as sugar capitalists in Iloilo, remained in commodity production, but later moved into banking, the media and airlines. More broadly, the old oligarchy was a mix of Spanish mestizo and Chinese. It was involved in agriculture, commerce, real estate, agricultural processing and, later, manufacturing. The individual conglomerates possessed a bank or banks. They – Lopez, Cojuangco, Soriano – combined political and corporate power until the rise of Marcos from the late 1960s. There was a distinct regional identity within these families. The Cojuangco originated from Luzon, Lopez from Negros/Panay, Aboitiz and Osmena from Cebu, and Floirendo from Davao.

From the late 1950s, these oligarchs, with huge land and agrarian interests, moved into import-substitution manufacturing. Contracts were secured through political connections. But Marcos sought to disrupt these elite families, to undermine the landed aristocracy, seize its assets and create a new economic elite. He took control of the monopolies in sugar, coconut and grain, and distributed them to his cronies. He exploited divisions within the old elite. Eduardo Cojuangco and Ramon Cojuangco were provided with more concessions in the coconut industry, assisting the vertical integration and tightening the family's position, while the Aquino family was prosecuted.

The Lopez family, which had built a political-economic empire on sugar from the middle of the nineteenth century, had diversified into transport, airlines, shipping, the Manila Electricity Company, the Philippine Commercial and Industrial Bank, the media, newspapers and television, petroleum, construction and tourism by the 1970s. Marcos saw them as a threat, and expropriated many of their media interests.[5] Marcos created a disorganized business system, forced capitalists to compete for state favours, destabilized the old elite and created a new one, and adopted policies that encouraged the growth of corruption on a huge scale.

The third feature of the Philippine corporate structure is the high share of foreign interests. The US had interests in oil refining, banking, automobiles, insurance, commodity processing and, later, the semiconductor sector. Japanese investments grew from the 1970s, with the introduction of an export-oriented industrialization policy by Marcos. The Japanese developed a powerful presence in automobiles, retailing, petrochemicals, infrastructure and tourism. However, it was the arrival of Chinese interests from Indonesia and Malaysia from the 1980s that shaped the industrial growth of Filipino-Chinese capitalism, usurping the position of the traditional Spanish mestizo industrialists by the 1990s. Prominent here were Salim and Robert Kuok, and their alliances with Gokongwei and Henry Sy. By 1993, the Salim Group held investments in 25 countries, including the US. Its investments in the Philippines were through the Metro Pacific Group, which included 15 subsidiaries and four affiliates in consumer goods, pharmaceuticals, real estate, telecommunications and banking. Many of these interests were secured through direct acquisition. Salim took over the PDCP Bank in 1994 and thereby secured an interest in investment banking. This entry of Nanyang Chinese into the Philippine corporate economy led to accelerated growth among the local Filipino-Chinese capitalists, particularly through the privatization programmes of Aquino and Ramos, and through the earlier attempts of Marcos to destabilize the traditional oligarchy. These developments coincided with the rise of China and the China market, further assisting the rise of domestic Chinese capitalists in the Philippines and the recovery of the

Philippines' economy. These historical experiences have shaped the nature of the Philippine bourgeoisie, its structure and its competitiveness.

Corporate structure

The Philippine corporate economy has the following main characteristics. First, ownership is concentrated in a few large families. Second, affiliation with subsidiaries and with associate firms is strong, as in the *keiretsu* in Japan. The corporations are largely conglomerates, possessing both related and unrelated product firms. There is marked diversification into finance, and the majority of the corporations include one or more banks. Third, great use is made of holding companies and interlocking shareholdings to increase family dominance. There is relatively little public listing of companies; there is, therefore, only limited use of government and institutional shareholding.

Fourth, privatization in the 1980s and 1990s increased corporate concentration, through a major wave of mergers. Fifth, foreign capital inflows further concentrated corporate authority in the hands of a small elite, through capital abundance and access to new technologies in electronics and telecommunications. Financial liberalism, therefore, had a major impact in increasing corporate concentration. Foreign-country and mutual funds, as well as private capital inflows, targeted the corporate elite in specific capital- and technology-intensive sectors.

Horizontal and vertical subsidiaries were interlocked through family ownership and control. There was manipulation of the bureaucracy and politicians to secure further concentration. The legal infrastructure was weak and the conglomerates lacked financial transparency, since the banks were held within the group. For both these reasons, the effective assessment of corporate growth and performance was extremely difficult. And, more broadly, monitoring was flimsy. The corporate family was often more concerned with the scale of growth, rather than profitability and efficiency.

Finally, the dominance of family management, cross-shareholdings and preferential transactions accorded to a small elite, hindered competition and encouraged the growth of monopolies. The dominance of the family – 50 families controlled more than 40 per cent of corporate assets – continued after 2000.[6] High concentration was also present in listed firms: 60 to 90 per cent of listed firms were owned by the top 20 shareholders, while 50 per cent of publicly listed firms were held by a mere five major shareholders. Only 22 per cent of the top 100 corporations in the Philippines were publicly traded, but even here, family ownership is pervasive. Once again, direct lending by banks, the state and foreign investors increases family concentration. Thirty per cent of total bank loans – US$10.7 billion in 1999[7] – for the top 100 corporations ensured the continuation of concentrated growth.

Concentration within sectors was also striking. In 1980, 98 per cent of all economic sectors had four or fewer companies controlling at least 35 per cent of sales output. This level of concentration in corporate output grew with privatization from the early 1990s.[8] These large, family-owned corporations survived in part because of the absence of a strong institutional framework, such as the bureaucracy, but principally because each conglomerate possessed a bank or banks at its core, and because abundant finance fed ambitious growth. There was no institutional or financial restraint.[9] Tables 12.1–12.4 further illustrate this concentrated ownership, output and dominance in specific industrial and economic sectors.

Table 12.1 demonstrates the impressive growth in sales output of the top 1,000 corporations between 1988 and 1997, an increase of 17.5 per cent. Retained earnings registered a compound growth of 27.2 per cent over the same period. These corporations were, therefore, highly profitable. This is confirmed by Table 12.2, which contains important performance indicators for different categories of a corporation. A few large conglomerates were responsible for a major part of sales. Privately owned corporations accounted for 42.8 per cent of sales by corporations in the period 1988–97. These private companies had a leverage ratio of 158 per cent. Their return on assets and return on equity were more than twice that of state-owned corporations but lower than that of foreign firms and publicly listed firms. The net profit margin of listed firms was high, 15.5 per cent, reflecting the large revenues accumulated by this group.

Table 12.3 provides further evidence of the concentration of production and sales within a few large companies. These large companies accounted for only 8.8 per cent of the total number of companies on the list yet were responsible for 56.1 per cent of the total sales of the corporate sector. Leverage was high among these companies, 158 per cent in the period 1988–97, although lower than that in other parts of Southeast Asia.

Table 12.4 provides a detailed breakdown of shareholding and ownership for publicly listed corporations. The concentration in ownership is dramatically clear. A single shareholder, often the family, holds 27.2 per cent of equity in a financial firm, and 40.8 per cent in non-financial corporations. The top five largest shareholders held 59.2 per cent in financial institutions, and 65.3 per cent in non-financial institutions. The top 20 largest shareholders held 76.2 per cent in the financial firms, and the average shareholding of the top 20 in the non-financial firms was 75.9 per cent. The control of corporations by a small elite edged out any opportunity for significant shareholding by the public, or shareholder activism.

The concentration in ownership was particularly marked within holding companies, although it varied between sectors. In 1997, it was highest in construction (74 per cent), property (69.8 per cent), manufacturing and trading (68.4 per cent) and communications (67.3 per cent). The concentration in ownership was facilitated by the dominance of family shareholdings, and by the low volume of shares issued to the public. The shares in publicly listed companies are thinly traded and illiquid. Share prices respond to movements in foreign funds, since domestic capital circulation is limited to the elite families, or is low in comparison to other stock markets in Southeast

Table 12.1 Growth and financial performance of the top 1,000 Philippine companies, 1988–97

Indicators	*1988*	*1989*	*1990*	*1991*	*1992*	*1993*	*1994*	*1995*	*1996*	*1997*	*Compound growth (%)*
Growth indicators (Peso billion)											
Net sales	464.7	519.1	629.6	741.3	862.3	954.1	1,177.60	1,394	1,697.50	1,978.90	17.5
Net income	28.4	33.6	35.2	46.5	64.8	72.9	144.4	148.3	193.5	96.5	14.6
Fixed assets	260.8	290.2	378.4	411.9	480.9	617.2	776.9	941.2	1,191.40	1,225.90	18.8
Total assets	618.6	707.1	861.4	952.6	1,123.50	1,317.10	1,781.20	2,341.10	3,160.10	3,893.90	22.7
Total liabilities	426.5	468.7	555.3	570.1	615.3	714.4	900.1	1,209.70	1,647.50	2,332.40	20.8
Stockholders' equity	192.1	238.4	306.1	382.5	508.2	602.7	881.2	1,131.40	1,512.70	1,561.50	26.2
Retained earning	51.4	63.1	95.8	136.4	188.6	218.0	338.0	411.7	443.6	446.9	27.2
Financial ratios (%)											
Leverage	222	197	181	149	121	119	102	107	109	149	146
ROE	14.8	14.1	11.5	12.2	12.8	12.1	16.4	13.1	12.8	6.2	12.6
ROA	4.6	4.7	4.1	4.9	5.8	5.5	8.1	6.3	6.1	2.5	5.3
Turnover	75	73	73	78	77	72	66	60	54	51	68
Net profit margin	6.1	6.5	5.6	6.3	7.5	7.6	12.3	10.6	11.4	4.9	7.9
Other indicators											
No. of companies	899	887	896	903	902	900	898	900	898	896	898
Sales per company (Peso billion)	0.5	0.6	0.7	0.8	1	1.1	1.3	1.6	1.9	2.2	1.2

Notes:
Leverage = total liabilities/stockholders' equity; net profit margin = net income/net sales; ROA (return on assets) = net income/total assets; ROE (return on equity) = net income/stockholders' equity; turnover = net sales/total assets.

Source: *SEC-Businessworld Annual Survey of Top 1,000 Corporations in the Philippines*, ADB, 2001, Chapter 3

Table 12.2 Growth and financial performance of the Philippines' corporate sector by firm ownership, 1988–97

Indicators	*Publicly listed*	*Privately owned*	*Foreign-owned*	*Government-owned*
Growth indicators (compound annual growth rate, %)				
Net sales	20.0	17.3	21.8	4.0
Net income	19.4	22.0	3.9	4.3
Fixed assets	19.6	28.4	26.3	9.8
Total assets	29.4	28.5	22.8	14.1
Total liabilities	26.4	27	22.9	12.9
Stockholders' equity	32.5	31.8	22.7	17.0
Retained earning	30.1	2.9	22	5.4
Financial ratios (%)				
Leverage	89	158	142	190
ROE	15.1	13.0	22.2	5.7
ROA	8.0	5.2	9.3	2.1
Turnover	53	103	146	22
Net profit margin	15.5	5.3	6.3	10.3
Other indicators				
Share in sales (%)	17.8	42.8	27.9	11.5
No. of companies	73	606	196	23
Sales per company (Peso billion)	2.5	0.8	1.5	4.8

Source: *SEC-Businessworld Annual Survey of Top 1,000 Corporations in the Philippines*, various years, ADB, 2001, p. 161

Table 12.3 Growth and financial performance of the Philippines' corporate sector by firm size, 1988–97

Indicators	*Large*	*Medium*	*Small*
Growth indicators (compound annual growth rate, %)			
Net sales	15.7	19.6	19.9
Net income	1.3	47.2	26.2
Fixed assets	15.5	29.9	25.4
Total assets	18.4	32.5	28.1
Total liabilities	18.2	25.6	25.0
Stockholders' equity	18.9	49.6	32.7
Retained earning	13.9	36.0	44.5
Financial ratios (%)			
Leverage	158	156	128
ROE	13.1	16	10.1
ROA	5.3	7.1	4.5
Turnover	65	81	73
Net profit margin	8.2	9.5	6.6
Other indicators			
Share in sales (%)	56.1	12.9	31.0
No. of companies	79	89	730
Sales per company (Peso billion)	7.3	1.6	0.5

Source: *SEC-Businessworld Annual Survey of Top 1,000 Corporations in the Philippines*, various years, ADB, 2001, p. 164

Table 12.4 Ownership concentration of Philippine publicly listed companies by sector, 1997

Sector	*Top 1*	*Top 5*	*Top 20*[a]
Financial institution			
Banks	26.9	59.2	76.4
Financial services	41.3	63.2	65.8
Average shareholding[b]	27.2	59.2	76.2
Non-financial company			
Communications	35.4	67.3	76.9
Power and energy	21.5	55.4	72.1
Transportation services	23.8	48.4	69.2
Construction and other related products	47.7	74	86.2
Food, beverage and tobacco	22.7	44.1	69.7
Holding companies	53.0	78.4	86.0
Manufacturing, distribution and trading	37.4	68.4	42.6
Hotel, recreation and other services	28.9	55.3	68.0
Property	54.8	69.8	74.5
Mining	23.4	56.0	51.9
Oil	19.9	45.1	64.3
Average shareholding[b]	40.8	65.3	75.9

Notes:

a Information on the top 20 shareholders is not available for five holding companies, ten manufacturing companies and two property companies.

b Weighted by market capitalization.

Source: *PSE databank*, ADB, 2001, p. 173

Asia. Dispersed, individual shareholding is insignificant. Family corporations, holding companies and the subsidiaries of conglomerates dominate shareholdings. Privately owned holding companies reinforce concentration or the pooling of family shareholdings, though they may be distributed over many companies through interlocking arrangements.

Thus, holding companies possessed the largest share in market capitalization on the Philippines stock exchange, accounting for 26.7 per cent of total market capitalization – a holding of P258.6 billion in non-financial publicly listed firms. They were also responsible for 66 per cent of the non-financial corporations within privately owned conglomerates. This structure of private ownership was disguised by the multi-layered nature of interlocking shareholdings. The weakness of institutional shareholding further facilitated the concentration of family ownership. The only significant institutional investors were investment trust funds. But these were concentrated in only a few elite firms – the Philippine Long Distance Telephone Company, Petron and Meralco in power and energy, and San Miguel in food and beverages.

The concentration was further enhanced through the control of management on the Board of Directors. The confusion in property rights caused difficulties in maintaining an independent audit. Many of the auditing companies had close connections with the corporations for 20 years or more, and this familiarity made disclosure more difficult. The close relations between corporations and their bank meant that creditors could exercise little restraint on management. The law, too, could impose little restraint. Moreover, since the banks were dominant, holding three-quarters of the resources in the financial system because of the weaknesses of capital markets in corporate finance, once again there was little restraining agency. Firms used bank loans and retained earnings, together with generous state credit, to finance growth. The ability of conglomerates to secure external capital was restricted to joint-ventures with foreign multinationals. It was only after 1993 that foreign capital markets became responsive to the potential for investment in the Philippines. Thus, debt financed a major share of growth, an increase of 34 per cent between 1994 and 1997. Yet the debt burden was low by Asian standards, since much of the foreign borrowing took place only after 1993, when stable economic conditions were secured by the Ramos administration.[10]

The Philippine Stock Exchange (PSE) was small in terms of market capitalization. In August 1997 it was roughly the same size as the SET, at US$47.7 billion. In comparison, the stock market in Malaysia was US$186 billion, South Korea US$143 billion and Indonesia US$61.5 billion. The PSE remained depressed from the 1970s to the 1990s, but rose from 1993 to 1997. The 1997 crisis was not particularly serious.

Market capitalization has been used by Claessens to identify the concentrated strength and volume of corporate assets within the single-family corporation.[11] But market capitalization is not an effective indicator when, as in the Philippines, the capital market is not fully developed. Listing is not widespread and the majority of corporations are held by the family-owner. In 1979, only 60 out of the 1,000 top corporations were listed. And even among those 60, family shareholdings remained significant. In contrast, for example, Malaysia's high concentration of corporate assets in the hands of a small elite – 76.2 per cent – should be analysed with a clearer perception of the institutional and state shareholdings on the KLSE.

These characteristics are clearly evident in the structure of the Ayala Corporation, which, in 1979, possessed 24 large firms in petrochemicals, mining, machine production, automobiles, textiles, pulp and paper, real estate, hotels and telecommunications. The Ayala Corporation, the holding company, was dominated by the family, although in 1973 the Mitsubishi Group acquired a 20 per cent stake. The Corporation was listed on the Manila Stock Exchange in 1976. Its largest subsidiary, Ayala Land, absorbed many of its smaller subsidiaries in construction, retailing, hotels, resorts and transport to become the largest publicly listed firm in terms of market capitalization on the stock exchange in July 1991. The group's main bank, the Bank of the Philippine Islands, was the third largest commercial bank in the country in terms of total assets, loans and deposits, and was listed in October 1991. It had mounted aggressive mergers in the early 1970s to compete with the Filipino-Chinese banks.[12] It purchased Peoples Bank and

Trust in 1974, Commercial Bank and Trust in 1981, Family Bank and Trust in 1984, and established a joint-venture with Morgan Guarantee Trust. It also possessed three insurance firms.[13]

The interlocking structures between the main corporation and its several subsidiaries increased the family's control. Ayala Corporation held 69 per cent of the cash flow rights and 77 per cent of voting rights in Ayala Land, and Ayala Land possessed 5 per cent of the cash flow and control of Ayala Corporation. Ayala Corporation had 90 per cent equity in Ayala Foundation and 34 per cent equity in the Bank of the Philippine Islands (BPI). The Ayala Foundation had 9 per cent of the shares in BPI.

Ayala Corporation is itself owned by Mermac Inc., formed in 1960, which holds 58 per cent of the equity. The Mitsubishi Bank (Meiji Life Insurance) has 20 per cent ownership and 23 per cent control. The opening of Ayala to Japanese investment in 1973 was a defensive move to protect the family interests from the demands of the Marcos family, which had already savaged the Lopez Group. The Ayala family held 100 per cent of the equity in Mermac.

With respect to Globe Telecom, 32 per cent of the equity was held by ITT, the Ayala Corporation holding 40 per cent. Once again, family ownership was at the core. With respect to Automated Electronics within the Ayala Group, the IFC had 20 per cent of the equity, Japan Asia Inc. a further 20 per cent and Assemblers Inc. 30 per cent. Automated Electronics has a subsidiary, I Micro Electronics, which is family owned and produces semiconductors for IBM.[14] Such cross-holdings and high family concentration are viable because the state and institutional stakes are meagre, certainly in comparison to Malaysia and Singapore in the same period. There was pressure from Marcos, challenging the position of these oligarchs. Ayala's support for Marcos' rival Aquino was obvious, and he kept his distance from Marcos and his cronies. The Spanish mestizo groups, including Soriano, Elizalde and Ayala, declined under Marcos, while the new elite, including Gokongwei (food, textiles, real estate and banking), Henry Sy (finance and retailing), Yuchengco (finance and insurance), George Ty (finance and automobiles), Uytengsu (flour milling, foods), Concepcion (flour milling, electrical appliances) and Lucio Tan (tobacco, banking and beer) made substantial advances.

Ayala sought protection through joint-ventures with foreign investors, principally Japanese *sogo shoshas*. It developed industrial estates and export processing zones with Japanese multinationals and Korean investors in Cebu City and Manila, and with Robert Kuok in Cebu Province. Ayala's finance and real-estate development had Indonesian and Korean partners. Its presence in the Manila district of Makati since 1851 was expanded into housing, shopping malls and hotels. With foreign multinationals expanding their interests in the Philippines after 1997, in oil refining, banking, commodity processing, automobiles and electronics, the Ayala Group was in a strong position.

The Ayala Corporation is distinctive in possessing both family and professional managers. The professionals were introduced in the 1970s, at a time when the corporation was wooing the Japanese *sogo shoshas*. It installed professional managers in its export-oriented industrial firms, while the holding company remained in the hands of the family. Consequently, the Ayala Corporation had eight non-Ayala managers, five professional managers, and three family members. The Chairman was a finance officer, so that the family retained control. Jaime Zobel retained control of decision-making. There was a pattern of appointing specialist managers – Jaime in banking, Estrada in insurance, Licuanan in real estate, Buhain in foods and Berba in export-directed manufacturing. A reduction in the size of the executive committee increased the influence of Jaime and his eldest son, Augusto.[15]

As noted earlier, the positioning of banks within these conglomerates shaped the pattern of corporate growth; indeed, it led to volatile bank and corporate performance in the Philippines, and, ultimately, distorted corporate governance. In 1949 there was only one private Filipino bank, the Philippine Bank of Commerce, established in 1938.[16] There were ten other banks, including one state-owned bank (Philippine National Bank), four branches of foreign banks, two controlled by the Church, and three controlled by American or Chinese interests. However, a decline in foreign banks by 1960 ushered in a growth in the number of domestic banks owned by Filipino conglomerates. This expansion was assisted by the 1948 General Banking Act, which required 60 per cent Filipino ownership for new banks. Furthermore, foreign banks could not accept government deposits or rediscount with the Central Bank. Foreign bank assets declined by half between 1950 and 1960, while the number of banks owned by industrial groups grew by more than 60 per cent.[17] Two mestizo groups did not establish their own banks – Soriano and Elizalde – because they had access to funds from other domestic capitalists, and from foreign banks. A further crucial change was an increase in Chinese banking. Also striking was a major shift in the ownership of banks, from the old capitalists to the relatives and cronies of Marcos, secured largely through political pressures.

The situating of private banks within large, highly concentrated industrial conglomerates unleashed excessive lending to shareholders within the group, which a fragile regulatory regime could do little to restrain. The banks were weakly capitalized, particularly so during a period of diversified and rapid growth. There were a number of bank failures, going back to the 1960s. The Continental Bank failed in 1974, and the General Bank and Trust closed in 1976. The financing of real-estate and stock market investments by these banks added to the instability.

The instability was aggravated in the 1970s by the transfer of banks to new owners, often the cronies or relatives of Marcos. Twelve banks changed hands in this decade. The Philippine Commercial and Industrial Bank of Eugenio Lopez passed to Ben Romualdez, the brother of Imelda Marcos.

Republic Bank was transferred to a Marcos relative, Roberto Benedicto, in 1978, and became the Republic Planters Bank.

The banks in industrial clusters were used primarily to support the conglomerate's interests. The conglomerate had access to foreign loans, government deposits, equity from state banks and subsidized credit from the state. The Republic Planters Bank had assets secured principally through subsidized credit. The Allied Bank of Lucio Tan, a Marcos crony, enjoyed selective credit allocations in the late 1970s.[18] This distribution of loans and foreign exchange swaps was facilitated by a weak Central Bank. Governor Licaros resigned in 1981 in view of a deteriorating financial sector. The fragility of the financial system often resulted in runs on banks, as for example Yujengco's General Bank and Trust Company in 1976.

The banks operated in a protected market, since foreign entry was restricted by legislation in 1948. A stronger regulation of the domestic banks was difficult to achieve. Legislation in 1973 requiring minimum levels of capitalization led briefly to an increase in foreign equity in local banks, but rampant corruption led to a swift exit. By 1975, a third of the foreign investors had divested. However, local banks still had access to foreign capital through the state. Marcos attracted an inflow of foreign capital through a package of financial reforms – although, in fact, many of the reforms were not implemented or, if put in place, were ineffective. Wide-scale abuse left both state and private banks holding an extraordinary volume of bad loans – US$5.9 billion in 1983. But the financial and corporate reforms of the Aquino and Ramos administrations ensured a less turbulent experience for the Philippines in the 1997 financial crisis. Aquino established the Philippine Commission on Good Government that acquired a controlling stake in private banks. It closed failing banks, such as the Manila Bank, and tightened the sanctions against specific financial violations with respect to the capitalization of banks, minimum adequacy ratios and excessive lending to single borrowers. The state replaced loans and subsidized credit with high yielding government securities. These reforms not only led to greater financial stability but also improved relations with the state. The government identified five large private banks to operate government deposits, and also removed the abuses in currency swaps and the rediscounting of Central Bank and Treasury bills. The merger of smaller banks and the competitive licensing of new banks reduced existing monopolies, in which banks were affiliated to large conglomerates. Moves to privatize state-owned banks led to the PNB emerging as a powerful private bank in 1995. The programme of privatization also led to the increasing importance of Filipino Chinese in the domestic bank sector, some in joint-ventures with Taiwanese, Hong Kong and Singapore financiers. Foreign banks were allowed to open more branches. These changes permitted eight new banks to operate, ten by 1995, including Citibank.[19] Fidel Ramos embarked on more radical reforms by closing down the Central Bank, whose debts were absorbed by the Treasury. In its place he established the Bangko Sentral ng Pilipinas.[20]

Despite these reforms, monopolistic structures remained. The excessive concentration of wealth in a small elite remained and in fact privatization enhanced rather than eroded the elite's power. The oligarch's links to the state ensured that the regulatory framework remained weak. Public bail-outs of failing banks continued, while selected individuals were able to survive by finding new joint-venture partners. The growth of the stock market in the 1990s, and the liberalization of the foreign exchange market in 1992 facilitated this globalization. In brief, there were serious structural obstacles to effective reform. If change were to be achieved, it had to sever the legacy of patrimonialism and cronyism.

The open economy meant a continued threat of capital flight, both domestic capital and foreign. Consequently, the growth of fixed capital was extremely modest. The percentage of gross domestic fixed capital formation was just 0.4 in 1980–4 and 6.2 in 1985–9, although it did move higher in the mid-1990s.[21] Consequently, most of the foreign capital flows were in the form of loans, both private and from foreign sources (see Table 12.5 for a perspective on FDI flows into the Philippines). Thus, the difficulties in mobilizing capital to fund growth is seen not just in poor returns on investment but crucially in poor GDP growth.

An important brake on effecting change was the impotency of the Philippine bureaucracy. Kang has argued that bureaucracies are more efficient in rapid growth than backward economies.[22] But it is also possible to argue that the autonomous character of a bureaucracy can also be undermined during periods of rapid growth, as witnessed in both Thailand and Indonesia in the 1980s and 1990s. There, the bureaucracy became increasingly politicized because of the high rewards on offer when the economy was growing rapidly. Patronage and politicization occlude, rather than are differentiated, as claimed by Kang. The Philippine bureaucracy, built on the American model that allows for political appointments to the most senior positions, provided considerable opportunities for the merging of patronage and politicization, and for the preservation of special interests. Marcos may have sought to break the position of existing interests but, in constructing new interests to replace the old, he simply created more areas of patronage, more rent-seeking entrepreneurs, more nepotism, clientelism, corruption and factionalism. It is only autonomy and distance between the state and business that can break these cycles. This did not occur in the Philippines.[23]

Patronage dominated the entire bureaucratic infrastructure, and during his presidency, Marcos used the judicial system to buttress his patronage distribution. During the period 1946 to 1972, the bureaucracy had already been riven by factional and clientelist loyalties. There were powerful cronies in key sections of the bureaucracy, notably in the central bank and in the important ministries. For example, the Board of Investment (BOI), established in 1966 and with a clear programme to promote rapid industrialization, was constantly thwarted by powerful bureaucrats supported by Marcos.

Table 12.5 Ownership concentration by selected industries in Philippines, 1997

Industry	*Top 20 stockholders*	*Top 5 stockholders*
Banks		
Bank of the Philippine Islands	90.7	75.9
Far East Bank and Trust	81.4	58.2
Metropolitan Bank and Trust	69.1	57.3
Philippine Commercial and Industrial Bank	80.8	63.3
Philippine National Bank	66.2	53.8
Rizal Commercial Bank	85.3	76.8
Union Bank of the Philippine	81.5	59.3
Communications		
ABS-CBN	84.6	79.9
Philippine Long Distance	75.4	66.0
Power and energy		
Manila Electric Corporation	68.2	46.2
Petro Corporation	82.8	80.8
Transportation		
Keppel Shipyard	83.6	73.6
Asian Terminals, Inc.	78.8	47.8
Construction		
Alsons Cement	88.1	68.3
Mariwasa Manufacturing	99.1	83.9
Food and beverages		
Jollibee Foods	92.7	61.0
San Miguel Corporation	59.0	28.8
Manufacturing		
Atlas Fertillizer	81.3	72.5
Pryce Corporation	74.8	50.6
Property		
Ayala Land	66.3	63.9
C&P Homes	83.1	79.3
Filinvest Land	66.8	62.1
Megaworld Properties	90.5	82.2
Oil		
Sinophil Corporation	68.9	38.5
Oriental Petroleum	61.3	52.1

Source: Figures derived from Cheng Hoon Lim and Charles Woodruff, 'Managing Corporate Distress in the Philippines: Some Policy Recommendations', IMF Working Paper 1998/138, p. 11; *SEC, Philippine Top 1,000 Corporations, 1997*, Manila: Securities and Exchange Commission, 1998; and company annual reports, cited in David C. Kang *Crony Capitalism Corruption and Development in South Korea and the Philippines*, Cambridge, Cambridge University Press, 2002, p. 177

Marcos ignored the BOI, except to use it to formulate policies that would be acceptable to the IMF and thus secure foreign aid.

Marcos used different governmental institutions to erode the power of the agrarian elites and the technocrats. He weakened Congress by packing it with oligarchs amenable to his views. With American military aid, he restructured the military and the police, which were both placed under his control. He created new cronies through the construction of new monopolies, under the guise of 'economic rationalization'. Although political power flowed through the president's Malacañang Palace, there were huge divisions between General Vera, Imelda Marcos and Juan Ponce Enrile, the Minister of Defence who finally rose against Marcos in February 1986.

The economic liberalization under Aquino and Ramos produced a firm break with the powerful oligarchs, and introduced serious measures to eliminate the monopolies, the opening of protected sectors of the economy to foreign participation, a reduction of tariff barriers, privatization, the decentralization of economic power, the simplification of tax processes and an improved regulation of financial institutions. Corporate reforms included an increased separation of ownership and control, improved debt-equity ratios, firmer oversight practices through the introduction of American accounting methods, a greater use of consolidated balance sheets and the regular filing of accounts with the SEC.

Thus, a central factor shaping corporate growth and governance in the Philippines has been the distinctive forms of Philippine corruption and cronyism. The Philippines is rich in natural resources, but the authority of government is weak and power is distributed across regional and metropolitan economic and political oligarchs. The result is a largely autonomous business class, a structure disturbed only briefly by Marcos and his attempts to centralize authority during his period of martial rule. The structure is marked by highly unstable patron–client networks and state–business relations. The highly insecure economic and political environment nurtures corrupt practices which, according to Hutchcroft, have seriously obstructed Philippine economic growth.[24]

But this rather pessimistic view should be balanced with the fact that while the 1997 financial crisis shattered most of the ASEAN economies, the Philippine experience was notably less traumatic. However, the Philippine economy did possess a high level of NPLs – 2.8 per cent in December 1996 rising to 3.4 per cent in June 1997[25] – and a contraction in loan loss provisions. There was also unhedged dollar debt, a high exposure of the banks to volatile real-estate investment and a depreciating peso. Corporate debt was also high, the liabilities of private firms increasing from 15 per cent in 1993 to 27 per cent in 1997.[26] But the Philippines was less scarred by the 1997 crisis than Thailand, Indonesia or Malaysia. Why this exceptionalism?

First, the Aquino government had introduced important reforms in economic liberalization, reducing quotas and credit subsidies, and undertaking reforms of the tax system. Moreover, privatization had reduced the state sector, and with de-regulation in such crucial sectors as banking and telecommunications, the capital market had become more active. However, the foreign debt crisis, high interest rates and the tight money policy imposed by the IMF and the Central Bank made recovery under Aquino difficult.

It was Ramos, from 1992, who took the dramatic measures. He dissolved the Central Bank and replaced it with the Bangko Sentral ng Philipinas. The entry of foreign banks and the liberalization of the capital account stabilized capital flows. But, most importantly, an export recovery secured macroeconomic stability. That export growth was dominated by the electronics and telecommunications sector, which accounted for 30 per cent of total exports in 1992 but 50 per cent in 1997. There was also impressive expansion in construction and finance, transportation and utilities (energy, water and gas).

However, financial liberalization introduced a measure of risk, since the regulatory framework remained weak. Speculative bubbles appeared in the real-estate and financial markets, as a result of excessive investment and the running of large deficits on current account. Since the regulatory framework was so weak, divided as it was between the Central Bank, the IMF and the ministries, the warning signs were not picked up.[27]

Although the 1997 financial crisis had less severe consequences for the Philippines, recovery was slow and NPLs and corporate defaults rose. The obstacles to recovery were, first, that the creation of asset management companies to absorb weak corporate assets went ahead too slowly. In 2002, Metropolitan Bank and Trust Company sold NPLs to an asset management company owned by a foreign bank. Second, capitalization and asset quality were poor, exacerbated by the low profitability of the banks and a weak domestic capacity to generate capital.

But there were also more positive signs. The reforms introduced by the Central Bank included the issuing of guidelines for the supervision and regulation of banks, the publication of reports on non-performing assets and improvements in management practices. The Philippine Deposit Insurance Corporation assumed a regulatory role. It was empowered to assist troubled financial institutions, such as the Philippine National Bank in 2000. It could also liquidate banks.

Banks were able to ride the turbulence of 1997 because the reforms of the late 1980s had strengthened their capital position. NPLs were high by September 1998, amounting to 11.5 per cent. The government's immediate response was to restrict foreign exchange trading, control inflation, reduce bank lending to volatile sectors such as real estate, and restructure or encourage the takeover of failing groups. In 1999, Philippine Airlines was restructured because of its high level of debt. Other groups faced takeover by domestic or foreign investors. Philippine Long Distance Telephone was taken over by First Pacific Corporation and restructured. The Soriano family's San Miguel Corporation was taken over by Cojuangco; it was then restructured, retaining its core brewing business but disposing of many of its local and foreign subsidiaries.

An amendment, in 2000, to the 1980 Corporation Code contained provisions to broaden corporate ownership. It encouraged new organizational structures and operations, as well as corporate dissolution. But implementation of the last was difficult. The insolvency law was biased towards the rescue and reform of corporations rather than allowing failing firms to fail. It was felt that insolvent corporations should be dealt with by the commercial courts and not by the Securities Commission. There were also provisions for the disclosure of ownership in holding companies and listed corporations. There was pressure to improve the accountability of directors and to strengthen the authority of corporate boards. Minority shareholders were to be protected to prevent large shareholders from engaging in risky ventures without disclosing information. Limits were placed on the links between financial and non-financial corporate institutions, notably by limiting the extent of cross-shareholding and the volume of connected lending. The Central Bank was given the power to limit loans to directors of connected corporations. The 2000 amendment also sought to establish adequate capital ratios and limits on cross-guarantees between firms in the same group.

A Banking Law in 2000 improved the monitoring of bank activities, increased the role of institutional investors, and sought to reform the employment of investment funds and venture capital. There was recognition that the financing of corporations through bonds and treasury bills would lessen the concentration on bank loans. There were also moves to stimulate the stock market. The elimination of private deals and insider trading, and the protection of minority shareholding interests was sought. The Central Bank was given the authority to limit loans to directors of corporations. An important argument so far has commented on the rise of the Filipino-Chinese capitalist and the implications of this for Philippine corporate transformation. It would be useful here to explore in detail the growth of this capitalist minority.

Chinese entrepreneurship

The rise of Chinese capitalist groups can be traced to the period of American rule, 1898–1946. Under the Spanish, the Chinese had remained a marginal group, restricted to provincial trade, some import-export trading and the manufacture of alcohol. Although Dee C. Chuan had founded the China Banking Corporation in 1920, it was only with the ISI of the period after 1950 that Chinese industrial interests had really grown. In the 1960s, Uytengsu moved into flour milling and food manufacturing, and John Gokongwei emerged in agri-business and food manufacturing. But the Chinese were still small in comparison with the Spanish mestizo and foreign groups. However, by 1990 they accounted for 37 per cent of manufacturing output.[28] It was the Marcos era that had secured the dominance of the Chinese in export-led industrialization. Only a small segment of these Chinese industrialists had emerged from existing interests, one exception being the

Yuchengco group that had long been found in tobacco manufacture, trade and insurance. The new Chinese bourgeoisie included Lucio Tan, whose interests were centred on the Fortune Tobacco Corporation.

The concentration of Chinese wealth in real estate, retailing, banking and manufacturing was boosted by privatization, which provided opportunities for the new Chinese to enter sectors dominated by the state and by Spanish mestizo entrepreneurs, notably mining and heavy industrialization. Economic liberalization, de-regulation and privatization from the 1980s took place simultaneously with an inflow of Asian capital into joint-ventures with Chinese Filipinos. Ramos pushed for a more aggressive form of de-regulation and for the privatization of government-owned and government-controlled corporations, particularly their non-performing sectors. His aim was to strengthen the private sector and to broaden ownership, partly through the creation of a more virile capital market. But, ironically, privatization produced a greater degree of concentration, with single families dominating specific corporate sectors.

By May 1994, 32 of the government-owned, controlled corporations had been sold to the private sector, and 16 partially sold. These included airlines, shipyards, shipping, petroleum and mining. The Chinese were the major beneficiaries of this privatization. With Philippine Airlines, 67 per cent of the equity was transferred to PR Holding of Lucio Tan in 1992. In 1994, the Philippine Shipyard and Engineering Corporation was sold to Keppel Singapore and Henry Sy. The National Shipping Corporation was sold to a Taiwanese Corporation in a joint-venture with Madrigal Shipping for US$18.5 million. John Gokongwei purchased the largest oil exploration company in 1994.[29]

In banking, the largest investors were Filipino-Chinese. Associated Bank was sold to Leonardo Ty. In telecommunications, privatization was aimed at breaking the monopoly held by the Philippine Long Distance Telephone Company, and thus to create greater localization of telephone exchanges, cellular mobile telephone systems and the modernization of international telephone networks. Two Chinese capitalists dominated: Alfonso Yuchengco (PLDD) and John Gokongwei (Digital Telecoms Philippines). Privatization achieved two goals. First, it brought capital- and technology-intensive industries within labour-intensive conglomerates. Second, it brought Chinese capitalists into closer relationships with the Spanish mestizo capitalists. For example, in telecommunications, the existing monopoly was split between Filipino-Chinese and Spanish mestizo groups. International capital, here American, Korean and Japanese, was also brought into the industry. Ayala established Globe Telecom, and Lopez created the International Communication Corporation and Radio Communication Philippines.

Filipino-Chinese were the major entrants in the banking sector. By 1994, only four foreign banks – Citibank, Bank of America, HSBC and Standard Chartered – were allowed to take deposits. The other foreign banks were permitted to own 30–40 per cent of the voting stock in local banks. By 1995, further foreign banks – from Japan, Australia, Korea, Taiwan, Thailand, Singapore, the US, the Netherlands and Germany – had entered the Philippines. These arrivals made the banking sector more competitive and more stable.[30]

In entering the heavy industry, energy, mining and shipping sectors, the Chinese were entering areas dominated by the state and Spanish mestizo capitalists.

The Filipino-Chinese family business used the holding company structure to expand activities without diluting family ownership and control. In this they were assisted by the foreign multinationals and, in particular, Japanese, Taiwanese and overseas Chinese from Singapore, Malaysia, Indonesia and Thailand. But crucial to the growth of the Filipino-Chinese were their ties to the state and to the bureaucracy. Boards of Directors were packed not only with family members but also former Cabinet members and bureaucrats. Ty had Pio Pedrosa, Placido Mapa and Cesar Virata (former Cabinet members, and a Chief Justice). Yuchengco had Carlos Romulo (an ambassador), Virata and prominent lawyers. The management excluded non-family members from decision-making. John Gokongwei Jr, aged 62, was Chairman of J. G. Summit Holdings and Vice Chairman of the Philippine Commercial International Bank. Three professional managers recruited in the 1980s in finance and industry were excluded from the decision-making structures. There were kinship ties with other Filipino-Chinese capitalists: the Dees, Sycip and Yuchengco groups were close, despite tight family control.

It was inevitable that such growth would result in further concentration of wealth and industrial power for both the Filipino-Chinese and the Spanish mestizo elites. In 1993, Filipino-Chinese banks controlled 38.43 per cent of the total assets of private commercial banks in the Philippines.[31] The Chinese also dominated telecommunications, where Alfonso Yuchengco and the PLDT controlled 90.46 per cent of the international telecommunications sector.[32] Chinese concentration in real estate grew through joint-ventures with Salim (Indonesia) and Japanese retailing groups, although in telecommunications and real estate they faced serious competition from Ayala and Lopez.

However, contrary to the view advanced by Daniel van den Bulcke and Zhang Hai Yan, the Filipino-Chinese were constrained by their rent-seeking culture within the Philippines to develop any specialism, brand reputation, or a coherent business organization and management structure to attempt successful internationalization.[33] Their success in the Philippines was built on shrewd alliances with specialist multinationals, principally Japanese, Southeast Asian and Taiwanese, in semiconductors, automobiles, shipping and petrochemicals.

Their growth was essentially through acquisitions, either as a consequence of state divestment or from Filipino industrialists. Their corporate structure facilitated diversification through separate holding companies, which made it possible to integrate specific sectors and subsidiaries, expanding without loss of family ownership and control. These holding companies were ultimately responsible for their diverse investments. Listing was used primarily to raise capital and to attract foreign joint-venture partners, and also to secure expansion through regional stock markets. The SMPH of Henry Sy was listed in 1994 and diversified rapidly. The privatization schemes of the 1990s attracted some listing of technology-intensive firms within these conglomerates. However, there were serious weaknesses in the privatization programme, arising out of patronage politics, cronyism, the weak capital markets and the absence of stable institutional investors. This implied that listing and the acquisition of privatized assets allowed the Filipino-Chinese capitalists to carve out lucrative niches in capital- and technology-intensive sectors, and to diversify away from their traditional base in labour-intensive textiles, food manufacturing and commodity production and trade.[34]

Thus, there was limited growth of the Manila Stock Exchange. By 2000, the Philippines had just 228 listed companies, the lowest in Asia.[35] Market valuation was a mere 0.25 per cent of GDP. On the stock market, 70 per cent of the assets in 1996 were held by foreign funds, many of whom retreated with the financial crisis in 1997.[36]

Therefore, there was, in addition, an uneven distribution of assets in terms of sectors and ownership. The concentration of ownership in certain sectors contributed to the uneven development of capital markets in the Philippines, undermining the potential for global expansion. It follows that there is insufficient empirical evidence to demonstrate that Filipino-Chinese multinationals were successful abroad because of their ethnic and family networks. The vertical integration of production and marketing units of subsidiaries with those of the parent company brought considerable difficulties to initiatives in Singapore and Hong Kong. Gokongwei and Sycip faced difficulties throughout Southeast Asia and China. If the free-standing firm structure had been adopted, it may well have produced a greater concentration of manufacturing and financial activities overseas.

Their entry into the US, through the acquisition of failing banks and firms, revealed the same obstacles to successful globalization. The lack of special expertise, absence of a brand name and capital deficiencies thwarted their ambitions. Centralized ownership and control, and the manipulation of politicians and bureaucrats, are not secure foundations for growth outside a patrimonial, clientelist environment. They failed to attract state or foreign multinational support abroad. Taiwanese multinationals possessed specialist knowledge, capital and viable international partners to expand in Asia, Australia and the West.

The period of import controls provided Filipino oligarchs with the structure to diversify in the 1960s, protected by a patrimonial state. Able to exploit loopholes in state regulations, they attracted credit and expanded. The state shared a major part of the risk.[37] There were no such advantages when they ventured abroad.

Ayala Land expanded in real estate in Hong Kong through joint ventures with Hong Kong Land. The International Container Terminal Services

(ICTS) operated in Argentina, Mexico and Pakistan, in less productive, more politically volatile areas. Their domestic operations in the Philippines remained the main revenue generator for ICTS.[38]

Gokongwei had limited success overseas in textiles, manufacturing and real estate. Jollibee foods in Brunei, Malaysia and Hong Kong faced difficulties in local tastes and local competition in the fast food sector. The Metro Pacific Corporation of Manuel Panglinan and Salim had limited success in Hong Kong, and in the 1990s they concentrated on the Philippines in telecommunications, banking, real estate, the Bonifacio Land Project and in light industry. George Ty's Metropolitan Bank and Trust had branches in Tokyo, Seoul and Taiwan, catering to Filipino migrant workers and their remittances.

The Philippine National Bank, privatized in 1995, has branches in California, Hong Kong, Guam and Italy, operating as a remittance house for migrant workers and as a merchant bank for Filipino industrialists seeking markets abroad. It is less successful in the latter, since competition in merchant banking is acute in the US, Europe and East Asia. In 1997, the Philippine National Bank sold 60 per cent of its equity to Maybank because of huge losses.

The only successes have been San Miguel of Soriano, which acquired 25 per cent equity in Australian Coco Cola Amatil, and in a joint-venture with Nestlé of Switzerland.[39] In these cases, the San Miguel brand name and Soriano's long-term relationships provided a secure basis for growth overseas.

Van Den Bulcke and Zhang have relied solely on questionnaires to build their hypothesis. This needs support from empirical sources. The theoretical assertions on multinational ownership, location and internationalization advantages cannot be substantiated by boasts from the very capitalists who are being investigated. Hence, their conclusions as to how overseas Chinese entrepreneurs from the Philippines successfully expanded, while maintaining family control through managerial structures that incorporated family and friends, is highly flawed.[40]

Conclusion

The Philippines had a unique colonial legacy, in contrast to Indonesia and Malaysia. The Spanish settler community is a highly distinctive feature of the Philippine political and economic infrastructure. British and Dutch colonialism left no such imprint. The Spanish mestizo community through further assimilation provided the basis for a Spanish mestizo capitalist oligarchy. The succeeding American colonial power, with its ambivalent attitude to imperialism, swiftly recognized this elite and transferred administrative and political power to it. These local *caciques* absorbed further economic power and dominated the capitalist transformation of the Philippine Islands. This entrenched provincial elite posed an uneasy experience for

Marcos, who sought to destabilize the group through political centralization, and by supplanting them with Chinese tycoons. But he had limited success. This enduring persistence of a small group of Spanish mestizo businessmen is in direct contrast to Indonesia, Thailand and Malaysia, where each period has seen the rise of new capitalist groups. In Malaysia, Tan Kah Kee in the interwar period was followed by Quek Leng Chan in the 1960s. In Indonesia, the fall of Oei Tiong Ham was followed by the rise of Salim.

First, in the Philippines, there was strong continuity of the Spanish mestizo capitalist elite. Even when shunned by Marcos in the 1970s, these oligarchs were able to survive by creating lucrative alliances with foreign capital, in particular with Japanese and American multinationals. The Chinese, who had been more subservient in this capitalist transformation, now assumed a pivotal role, through their internal and external ethnic networks.

Second, the structures of state and bureaucratic authority in the Philippines were weaker than those in Thailand, Malaysia and Indonesia. The establishment of a strong 'developmental state' depends on an efficient bureaucracy that creates institutions and policies critical for rapid economic growth. The disjuncture between authority and power is acute in the Philippines and weakens policy making. In restructuring agrarian and industrial linkages to secure productivity gains and a more efficient distribution of wealth, the state is constantly undermined by these oligarchs. The bureaucracy assists in the implementation of sound macro-economic policy, and rents can be kept low if growth is dramatic and rent-seeking costs can be contained. However, when the state turns predatorial, as under Marcos, then growth is undermined and the adverse costs of rents rise. In Malaysia, Indonesia and Thailand, the state directed planning and provided greater security and firmer long-term targets, even though cronyism was rife. De-regulation and liberalization under Aquino and Ramos provided only a breathing space. The incentive for corporate reform and improved corporate governance could only come from increased international competition and fuller integration into the international economy.

13 Conclusion

Lost in translation: reinterpreting the rise of the corporate order in Southeast Asia

This book is concerned with the growth of large corporations in Southeast Asia, focusing on corporate organization, methods of financing, business environment and corporate governance. It seeks to understand their role in the dynamic growth of that region and those same factors that unleashed the crisis in 1997. The usefulness of such a study of large corporations is that it will assist in unravelling this rise and collapse within three decades. Although Radelet and Sachs attributed the crisis to volatile international financial markets, irrational speculation and contagion, this volume subscribes to the Krugman hypothesis of endogenous structural defects escalating into crisis.[1]

A detailed analysis of macro-economic growth is essential in understanding corporate development in the region. Agricultural growth, industrialization, levels of FDI, technology, R&D and competitive pressures all influence and are, in turn, affected by, patterns of corporate development and strategies.

In the late 1930s agricultural output accounted for more than half the national product in the major economies of Southeast Asia, except in Singapore. By 1960 this share of agriculture in GDP declined and by 1988 it accounted for less than 25 per cent of the GDP in the major ASEAN countries. Concurrently, manufacturing as a share of GDP rose from 9 per cent in 1965, to 32 per cent in 1990, in Malaysia; in Indonesia it was an increase from 8 per cent to 20 per cent, and 14 to 26 per cent in Thailand in the same years. With heavy inflow of FDI from the 1970s, the expansion in manufacturing was achieved more from capital investments, rather than from an increase in total factor productivity. FDI also had an impact on industrial restructuring, a move from labour-intensive to capital-intensive industrialization between the 1970s and the 1990s. This was accompanied by a defined increase in corporate growth, diversification and globalization. Corporate structures were critical in the selection of industry and appropriate markets. The Japanese model of diversification possessed clusters of competitive advantages in product selection, technology, capital accumulation and markets and was achieved through horizontal mergers as in the *keiretsu*. In contrast, Southeast Asian corporations sought diversification through vertical and horizontal subsidiaries, all managed by the family. Diversification was achieved through access to state contracts, licences and joint-venture relations with foreign multinationals. This internalization of growth, without a Chandlerian multi-divisional structure or a *keiretsu* meant firms with power in one industrial sector could move into all other unrelated sectors, through connections to the state. Costs of R&D and risks were often absorbed by the state. The monopolies that were erected, then mounted acquisitions and mergers with further soft loans from the state. Such factor accumulation both from the state and foreign capital had more impact on trade, regional division of labour, labour productivity and technology transfer but less on corporate efficiency.

Market liberalization from the late 1980s was not releasing competitive pressures. Privatization, too, changed little of the existing oligopolistic corporate structures. Public monopolies frequently became private monopolies. These changes in the economy, the increased role of foreign investment, the de-regulation, privatization, all should have been reflected in changes in corporate organization and, above all, on corporate governance. Instead, corporations became more concentrated in ownership, and amassed within specific industrial sectors. Tables 13.1–13.3 demonstrate the significance of FDI in investment growth.

This East Asian Model of rapid economic growth since 1960 was sustained by an export-led industrialization with huge capital inflows, both within an intra-Asian basin of investments, production and trade, as well as through global expansion westward. This model places corporate growth at the centre of this dramatic transformation. It is also aware of seething corporate volatility in this intensive growth and diversification. This emphasis on individual corporate case studies within a sharper, regional and issue-based analysis, is carefully structured to identify core institutions that shape both macro-economic growth and corporate evolution and change.

The emergence of these diversified corporations, their organizational structures and performance are delineated through individual country analysis. This is not to assert that each country did not possess distinct structural and environmental features, but only to identify some of the similarities. The internal and external dimensions of their specific growth are traced over a period of three decades, identifying particular cycles of growth or decline.

The focus is on ownership structure, the distribution of control and how they combine concentrated family ownership and control through corresponding densities of economic power in particular industrial sectors. This ownership concentration and economic concentration, distort competition, weakening internal and external corporate governance.

Concentrated family ownership was assisted by the creation of holding companies, controlling diverse subsidiaries specializing in various products and regional sectors. This pattern of corporate evolution is replicated throughout the region from the 1960s and even after the 1997 crisis.

Family-owned corporations were, ironically, the main beneficiaries of nationalization after decolonization in the 1950s. Though the state emerged

Table 13.1 FDI as a percentage of total investment

	1980	*1998*
Indonesia	1.0	–2.7
Malaysia	12.5	25.8
Philippines	–1.1	12.8
Thailand	2.0	24.7
Singapore	22.8	25.5

Source: Asian Development Bank, *Key Indicators for Developing Asian and Pacific Countries*, ADB, Manila, 2002

Table 13.2 FDI in ASEAN (US$ million)

	1989	*1996*	*1997*	*1998*	*1999*
Indonesia	682.0	6,194.0	4,677.0	–356.0	–2,745.0
Malaysia	1,667.9	5,078.0	5,136.5	2,163.4	1,552.9
Philippines	563.0	1,517.0	1,220.0	2,287.0	573.0
Thailand	1,775.5	2,335.9	3,894.7	7,315.0	6,213.0
Singapore	2,886.6	8,984.1	8,085.2	5,492.9	6,984.3

Source: World Bank, *World Development Indicators*, Washington, DC, 2002

Table 13.3 GDP growth rates (five-year averages in percentages)

	1970–4	*1975–9*	*1980–4*	*1985–9*	*1990–4*	*1995–9*
Indonesia	8.2	7.4	6.7	6.0	8.0	1.6
Malaysia	8.2	7.2	6.9	4.9	9.3	5.1
Philippines	5.4	6.2	1.3	2.7	1.9	3.6
Singapore	11.5	7.4	8.5	6.3	9.4	5.9
Thailand	7.1	8.0	5.6	9.0	9.0	1.4

Source: World Bank, *World Development Indicators*, Washington, DC, 2001; ADB, *Key Indicators for Developing Asian and Pacific Countries*, Manila, 2002

as a major economic player, it shared corporate wealth creation with existing private capitalists. With ISI and, later, export-oriented industrialization, competition was eschewed and oligopolies preferred in the belief that they were more efficient and achieved fast growth. From the mid-1980s privatization programmes were mooted as an indispensable route to improving productivity, attracting foreign capital and relevant technology. This structural transformation of SOEs in public utilities and manufacturing and their divestment led to these large family-dominated conglomerates absorbing these elite state corporations as well as banks.

The heavy influx of foreign capital from 1970s to the mid-1980s, when FDI from Japan and the US grew at an average rate of 21 per cent per annum, and accelerated further after 1987, reflected partial re-direction of manufacturing from Japan to Southeast Asia. The portfolio element of foreign investment increased in the 1990s; the primary targets were the stock market and real estate. This influx of foreign capital stimulated more corporate diversification into capital- and R&D-intensive sectors – into telecommunications and electronics. The final feature of this corporate transformation was its global expansion into East Asia, Central Asia and into the US and Europe. Between 1981 and 1995 trade between China and Southeast Asia increased tenfold and here the main beneficiaries were large private corporations.

Although diversified commercial–industrial structures were common in Japan (*zaibatsu* in pre-war period and later the *keiretsu*) and in Korea (*chaebols*), the Southeast Asian conglomerate was distinctive. First, *chaebols* possessed a tiny family ownership, as seen in Samsung. The Lee family held 100 per cent ownership of an unlisted firm, and used that to establish family ownership and control over other subsidiaries. This is similar to the holding company in Southeast Asia. The Japanese *zaibatsu* and, later, the *keiretsu*, held interlocking ownership with reduced family stake and managerial control.

Second, the Japanese conglomerate included banks, insurance companies and trusts, linked to the industrial and commercial subsidiaries in the group. Southeast Asian conglomerates possessed banks and financial institutions, but there was a difference. Japanese banks held shares in the non-financial subsidiaries and sought to monitor the activities of the group. Within the Southeast Asian group, the ownership was centralized in one major shareholder, often the founding family, and monitoring was difficult. The *chaebols* had owned banks in the late 1950s but banking was renationalized in 1961 and the *chaebols* were banned from retail banking. They then established merchant banks, securities units and insurance firms. However, this distinctiveness was eroded by the early 1980s with the privatization of banks. The *chaebols* throughout had access to government-directed credit and credit from Japanese and American banks.[2]

The third difference between the Southeast Asian conglomerate and the East Asian corporation is the nature of the relationship to the state. Although the *chaebols* exhibited the strong government–business partnership, as in the Southeast Asian case, there is a difference.[3] The democratic reforms in Korea in 1987 changed the existing collusive ties. There was increasing disengagement by the state with large business, and the revival of state power corresponded with economic de-regulation and financial liberalization. This pushed the *chaebols* to seek markets overseas.[4]

In contrast, de-regulation and financial liberalization in Southeast Asia intensified state–business links from 1989. This undeviating, unswerving state patronage remained both at home and abroad. Globalization presented no serious rupture.

The major theoretical contribution of this volume has been an analysis of the concentrated nature of corporate structure and the impact on corporate governance. First, the high concentration of ownership and management by the family distorted the transparency of corporations and accountability of controlling shareholders and managers. The high levels of industrial concentration, and the privileged relationship with the state, meant there was little incentive to change. The non-competitive market structure for these large conglomerates made few demands for improved efficiency. Focus is on growth.

Second, the financial institutions, the banks and the stock market are important extensions of this type of growth. The risks the conglomerate confronted were located principally in their relationship to banks and financial institutions in the group. The links introduced structural weaknesses in the high levels of connected lending, in high debt-equity ratios and the lack of financial supervision, and thereby confused the measures aimed at financial liberalization introduced in the late 1980s. The spill-over effects of this confused the relationship between non-financial and financial units in the group. This increased risk of a misallocation of financial resources was heightened by government guarantees. This moral hazard is clear from all the country studies in this volume.

The corporate vulnerability marked during the 1997 crisis was associated with high debt from banks within the group and borrowing from abroad. Such dependence was present since the mid-1980s but it was the financial liberalization that exposed the economies to speculative attacks and instability. Weak regulation and lack of prudent supervision further destabilized these highly leveraged corporations.

The book also explores the ways in which the region's stock exchanges have determined which industrial and commercial initiatives have found favour and led to a concentration of ownership and monopolistic power. The broad reshaping of corporate finance through the stock exchanges coincided with detailed changes in corporate structures, the creation of holding companies, integrating newly acquired firms into large MNEs with global ambitions. This rapid growth in economic diversification and globalization was coordinated through large inflows of foreign capital into the region from the 1970s. The effects of large concentrated positions of portfolio capital in targeting specific sectors of the economy (property, finance and currency markets), their herding and manipulative activities not only increased speculation but assisted in creating large, diversified corporations in Southeast Asia that were reluctant to specialize because diversification provided revenues, reduced risks and concealed problems of quality. They were also confident to mount global initiatives while lacking technological and innovative experience. Thus, Renong (Malaysia), Salim (Indonesia) and Shinawatra (Thailand) expanded into Vietnam, Cambodia, China, Bangladesh, India, Uzbekistan, South Africa, Australia and Uruguay in telecommunications, the hotel industry, infrastructural growth, finance and petroleum refining.

This book has sought to study the behaviour of the portfolio and direct investment that sustained the globalization of Southeast Asian corporations.

Within this portfolio capital, two important issues had to be disentangled. Who are the providers of long-term portfolio capital, as distinct from the short-term portfolio investors? The source of this portfolio investment in equities, bonds and derivatives is central to clarifying the background to the institutions responsible for the expansion and volatility of the stock market and, ultimately, the instability of the corporate economy.

Moreover, an important development in the 1980s and 1990s was the move towards aggressive takeovers, assisted by the state, by the inflows of foreign capital and the boom in stock markets across Asia, with serious implications for the concentration of ownership, as well as changes in the treatment of minority shareholders. This frantic wave of merger activity, though subdued briefly in 1997, was encouraged by the government from 1998 as part of the successful restructuring of failed corporations. Thus, this volume concentrates on understanding in detail how regional governments in Southeast Asia have responded to the crisis and undertaken the necessary financial and corporate restructuring.

In addition, the presence of government intervention in Southeast Asia's stock markets and their coteries of crony capitalists have important implications for the pricing of IPOs and the creation of crony capitalism, since the share issues are targeted at specific client groups, particularly in Malaysia, Thailand, the Philippines and Indonesia. This under-pricing of new issues by the Malaysian government to improve investment opportunities has attracted short-term speculators, and adds to the risk and volatility of the stock exchanges in the region. This is not a study of efficient markets but is one that seeks principally to identify the major actors in the stock exchanges and stock behaviour over the 1980s and 1990s. Again, the focus of attention is on the impact it had on corporate growth and corporate governance.

As a direct consequence of the dominance of government, bureaucrats and major capitalists in the stock exchanges of Southeast Asia, their impact on stock market behaviour is clear. Information is available and taken advantage of. Hence, the complex, intricate relationships of these government and crony shareholders has intrinsic value both in identifying patterns of probable insider-trading, as well as close interlocking ties between major business groups listed on the stock exchanges and the state, adding to corporate concentrations. This explains, in part, the meteoric rise of hitherto unknown capitalists in Malaysia, Indonesia, Thailand and the Philippines in this period.

The increase in stock market capitalization is particularly pronounced between 1990 and 1994. Malaysia experienced an increase from US$48.6 billion in 1990 to US$199.3 billion in 1994. Indonesia saw an increase from US$8.1 billion to US$47.2 billion between 1990 and 1994. The Philippines witnessed a growth from US$5.9 billion to US$55.5 billion in the same years. Singapore had a growth from US$34.3 billion to US$134.5 billion, and Thailand grew with an increase from US$23.9 billion to US$131.5 billion. In comparison, Japan's stock market rose slightly from US$2,917.7

billion to US$3,719.9 billion.[5] This increase in listing was fuelled by the explosion in portfolio capital and by an increase in corporate bonds.

Another major factor for the growth of the stock market in the period after 1986 was the privatization of SOEs. The privatization of state corporations in large infrastructural projects in road, rail and telecommunications involved the flotation of new and existing companies, absorbing some of the huge inflows of FDI and portfolio investment in the period. These privatized firms also exploited the rising demand for equity-related derivatives – swaps, options, equity warrants, futures, forwards etc. Yet, ownership remained with the select individuals and family and state institutional holdings. This new founding group reinforced their ownership further through rights issues and bonus issues. Wide public shareholding was limited in these newly privatized corporations. Hence, the increased participation on the stock market was not reproduced in any visible ownership restructuring. This is clear in all the major corporations studied in this volume. Even the mergers and acquisitions merely intensified the existing ownership, creating larger concentrated enterprises. The 1997 crisis did introduce reforms that involved institutional changes. However, many of such corporate changes were to save the firms rather than create greater transparency.

The sale of unrelated divisions and units paved the way for a focused strategy, but it still did not create the sharper, focused integration that could have shaped the highly diversified industrial conglomeration. Both before and after the 1997 crisis, the stock market was the instrument used by powerful capitalists to diversify into the hi-tech and R&D- and capital-intensive sector. No real discipline in resource allocation was necessary since the state and foreign partner provided capital, R&D and guarantees both on contracts and markets.

There was a palpable increase after 1997 in foreign equity in these large, listed corporations in the region, with many foreign partners accepting debt swaps for equity participation. In Indonesia and Thailand there is a substantial increase in outsiders participating on the stock market, both foreign institutional and multinational groups. There was an increase in intra-regional investment by Singapore, exploiting the potential in the restructuring of failing banks and corporations in Indonesia, Thailand and even in Malaysia.

This rescue and recapitalization of failing banks and industrial corporations after 1997 introduced an interesting dimension to stock market activities. Since the initial rescue was in a period of imperfect information on NPLs, much of the equity purchases by foreign investors were in convertible financial instruments which provided greater security in a volatile environment, before a sharper judgement could be made on profitability. This interim measure did not need managerial changes.[6]

These regional stock markets had already been associated with an increase in takeovers and mergers since the early 1980s. This then involved restructuring through multiple holding companies and mergers of related subsidiaries. Growth in scale and scope resulted. The issuing of new stock, raising money for new and diverse financial instruments added to the debt burden. This volume of new shares grew, particularly between 1990 and 1993.

Acquiring new firms, tapping into new markets and new products, led to listings on multiple stock exchanges in the region and in Hong Kong and in the US. However, the overriding impression of the stock markets in Southeast Asia is that active trading is often limited to a small number of elite stocks – SingTel, Telekom Malaysia and Indosat. These large issues crowded out other private issues. Even with privatization, shares available for public purchase were limited.

The importance of foreign capital for these regional stock exchanges was not only for an increase in active trading of shares but also in prospects for monitoring performance, and for rigorous corporate governance. Inversely, when secondary trading rose with venture capital participation after 1989, increases in volatility were inevitable. Surges of portfolio capital targeted the stock market and real estate, adding to this volatility.

Another obsessive theme here is that institutional shareholding, which could have provided stability, in fact, lacked autonomy and was also small. Principal institutional investors were from the state, political parties, the military, pension funds and, after 1997, insurance groups and investment groups belonging to foreign multinationals. In Malaysia, institutional investment groups belonged to state and to an ethnic group (*bumiputra*), and its main aim was achieving economic redistribution in favour of *bumiputras*. This institutional shareholding thus did not seek nor achieve financial prudence. An ill-disciplined culture of financial indulgence permeated them, contributing to magnificent failures such as Renong and Arab – Malaysia Bank in 1998.

The extent of this institutional shareholding in Malaysia and Singapore is difficult to unravel because of the interlocks between these several institutional groups. Adam and Cavendish provide estimates on institutional holdings that are very high, equal to almost 70 per cent of total equity, while individual stakes accounted for only 19 per cent on the KLSE between 1987 and 1992.[7]

My perception is that this was constantly changing; by 1991 single family ownership was rising. The interlocking holdings of Halim Saad, Tajuddin Ramli, Azman Hashim, Mirzan Mahatir, Vincent Tan and Quek Leng Chan were large. Malaysian institutional shareholding distorted the stock market by securing low-priced IPOs, which were sold below value to *bumiputra* institutional shareholding groups, such as PNB, ASN and ASB. In 1990 this under-pricing of IPOs of 14 SOEs may have amounted to a loss of 4.25 billion ringgit.[8]

The majority of the corporations covered in this volume reveal high debt-equity ratio, concentrated ownership and rapid diversification. They use size and diversified growth as a proxy for this fundamental risk of high debt burdens. This risk is further aggravated by the organizational devices used by the family firms to go public, without losing control. The use of holding companies, listing some, not others, switching between listing and private ownership and maintaining 100 per cent family-owned investment companies – all this complicated the corporate landscape and impaired corporate governance.

The stock market, its share prices and dividend payments were not always efficient indicators for predicting the value of the firm. Firm size and political contacts bestowed higher status. Only the 1997 crisis exposed the true debt position. The market is not efficient in the short term. It does even out when better information becomes available. These inherent difficulties partly explain why the stock markets in Southeast Asia were never a critical source of corporate finance. Retained earnings, followed by bank loans, then equity, were the predominant patterns of finance, both before and after 1997.

Corporate governance was characterized by a concentrated ownership, tight insider control with weak monitoring in an environment of weak legal infrastructure and weak implementation. The Board of Directors lacked sufficient number of independent directors, and there were few limits on interlocking directorships. Even in Singapore where corporate governance disclosures and practices were higher than elsewhere, an elite corps of technocrats and politicians dominated the management of the large corporations there.

In fact, the separation of CEO and Chairman was more rigorously pursued in Malaysia, in comparison with Singapore, while Thailand maintained greater independence on the corporation's Board of Directors after 1997. There were, throughout Southeast Asia, restrictions on the use of nominees in ownership but there were difficulties in implementation.

Audits were pursued with greater vigour after 1998, with increased communications with shareholders. Improved investor relations included regular reports, websites and surveys with an increased use of technology. The annual general meeting was regularly scheduled, but minority shareholders were largely absent. Senior management and owners made the decisions. This lack of separation between strategic planning and operational decision-making made this over-centralized ownership and management untenable, confusing growth, as well as capital allocation and allowing occasional fraud; the only exception, where despite such concentrated ownership fraud was inconceivable, was in Singapore, though there too, Sinar Mas did indulge in a cleverly hatched swindle through listings in Singapore, China and New York, in 1994 (see Chapter 2). It is this weak corporate governance and weak financial regulation that were perceived by Montes as the primary reasons for the distress in 1997.[9]

Krugman hints at crony capitalism as the major cause of this meltdown.[10] These enduring influences of business–state relationships are captured in all the regional studies in this volume. The long and tenacious relationship of these large corporations to the state encouraged factor accumulation rather than efficiency. The state is a critical force in development but it must promote competition not provide a perfect patronage.

Throughout, the analysis is historical. A micro-analysis of state–business relations is attempted through detailed historical case studies, balanced within the larger institutional environment. It assesses the importance of cronyism in business contracts, decision-making, and the interpenetration of the bureaucracy, politicians and military within the corporate sector, either through board representations, or ownership and management. The reform of such cronyistic links, attempted after 1997, involved independent audits, reduction of interlocking shareholding between firms, loosening state ties, improvement in insolvency laws and easing corporations into a regulated infrastructure. Implementation of such real change remains uncertain.

One aspect of this cronyism is captured in the privatization pacts of the late 1980s and early 1990s. Since 1983 there was an increasing awareness that SOEs were inefficient and a redistribution of ownership was essential to attract foreign capital and technology. This led to the establishment of crucial committees empowered to produce guidelines for the divestment of state ownership of large public utilities in infrastructural programmes, telecommunication, electricity and water. Initiatives in privatization were launched in Malaysia in 1985, Singapore in 1986, the Philippines in 1987, and Indonesia and Thailand in 1989.

The methods of privatization were diverse. One strategy was to retain ownership by the state but to lease management of operations to the private sector. A second strategy was to seek private finance and operational skills through BOT (build, operate, transfer) and BT (build and transfer) schemes. A third involved joint-ventures between private enterprises and foreign multinationals, supported also by the state. A fourth tactic was to introduce competition into state monopolies. A fifth strategy was to create mergers or de-mergers between existing corporations, spinning off newly privatized units in that process.

In Thailand, failing SOEs were either sold or partial sectors of them were privatized. In the case of a capital-intensive project such as Bangkok Mass Transit System, there was a clear transfer of control and management. Equally in the Philippines, weak performers were sold. The Philippines National Bank was privatized by Aquino after it was defrauded by politicians and crony capitalists. The political uncertainties persisted even under Aquino and Ramos from 1983 to 1992 and led to the use of a variety of options to transfer ownership. These ranged from public auctions, direct debt–equity swaps and negotiated sales of airlines and other large enterprises. The transfers were ad hoc, benefiting those with access to network capital, such as ethnic Chinese in the Philippines. In Malaysia there were direct sales to political cronies who were attracted by the prospect of subsidized state credit, provision of technology, work guarantees, exchange rate assistance and a stable share of profits.

In the case of Singapore, divestment to government-dominated investment companies such as Temasek Holdings and MND holdings did not constitute any radical change of ownership from the state to private capitalists. Strategic industries such as defence and water, were retained by the state, while corporations in airlines, shipping, property and ports were privatized, though the state preserved a controlling stake. Thus, SingTel, the telecommunications group, had, after ten years of privatization, still revealed a government equity ownership of 83 per cent.

According to Claessens and others, the state held 10.2 per cent of the 100 top corporations and banks in Indonesia, 18.2 per cent in Malaysia, 23.6 per cent in Singapore, 7.5 per cent in Thailand and 3.6 per cent in the Philippines after privatization.[11] These figures cannot be strictly accurate since the state throughout Southeast Asia held both direct and indirect holdings through institutional groups, political parties and cronies. Both in Malaysia and Singapore the governments retained voting rights, allowing them a crucial veto on mergers, liquidation and global moves.

In Singapore the investment companies held major shareholdings as well as senior managerial positions. These investment companies, even after privatization, were managed by state-appointed technocrats and former Cabinet ministers. Political cronyism, which is rife in Indonesia, Thailand and the Philippines, also obscured the true extent of state holdings and influence. The use of nominee companies disguised and confused the true identity of the stakeholders.

The motive behind such large-scale privatization was to improve competition and efficiency. However, these newly privatized corporations were mainly monopolies, revealing high leverage and high debt burdens. This challenges the orthodoxy that privatization bequeaths greater competition and greater efficiency.[12]

In the case of Southeast Asia, privatization should have been accompanied by effective de-regulation and reforms in competition. Change in ownership is not sufficient to improve performance. Gains from privatization are derived from a combination of ownership changes, incentives for institutional reform, contractual issues, removal of artificial barriers to entry and exit in particular industrial sectors, and a legal framework supporting competition and corporate governance.

In the absence of these conditions, privatization merely deepened the embedded weaknesses within the corporate economy. The only notable success was in telecommunications. The industry possessed a natural monopoly and the rapid technological change ensured the emergence of powerful domestic telecommunication specialists. In Malaysia, Thailand, Singapore and the Philippines there were impressive increases in income between 1983 and 1997. There was improved operating efficiency, partly because of de-regulation but crucially because of increased inputs of technology. There was an increase in capital investment of 11.24 per cent between 1983 and 1997 in Malaysia.[13] Increases in fixed line subscriptions, increase in output in international traffic, productivity improvements and increase in R&D inputs, all followed this growth in capital investment.[14]

A final transition in this phase of ambitious privatization was for these regional monopolies to chart the takeover of related groups in Central Asia, Southeast Asia and South Africa. Their regional initiatives in Vietnam, Cambodia and Burma were more lucrative than their adventures into Uzbekistan and Kazakhstan.[15]

These third world multinationals saw the rise of China and Central Asia as an opportunity for growth. They invested in both capital- and labour-intensive industries in China, Uzbekistan, India and even the US and Europe. They faced operational and legal difficulties besides serious competitive pressures from Japanese, Korean, Taiwanese as well as Western multinationals. This transformation into third world multinationals is occurring while corporations are strictly family owned.

One of the major debates in business history has been the alleged failure of British personal capitalism to transform into managerial capitalism with a clear separation of ownership from control.[16] How does Southeast Asia fit into this debate? This volume clearly demonstrates that they are totally committed to personal capitalism.

Personal capitalism remains triumphant in Southeast Asia as it has been for much of the modern period. That triumph has not been disturbed, despite the emergence by the 1970s of state and institutional share ownership. Scale and scope of industrial production, too, has conformed to this continuity in personal capitalism. This is not a culturally induced differentiation but a development shaped by complex interactions between these business dynasties, the state and foreign capital, in a resource-rich environment where no constellation or web of institutional investors can usurp the pre-eminence of these capitalist barons. The commitment to personal capitalism is, ironically, assisted by the state, institutional shareholders and foreign multinationals.

In contrast, British capitalists had, by the last decade of the nineteenth century, accepted that growth and innovation could only be guaranteed through a radical transformation in ownership, structure and strategy. They had moved to a more diversified form of ownership with powerful, dispersed institutional shareholding held by financial institutions, banks, insurance houses and, later, by pension funds.[17]

Southeast Asian capitalists confronted no obstacles to this presentation of personal capitalism and made no compromises. They held a clear vision that harnessing new finance, new organizational structures, new forms of acquisition of R&D and new patterns of operational management could secure the permanence of this personal capitalism.

The Japanese corporate system with the main bank emerged as a decentralized formation with *kigyo shudan* firms, joined by a web of cross-shareholdings.[18] *Sogo Shosha* trading firms joined these banking, trade and marketing networks. Family remained a shadowy figure. In the Southeast Asian model, preservation of family enterprise was sacrosanct. Chains of state and investment groups, including the World Bank and IMF, participated to facilitate family groups to operate across a range of industries and regions. Privatization and economic de-regulation did not mark a transition to a market-oriented model but merely offered more opportunities for the growth of personal capitalism.

This system of capital mobilization and the embeddedness of personal capitalism is thus complex. Abstractions of culture and cultural idealizations may prove only a distraction.

Notes

1 Introduction

1 Eduardo D. Roca, *Price Interdependence Among Equity Markets in the Asia Pacific Region, Focus on Australia and ASEAN*, Aldershot: Ashgate, 2000, pp. 82–3.
2 A. Shleifer and Vishny, R. 'The limits of arbitrage', *Journal of Finance*, 52, 1997, pp. 35–55. Andrei Shleifer, *Inefficient Markets: An Introduction to Behavioural Finance*, Oxford: Oxford University Press, 2000.
3 J. A. Schumpeter, *Capitalism, Socialism and Democracy*, London: Unwin University Books, 1943.
4 Moha Asri Abdullah, 'An overview of the macroeconomic contribution of small and medium enterprise in Malaysia', in Charles Harvie and Boon-Chye Lee (eds), *The Role of SMEs in National Economies in East Asia*, Cheltenham: Edward Elgar, 2002, pp. 182–204.
5 Ibid., pp. 188–9.
6 Harvie and Lee, *The Role of SMEs in National Economies in East Asia*, pp. 32–5.
7 Stijn Claessens *et al.*, 'How does foreign entry affect the domestic banking market?', *World Bank Working Paper*, May 1998. Stijn Claessens *et al.*, 'The separation of ownership and control in East Asian corporations', *Journal of Financial Economics*, 58, 2000, pp. 81–112.
8 Paul D. Hutchcroft, *Booty Capitalism: The Politics of Banking in the Philippines*, Ithaca, NY: Cornell University Press, 1998. Richard Robison, *Indonesia: The Rise of Capital*, St Leonard: Allen & Unwin, 1986. E. T. Gomez and Jomo K. S., *Malaysia's Political Economy: Politics, Patronage, and Profits*, Cambridge: Cambridge University Press, 2nd edn, 1999. Yoshihara K., *The Nation and Economic Growth: The Philippines and Thailand*, Singapore: Oxford University Press, 1994. Ruth T. McVey (ed.) *South East Asian Capitalists*, Ithaca, NY: Cornell South East Asia Program, 1992. Yoshihara K., *The Rise of Ersatz Capitalism in South East Asia*, Singapore: Oxford University Press, 1988.
9 See Brown, 2000, conclusion.
10 Wang Gungwu, *Trade and Cultural Values: Australia and the Four Dragons*, Sydney: Asian Studies Association of Australia, 1988. Suehiro Akira, *Capital Accumulation in Thailand 1885–1985*, Tokyo: East Asian Cultural Studies, 1989. Wang Gungwu, *Don't Leave Home: Migration and the Chinese*, Singapore Times Academic Press, 2001.
11 Sato Yuri, 'The Astra Group: a pioneer of management modernization in Indonesia', *The Developing Economies*, 34, 3, 1996. Sato Yuri, 'The Salim Group in Indonesia: the development and behaviour of the largest conglomerate in SE Asia', *The Developing Economies*, 31, 4, 1993, pp. 408–41.

2 Indonesian conglomerates

1 Hal Hill, *Indonesia's Industrial Transformation*, Singapore: ISEAS, 1997, pp. 46–317. Kelly Bird, 'Concentration in Indonesian Manufacturing, 1975–93', *Bulletin of Indonesian Economic Studies*, 35, 1, 1999, p. 57.
2 In 1993–7, two-thirds of large Indonesian corporations were held by a single family: the public stake was a meagre 1–5 per cent: ICMD, 1992–8.
3 On the whole, privatization was not successful, although some Chinese conglomerates and the family benefited from it.
4 Bapepam (Badan Pelaksana Pasar Modal (Capital Market Supervisory Agency)), *Annual Reports*, 1990–5. See also David George McKendrick, 'Acquiring technological capabilities: aircraft and commercial banking in Indonesia', Ph.D. thesis, University of California at Berkeley, 1989, p. 2.
5 Indonesian Securities, Clearing and Depository Institutions Periodic Report, September 1995, p. 6.
6 For more details on BCA, see Chapter 3.
7 Philippe F. Delhaise, *Asia in Crisis: Implosion of the Banking and Finance Systems*, Singapore: John Wiley Asia, 1998, p. 130. See also Baring Securities, *Report on P. T. Astra International*, 1996, p. 6.
8 Infobank 1995, p.26, cited in Ross H. McLeod and Ross Garnaut (eds), *East Asia in Crisis: From Being a Miracle to Needing One?*, London: Routledge, 1998, p. 295.
9 In July 1997, the Jakarta Stock Exchange sent a second warning because of four mistakes made in buying own shares and transactions on affiliated shares. If it made another mistake, the group would be delisted. Director Charles de Queljoe resigned in February 1998. *Indonesian Capital Market Directory 2002*, p. 550.
10 Badan Koordinasi Penanaman Modal (BKPM) (Capital Investment Coordinating Board). Republik Indonesia, Trend of Investments, August 1987–99.
11 Ibid. Mohammad Rosul, 'Coping with capital flows and the monetary policy framework: the case of Indonesia', in C. H. Kwan, Donna Vandenbrink and Chia Siow Yue (eds), *Coping with Capital Flows in East Asia*, Singapore: Nomura Research Institute and Institute of Southeast Asian Studies, 1998, p. 246.
12 Hal Hill, 'Indonesia: the strange and sudden death of a tiger economy', *Oxford Development Studies*, 28, 2, 2000, p. 92.
13 IFC, *1998 Factbook*, Washington, DC, Emerging Markets Data Base, 1998. Bank Indonesia, *Indonesia Financial Statistics 2002*. Siregar, A., 'Demokratisasi dan Ekonomi Pasar' (Democratization and the market economy), *Warta Ekonomi*, 2000.
14 BKPM, Trend of Investment Approvals and Permanent Licences, 1989–99, *Annual Report 1999*, pp. 9–61. Badan Pengawas Pasar Modal (Indonesian Capital Market), *Annual Reports*, 1990–9. Jakarta Stock Exchange, *Factbook*, 1989–95.
15 BKPM, August 1997–2003, Jakarta Stock Exchange pp. 16–61. *Report on P. T. Astra International*, 1996, Jakarta Baring Securities.
16 BKPM, *Annual Report*, 1990, p. 5.
17 Bapepam, *Annual Reports*, 1990–3.
18 BKPM, August 1990–2003.
19 Ibid.
20 Ibid.
21 Moody Investors Service, Global Credit Research, 24 October 1997, teleconference proceedings, 'The impact of market turmoil in SE Asia and Korea on Japanese banks and other financial institutions, October 1997'.
22 Bank Indonesia and Central Bureau of Statistics, *Annual Reports*, 1990–2000.
23 Mergers and acquisitions by foreign MNEs increased FDI value from US$36 million in 1998 to US$1,441 million in 2000. BKPM, August 1997–August 2003.

24 Indocement, *Annual Report*, 2000, p. 16.
25 Astra International, *Annual Report*, 2000. A consortium led by Cycle and Carriage won the tender, offering 39.5 per cent equity for US$506 million to be paid to BPPN (IBRA). This was equivalent to Rp3.77 trillion, to cover part of the debt owed to IBRA of Rp5.59 trillion. Sales of other subsidiaries to cover the remaining debt (US$160 million) were due in 2000.
26 Bank Indonesia statistics, 1997–2001. These are only crude estimates, since even Bank Indonesia does not possess accurate statistics on capital outflows. IFC statistics may be more accurate, but even that is not certain.
27 ING Barings, Indonesia Stock Market Review, May 2000, Report on Tirtamas Concern. Also see IBRA, July 2002 monthly, 28th edition, p. 2, and *Koran Tempo*, 19 October 2001.
28 FPH 1990–5, *Consolidated Profit and Loss Accounts.*
29 FPH, *Annual Report and Consolidated Financial Statement*, 15 May 1995.
30 Ibid.
31 Ibid.
32 McKendrick, 'Acquiring technological capabilities', p. 394; Yuri Sato, 'The Salim Group in Indonesia: the development and behaviour of the largest conglomerate in South-East Asia', *The Developing Economies*, 31, 4, 1993, p. 417. Salim Group accounts, contained in FPH, *Annual Report*, 15 May 1995.
33 IBRA, *Monthly Report*, April 2000, December 2000. See also *International Herald Tribune*, 17 May 1999.
34 Indonesian Cement Association Reports, 1994–2001.
35 Ibid.
36 IBRA, *Monthly Report*, 1, April 2000, p. 2.
37 Indocement Tunggal Prakarsa, *Annual Report*, 29 December 2000. (Independent auditor A. Anderson and Prasetio Utomo and Co.) The Indocement sale in May 2001 involved a rights issue, debt to equity swap, and option rights.
38 P. T. Semen Gresik, *Annual Report*, 31 December 2001.
39 Ibid.
40 Semen Gresik, *Annual Report*, December 1996–December 2000.
41 IBRA, *Monthly Report*, 28th edition, July 2002, p. 2. See also Kees van Dijk, *A Country in Despair: Indonesia between 1997 and 2000*, Leiden: KITLV Press, 2000, p. 415.
42 IBRA, *Monthly Report*, May 2000, p. 2; Semen Cibinong, *Annual Report and Consolidated Financial Statement*, 31 December 1994–5 (Prasetio Utomo), 31 December 1995–6 (Prasetio Utomo), 2000–1 (Deloitte Touche Tohmatsu), 2001–2 (Deloitte Touche Tohmatsu).
43 Institute of Economic and Financial Research, *Indonesian Capital Market Directory*, 2002, p. 76.
44 Indofood Sukses Makmur, *Consolidated Financial Statement*, 1998–2000.
45 IBRA, *Monthly Report*, 12, March 2001, pp. 1–2; 14, May 2001, p. 1.
46 IBRA, *Monthly Report*, 21, December 2001, p. 2.
47 IBRA, *Monthly Report*, 9, December 2000, p. 1.
48 Ibid.
49 IBRA, *Monthly Report*, 12, March 2001.
50 Ibid., p. 2.
51 ICMD, pp. 546, 548 for Bhakti Capital Indonesia.
52 Ibid.
53 The Oversight Committee for IBRA (Komite Pemantau Pelaksanaan Tugas, BPPN), September 2000.
54 ICMD, 2002, p. 556.
55 Singapore Exchange Ltd., *Companies Handbook 2001*, part 2, pp. 541–3.

56 Ibid.
57 IBRA, *Monthly Report*, 6, September 2000, pp. 1–2.
58 Ibid.
59 IBRA, *Monthly Report*, 16, July 2001, p. 3.
60 *China Foreign Economic Statistical Yearbook*, Beijing: China Statistics Press, 2002, pp. 117–221. See also Curt Weldon, *The China Connection*, Washington, DC, December 2003.
61 Singapore Exchange Ltd., *Companies Handbook*, p. 542.
62 Jim Erickson and Keith Loveard, 'Hot-noodle take-away', *Asiaweek*, 8 January 2004.
63 Law of the Republic of Indonesia, No. 5, 5 March 1999, Prohibition against Monopolistic Practices and Unfair Business Competition.
64 IBRA, *Monthly Report*, 34, January 2003, p. 2.
65 Ibid. Indah Kiat, Pulp and Paper (IKPP), *Annual Report*, Pulp and Paper, December 2001, December 2002.
66 IKPP, *Consolidated Financial Statement*, 31 December 2000, 31 December 2001.
67 IKPP, *Consolidated Financial Statement*, 31 December 1999, 31 December 2000, 31 December 2001.
68 Ibid.
69 Tjiwi Kimia, *Annual Report*, 31 December 2001.
70 Tjiwi Kimia, *Directors' Reports and Consolidated Financial Statements*, December 1994–December 2000.
71 Ibid.
72 IBRA, *Monthly Report*, May 2001, p. 2.
73 Tjiwi Kimia, *Directors' Report and Financial Statements*, 31 December 1999–2001.
74 ICMD 2002, p. 182.
75 Tjiwi Kimia, *Directors' Report and Financial Statements*, 31 December 2000–December 2001.
76 ICMD, 1998, volume 1, pp. 88–9.
77 The Oversight Committee Report in June 2003, of debt restructuring of December 2002 of APP's US$6.5 billion.
78 APP, *Financial Statement for Year ending 31 December 1997*, pp. 4–5.
79 APP, *Financial Statement*, 31 December 1997, p. 4; 31 December 1999, p. 6.
80 US Securities and Exchange Commission 1999, *Prospectus, Asia Pulp and Paper Co.*, File 333–12554, 26 April 1999.
81 Ibid.
82 Ibid.
83 APP, *Financial Statement*, December 1999, pp. 12–13.
84 Ibid.
85 This was part of a value-added production strategy, distinguished from Tjiwi Kimia, which focused on the domestic market and the Asian export market, while production in China was for the Australian, American and European markets. In Indonesia, the advantages for the group were that it was allowed to defer taxes, had access to cheap timber (because of low royalties) and it enjoyed tariff incentives.
86 IBRA, *Monthly Report*, 15, June 2001, p. 2; 33, December 2002, p. 1.
87 The Oversight Committee Report in June 2003 of the debt restructuring of December 2002 of APP, pp. 2–3.
88 Ibid. IBRA, June 2003, p. 4.
89 IBRA, *Monthly Report*, 21, December 2001, p. 1.
90 Money-Laundering Crimes Law, 15, 17 April 2002.
91 The Oversight Committee Report in June 2003 of debt restructuring of December 2002 of APP, pp. 2–3.

92 Chip Dillon and Norman Waite, 'Asia Pulp and Paper IQ deceptive: earnings power still strong', Saloman Smith Barney, 1 July 1998.
93 Charles C. Spencer *et al.*, 'Asia Pulp and Paper: well-positioned for Asia's recovery', Morgan Stanley Dean Witter, 28 June 1999.
94 Andy Choi, Charles Spencer and Nira Tanoko, 'Asia Pulp and Paper: here comes the cash flow!', Morgan Stanley Dean Witter, 12 November 1999.
95 US Securities and Exchange Commission 1999, *Prospectus, Asia Pulp and Paper Co.*, File 333–12554, 26 April 1999.
96 Oversight Committee, June 2003, op. cit.
97 IBRA, *Monthly Report*, March 2000. The APP report for 1999 appeared only after pressure from the NYSEC. The report of 6 April 1999 was incomplete.
98 US Securities and Exchange Commission 1999, *Prospectus, Asia Pulp and Paper*, 26 April 1999; Oversight Committee, June 2003, op. cit.; Ben Dolven and Sara Webb, 'Pulp fiction', *Far Eastern Economic Review*, 14 February 2002; Ruben David, 'Asia Pulp and Paper Co Ltd.', P T Nomura Indonesia, 24 August 2000; Lee Dennis, 'Asia Pulp and Paper: coping with growing pains', ABN-AMRO, 30 January 2001.
99 See ICMD, 1990–2002, BOD BOC shareholding structure for the different members of the family. Even after the delisting of APP in Singapore and New York, family control was retained.
100 IBRA, *Monthly Report*, June 2000, p. 2. Agreement of 2 November 2001, in *Monthly Report*, December 2001, p. 1.
101 IBRA, *Monthly Report*, 38, May 2003, pp. 1–2.
102 Ibid. IBRA, *Monthly Report*, 43, October 2003, pp. 1–2.
103 IBRA, *Monthly Report*, 46, January 2004, p. 2.
104 Indonesian Financial Sector, *Monthly Report*, 40, December 2003.
105 Financial Debt Restructuring, October 2002, Bank Mandiri Agreement with Indah Kiat Pulp and Paper, Tjiwi Kimia.
106 See Texmaco Jaya, *Annual Report*, December 2000–December 2001, prepared by auditors Grant Thornton and Hendrawinata.
107 Indorama Synthetics, *Annual Reports*, 1996–9. Indorama Synthetics was one of Indonesia's largest producers of polyester, established in 1974. Sixty-six per cent of its production was exported to the European Union, Australia and the US. The Lohia family control and manage the firm. It has equity holdings by IFC.
108 Hal Hill, *Indonesia's Industrial Transformation*, Singapore: Institute of Southeast Asian Studies, 1997, 83–121.
109 Peter Van Diermen, *Small Business in Indonesia*, Aldershot: Ashgate, 1997, pp. 69–70.
110 Texmaco Jaya, *Annual Report and Consolidated Financial Statement*, December 2001–December 2003.
111 IBRA, *Monthly Report*, July 2000, p. 2.
112 Oversight Committee (KPPT), September 2000, pp. 1–2.
113 Oversight Committee to IBRA, July 2000 Report, p. 5.
114 IBRA, *Monthly Report*, 37, April 2003, pp. 2–3.
115 Ibid.
116 IBRA, *Monthly Report*, 39, June 2003, p. 2. Annual Reports of Polysindo Eka Perkasa and Texmaco Perkasa Engineering, 1999–2003.
117 Kees van Dijk, *A Country in Despair*, pp. 485, 509, 528.
118 Ibid.
119 Ibid., pp. 486–8. For more details on the Tanri Abeng episode, see Kees van Dijk, *A Country in Despair*, pp. 419–20, 486–8, and *Forum Keadilan*, 6 April 1998, p. 16.

120 Ibid., pp. 424, 485–6, 531. See also *Jakarta Post*, 7 August 1999. Kwik Kian Gie was State Minister for Development, and Planning Chairman of BAPPENAS. Glen Yusuf was the Chairman of BPPN in August 1998. The English name for BPPN is IBRA, the Indonesian Bank Restructuring Agency. Bambang Subianto had been Chairman of IBRA, and he became Minister of Finance under Habibie. Tanri Abeng was Minister for Efficiency of State Companies in April 1998.

121 Amendment to Law on Bankruptcy Government Regulation No. 1, 22 April 1998.

122 Kees van Dijk, *A Country in Despair*, p. 528; *Far Eastern Economic Review*, 19 October 2000, p. 76. Abdurrahman Wahid had negotiated a private deal to allow Sinivasan, Nursalim and Prajogo Pangestu to continue with their business despite the massive debts.

123 Restructuring of SOE, Law No. 19, June 2003; Law No. 5, March 1999; and Law No. 30 of 2000, were all part of this effort to improve competition and corporate governance.

124 Statement by Mark Baird, Country Director World Bank, at the JITF/IBRA Conference on Corporate Debt Restructuring, 2 November 2000.

125 Montreevat and Hew, 'Commercial bank lending and restructuring in the ASEAN countries', in Nick Freeman (ed.), *Financing South East Asia's Economic Development*, Singapore: ISEAS, 2003, pp. 60–96.

126 See Pangestu and Habir, 'The boom, bust, and restructuring of Indonesian banks', in Gordon de Brouwer (ed.), *Financial Markets and Policies in East Asia*, London: Routledge, 2002, pp. 122–56.

127 Ibid., p. 145.

128 IBRA, *Monthly Report*, January 2004, p. 2.

129 Kees van Dijk, *A Country in Despair*, pp. 251–3, 403–4.

130 The Corporate Debt Restructuring Committee successfully completed the restructuring of 19 companies involving debt of Rm14.1 billion. Restructuring of another 25 involved Rm16.2 billion. The banks were restructured by Danamodal, which invested Rm5.3 billion in ten banks.

131 Kees van Dijk, *A Country in Despair*, pp. 424–46, 484–6, 489–92.

132 Ibid., pp. 424–45, 429, 531.

133 *Tempo*, 24 October 1999; *Panji Masyarakat*, 27 October 1999; *Jakarta Post*, 16 September 1999; *Kompas*, 2 November 2000; *Forum Keadilan*, 27 February 2000.

134 There was serious corruption in Bank Bali, where Djaja Ramli and three other directors of the bank were arrested in December 1999. Consequently, Standard Chartered withdrew, removing its equity from the bank.

135 Kees van Dijk, *A Country in Despair*, pp. 485, 509, 528.

136 Ibid.

137 See William Mako, 'Corporate restructuring and reform: lessons from Korea', Paper presented at the Conference on the Korean Crisis and Recovery, Seoul, 18 May 2001.

138 Hal Hill, 'Indonesia: the strange and sudden death of a tiger economy', pp. 99–101.

3 Irrational exuberance

1 Pierre-Richard Agénor, Marcus Miller, David Vines and Axel Weber (eds), *The Asian Financial Crisis: Causes, Contagion and Consequences*, Cambridge: Cambridge University Press, 1999; Gordon de Brouwer and Wisarn Pupphavesa (eds), *Asia Pacific Financial Deregulation*, London: Routledge, 1999; Stephanie

Griffith Jones, Manuel F. Montes and Anwar Nasution (eds), *Short-term Capital Flows and Economic Crisis*, Oxford: Oxford University Press, 2001. Nasution's chapter 'Capital inflows and policy responses: the case of Indonesia in the 1990s', pp. 117–43, covers only the period 1990–4, neglecting the period 1994–96 which is the most critical phase in determining how portfolio inflows distorted the financial system. The neglect of this crucial period affects the entire analysis. See also Masayoshi Tsurumi (ed.), *Financial Big Bang in Asia*, Aldershot: Ashgate, 2001; Sebastian Edwards, *Capital Flows and the Emerging Economies: Theory, Evidence and Controversies*, Chicago, IL: University of Chicago Press, 2000; Jomo K. S. (ed.), *Tigers in Trouble: Financial Governance, Liberalization and Crises in East Asia*, London: Zed, 1998; Steven Radelet and Jeffrey D. Sachs, 'The East Asian financial crisis: diagnosis, remedies, prospects', *Brookings Papers on Economic Activity*, 1, 1998, pp. 1–74, 88–90; Peter G. Warr, 'What happened to Thailand?', *World Economy*, 22, 5, 1999, pp. 631–50; Shalendra D. Sharma, 'The Indonesian financial crisis', in *Indonesia in Crisis: A Macroeconomic Update*, Washington, DC: The World Bank, 1998, pp. 1–32. Sharma's paper contains good information on the banks and their difficulties.

2 Stijn Claessens, Djankov Simeon and Larry H. P. Lang, 'Separation of ownership and control in East Asian Corporations', *Journal of Financial Economics*, 58, 2000, pp. 81–112; Stijn Claessens, Djankov Simeon and Lixin Colin Xu, 'Corporate performance in the East Asian financial crisis', *World Bank Research Observer*, 15, 1, 2000, pp. 23–46.

3 Robert J. Shiller, *Irrational Exuberance*, Princeton, NJ: Princeton University Press, 2000, pp. 44, 135, 191, 203.

4 For an excellent study on the Indonesian financial system see David C. Cole and Betty F. Slade, *Building a Modern Financial System*, Cambridge: Cambridge University Press, 1996. See also David George McKendrick, 'Acquiring technological capabilities: aircraft and commercial banking in Indonesia', Ph.D. dissertation, University of California at Berkeley, 1989; and Rajeswary Ampalavanar Brown, *Chinese Big Business and the Wealth of Asian Nations*, Basingstoke: Palgrave, 2002, chapter 10.

5 Indonesian Securities, Clearing and Depository Institution, *Periodic Reports*, 1993–5; Bapepam, *Annual Reports*, 1993–5. See also, Institute for Economic and Financial Research, *Indonesian Capital Market Directory* (hereafter *ICMD*), 1993–2002; and Claessens, Djankov and Lang, 'The separation of ownership and control', p. 103.

6 McKendrick, 'Acquiring technological capabilities', p. 192.

7 Moody Investors Service, Global Credit Research, 24 October 1997, teleconference proceedings, 'The impact of market turmoil in South East Asia and Korea on Japanese banks and other financial institutions'.

8 ADB, *Asia Development Outlook*, 1999, p. 26. *Panji Masyarakat*, 24 June 1998, p. 69. *Jakarta Post*, 9 October 1999. See also Stijn Claessens, Djankov Simeon and Daniel Klingebiel, 'Financial restructuring in East Asia: halfway there?', World Bank, Financial Sector Discussion Paper, 3, 1999, pp. 5–6.

9 Bank Summa had losses of Rp591 billion. Baring Securities, *Report on P.T. Astra International*. Its NPLs were valued at Rp1.5 billion (US$720 million). See Brown, *Chinese Big Business*, p. 64.

10 Sharma, 'The Indonesian financial crisis', p. 29. ING Barings Indonesia Research, Stock Market Review, Slow Road to Recovery, Company Review, May 2000, pp. 30–94.

11 *Tempo*, 20 February 2000, p. 31.

12 Claessens, Djankov and Lang, 'Separation of ownership and control', p. 11; Paola Bongini, Stijn Claessens and Giovarni Ferri, 'The political economy of

distress in East Asian financial institutions', *Journal of Financial Services*, 19, 1, 2001, pp. 5–25.

13 *ICMD*, 2002, pp. 469–559; BKPM, *Annual Report*, 1999.

14 The composite index of the Jakarta Stock Exchange rose from 66.35 to 305.12 per cent in 1988, to 588.765 in 1993 and 637.43 in 1996 before collapsing to 401.71 in 1997, to 398.038 in 1998, followed by an artificially supported rise to 679.919 in 1999. Bank Indonesia, *Indonesia Financial Statistics*, 2002; Jakarta Stock Exchange, *Factbook*, 2000 and 2002; A. Siregar, 'Demokratisasi dan Ekonomi Pasar' [Democratization and Market Economy], *Warta Ekonomi*, 2000.

15 Jakarta Stock Exchange, *Factbook*, 1989–95.

16 Bapepam, *Factbook of the Indonesian Capital Market*, 1990; *Annual Report*, 1992, 1993.

17 Carl Johan Lindgren *et al.*, *Financial Sector Crisis and Restructuring: Lessons from Asia*, Washington, DC: IMF Occasional Paper 188, 1999, p. 13.

18 *ICMD*, 2002, pp. 490–1.

19 Takatoshi Ito, 'Capital flows in Asia', in Sebastian Edwards (ed.), *Capital Flows and the Emerging Economies: Theory, Evidence, and Controversies*, Chicago, IL: University of Chicago Press, 2000, p. 264. See also IMF, *International Capital Markets*, September 1998.

20 Ito, 'Capital flows in Asia', p. 258.

21 Bank for International Settlements, 'The maturity, sectoral and nationality distribution of International Bank lending', Basel, January 1998, cited in Ito, 'Capital flows in Asia', p. 277.

22 Bank lending to property and real-estate sectors increased by 40 per cent between 1995 and 1996, again rising in 1996–7, a 21 per cent increase from 1996. Sharma, 'The Indonesian financial crisis', pp. 9–13.

23 After 1997, foreign investors were allowed to form holding companies, could absorb equity in pioneer industries outside Java and were given fiscal incentives to encourage investments. BKPM, *Annual Reports*, 1999–2000.

24 BKPM, *Annual Report*, 1999.

25 ADB, *Annual Report*, 2001, p. 83, cited in P. C. Athukorala, 'Foreign direct investment in crisis and recovery: lessons from the Asian economic crisis', Paper presented at XIII International Economic History Congress, Buenos Aires, 2002, p. 27. These figures are only announced values. The Coordinating Body for Investment (BKPM) noted an increase of 37 per cent of FDI approvals for 2000. Yet, Japanese inward investment for 2001 dropped to 1 per cent from 5 per cent for 2000.

26 BKPM is Badan Koordinasi Penaman Modal (Investment Coordination Board) while BPPN is Badan Penyehatan Perbankan Nasional (Indonesian Bank Restructuring Agency).

27 Bongini, Claessens and Ferri, 2001; Claessens, Djankov and Xu, 2000.

28 Short-term debt owed to foreign commercial banks was US$33 billion, which was 1.75 times that of Indonesian foreign exchange reserves in 1998. Steven Radelet, 'Indonesia: long road to recovery', Unpublished paper, Harvard Institute for International Development, March 1999, pp. 3–4. Japan provided more than 40 per cent of total foreign credit and their reduction increased distress for Indonesian banks.

29 BCA, Balance sheets and *Annual Reports*, 1970–91. See Table 3.5.

30 See FPH, *Annual Report*, 1995 for Salim Group's consolidated group accounts. See also Sato Yuri, 'The Salim Group in Indonesia: the development and behaviour of the largest conglomerate in South East Asia', *Developing Economies*, 21, 4, 1993, pp. 408–41.

31 FPH, *Annual Report*, 1995.

32 Sharma, 'The Indonesian financial crisis', pp. 26–7.
33 *Forum Keadilan*, 15 December 1997; *Suara Pembaruan*, 12 January 1998; Kees van Dijk, *A Country in Despair: Indonesia between 1997 and 2000*, Leiden: KITLV Press, 2000, p. 90.
34 *ICMD*, 2002, pp. 476–7.
35 *International Herald Tribune*, 17 May 1999.
36 *Far Eastern Economic Review*, 12 March 1998.
37 *Indonesian Financial Statistics*, monthly and annual reports 1990–8.
38 Key Indicators of Developing Asian and Pacific Countries, 18, 1997, pp. 136–7.
39 *ICMD*, 2002, pp. 490–1.
40 *South China Morning Post*, International Weekly, 8 October 1994.
41 *ICMD*, 2002, pp. 490–1.
42 *Merdeka*, Minggu ke, Julai 1998.
43 Bank Umum Nasional, *Annual Report*, December 1996; *Merdeka*, Julai 1998.
44 *Jakarta Post*, 15 June 1999; *Kompas*, 30 September 1999; *Panji Masyarakat*, 24 June 1998, p. 69.
45 *Forum Keadilan*, 14, 12, 1998, p. 83; *Panji Masyarakat*, 26 June 1998, p. 69.
46 Van Dijk, *A Country in Despair*, pp. 276, 408.
47 *Kompas*, 30 September 1999.
48 *Panji Masyarakat*, 24 June 1998, p. 69.
49 Data from balance sheets of Bank Indonesia and Bank International Indonesia, 1993–8.
50 Bank International Indonesia, *Annual Reports*.
51 Rajeswary Ampalavanar Brown, *Capital and Entrepreneurship in South East Asia*, Basingstoke: Macmillan, 1994, pp. 142–50.
52 *Ummat*, 8 March 1999, pp. 31–2; *Media Indonesia*, 30 March 1999, 31 March 1999.
53 *ICMD*, 2002, pp. 498–9; Bank Niaga, financial accounts for 2001.
54 Standard and Poor, *Country Reports: Indonesia*, 1995, 2003.
55 Reiny Iriana and Fredrik Sjoholm, 'Indonesia's economic crisis: contagion and fundamentals', *Developing Economies*, 2, 2002, pp. 149–50.
56 Hal Hill, 'Indonesia: the strange and sudden death of a tiger economy', *Oxford Development Studies*, 2, 28, 2000, pp. 117–39.
57 Ibid., p. 124.
58 Ibid., pp. 91–2.
59 *Panji Masyarakat*, 24 June 1998, p. 69; *Far Eastern Economic Review*, 17 December 1998, pp. 51–2.
60 Hill, 'Indonesia: the strange and sudden death', p. 94.
61 Claessens, Djankov and Xu, 'Corporate performance in the East Asian financial crisis', pp. 2, 19.
62 *ICMD*, 2002, pp. 476, 480, 488, 490.
63 Van Dijk, *A Country in Despair*, p. 531.
64 *Tempo*, 20 February 2000, p. 31.
65 Bank Indonesia, *Indonesia Financial Statistics*, 2000.
66 Bank Indonesia, *Indonesia Financial Statistics*, 2000; *Annual Reports*, 1995–9. NPLs were calculated to account for 60–85 per cent of all loans, bank recapitalization would cost Rp643 trillion (US$89 billion). By November 1998 it was clear that private corporations held US$118 billion debt, 60 per cent of this owed to foreign creditors, 40 per cent of debt was in foreign currency. See Sharma, 'The Indonesian Financial Crisis', pp. 29–30. See also Lindgren *et al.*, 'Financial sector crisis and restructuring', p. 13. 'Memo-lending' is moneylending based on close contacts between lender and borrower.
67 Sharma, 'The Indonesian financial crisis', p. 29.

68 Van Dijk, *A Country in Despair*, p. 401.
69 Bongini, Claessens and Ferri, 'The political economy of distress', pp. 5–25; Claessens, Djankov and Lang, 'The separation of ownership and control', pp. 81–112. See also Lindgren *et al.*, 'Financial sector crisis and restructuring', p. 65.
70 Bank Indonesia, *Financial Statistics*, 2000; Sharma, 'The Indonesian financial crisis', p. 29.
71 *ICMD*, 2002, p. 514.
72 *Jakarta Post*, 16 August 1999, 21 September 1999.
73 *Jakarta Post*, 17 December 1999.
74 *ICMD*, 2002, p. 472.
75 See Chapters 5 and 8.
76 McKendrick, 'Acquiring technological capabilities', p. 174.
77 Cole and Slade, *Building a Modern Financial System*, pp. 85, 137, 182, 277, 340.

4 Indonesian corporations, cronyism and corruption

1 Richard Robison, *Indonesia: The Rise of Capital*, Sydney: Allen & Unwin, 1986; Andrew MacIntyre, 'Funny money: fiscal policy, rent seeking and economic performance', in Mushtaq H. Khan and Jomo K. S. (eds), *Rents, Rent Seeking and Economic Development: Theory and Evidence*, Cambridge: Cambridge University Press, 2000, pp. 248–73.
2 Raymond Fisman, 'Estimating the value of political connections', *American Economic Review*, September 2001, pp. 1095–1102.
3 Stijn Claessens, Simeon Djankov and Larry H. P. Lang, 'Who controls East Asian corporations?', Financial Economics Unit, Financial Sector Practice Department, World Bank, February 1999.
4 See also, Robert Wade, 'The market for public office: why the Indian State is not better at development', *World Development*, 13, 4, April 1985, pp. 467–97.
5 Charles Perrow, 'Economic theories of organization', *Theory and Society*, 15, 1986, pp. 11–45.
6 IFC loans resulted in such corruption that in September 2001, it petitioned the Indonesian government and withheld US$250 million in FDI. For IFC equity involvement in large corporations, see Rajeswary Ampalavanar Brown, *Chinese Big Business and the Wealth of Asian Nations*, London: Palgrave, 2000, pp. 69–70.
7 Takatoshi Ito, 'Capital flows in Asia', in Sebastian Edwards (ed.), *Capital Flows and the Emerging Economies: Theory, Evidence and Controversies*, Chicago, IL: University of Chicago Press, 2000.
8 Hal Hill, *The Indonesian Economy in Crisis: Causes, Consequences, and Lessons*, Singapore: ISEAS, 1999, pp. 8–9.
9 Hal Hill, *The Indonesian Economy in Crisis*, pp. 23–37; P. Krugman, 'The myth of Asia's miracle', *Foreign Affairs*, 73, 6, 1994, pp. 62–78; P. Krugman, 'Latin lessons for Asia', *Far Eastern Economic Review*, 25 October 1999.
10 Alice Amsden, *Asia's Next Giant*, Cambridge: Cambridge University Press, 1989, p. 8.
11 Paul D. Hutchcroft, *Booty Capitalism: The Politics of Banking in the Philippines*, Ithaca, NY: Cornell University Press, 1998.
12 Hal Hill, *The Indonesian Economy in* Crisis, 1999, p. 69.
13 See IBRA, *Monthly Report*, September 1999.
14 Hutchcroft, *Booty Capitalism*, pp. 170–81.
15 Ibid., pp. 130, 155.

16 For an excellent appraisal of Soeharto, see R. E. Elson, *Suharto: A Political Biography*, Cambridge: Cambridge University Press, 2001, pp. 257–64.
17 David C. Cole and Betty F. Slade, *Building a Modern Financial System: The Indonesian Experience*, Cambridge: Cambridge University Press, 1996; Lloyd R. Kenward, 'What has been happening at Bank Indonesia?', *Bulletin of Indonesian Economic Studies*, 35, 1, April 1999, pp. 121–7.
18 David C. Kang, *Crony Capitalism: Corruption and Development in South Korea and the Philippines*, Cambridge: Cambridge University Press, 2002, pp. 96–121.
19 Hal Hill, *The Indonesian Economy in Crisis*, pp. 70–8.
20 For a detailed analysis of the rise and decline of the Indonesian military in economic activities, see Dr Indria Sameyo *et al.*, *Berbisnis, Buku Pertama Yang Menyingkap data dan Kasus Penyimpangan dalam Praktik Bisnis Kalangan militer*, Mizan Pustaka Kronik Indonesia Baru, September 1998.
21 *Tempo*, 26 July 1980. *Soeharto, Pikiran, ucapan dan tindakan: otobiografi seperti di paparkan kepada G Dwipayana dan Ramadhan KH*, Jakarta: Citra Lamtoro Gung Persada, 1989, pp. 459–60. In English: *Soeharto, My Thoughts, Words and Deeds: An Autobiography as Told to G. Dwipayana and Ramadhan K. H.*, translated by Sumadi, edited by Muti'ah Lestiono, Jakarta: Citra Lamtoro Gung Persada, 1991.
22 *Conglomeration Indonesia: Regeneration and Transformation into World Class Corporate Entities*, Pusat Data Business Indonesia, vol. 1–3, 1997. ICMD, 2001, 2002. Institute for Economic and Financial Research, Jakarta, 2001, 2002.
23 'The army's dirty war', *Tapol Bulletin*, 153, July 1999; Liem Soei Liong, 'It's the military stupid', in Freek Colombijn and J. Thomas Lindblad, *Roots of Violence in Indonesia*, Singapore: ISEAS, 2002, pp. 197–226.
24 Aditjondro George Junus, 'Guns, pamphlets, and handie-talkies: how the military exploited local ethno religious tensions in Maluku to preserve their political and economic privileges', in Ingrid Wessel and George Wimhofer (eds), *Violence in Indonesia*, Hamburg: Abera, 2001, pp. 100–28.
25 *Republika*, 6 June 1998; *Kompas*, 12 June 1998, 27 November 1998; *Business Times*, 18 September 1999; *Suara Pembaruan*, 23 April 1995; *Suara Karya*, 6 June 1998; *Suara Pembaruan*, 25 June 1998; *Merdeka*, 9 July 1998; *Bisnis*, 1 June 1998; *Jakarta Post*, 15 February 2003, 24 May 2004.
26 Sudharmono, *Pengalaman dalam masa pengabdian: sebuah otobiografi*, Jakarta: Grasindo, 1997.
27 *Media Indonesia*, 2 August 1998.
28 Kelly Bird, 'Survey of recent development', *Bulletin of Indonesian Economic Studies*, 32, 1, 1996.
29 *Kompas*, 6, 12 June 1998. , 27 November 1998.
31 *Jakarta Post*, 15 February 2003.
30 *Kompas*, 2 September 1998; *Republika*, 6, 19 June 1998.
32 For more details on the military and the *yayasan*, see Indria Samego, *Bila ABRI Berbisnis*, *Buku Pertama Yang Menyingkap data dan Kasus Penyim pangan dalam Praktik Bisnis Kalangan militer*, Bandung Mizan 1998 (*when the armed forces entered business.*) First book to shed light on the business practices of the armed forces. *Kontan*, 31, 3, 3 May 1999, 'Bisnis Prajunt di Hutan Rimba Yayasan ABRI menguasai dua juta hectare HPH'; Bisnis Militer Orde Baru Iswandi, October 1998, *Ekonomi Indonesia Di Tangan Para Jenderal.*
33 John McBeth, 'Techno-battles', *Far Eastern Economic Review*, 7 April 1994.
34 ICMD, 1990–4, Jakarta, Institute for Economic and Social Research.
35 *Conglomeration Indonesia*, Pusat Data Business Indonesia, vol. II, pp. 629–37.
36 Jeffrey A. Winters, *Power in Motion: Capital Mobility and the Indonesian State*, Ithaca, NY: Cornell University Press, 1996; R. Pangaribuan, *The Indonesian*

State Secretariat, 1945–93, Perth: Asia Research Centre on Political and Economic Change, 1995.

37 Bank Indonesia, *Indonesian Financial Statistics*, 1988–96.

38 Ibid., 1982–96.

39 Elson, *Suharto*, pp. 192, 196, 250, 281.

40 Ibid., p. 280.

41 Adam Schwarz, *A Nation in Waiting: Indonesia in the 1990s*, Sydney: Allen & Unwin, 2nd edn, 1999; Michael Backman, *Asian Eclipse: Exposing the Dark Side of Business in Asia*, Singapore: John Wiley, 1999.

42 Claessens, 1999, 'Who controls East Asia corporations'.

43 The following account draws on P. T. Bimantara Citra and its subsidiaries for the years ended 31 December 1995–2003: prior to 1998, the accountants were Indonesian: after that date, the accountants were Deloitte Touche Tohmatsu.

44 Telekom Indonesia, 2000.

45 See Bimantara Citra, Consolidated Financial Statements for 2001 and 2002.

46 Humpuss Intermoda Transportasi Tbk, 1993–2002, ICMD, 1993–2002.

47 David Jenkins, 'After Marcos: now for the Soeharto billions', *Sydney Morning Herald*, 10 April 1986; John Mcbeth, 'New kids on the Block', *Far Eastern Economic Review*, 25 November 1993; *Tempo*, 10 September 2000; *South China Morning Post*, 19 February 1999.

48 Claessens, 1999, 'Who controls East Asia corporations'.

49 Bakrie Bros, Balance Sheets and Annual Reports, 1997–2001.

50 ICMD, 1989–2003.

51 Cole and Slade, *Building a Modern Financial System*, p. 355.

52 See Juzhong Zhuang, David Edwards and Virginia Capulong (eds), *Corporate Governance and Finance in East Asia: A Study of Indonesia, Republic of Korea, Malaysia, Philippines, and Thailand*, ADB Report, Manila, 2001, vols 1, 2.

53 *Tempo*, 27 November 2000.

54 Ibid.

55 This was not always a success, as shown in Chapter 7. However, it does encourage indigenous entrepreneurship.

56 Marshall I. Goldman, *The Piratization of Russia: Russian Reform goes Awry*, London: Routledge, 2003.

57 Direktorat Jenderal Pembinaan BUMN Departmen Keuangan Republik Indonesia, April 2001.

58 Daniel Fitzpatrick, 'Indonesian corporate governance: would outside directors or commissioners help?', in Chris Manning and Peter van Dierman, *Indonesia in Transition*, Singapore: ISEAS, 2000, pp. 293–308.

59 *Kompas*, 21 July 2000.

60 *Kompas*, 18 July 2000.

61 *Straits Times*, 26 August 2000.

62 *Tempo Interaktif*, 30 November 2000.

63 John Scott, *Corporate Business and Capitalist Classes*, Oxford: Oxford University Press, 1997, p. 229.

5 Malaysian banking

1 Lee Sheng-Yi, *The Monetary and Banking Development of Malaysia and Singapore*, Singapore: Singapore University Press, 1974, p. 88.

2 Natasha Hamilton-Hart, *Asian States, Asian Bankers: Central Banking in Southeast Asia*, Ithaca, NY and London: Cornell University Press, 2002, p. 146.

3 Bank Negara Malaysia, *Quarterly Bulletin*, 1995.

4 See Stijn Claessens, Simeon Djankov and Larry H. P. Lang, 'The separation of ownership and control in East Asian corporations', *Journal of Financial Economics*, 58, October 2000, pp. 81–112; Stijn Claessens, Simeon Djankov, Joseph Fan and Larry Lang, *Corporate Diversification in East Asia: The Role of Ultimate Ownership Structure and Grand Affiliation*, Washington, DC: World Bank, Policy Research Working Paper 2089, 1999.
5 See Christopher Adam and William Cavendish, 'Early privatization', in Jomo K. S. (ed.), *Privatizing Malaysia: Rents, Rhetoric, Realities*, Boulder, CO and London: Westview Press, 1995, p. 38.
6 Ibid., p. 28.
7 Ibid., p. 39.
8 Hamilton-Hart, *Asian States, Asian Bankers*, p. 148.
9 Edmund Terence Gomez, *Political Business: Corporate Involvement of Malaysian Political Parties*, Cairns: James Cook University Press, 1994, p. 60; Hamilton-Hart, *Asian States, Asian Bankers*, p. 149.
10 Bank Negara Malaysia, *Annual Report, 1994*, pp. 249–55.
11 See J. Pound, 'Proxy contents and the efficiency of shareholder oversight', *Journal of Financial Economics*, 20, 1988, pp. 237–55.
12 The stock market in Kuala Lumpur suffered heavy losses between March and July 1997 despite the increased activities of EPF and state unit trusts.
13 John Kay, *Foundations of Corporate Success*, Oxford: Oxford University Press, 1994.
14 J. E. Stiglitz, 'Credit markets and the control of capital', *Journal of Money, Credit, and Banking*, 17, 2, 1985, pp. 133–52.
15 KLSE, *Annual Reports*, 1970–99.
16 Ibid.
17 In the mid-1970s, not one private Malay firm was in the top 100 firms listed on the KLSE. In 2001, the number of top Malay firm was three out of 20. Meanwhile, Chinese held 16 and Indians had one. Thus, despite two decades of ethnic restructuring, Chinese still dominated the Malaysian corporate economy. *Malaysian Business*, 1 February 2001. A word of caution, though: SOEs were still dominant in terms of assets.
18 Hamilton-Hart, *Asian States, Asian Bankers*, p. 125.
19 E. T. Gomez and Jomo K. S., *Malaysia's Political Economy: Politics, Patronage, and Profits*, Cambridge: Cambridge University Press, 1999, pp. 61–2.
20 *Asia Week*, 5 January 1994; Peter Searle, *The Riddle of Malaysian Capitalism: Rent Seekers or Real Capitalists?*, St Leonard's, Australia: Allen & Unwin, 1999, p. 169.
21 *Malaysian Business*, 16 January 1995.
22 Arab Malaysian Bank, *Balance Sheet* 1992–7; *Annual Report*, June 1997.
23 *Far Eastern Economic Review*, 19 February 1998, 20 May 1999.
24 Danaharta, *Operations Report*, Kuala Lumpur, 2000, Appendix 1.
25 Standard and Poor Report, 1999.
26 Maybank, *Annual Report*, 30 June 1996.
27 Maybank, *Annual Report*, 30 June 1998.
28 Mercantile Bank correspondence, 6 February 1963.
29 Letter from P. T. Lamb, Kuala Lumpur, Mercantile Bank to C. F. Pow, Mercantile Bank London, 5 March1965; 26 March 1963. Letter from Mercantile Bank KL, I. J. McGwilke to S. J. Elgar London (Mercantile Bank History 2939), Mercantile Bank Kota Bharu 19 January 1969 Letter from R. C. Bowley to P. T. Lamb, Kuala Lumpur.
30 KL Mercantile Bank 13 September 1963 Letter I. J. McGwilke to S. J. Elgar, London.

31 Correspondence, Mercantile Bank Penang, 28 January 1966, 5 January 1966. Mercantile Bank, Letter from I. P. MacFarlane to C. F. Pow of London, 15 January 1969 Mercantile Bank Singapore.
32 Mercantile Bank correspondence, 26 March 1963; 28 January 1966; 8 March 1966.
33 Mercantile Bank correspondence 9 February 1965.
34 Letter I. P. MacFarlane to C. F. Pow of London 15 January 1965. Mercantile Bank Singapore.
35 Mercantile Bank Penang, 5 July 1965.
36 'Mobile Banks in the East Coast', Letter 5 February 1963 from P. T. Lamb to C. F. Pow London.
37 I. H. Imlach to D. L. Coure, 22 January 1965, Kuala Lumpur Mercantile Bank.
38 *Straits Times*, 23 December 1976.
39 Lee Sheng-Yi, *The Monetary and Banking Development of Malaysia and Singapore*, p. 274. Malayan Banking was renamed Maybank in the 1970s.
40 *Bumiputra* investment was held through Amanah Raya Bhd (29.6 per cent), PNB (20 per cent), Khazanah Nasional (5 per cent) and FELDA (2 per cent).
41 Maybank, *Annual Report*, 9 September 1995.
42 Directors' Report, 8 April 2002.
43 Maybank, *Annual Report*, 28 August 1995, 6 June 1996.
44 Maybank, *Managing Director's Report* for 1999, and *Annual Report*, 17 September 1998. Number of Maybank branches in 1996: Malaysia 336, Singapore 22, Brunei 3, China 3, Papua New Guinea 2, Hong Kong 1, Vietnam 2, United Kingdom 1, Cambodia 1, Uzbekistan 1.
45 Maybank, *Annual Report*, 6 June 1996, p. 19.
46 Maybank, *Managing Director's Report*, 27 September 1995, p. 20.
47 Maybank, *Managing Director's Report* for 1995, and *Annual Report*, 27 September 1995.
48 Maybank, *Annual Reports*, 1997, 1998. NPLs of Maybank were 14.9 per cent at the end of June 1999, rising from 10.9 per cent in 1998. Loan recoveries were 45.8 per cent of total debt, so moderate progress was achieved in the restructuring of debt. In 1997 and 1998, all banks in Malaysia saw loan growth fall from 35.6 per cent to 10.3 per cent. Deposits growth fell from 26.6 per cent to 6.1 per cent. Loan/deposit ratio remained 95.2 per cent. NPLs to total loans increased from 2.1 per cent in June 1997 to 8.9 per cent in June 1998.
49 Maybank's subidiaries in Indonesia declined by 23 per cent in 1999, while their loan growth was 7 per cent.
50 Maybank, *Annual Report*, 29 August 2001, p. 44.
51 Much of these investments were in the purchase of shares for institutional investor ASB, meaning there was less speculation.
52 Maybank, *Annual Report*, 29 August 2001. See also Managements' Discussion and Analysis of Financial Performance Year Ending June 2002.
53 Maybank, *Directors' Report*, 2001–2, 30 June 2002.
54 Maybank, *Annual Report*, 30 August 2000. The merged banks alone revealed assets of RM133 billion.
55 *The Edge*, 29 August 2002.
56 *The Edge*, 31 May 2000.
57 It had a fair distribution of Malay and non-Malay owners, directors and managers: Ahmad Abdullah, Taib bin Abdul Hamid, Tong Kooi Ong and Ng Seng Hin. PAB Group, *Financial Statements*, 19 April 2000.
58 PAB, *Annual Report*, 20 May 1997, p. 16.
59 PAB, *Report*, 14 November 2000.
60 PAB, *Report*, 28 April 1999.

61 PAB, *Annual Report*, 1 July 1999, p. 17.
62 Phileo Allied Bhd, *Annual Report*, 28 April 1999, 1 July 1999, p. 17; Phileo Allied Bhd, *Directors' Report*, May 2000.
63 PAB, *Annual Reports*, 26 April 2000, 28 May 2001.
64 Danaharta was an asset management company to whom bad debt and NPLs were transferred. Danamodal was a special institution for the recapitalization of banks. It pursued prudent classification of loans, provisions for bad debt, capital adequacy ratio, limits to single exposures and a rigorous liquidity framework before embarking on recapitalization of these failing financial institutions.
65 Prema-chandra Athukorala, 'Capital account regimes, crisis and adjustment in Malaysia', *Asian Development Review*, 18, 1, 2000, p. 92.
66 Connected lending and fraud was revealed in the case of a RM3 billion loan by four Malaysian banks to a protégé of Daim, the Finance Minister, for the acquisition of a Philippines steel plant. The borrower then defaulted. Hamilton-Hart, *Asian States, Asian Bankers*, p. 125; *Business Times*, 17 March 1999.
67 Athukorala, 'Capital account regimes, crisis and adjustment in Malaysia', p. 94.
68 Ibid., p. 96.
69 Ibid.
70 Ibid.
71 Edmund Terence Gomez, *Chinese Business in Malaysia: Accumulation, Accommodation, and Ascendance*, Honolulu, HA: University of Hawaii Press, 1999, p. 2.
72 Bank Negara Malaysia, *Annual Report*, 1997, pp. 192–3.
73 Hamilton-Hart, *Asian States, Asian Bankers*, p. 126.
74 Ibid., pp. 115–16.
75 The Banking and Finance Industry Act of 1989 prohibited loans to companies in which directors had interests and required senior bankers to declare their assets. However, this remained only in law and was ignored in practice. There were no restrictions on Malaysian banks' involvement in stockbroking and property, trust management and nominee services were also permitted. *The Star*, 11 July 1991.
76 Hamilton-Hart, *Asian States, Asian Bankers*, p. 164.
77 Bank Negara Malaysia, Press Release, 31 December 2000.
78 Danaharta, *Operations Report*, Kuala Lumpur, 2000, Appendix 1.
79 *Bernama*, 26 November 1999.
80 *New Straits Times*, 15 August 2000; *Business Times*, 2 July 2001.
81 *New Straits Times*, 31 August 2000.
82 Danaharta, *Operations Report*, Kuala Lumpur, 2000, Appendix 1.
83 *Business Times Malaysia*, 31 March 2000.
84 *Business Times Malaysia*, 15 November 1999.

6 Capital structure puzzle

1 Malaysia possessed the highest ratio of stocks as a share of GNP between 1989 and 1996 in Asia. In 1996 the Malaysian ratio was 299 per cent, while for Hong Kong it was 296 per cent and for Korea, 30 per cent. International Finance Corporation, *Emerging Stock Market Factbook, 1997*, Washington, DC, 1997.
2 Economic Planning Unit, *Mid-Term Review of the Seventh Malaysia Plan 1996–2000*, Kuala Lumpur: Government Printers, 2000.
3 Christopher Adam and William Cavendish, 'Background', in Jomo K.S. (ed.), *Privatising Malaysia: Rents, Rhetoric, Realities*, Boulder, CO: Westview, 1995, p. 29.

4 The connection between stock market performance and political connections of major corporations in Indonesia is discussed in Raymond Fisman, 'Estimating the value of political connections', *The American Economic Review*, 91, 4, September 2001, pp. 1095–1102; *The Suharto Dependency Index*, The Castle Group, Jakarta, 1995; Anne O. Kruegar, 'The political economy of the rent seeking society', *The American Economic Review*, 64, 3, June 1974, pp. 291–303.

5 *The Suharto Dependency Index*, p.33.

6 See also KLSE, *Investing in the Stock Market in Malaysia*, 12 February 2001.

7 Philippe F. Delhaise, *Asia in Crisis: The Implosion of the Banking and Finance Systems*, Singapore: John Wiley & Son, 1998, p. 150. Investment in equity markets formed 24.4 per cent of NPLs of Malaysian commercial banks while finance houses' NPLs were 17 per cent, those of merchant banks account for 20.4 per cent and purchase of securities accounted for 17.1 per cent of total NPLs: of this the property sector held 21.0 per cent. Bank Negara Malaysia, *Annual Report*, 1999.

8 There was a serious case of market manipulation on the Second Board in June 1993 when Union Paper Holdings attempted to rig the price by circulating rumours of a reverse takeover by Kewangan Usaha Bhd. This excessive speculation led to conviction in August 1993 of prominent individuals on the offence of short-selling and market manipulation. This seems to suggest that the regulation does sometimes work.

9 Mansor Md. Isa and Tan Kok Hong, 'The announcement effects of rights and bonus issues on Malaysian stock prices', *Capital Markets Review*, 5, 2, 1997, pp. 45–58.

10 M. Ariff and L. W. Johnson, *Securities Markets and Stock Pricing: Evidence from a Developing Capital Market in Asia*, Singapore: Longman, 1990, pp. 289–95.

11 Ibid.

12 Ibid.

13 K. S. Jomo, *Malaysian Eclipse, Economic Crisis and Recovery*, London: Zed Books, 2001, pp. 147–50.

14 Ong Hong Cheong, 'Coping with capital flows and the role of monetary policy: the Malaysian experience, 1990–95', in C. H. Kwan, Donna Vandenbrink and Chia Siow Yue, *Coping with Capital Flow in East Asia*, Institute of Southeast Asian Studies, 1998, pp. 220–43.

15 KLSE, *KLSE Statistics*, various years; Bank Negara Malaysia, *Annual Report*, various issues 1995–2001; Bank Negara Malaysia, *Monthly Statistical Bulletin*, various issues 1995–2000; Bank Negara Malaysia, *Quarterly Economic Bulletin*, various issues 1990–2001.

16 Bank Negara Malaysia, *Quarterly Bulletin*, 2, 3,1987.

17 Yoshihara Kunio, *Sogo Shosha: The Vanguard of the Japanese Economy*, Oxford: Oxford University Press, 1982.

18 Hong Leong Credit Bhd, *Financial Statements and Profit and Loss Accounts*, 1971–95.

19 Ibid.

20 Ibid.

21 *Business Times*, 3 July 1984.

22 Dao Heng Bank, *Annual Report*, 12 November 1990. In 1994 Dao Heng Bank had assets of US$4,224 million and profits of US$51.5 million. See *Consolidated Profit and Loss Accounts*, *Balance Sheet* and *Financial Summaries*, 1986–94.

23 Hong Leong Malaysia, *Balance Sheet*, *Annual Reports* and *Profit and Loss Accounts*, 1987–97.

24 *Far Eastern Economic Review*, 8 September 1994.

25 *Malaysian Business*, 1 March 1994.
26 *Business Times*, 3–4 September 1994.
27 *Business Times*, 13 April 1992.
28 *Business Times*, 30 July 1990.
29 Ibid.
30 *Business Times*, 9 November 1994.
31 *KLSE Handbook 1997*, pp. 86–7.
32 Ibid., p. 121.
33 *Far Eastern Economic Review*, 11 March 1993; *Malaysian Business*, 16 April 1992.
34 Paul Zarowin, 'Does the stock market overreact to corporate earnings information?', *The Journal of Finance*, XLIV, 5, December 1989, pp. 1385–99.
35 Hong Leong has three main listed companies in Malaysia, Hong Leon Credit ranked 24th on the KLSE with listed capital of RM305,706,400, average annual share price 12.6 ringgit, and market valuation of RM3,835,366,054. Hong Leong Bank is ranked 28th on the KLSE while Hume Industries is ranked 31st with paid-up capital of RM247,781,830, share price 12.2 ringgit and market valuation of RM3,022,938,326. KLSE, *Annual Report*, 31 December 1996.
36 Hong Leong Bank, *Balance Sheet*, 2 September 1996, 24 August 2000, 5 June 2001.
37 Ibid.
38 KLSE, *Annual Report*, 31 December 1996. Andrei Shleifer and Robert W. Vishny, 'A survey of corporate governance', *Journal of Finance*, 52, 1997, pp. 737–83.
39 Ibid.
40 Hong Leong Bank, *Directors' Report*, 30 June 1998, 30 June 2001.
41 KLSE, *Annual Companies Handbook*, 1995; Hong Leong Bank, *Directors' Report*, 30 June 1998, 30 June 2001. Hong Leong Bank maintained a capital adequacy ratio of 10.3 per cent in 1997, 12.9 per cent in 1998, contrasting with the majority of Malaysian banks which held a capital adequacy ratio of 8 per cent in this period.
42 See also R. La Porta, 'Expectations and the cross-section of stock returns', *Journal of Finance*, 51, 1996, pp. 1715–42.
43 *Asian Wall Street Journal*, 6 January 1993; Peter Searle, *The Riddle of Malaysian Capitalism*, p. 218. *Far Eastern Economic Review*, 4 February 1993.
44 Hong Leong Bank, *Directors' Report*, 30 June 1998. The four Malay executives were Mohd Noor Mutalib, Senior Group Manager NSTP, Ahmad Nazri Abdullah, Group Editor Malay Language Publications, Abdul Kadir Jasin, Group Editor of English Language Publications, and Khalid Ahmad, Managing Director, NSTP Group.
45 KLSE, *Annual Companies Handbook*, 1996–2001. Linkages between UMNO and Hong Leong are identifiable since the 1980s. Hume Industries, a construction subsidiary of Hong Leong, worked with UMNO, buying shares in Jaguh Mutiara Sdn Bhd, an UMNO owned company connected to its Fleet Group. Hume's links strengthened when the Fleet Group was taken over by Renong. In 1991, Hume acquired a 49 per cent stake in Nanyang Press, the largest Chinese-language daily, purchased from Wan Azmi, an Anwar protégé. Another link to Malay capital was in the establishment of KLOFFE, an options and financial futures consortium with Renong and Rashid Hussein in 1991. In January 1993 Hong Leong's financing of the takeover of NSTP/TV3 further reinforced these connections with the ruling Malay elite. See Searle, *The Riddle of Malaysian Capitalism*, pp. 216–20.

46 See *Straits Times*, 18 May 1994, 28 February 1995, 28 March 1995. Yeo Hiap Seng, *Annual Reports*, 1995, 1996.

47 There is no attempt here to analyse in depth and rigour the efficient markets hypothesis. What is sought is to show how social, political factors confuse share pricing and performance. Paul Zarowin, 'Does the stock market overreact to corporate earnings information?', pp. 1388–99. Lok Kong Sing and G. S. Gupta, 'Dividend behaviour in Malaysia', *Capital Markets Review*, 3, 1, 1995, pp. 73–83.

48 Mary A. O'Sullivan, *Contests for Corporate Control: Corporate Governance and Economic Performance in the United States and Germany*, Oxford: Oxford University Press, 2000.

49 M. N. Annuar, M. Ariff and M. Shamsher, 'Is Kuala Lumpur's emerging share market efficient?', *Journal of International Financial Markets*, 4, 1994, pp. 61–71.

50 S. M. Dawson, 'Secondary stock market performance of initial public offers, Hong Kong, Singapore, and Malaysia, 1978–84', *Journal of Business Finance and Accounting*, 14, 1987, pp. 67–76.

51 A. Shleifer and L.H. Summers, 'The noise trader approach to finance', *Journal of Economic Perspectives*, 4, 1990, pp. 19–33.

52 Brown, *Chinese Big Business*, Chapter 5.

7 Renong

1 Renong Bhd, *Annual Report*, 31 October 2000.

2 Ibid., 10 November 1986.

3 Renong Bhd, *Annual Report*, June 1991.

4 Renong Bhd, *Annual Report*, 19 April 2000.

5 Executive Chairman, Halim Saad, Statement, 4 December 1990.

6 Renong Bhd, *Annual Report*, 3 March 1997.

7 A large majority of Renong's warrants throughout the 1990s were held by the Central Depository, a subsidiary of the KLSE. The rest were with other *bumiputra* institutional investors. Substantial bondholders were EPF (47.17 per cent), Mayban Nominees (10.4 per cent), Permodalan Nasional Bhd (6.79 per cent) and Bank Pertanian Malaysia (6.11 per cent). Foreign warrant holders in October 1997 included Hwang DBS Nominees (23.59 per cent) and Chung Khiaw Nominees (5.09 per cent).

8 Renong Bhd, *Annual Report*, 15 October 1998.

9 R. E. Caves, 'Corporate strategy and structure', *Journal of Economic Literature*, 18, 1980, pp. 64–92.

10 Raghuram G. Rajan and Luigi Zingales, 'The governance of the new enterprise', in Xavier Vives (ed.), *Corporate Governance: Theoretical and Empirical Perspectives*, Cambridge: Cambridge University Press, 2000, pp. 201–32. See also Luigi Zingales, *Corporate Governance*, Cambridge, MA: National Bureau of Economic Research, 1997.

11 KLOFFE, a consortium trading in futures, was established in 1991. Renong held a share of 33.3 per cent, Rashid Hussein 22.2 per cent, Zalik Securities 22.2 per cent and NSTP 22.2 per cent. All trade was in domestic derivatives.

12 Renong Bhd, *Annual Report*, 10 November 1986.

13 Renong Bhd, *Annual Report*, 30 June 1990.

14 Renong Bhd, *Annual Report*, 30 June 1991, p. 700.

15 *KLSE Handbook 1997*, volume 2, p. 552.

16 Ibid., p. 240.

17 Renong Bhd, *Annual Report*, 1997, pp. 150–61.

18 Renong Bhd, *Annual Report*, 1997, pp. 162–3.
19 *KLSE Handbook 1997*, volume 2, p. 240 and volume 3, p. 208.
20 UEM, *Annual Report*, 1997.
21 UEM, *Annual Report*, 1997, pp. 149–55. His links to Hong Leong Group were reflected in his shareholding in that group's subsidiaries. He also had direct links to the Berjaya Group and Vincent Tan.
22 *Malaysian Business*, 10 October 1993.
23 Renong Bhd, *Annual Report*, 1999, p. 136.
24 Renong Bhd, *Annual Report*, 19 October 1999, and *Statement of Directors*, 27 October 1999, p. 136.
25 By May 1999, the Renong Group owed banks RM28 billion (US$7.3 billion). This was five per cent of Malaysia's total bank loans. *Far Eastern Economic Review*, 1 February 1998, 6 May 1999. The state issued bonds of RM11.3 billion (US$3 billion) to the creditor banks of Renong.
26 Renong Bhd, *Annual Report*, 2000, p. 30.
27 Renong Bhd, *Annual Report*, 1999, p. 122.
28 Ibid., p. 123.
29 Renong Bhd, *Annual Report*, 13 March 2000.
30 Ibid., 2000, *Chairman's Statement*, p. 22.
31 UEM World, *Inaugural Annual Report*, 31 March 2004.
32 Ibid.
33 Mushtaq Khan and K. S. Jomo (eds), *Rents, Rent-Seeking and Economic Development: Theory and Evidence in Asia*, Cambridge: Cambridge University Press, 2000.

8 The emergence and development of Singapore as a regional/international financial centre

1 *Singapore Corporate Handbook*, 2000, pp. xix–xxviii.
2 *Singapore Corporate Handbook*, 1990, 1998 and 2002.
3 *Singapore Corporate Handbook*, 2000, pp. xix–xx.
4 See Peter G. Zhang, *Barings Bankruptcy and Financial Derivatives*, Singapore: World Scientific, 1995.
5 MAS, *Annual Reports*, 1990, 1996 and 1997, (Commodities Quotations).
6 *Yearbook of Statistics, Singapore*, 1990, 1994 and 1995. See also *International Financial Statistics*, 1994, 1996 and 1997, The International Monetary Fund, Washington, DC.
7 See Chapter 2.
8 Gordon de Brouwer, *Hedge Funds in Emerging Markets*, Cambridge: Cambridge University Press, 2001, p. 118.
9 Natasha Hamilton Hart, *Asian States, Asian Bankers: Central Banking in South East Asia*, Ithaca, NY: Cornell University Press, 2002, p. 137.
10 Department of Statistics, *Economic Survey of Singapore*, 2000, p. 85 Occasional Paper on Economic Statistics, Singapore, 2001.
11 *Business Times*, 27 April 1985, 15 August 1986.
12 *Business Times*, 27 February 1985, 20 March 1987.
13 *Straits Times*, 27 June 1996, 6 May 1993, 20 March 1987.
14 *Business Times*, 18 January 1993.
15 Toyo Keizai Inc., *Asian Company Handbook* 1998, p. 484.
16 DBS, *Annual Report*, May 1998. See Chapter 10.
17 *Business Times*, 22 September 1986.
18 *Straits Times*, 25 November 1996.
19 *Business Times*, 16 September 1994.

20 DBS, *Annual Report*, December 1997, December 1998, December 1999. See also *Straits Times*, 9 March 1999.

9 Dead calm

1 W. G. Huff, *The Economic Growth of Singapore: Trade and Development in the Twentieth Century*, Cambridge: Cambridge University Press, 1994, p. 321.
2 Department of Statistics: Singapore, 2001, p.3, and p. 8. See also, Gavin Peebles and Peter Wilson, *Economic Growth and Development in Singapore: Past and Future*, Edward Elgar, 2002, p. 14.
3 Peebles and Wilson, *Economic Growth and Development in Singapore*, p. 115.
4 Department of Statistics Singapore, 2001, p. 8.
5 Huff, *The Economic Growth of Singapore*, p. 319.
6 Peebles and Wilson, *Economic Growth and Development in Singapore*, p. 44. See also, Alwyn Young, 'A tale of two cities: factor accumulation and technical change in Hong Kong and Singapore', in Stanley Fischer and Olivier Blanchard (eds), *NBER Macroeconomics Annual 1992*, no. 7, Cambridge, MA: MIT Press, p. 43.
7 Peebles and Wilson, *Economic Growth and Development in Singapore*, p. 44.
8 Ibid., p. 165.
9 Ibid., p. 170.
10 Huff, *The Economic Growth of Singapore*, p. 338 and Peebles and Wilson, *Economic Growth and Development in Singapore*, pp. 170, 172–3.
11 Huff, *The Economic Growth of Singapore*, pp. 169–70.
12 Ibid., pp. 330–1.
13 Peebles and Wilson, *Economic Growth and Development in Singapore*, pp. 100–1.
14 Ibid., pp. 194–5.
15 Huff, *The Economic Growth of Singapore*, p. 428.
16 Henry Wai Chung Yeung, 'Governing investment in China? The experience of government linked companies from Singapore', unpublished paper, n.d., p. 6.
17 W. G. Huff, 'What is the Singapore model of economic development?', *Cambridge Journal of Economics*, 19, 1994, p. 1428.
18 Annual Report of the Department of Statistics, Singapore, *Investments Abroad 1976–2003*, contains vital information on the initiatives abroad. In addition, for China, see *China Foreign Economic Statistical Yearbook 1990–2004*, Hong Kong: China Resources Publications.
19 Peebles and Wilson, *Economic Growth and Development in Singapore*, p. 224.
20 Ibid., p. 230.
21 Capita Land capitalization in September 2004 was S$7.2 billion. In 1989 Raffles Holdings created international resorts in Asia and Australia. It was listed in 1995. In June 2001 it acquired Surrsotel Holdings for S$420.1 million. Raffles Shareholding breakdown: Capita Land 38 per cent; Singapore Technologies and Temasek Holdings over 30 per cent; OCBC 3 per cent. Public holding in Raffles was 23.94 per cent on 24 February 2004. Prince Alwaleed's bid for Savoy Hotel was £250 million in January 2005. This bid was contested by GIC Singapore, *The Times*, UK, 15 January 2005.
22 *Economic Survey of Singapore*, 2000, Table 9.2.
23 Keppel Corporation, Singapore, *Annual Report*, various years.
24 In May 1999, Sembawang sold its entire stake in Wah Kwong Shipping of Hong Kong and acquired an increased holding in offshore petroleum services in the Far East.
25 SembCorp, *Annual Report*, April 2003.

26 Harry Bloch and Sam Tang, 'Estimating technical change, economies of scale and degree of competition for manufacturing industries in Singapore', *The Singapore Economic Review*, 45(1), 2000, p. 52; See also Peebles and Wilson, *Economic Growth and Development in Singapore*, p. 61; Paul Krugman, 'The myth of Asia's miracle', *Foreign Affairs*, November–December 1994, pp. 62–78.
27 Peebles and Wilson, *Economic Growth and Development in Singapore*, pp. 58–66, 157–8.
28 Peebles and Wilson, *Economic Growth and Development in Singapore*, p. 129.
29 Singapore Stock Exchange, *Singapore Companies Handbook* 2001, Part 1 pp. 194–6.
30 Henry Wai Chung Yeung, 'Governing investment in China? The experience of government-linked companies from Singapore', unpublished paper, n.d., p. 43.
31 Singapore Department of Statistics, 1988–2001.
32 *Emerging Stock Markets Fact Book* 1998.
33 *Emerging Stock Markets Fact Book* 1998. See also Eduardo D. Roca, *Price Interdependence among Equity Markets in the Asia Pacific Region*, Aldershot: Ashgate, 2000.
34 *Business Times Singapore*, 8 March 2000.
35 Nick J. Freeman and Frank L. Bartels, *Portfolio investment in South East Asia's Stock Markets: A Survey of Institutional Investors Current Perceptions and Practices*, Institute of South East Asian Studies, Working Paper, Economics and Finance, No. 3, April 2000.
36 *Yearbook of Statistics*, Singapore, 2000, p. 72. *Economic Survey of Singapore*, 1994, tables.
37 *Yearbook of Statistics*, Singapore, 2000, p. 72.
38 Department of Statistics Singapore, *Singapore's Investments Abroad*, 1976–89, 1990–2003, various years Singapore National Printers. *Yearbook of Statistics*, Singapore, various years. See also Lee Tsao Yuan, *Overseas Investment Experience of Singapore Manufacturing Companies*, Singapore: McGraw Hill, 1994. See also, Peebles and Wilson, *Economic Growth and Development in Singapore*, p. 189.
39 Peebles and Wilson, *Economic Growth and Development in Singapore*, p. 190.
40 Department of Statistics Singapore Investments Abroad 1990–2003.
41 *Yearbook of Statistics*, Singapore 2000, pp. 13 and 72.
42 Peebles and Wilson, *Economic Growth and Development in Singapore*, p. 63. See also the TFP debate on pages 60–6.
43 R. J. Gobat Cardarelli and J. Lee., *Singapore: Selected Issues*. International Monetary Fund, Staff Country Report No. 00/03, Washington, DC, 2000.

10 Thai financial institutions

1 Bank of Thailand, *Annual Report*, 1997.
2 Piman Limpaphayom, 'Chapter 4 – Thailand', in David Edwards, Juzhong Zhuang and Virginia A. Capulong (eds), *Corporate Governance and Finance in East Asia: A Study of Indonesia, the Republic of Korea, Malaysia, the Philippines, and Thailand. Volume 2: Country Studies*, Manila: ADB, 2001, p. 241.
3 Ibid.
4 Ibid.
5 Estimated from Bank of Thailand, *Economic Reports*, 1990–7.
6 Bangkok Bank, *Annual Report*, 1960, 1965, 1993, 1996 and 1997.
7 David Edwards, Juzhong Zhuang and Virginia A. Capulong (eds), *Corporate Governance and Finance in East Asia*, p. 261.
8 Estimates from Pacific Basin Capital Markets Database compiled by the University of Rhode Island, USA, cited in David Edwards, Juzhong Zhuang and

Virginia A. Capulong (eds), *Corporate Governance and Finance in East Asia*, p. 261. See also Merrill Lynch Phatra reports 1990–7.

9 *South China Morning Post*, 18 January 1994; *Business Times*, 17 March 1995.

10 Bank of Thailand, *Annual Reports on Commercial Banks*, various years.

11 Gordon de Brouwer with Wisarn Pupphavesa, *Asia Pacific Financial Deregulation*, London: Routledge, 1999, p. 45.

12 Ibid., p. 47.

13 *South China Morning Post*, 19 December 1995.

14 Thai commercial banks' foreign currency loans rose at the end of 1996 to US$31.5 billion, or 17 per cent of total private sector loans.

15 Bank of Thailand, *Economic Reports*, 1990–7.

16 45 per cent of total net capital movements in 1985 creating debt inflows, rose to 65 per cent in 1990 and to 84 per cent in 1994. The proportion of external debt as a percentage of GDP grew from 42.2 per cent in 1986 to 251.9 per cent in 1997. David Edwards, Juzhong Zhuang and Virginia A. Capulong (eds), *Corporate Governance and Finance in East Asia*, pp. 261–2.

17 Yoshiro Miwa, *Firms and Industrial Organisations in Japan*, London: Macmillan, 1996, pp. 96, 112 and 114.

18 P. Collier and C. Mayer, 'The assessment: financial liberalization, financial systems and economic growth', *Oxford Review of Economic Policy*, 5, 1989, pp. 1–2. See also C. Mayer, 'Financial systems, corporate finance and economic development', in R. G. Hubbard (ed.), *Asymmetric Information, Corporate Finance and Investment*, Chicago, IL: Chicago University Press, 1990.

19 Varaphat Chensavasdijai, 'The effect of financial liberalization on investment behaviour of Thai manufacturing firms', D.Phil. thesis, University of Oxford, 1999, pp. 96 and 101.

20 Bank of Thailand, *Annual Report*, 1982–95; Bank of Thailand, *Quarterly Bulletin*, 1985–95. See also National Economic and Social Development Board, *Flow of Funds Accounts of Thailand*, 1970–95; after March 1993, BIBF accounts are included.

21 Bank of Thailand, *Quarterly Bulletin*, 1995. See also Bank of Thailand, *Annual Report*, 1982–96.

22 Bank of Thailand, *Annual Report*, 1991–5. See also World Bank, *The Emerging Asian Bond Market 1995*, Washington, DC: World Bank, 1995, which reported that bond issues as a percentage of GDP were lowest in this period in East Asia.

23 R. I. McKinnon, 'Financial repression and the liberalization problem within less-developed countries', in S. Grassman and E. Lundberg (eds), *The World Economic Order: Past and Present Prospects*, London: Macmillan, 1981; E. S. Shaw, *Financial Deepening in Economic Development*, New York: Oxford University Press, 1973.

24 Thailand, Board of Investment, *Annual Report*, various years; Bank of Thailand, *Quarterly Bulletin*, 1987–97.

25 Thailand, Board of Investment, *Annual Report*, 1985–97.

26 Moody Investors Service, Global Credit Research, 24 October 1997, teleconference proceedings, 'The impact of market turmoil in South East Asia and Korea on Japanese banks and the Asian financial institutions'.

27 Bank of Thailand, *Quarterly Bulletin*, various issues; National Economic and Social Development Board (NESDB), *Flow of Funds Accounts of Thailand*, 1990–6.

28 *Business Times*, 16 April 1998.

29 Bank of Thailand, *Annual Report*, 1993–6; Bank of Thailand, *Quarterly Bulletin*, 1993–6.

30 Akira Kohsaka, 'Interdependence through capital flows in Pacific Asia and the role of Japan', in Takatoshi Ito and Anne O. Krueger (eds), *Financial Deregulation and Integration in East Asia*, Chicago, IL: University of Chicago Press, 1996, p. 120. Bank of Thailand data in December 1997 shows the increase in portfolio investment in November 1996: foreign debt amounted to US$93.4 billion. Fifty per cent of the latter was short-term. Bank of Thailand, *Quarterly Bulletin*, 1997 and 1998.

31 *Bangkok Post*, 'Week in review', 14–20 March 1999. In December 1998, NPLs accounted for 46 per cent of all lending by the Thai financial sector.

32 *Far Eastern Economic Review*, 12 June 1997.

33 J. D. Glen and M. A. Sumbinski, 'Trends in private investment in developing countries', Washington, DC: World Bank, International Finance Corporation Discussion Paper 34, 1998. In 1997, Thailand registered negative net private capital outflows of US$8.1 billion, rising to US$15.6 billion in 1998.

34 *South China Morning Post*, 5 April 1994.

35 Ibid. See also IMF, *International Financial Statistics*, Washington, DC, 1993 and 1994; Bank of Japan, Research and Statistics Department, *Economic Statistics Monthly*, 1993 and 1996.

36 Bank of Thailand, *Annual Report*, 1990 and 1997.

37 Hongkong and Shanghai Bank in Hong Kong, Internal correspondence, 6 July 1995, Midland Bank Archives, London.

38 Data Stream, Database 1996 and Capital Data Bondware Database 1996; J.P. Morgan, *World Financial Markets, 1998*, Q1 report on Thailand, 1998.

39 Bank of Thailand, *Report on Finance One*, March 1998.

40 See *International Herald Tribune*, 5 January 1998; *Financial Times*, 12 January 1998; D. Robinson, Y. Byeon and R. Teja with W. Tseng, *Thailand: Adjusting to Success, Current Policy Issues*, Washington, DC: International Monetary Fund, 1991; J. Corbett and T. J. Jenkinson, 'How is investment financed? A study of Germany, Japan, the United Kingdom, and the United States', *The Manchester School of Business Supplement*, 65, 1997, Table 1, p. 74.

41 Finance One, *Annual Reports* and *Balance Sheets*, 1990–7.

42 The Stock Exchange of Thailand, *Key Statistics*, 1994–2000.

43 Department of Commercial Registration, Ministry of Commerce 1991–2000. See also David Edwards, Juzhong Zhuang and Virginia A. Capulong (eds), *Corporate Governance and Finance in East Asia*, p. 235. Total paid up capital on the SET rose to 1291.2 billion baht in 2000.

44 'Monthly corporate securities trading 1993–8 by groups of investors', in *Reports of Department of Commercial Registration*, Ministry of Commerce.

45 'Monthly Corporate Securities Trading, 1993–2000', in Reports of Department of Commercial Registration, Ministry of Commerce. See also Reports of the Bank of Thailand and Reports of the Stock Exchange of Thailand, 1993–2000.

46 SET, *Key Financial Ratios*, 1992–9.

47 SET, *Annual Reports*, 1991–6 and Merrill Lynch Phatra, *Corporate Reports and Financial Statements*, 1990–7.

48 SET, *Key Financial Ratios* and *Annual Reports*, 1990–9.

49 Ibid.

50 Ibid.

51 David Edwards, Juzhong Zhuang and Virginia A. Capulong (eds), *Corporate Governance and Finance in East Asia*, pp. 253–4.

52 C. Mayer, 'Financial systems, corporate finance, and economic development', in R. Hubbard (ed.), *Asymmetric Information, Corporate Finance, and Investment*, Chicago, IL: University of Chicago Press, 1990; P. Collier and C. Mayer, 'The assessment: financial liberalization, financial systems, and economic growth', *Oxford Review of Economic Policy*, 5, 1989, pp. 1–12.

53 Securities One, 'Report on land and property', June 1997.
54 Ibid. See also Bank of Thailand, *Annual Report*, 1997.
55 The exposure of Thai banks to risky assets is clear from the following figures. Between 1991 and 1995, their property loans as a share of total loans were estimated at 20 per cent, while bonds and securities as a share of total assets grew from 7 per cent to 10 per cent. Goldman Sachs, 'Banking research, September 1997', cited in Pierre-Richard Agénor, Marcus Miller, David Vines and Axel Weber (eds), *The Asian Financial Crisis: Causes, Contagion and Consequences*, Cambridge: Cambridge University Press, 1999, p. 23.
56 UBS Global Research, May 1997, pp. 82–4.
57 Land and House, *Annual Reports* and *Balance Sheets*, 1990–6.
58 Securities One, 'Report on land and property', June 1997. This is a detailed study of the six largest land property specialists in Thailand.
59 Ibid.
60 *Far Eastern Economic Review*, 21 October 1999.
61 Bangkok Land, *Annual Reports* and *Balance Sheets*, 1993–7.
62 Bangkok Land, *Interim Report*, March 1998.
63 *Far Eastern Economic Review*, 21 October 1998.
64 Laurids S. Lauridsen, 'Thailand: causes, conduct, consequences', in Jomo K. S. (ed.), *Tigers in Trouble: Financial Governance, Liberalization and Crisis in East Asia*, London: Zed Books, 1998, p. 139.
65 Ibid., p. 138. External borrowing by the Thai private sector grew from US$40 billion in 1992 to US$80 billion in March 1997, and to US$90 billion in August 1997.
66 Ammar Siamwalla, 'Can a developing democracy manage its macroeconomy? The case of Thailand', *Thai Development Research Institute, Quarterly Review*, 12, 4, 1997, p. 3.
67 Bank of Thailand, *Annual Report*, 1995 and 1996.
68 Ruth McVey, 'Greed, violence and Thai politics', Paper presented to the Fifth International Conference on Thai Studies, London, 1993.
69 Thitinan Pongsudhirak, 'Autonomy, institutions, and the Baht crisis', in Dieter Mahncke, Kullada Kesboonchoo-Mead, Prathoomporn Vajrasthira and Rudolf Hrbek (eds), *ASEAN and the EU in the International Environment*, Baden-Baden: Nomos Verlagsgesellschaft, 1999, pp. 95–6.
70 Ammar Siamwalla, 'Can a developing democracy manage its macroeconomy?', p. 5.
71 *Bangkok Post*, 6, 7 October 1997. See also Peter G. Warr, 'Thailand', in Ross H. McLeod and Ross Garnaut, *East Asia in Crisis: From Being a Miracle to Needing One?* London: Routledge 1998, pp. 49–65.
72 Kitti Limskul and Thaneit Khantigaroon, 'Business cycle indicators for Thailand', in Hiroshi Osada and Daisuke Hiratsuka (eds), *Business Cycles in Asia*, Tokyo: Institute of Developing Economies, 1991, pp. 96–103.
73 ADB, Economics and Development Resource Center, *Key Indicators of Developing Asian and Pacific Countries, 1997*, Manila: Oxford University Press, 1997, vol. 28, pp. 328–9.
74 J. Schumpeter, *Business Cycles*, New York: McGraw Hill, 1939.
75 Pasuk Phongpaichit and Chris Baker, *Thailand's Crisis*, Chiang Mai: Silkworm Books, 2000, pp. 167–8, 171–2.
76 Reports used by CDRAC, August 4, 1998; Economic Reports 1999–2000; CDRAC Reports of March 2000; Merrill Lynch Reports November 1999, March 2000; IMF Report, February 2000; IMF Report 1999; 'Thailand Seventh Review Under the Stand by Arrangement', EBS 99/86; Moody's Investor Survey 1999; Nick J. Freeman, *Foreign Portfolio Investors Approaches to Thailand's Equity*

Market: Survey Findings and Preliminary Analysis, ISEAS Economics and Finance Working Papers, No. 2, 2000.

77 BOT Economic Reports 2000. See also Porametee Vimolsiri, *The Role of Foreign Investors in the Thai Currency Crisis of 1997*, ISEAS, Economics and Finance Working Papers, No. 4, 2001.

78 Standard and Poor (hereafter referred to as S & P) (Ian Thompson and Nancy Koh), *Thailand Banking Outlook*, 2003–4, p. 18.

79 Ibid., p. 24.

80 Ibid., p. 19.

81 Ibid., p. 26.

82 Ibid., p. 25.

83 See CDRAC, 2000; and Merrill Lynch Phatra Report, 2000.

84 The first bankruptcy court was opened in June 1999 and 80 cases were dealt with between June and September 1999.

85 IMF 1999, 'Financial sector crisis and restructuring: lessons from Asia', Economic Background Studies (EBS), 99/154.

86 S & P, *Thailand Banking Outlook*, p. 25.

87 Ibid., p. 8.

88 Porametee, *The Role of Foreign Investors in the Thai Currency Crisis of 1997*, p. 39.

89 In 1997, out of 15 Thai-owned commercial banks, one was state owned. By 2003, out of 12 banks, three were family controlled, four were foreign owned, and the remaining were in state hands poised for sale. The difficulties in privatization led to the postponement of the sale of Krung Thai and Bank Thai. Before 1997, foreign shareholding was from 9–10 per cent; at the end of 2002 it was 38 per cent. High levels of NPLs dissuaded many foreign banks from purchase. HSBC withdrew from the purchase of Bangkok Metropolitan Bank because of the high ratio of NPLs. In its purchase of Radanasin in 1999, United Overseas Bank (UOB) had underestimated the bank's NPLs distress; hence it continued to register losses into 2002. Similarly, DBS Thai Danu only became profitable from the second half of 2001, after enduring a loss of three-quarters of its original purchase price in disposing of NPLs.

90 Thai Farmers Bank Research Centre Database, May 2000.

91 *Bangkok Post*, 11 September 1999 and 13 October 1999.

92 SCNB, *Balance Sheets* and *Annual Reports*, 1998–2003.

93 TDDBS, *Annual Report*, 2000.

94 Bank of Thailand, *Annual Report*, July 2000.

95 CEIC, CEIC Database, Hong Kong, McGraw Hill, July 2000.

96 S & P, *Thailand Banking Outlook*; David Edwards, Juzhong Zhuang and Virginia A. Capulong (eds), *Corporate Governance and Finance in East Asia*.

11 The power of large single shareholding and industrial concentration in Thai corporate structure and performance

1 Richard F. Doner and Gary Hawes, 'The political economy of growth in East and South East Asia', in Manochehr Dorraj (ed.), *The Changing Political Economy of the Third World*, 1995, Boulder, CO: Lynne Rienner, 1995, pp. 9–10.

2 *World Bank Report*, 1997, p. 243.

3 William E. Brummit and Frank Flatters, *Exports, Structural Change and Thailand's Rapid Growth*, Bangkok: Thai Development Research Institute, 1992, p. 21.

4 Richard F. Doner and Ansil Ramsay, 'Rent seeking and economic development in Thailand', in Mushtaq H. Khan and Jomo K. S. (eds), *Rents, Rent Seeking*

and Economic Development: Theory and Evidence in Asia, Cambridge: Cambridge University Press, 2000, p. 147.

5 Stijn Claessens *et al.*, 'The separation of ownership and control in East Asian Corporations', *Journal of Financial Economics*, 58, 2000, pp. 81–112.

6 SET, Comprehensive Listed Company Information Database, 1990–9.

7 Ibid.

8 Thai employees were rarely offered stock options by Thai corporations, in contrast to the practice in Japanese corporations. This stakeholder culture was missing.

9 Reports of Securities and Exchange Commission of Thailand, 1993–2003. See also Piman Limpaphayom, 'Chapter 4 – Thailand', in David Edwards, Juzhong Zhuang and Virginia A. Capulong (eds), *Corporate Governance and Finance in East Asia: A Study of Indonesia, the Republic of Korea, Malaysia, the Philippines, and Thailand. Volume 2: Country Studies*, Manila: ADB, 2001, pp. 229–77. See also Stewart C. Myers, 'The capital structure puzzle', *The Journal of Finance*, Vol. XXXIX, No. 3, July 1984, pp. 575–92.

10 Securities and Exchange Commission of Thailand, *Key Capital Market Statistics, 1992–99*. See also the Pacific Basin Capital Market Database compiled by the University of Rhode Island, USA, cited in David Edwards, Juzhong Zhuang and Virginia A. Capulong (eds), *Corporate Governance and Finance in East Asia*, p. 239.

11 Pacific Basin Capital Market Database compiled by the University of Rhode Island, USA, cited in David Edwards, Juzhong Zhuang and Virginia A. Capulong (eds), *Corporate Governance and Finance in East Asia*, p. 240.

12 SET, *Listed Companies Profile Information and Index*, 1990–2001.

13 The performance of non-financial private corporations in Thailand is derived from Data on the Stock Exchange of Thailand and from the Merrill Lynch Phatra Report 1994–9. See also Bank of Thailand, *Annual Economic Reports 1990–99.*

14 Doner and Ramsay, 'Rent seeking and economic development in Thailand', pp. 145–81; Michael T. Rock, 'Thailand's old bureaucratic polity and its new semi-democracy', in Mushtaq K. Khan and Jomo K. S., *Rents, Rent-Seeking and Economic Development: Theory and Evidence in Asia*, Cambridge: Cambridge University Press, 2000, pp. 182–206.

15 Doner and Ramsay, 'Rent seeking and economic development in Thailand', p. 171; Rock, 'Thailand's old bureaucratic polity and its new semi-democracy', p. 185.

16 Rock, 'Thailand's old bureaucratic polity and its new semi-democracy', pp. 188–93.

17 Richard Doner, 'Politics and the growth of local capital in Southeast Asia: auto industries in the Philippines and Thailand', in Ruth McVey (ed.), *Southeast Asian Capitalists*, Ithaca, NY: Cornell University, Southeast Asia Program, 1992, p. 191.

18 Ibid., p. 214.

19 Ibid.

20 Shigeki Higashi, 'The automotive industry in Thailand: from protective promotion to liberalization', in IDE Spot Survey, *The Automotive Industry in Asia: The Great Leap Forward,* Tokyo: Institute of Developing Economies, 1995, pp. 16–25. See also Tara Siam Business Information Ltd, *Tara Siam Business Directory 1996/97*, Vol. 2, Bangkok, 1998, p. 340.

21 Tara Siam Business Directory 1996/97, Vol. 2, p. 341.

22 Ibid., p. 339.

23 The Boonsoong family had been involved in tin-mining and trade since 1800. In 1950, they moved into real estate and food and beverages. They took over

the East Asiatic Dredging Co in 1949. In 1957 they moved into importing cars and, later, into assembly in partnership with Isuzu and Mitsubishi. Since 1983, it absorbed 29 per cent of the commercial vehicles market in Thailand. The Boonsoong family was close to Pote Sarasin, the Minister of Economic Affairs during the 1970s. He was subsequently co-opted into the corporation as the largest shareholder of Bangchan General Assembly.

24 Shigeki Higashi, 'The automotive industry in Thailand', pp. 17, 23–4.
25 James Zhan and Terutomo Ozawa, *Business Restructuring in Asia: Cross Border Mergers and Acquisitions in the Crisis Period*, Arhus and Copenhagen, Denmark: Copenhagen Business School Press, 2001, p. 45.
26 Ibid.
27 United Communications Industry, *Annual Report*, 1999–2000.
28 Telecom Asia Ltd, *Annual Report*, 1998–2000.
29 *The Nation*, 27 July 1997.
30 *Far Eastern Economic Review*, 10 August 2000.
31 Shin Corp, *Annual Report*, 1998–2002.
32 *Far Eastern Economic Review*, 28 December 2001 and 4 January 2001. See also Duncan McCargo and Ukrist Pathmanand, *The Thaksinization of Thailand*, Copenhagen: NIAS Press, 2005, pp. 34–63.
33 McCargo and Pathmanand, *The Thaksinization of Thailand.*
34 *Myanmar Times*, 20–26 May 2002 and 15 July 2002; *Bangkok Business*, 16 May 2002.
35 Cambodia Telecommunications. See www.efinance.com, 30 January 2003; *Bangkok Post*, 23 June 2003.
36 McCargo and Pathmanand, *The Thaksinization of Thailand*, p. 57.
37 *The Nation*, 5 June 2003.
38 McCargo and Pathmanand, *The Thaksinization of Thailand*, pp. 179–82.
39 For more details on the nationalist ideology exploited by Thai business groups after the 1997 crisis see Pasuk Phongpaichet and Chris Baker, *Thailand's Crisis*, Chiang Mai, Thailand: Silkworm Books, 2000, pp. 161–3, 176–9, 188–90.
40 Paul Krugman 'What happened to Asia?', January 1998. http://web.mit.edu/Krugman/www/disinter.html, pp. 3–4.
41 *The Nation*, 22 July 1998.
42 Bank of Thailand, *Annual Economic Reports*, 1996–2002; *Reports of Securities and Exchange Commission 1995–2002*; SET, *Investment information 1999–2002.*
43 Bank of Thailand, *Annual Economic Reports*, 1990–7.
44 UNCTAD, *World Investment Report 2000: Cross Border Mergers and Acquisitions and Development*, Geneva: UNCTAD, 2000; UNCTAD, *World Investment Report 2003: Transnational Corporations and Export Competitiveness*, Geneva: UNCTAD, 2003. See also SET, *Investment Information, Listed companies*, 1996–2003, and Securities and Exchange Commission of Thailand, *Annual Reports*, 1993–2002.
45 *Bangkok Post*, 25 August 1998.
46 Zhan and Ozawa, *Business Restructuring in Asia*, p. 23.
47 Pasuk and Baker, *Thailand's Crisis*, p. 224.
48 Ibid.
49 *Far Eastern Economic Review*, 15 August 2002. See also Peter Brimble and James Sherman, *Mergers and Acquisitions in Thailand: The Changing Face of Foreign Direct Investment*, Report Prepared for the United Nations Conference on Trade and Development, 20 May 1999, p. 21; Chris Dixon 'Post crisis restructuring, foreign ownership, corporate resistance and economic nationalism in Thailand', in *Contemporary South East Asia*, 20, 1, 2004, pp. 45–72.

50 UNCTAD, *World Investment Report 2000: Cross Border Mergers and Acquisitions and Development*, Geneva: UNCTAD, 2000; UNCTAD, *World Investment Report 2003: Transnational Corporations and Export Competitiveness*, Geneva: UNCTAD, 2003; SET, *Investment Information, Listed Companies, Company Profile*, 4 July 2003.
51 David Edwards, Juzhong Zhuang and Virginia A. Capulong (eds), *Corporate Governance and Finance in East Asia*, pp. 222–3, 266 and 269.
52 Ibid., p. 245.
53 Pasuk and Baker, *Thailand's Crisis*, p. 167.

12 Philippines' corporate and financial institutions

1 John Larkin, 'Philippine history reconsidered: a socio-economic perspective', *American Historical Review*, 87, 1982, pp. 606–18.
2 Peter Krinks, *The Economy of the Philippines: Elites, Inequalities, and Economic Restructuring*, London: Routledge, 2002, p. 50.
3 Krinks, *The Economy of the Philippines*, pp. 9, 50; World Bank, 2000.
4 Cesar G. Saldaña, 'The Philippines', in *Corporate Governance and Finance in East Asia: A Study of Indonesia, Republic of Korea, Philippines, Malaysia, Thailand*, Manila: ADB, Economics and Development Resource Center, vol. 2, 2001.
5 In the same period, the Osmena family was forced into exile, and Vicente Tan, the owner of the Continental Bank and the Philippine Trust Company, was arrested (in 1974) for economic sabotage, and forced to sell the two banks. David C. Kang, *Crony Capitalism: Corruption and Development in South Korea and the Philippines*, Cambridge: Cambridge University Press, 2002.
6 See Table 12.2 for a perspective on ownership concentration in selected industries in 1997.
7 Kang, *Crony Capitalism*, pp. 175–7.
8 Ibid., pp. 135–6; SEC General Information 1994; Committee on Privatization Report 1994, cited in *Business World, 7th Anniversary Report 1994*, p. 96.
9 Concentration was 'just not a detriment to the evolution of a country's legal system but in fact emerged because of the lack of effective legal constraints', Stijn Claessen, Simeon Djankov and Larry H. P. Lang, 'The separation of ownership and control in East Asian corporations', *Journal of Financial Economics*, 58, October 2000, p. 109.
10 The large conglomerates with banks included Ayala, Gokongwei, Lopez and Henry Sy. In 1997 the Ayalas took the largest share of their profits from real estate and banking. For Gokongwei, it was manufacturing and banking. Lopez, too, took high profits from banking, but also the media. Only Henry Sy depended largely on retailing, almost 70 per cent of his profits.
11 Claessens *et al.*, 'The separation of ownership and control in East Asian corporations', 2000, p. 108.
12 K. Koike, 'The Ayala Group during the Aquino period: diversification along with a changing ownership and management structure', *The Developing Economies*, 31, 4, 1993, p. 454.
13 *Asian Company Handbook 1998*. Tokyo: Toyo Keizai, 1998, pp. 686–8.
14 Claessens *et al.*, October 2000, p. 97.
15 The Bank of the Philippine Islands was taken over by the Ayala Group in 1969 from the Manila Archdiocese. K. Koike, 'The Ayala Group during the Aquino period', pp. 442–64.
16 Paul D. Hutchcroft, *Booty Capitalism: The Politics of Banking in the Philippines*, Ithaca, NY: Cornell University Press, 1998, p. 78.

17 Ibid., p. 86.
18 Ibid., p. 137.
19 By 1989, Philippine banks were already recording higher profits, 271 per cent higher than in eight other Asian countries. Hutchcroft, *Booty Capitalism*, p. 197.
20 Paul D. Hutchcroft, *Booty Capitalism*, p. 221.
21 Hal Hill and P. Athukorala, 'Foreign investment in East Asia: a survey', *Asian Pacific Economic Literature*, 12, 2, 1998, pp. 23–50.
22 Kang, *Crony Capitalism*, pp. 61–3, 76–7, 80–4, 139, 148.
23 Benedict J. Kerkvliet and Resil B. Mojares (eds), *From Marcos to Aquino: Local Perspectives on Political Transition in the Philippines*, Quezon City: Ateneo de Manila University Press, 1991; Geoffrey Hiscock, *Asia's Wealth Club: Who's Really Who in Business*, London: Nicholas Breasley, 1997; Alfred W. McCoy (ed.), *An Anarchy of Families: State and Family in the Philippines*, Madison, WI: University of Wisconsin, Center for Southeast Asian Studies, 1993; Cesar G. Saldaña, 'Philippine corporate governance, environment, and policy, and their impact on corporate performance', Conference on corporate governance in Asia: a comparative perspective: Seoul, OECD, Korean Development Institute, Government of Japan, and World Bank, 1999; Cesar G. Saldaña, 'The Philippines', in *Corporate Governance and Finance in East Asia: A Study of Indonesia, Republic of Korea, Philippines, Malaysia, Thailand*, Manila: ADB, Economics and Development Resource Center, vol. 2, 2001; Peter Krinks, 'Fruits of independence? Philippine capitalists and the banana export industry', in Michael Taylor and Nigel Thrift (eds), *Multinationals and the Restructuiring of the World Economy*, London: Routledge, 1986, pp. 256–81; David Wurfel, 'Elites of wealth and elites of power, the changing dynamic: a Philippine case study', in *Southeast Asian Affairs, 1979*, Singapore: Institute of Southeast Asian Studies, Heinemann Educational Asia, 1979, pp. 233–45.
24 Hutchcroft, *Booty Capitalism*, pp. 166–9.
25 Joseph Y. Lim, 'The East Asian economic and financial crisis: the case of the Philippines', in Masayoshi Tsurumi (ed.), *Financial Big Bang in Asia*, Aldershot: Ashgate, 2001, p. 258.
26 Joseph Y. Lim, 'The East Asian economic and financial crisis', p. 264.
27 Paul D. Hutchcroft, 'Obstructive corruption: the politics of privilege in the Philippines', in Mushtaq H. Khan and Jomo K. S. (eds), *Rents, Rent-Seeking, and Economic Development: Theory and Evidence in Asia*, Cambridge University Press, 2000, pp. 207–47.
28 Business World, *Anniversary Report 1994, Philippine Inc.*, Manila, 1994; Yoshihara Kunio, *Philippine Industrialization: Foreign and Domestic Capital*, Quezon City: Ateneo de Manila University Press, 1985; Ellen H. Palanca, 'Chinese business families in the Philippines since the 1890s', in Rajeswary Ampalavanar Brown (ed.), *Chinese Business Enterprise in Asia*, London: Routledge, 1995, pp. 197–213.
29 Temario C. Rivera, 'The Chinese-Filipino Taipans and industrial reform in the Ramos administration', in Temano C. Rivera and Kenji Koike (eds), *The Chinese-Filipino Business Families under Ramos Government*, Tokyo: Institute of Developing Economies, JRP Series 114, 1995, pp. 28–9.
30 Acquisitions of banks by Chinese: Allied Bank, Lucio Tan; Banco de Oro, Henry Sy; China Banking Corporation, Henry Sy; Philippine National Bank and Far East Bank, Gokongwei; Philippine Commercial Bank, Gokongwei; Family Savings Bank and Insular Bank of Asia and America, Gotianun family. These last two were later sold.
31 Temario C. Rivera, 'The Chinese-Filipino business families and industrial reform in the Ramos administration', p. 23.

32 Ibid., p. 27.
33 Daniel van den Bulcke and Zhang Hai Yan, 'Chinese family-owned multinationals in the Philippines and the internationalisation process', in R. A. Brown (ed.), *Chinese Business Enterprise in Asia*, London: Routledge, 1995.
34 Ng Chee Yuen and Toh Kin Woon, 'Privatization in the Asia Pacific Region', *Asian Pacific Economic Literature*, 6, 2, 1992, pp. 42–68.
35 Peter Krinks, *The Economy of the Philippines*, p. 66.
36 Ibid., pp. 67, 95.
37 Hutchcroft, *Booty Capitalism*, p. 11.
38 ICTS, *Annual Report*, 1998.
39 San Miguel, *Directors' Report*, 1999–2000.
40 Daniel van den Bulcke and Zhang Hai Yan, 'Chinese family-owned multinationals in the Philippines', pp. 214–46. 'The comparative advantages of CHMNES are derived first from their multi-level business strategies which are appropriate to different segments of the market in terms of prices and quality and second from their intrinsic and effective business systems. These systems allow CHMNES to have superior business information systems and distribution networks than both local and other foreign subsidiaries.' There is no detailed corporate information, no quantitative or qualitative data, from which such conclusions might be drawn. The tables are derived from surveys that do not mention the types of products or the specific markets surveyed. And a one-year (1992) survey does not provide even longitudinal evidence. The tables 12.1–12.13 appear impressive but my micro-level study of Filipino groups in South East Asia and Hong Kong does not indicate such success. Rather cynically, they also maintain that the Filipino-Chinese enjoyed comparable success to Taiwanese firms. This can be accepted only with solid empirical evidence. See also Ellen H. Palance, 'Chinese business families in the Philippines since the 1890s', in R. A. Brown (ed.), *Chinese Business Enterprise in Asia*, London: Routledge, 1995, pp. 197–213; K. Koike, 'The Ayala Group during the Aquino period', pp. 442–64; Kenji Koike, 'Changing ownership and management structure of Taipans compared with Ayala Group', in Temario C. Rivera and Kenji Koike (eds), *The Chinese Filipino Business Families under the Ramos Government*, Tokyo: IDE, Joint Research Program Series no. 114, 1995. Koike and Rivera provide good empirical data.

Chapter 13 Conclusion

1 Radelet Steven and Jeffrey Sachs, *The East Asian Financial Crisis: Diagnosis, Remedies, Prospects*, Brookings Paper in Economic Activity, 1, 1998, pp. 1–74. Paul Krugman, 'What Happened to Asia?', Mimeograph 1998 http://web.mit.edu/krugman/www/disinter.html.
2 Stephan Haggard, Wonhyuk Lim and Euysung Kim (eds), *Economic Crisis and Corporate Restructuring in Korea*, Cambridge University Press, 2003, pp. 6–7.
3 Ibid., p. 308.
4 See Jongryn Mo and Chung-In Moon, 'Business–Government Relations under Kim Dae-jung', in Haggard, Lim and Kim, *Economic Crisis and Corporate Restructuring in Korea*, pp. 127–49.
5 Source: Statistical Data from these various stock markets for 1987–98.
6 See Steve Thompson and Mike Wright, 'Corporate governance: the role of restructuring transactions', *The Economic Journal*, 105, May 1995, pp. 690–703.
7 Christopher Adam and William Cavendish, 'Background', in Jomo, K.S., *Privatizing Malaysia, Rents, Rhetoric, Realities*, Boulder, CO: Westview Press, 1995, p. 34.

8 Ibid., p. 38.
9 Manuel Montes, *The Currency Crisis in Southeast Asia*, Singapore: Institute of South East Asian Studies, 1998.
10 Paul Krugman, 'The myth of Asia's miracle', *Foreign Affairs*, November–December 1994; Paul Krugman, 'What Happened to Asia?'.
11 Stijn Claessens, Simeon Djankov and Larry Lang, 'East Asian corporates: growth, financing and risks over the last decade', unpublished MS, World Bank, Washington, DC, 1998.
12 See J. A. Kay and P. J. Thompson, 'Privatization: a policy in search of a rationale', *The Economic Journal*, 96, 381, March 1986, p. 22.
13 Emilyn Cabanda and Mohamed Ariff, 'Performance gains through privatization and competition of Asian telecommunications', *ASEAN Economic Bulletin*, 19, 3, December 2002, pp. 254–79.
14 Ibid., p. 270.
15 For more details on Thai telecommunications, see Rajeswary Ampalavanar Brown, *Chinese Big Business and the Wealth of Asian Nations*, Palgrave, 2000, Chapter 7.
16 A. D. Chandler, *The Visible Hand: The Managerial Revolution in American Business*, Cambridge, MA: Harvard University Press, 1977. A. D. Chandler, *Scale and Scope : The Dynamics of Industrial Capitalism*, Cambridge, MA: Harvard University Press, 1990. Michael Useem, *Investor Capitalism*, New York, Basic Books, 1996. And Michael Useem, *Executive Defence : Shareholder Power and Corporate Reorganization*, Cambridge, MA: Harvard University Press, 1993.
17 John Kay, *Foundation of Corporate Success*, Oxford: Oxford University Press, 1993. M. W. Kirby and Mary B. Rose (eds), *Business Enterprise in Modern Britain from the Eighteenth to the Twentieth Centuries*, London: Routledge, 1994. S. R. H. Jones and S. P. Ville, 'Efficient transactions or rent seeking monopolists? The rationale for early chartered trading companies', *Journal of Economic History*, 56, 1996, pp. 818–915.
18 Morikawa Hidemasa, *Zaibatsu: The Rise and Fall of Family Enterprise groups in Japan*, Tokyo: University of Tokyo Press, 1992.

Bibliography

Primary sources

Indonesia

Bapepam (Indonesian Capital Market) Annual Reports, 1990–2001
Indonesian Stock Exchange Publications, 1988–2005
Indonesian Economic and Finance Research, Indonesian Capital Market Directory, 1989–2005
Publications of Badan Koordinasi Penaman Modal (BKPM)-Capital Investment Coordinating Board, Republik Indonesia, 1987–2003
Bank Indonesia Publications, 1980–2005
Jakarta Stock Exchange Publications, 1985–2005
IBRA (Indonesian Bank Restructuring Agency) Monthly Reports, 2000–February 2004
Indonesian Legal Publications, 1980–2005

Annual Reports of the following

Indonesian Cement Association
Indocement
Semen Gresik
Semen Cibinong
First Pacific Holdings
Astra International
Indofood Sukses Makmur
Indah Kiat Pulp and Paper
Texmaco Jaya
Gadjah Tunggal
Bank Central Asia
Lippo Bank
Bank Duta
Bank Bali
Bank Niaga
Bank International Indonesia
Bimantara Citra
Humpuss
Sinar Mas
Asia Pulp and Paper

Newspapers

Tempo
Far Eastern Economic Review
Republika
Business Times
Kompas
Tapol Bulletin
Media Indonesia
Forum Keadilan
Suara Pembaruan
Asia Week
International Herald Tribune
Merdeka
Jakarta Post
Straits Times
Panji Masyarakat
South China Morning Post

Publications of Asian Development Bank
IMF
World Bank
UNCTAD
BANKSTAT

Malaysia

Bank Negara Malaysia, 1980–2005
Malaysian Industrial Development Authority
Publications of Kuala Lumpur Stock Exchange
Publications of Arab Malaysia Bank
Maybank
Hong Leong
Renong Bhd
United Engineers Malaysia
United Engineers Malaysia World
Phileo Allied Bank
Archives of HSBC
Mercantile Bank
Standard Chartered
Overseas Chinese Banking Corporation
Publications of Danaharta
Bernama
The Edge
New Straits Times
Business Times Malaysia
Malaysian Business

Philippines

Publications of Manila Stock Exchange
Reports of Bank of Philippine Islands
San Miguel Corporation
Ayala Corporation
Philippine National Bank

Singapore

Publications of Singapore Stock Exchange
Monetary Authority of Singapore
Department of Statistics
Company reports of Overseas Union Bank, United Overseas Bank, Overseas Chinese Banking Corporation, Development Bank of Singapore, Keppel TatLee Bank, Keppel Corporation, SingTel, Sembawang Corporation

Thailand

Publications of the Stock Exchange of Thailand
Publications of the Ministry of Commerce and Industry
Securities and Exchange Commission of Thailand
Bank of Thailand
Tara Siam Business Directory, 1997–8, 3 volumes
United Communication Industry Reports
Siam Motors
Siam Cement
Telecom Asia
Shin Corp
Bangkok Bank
Bank of Asia
Thai Danu
Nakornthon Bank
Merrill Lynch Phatra Reports, 1990–7
The Nation
Bangkok Post

For all the countries

Moody Investors Service
Standard and Poor
Datastream
Bloomberg
Asian Wall Street Journal

Secondary sources

Abdullah, Moha Asri, 'An overview of the macroeconomic contribution of small and medium enterprise in Malaysia', in Charles Harvie and Boon-Chye Lee (eds), *The Role of SMEs in National Economies in East Asia*, Cheltenham: Edward Elgar, 2002, pp. 181–201.

Adam, Christopher S. and William Cavendish, 'Background', in Jomo K.S. (ed.), *Privatising Malaysia: Rents, Rhetoric, Realities*, Boulder, CO: Westview, 1995, pp. 11–41.

Agénor, Pierre-Richard, Marcus Miller, David Vines and Axel Weber (eds), *The Asian Financial Crisis: Causes, Contagion and Consequences*, Cambridge: Cambridge University Press, 1999.

Amsden, Alice, *Asia's Next Giant*, Cambridge: Cambridge University Press, 1989.

Annuar M. N., M. Ariff and M. Shamsher, 'Is Kuala Lumpur's emerging share market efficient?', *Journal of International Financial Markets*, 4, 1994, pp. 61–71.

Ariff, M. and L. W. Johnson, *Securities Markets and Stock Pricing: Evidence from a Developing Capital Market in Asia*, Singapore: Longman, 1990.

Athukorala, Prema-chandra, 'Capital account regimes, crisis and adjustment in Malaysia', *Asian Development Review*, 18, 1, 2000, pp. 17–48.

Backman, Michael, *Asian Eclipse: Exposing the Dark Side of Business in Asia*, Singapore: John Wiley, 1999.

Bird, Kelly, 'Concentration in Indonesian manufacturing, 1975–93', *Bulletin of Indonesian Economic Studies*, 35, 1, 1999, pp. 43–73.

——, 'Survey of recent development', *Bulletin of Indonesian Economic Studies*, 32, 1, 1996.

Bongini, Paola, Stijn Claessens and Giovanni Ferri, 'The political economy of distress in East Asian financial institutions', *Journal of Financial Services*, 19, 1, 2001, pp. 5–25.

Brimble, Peter and James Sherman, *Mergers and Acquisitions in Thailand: The Changing Face of Foreign Direct Investment*, Report prepared for the United Nations Conference on Trade and Development, 20 May 1999.

Brown, Rajeswary Ampalavanar, *Capital and Entrepreneurship in South East Asia*, Basingstoke: Macmillan, 1994.

——, *Chinese Big Business and the Wealth of Asian Nations*, London: Palgrave, 2000.

Brummit, William E. and Frank Flatters, *Exports, Structural Change and Thailand's Rapid Growth*, Bangkok: Thai Development Research Institute, 1992.

Cabanda, Emilyn and Mohamed Ariff, 'Performance gains through privatization and competition of Asian telecommunications', *ASEAN Economic Bulletin*, 19, 3, December 2002, pp. 254–79.

Castle Group, The, *The Suharto Dependency Index*, Jakarta, 1995.

Caves, R. E., 'Corporate strategy and structure', *Journal of Economic Literature*, 18, 1980, pp. 64–92.

Chandler, A. D., *The Visible Hand: The Managerial Revolution in American Business*, Cambridge MA: Harvard University Press, 1977.

——, *Scale and Scope: The Dynamics of Industrial Capitalism*, Cambridge, MA: Harvard University Press, 1990.

Chensavasdijai, Varaphat, 'The effect of financial liberalization on investment behaviour of Thai manufacturing firms', D.Phil. thesis, University of Oxford, 1999.

Cheong, Ong Hong, 'Coping with capital flows and the role of monetary policy: the Malaysian experience, 1990–95', in C. H. Kwan, Donna Vandenbrink and Chia Siow Yue, *Coping with Capital Flow in East Asia*, Institute of Southeast Asian Studies, 1998, pp. 220–43.

China Foreign Economic Statistical Yearbook, Beijing: China Statistics Press, 2002.

Choi, Andy, Charles Spencer and Nira Tanoko, 'Asia Pulp and Paper: here comes the cash flow!', Morgan Stanley Dean Witter, 12 November 1999.

Claessens, Stijn, Larry Lang, Simeon Djankov and Joseph Fan, 'How does foreign entry affect the domestic banking market?', *World Bank Working Paper*, May 1998.

——, Simeon Djankov and Daniel Klingebiel, 'Financial restructuring in East Asia: halfway there?', World Bank, Financial Sector Discussion Paper, 3, 1999, pp. 5–6.

——, —— and Larry Lang, 'East Asian corporates: growth, financing and risks over the last decade', unpublished MS, Washington, DC: World Bank, 1998.

——, —— and ——, 'Who controls East Asian corporations?', Financial Economics Unit, Financial Sector Practice Department, World Bank, February 1999.

——, ——, Simeon Djankov and Larry Lang, 'The separation of ownership and control in East Asian corporations', *Journal of Financial Economics*, 58, October 2000, pp. 81–112.

——, —— and Lixin Colin Xu, 'Corporate performance in the East Asian financial crisis', *World Bank Research Observer*, 15, 1, 2000, pp. 23–46.

——, ——, Joseph Fan and Larry Lang, *Corporate Diversification in East Asia: The Role of Ultimate Ownership Structure and Grand Affiliation*, Washington DC: World Bank, Policy Research Working Paper 2089, 1999.

Cole, David C. and Betty F. Slade, *Building a Modern Financial System*, Cambridge: Cambridge University Press, 1996.

Collier, P. and C. Mayer, 'The assessment: financial liberalization, financial systems, and economic growth', *Oxford Review of Economic Policy*, 5, 1989, pp. 1–12.

Corbett, J. and T.J. Jenkinson, 'How is investment financed? A study of Germany, Japan, the United Kingdom, and the United States', *The Manchester School of Business Supplement*, 65, 1997.

Dawson, S. M., 'Secondary stock market performance of initial public offers, Hong Kong, Singapore, and Malaysia, 1978–84', *Journal of Business Finance and Accounting*, 14, 1987, pp. 67–76.

de Brouwer, Gordon with Wisarn Pupphavesa, *Asia Pacific Financial Deregulation*, London: Routledge, 1999.

——, *Hedge Funds in Emerging Markets*, Cambridge: Cambridge University Press, 2001.

Delhaise, Philippe F., *Asia in Crisis: The Implosion of the Banking and Finance Systems*, Singapore: John Wiley & Son, 1998.

Dillon, Chip and Norman Waite, 'Asia Pulp and Paper IQ deceptive: earnings power still strong', Saloman Smith Barney, 1 July 1998.

Dixon, Chris, 'Post crisis restructuring, foreign ownership, corporate resistance and economic nationalism in Thailand', *Contemporary South East Asia*, 20, 1, 2004, pp. 45–72.

Doner, Richard F., 'Politics and the growth of local capital in Southeast Asia: auto industries in the Philippines and Thailand', in Ruth McVey (ed.), *Southeast Asian Capitalists*, Ithaca, NY: Cornell University, Southeast Asia Program, 1992, pp. 191–218.

—— and Ansil Ramsay, 'Rent seeking and economic development in Thailand', in Mushtaq H. Khan and Jomo K. S. (eds), *Rents, Rent-seeking and Economic Development: Theory and Evidence in Asia*, Cambridge: Cambridge University Press, 2000.

—— and Gary Hawes, 'The political economy of growth in Southeast and Northeast Asia', in Manochehr Dorraj (ed.), *The Changing Political Economy of the Third World*, Boulder, CO: Lynne Rienner, 1995, pp. 145–86.

Edwards, Sebastian, *Capital Flows and the Emerging Economies: Theory, Evidence and Controversies*, Chicago, IL: University of Chicago Press, 2000.

Elson, R. E., *Suharto: A Political Biography*, Cambridge: Cambridge University Press, 2001.

Fisman, Raymond, 'Estimating the value of political connections', *American Economic Review*, September 2001, pp. 1095–1102.

Fitzpatrick, Daniel, 'Indonesian corporate governance: would outside directors or commissioners help?', in Chris Manning and Peter van Dierman, *Indonesia in Transition*, Singapore: ISEAS, 2000, pp. 293–308.

Freek, Colombijn and J. Thomas Lindblad, *Roots of Violence in Indonesia*, Singapore: ISEAS, 2002.

Freeman, Nick J., *Foreign Portfolio Investors Approaches to Thailand's Equity Market: Survey Findings and Preliminary Analysis*, ISEAS Economics and Finance Working Papers, No. 2, 2000.

—— (ed.), *Financing South East Asia's Economic Development*, Singapore: ISEAS, 2003.

—— and Frank L. Bartels, *Portfolio Investment in South East Asia's Stock Markets: A Survey of Institutional Investors Current Perceptions and Practices*, Institute of Southeast Asian Studies, Working Paper Economics and Finance, No. 3, April 2000.

Glen, J. D. and M. A. Sumbinski, 'Trends in private investment in developing countries', Washington, DC: World Bank, International Finance Corporation Discussion Paper 34, 1998.

Goldman, Marshall I., *The Piratization of Russia: Russian Reform goes awry*, London: Routledge, 2003.

Gomez, Edmund Terence, *Political Business: Corporate Involvement of Malaysian Political Parties*, Cairns: James Cook University Press, 1994.

——, *Chinese Business in Malaysia: Accumulation, Accommodation, and Ascendance*, Honolulu, HA: University of Hawaii Press, 1999.

Gomez, E. T. and Jomo K. S., *Malaysia's Political Economy: Politics, Patronage, and Profits*, Cambridge: Cambridge University Press, 2nd edn, 1999.

Haggard, Stephan, Wonhyuk Lim and Euysung Kim (eds), *Economic Crisis and Corporate Restructuring in Korea*, Cambridge: Cambridge University Press, 2003.

Hamilton-Hart, Natasha, *Asian States, Asian Bankers: Central Banking in Southeast Asia*, Ithaca, NY and London: Cornell University Press, 2002.

Hidemasa, Morikawa, *Zaibatsu: The Rise and Fall of Family Enterprise groups in Japan*, Tokyo: University of Tokyo Press, 1992.

Higashi, Shigeki, 'The automotive industry in Thailand: from protective promotion to liberalization', in IDE Spot Survey, *The Automotive Industry in Asia: The Great Leap Forward*, Tokyo: Institute of Developing Economies, 1995, pp. 16–25.

Hill, Hal, *Indonesia's Industrial Transformation*, Singapore: ISEAS, 1997.

——, *The Indonesian Economy in Crisis: Causes, Consequences, and Lessons*, Singapore: ISEAS, 1999.

——, 'Indonesia: the strange and sudden death of a tiger economy', *Oxford Development Studies*, 28, 2, 2000, pp. 117–39.

—— and P. Athukorala, 'Foreign investment in East Asia: a survey', *Asian Pacific Economic Literature*, 12, 2, 1998, pp. 23–50.

Hiscock, Geoffrey, *Asia's Wealth Club: Who's Really Who in Business*, London: Nicholas Breasley, 1997.

Huff, W. G., *The Economic Growth of Singapore: Trade and Development in the Twentieth Century*, Cambridge: Cambridge University Press, 1994.

——, 'What is the Singapore model of economic development?', *Cambridge Journal of Economics*, 19, 1995.

Hutchcroft, Paul D., *Booty Capitalism: The Politics of Banking in the Philippines*, Ithaca, NY: Cornell University Press, 1998.

——, 'Obstructive corruption: the politics of privilege in the Philippines', in Mushtaq H. Khan and Jomo K. S. (eds), *Rents, Rent-Seeking, and Economic Development: Theory and Evidence in Asia*, Cambridge: Cambridge University Press, 2000, pp. 207–47.

International Finance Corporation, *Emerging Stock Market Factbook*, Washington, DC, 1997.

Iriana, Reiny and Fredrik Sjoholm, 'Indonesia's economic crisis: contagion and fundamentals', *Developing Economies*, 12, 2, 2002, pp. 135–51.

Isa, Mansor Md. and Tan Kok Hong, 'The announcement effects of rights and bonus issues on Malaysian stock prices', *Capital Markets Review*, 5, 2, 1997, pp. 45–58.

Ito, Takatoshi, 'Capital flows in Asia', in Sebastian Edwards (ed.), *Capital Flows and the Emerging Economies: Theory, Evidence, and Controversies*, Chicago, IL: University of Chicago Press, 2000.

Jomo K. S. (ed.), *Tigers in Trouble: Financial Governance, Liberalization and Crises in East Asia*, London: Zed, 1998.

——, *Malaysian Eclipse, Economic Crisis and Recovery*, London: Zed Books, 2001.

Jones, S. R. H. and S. P. Ville, 'Efficient transactions or rent seeking monopolists? The rationale for early chartered trading companies', *Journal of Economic History*, 56, 1996 pp. 818–915.

Jones, Stephanie Griffith, Manuel F. Montes and Anwar Nasution (eds), *Short-term Capital Flows and Economic Crisis*, Oxford: Oxford University Press, 2001.

Jongryn, Mo and Chung-In Moon, 'Business–Government relations under Kim Dae-jung', in Stephan Haggard, Wonhyuk Lim and Euysung Kim (eds), *Economic Crisis and Corporate Restructuring in Korea*, Cambridge: Cambridge University Press, 2003, pp. 127–49.

Junus, Aditjondro George, 'Guns, pamphlets, and handie-talkies: how the military exploited local ethno religious tensions in Maluku to preserve their political and economic privileges', in Ingrid Wessel and George Wimhofer (eds), *Violence in Indonesia*, Hamburg: Abera, 2001, pp. 100–28.

Kang, David C., *Crony Capitalism: Corruption and Development in South Korea and the Philippines*, Cambridge: Cambridge University Press, 2002.

Kay, J. A. and P. J. Thompson, 'Privatization: a policy in search of a rationale', *The Economic Journal*, 96, 381, 1986, pp. 18–38.

Kay, John, *Foundation of Corporate Success*, Oxford: Oxford University Press, 1993.

Kenward, Lloyd R., 'What has been happening at Bank Indonesia?', *Bulletin of Indonesian Economic Studies*, 35, 1, 1999, pp. 121–7.

Kerkvliet, Benedict J. and Resil B. Mojares (eds), *From Marcos to Aquino: Local Perspectives on Political Transition in the Philippines*, Quezon City: Ateneo de Manila University Press, 1991.

Khan, Mushtaq H. and Jomo K. S. (eds) *Rents, Rent Seeking and Economic Development: Theory and Evidence in Asia*, Cambridge: Cambridge University Press, 2000.

Kirby, M.W. and Rose, Mary B. (eds), *Business Enterprise in Modern Britain from the Eighteenth to the Twentieth Centuries*, London: Routledge, 1994.

Kohsaka, Akira, 'Interdependence through capital flows in Pacific Asia and the role of Japan', in Takatoshi Ito and Anne O. Krueger (eds), *Financial Deregulation and Integration in East Asia*, Chicago, IL: University of Chicago Press, 1996, pp. 107–46.

Koike, K., 'The Ayala Group during the Aquino period: diversification along with a changing ownership and management structure', *The Developing Economies*, 31, 4, 1993, pp. 442–64.

——, 'Changing ownership and management structure of Taipans compared with Ayala Group', in Temario C. Rivera and Kenji Koike (eds), *The Chinese Filipino Business Families under the Ramos Government*, Tokyo: IDE, Joint Research Program Series no. 114, 1995, pp. 35–65.

Krinks, Peter, 'Fruits of independence? Philippine capitalists and the banana export industry', in Michael Taylor and Nigel Thrift (eds), *Multinationals and the Restructuring of the World Economy*, London: Routledge, 1986, pp. 256–81.

——, *The Economy of the Philippines: Elites, Inequalities, and Economic Restructuring*, London: Routledge, 2002.

Krueger, Anne O., 'The political economy of the rent seeking society', *The American Economic Review*, 64, 3, June 1974, pp. 291–303.

Krugman, P., 'The Myth of Asia's Miracle', *Foreign Affairs*, 73, 6, 1994, pp. 62–78.

——, 'What happened to Asia?', Mimeograph 1998, downloaded on 16 December 2005 from http://web.mit.edu/Krugman/www/disinter.html.

——, 'Latin Lessons for Asia', *Far Eastern Economic Review*, 25 October 1999.

Larkin, John, 'Philippine history reconsidered: a socioeconomic perspective', *The American Historical Review*, 87, 1982, pp. 595–628.

Lauridsen, Laurids S., 'Thailand: causes, conduct, consequences', in Jomo K. S. (ed.), *Tigers in Trouble: Financial Governance, Liberalization and Crisis in East Asia*, London: Zed Books, 1998, pp. 137–61.

Lee Tsao Yuan, *Overseas Investment Experience of Singapore Manufacturing Companies*, Singapore: McGraw-Hill, 1994.

Lee, Sheng-Yi, *The Monetary and Banking Development of Malaysia and Singapore*, Singapore: Singapore University Press, 1974.

Lim, Joseph Y., 'The East Asian economic and financial crisis: the case of the Philippines', in Masayoshi Tsurumi (ed.), *Financial Big Bang in Asia*, Ashgate, 2001, pp. 251–90.

Limpaphayom, Piman, 'Chapter 4 – Thailand', in David Edwards, Juzhong Zhuang and Virginia A. Capulong (eds), *Corporate Governance and Finance in East Asia: A Study of Indonesia, the Republic of Korea, Malaysia, the Philippines, and Thailand. Volume 2: Country Studies*, Manila: Asian Development Bank, 2001.

Limskul, Kitti and Thaneit Khantigaroon, 'Business cycle indicators for Thailand', in Hiroshi Osada and Daisuke Hiratsuka (eds), *Business Cycles in Asia*, Tokyo: Institute of Developing Economies, 1991, pp. 96–103.

Lindgren, Carl Johan and I. Filatotchev, *Financial Sector Crisis and Restructuring: Lessons from Asia*, Washington, DC: IMF Occasional Paper 188, 1999.

McCargo, Duncan and Ukrist Pathmanand, *The Thaksinization of Thailand*, Copenhagen: NIAS Press, 2005.

McCoy, Alfred W. (ed.), *An Anarchy of Families: State and Family in the Philippines*, Madison, WI: University of Wisconsin, Center for Southeast Asian Studies, 1993.

MacIntyre, Andrew, 'Funny money: fiscal policy, rent seeking and economic performance', in Mushtaq H. Khan and Jomo K. S. (eds), *Rents, Rent Seeking and Economic Development: Theory and Evidence*, Cambridge: Cambridge University Press, 2000, 248–73.

McKendrick, David George, 'Acquiring technological capabilities: aircraft and commercial banking in Indonesia', Ph.D. thesis, University of California at Berkeley, 1989.

McKinnon, R. I., 'Financial repression and the liberalization problem within less-developed countries', in S. Grassman and E. Lundberg (eds), *The World Economic Order: Past and Present Prospects*, London: Macmillan, 1981.

McLeod, Ross H. and Ross Garnaut (eds), *East Asia in Crisis: From Being a Miracle to Needing One?*, London: Routledge, 1998.

McVey, Ruth (ed.), *South East Asian Capitalists*, Ithaca, NY: Cornell South East Asia Program, 1992.

——, 'Greed, violence and Thai politics', Paper presented to the Fifth International Conference on Thai Studies, London, 1993.

Masayoshi, Tsurumi (ed.), *Financial Big Bang in Asia*, Aldershot: Ashgate, 2001.

Mayer, C., 'Financial systems, corporate finance and economic development', in R. G. Hubbard (ed.), *Asymmetric Information, Corporate Finance and Investment*, Chicago, IL: Chicago University Press, 1990.

Miwa,Yoshiro, *Firms and Industrial Organisations in Japan*, London: Macmillan, 1996.

Mohammad Rosul, 'Coping with capital flows and the monetary policy framework: the case of Indonesia', in C. H. Kwan, Donna Vandenbrink and Chia Siow Yue (eds), *Coping with Capital Flows in East Asia*, Singapore: Nomura Research Institute and Institute of Southeast Asian Studies, 1998.

Montes, Manuel, *The Currency Crisis in Southeast Asia*, Singapore: Institute of Southeast Asian studies, 1998.

Myers, Stewart C., 'The capital structure puzzle', *The Journal of Finance*, XXXIX, 3, July 1984, pp. 575–92.

Ng Chee Yuen and Toh Kin Woon, 'Privatization in the Asia Pacific Region', *Asian Pacific Economic Literature*, 6, 2, 1992, pp. 42–68.

O'Sullivan, Mary A., *Contests for Corporate Control: Corporate Governance and Economic Performance in the United States and Germany*, Oxford: Oxford University Press, 2000.

Palanca, Ellen H., 'Chinese business families in the Philippines since the 1890s', in Rajeswary Ampalavanar Brown (ed.), *Chinese Business Enterprise in Asia*, London: Routledge, 1995, pp. 197–213.

Pangaribuan, R., *The Indonesian State Secretariat, 1945–93*, Perth: Asia Research Centre on Political and Economic Change, 1995.

Pangestu, Mari and Manggi Habir, 'The boom, bust, and restructuring of Indonesian banks', in Gordon de Brouwer (ed.), *Financial Markets and Policies in East Asia*, London: Routledge, 2002, pp. 122–56.

Peebles, Gavin and Peter Wilson, *Economic Growth and Development in Singapore: Past and Future*, Cheltenham: Edward Elgar, 2002.

Perrow, Charles, 'Economic theories of organization', *Theory and Society*, 15, 1986, pp. 11–45.

Phongpaichit, Pasuk and Chris Baker, *Thailand's Crisis*, Chiang Mai, Thailand: Silkworm Books, 2000.

—— and ——, 'The Thai economic crisis: new ideals of liberalism and the reaction of Thai society', in Praipol Khumsap (ed.), *Articles Commemorating the Sixtieth Anniversary of Acharn Ammar Siamwalla*, Faculty of Economics, Thammasat University, 1999.

Pongsudhirak, Thitinan, 'Autonomy, institutions, and the baht crisis', in Dieter Mahncke, Kullada Kesboonchoo-Mead, Prathoomporn Vajrasthira and Rudolf Hrbek (eds), *ASEAN and the EU in the International Environment*, Baden-Baden: Nomos Verlagsgesellschaft, 1999, pp. 85–96.

Porametee,Vimolsiri, *The Role of Foreign Investors in the Thai Currency Crisis of 1997*, ISEAS, Economics and Finance Working Papers, No. 4, 2001.

Porta, R. La, 'Expectations and the cross-section of stock returns', *Journal of Finance*, 51, 1996, pp. 1715–42.

Pound, J., 'Proxy contents and the efficiency of shareholder oversight', *Journal of Financial Economics*, 20, 1988, pp. 237–55.

Radelet, Steven and Jeffrey D. Sachs, 'The East Asian financial crisis: diagnosis, remedies, prospects', *Brookings Papers on Economic Activity*, 1, 1998, pp. 1–74, 88–90.

Rajan, Raghuram G. and Luigi Zingales, 'The governance of the new enterprise', in Xavier Vives (ed.), *Corporate Governance: Theoretical and Empirical Perspectives*, Cambridge: Cambridge University Press, 2000, pp. 201–32.

Rivera, Temario C., 'The Chinese-Filipino business families and industrial reform in the Ramos administration', in Temario C. Rivera and Kenji Koike (eds), *The Chinese Filipino Business Families under the Ramos Government*, Tokyo: IDE, Joint Research Program Series no. 114, 1995, pp. 1–33.

Robinson, D., Y. Byeon and R. Teja with W. Tseng, *Thailand: Adjusting to Success, Current Policy Issues*, Washington, DC: International Monetary Fund, 1991.

Robison, Richard, *Indonesia: The Rise of Capital*, St Leonard: Allen & Unwin, 1986.

Roca, Eduardo D., *Price Interdependence among Equity Markets in the Asia Pacific Region, Focus on Australia and ASEAN*, Aldershot: Ashgate, 2000.

Rock, Michael T., 'Thailand's old bureaucratic polity and its new semi-democracy', in Mushtaq H. Khan and Jomo K. S. (eds), *Rents, Rent-Seeking, and Economic Development: Theory and Evidence in Asia*, Cambridge: Cambridge University Press, 2000, pp. 182–206.

Saldaña, Cesar G., 'Philippine corporate governance, environment, and policy, and their impact on corporate performance', Conference on corporate governance in Asia: a comparative perspective: Seoul, OECD, Korean Development Institute, Government of Japan and World Bank, 1999.

——, 'The Philippines', in *Corporate Governance and Finance in East Asia: A Study of Indonesia, Republic of Korea, Philippines, Malaysia, Thailand*, Manila: Asia Development Bank, Economics and Development Resource Center, vol. 2, 2001.

Samego, Indria, *Berbisnis, Buku Pertama Yang Menyingkap data dan Kasus Penyimpangan dalam Praktik Bisnis Kalangan militer*, (ed. Bila Abri), Mizan Pustaka Kronik Indonesia Baru, September 1998.

Sato, Yuri, 'The Salim Group in Indonesia: the development and behaviour of the largest conglomerate in SE Asia', *The Developing Economies*, 31, 4, 1993, pp. 408–41.

——, 'The Astra Group: a pioneer of management modernization in Indonesia', *The Developing Economies*, 34, 3, 1996, pp. 247–80.

Schumpeter, J. A., *Business Cycles*, New York: McGraw-Hill, 1939.

——, *Capitalism, Socialism and Democracy*, London: Unwin University Books, 1943.

Schwarz, Adam, *A Nation in Waiting: Indonesia in the 1990s*, Sydney: Allen & Unwin, 2nd edn, 1999.

Scott, John, *Corporate Business and Capitalist Classes*, Oxford: Oxford University Press, 1997.

Searle, Peter, *The Riddle of Malaysian Capitalism: Rent Seekers or Real Capitalists?*, St Leonard's, Australia: Allen & Unwin, 1999.

Sharma, Shalendra D., 'The Indonesian financial crisis', in World Bank, *Indonesia in Crisis: A Macroeconomic Update*, Washington, DC: The World Bank, 1998, pp. 1–32.

Shaw, E. S., *Financial deepening in economic development*, New York: Oxford University Press, 1973.

Shiller, Robert J., *Irrational Exuberance*, Princeton, NJ: Princeton University Press, 2000.

Shleifer, Andrei, *Inefficient Markets: An Introduction to Behavioural Finance*, Oxford: Oxford University Press, 2000.

—— and L. H. Summers, 'The noise trader approach to finance', *Journal of Economic Perspectives*, 4, 1990, pp. 19–33.

—— and Robert W. Vishny, 'The limits of arbitrage', *Journal of Finance*, 52, 1997, pp. 35–55.

—— and ——, 'A survey of corporate governance', *Journal of Finance*, 52, 1997, pp. 737–83.

Siamwalla, Ammar, 'Can a developing democracy manage its macroeconomy? The case of Thailand', *Thai Development Research Institute, Quarterly Review*, 12, 4, 1997, pp. 3–10.

Sing, Lok Kong and G. S. Gupta, 'Dividend behaviour in Malaysia', *Capital Markets Review*, 3, 1, 1995, pp. 73–83.

Siregar, A., 'Demokratisasi dan Ekonomi Pasar [Democratization and the market economy]', *Warta Ekonomi*, 2000.

Spencer, Charles C., 'Asia Pulp and Paper: well-positioned for Asia's recovery', Morgan Stanley Dean Witter, 28 June 1999.

Stiglitz, J. E., 'Credit markets and the control of capital', *Journal of Money, Credit, and Banking*, 17, 2, 1985, pp. 133–52.

Suehiro, Akira, *Capital Accumulation in Thailand 1885–1985*, Tokyo: East Asian Cultural Studies, 1989.

Thompson, Steve and Mike Wright, 'Corporate governance: the role of restructuring transactions', *The Economic Journal*, 105, 1995, pp. 690–703.

Useem, Michael, *Executive Defence: Shareholder Power and Corporate Reorganization*, Cambridge, MA: Harvard University Press, 1993.

——, *Investor Capitalism*, New York: Basic Books, 1996.

van den Bulcke, Daniel and Zhang Hai Yan, 'Chinese family-owned multinationals in the Philippines and the internationalisation process', in R. A. Brown (ed.), *Chinese Business Enterprise in Asia*, London: Routledge, 1995, pp. 214–46.

van Diermen, Peter, *Small Business in Indonesia*, Aldershot: Ashgate, 1997.

van Dijk, Kees, *A Country in Despair: Indonesia between 1997 and 2000*, Leiden: KITLV Press, 2000.

Wade, Robert, 'The market for public office: why the Indian State is not better at development', *World Development*, 13, 4, 1985, pp. 467–97.

Wang, Gungwu, *Trade and Cultural Values: Australia and the Four Dragons*, Sydney: Asian Studies Association of Australia, 1988.

——, *Don't Leave Home: Migration and the Chinese*, Singapore Times Academic Press, 2001.

Warr, Peter G., 'Thailand', in Ross H. McLeod and Ross Garnaut, *East Asia in Crisis: From Being a Miracle to Needing One?*, London: Routledge, 1998, pp. 49–65.

——, 'What happened to Thailand?', *World Economy*, 22, 5, 1999, pp. 631–50.

Weldon, Curt, *The China Connection*, Washington, DC, December 2003.

Winters, Jeffrey A., *Power in Motion: Capital Mobility and the Indonesian State*, Ithaca, NY: Cornell University Press, 1996.

World Bank, *The Emerging Asian Bond Market*, 1995, Washington, DC: World Bank, 1995.

Wurfel, David, 'Elites of wealth and elites of power, the changing dynamic: a Philippine case study', in *Southeast Asian Affairs, 1979*, Singapore: Institute of Southeast Asian Studies, Heinemann Educational Asia, 1979, pp. 233–45.

Yoshihara, K., *Sogo Shosha: The Vanguard of the Japanese Economy*, Oxford: Oxford University Press, 1982.

——, *Philippine Industrialization: Foreign and Domestic Capital*. Quezon City: Ateneo de Manila University Press, 1985.

——, *The Rise of Ersatz Capitalism in South East Asia*, Singapore: Oxford University Press, 1988.

——, *The Nation and Economic Growth: the Philippines and Thailand*, Singapore: Oxford University Press, 1994.

Young, Alwyn, 'Lessons from the East Asian NICs: a contrarian view', *European Economic Review*, 38, 1994, pp. 964–73.

——, 'The tyranny of numbers: confronting the statistical realities of the East Asian growth experience', *Quarterly Journal of Economics*, 110, 1995, pp. 641–80.

——, 'A tale of two cities: factor accumulation and technical change in Hong Kong and Singapore', in Stanley Fischer and Olivier Blanchard (eds), *NBER Macroeconomic Annual 1992*, No. 7, Cambridge, MA: MIT Press.

Zarowin, Paul, 'Does the stock market overreact to corporate earnings information?', *The Journal of Finance*, XLIV, 5, 1989, pp. 1385–99.

Zhan, James and Terutomo Ozawa, *Business Restructuring in Asia: Cross Border Mergers and Acquisitions in the Crisis Period*, Arhus and Copenhagen, Denmark: Copenhagen Business School Press, 2001.

Zhuang, Juzhong, David Edwards and Virginia Capulong (eds), *Corporate Governance and Finance in East Asia: A Study of Indonesia, Republic of Korea, Malaysia, Philippines, and Thailand*, ADB Report, Manila, 2001, vols 1, 2.

Zingales, Luigi, *Corporate Governance*, Cambridge, MA: National Bureau of Economic Research, 1997.

Index